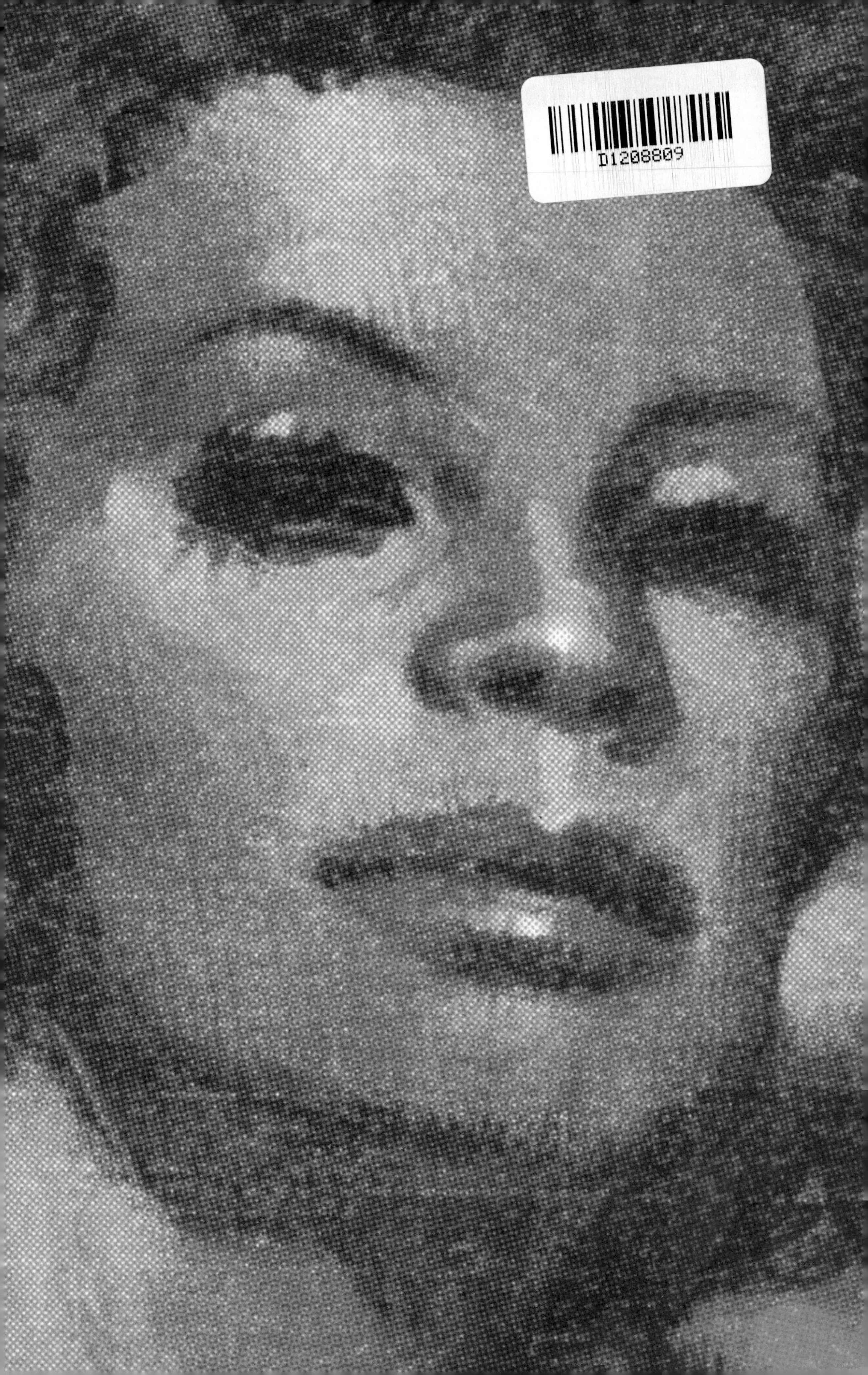

CRIMINAL

The Deluxe Edition

CRIMINAL
The Deluxe Edition

Ed Brubaker Sean Phillips
Colors by Val Staples

ICON

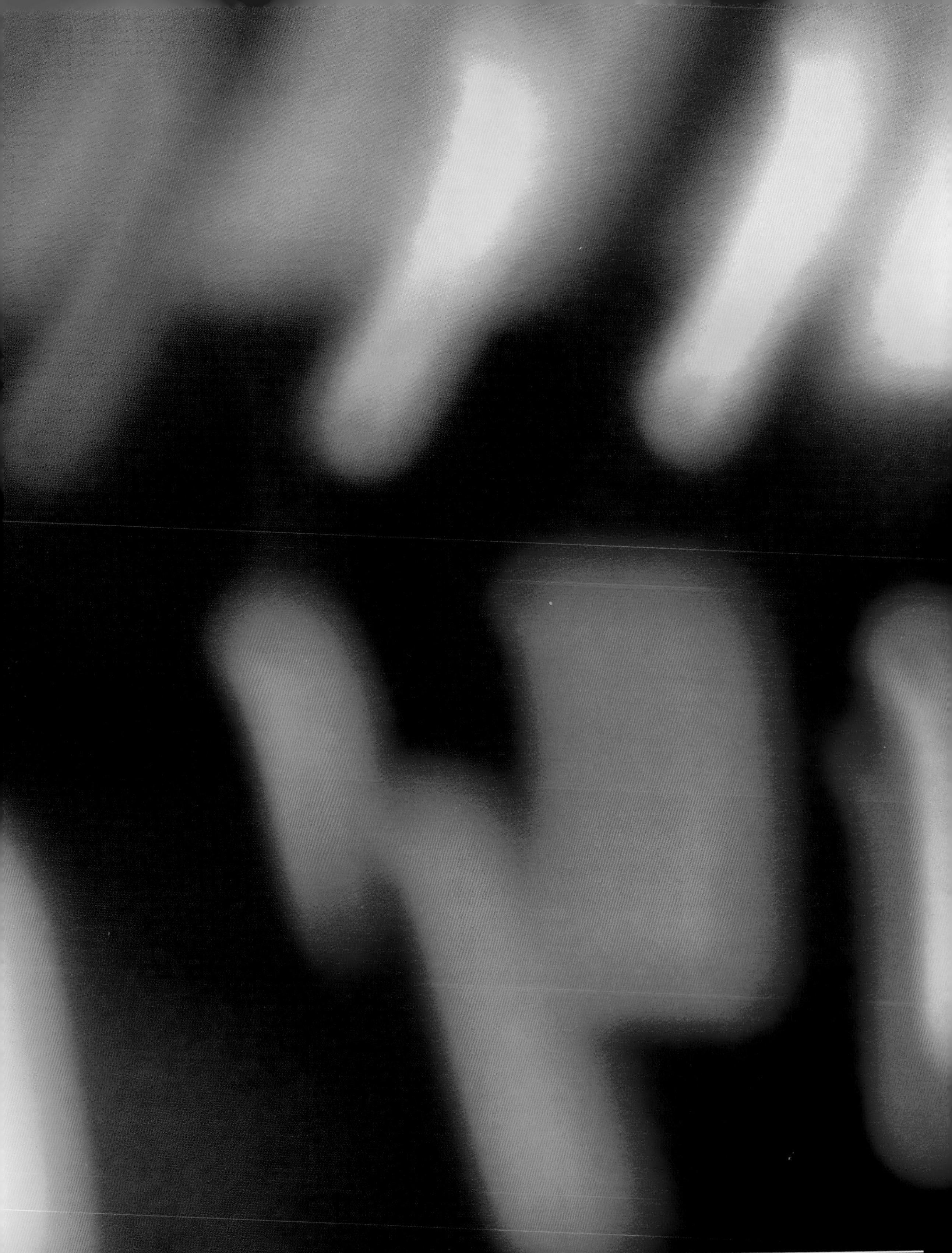

CRIMINAL DELUXE EDITION. Contains material originally published in magazine form as CRIMINAL Vol 1 #1-10 and CRIMINAL Vol 2 #1-3. First printing 2009.
ISBN# 978-0-7851-4229-4.
Published by MARVEL PUBLISHING. INC., a subsidiary of MARVEL ENTERTAINMENT INC. OFFICE OF PUBLICATION: 417 5th Avenue, New York, NY 10016.

Contents

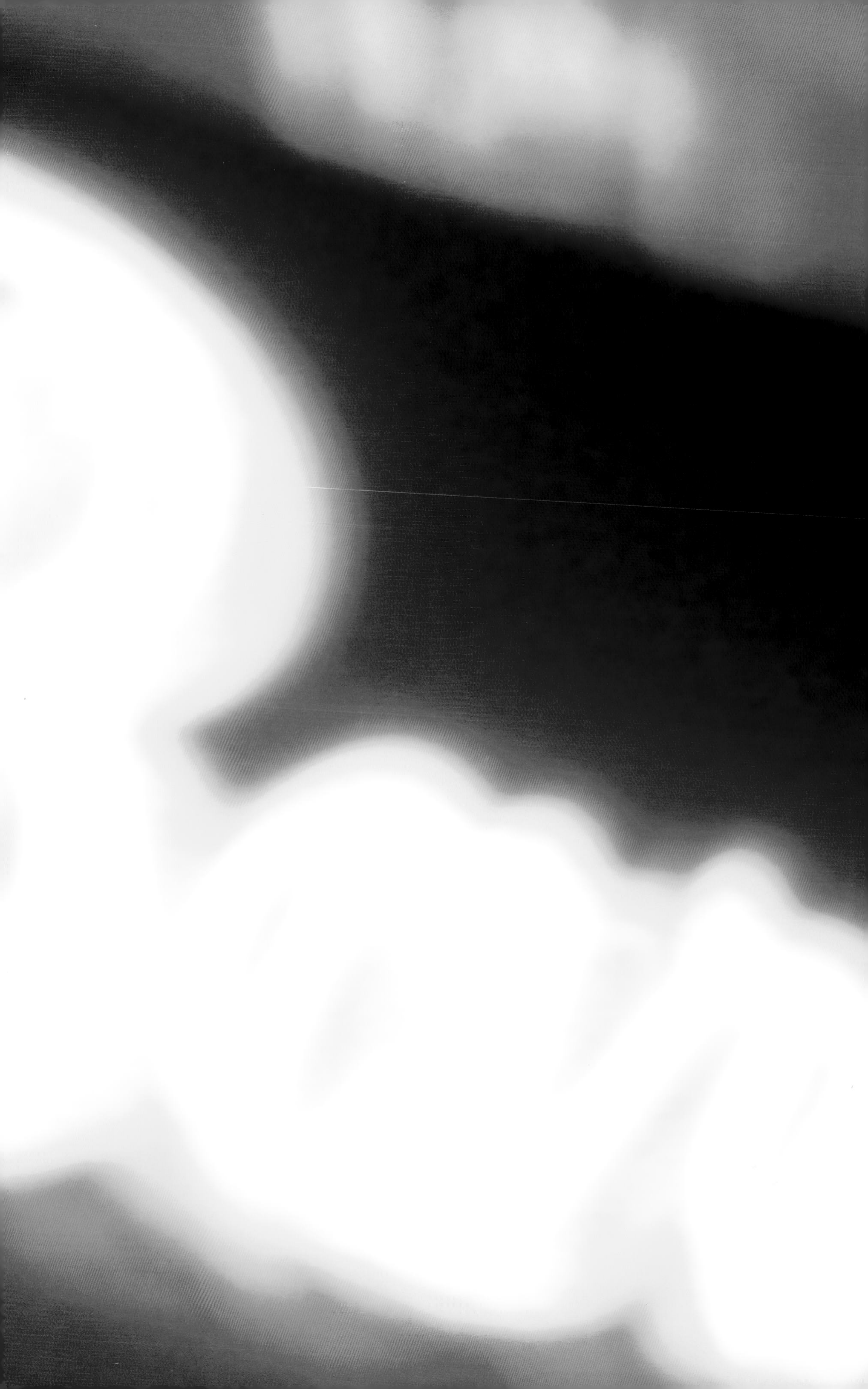

Introduction

Those of us who grow up loving stories seem to follow an evolutionary path. At the start, we love fantasy, science fiction, tall tales of derring-do and the supernatural. Our eyes grow wide at talk of magic kingdoms, galactic empires and superhuman beings. The early fictional view of humanity is polarized into categories of good and evil, hero and villain, right and wrong.

But, as we continue growing, we start to see that, beneath their colorful and detailed trappings, these fables are often threadbare, inaccurate, ultimately unsatisfying. As our own lives become more difficult and confusing, our problems more subtle and ungraspable, so we begin to yearn for stories that will illuminate our confusion, that will resonate with the conflicting chords of adolescence and impending adulthood.

In my own case, a love of Asimov, Heinlein, Niven and Clarke, Howard and Leiber was abandoned for that of Leonard, Higgins, Thompson and Wambaugh, Chandler and Hammett.

I suspect the same is true for many of you reading this introduction.

My newly-found tales of crime and corruption were arguably still melodrama; human frailty and complexity writ large, with life or death consequences for the protagonists, but they fitted the world I perceived around me, the headlines in the newspapers and the images on TV.

It occurs to me that this progression represents a shift from outer to inner preoccupations. From the mysteries and terrors of deep space or the dark wood, our fears move to the even more worrying and shadowy depths of our secret lives; the battles not with aliens or monsters out there but the daily struggle with our own conscience and the emotions we harbor within.

Another suspicion I harbor about you, reader, is that you love comic strips.

Doesn't take a great detective to piece that one together, I'll admit.

Let me go further, though. Just as your preference for stories has mutated, I'm betting your taste in imagery has changed similarly. Once fascinated by detail, decoration, bright color and exaggeration, I'm pretty sure that you now find yourself increasingly drawn to efficient composition, economy of line, focused narrative and subtlety of draftsmanship.

I think we all know who the main suspects are, here. Let's just say that Krigstein, Craig, Toth and, yes, Miller are, if you like, in the frame.

Their skills honed on early tales of blood and thunder, such artists have brought new dimensions to the comic page. They have discovered that to depict titanic, yet largely internal, human conflicts in the purely external medium of the comic strip is a far greater challenge than enlivening even the most extravagant star fleet or goblin horde. We are all familiar with real life; its detail, its texture and its language.

One wrong word, one wrong look and the game's up.

Fortunately, Brubaker and Phillips (or Ed and Sean, as they're known to their associates) are hardened professionals, too.

Ed's dialogue is pitch perfect, crackling with the rhythms and accents of real flesh and blood and his narratives unfold with the unexpected inevitability of the truth. Working in utter harmony, Sean's seemingly effortless bands of pictures unerringly bring settings and characters to life with subtlety and, when needed, with explicit and convincing brutality.

The Criminal line-up wouldn't be complete without Val Staples, whose colors, equally flexible and sympathetic, add atmosphere and drama in exactly the right measure.

Not only are the stories this trio weaves individually enthralling and compelling but, collected together in this present volume, the larger tapestry becomes apparent as characters stumble in and out of each other's stories and a rich shared history emerges from the interplay of incidents.

The effect is mesmerizing and, in re-reading the material for this introduction, I have become lost many times in the narrative, often forgetting that I'm reading a story on a printed page. That's something that happened to me often in my early days of enjoying stories but, with age and professional detachment, happens very rarely now.

Paradoxically, the highest compliment I can pay Ed, Sean and Val, as a lifelong lover of stories, is that what follows never seems like one.

Dave Gibbons
July 2009

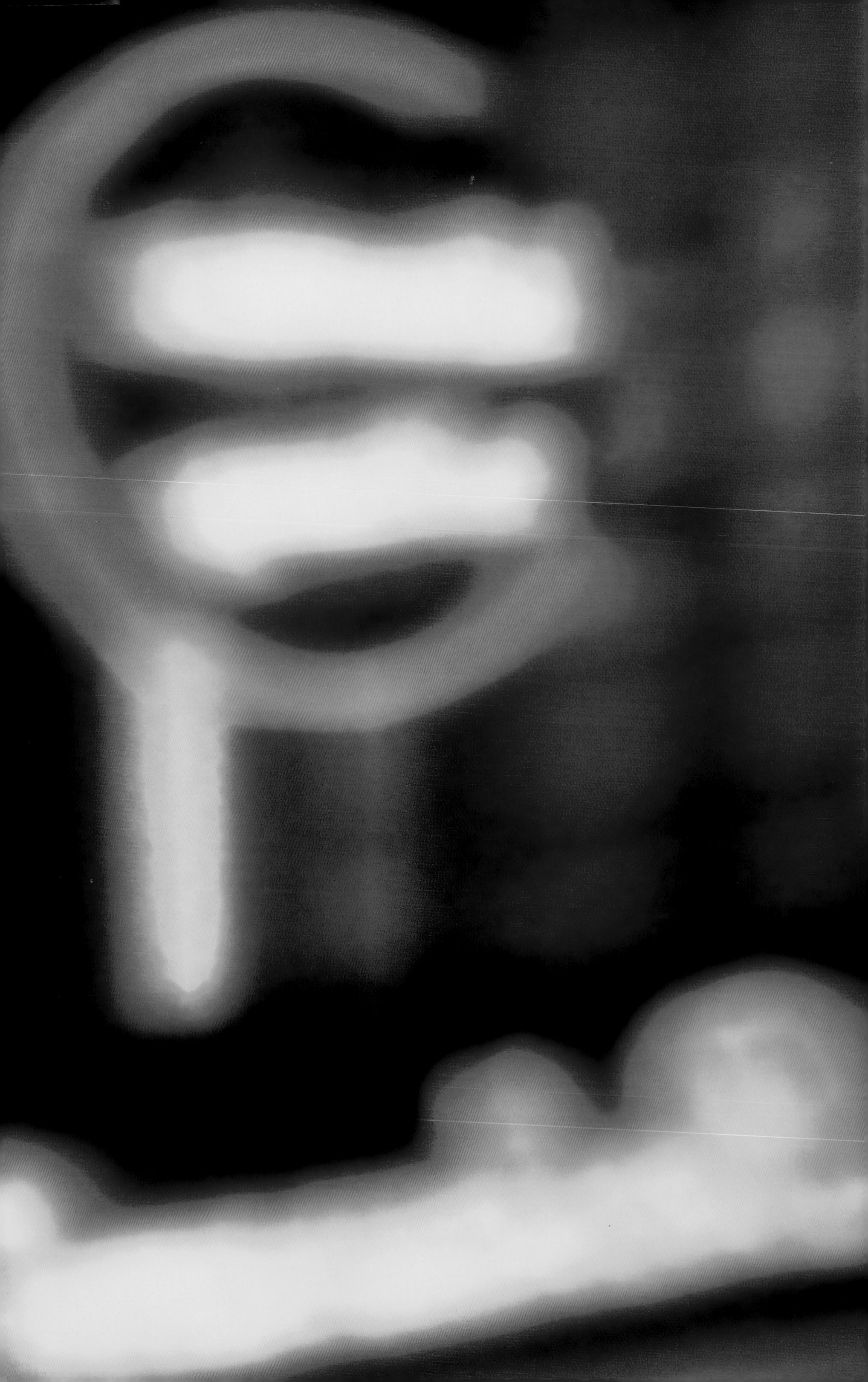

Coward

CRIMINAL: Coward

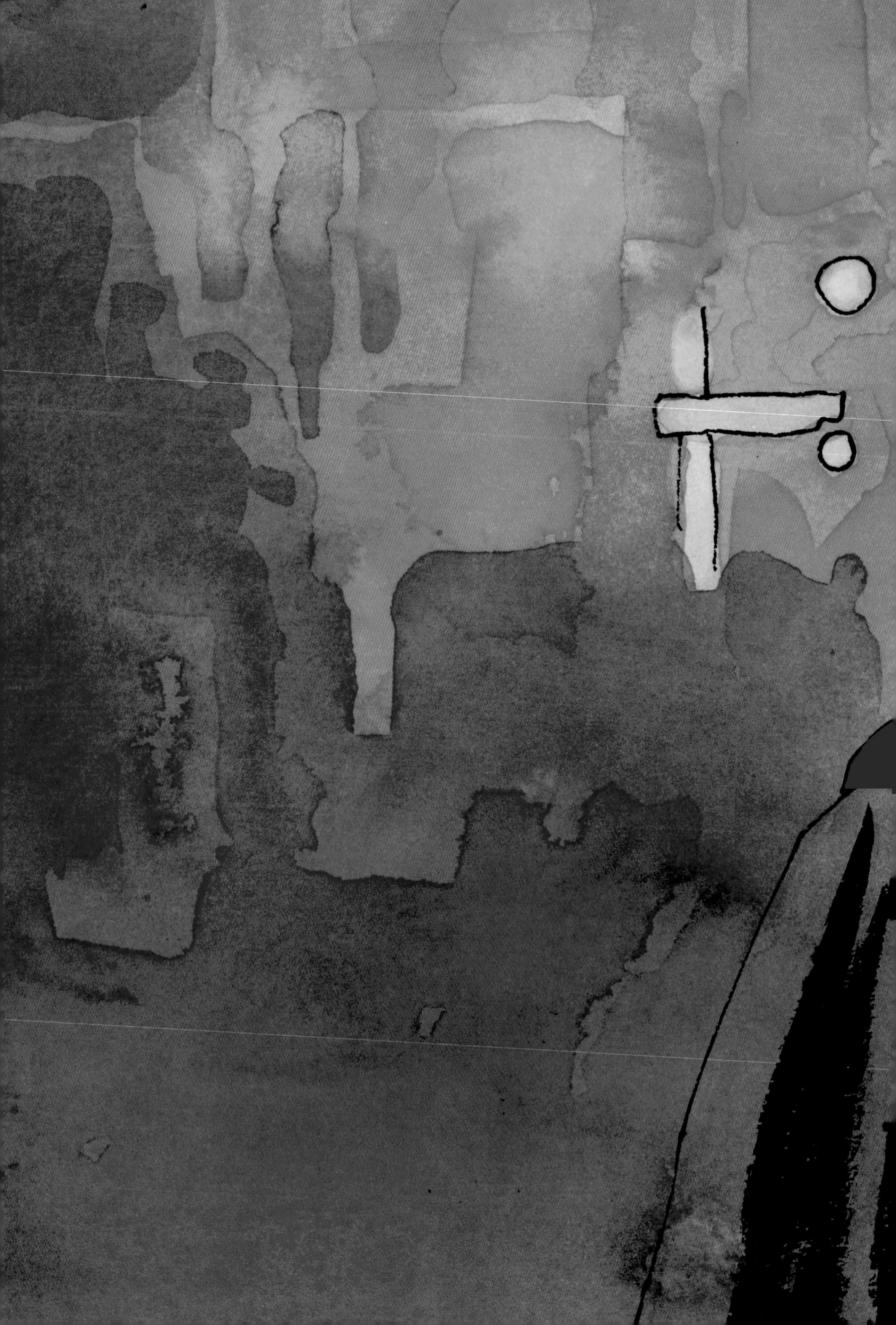

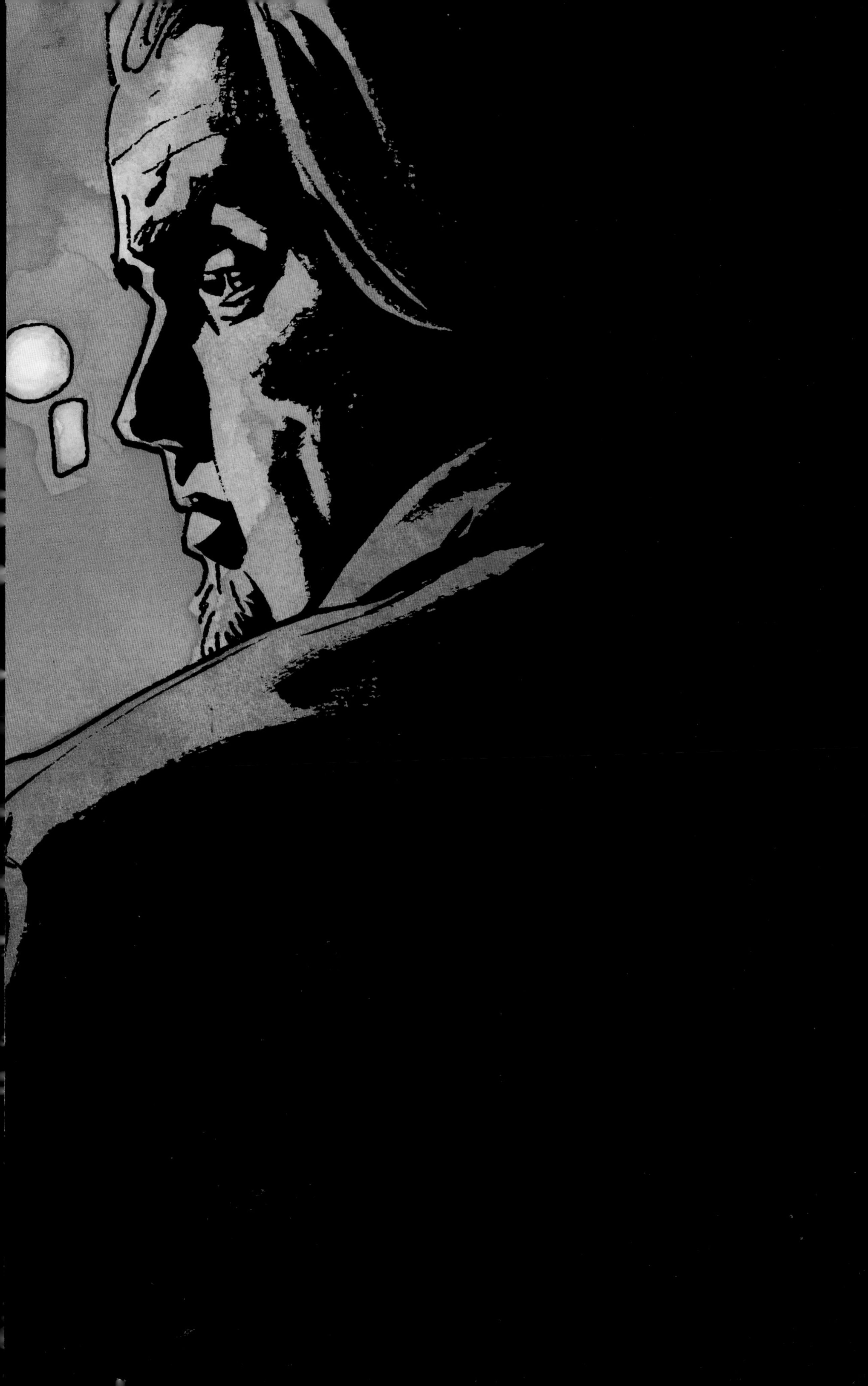

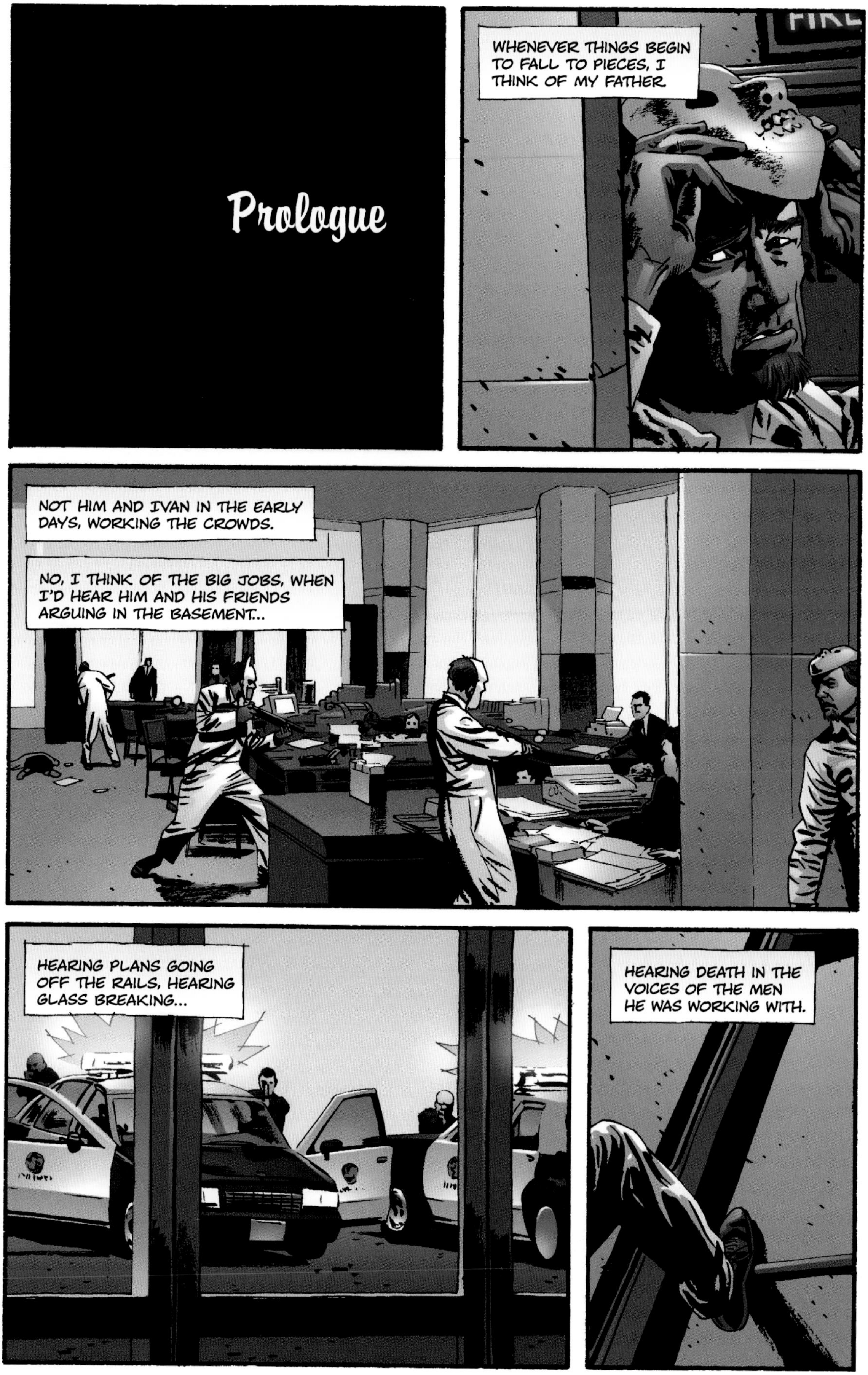
Prologue
WHENEVER THINGS BEGIN TO FALL TO PIECES, I THINK OF MY FATHER
NOT HIM AND IVAN IN THE EARLY DAYS, WORKING THE CROWDS.
NO, I THINK OF THE BIG JOBS, WHEN I'D HEAR HIM AND HIS FRIENDS ARGUING IN THE BASEMENT...
HEARING PLANS GOING OFF THE RAILS, HEARING GLASS BREAKING...
HEARING DEATH IN THE VOICES OF THE MEN HE WAS WORKING WITH.

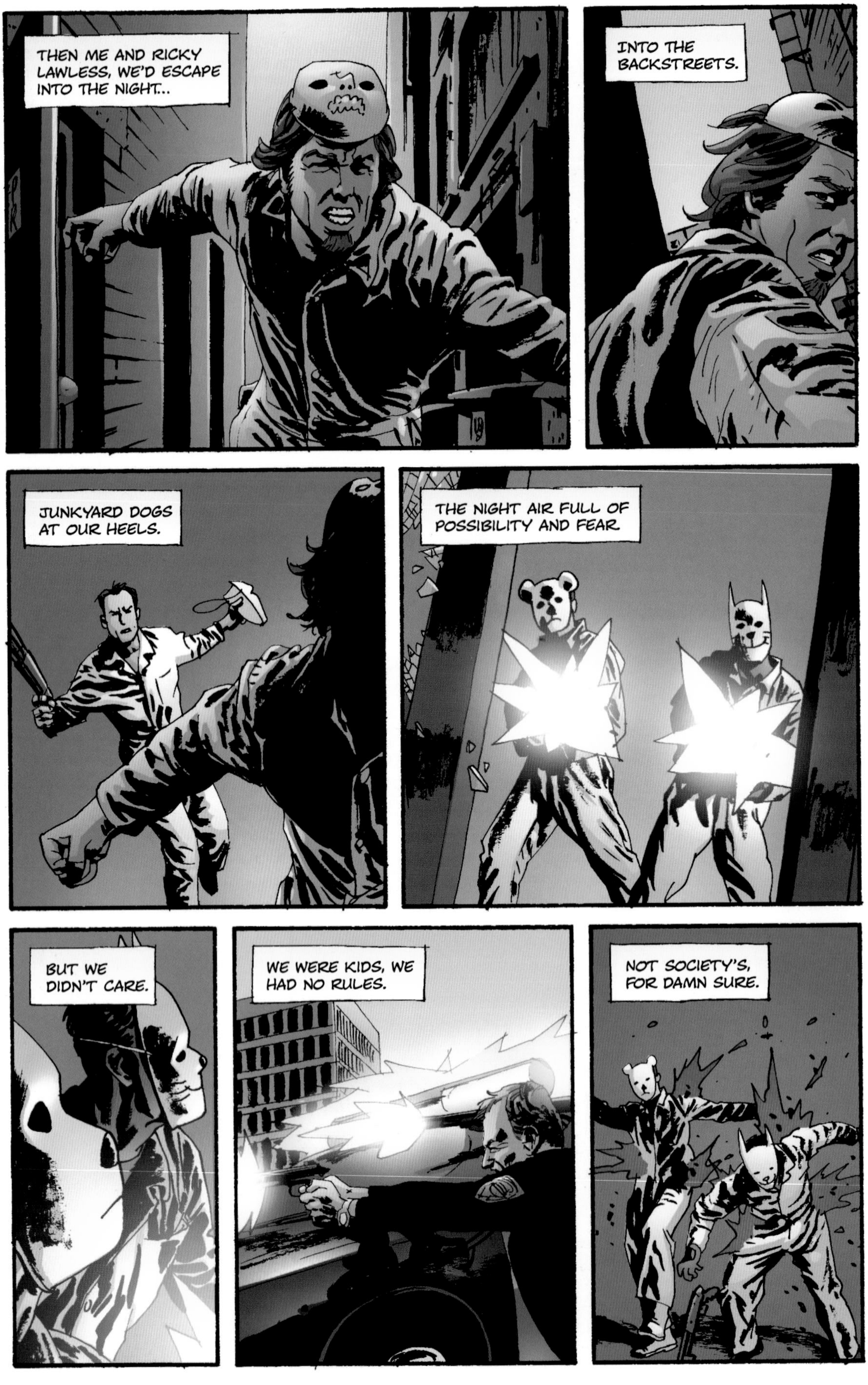
THEN ME AND RICKY LAWLESS, WE'D ESCAPE INTO THE NIGHT...
INTO THE BACKSTREETS.
JUNKYARD DOGS AT OUR HEELS.
THE NIGHT AIR FULL OF POSSIBILITY AND FEAR
BUT WE DIDN'T CARE.
WE WERE KIDS, WE HAD NO RULES.
NOT SOCIETY'S, FOR DAMN SURE.

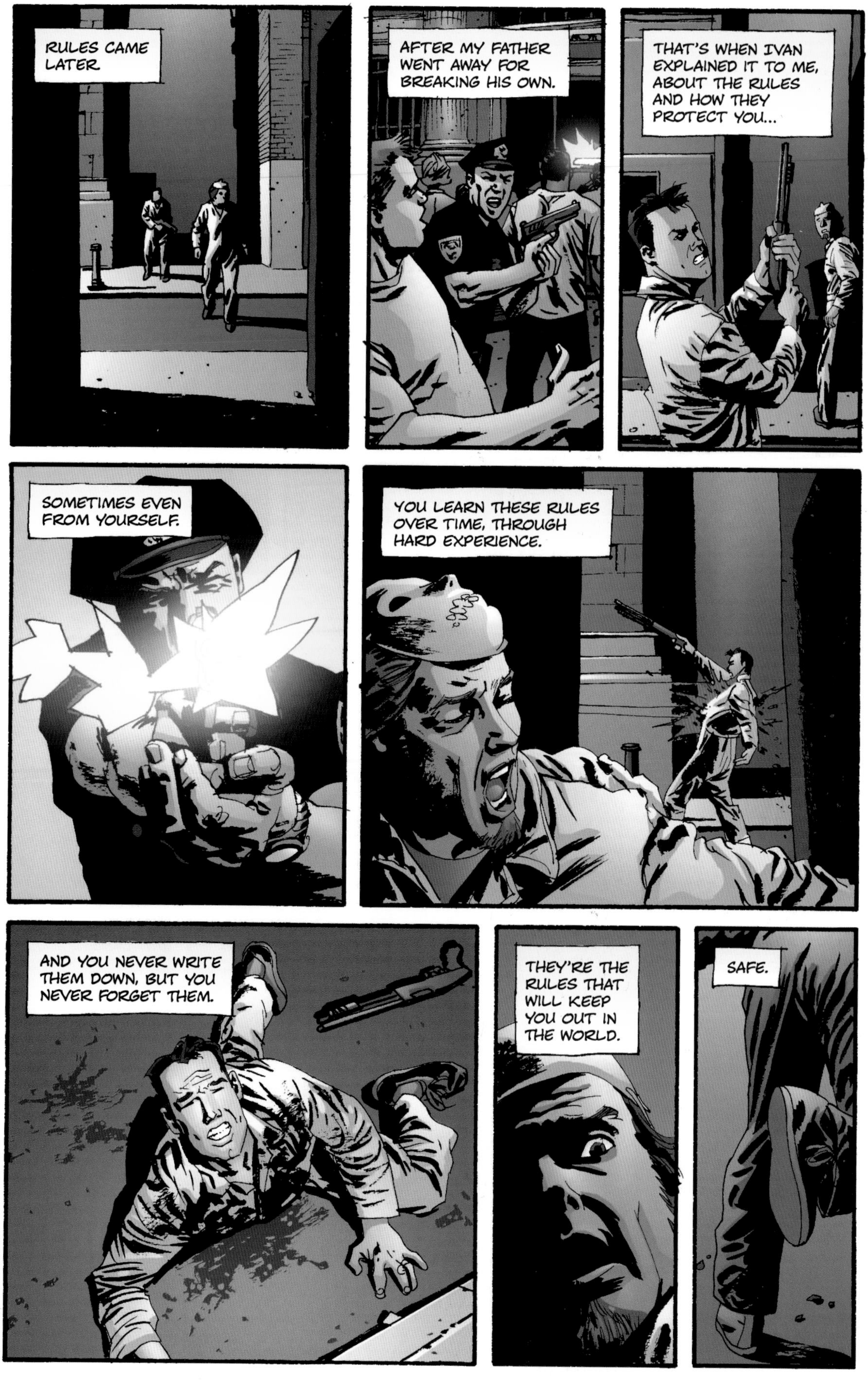
RULES CAME LATER.
AFTER MY FATHER WENT AWAY FOR BREAKING HIS OWN.
THAT'S WHEN IVAN EXPLAINED IT TO ME, ABOUT THE RULES AND HOW THEY PROTECT YOU...
SOMETIMES EVEN FROM YOURSELF.
YOU LEARN THESE RULES OVER TIME, THROUGH HARD EXPERIENCE.
AND YOU NEVER WRITE THEM DOWN, BUT YOU NEVER FORGET THEM.
THEY'RE THE RULES THAT WILL KEEP YOU OUT IN THE WORLD.
SAFE.

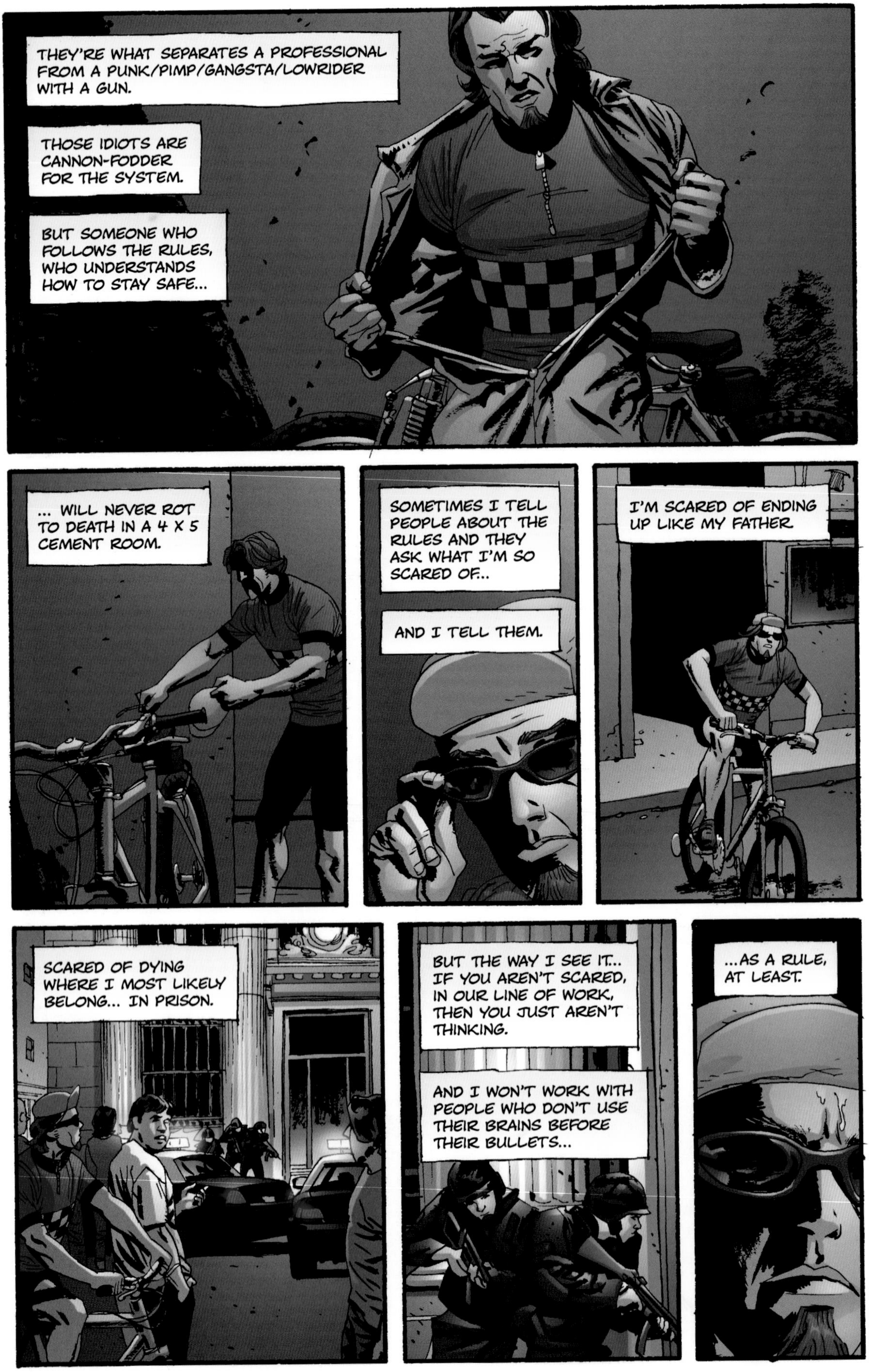
THEY'RE WHAT SEPARATES A PROFESSIONAL FROM A PUNK/PIMP/GANGSTA/LOWRIDER WITH A GUN.
THOSE IDIOTS ARE CANNON-FODDER FOR THE SYSTEM.
BUT SOMEONE WHO FOLLOWS THE RULES, WHO UNDERSTANDS HOW TO STAY SAFE...
... WILL NEVER ROT TO DEATH IN A 4 X 5 CEMENT ROOM.
SOMETIMES I TELL PEOPLE ABOUT THE RULES AND THEY ASK WHAT I'M SO SCARED OF...
AND I TELL THEM.
I'M SCARED OF ENDING UP LIKE MY FATHER.
SCARED OF DYING WHERE I MOST LIKELY BELONG... IN PRISON.
BUT THE WAY I SEE IT... IF YOU AREN'T SCARED, IN OUR LINE OF WORK, THEN YOU JUST AREN'T THINKING.
AND I WON'T WORK WITH PEOPLE WHO DON'T USE THEIR BRAINS BEFORE THEIR BULLETS...
...AS A RULE, AT LEAST.

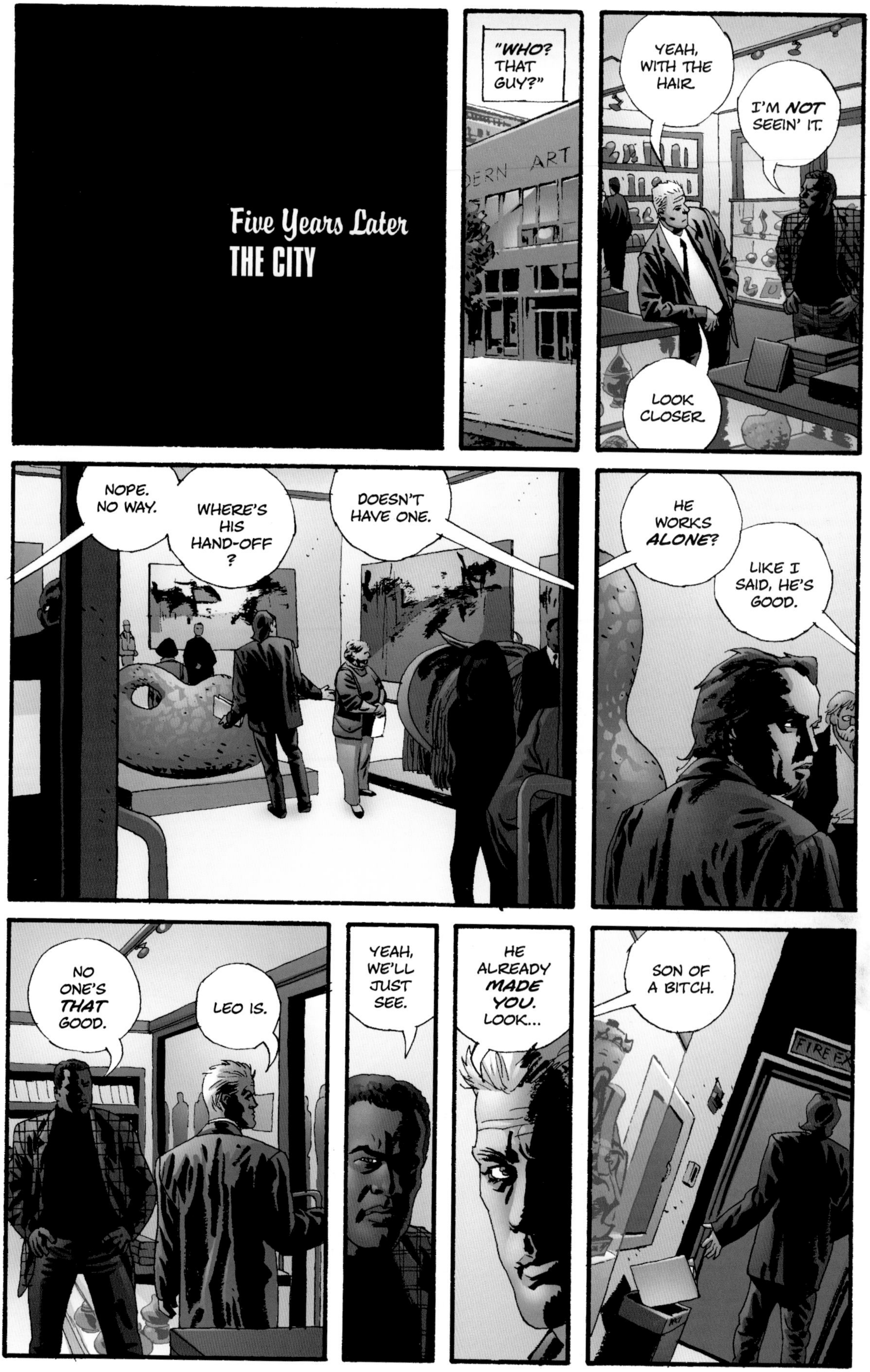
Five Years Later
THE CITY
"WHO? THAT GUY?"
YEAH, WITH THE HAIR
I'M NOT SEEIN' IT.
LOOK CLOSER
NOPE. NO WAY.
WHERE'S HIS HAND-OFF?
DOESN'T HAVE ONE.
HE WORKS ALONE?
LIKE I SAID, HE'S GOOD.
NO ONE'S THAT GOOD.
LEO IS.
YEAH, WE'LL JUST SEE.
HE ALREADY MADE YOU. LOOK...
SON OF A BITCH.

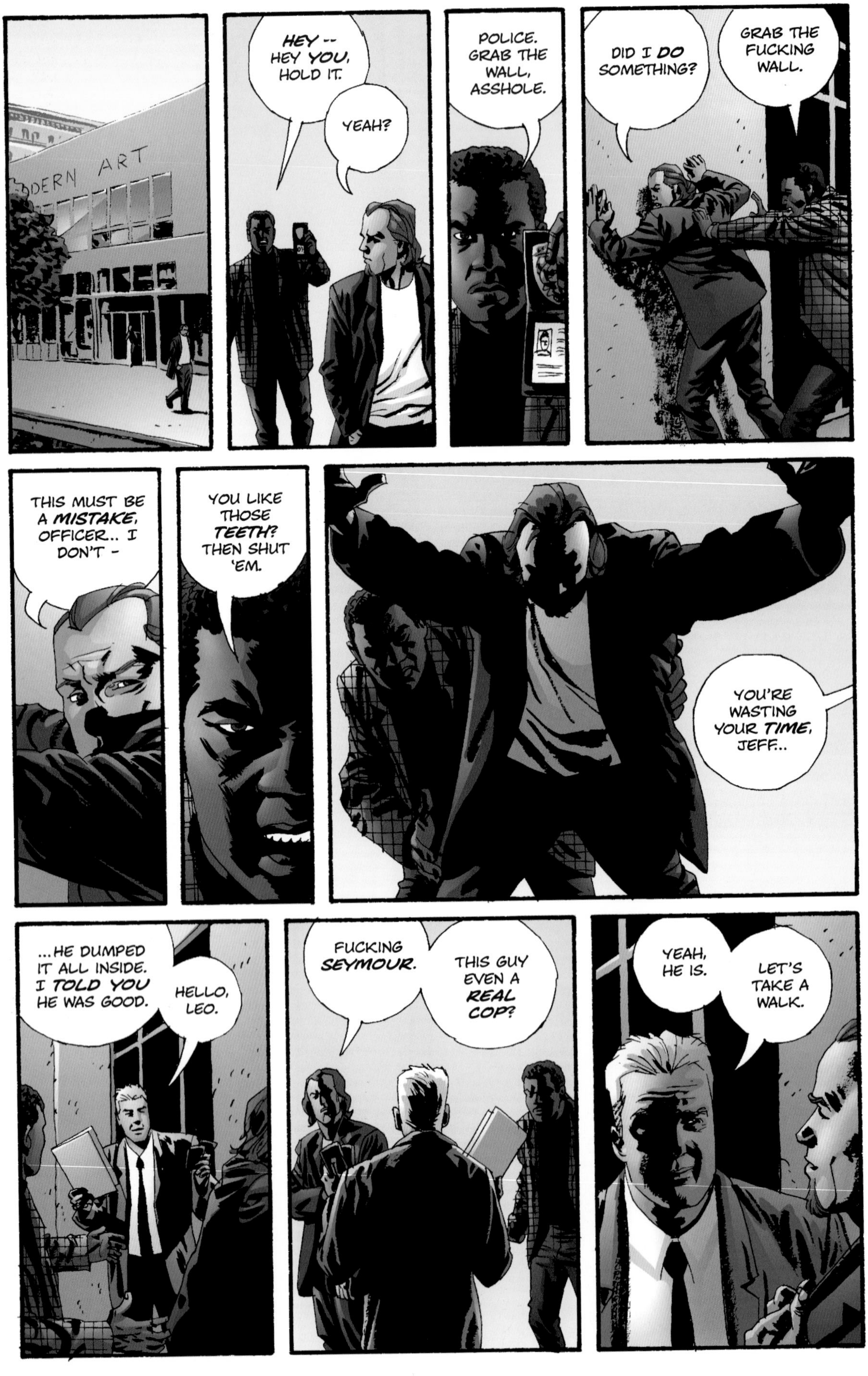

DERN ART
HEY -- HEY YOU, HOLD IT.
YEAH?
POLICE. GRAB THE WALL, ASSHOLE.
DID I DO SOMETHING?
GRAB THE FUCKING WALL.
THIS MUST BE A MISTAKE, OFFICER.. I DON'T -
YOU LIKE THOSE TEETH? THEN SHUT 'EM.
YOU'RE WASTING YOUR TIME, JEFF..
...HE DUMPED IT ALL INSIDE. I TOLD YOU HE WAS GOOD.
HELLO, LEO.
FUCKING SEYMOUR.
THIS GUY EVEN A REAL COP?
YEAH, HE IS.
LET'S TAKE A WALK.

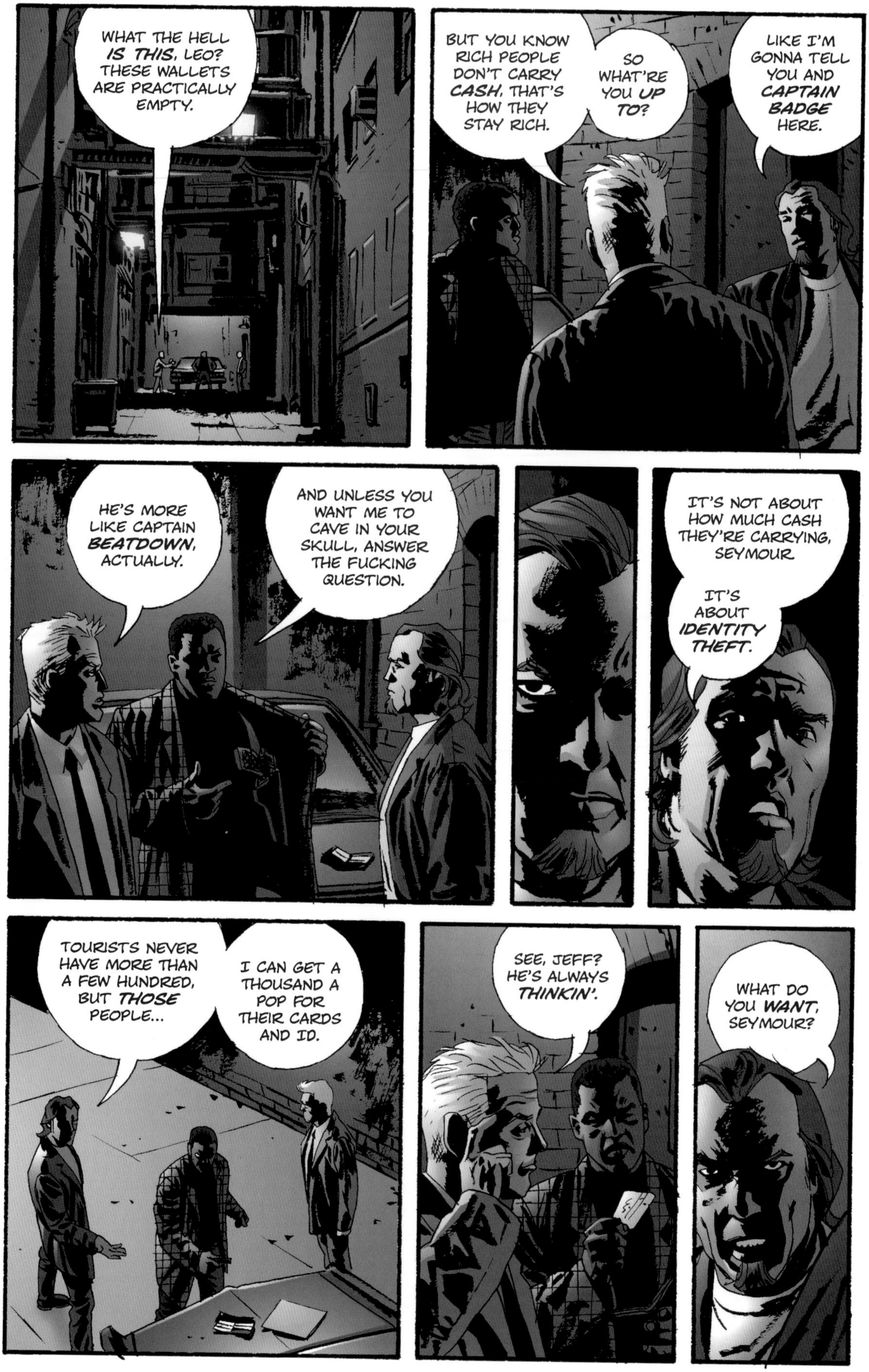
WHAT THE HELL IS THIS, LEO? THESE WALLETS ARE PRACTICALLY EMPTY.
BUT YOU KNOW RICH PEOPLE DON'T CARRY CASH. THAT'S HOW THEY STAY RICH.
SO WHAT'RE YOU UP TO?
LIKE I'M GONNA TELL YOU AND CAPTAIN BADGE HERE.
HE'S MORE LIKE CAPTAIN BEATDOWN, ACTUALLY.
AND UNLESS YOU WANT ME TO CAVE IN YOUR SKULL, ANSWER THE FUCKING QUESTION.
IT'S NOT ABOUT HOW MUCH CASH THEY'RE CARRYING, SEYMOUR.
IT'S ABOUT IDENTITY THEFT.
TOURISTS NEVER HAVE MORE THAN A FEW HUNDRED, BUT THOSE PEOPLE...
I CAN GET A THOUSAND A POP FOR THEIR CARDS AND ID.
SEE, JEFF? HE'S ALWAYS THINKIN'.
WHAT DO YOU WANT, SEYMOUR?

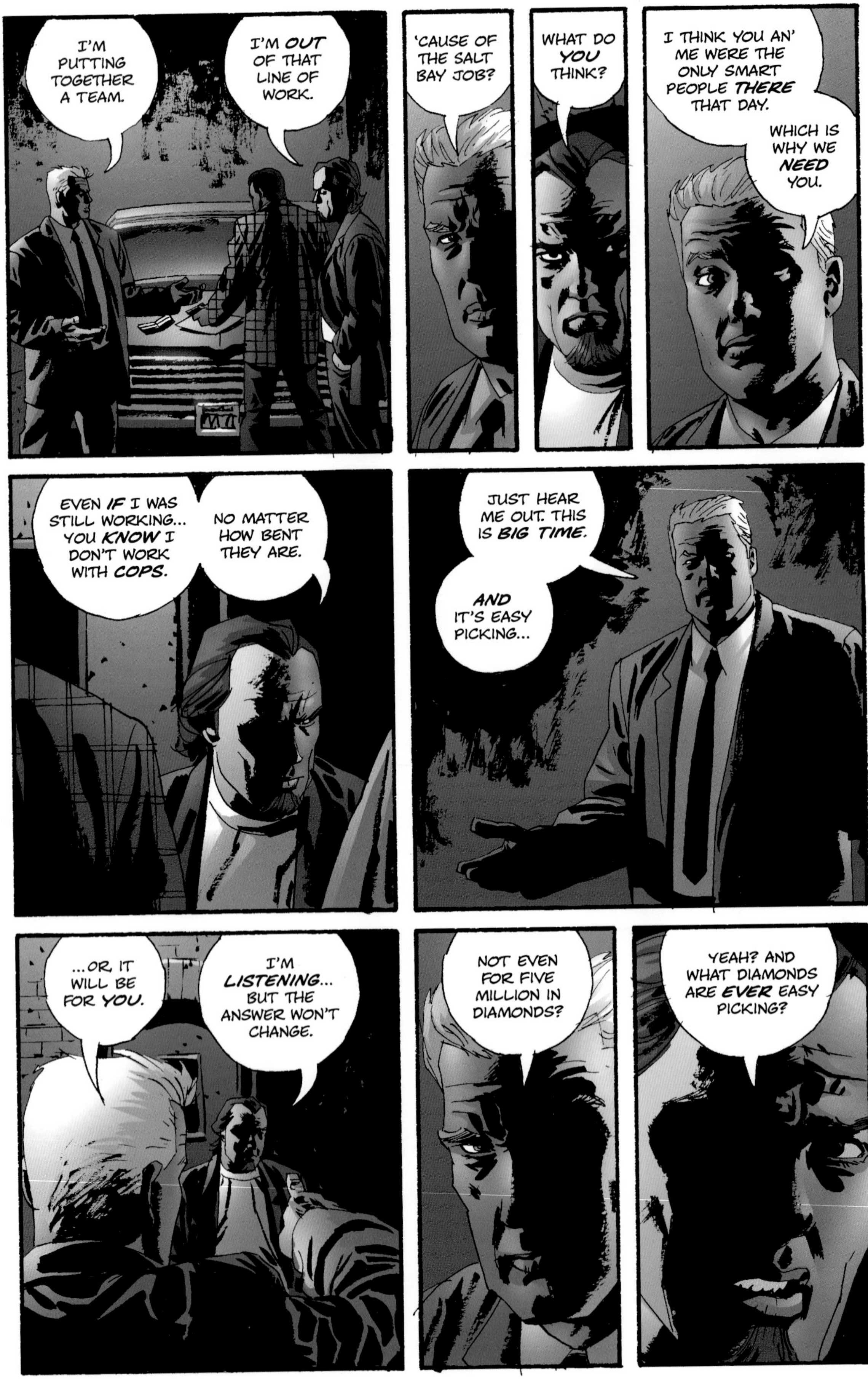
I'M PUTTING TOGETHER A TEAM.
I'M OUT OF THAT LINE OF WORK.
'CAUSE OF THE SALT BAY JOB?
WHAT DO YOU THINK?
I THINK YOU AN' ME WERE THE ONLY SMART PEOPLE THERE THAT DAY.
WHICH IS WHY WE NEED YOU.
EVEN IF I WAS STILL WORKING... YOU KNOW I DON'T WORK WITH COPS.
NO MATTER HOW BENT THEY ARE.
JUST HEAR ME OUT. THIS IS BIG TIME.
AND IT'S EASY PICKING...
...OR, IT WILL BE FOR YOU.
I'M LISTENING... BUT THE ANSWER WON'T CHANGE.
NOT EVEN FOR FIVE MILLION IN DIAMONDS?
YEAH? AND WHAT DIAMONDS ARE EVER EASY PICKING?

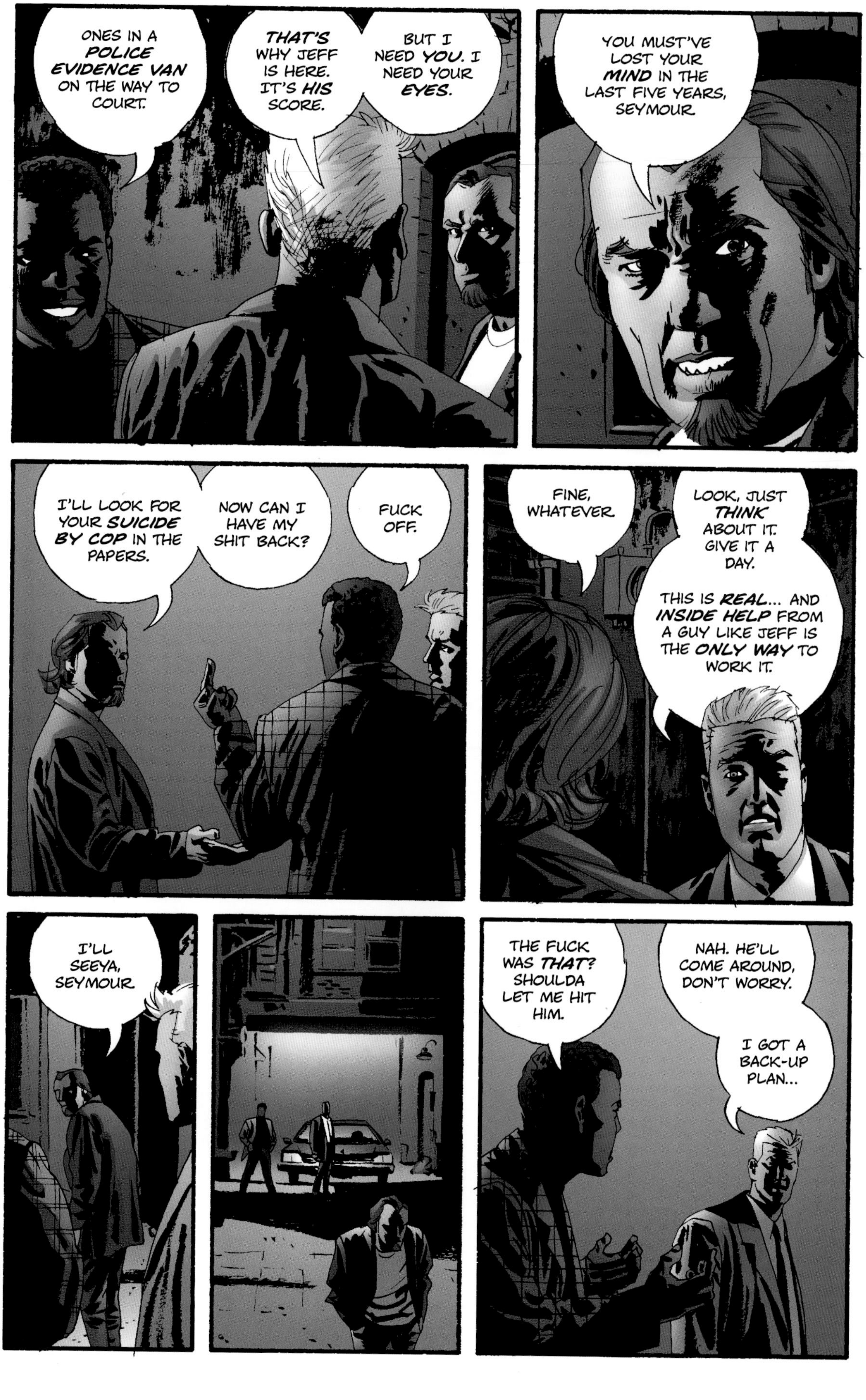
ONES IN A POLICE EVIDENCE VAN ON THE WAY TO COURT.
THAT'S WHY JEFF IS HERE. IT'S HIS SCORE.
BUT I NEED YOU. I NEED YOUR EYES.
YOU MUST'VE LOST YOUR MIND IN THE LAST FIVE YEARS, SEYMOUR.
I'LL LOOK FOR YOUR SUICIDE BY COP IN THE PAPERS.
NOW CAN I HAVE MY SHIT BACK?
FUCK OFF.
FINE, WHATEVER.
LOOK, JUST THINK ABOUT IT. GIVE IT A DAY.
THIS IS REAL... AND INSIDE HELP FROM A GUY LIKE JEFF IS THE ONLY WAY TO WORK IT.
I'LL SEEYA, SEYMOUR.
THE FUCK WAS THAT? SHOULDA LET ME HIT HIM.
NAH. HE'LL COME AROUND, DON'T WORRY.
I GOT A BACK-UP PLAN...

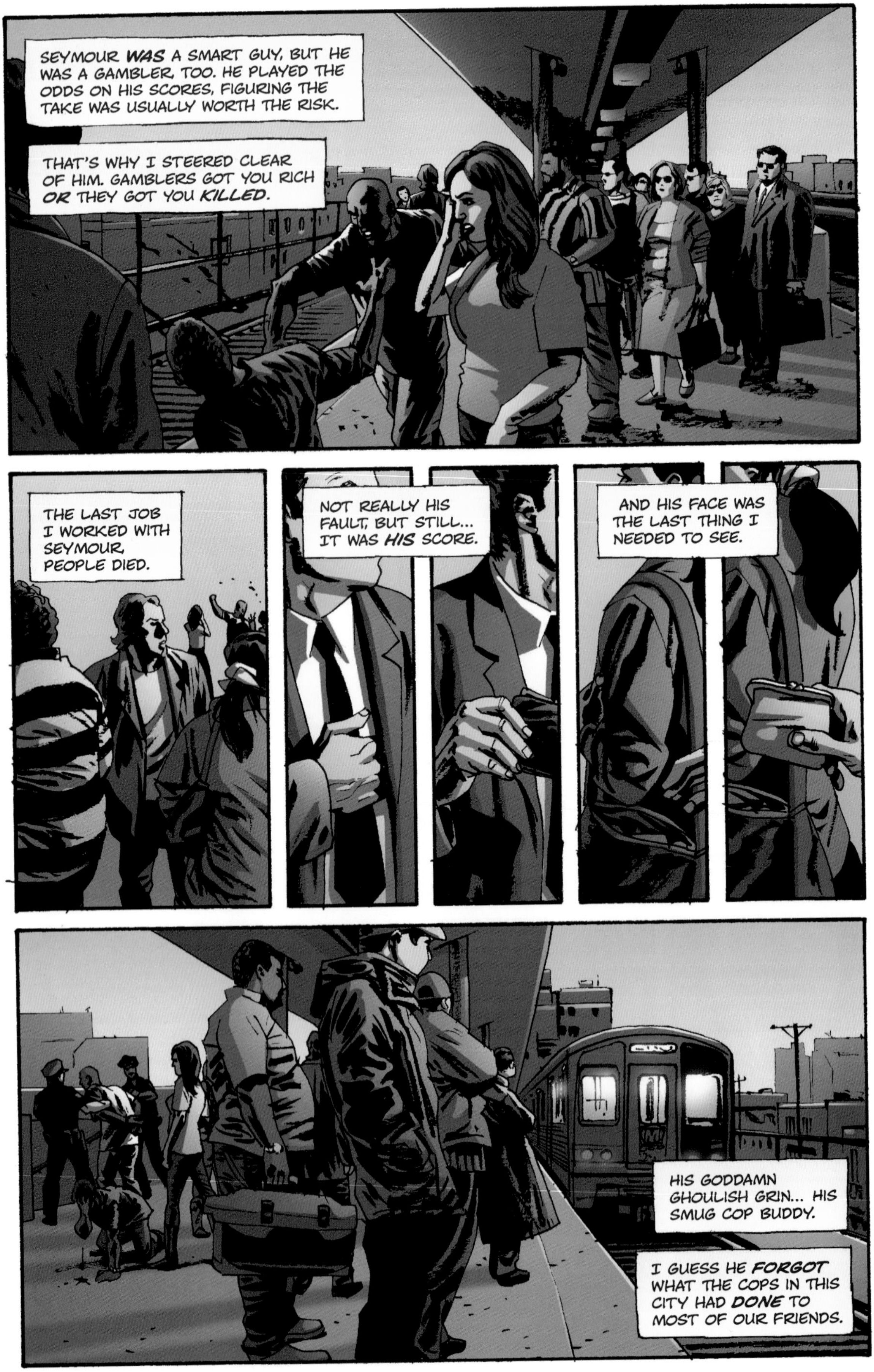
SEYMOUR WAS A SMART GUY, BUT HE WAS A GAMBLER, TOO. HE PLAYED THE ODDS ON HIS SCORES, FIGURING THE TAKE WAS USUALLY WORTH THE RISK.
THAT'S WHY I STEERED CLEAR OF HIM. GAMBLERS GOT YOU RICH OR THEY GOT YOU KILLED.
THE LAST JOB I WORKED WITH SEYMOUR, PEOPLE DIED.
NOT REALLY HIS FAULT, BUT STILL... IT WAS HIS SCORE.
AND HIS FACE WAS THE LAST THING I NEEDED TO SEE.
HIS GODDAMN GHOULISH GRIN... HIS SMUG COP BUDDY.
I GUESS HE FORGOT WHAT THE COPS IN THIS CITY HAD DONE TO MOST OF OUR FRIENDS.

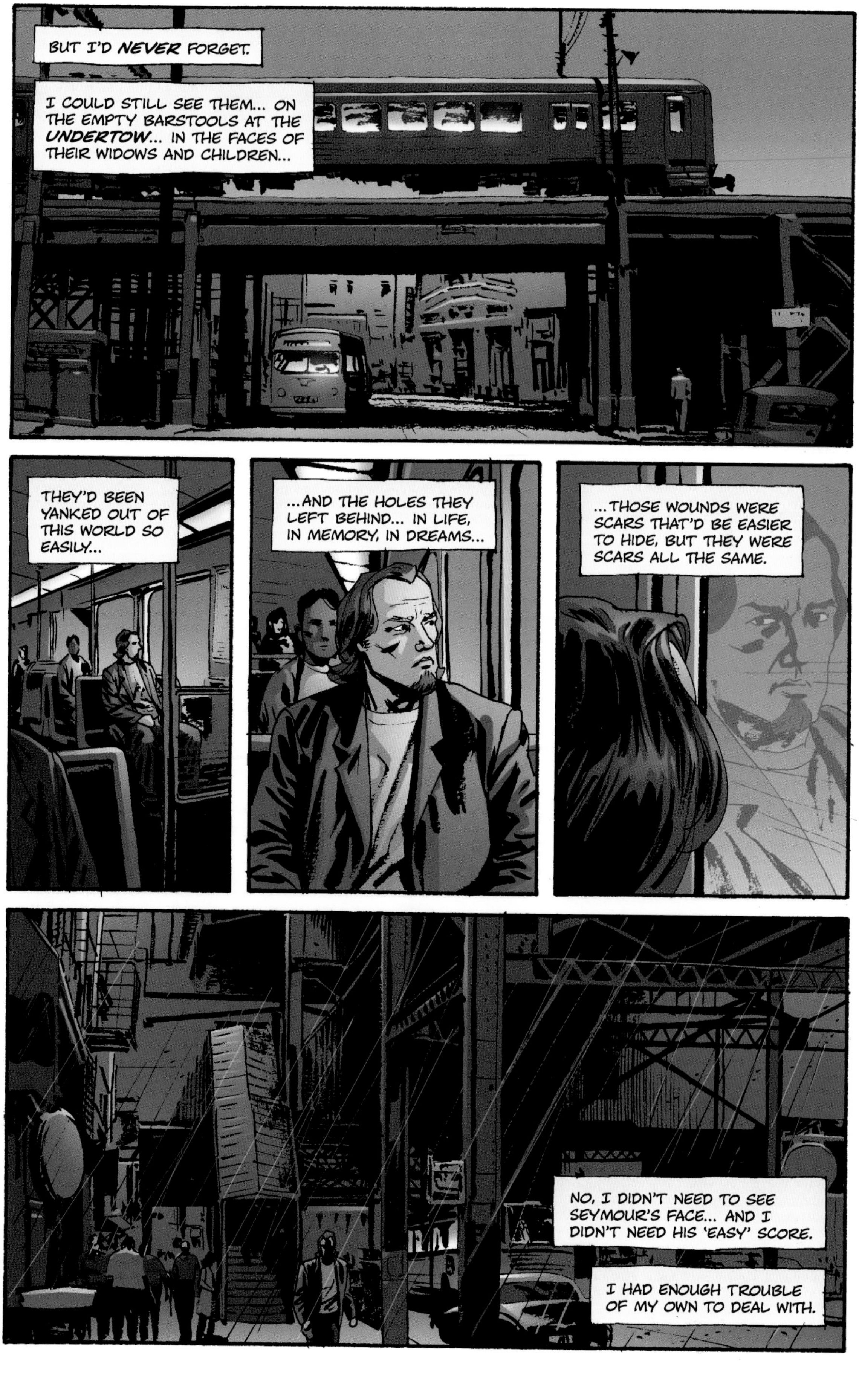
BUT I'D NEVER FORGET.
I COULD STILL SEE THEM... ON THE EMPTY BARSTOOLS AT THE UNDERTOW... IN THE FACES OF THEIR WIDOWS AND CHILDREN...
THEY'D BEEN YANKED OUT OF THIS WORLD SO EASILY...
...AND THE HOLES THEY LEFT BEHIND... IN LIFE, IN MEMORY, IN DREAMS...
...THOSE WOUNDS WERE SCARS THAT'D BE EASIER TO HIDE, BUT THEY WERE SCARS ALL THE SAME.
NO, I DIDN'T NEED TO SEE SEYMOUR'S FACE... AND I DIDN'T NEED HIS 'EASY' SCORE.
I HAD ENOUGH TROUBLE OF MY OWN TO DEAL WITH.

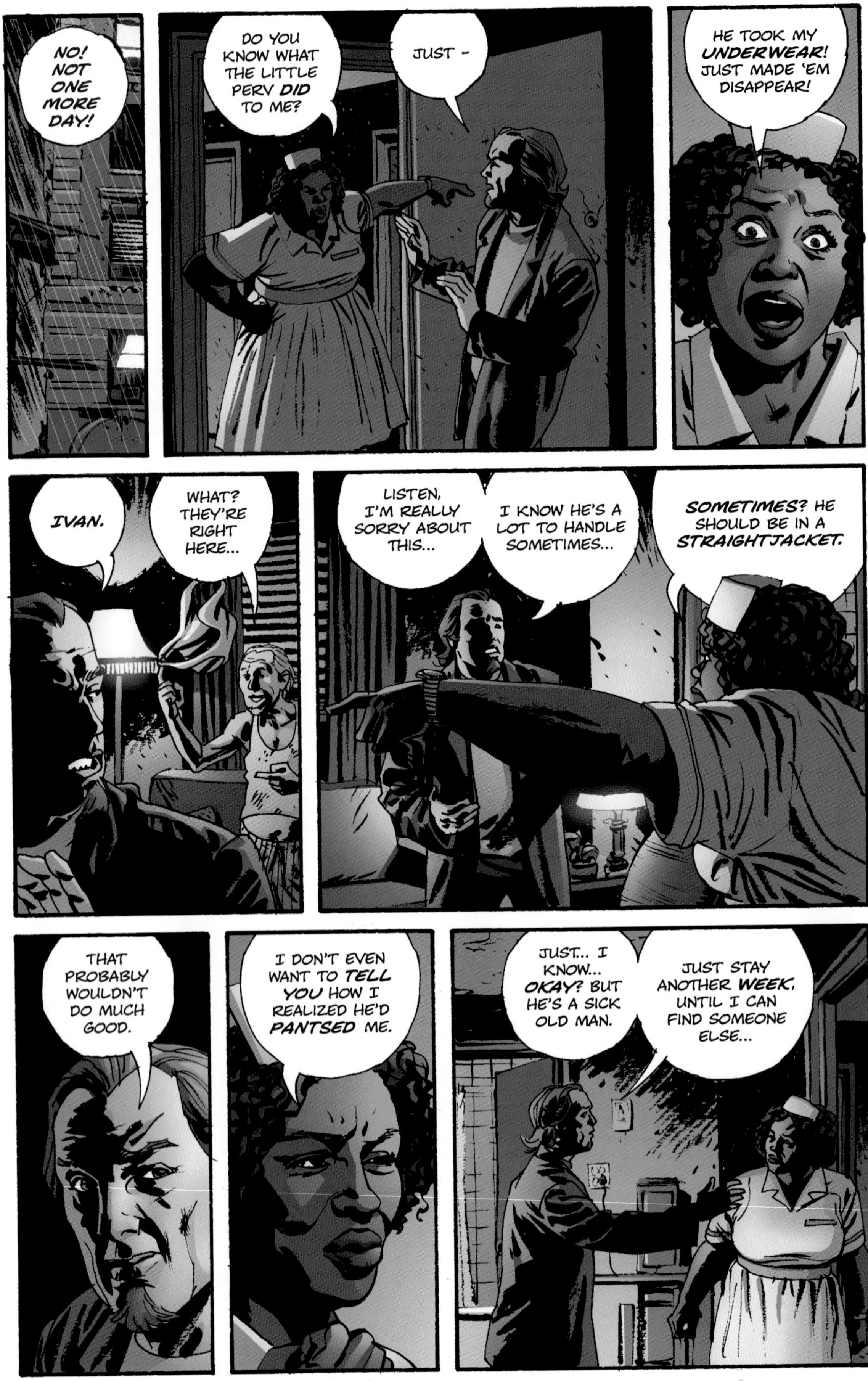
NO! NOT ONE MORE DAY!
DO YOU KNOW WHAT THE LITTLE PERV DID TO ME?
JUST -
HE TOOK MY UNDERWEAR! JUST MADE 'EM DISAPPEAR!
IVAN.
WHAT? THEY'RE RIGHT HERE...
LISTEN, I'M REALLY SORRY ABOUT THIS...
I KNOW HE'S A LOT TO HANDLE SOMETIMES...
SOMETIMES? HE SHOULD BE IN A STRAIGHTJACKET.
THAT PROBABLY WOULDN'T DO MUCH GOOD.
I DON'T EVEN WANT TO TELL YOU HOW I REALIZED HE'D PANTSED ME.
JUST... I KNOW... OKAY? BUT HE'S A SICK OLD MAN.
JUST STAY ANOTHER WEEK, UNTIL I CAN FIND SOMEONE ELSE...

I'M SORRY, LEO... HE'S JUST TOO MUCH.

HE SHOULD BE IN A *HOME*... ONE WITH ALL *MALE* NURSES.

I CAN'T AFFORD THAT... NOT THE KIND OF PLACE HE'D NEED.

WITH HIS... *QUIRKS*.

THEN YOU NEED TO GET HIM CLEAN, LEO.

BUT WHATEVER YOU DO, YOU'LL HAVE TO FIND SOMEONE *ELSE* FOR TOMORROW.

'CAUSE IF HE TOUCHED ME AGAIN, I'M AFRAID I'LL KILL HIM.

NICE, IVAN... REAL NICE.

WHAT DID I *DO*, TOMMY?

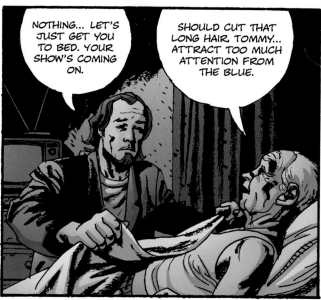

NOTHING... LET'S JUST GET YOU TO BED. YOUR SHOW'S COMING ON.

SHOULD CUT THAT LONG HAIR, TOMMY... ATTRACT TOO MUCH ATTENTION FROM THE BLUE.

I WILL... TOMORROW.

I PROMISE.

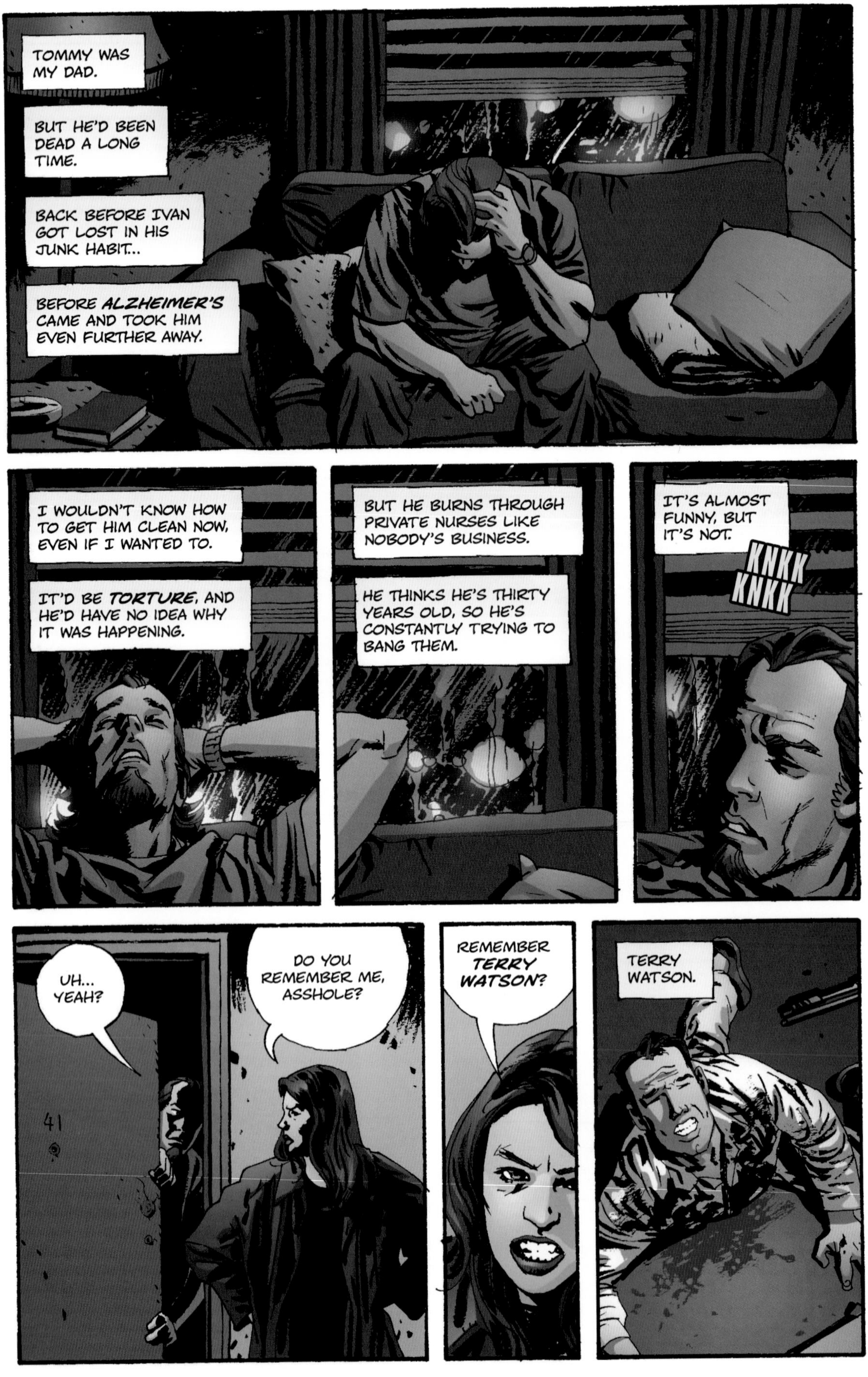
TOMMY WAS MY DAD.
BUT HE'D BEEN DEAD A LONG TIME.
BACK BEFORE IVAN GOT LOST IN HIS JUNK HABIT...
BEFORE ALZHEIMER'S CAME AND TOOK HIM EVEN FURTHER AWAY.
I WOULDN'T KNOW HOW TO GET HIM CLEAN NOW, EVEN IF I WANTED TO.
IT'D BE TORTURE, AND HE'D HAVE NO IDEA WHY IT WAS HAPPENING.
BUT HE BURNS THROUGH PRIVATE NURSES LIKE NOBODY'S BUSINESS.
HE THINKS HE'S THIRTY YEARS OLD, SO HE'S CONSTANTLY TRYING TO BANG THEM.
IT'S ALMOST FUNNY, BUT IT'S NOT.
KNKK KNKK
UH... YEAH?
DO YOU REMEMBER ME, ASSHOLE?
41
REMEMBER TERRY WATSON?
TERRY WATSON.

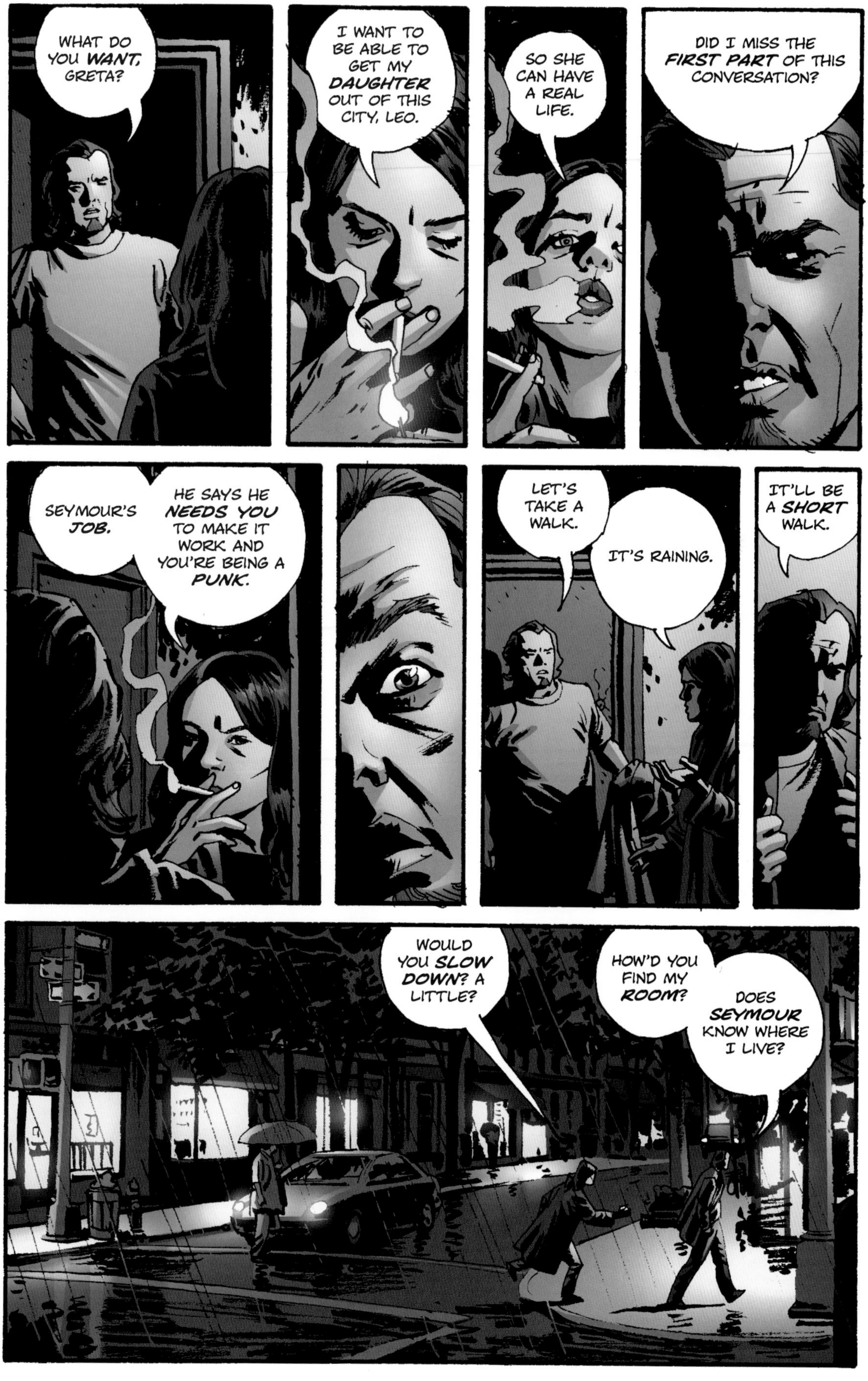
WHAT DO YOU WANT, GRETA?
I WANT TO BE ABLE TO GET MY DAUGHTER OUT OF THIS CITY, LEO.
SO SHE CAN HAVE A REAL LIFE.
DID I MISS THE FIRST PART OF THIS CONVERSATION?
SEYMOUR'S JOB.
HE SAYS HE NEEDS YOU TO MAKE IT WORK AND YOU'RE BEING A PUNK.
LET'S TAKE A WALK.
IT'S RAINING.
IT'LL BE A SHORT WALK.
WOULD YOU SLOW DOWN? A LITTLE?
HOW'D YOU FIND MY ROOM?
DOES SEYMOUR KNOW WHERE I LIVE?

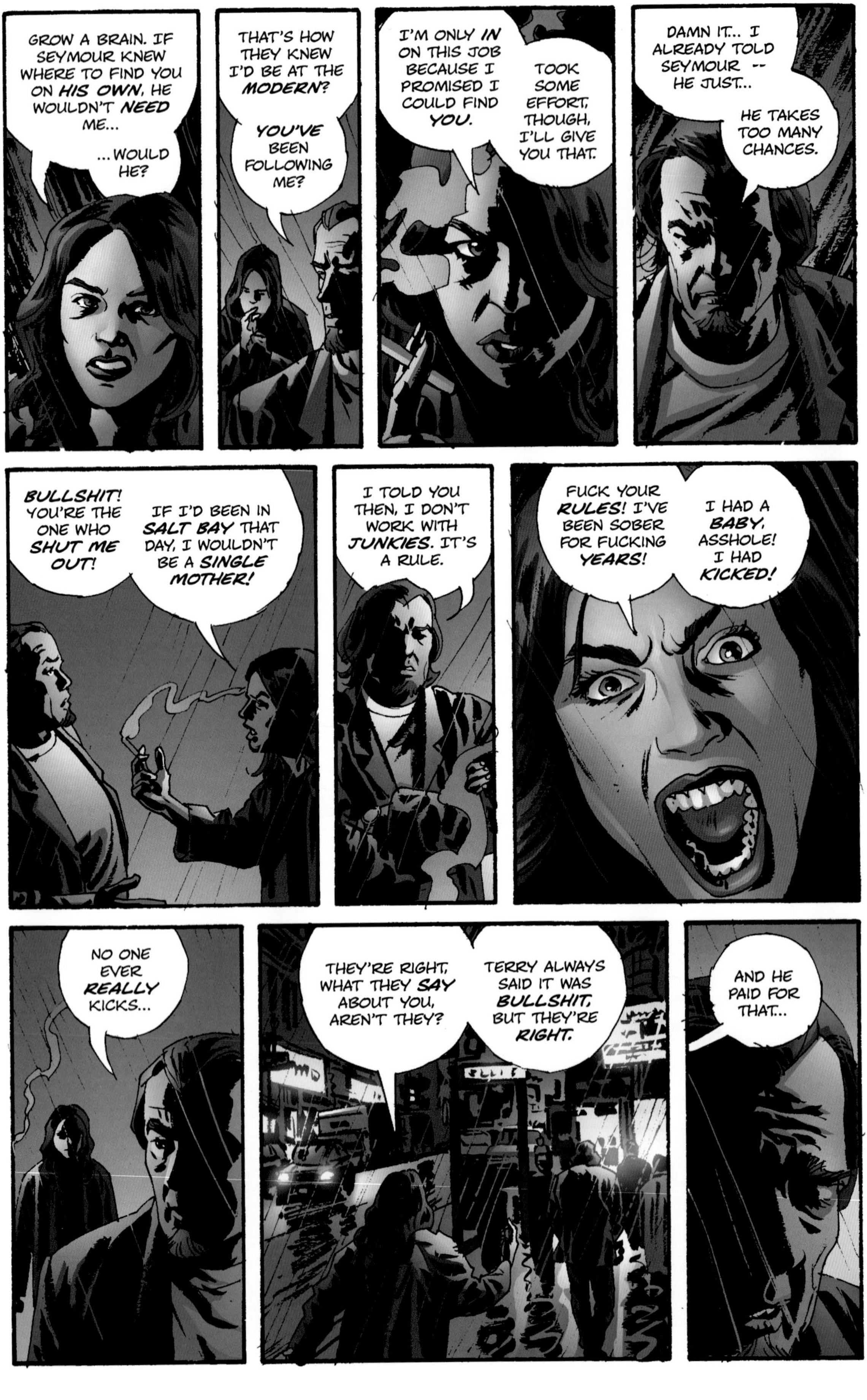
GROW A BRAIN. IF SEYMOUR KNEW WHERE TO FIND YOU ON HIS OWN, HE WOULDN'T NEED ME...
...WOULD HE?
THAT'S HOW THEY KNEW I'D BE AT THE MODERN?
YOU'VE BEEN FOLLOWING ME?
I'M ONLY IN ON THIS JOB BECAUSE I PROMISED I COULD FIND YOU.
TOOK SOME EFFORT, THOUGH, I'LL GIVE YOU THAT.
DAMN IT... I ALREADY TOLD SEYMOUR -- HE JUST...
HE TAKES TOO MANY CHANCES.
BULLSHIT! YOU'RE THE ONE WHO SHUT ME OUT!
IF I'D BEEN IN SALT BAY THAT DAY, I WOULDN'T BE A SINGLE MOTHER!
I TOLD YOU THEN, I DON'T WORK WITH JUNKIES. IT'S A RULE.
FUCK YOUR RULES! I'VE BEEN SOBER FOR FUCKING YEARS!
I HAD A BABY, ASSHOLE! I HAD KICKED!
NO ONE EVER REALLY KICKS...
THEY'RE RIGHT, WHAT THEY SAY ABOUT YOU, AREN'T THEY?
TERRY ALWAYS SAID IT WAS BULLSHIT, BUT THEY'RE RIGHT.
AND HE PAID FOR THAT...

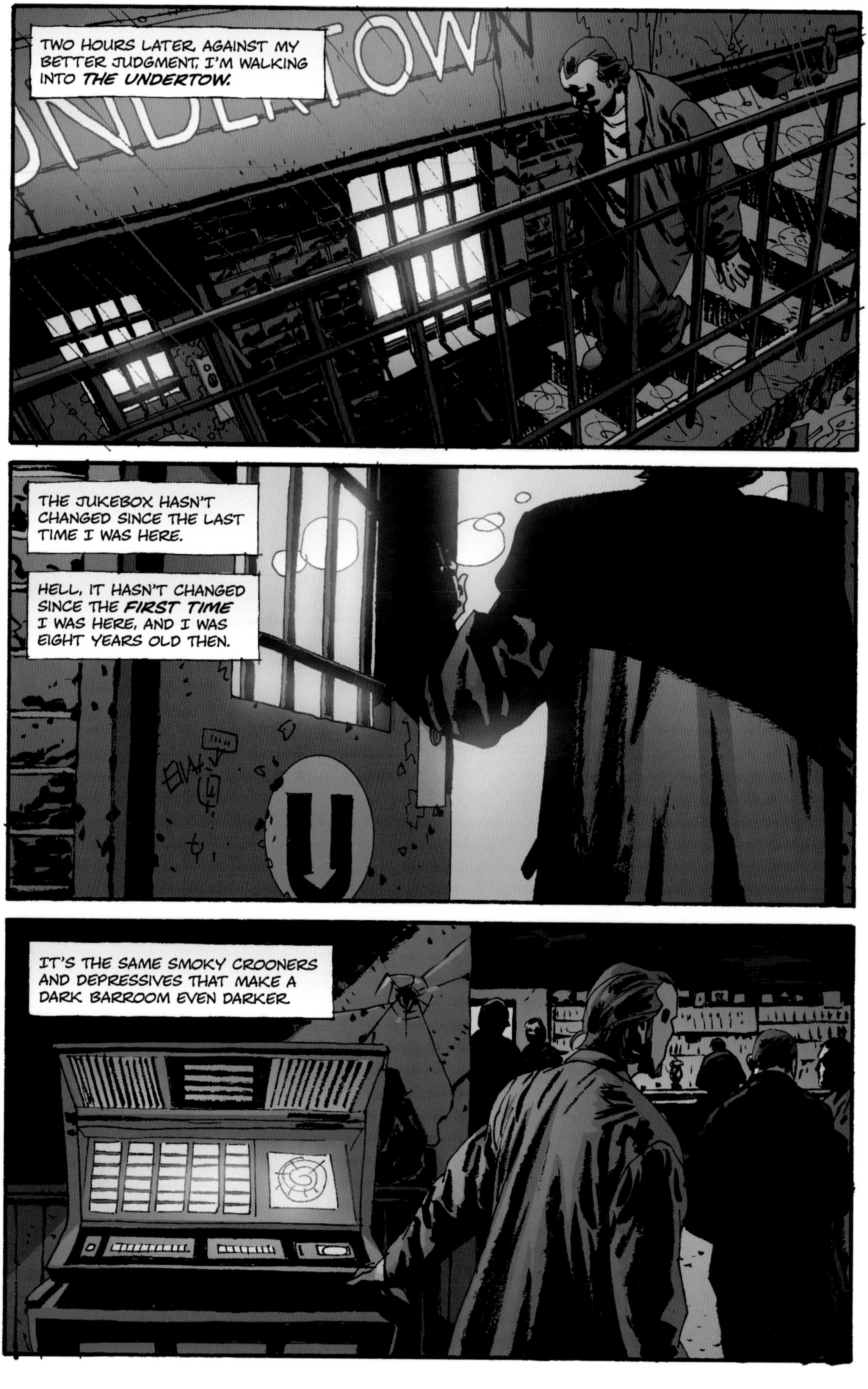
TWO HOURS LATER, AGAINST MY BETTER JUDGMENT, I'M WALKING INTO *THE UNDERTOW.*
THE JUKEBOX HASN'T CHANGED SINCE THE LAST TIME I WAS HERE.
HELL, IT HASN'T CHANGED SINCE THE *FIRST TIME* I WAS HERE, AND I WAS EIGHT YEARS OLD THEN.
IT'S THE SAME SMOKY CROONERS AND DEPRESSIVES THAT MAKE A DARK BARROOM EVEN DARKER.

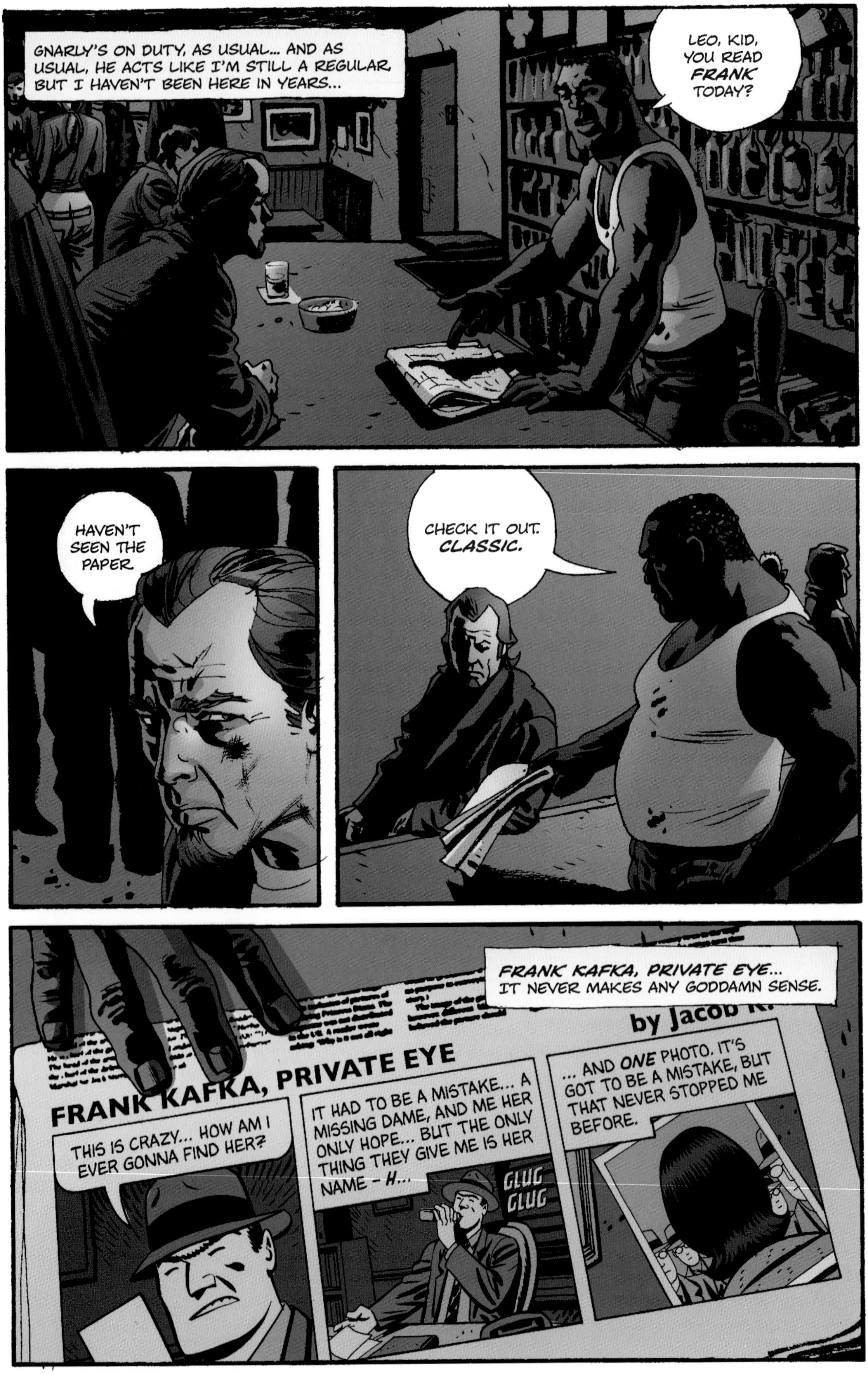
GNARLY'S ON DUTY, AS USUAL... AND AS USUAL, HE ACTS LIKE I'M STILL A REGULAR, BUT I HAVEN'T BEEN HERE IN YEARS...
LEO, KID, YOU READ FRANK TODAY?
HAVEN'T SEEN THE PAPER.
CHECK IT OUT. CLASSIC.
FRANK KAFKA, PRIVATE EYE... IT NEVER MAKES ANY GODDAMN SENSE.
by Jacob K.
FRANK KAFKA, PRIVATE EYE
THIS IS CRAZY... HOW AM I EVER GONNA FIND HER?
IT HAD TO BE A MISTAKE... A MISSING DAME, AND ME HER ONLY HOPE... BUT THE ONLY THING THEY GIVE ME IS HER NAME – H...
GLUG GLUG
... AND ONE PHOTO. IT'S GOT TO BE A MISTAKE, BUT THAT NEVER STOPPED ME BEFORE.

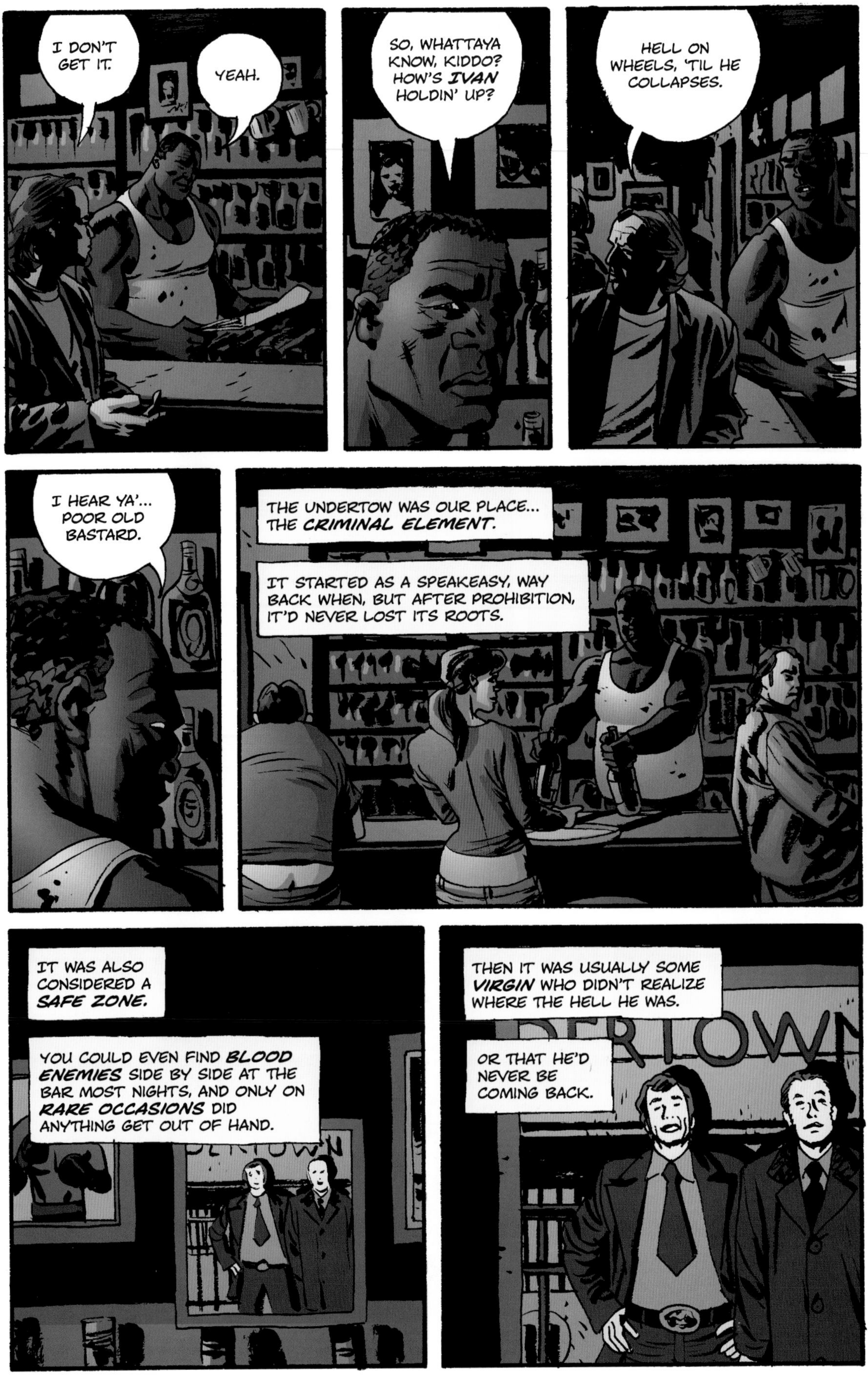
I DON'T GET IT.
YEAH.
SO, WHATTAYA KNOW, KIDDO? HOW'S IVAN HOLDIN' UP?
HELL ON WHEELS, 'TIL HE COLLAPSES.
I HEAR YA'... POOR OLD BASTARD.
THE UNDERTOW WAS OUR PLACE... THE CRIMINAL ELEMENT.
IT STARTED AS A SPEAKEASY, WAY BACK WHEN, BUT AFTER PROHIBITION, IT'D NEVER LOST ITS ROOTS.
IT WAS ALSO CONSIDERED A SAFE ZONE.
YOU COULD EVEN FIND BLOOD ENEMIES SIDE BY SIDE AT THE BAR MOST NIGHTS, AND ONLY ON RARE OCCASIONS DID ANYTHING GET OUT OF HAND.
THEN IT WAS USUALLY SOME VIRGIN WHO DIDN'T REALIZE WHERE THE HELL HE WAS.
OR THAT HE'D NEVER BE COMING BACK.

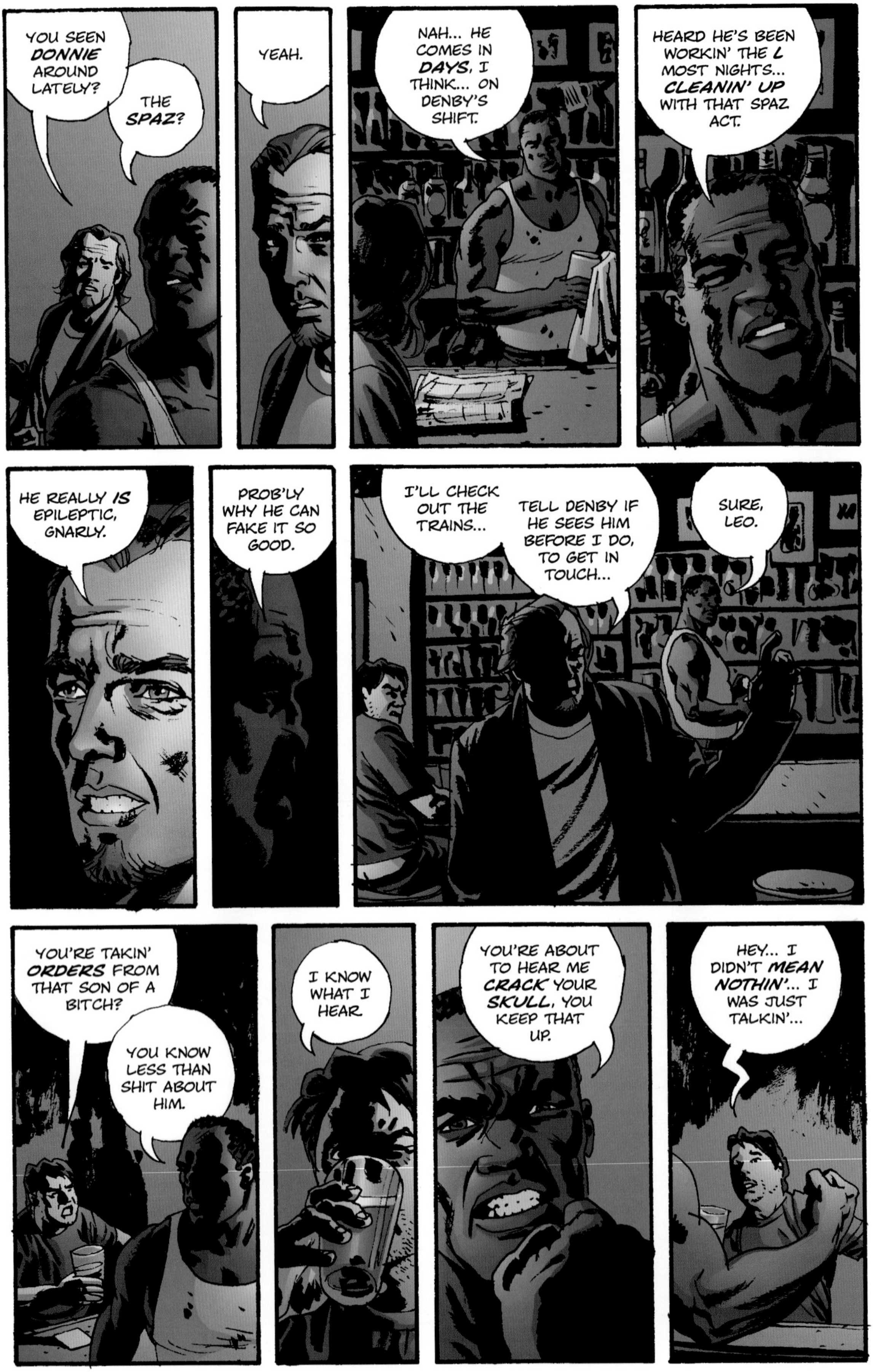
YOU SEEN DONNIE AROUND LATELY?
THE SPAZ?
YEAH.
NAH... HE COMES IN DAYS, I THINK... ON DENBY'S SHIFT.
HEARD HE'S BEEN WORKIN' THE L MOST NIGHTS... CLEANIN' UP WITH THAT SPAZ ACT.
HE REALLY IS EPILEPTIC, GNARLY.
PROB'LY WHY HE CAN FAKE IT SO GOOD.
I'LL CHECK OUT THE TRAINS...
TELL DENBY IF HE SEES HIM BEFORE I DO, TO GET IN TOUCH...
SURE, LEO.
YOU'RE TAKIN' ORDERS FROM THAT SON OF A BITCH?
YOU KNOW LESS THAN SHIT ABOUT HIM.
I KNOW WHAT I HEAR.
YOU'RE ABOUT TO HEAR ME CRACK YOUR SKULL, YOU KEEP THAT UP.
HEY... I DIDN'T MEAN NOTHIN'... I WAS JUST TALKIN'...

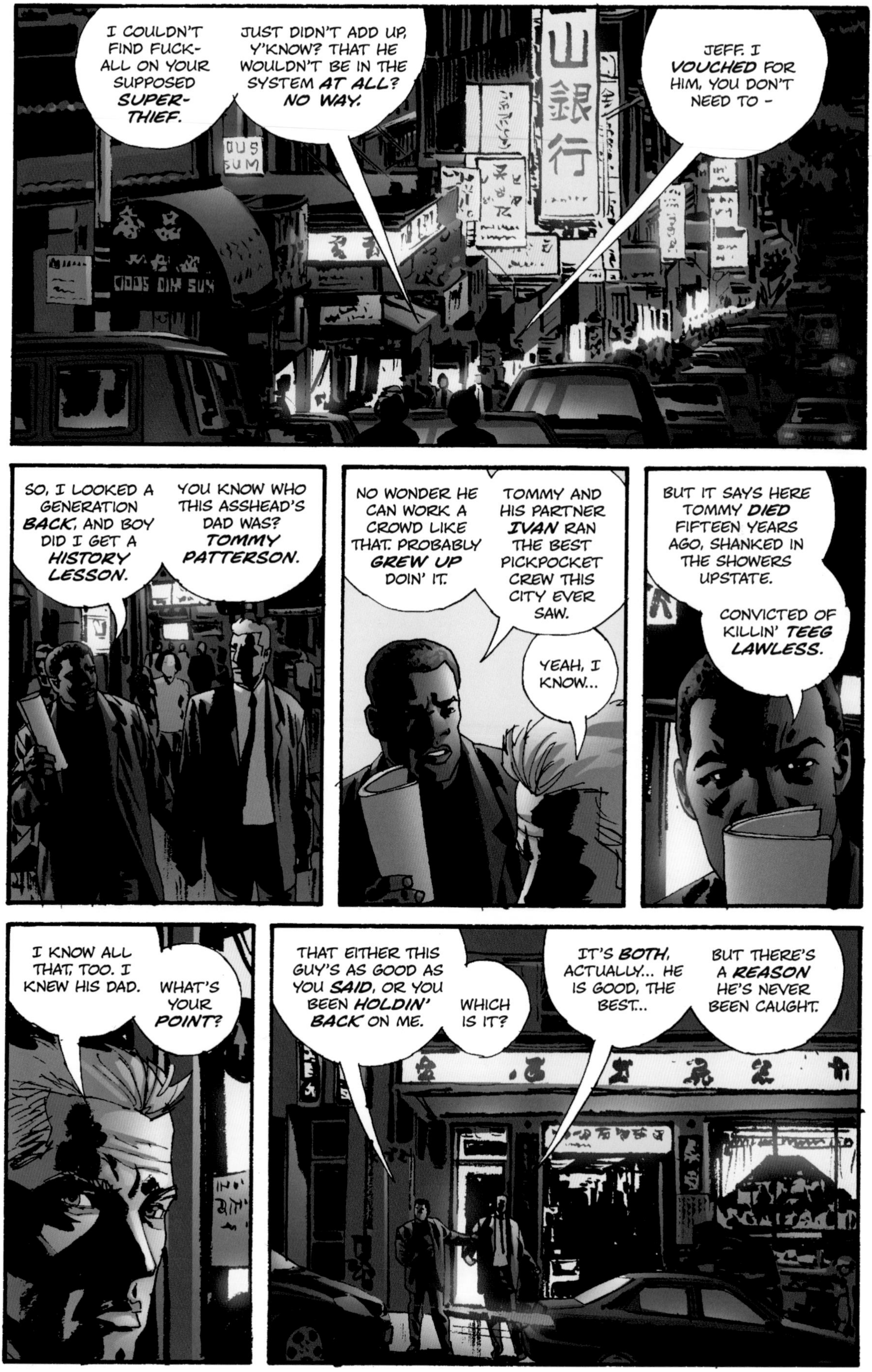
I COULDN'T FIND FUCK-ALL ON YOUR SUPPOSED SUPER-THIEF.
JUST DIDN'T ADD UP, Y'KNOW? THAT HE WOULDN'T BE IN THE SYSTEM AT ALL? NO WAY.
JEFF. I VOUCHED FOR HIM, YOU DON'T NEED TO -
SO, I LOOKED A GENERATION BACK, AND BOY DID I GET A HISTORY LESSON.
YOU KNOW WHO THIS ASSHEAD'S DAD WAS? TOMMY PATTERSON.
NO WONDER HE CAN WORK A CROWD LIKE THAT. PROBABLY GREW UP DOIN' IT.
TOMMY AND HIS PARTNER IVAN RAN THE BEST PICKPOCKET CREW THIS CITY EVER SAW.
YEAH, I KNOW...
BUT IT SAYS HERE TOMMY DIED FIFTEEN YEARS AGO, SHANKED IN THE SHOWERS UPSTATE.
CONVICTED OF KILLIN' TEEG LAWLESS.
I KNOW ALL THAT, TOO. I KNEW HIS DAD.
WHAT'S YOUR POINT?
THAT EITHER THIS GUY'S AS GOOD AS YOU SAID, OR YOU BEEN HOLDIN' BACK ON ME.
WHICH IS IT?
IT'S BOTH, ACTUALLY... HE IS GOOD, THE BEST...
BUT THERE'S A REASON HE'S NEVER BEEN CAUGHT.

"LEO'S A **COWARD**.

"HE DOESN'T JUST WALK AWAY FROM TROUBLE, HE **RUNS**."

AND AS GOOD AS HE IS AT SEEING HOLES IN SECURITY AND MAPPING OUT SCORES...

...HE'S JUST THAT GOOD AT **SLIPPING AWAY**, TOO.

"THAT'S ONE OF THE REASONS WE NEED HIM, JEFF."

IF YOU GET MY MEANING.

SO THEN, YOU GUYS AREN'T EXACTLY FRIENDS?

LEO DOESN'T **HAVE** ANY FRIENDS...

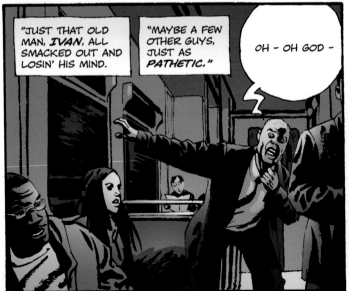

"JUST THAT OLD MAN, **IVAN**, ALL SMACKED OUT AND LOSIN' HIS MIND.

"MAYBE A FEW OTHER GUYS, JUST AS **PATHETIC**."

OH – OH GOD –

GGUUUGGG! GGUUGG!

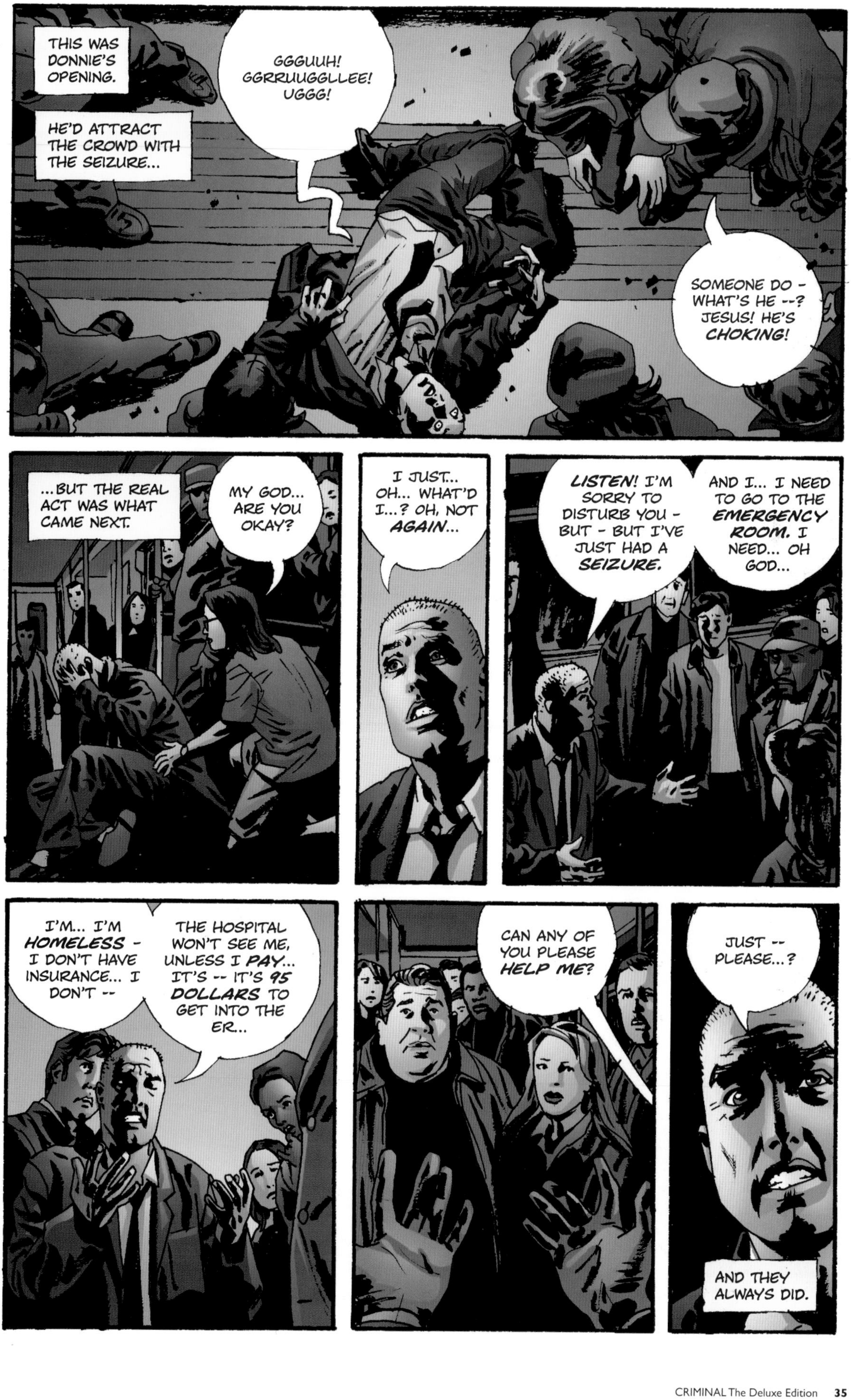
THIS WAS DONNIE'S OPENING.
HE'D ATTRACT THE CROWD WITH THE SEIZURE...
GGGUUH! GGRRUUGGLLEE! UGGG!
SOMEONE DO - WHAT'S HE --? JESUS! HE'S CHOKING!
...BUT THE REAL ACT WAS WHAT CAME NEXT.
MY GOD... ARE YOU OKAY?
I JUST... OH... WHAT'D I...? OH, NOT AGAIN...
LISTEN! I'M SORRY TO DISTURB YOU - BUT - BUT I'VE JUST HAD A SEIZURE.
AND I... I NEED TO GO TO THE EMERGENCY ROOM. I NEED... OH GOD...
I'M... I'M HOMELESS - I DON'T HAVE INSURANCE... I DON'T --
THE HOSPITAL WON'T SEE ME, UNLESS I PAY... IT'S -- IT'S 95 DOLLARS TO GET INTO THE ER..
CAN ANY OF YOU PLEASE HELP ME?
JUST -- PLEASE...?
AND THEY ALWAYS DID.

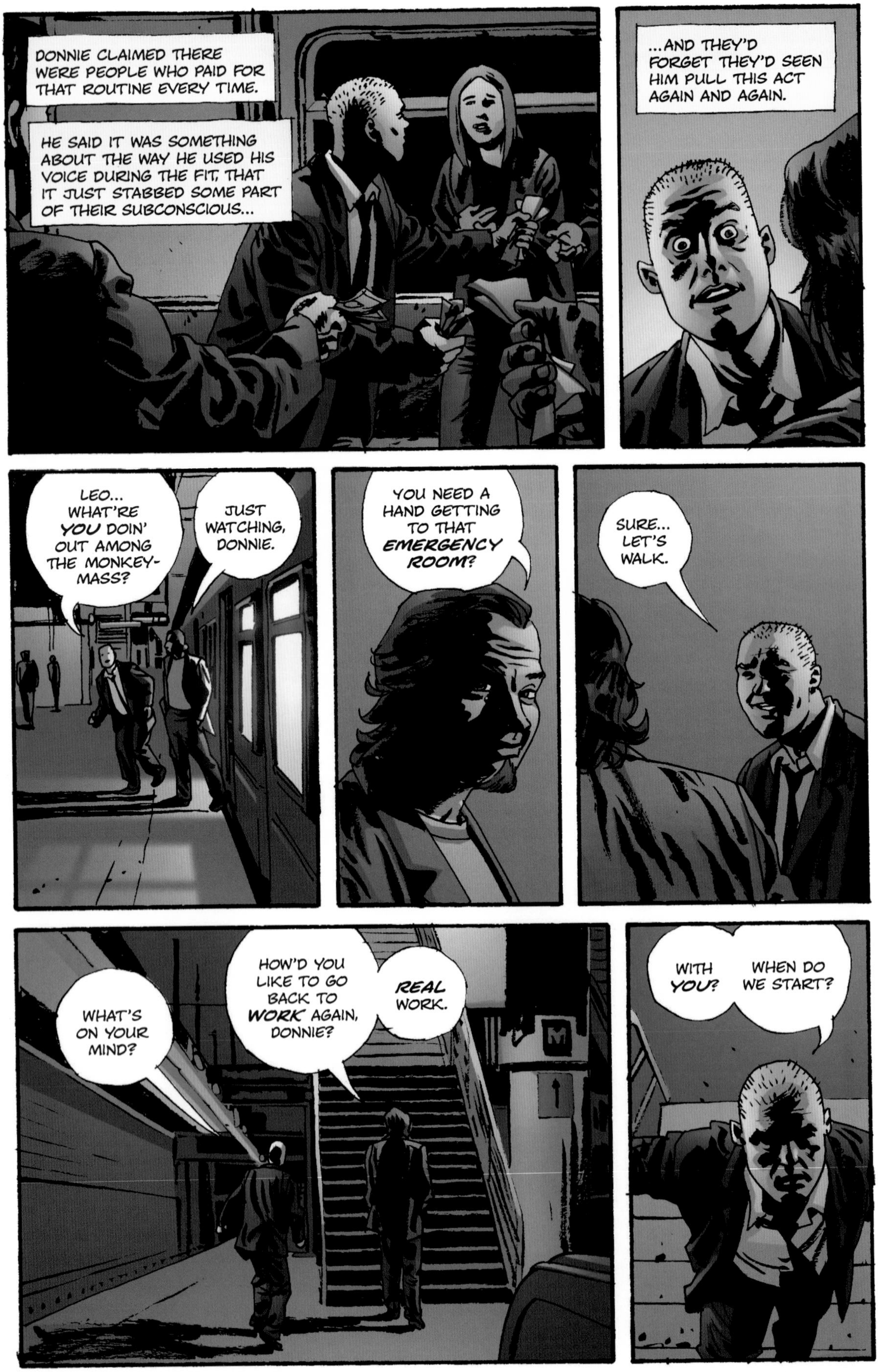
DONNIE CLAIMED THERE WERE PEOPLE WHO PAID FOR THAT ROUTINE EVERY TIME.
HE SAID IT WAS SOMETHING ABOUT THE WAY HE USED HIS VOICE DURING THE FIT, THAT IT JUST STABBED SOME PART OF THEIR SUBCONSCIOUS...
...AND THEY'D FORGET THEY'D SEEN HIM PULL THIS ACT AGAIN AND AGAIN.
LEO... WHAT'RE *YOU* DOIN' OUT AMONG THE MONKEY-MASS?
JUST WATCHING, DONNIE.
YOU NEED A HAND GETTING TO THAT *EMERGENCY ROOM?*
SURE... LET'S WALK.
WHAT'S ON YOUR MIND?
HOW'D YOU LIKE TO GO BACK TO *WORK* AGAIN, DONNIE?
REAL WORK.
WITH *YOU?*
WHEN DO WE START?

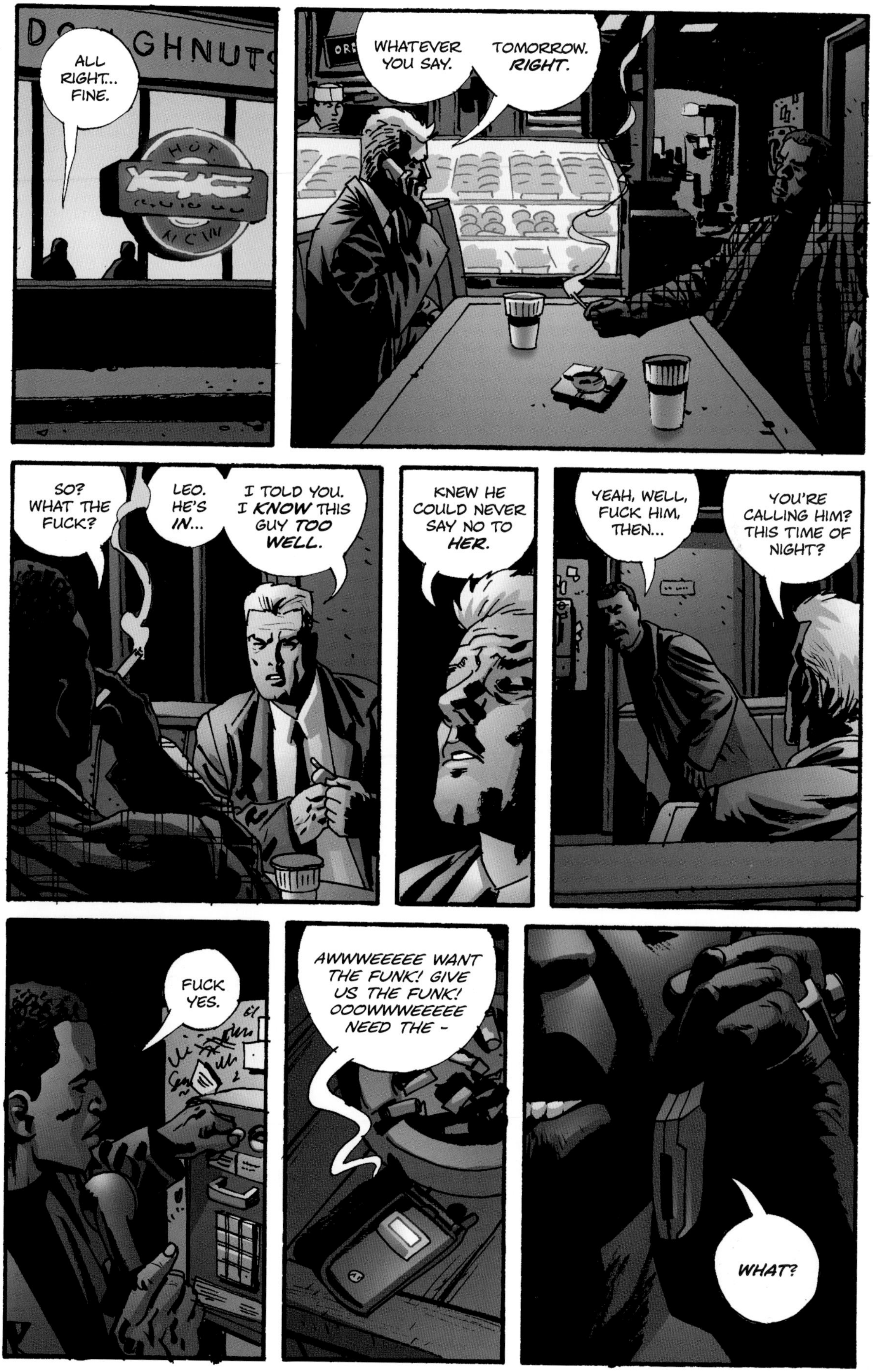
DOUGHNUTS
ALL RIGHT... FINE.
WHATEVER YOU SAY.
TOMORROW. RIGHT.
SO? WHAT THE FUCK?
LEO. HE'S IN...
I TOLD YOU. I KNOW THIS GUY TOO WELL.
KNEW HE COULD NEVER SAY NO TO HER.
YEAH, WELL, FUCK HIM, THEN...
YOU'RE CALLING HIM? THIS TIME OF NIGHT?
FUCK YES.
AWWWEEEEE WANT THE FUNK! GIVE US THE FUNK! OOOWWWEEEEE NEED THE -
WHAT?

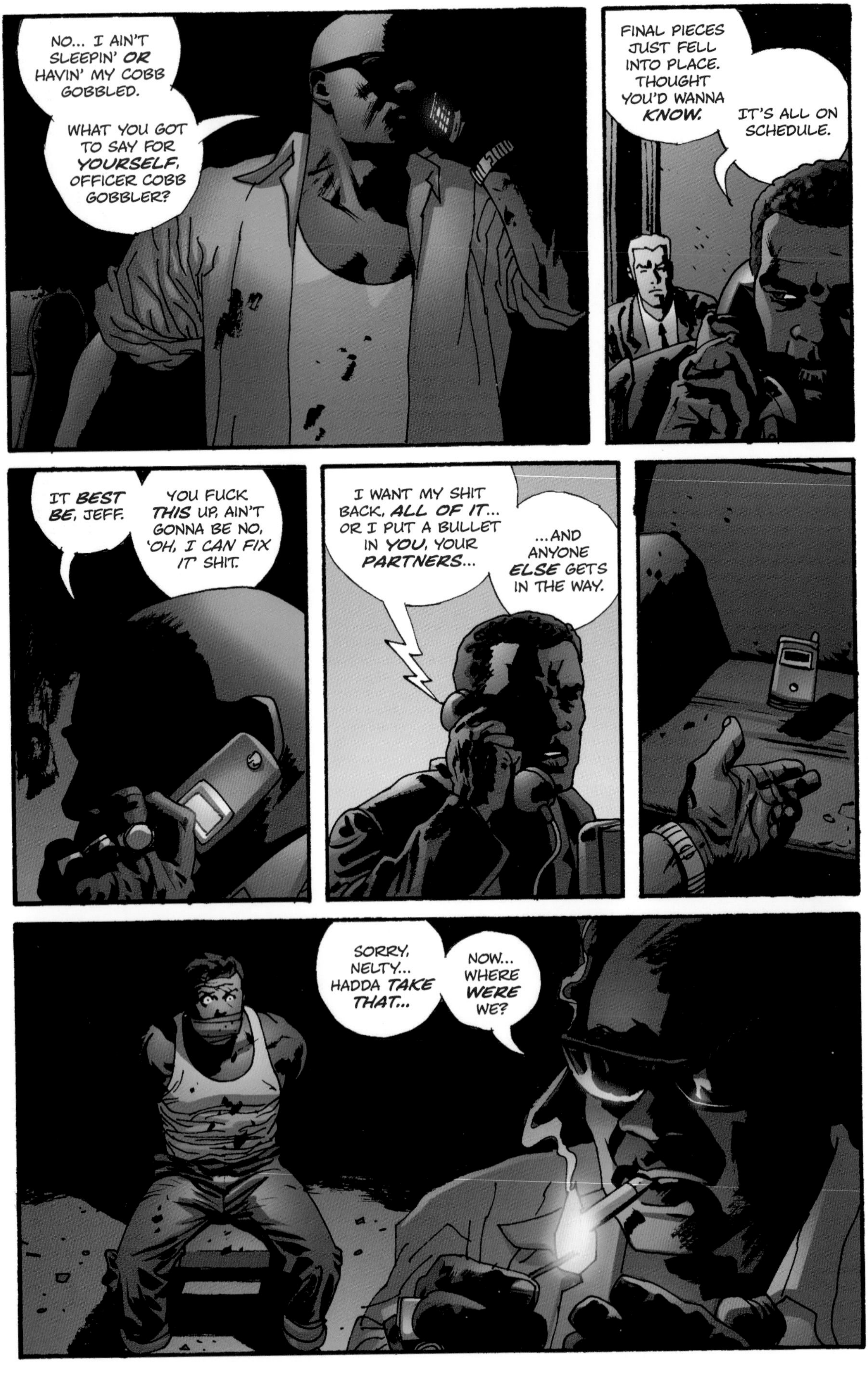

NO... I AIN'T SLEEPIN' OR HAVIN' MY COBB GOBBLED.
WHAT YOU GOT TO SAY FOR YOURSELF, OFFICER COBB GOBBLER?
FINAL PIECES JUST FELL INTO PLACE. THOUGHT YOU'D WANNA KNOW.
IT'S ALL ON SCHEDULE.
IT BEST BE, JEFF.
YOU FUCK THIS UP, AIN'T GONNA BE NO, 'OH, I CAN FIX IT' SHIT.
I WANT MY SHIT BACK, ALL OF IT... OR I PUT A BULLET IN YOU, YOUR PARTNERS...
...AND ANYONE ELSE GETS IN THE WAY.
SORRY, NELTY... HADDA TAKE THAT...
NOW... WHERE WERE WE?

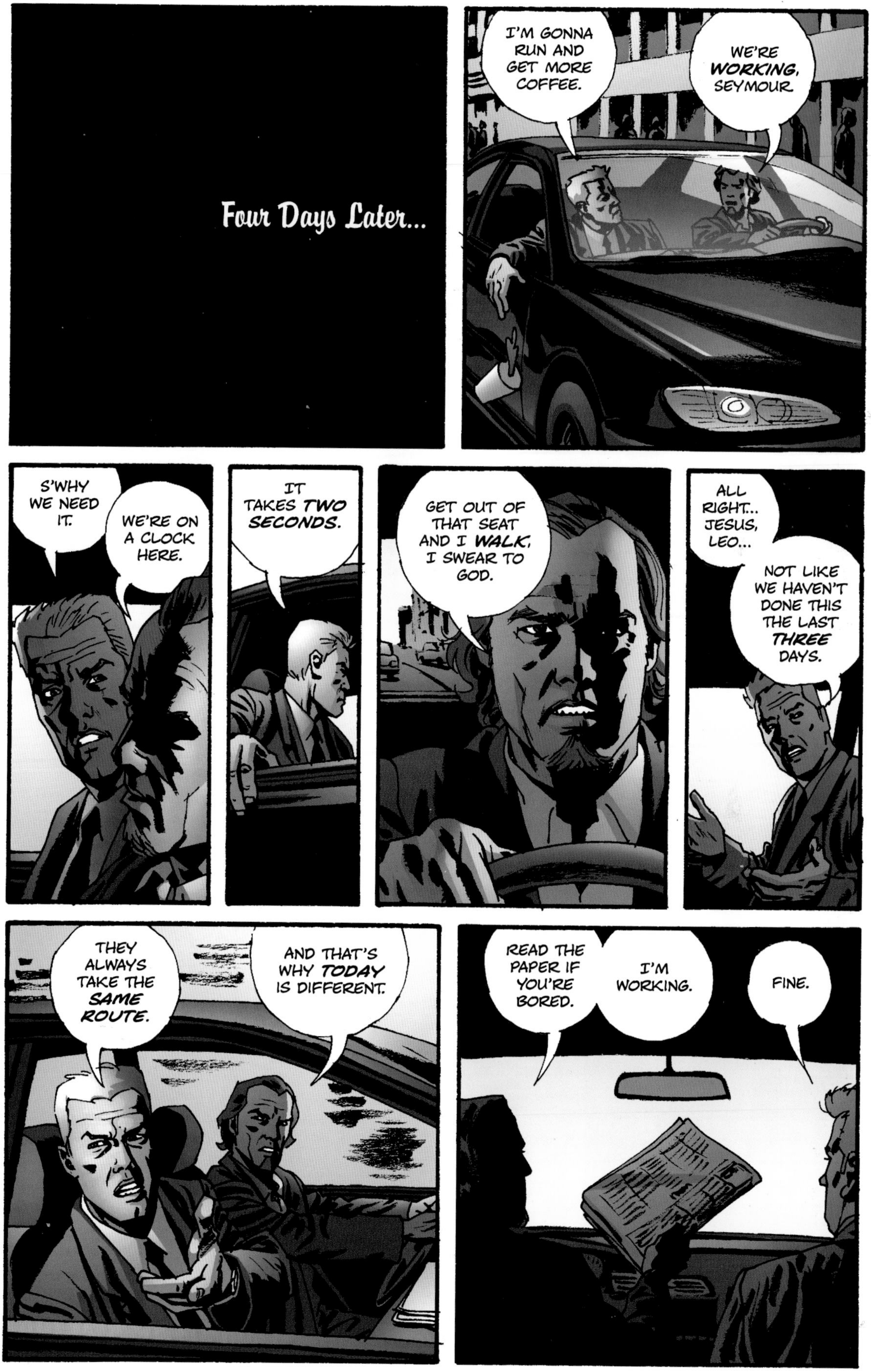
Four Days Later...
I'M GONNA RUN AND GET MORE COFFEE.
WE'RE WORKING, SEYMOUR
S'WHY WE NEED IT.
WE'RE ON A CLOCK HERE.
IT TAKES TWO SECONDS.
GET OUT OF THAT SEAT AND I WALK, I SWEAR TO GOD.
ALL RIGHT... JESUS, LEO...
NOT LIKE WE HAVEN'T DONE THIS THE LAST THREE DAYS.
THEY ALWAYS TAKE THE SAME ROUTE.
AND THAT'S WHY TODAY IS DIFFERENT.
READ THE PAPER IF YOU'RE BORED.
I'M WORKING.
FINE.

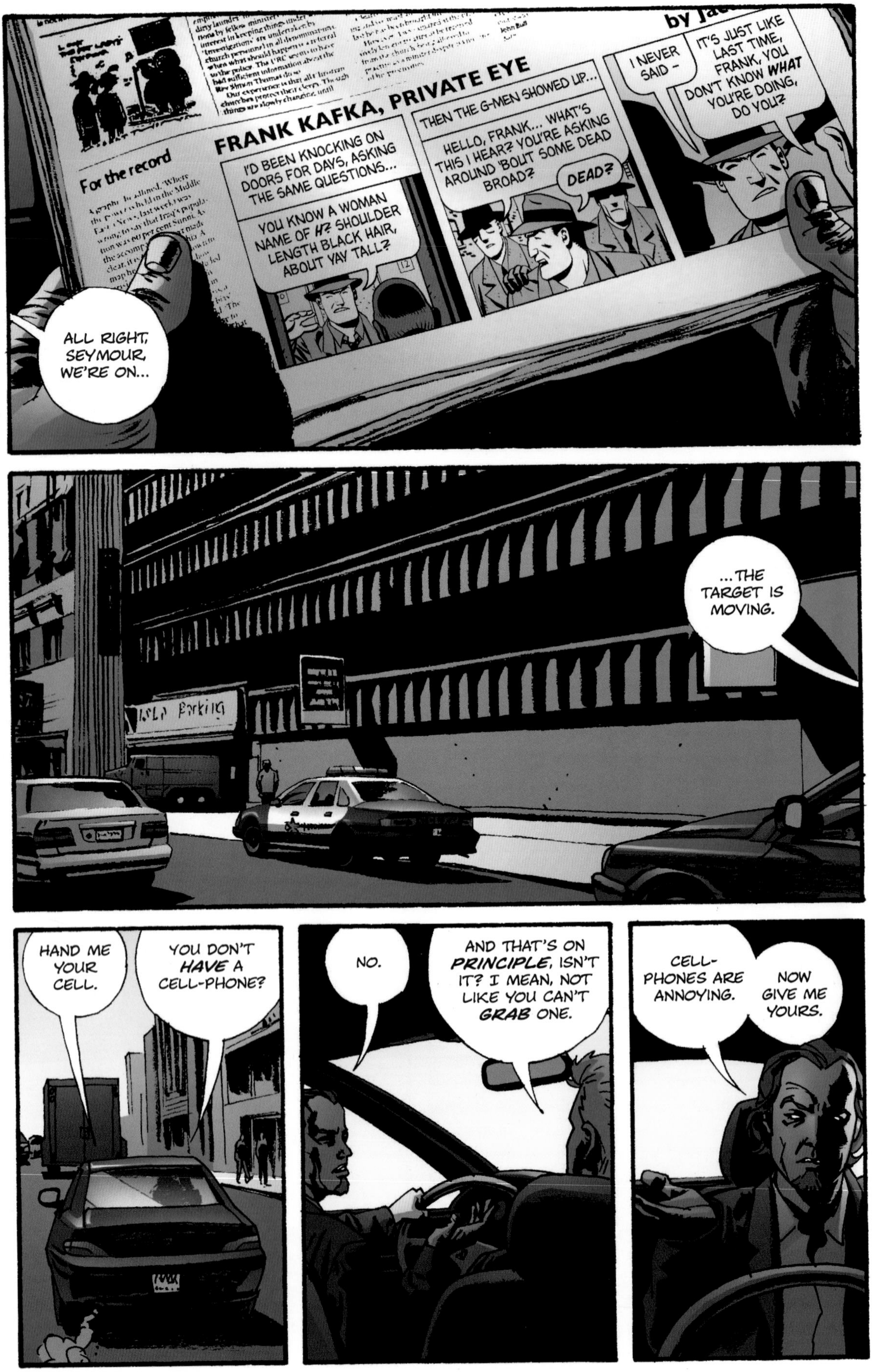

For the record
FRANK KAFKA, PRIVATE EYE
I'D BEEN KNOCKING ON DOORS FOR DAYS, ASKING THE SAME QUESTIONS...
YOU KNOW A WOMAN NAME OF H? SHOULDER LENGTH BLACK HAIR, ABOUT YAY TALL?
THEN THE G-MEN SHOWED UP...
HELLO, FRANK... WHAT'S THIS I HEAR? YOU'RE ASKING AROUND 'BOUT SOME DEAD BROAD?
DEAD?
I NEVER SAID -
IT'S JUST LIKE LAST TIME, FRANK, YOU DON'T KNOW WHAT YOU'RE DOING, DO YOU?
ALL RIGHT, SEYMOUR, WE'RE ON...
...THE TARGET IS MOVING.
HAND ME YOUR CELL.
YOU DON'T HAVE A CELL-PHONE?
NO.
AND THAT'S ON PRINCIPLE, ISN'T IT? I MEAN, NOT LIKE YOU CAN'T GRAB ONE.
CELL-PHONES ARE ANNOYING.
NOW GIVE ME YOURS.

EVERY DAY AT 4:30 PM, THE VAN LEFT THE **EVIDENCE STORAGE FACILITY** AND DROVE TWO MILES TO THE DOWNTOWN COURTHOUSE.

THEY DELIVERED EVIDENCE FOR TRIAL THE NEXT DAY, WHICH NEEDED TO BE PROCESSED BEFORE IT COULD BE PRESENTED IN COURT.

SEYMOUR AND HIS CROOKED COP BUDDY JEFF WERE RIGHT...

THE TRANSPORT VAN WAS THE WEAK LINK.

BECAUSE NO ONE EVER KNEW WHAT IT WAS CARRYING, SO WHO WAS GOING TO TAKE DOWN A **POLICE TRANSPORT VEHICLE** ON THE OUTSIDE CHANCE OF A BIG SCORE?

NOT EVEN JUNKIES WERE THAT DESPERATE.

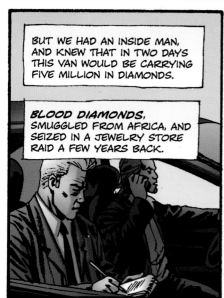

BUT WE HAD AN INSIDE MAN, AND KNEW THAT IN TWO DAYS THIS VAN WOULD BE CARRYING FIVE MILLION IN DIAMONDS.

BLOOD DIAMONDS, SMUGGLED FROM AFRICA, AND SEIZED IN A JEWELRY STORE RAID A FEW YEARS BACK.

THE ACCUSED WERE FINALLY GETTING THEIR DAY IN COURT, AND THEIR LAWYER WAS SMART ENOUGH TO DEMAND ALL EVIDENCE BE PRESENT.

GREAT WAY TO INFLUENCE A JURY... SHOW THEM WHAT FIVE MIL IN GEMS LOOKS LIKE, AND ASK WHAT THEY'D DO IN THE DEFENDANT'S PLACE.

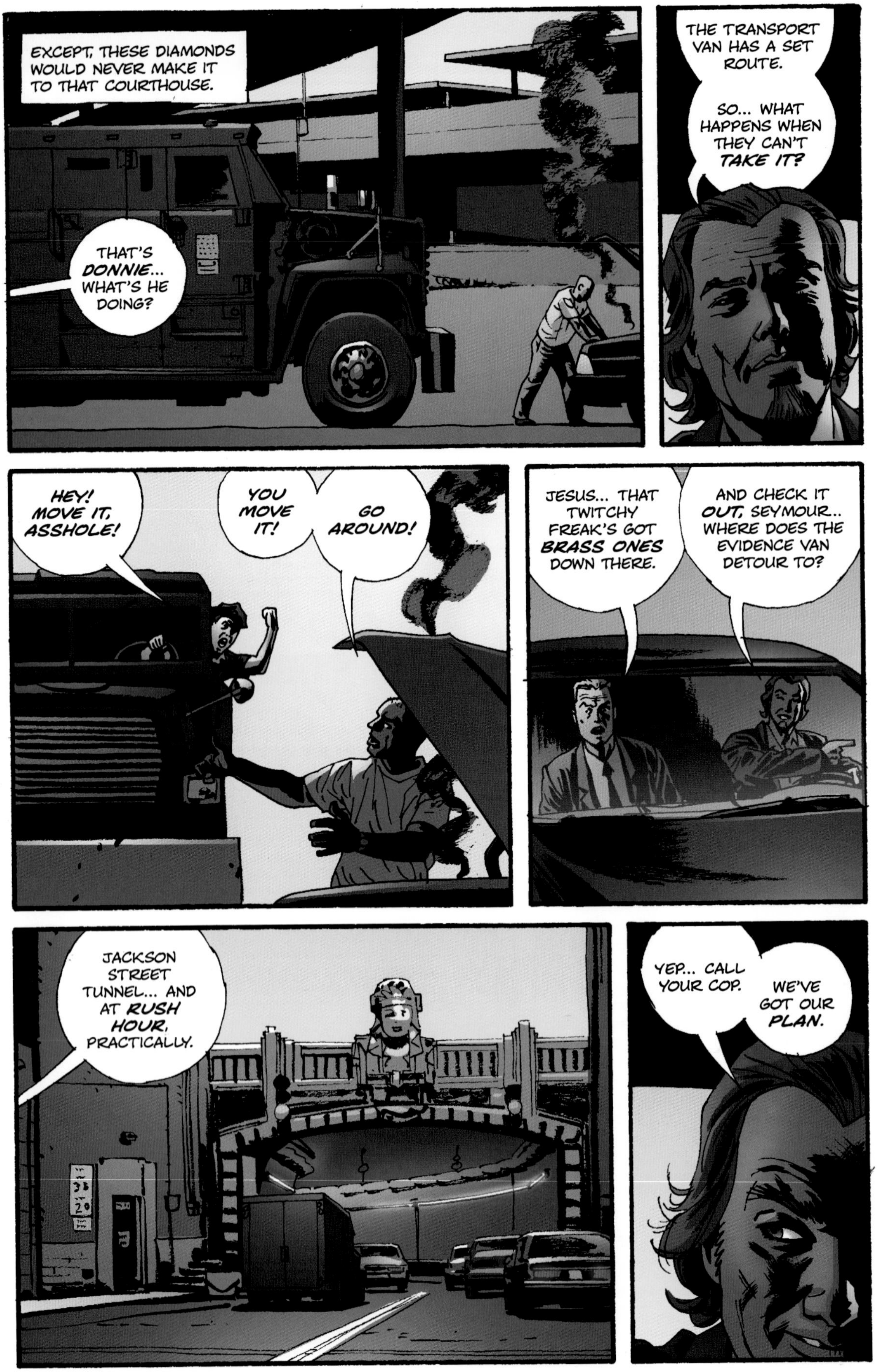
EXCEPT, THESE DIAMONDS WOULD NEVER MAKE IT TO THAT COURTHOUSE.
THAT'S DONNIE... WHAT'S HE DOING?
THE TRANSPORT VAN HAS A SET ROUTE.
SO... WHAT HAPPENS WHEN THEY CAN'T TAKE IT?
HEY! MOVE IT, ASSHOLE!
YOU MOVE IT!
GO AROUND!
JESUS... THAT TWITCHY FREAK'S GOT BRASS ONES DOWN THERE.
AND CHECK IT OUT, SEYMOUR... WHERE DOES THE EVIDENCE VAN DETOUR TO?
JACKSON STREET TUNNEL... AND AT RUSH HOUR, PRACTICALLY.
YEP... CALL YOUR COP.
WE'VE GOT OUR PLAN.

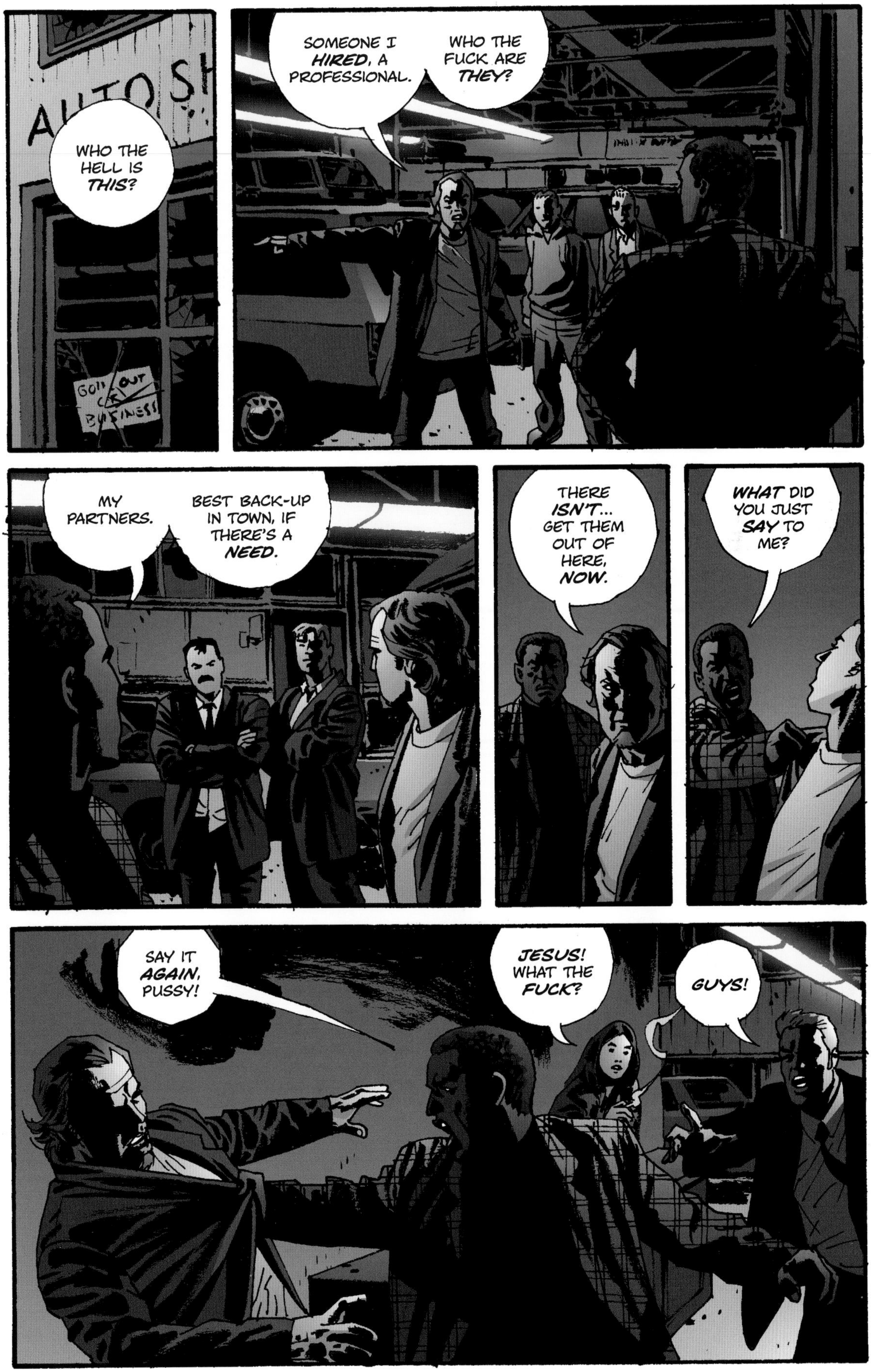
AUTO SH
WHO THE HELL IS THIS?
GOIN OUT OF BUSINESS
SOMEONE I HIRED, A PROFESSIONAL.
WHO THE FUCK ARE THEY?
MY PARTNERS.
BEST BACK-UP IN TOWN, IF THERE'S A NEED.
THERE ISN'T... GET THEM OUT OF HERE, NOW.
WHAT DID YOU JUST SAY TO ME?
SAY IT AGAIN, PUSSY!
JESUS! WHAT THE FUCK?
GUYS!

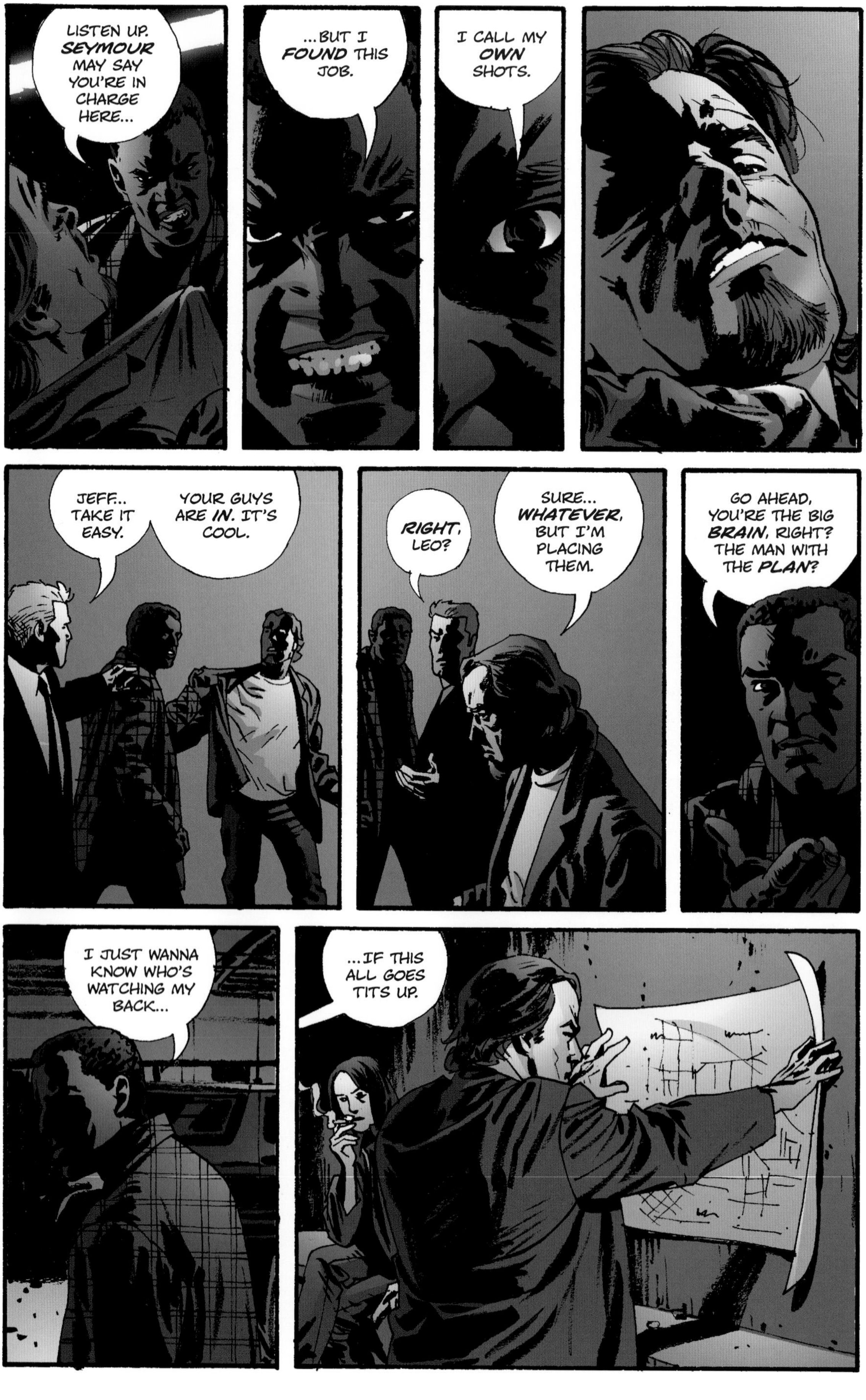
LISTEN UP. SEYMOUR MAY SAY YOU'RE IN CHARGE HERE...
...BUT I FOUND THIS JOB.
I CALL MY OWN SHOTS.
JEFF.. TAKE IT EASY.
YOUR GUYS ARE IN. IT'S COOL.
RIGHT, LEO?
SURE... WHATEVER, BUT I'M PLACING THEM.
GO AHEAD, YOU'RE THE BIG BRAIN, RIGHT? THE MAN WITH THE PLAN?
I JUST WANNA KNOW WHO'S WATCHING MY BACK...
...IF THIS ALL GOES TITS UP.

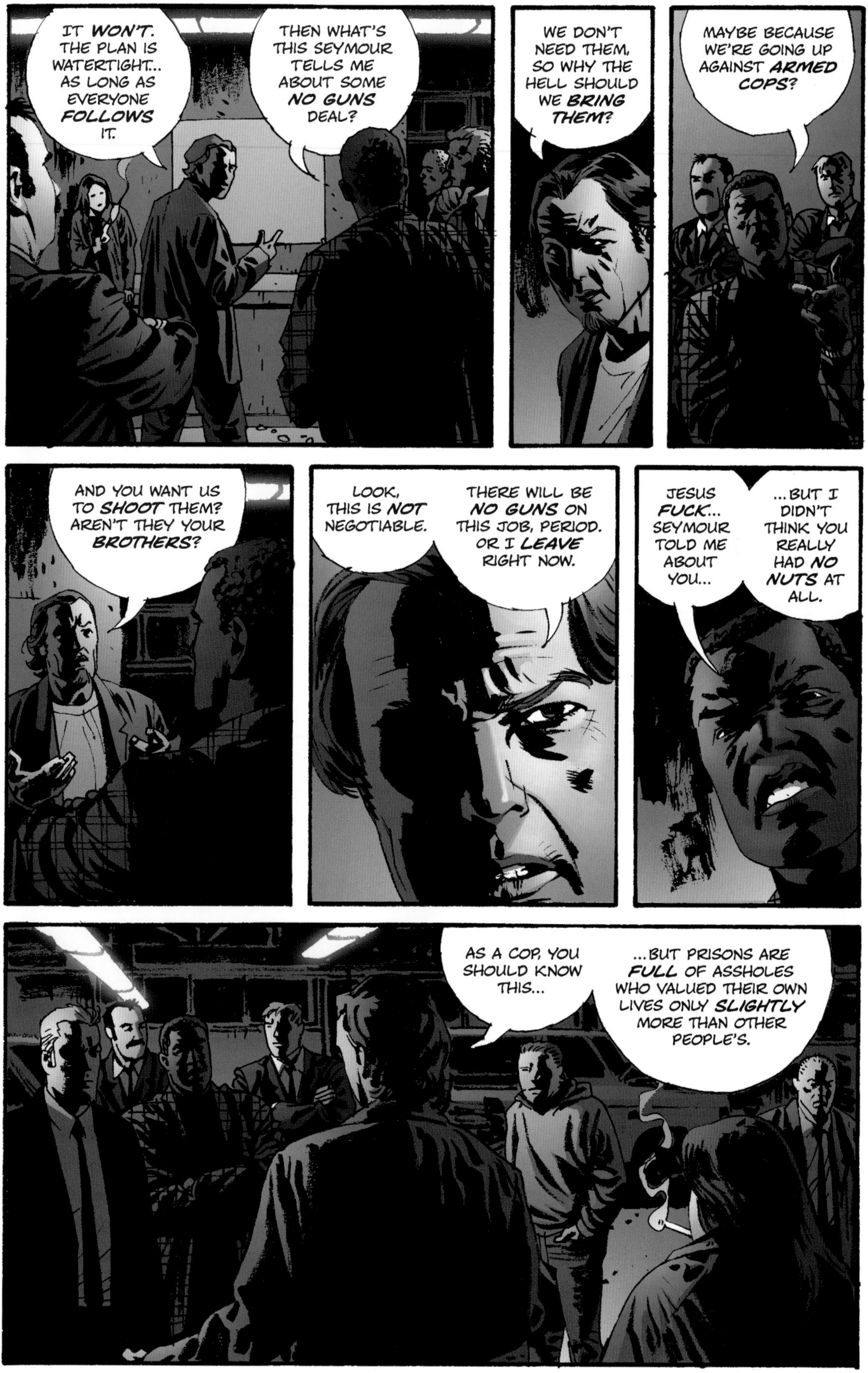
IT WON'T. THE PLAN IS WATERTIGHT... AS LONG AS EVERYONE FOLLOWS IT.
THEN WHAT'S THIS SEYMOUR TELLS ME ABOUT SOME NO GUNS DEAL?
WE DON'T NEED THEM, SO WHY THE HELL SHOULD WE BRING THEM?
MAYBE BECAUSE WE'RE GOING UP AGAINST ARMED COPS?
AND YOU WANT US TO SHOOT THEM? AREN'T THEY YOUR BROTHERS?
LOOK, THIS IS NOT NEGOTIABLE.
THERE WILL BE NO GUNS ON THIS JOB, PERIOD. OR I LEAVE RIGHT NOW.
JESUS FUCK... SEYMOUR TOLD ME ABOUT YOU...
...BUT I DIDN'T THINK YOU REALLY HAD NO NUTS AT ALL.
AS A COP, YOU SHOULD KNOW THIS...
...BUT PRISONS ARE FULL OF ASSHOLES WHO VALUED THEIR OWN LIVES ONLY SLIGHTLY MORE THAN OTHER PEOPLE'S.

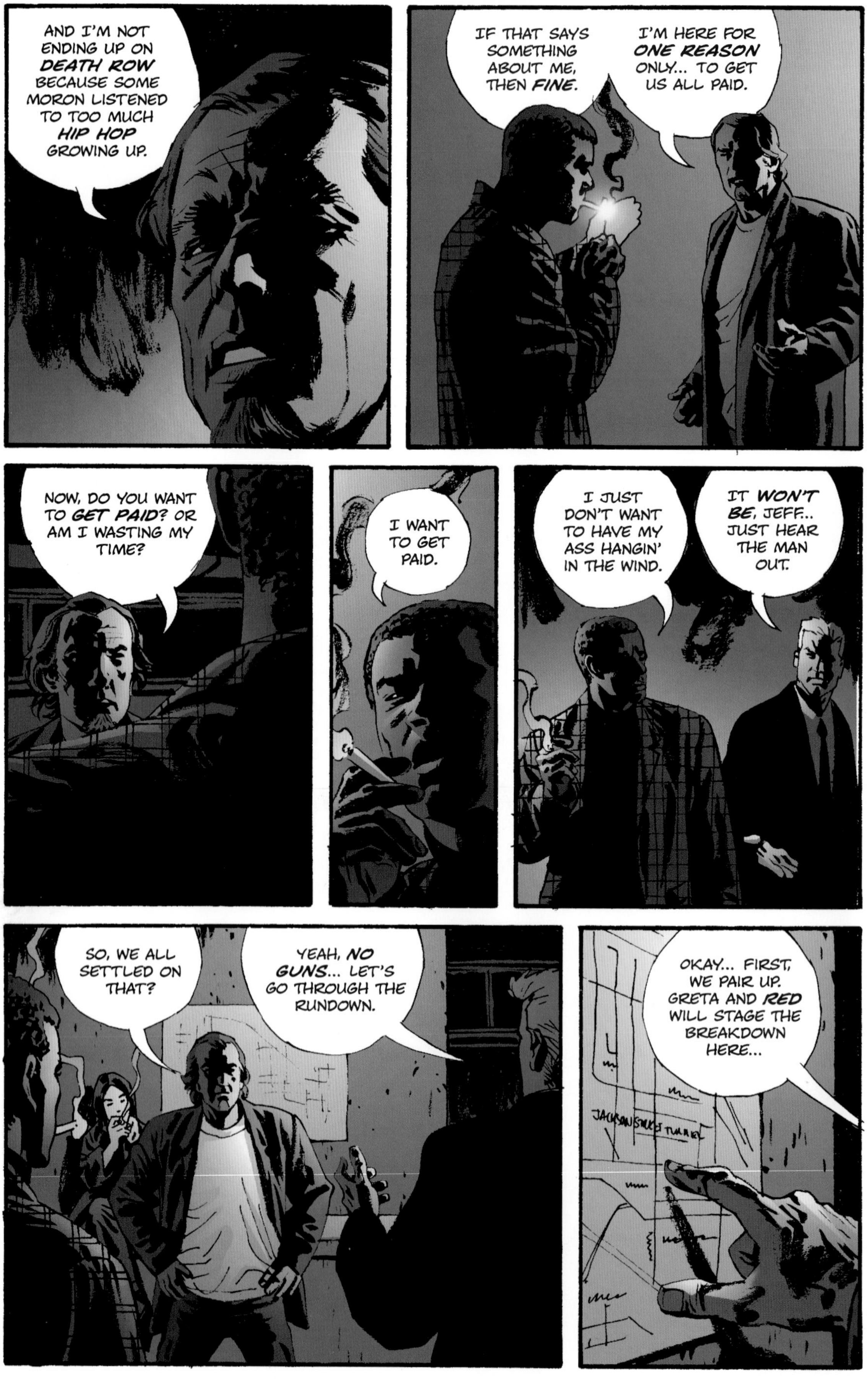
AND I'M NOT ENDING UP ON DEATH ROW BECAUSE SOME MORON LISTENED TO TOO MUCH HIP HOP GROWING UP.
IF THAT SAYS SOMETHING ABOUT ME, THEN FINE.
I'M HERE FOR ONE REASON ONLY... TO GET US ALL PAID.
NOW, DO YOU WANT TO GET PAID? OR AM I WASTING MY TIME?
I WANT TO GET PAID.
I JUST DON'T WANT TO HAVE MY ASS HANGIN' IN THE WIND.
IT WON'T BE, JEFF... JUST HEAR THE MAN OUT.
SO, WE ALL SETTLED ON THAT?
YEAH, NO GUNS... LET'S GO THROUGH THE RUNDOWN.
OKAY... FIRST, WE PAIR UP. GRETA AND RED WILL STAGE THE BREAKDOWN HERE...
JACKSON STREET TUNNEL

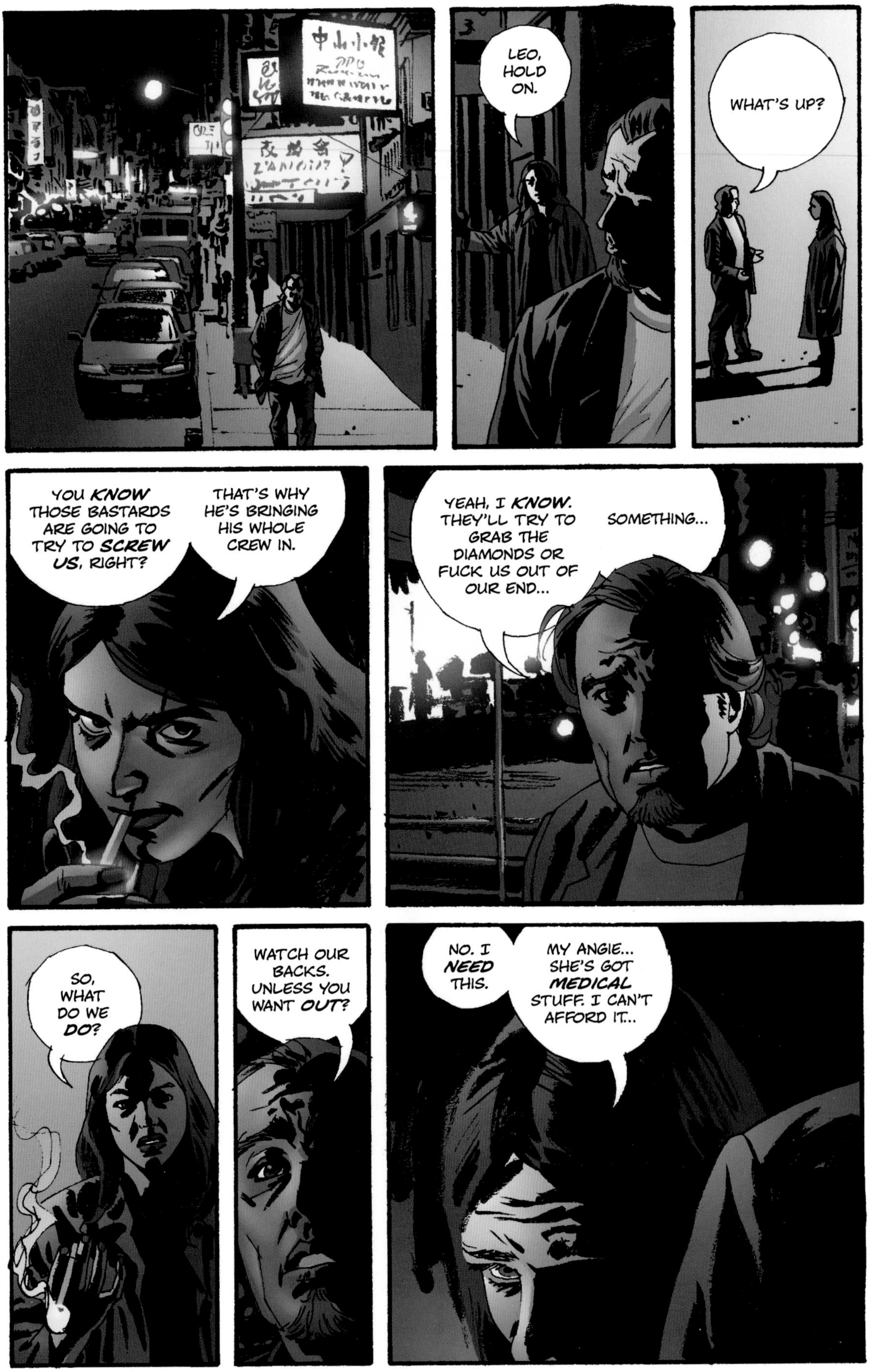
LEO, HOLD ON.
WHAT'S UP?
YOU KNOW THOSE BASTARDS ARE GOING TO TRY TO SCREW US, RIGHT?
THAT'S WHY HE'S BRINGING HIS WHOLE CREW IN.
YEAH, I KNOW. THEY'LL TRY TO GRAB THE DIAMONDS OR FUCK US OUT OF OUR END...
SOMETHING...
SO, WHAT DO WE DO?
WATCH OUR BACKS. UNLESS YOU WANT OUT?
NO. I NEED THIS.
MY ANGIE... SHE'S GOT MEDICAL STUFF. I CAN'T AFFORD IT...

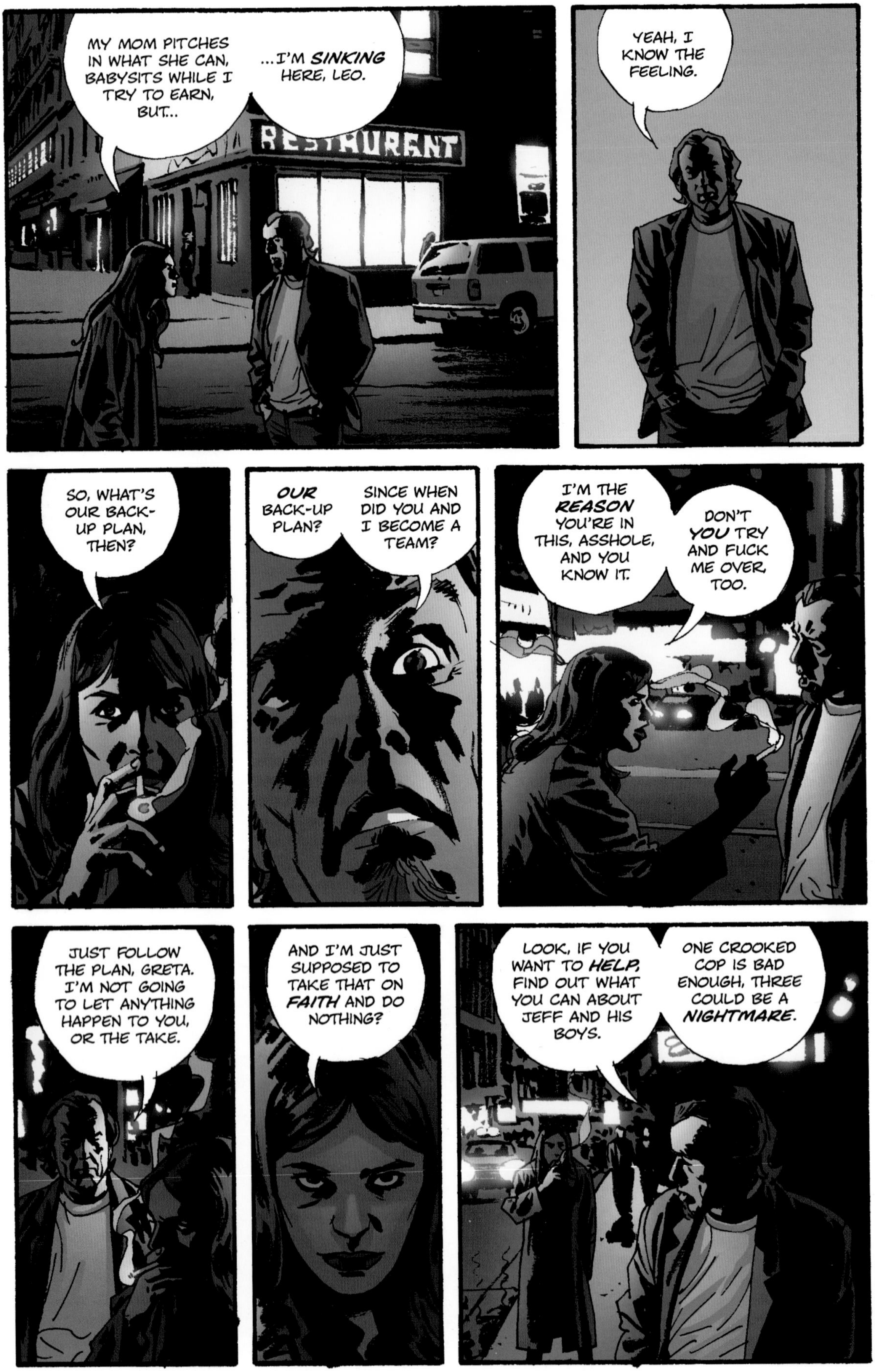
MY MOM PITCHES IN WHAT SHE CAN, BABYSITS WHILE I TRY TO EARN, BUT...
...I'M SINKING HERE, LEO.
RESTAURANT
YEAH, I KNOW THE FEELING.
SO, WHAT'S OUR BACK-UP PLAN, THEN?
OUR BACK-UP PLAN?
SINCE WHEN DID YOU AND I BECOME A TEAM?
I'M THE REASON YOU'RE IN THIS, ASSHOLE, AND YOU KNOW IT.
DON'T YOU TRY AND FUCK ME OVER, TOO.
JUST FOLLOW THE PLAN, GRETA. I'M NOT GOING TO LET ANYTHING HAPPEN TO YOU, OR THE TAKE.
AND I'M JUST SUPPOSED TO TAKE THAT ON FAITH AND DO NOTHING?
LOOK, IF YOU WANT TO HELP, FIND OUT WHAT YOU CAN ABOUT JEFF AND HIS BOYS.
ONE CROOKED COP IS BAD ENOUGH, THREE COULD BE A NIGHTMARE.

BUT WITH THE JOB A DAY AWAY, I KNEW THERE WAS NO TIME LEFT TO DIG UP ANYTHING THAT'D MAKE A DIFFERENCE.

WE'D ALREADY ROLLED THE DICE, AND NOW WE HAD TO WAIT AND SEE HOW THEY CAME UP.

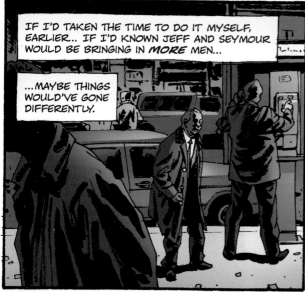

IF I'D TAKEN THE TIME TO DO IT MYSELF, EARLIER... IF I'D KNOWN JEFF AND SEYMOUR WOULD BE BRINGING IN *MORE* MEN...

...MAYBE THINGS WOULD'VE GONE DIFFERENTLY.

BUT I WAS DISTRACTED...

YOU *SURE*, GNARLY?

YEAH, NO PROBLEM... DON'T SWEAT IT.

I JUST NEED SOMEONE I CAN *TRUST*, Y'KNOW?

IT'LL BE A DAY, MAYBE TWO AT THE MOST, JUST IN CASE.

LOOK, DAGMAR LOVES IVAN, KIDDO, SO IT'S *NOT* A PROBLEM.

WELL, SHE HASN'T HAD TO DEAL WITH HIM *LATELY*.

JUST TELL HER TO *SLAP HIM* IF HE GETS OUTTA LINE.

BUT THANKS... HOPEFULLY AFTER THIS, I CAN GET HIM SOME *REAL* HELP...

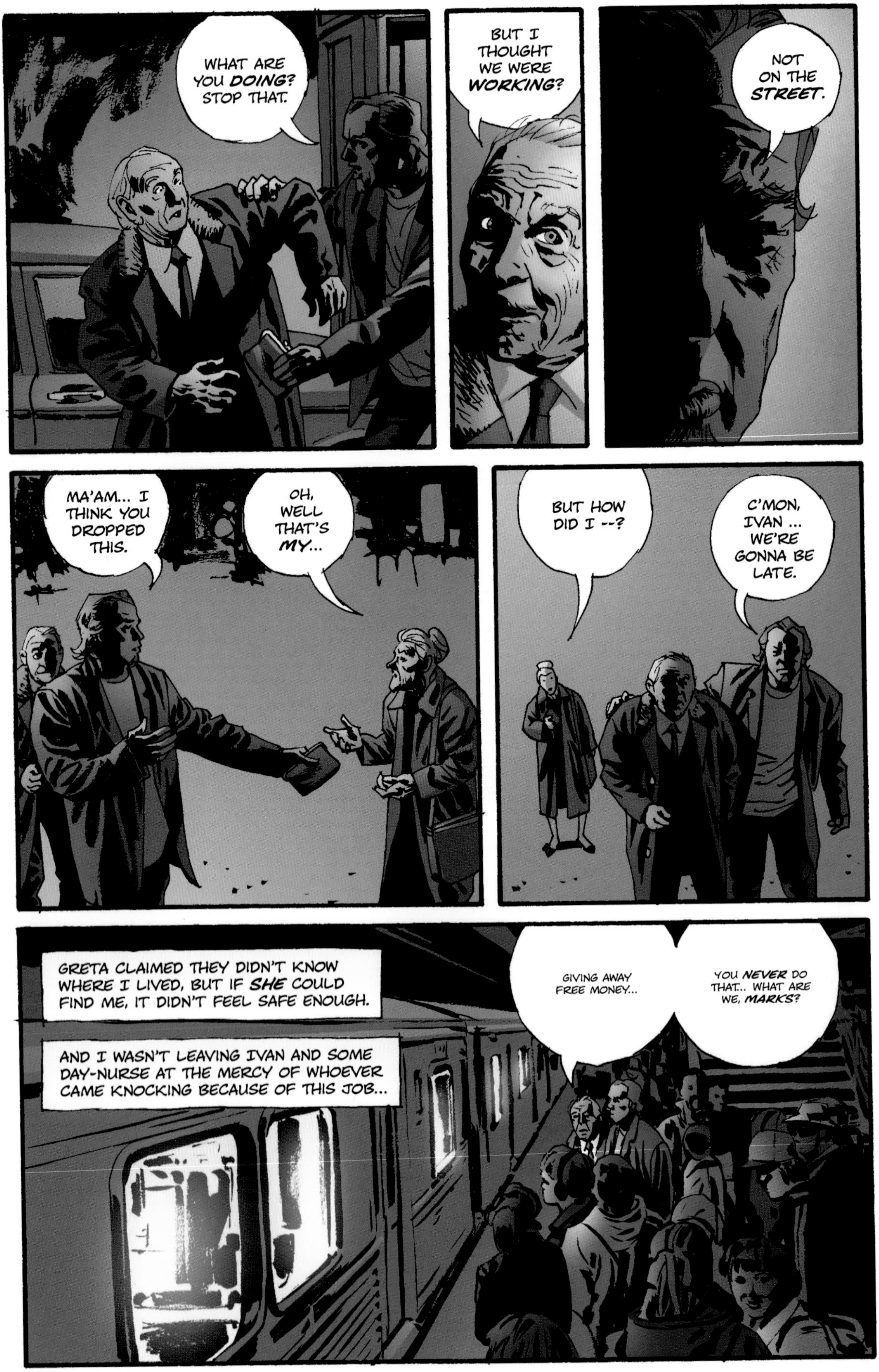
WHAT ARE YOU DOING? STOP THAT.
BUT I THOUGHT WE WERE WORKING?
NOT ON THE STREET.
MA'AM... I THINK YOU DROPPED THIS.
OH, WELL THAT'S MY...
BUT HOW DID I --?
C'MON, IVAN ... WE'RE GONNA BE LATE.
GRETA CLAIMED THEY DIDN'T KNOW WHERE I LIVED, BUT IF SHE COULD FIND ME, IT DIDN'T FEEL SAFE ENOUGH.
AND I WASN'T LEAVING IVAN AND SOME DAY-NURSE AT THE MERCY OF WHOEVER CAME KNOCKING BECAUSE OF THIS JOB...
GIVING AWAY FREE MONEY...
YOU NEVER DO THAT... WHAT ARE WE, MARKS?

OF **COURSE** WE'RE NOT, BUT WE'RE ON A **MISSION** RIGHT NOW.

WHAT MISSION?

LOOKING FOR THE RICHEST MAN IN THE CITY.

SEBASTIAN HYDE? ON THE SUBWAY? I DON'T THINK SO, LEO.

OKAY, HOW ABOUT THE MAN WHO'S CARRYING THE MOST **CASH**, THEN? THINK YOU CAN SPOT **HIM**?

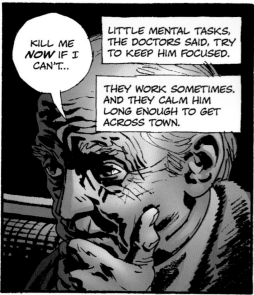

KILL ME **NOW** IF I CAN'T...

LITTLE MENTAL TASKS, THE DOCTORS SAID, TRY TO KEEP HIM FOCUSED.

THEY WORK SOMETIMES. AND THEY CALM HIM LONG ENOUGH TO GET ACROSS TOWN.

I WORRY MORE THAN I **SHOULD**. HE'S BEEN IN THE GAME SINCE HE WAS EIGHT, WEAVING THROUGH THE CROWDS ON THE CARNIVAL GROUNDS WHERE HE WAS RAISED.

BUT IF HE GOT CAUGHT, IT WOULD BE **WORSE** THAN A NIGHTMARE.

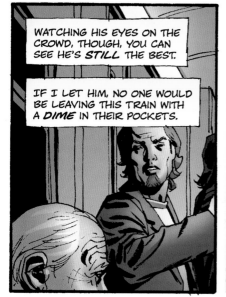

WATCHING HIS EYES ON THE CROWD, THOUGH, YOU CAN SEE HE'S **STILL** THE BEST.

IF I LET HIM, NO ONE WOULD BE LEAVING THIS TRAIN WITH A **DIME** IN THEIR POCKETS.

THOSE LITTLE SPARKS OF WHO HE **USED TO BE** MAKE ALL THE DIFFERENCE, BUT THEY CUT BOTH WAYS.

THIS IS OUR STOP, IVAN.

SURE, I... I ...

WHERE **ARE** WE...?

The Job

HERE'S THE THING... MOST HEISTS, EVEN GOOD ONES, ARE LIKE A *HOUSE OF CARDS.*

ONE MINOR DETAIL GOES WRONG, AND THEY COLLAPSE ALL AROUND YOU.

BUT I PLANNED FOR CONTINGENCIES. I *ORCHESTRATED.*

SO, MY SCORES BEGAN WITH A WELL-PLACED *DISTRACTION* FOR THE POLICE.

THIS TIME IT WAS DONNIE LEAVING A *SUSPICIOUS* PACKAGE IN A *JEWISH DELI* ON BROADWAY...

WE GOOD?

LET'S HIT IT...

THEY GOT A PICTURE OF THE MAYOR IN THERE, TAKIN' A BITE OUT OF A *PICKLE.*

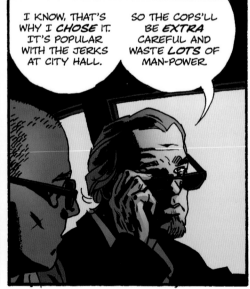

I KNOW, THAT'S WHY I *CHOSE* IT. IT'S POPULAR WITH THE JERKS AT CITY HALL.

SO THE COPS'LL BE *EXTRA* CAREFUL AND WASTE *LOTS* OF MAN-POWER

GOTTA LOVE THE *WAR ON TERROR,* HUNH?

YEP... ONLY WINNERS ARE THE *THIEVES.*

SEYMOUR DID WHAT HE ALWAYS DID BEST, KEEPING THE CLOCK AND CALLING "GO" TIMES.

THE MOMENT THE EVIDENCE TRANSPORT TURNED ITS FIRST CORNER, HE WAS ON THE PHONE TO 911 REPORTING A BOMB THREAT AT THE DELI WE'D JUST LEFT.

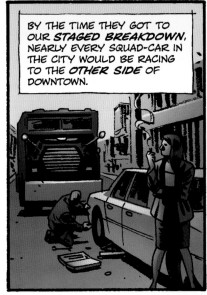

BY THE TIME THEY GOT TO OUR *STAGED BREAKDOWN*, NEARLY EVERY SQUAD-CAR IN THE CITY WOULD BE RACING TO THE *OTHER SIDE* OF DOWNTOWN.

AND WHEN THEY PULLED INTO THE *JACKSON STREET TUNNEL*, THANKS TO CAREFUL TIMING AND SEYMOUR'S WATCHFUL EYE...

...THEY WERE PULLING IN *RIGHT BEHIND* ME AND DONNIE.

OKAY, HOW ABOUT THIS ONE...

YOU WILL DRINK THE BLACK SPERM OF MY VENGEANCE!

TOO EASY... *BEYOND THE VALLEY OF THE DOLLS.*

GRETA AND RED WOULD BE TWO OR THREE CARS BEHIND THEM, HAVING RELEASED THE JACK AND RACED BACK AROUND.

AND JEFF'S PARTNERS WERE CREATING A *TRAFFIC JAM* TWENTY YARDS AHEAD...

HNNK
BLLEEP
HOONK
BREEETT

...NEXT TO AN *ABANDONED* CAR THAT DONNIE AND I PLACED THIRTY MINUTES EARLIER

OUT OF GAS
PLEASE
DON'T TOW

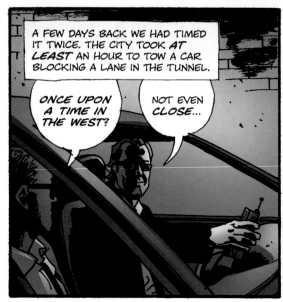

A FEW DAYS BACK WE HAD TIMED IT TWICE. THE CITY TOOK *AT LEAST* AN HOUR TO TOW A CAR BLOCKING A LANE IN THE TUNNEL.

ONCE UPON A TIME IN THE WEST?

NOT EVEN *CLOSE*...

AND WITH SEYMOUR AND JEFF IN THE GETAWAY CAR NEARBY, MONITORING POLICE TRAFFIC...

ALL CLEAR, LEO. THEY JUST CORDONED OFF *SIX BLOCKS* OF BROADWAY, *BOMB SQUAD* AND EVERYTHING.

RIGHT.

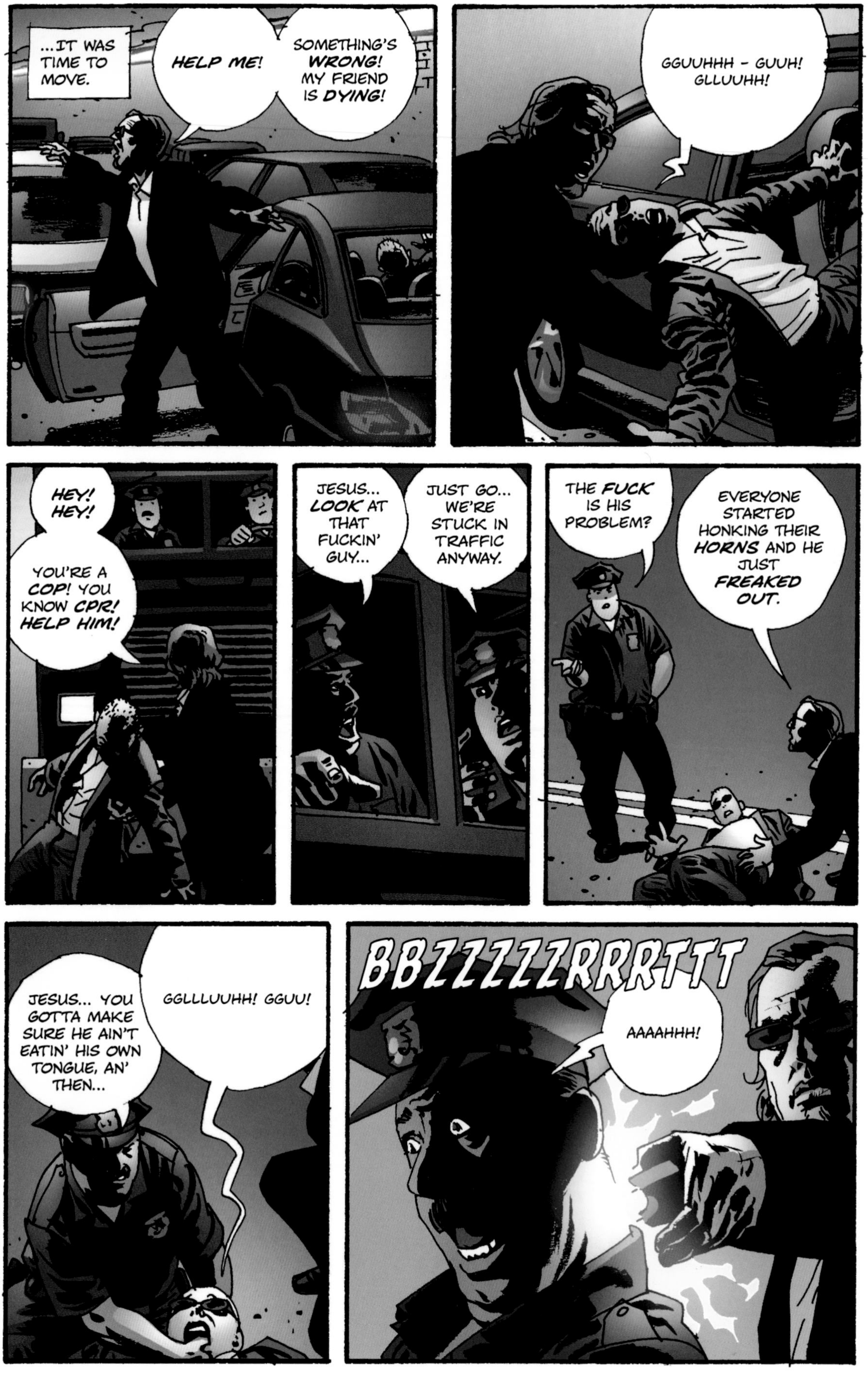
...IT WAS TIME TO MOVE.
HELP ME!
SOMETHING'S WRONG! MY FRIEND IS DYING!
GGUUHHH - GUUH! GLLUUHH!
HEY! HEY!
YOU'RE A COP! YOU KNOW CPR! HELP HIM!
JESUS... LOOK AT THAT FUCKIN' GUY...
JUST GO... WE'RE STUCK IN TRAFFIC ANYWAY.
THE FUCK IS HIS PROBLEM?
EVERYONE STARTED HONKING THEIR HORNS AND HE JUST FREAKED OUT.
JESUS... YOU GOTTA MAKE SURE HE AIN'T EATIN' HIS OWN TONGUE, AN' THEN...
GGLLLUUHH! GGUU!
BBZZZZZZRRRRTTT
AAAAHHH!

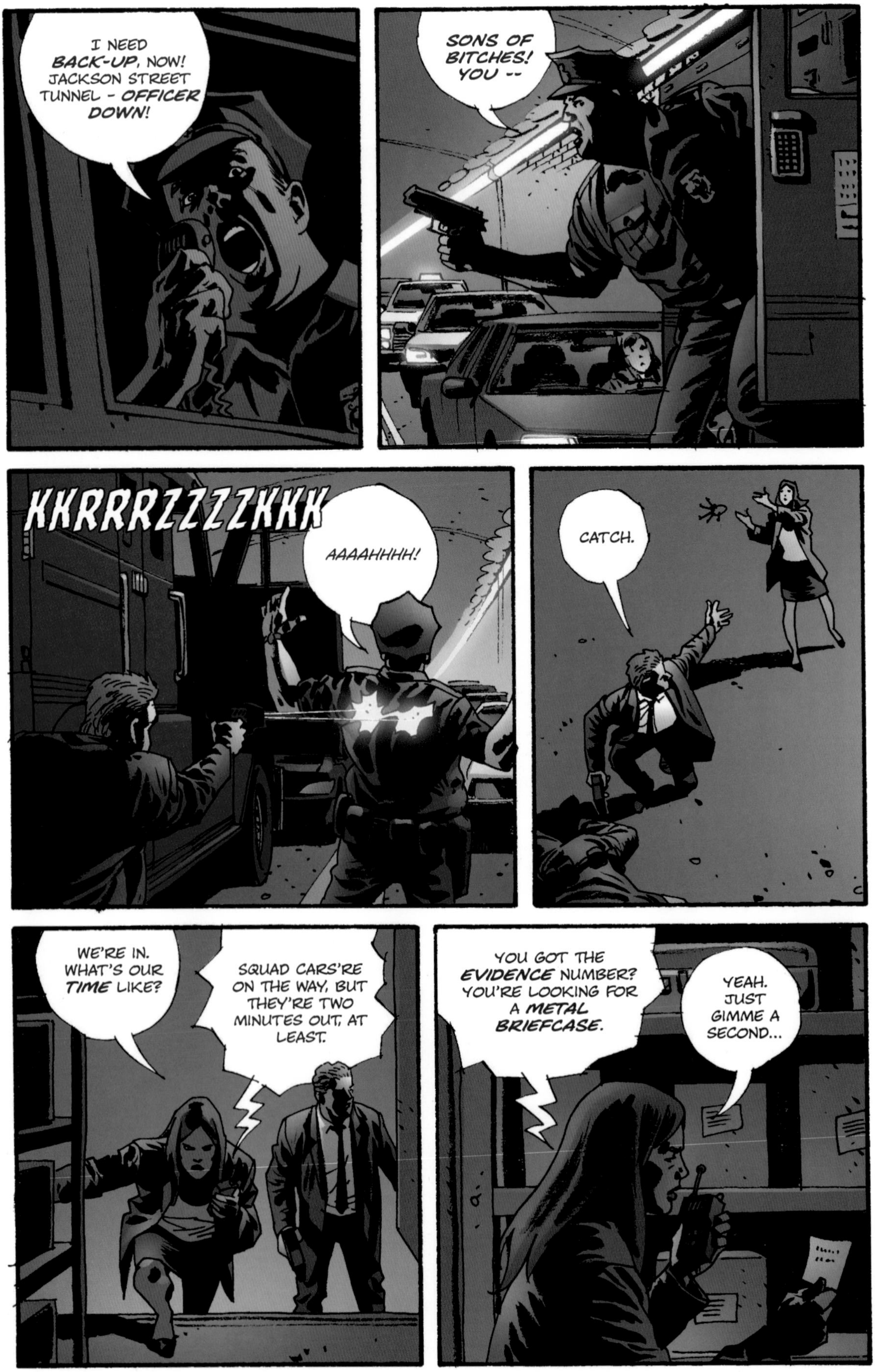
I NEED BACK-UP, NOW! JACKSON STREET TUNNEL - OFFICER DOWN!
SONS OF BITCHES! YOU --
KKRRRZZZZKKK
AAAAHHHH!
CATCH.
WE'RE IN. WHAT'S OUR TIME LIKE?
SQUAD CARS'RE ON THE WAY, BUT THEY'RE TWO MINUTES OUT, AT LEAST.
YOU GOT THE EVIDENCE NUMBER? YOU'RE LOOKING FOR A METAL BRIEFCASE.
YEAH. JUST GIMME A SECOND...

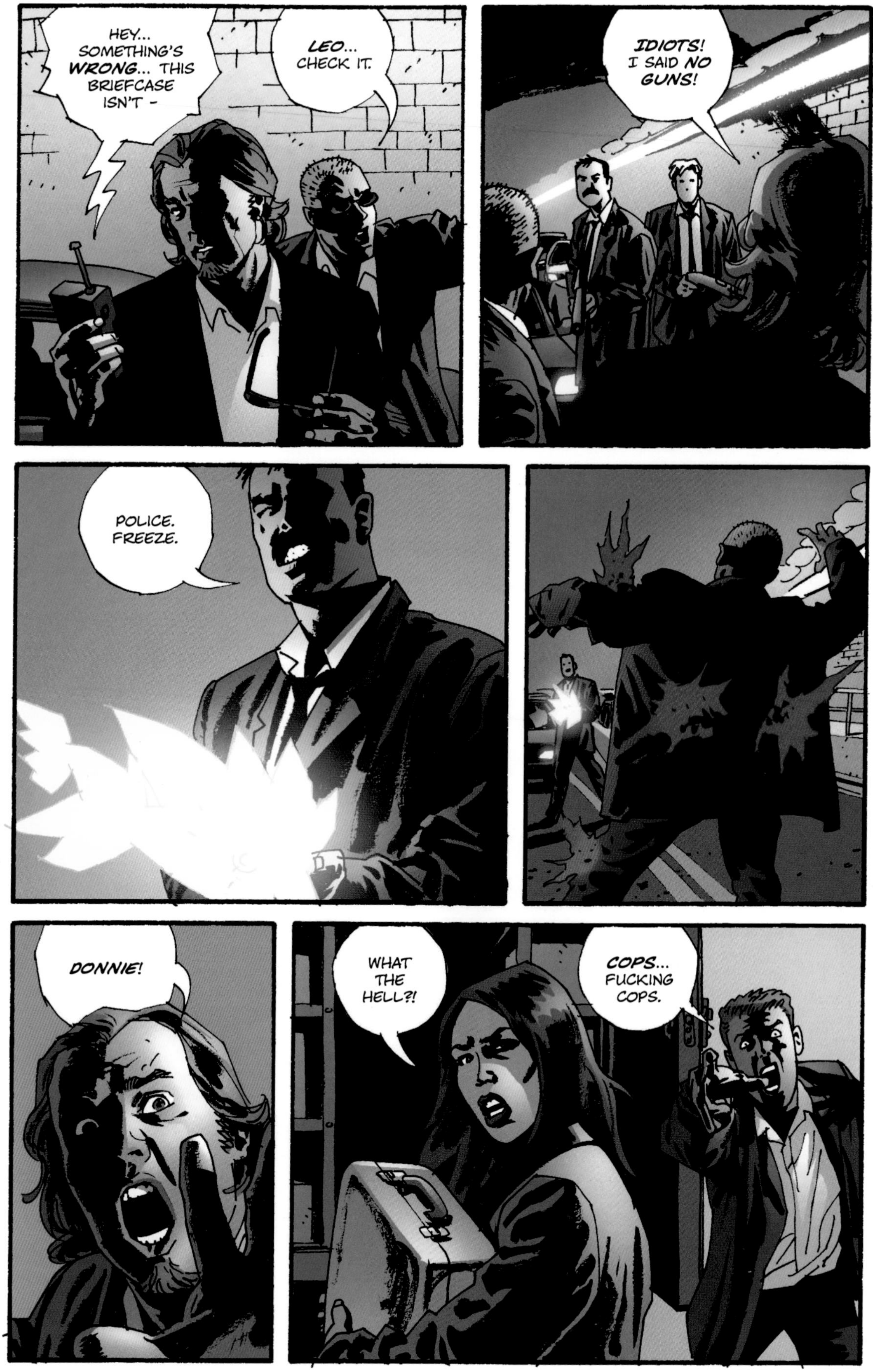
HEY... SOMETHING'S WRONG... THIS BRIEFCASE ISN'T -
LEO... CHECK IT.
IDIOTS! I SAID NO GUNS!
POLICE. FREEZE.
DONNIE!
WHAT THE HELL?!
COPS... FUCKING COPS.

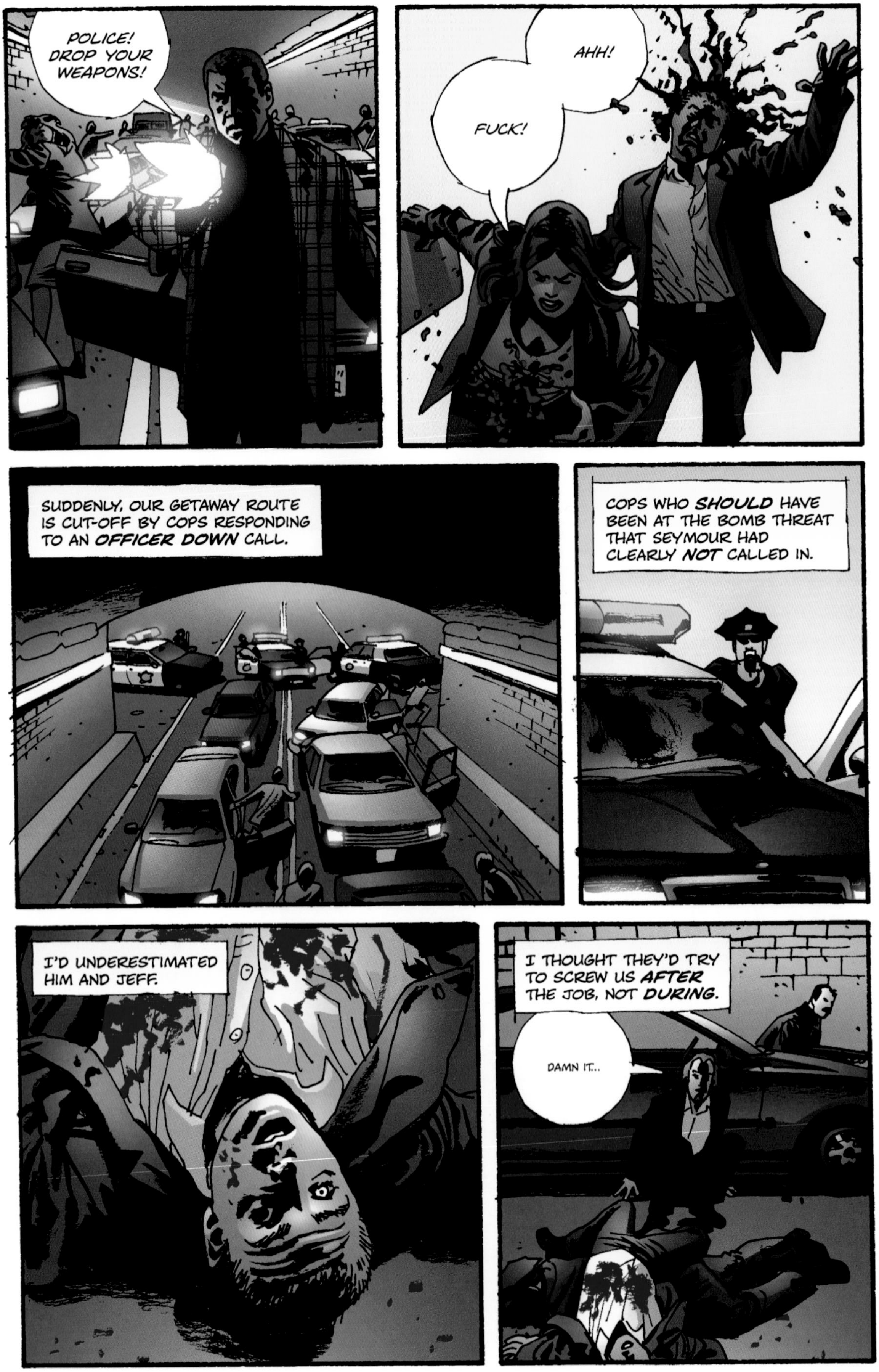
POLICE! DROP YOUR WEAPONS!
AHH!
FUCK!
SUDDENLY, OUR GETAWAY ROUTE IS CUT-OFF BY COPS RESPONDING TO AN *OFFICER DOWN* CALL.
COPS WHO *SHOULD* HAVE BEEN AT THE BOMB THREAT THAT SEYMOUR HAD CLEARLY *NOT* CALLED IN.
I'D UNDERESTIMATED HIM AND JEFF.
I THOUGHT THEY'D TRY TO SCREW US *AFTER* THE JOB, NOT *DURING*.
DAMN IT...

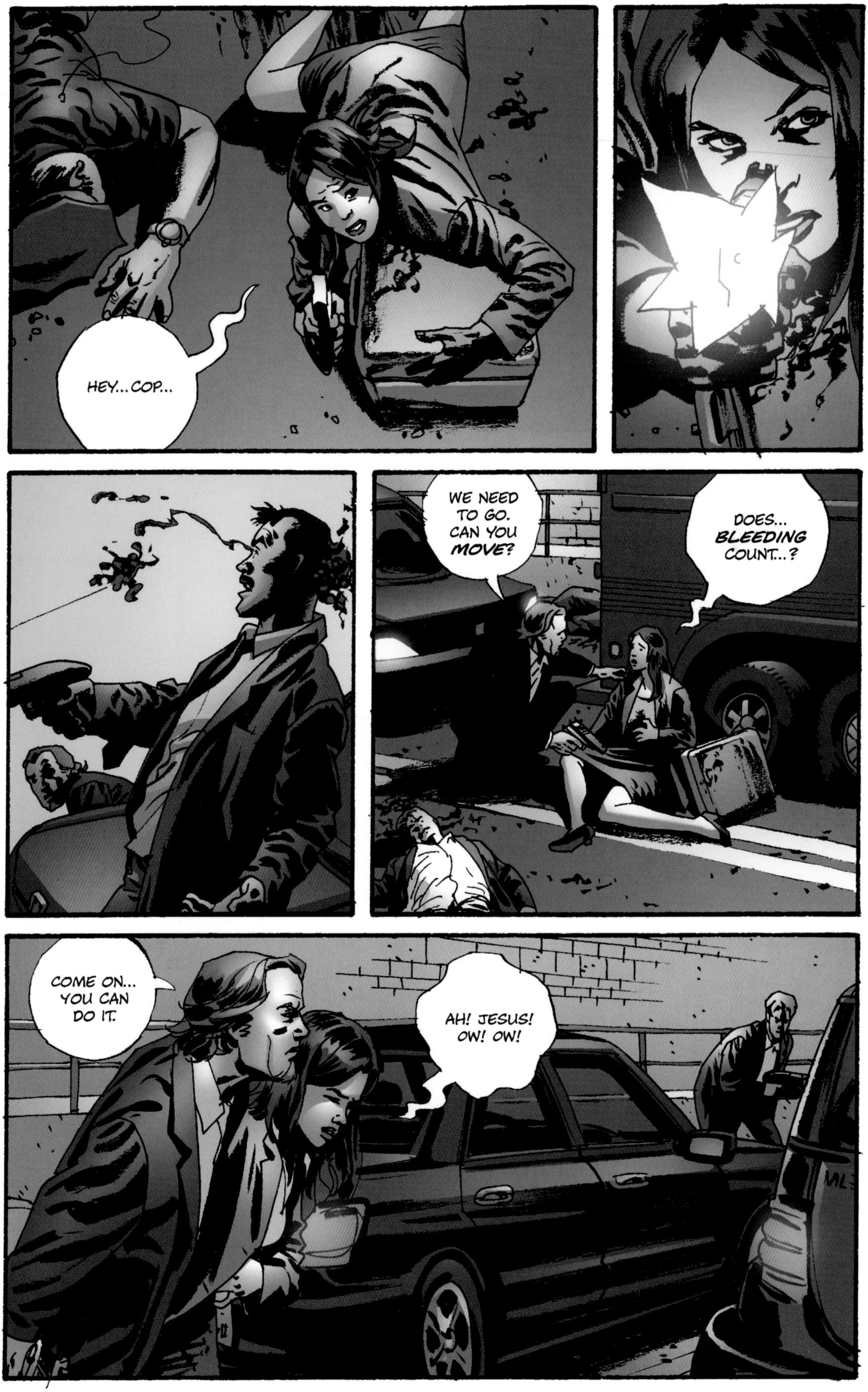
HEY... COP...
WE NEED TO GO. CAN YOU *MOVE*?
DOES... **BLEEDING** COUNT...?
COME ON... YOU CAN DO IT.
AH! JESUS! OW! OW!

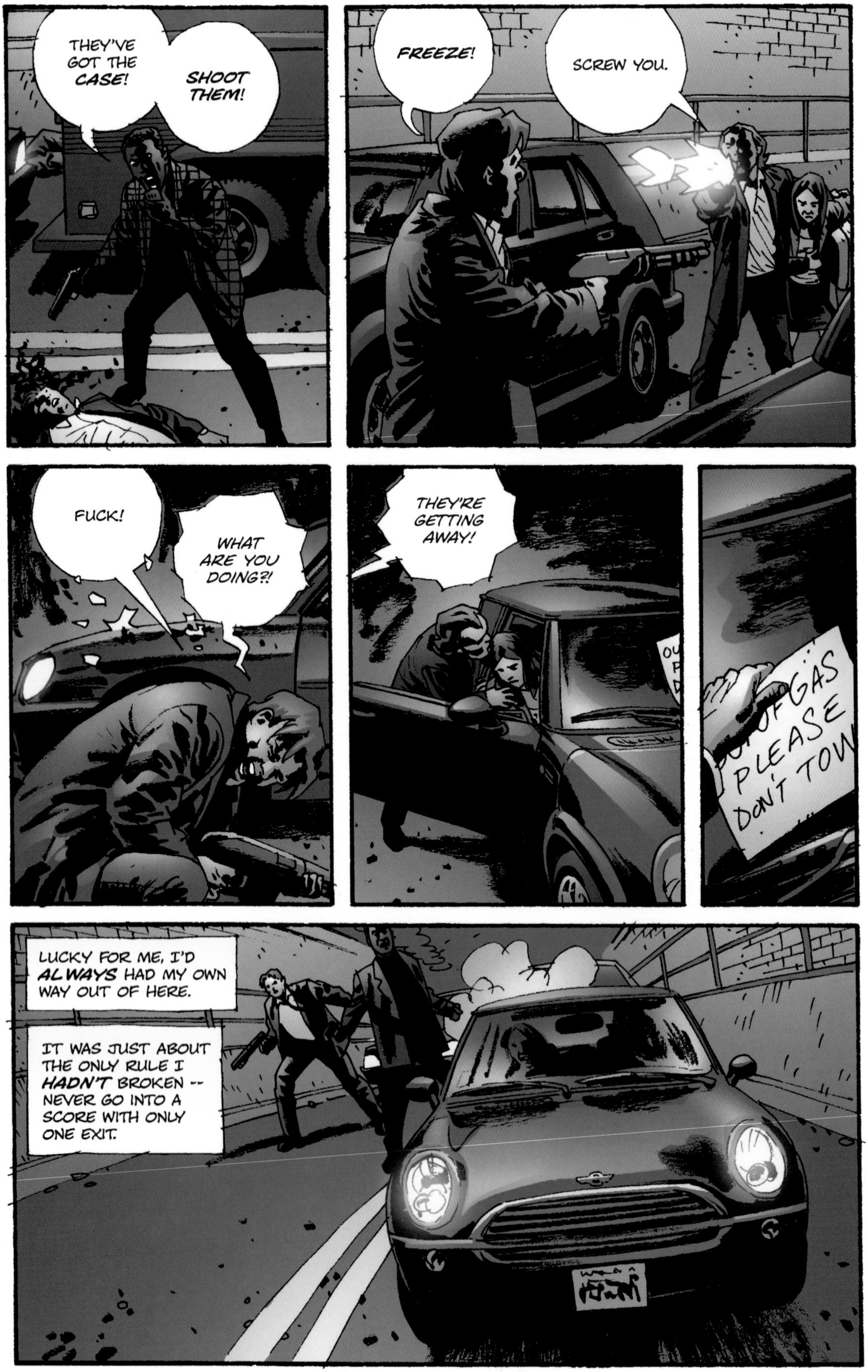
THEY'VE GOT THE CASE!
SHOOT THEM!
FREEZE!
SCREW YOU.
FUCK!
WHAT ARE YOU DOING?!
THEY'RE GETTING AWAY!
OUT OF GAS PLEASE DON'T TOW
LUCKY FOR ME, I'D ALWAYS HAD MY OWN WAY OUT OF HERE.
IT WAS JUST ABOUT THE ONLY RULE I HADN'T BROKEN -- NEVER GO INTO A SCORE WITH ONLY ONE EXIT.

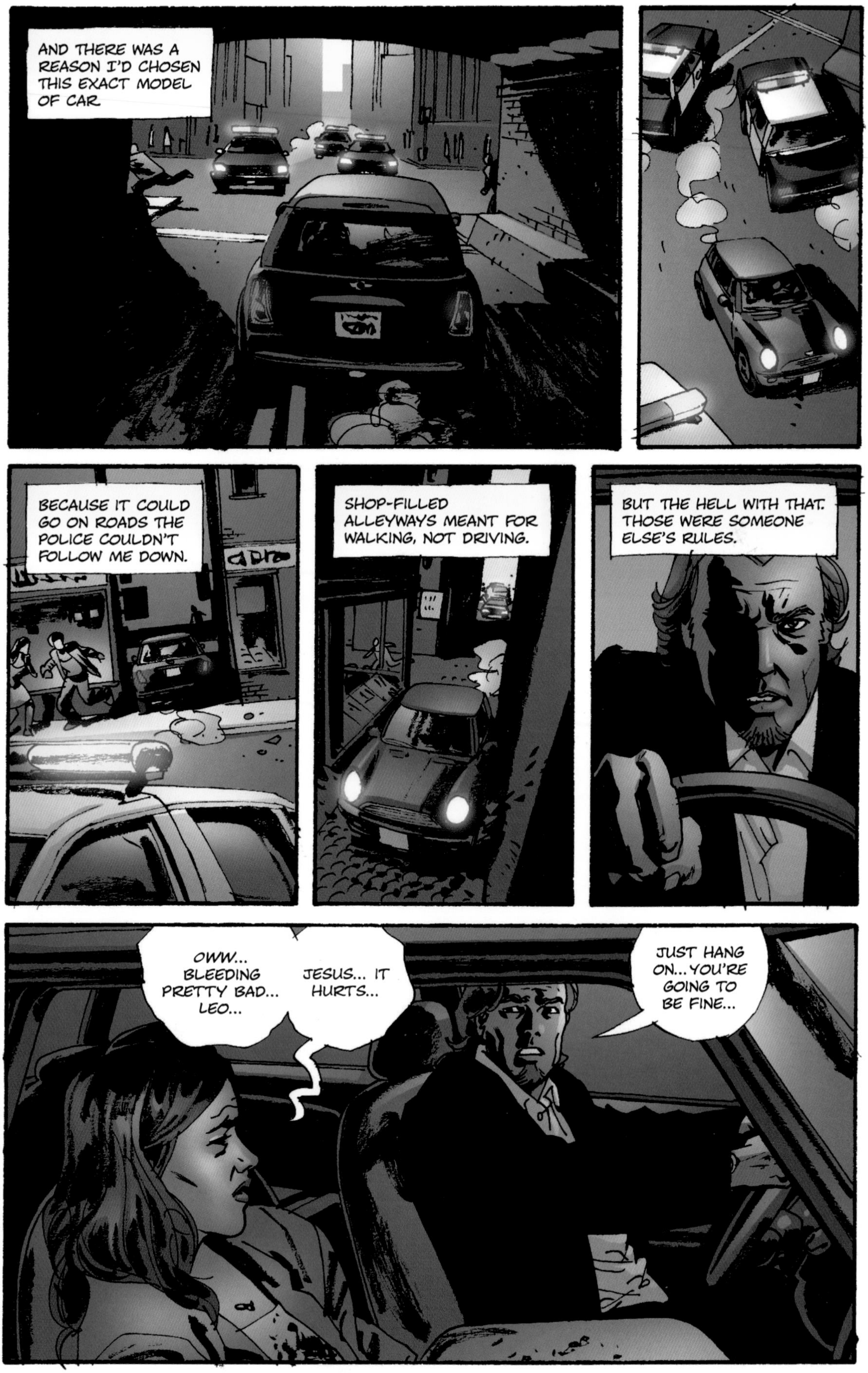
AND THERE WAS A REASON I'D CHOSEN THIS EXACT MODEL OF CAR
BECAUSE IT COULD GO ON ROADS THE POLICE COULDN'T FOLLOW ME DOWN.
SHOP-FILLED ALLEYWAYS MEANT FOR WALKING, NOT DRIVING.
BUT THE HELL WITH THAT. THOSE WERE SOMEONE ELSE'S RULES.
OWW... BLEEDING PRETTY BAD... LEO...
JESUS... IT HURTS...
JUST HANG ON... YOU'RE GOING TO BE FINE...

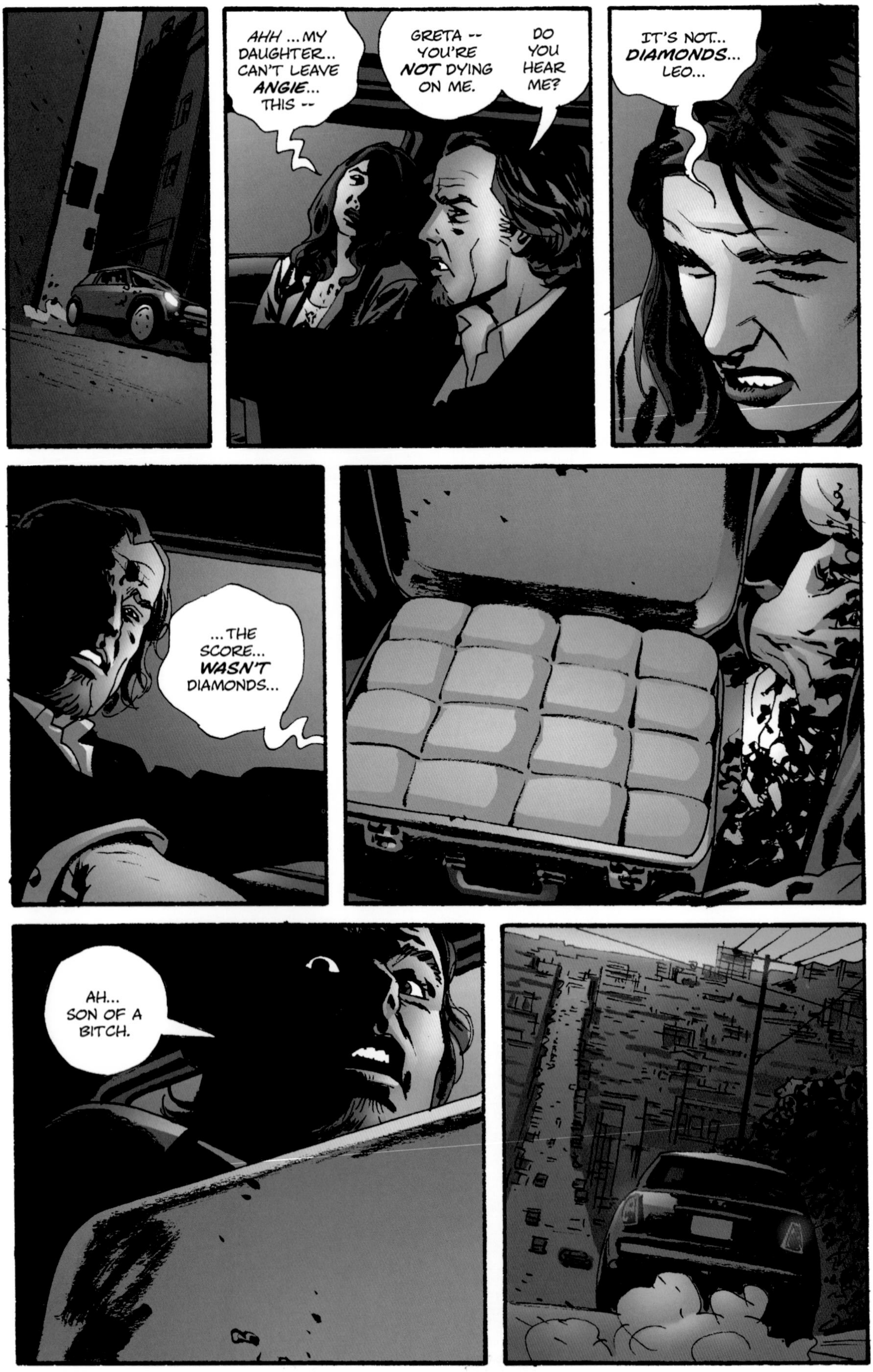
AHH ...MY DAUGHTER.. CAN'T LEAVE ANGIE... THIS --
GRETA -- YOU'RE NOT DYING ON ME.
DO YOU HEAR ME?
IT'S NOT... DIAMONDS... LEO...
...THE SCORE... WASN'T DIAMONDS...
AH... SON OF A BITCH.

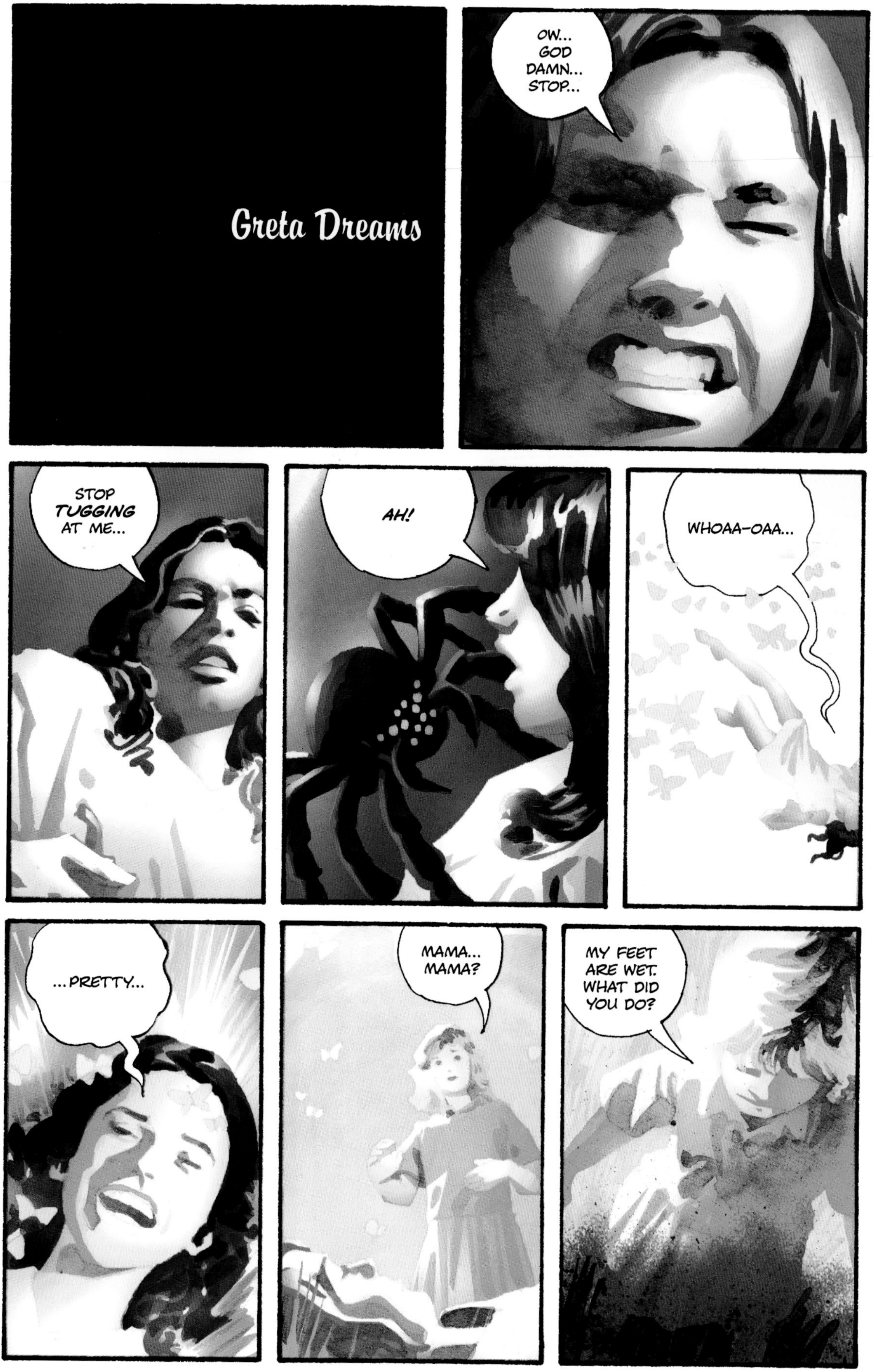
Greta Dreams
OW... GOD DAMN... STOP...
STOP TUGGING AT ME...
AH!
WHOAA-OAA...
...PRETTY...
MAMA... MAMA?
MY FEET ARE WET. WHAT DID YOU DO?

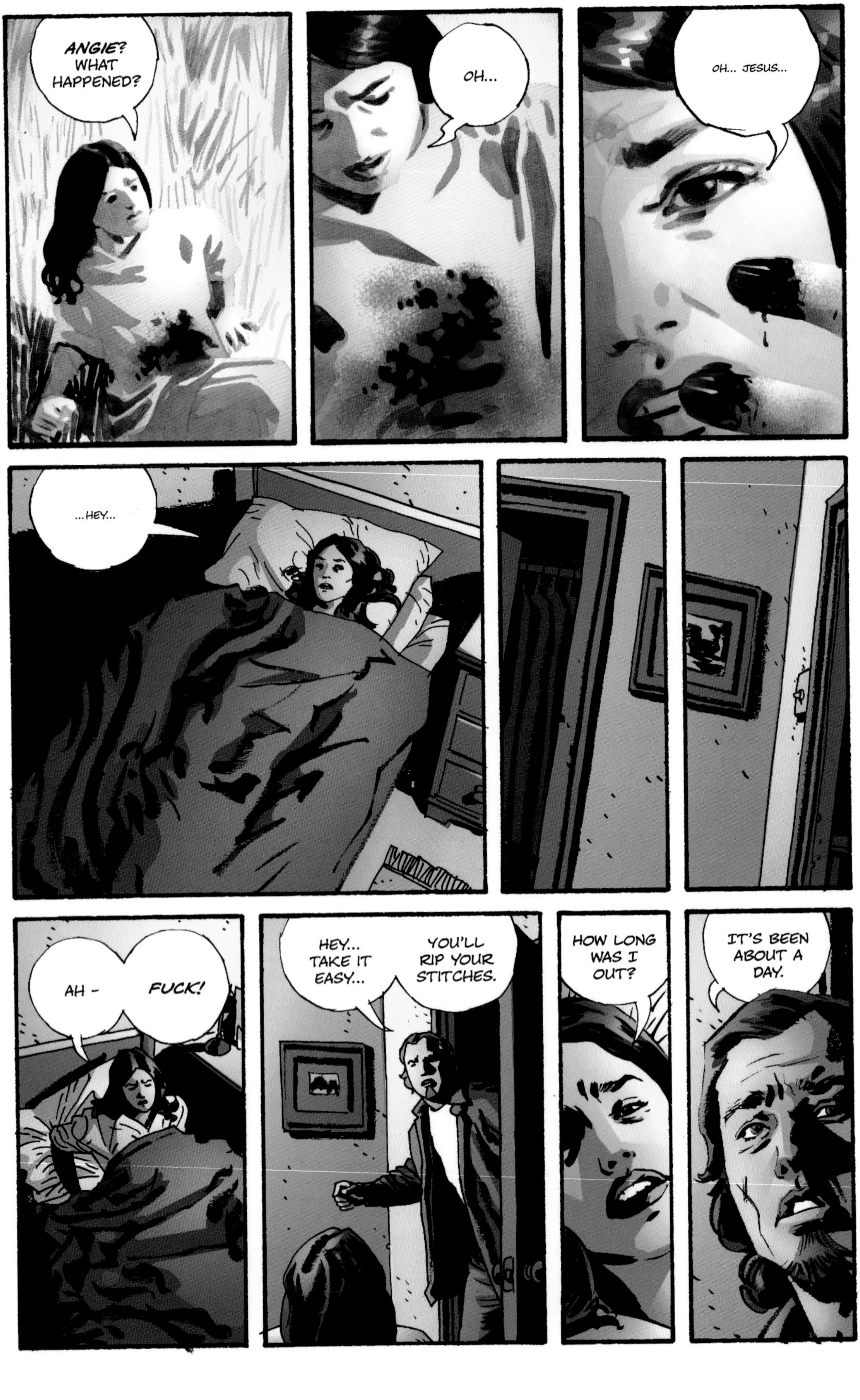
ANGIE? WHAT HAPPENED?
OH...
OH... JESUS...
...HEY...
AH -
FUCK!
HEY... TAKE IT EASY...
YOU'LL RIP YOUR STITCHES.
HOW LONG WAS I OUT?
IT'S BEEN ABOUT A DAY.

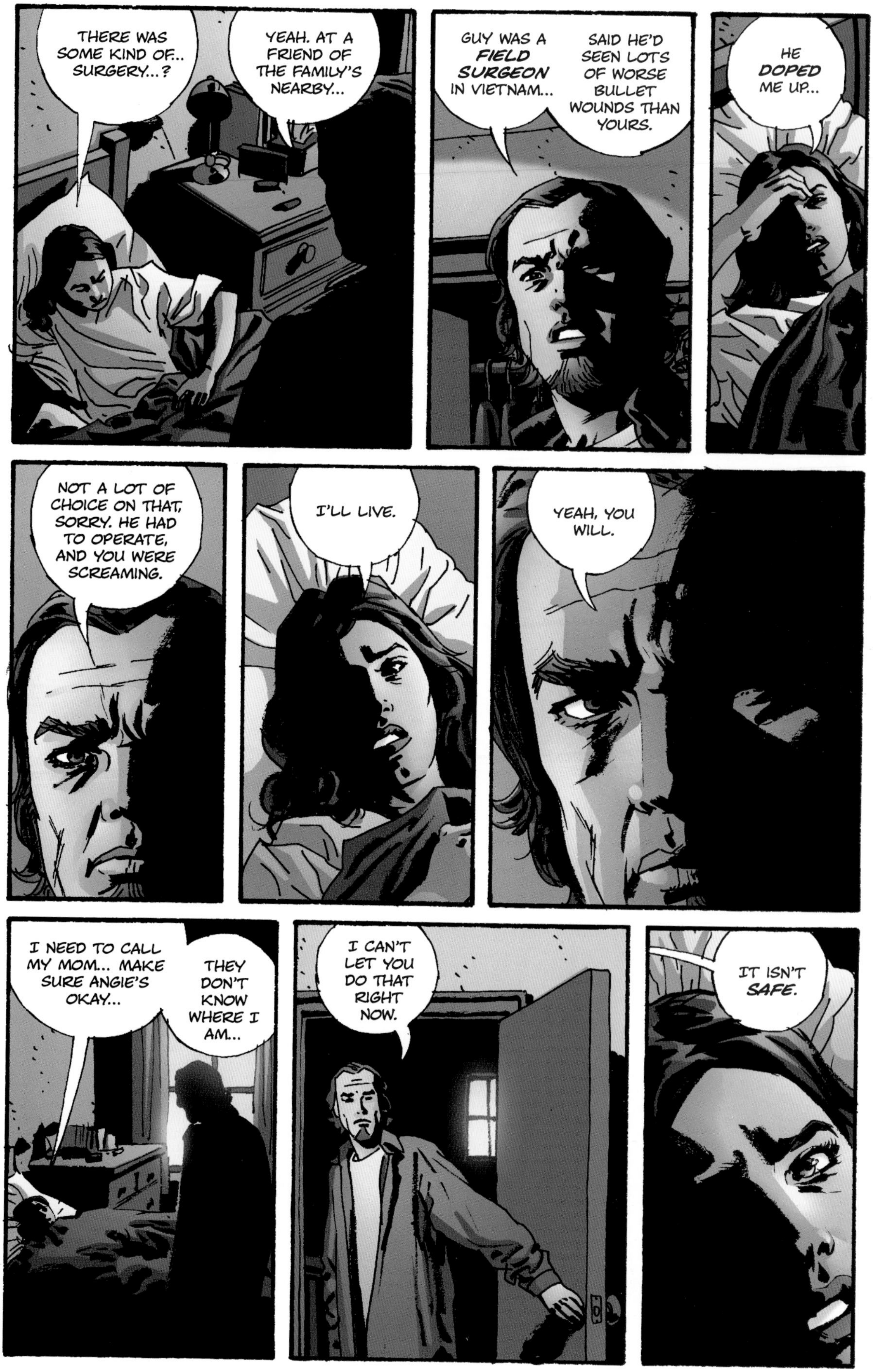
THERE WAS SOME KIND OF... SURGERY...?
YEAH. AT A FRIEND OF THE FAMILY'S NEARBY...
GUY WAS A FIELD SURGEON IN VIETNAM...
SAID HE'D SEEN LOTS OF WORSE BULLET WOUNDS THAN YOURS.
HE DOPED ME UP...
NOT A LOT OF CHOICE ON THAT, SORRY. HE HAD TO OPERATE, AND YOU WERE SCREAMING.
I'LL LIVE.
YEAH, YOU WILL.
I NEED TO CALL MY MOM... MAKE SURE ANGIE'S OKAY...
THEY DON'T KNOW WHERE I AM...
I CAN'T LET YOU DO THAT RIGHT NOW.
IT ISN'T SAFE.

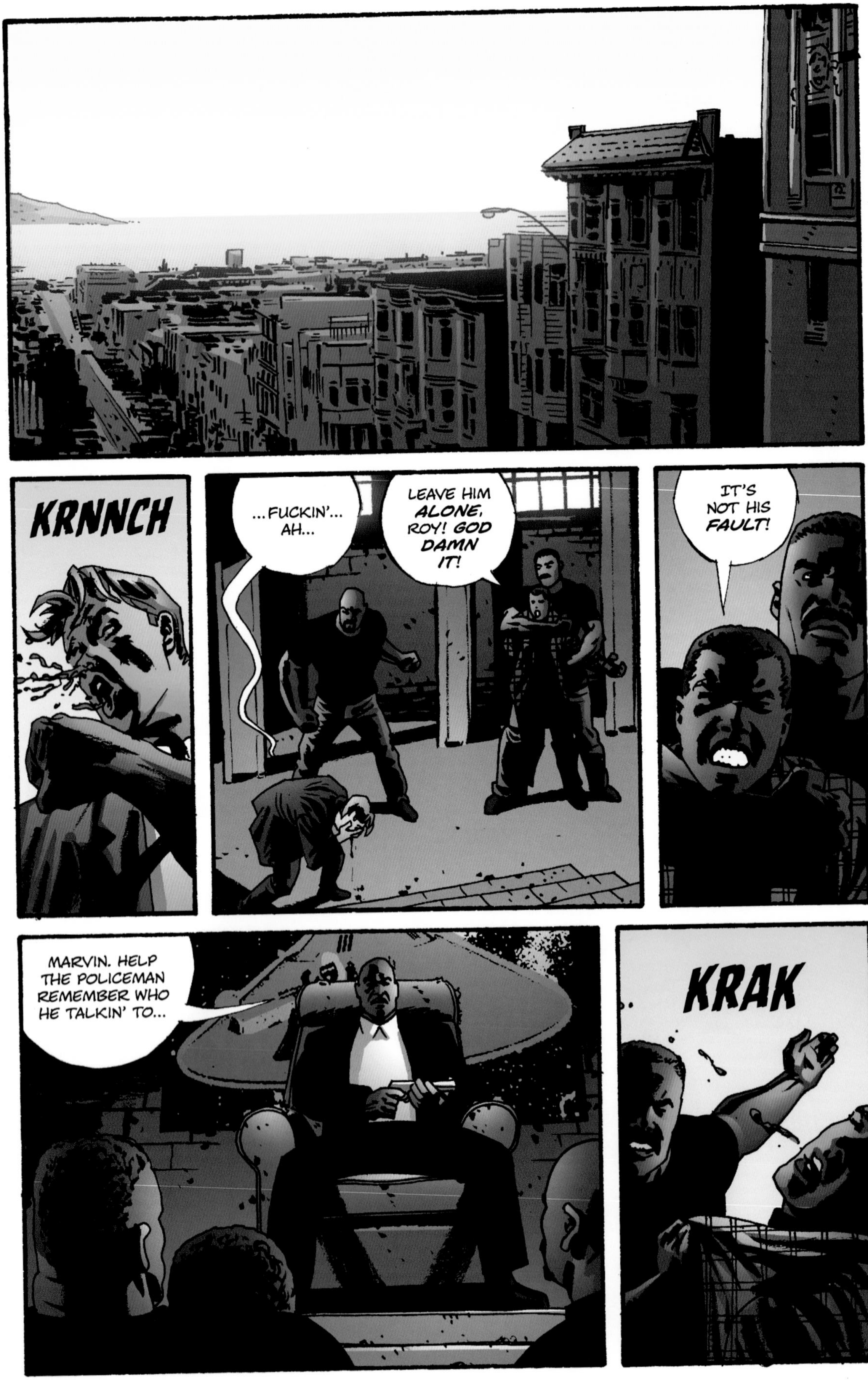
KRNNCH
...FUCKIN'... AH...
LEAVE HIM ALONE, ROY! GOD DAMN IT!
IT'S NOT HIS FAULT!
MARVIN. HELP THE POLICEMAN REMEMBER WHO HE TALKIN' TO...
KRAK

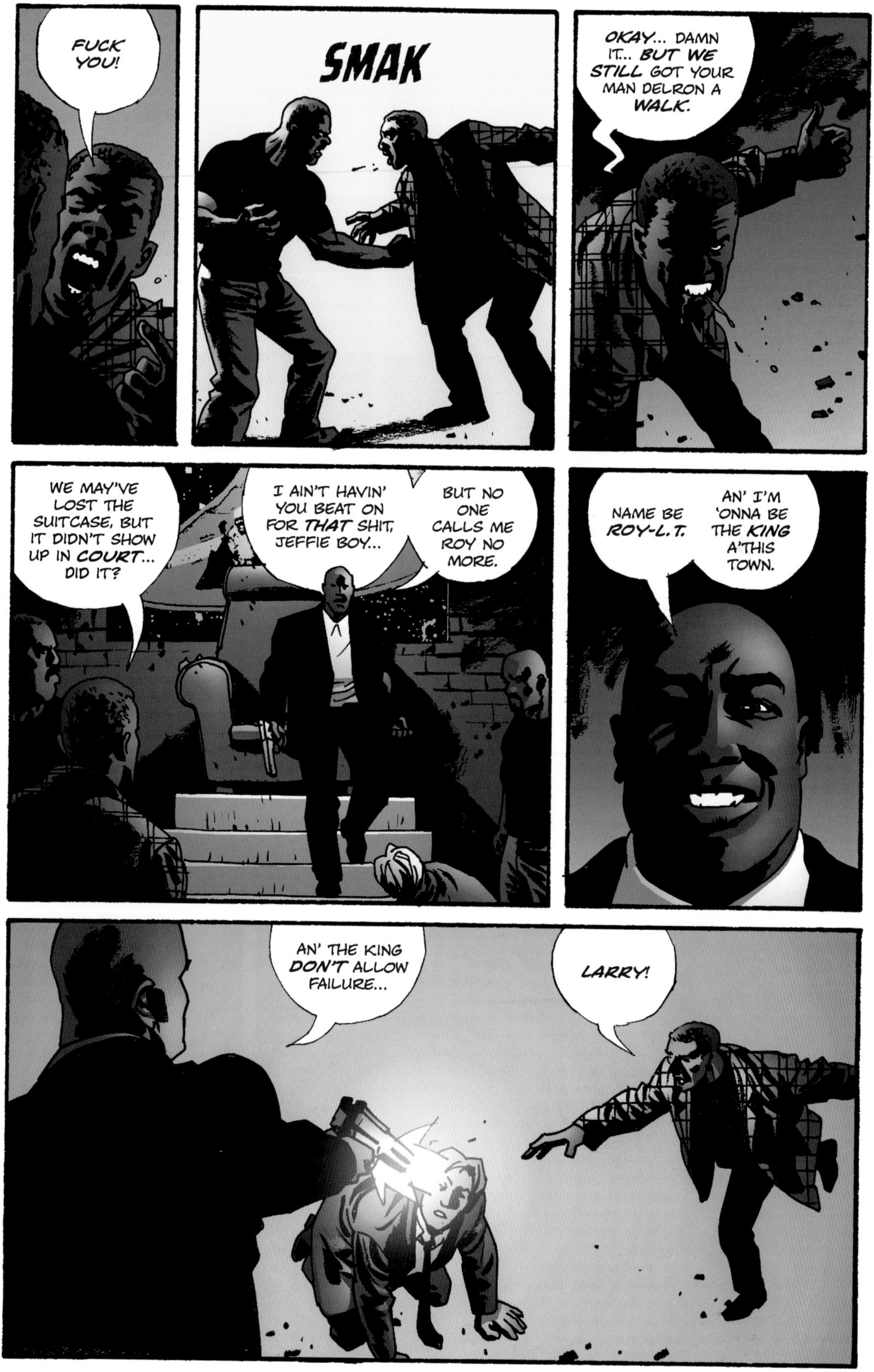
FUCK YOU!
SMAK
OKAY... DAMN IT... BUT WE STILL GOT YOUR MAN DELRON A WALK.
WE MAY'VE LOST THE SUITCASE, BUT IT DIDN'T SHOW UP IN COURT... DID IT?
I AIN'T HAVIN' YOU BEAT ON FOR THAT SHIT, JEFFIE BOY...
BUT NO ONE CALLS ME ROY NO MORE.
NAME BE ROY-L.T.
AN' I'M 'ONNA BE THE KING A'THIS TOWN.
AN' THE KING DON'T ALLOW FAILURE...
LARRY!

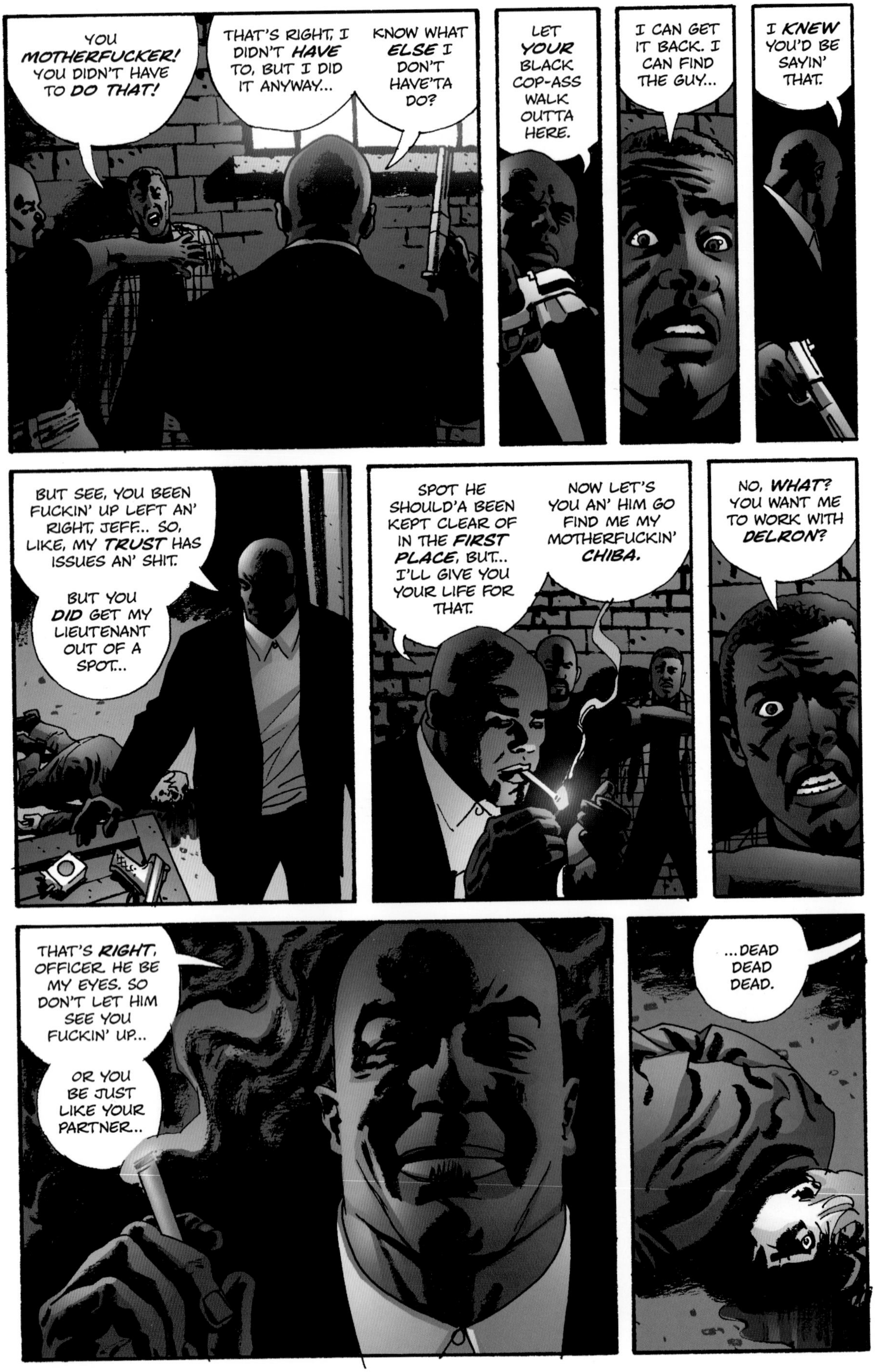
YOU MOTHERFUCKER! YOU DIDN'T HAVE TO DO THAT!
THAT'S RIGHT, I DIDN'T HAVE TO, BUT I DID IT ANYWAY...
KNOW WHAT ELSE I DON'T HAVE'TA DO?
LET YOUR BLACK COP-ASS WALK OUTTA HERE.
I CAN GET IT BACK. I CAN FIND THE GUY...
I KNEW YOU'D BE SAYIN' THAT.
BUT SEE, YOU BEEN FUCKIN' UP LEFT AN' RIGHT, JEFF... SO, LIKE, MY TRUST HAS ISSUES AN' SHIT.
BUT YOU DID GET MY LIEUTENANT OUT OF A SPOT...
SPOT HE SHOULD'A BEEN KEPT CLEAR OF IN THE FIRST PLACE, BUT... I'LL GIVE YOU YOUR LIFE FOR THAT.
NOW LET'S YOU AN' HIM GO FIND ME MY MOTHERFUCKIN' CHIBA.
NO, WHAT? YOU WANT ME TO WORK WITH DELRON?
THAT'S RIGHT, OFFICER. HE BE MY EYES. SO DON'T LET HIM SEE YOU FUCKIN' UP...
OR YOU BE JUST LIKE YOUR PARTNER...
...DEAD DEAD DEAD.

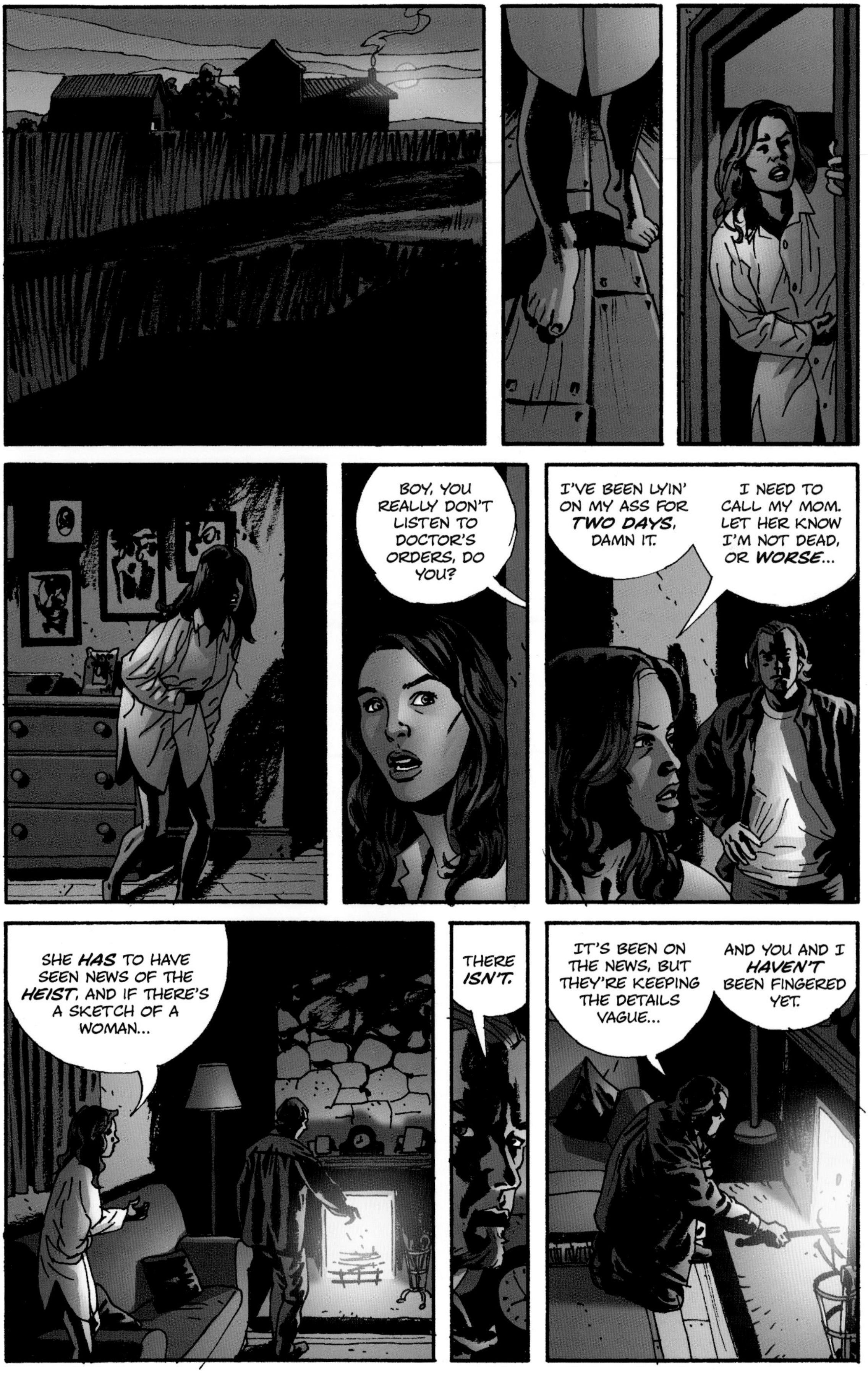
BOY, YOU REALLY DON'T LISTEN TO DOCTOR'S ORDERS, DO YOU?
I'VE BEEN LYIN' ON MY ASS FOR TWO DAYS, DAMN IT.
I NEED TO CALL MY MOM. LET HER KNOW I'M NOT DEAD, OR WORSE...
SHE HAS TO HAVE SEEN NEWS OF THE HEIST, AND IF THERE'S A SKETCH OF A WOMAN...
THERE ISN'T.
IT'S BEEN ON THE NEWS, BUT THEY'RE KEEPING THE DETAILS VAGUE...
AND YOU AND I HAVEN'T BEEN FINGERED YET.

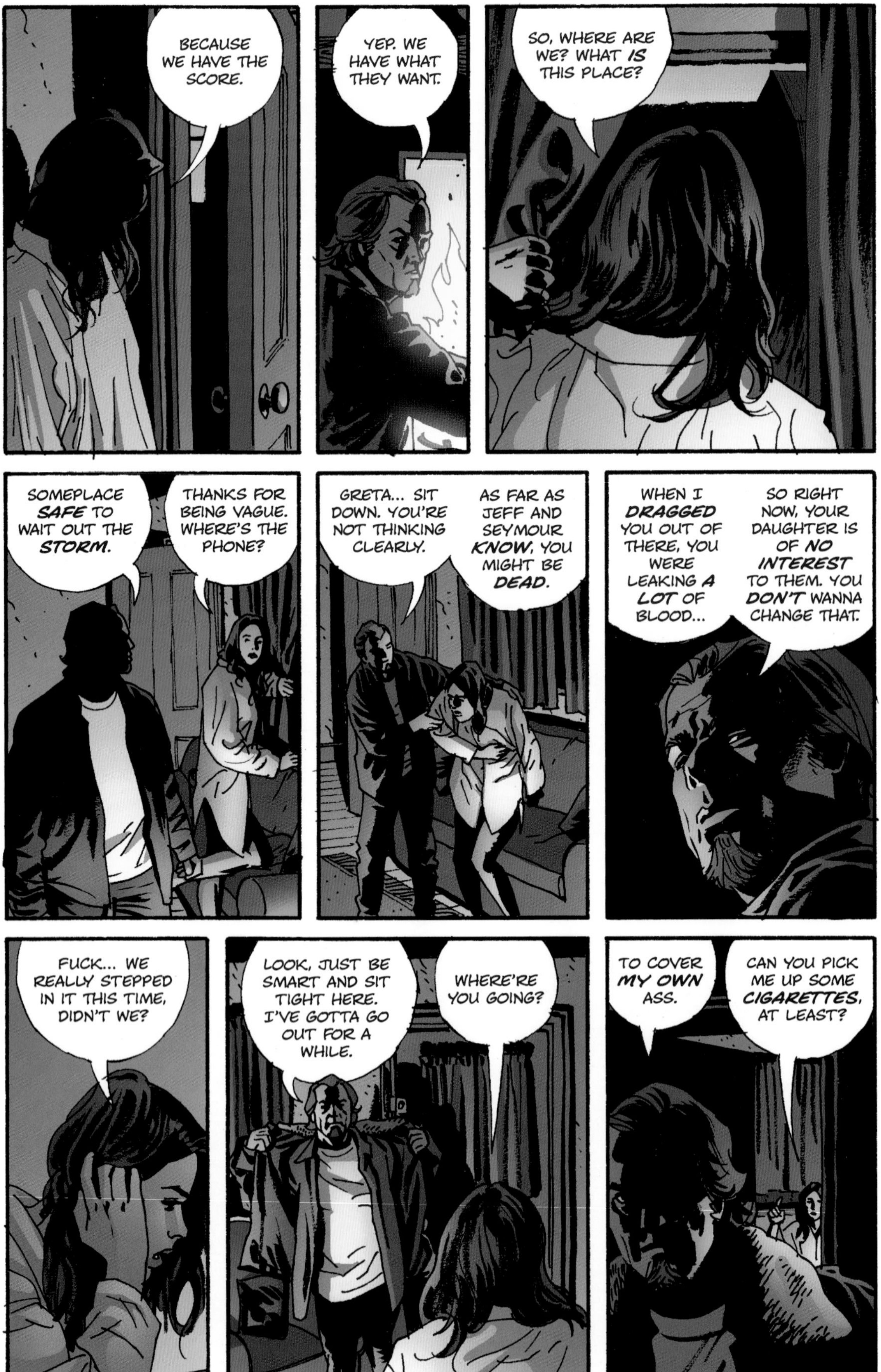
BECAUSE WE HAVE THE SCORE.
YEP. WE HAVE WHAT THEY WANT.
SO, WHERE ARE WE? WHAT IS THIS PLACE?
SOMEPLACE SAFE TO WAIT OUT THE STORM.
THANKS FOR BEING VAGUE. WHERE'S THE PHONE?
GRETA... SIT DOWN. YOU'RE NOT THINKING CLEARLY.
AS FAR AS JEFF AND SEYMOUR KNOW, YOU MIGHT BE DEAD.
WHEN I DRAGGED YOU OUT OF THERE, YOU WERE LEAKING A LOT OF BLOOD...
SO RIGHT NOW, YOUR DAUGHTER IS OF NO INTEREST TO THEM. YOU DON'T WANNA CHANGE THAT.
FUCK... WE REALLY STEPPED IN IT THIS TIME, DIDN'T WE?
LOOK, JUST BE SMART AND SIT TIGHT HERE. I'VE GOTTA GO OUT FOR A WHILE.
WHERE'RE YOU GOING?
TO COVER MY OWN ASS.
CAN YOU PICK ME UP SOME CIGARETTES, AT LEAST?

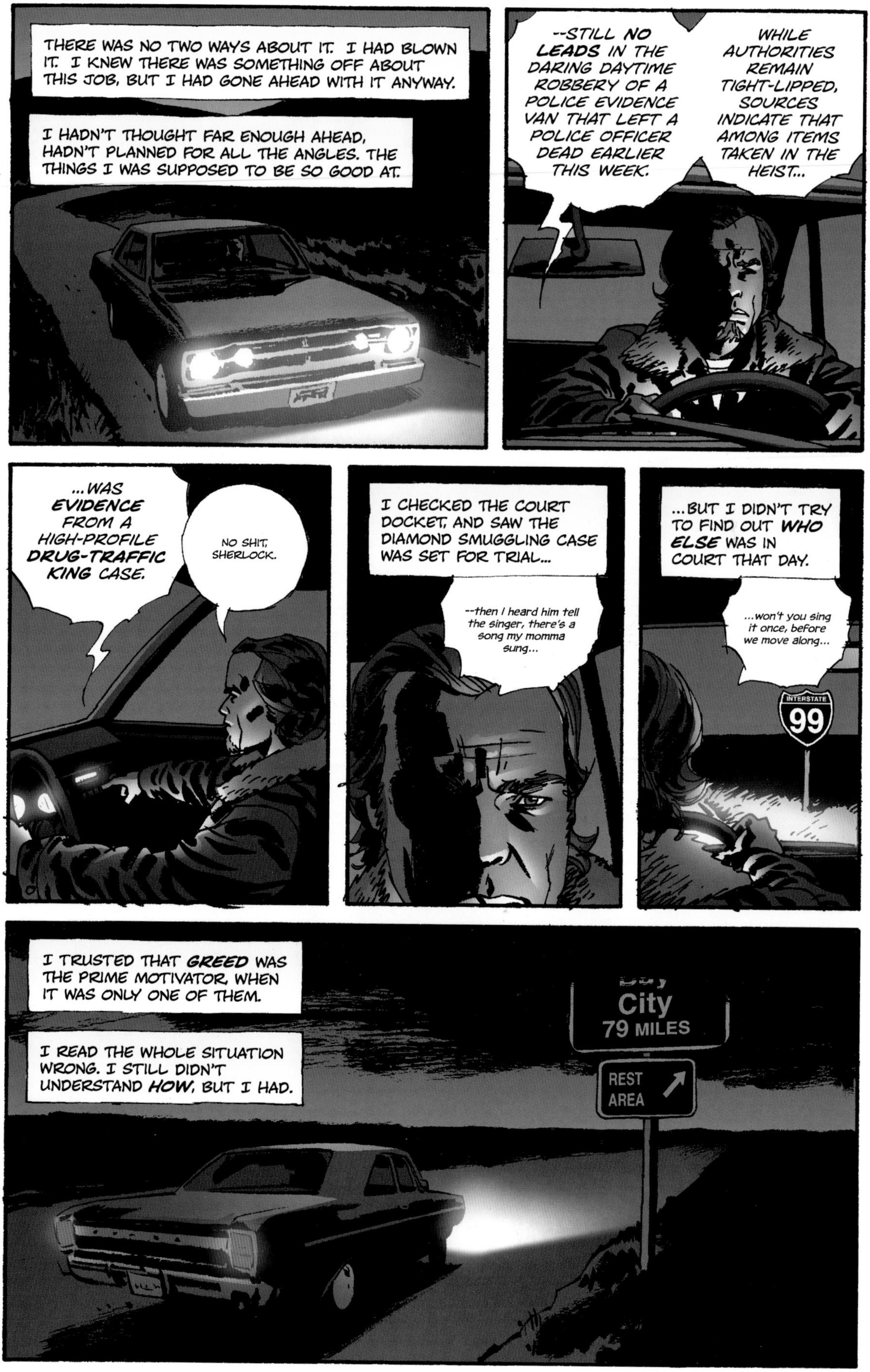
THERE WAS NO TWO WAYS ABOUT IT. I HAD BLOWN IT. I KNEW THERE WAS SOMETHING OFF ABOUT THIS JOB, BUT I HAD GONE AHEAD WITH IT ANYWAY.
I HADN'T THOUGHT FAR ENOUGH AHEAD, HADN'T PLANNED FOR ALL THE ANGLES. THE THINGS I WAS SUPPOSED TO BE SO GOOD AT.
--STILL NO LEADS IN THE DARING DAYTIME ROBBERY OF A POLICE EVIDENCE VAN THAT LEFT A POLICE OFFICER DEAD EARLIER THIS WEEK.
WHILE AUTHORITIES REMAIN TIGHT-LIPPED, SOURCES INDICATE THAT AMONG ITEMS TAKEN IN THE HEIST...
...WAS EVIDENCE FROM A HIGH-PROFILE DRUG-TRAFFIC KING CASE.
NO SHIT, SHERLOCK.
I CHECKED THE COURT DOCKET, AND SAW THE DIAMOND SMUGGLING CASE WAS SET FOR TRIAL...
--then I heard him tell the singer, there's a song my momma sung...
...BUT I DIDN'T TRY TO FIND OUT WHO ELSE WAS IN COURT THAT DAY.
...won't you sing it once, before we move along...
INTERSTATE
99
I TRUSTED THAT GREED WAS THE PRIME MOTIVATOR, WHEN IT WAS ONLY ONE OF THEM.
I READ THE WHOLE SITUATION WRONG. I STILL DIDN'T UNDERSTAND HOW, BUT I HAD.
City
79 MILES
REST AREA

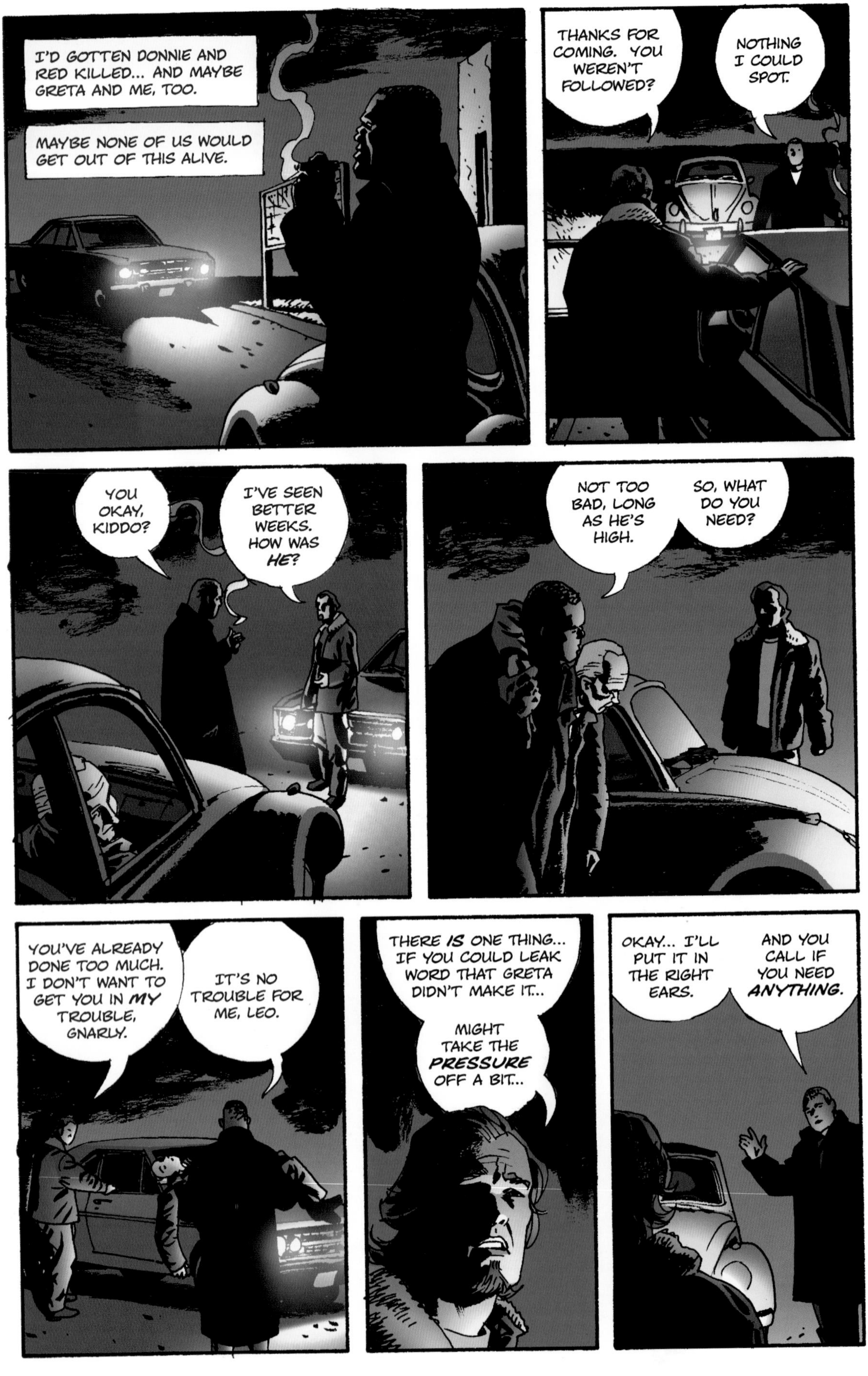
I'D GOTTEN DONNIE AND RED KILLED... AND MAYBE GRETA AND ME, TOO.
MAYBE NONE OF US WOULD GET OUT OF THIS ALIVE.
THANKS FOR COMING. YOU WEREN'T FOLLOWED?
NOTHING I COULD SPOT.
YOU OKAY, KIDDO?
I'VE SEEN BETTER WEEKS. HOW WAS HE?
NOT TOO BAD, LONG AS HE'S HIGH.
SO, WHAT DO YOU NEED?
YOU'VE ALREADY DONE TOO MUCH. I DON'T WANT TO GET YOU IN MY TROUBLE, GNARLY.
IT'S NO TROUBLE FOR ME, LEO.
THERE IS ONE THING... IF YOU COULD LEAK WORD THAT GRETA DIDN'T MAKE IT...
MIGHT TAKE THE PRESSURE OFF A BIT...
OKAY... I'LL PUT IT IN THE RIGHT EARS.
AND YOU CALL IF YOU NEED ANYTHING.

WHAT I *NEEDED* WAS A TIME MACHINE, TO GO BACK AND NOT MAKE ALL THE SAME MISTAKES OVER AGAIN...

...BUT I'D PROBABLY MAKE NEW ONES THAT WERE JUST AS BAD.

HEY LEO... THERE'S A *GIRL* SLEEPIN' ON THE COUCH. A HOT ONE.

YOU GETTIN' SOME *NOOKIE* OUT HERE?

M'NOT ASLEEP... I'M –

OW! FUCK!

AND SHE'S GOT *MY* KINDA MANNERS.

YOU MUST BE *IVAN*.

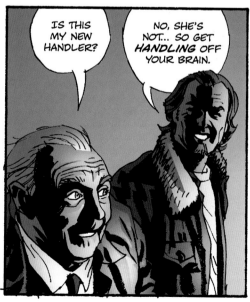

IS THIS MY NEW HANDLER?

NO, SHE'S NOT... SO GET *HANDLING* OFF YOUR BRAIN.

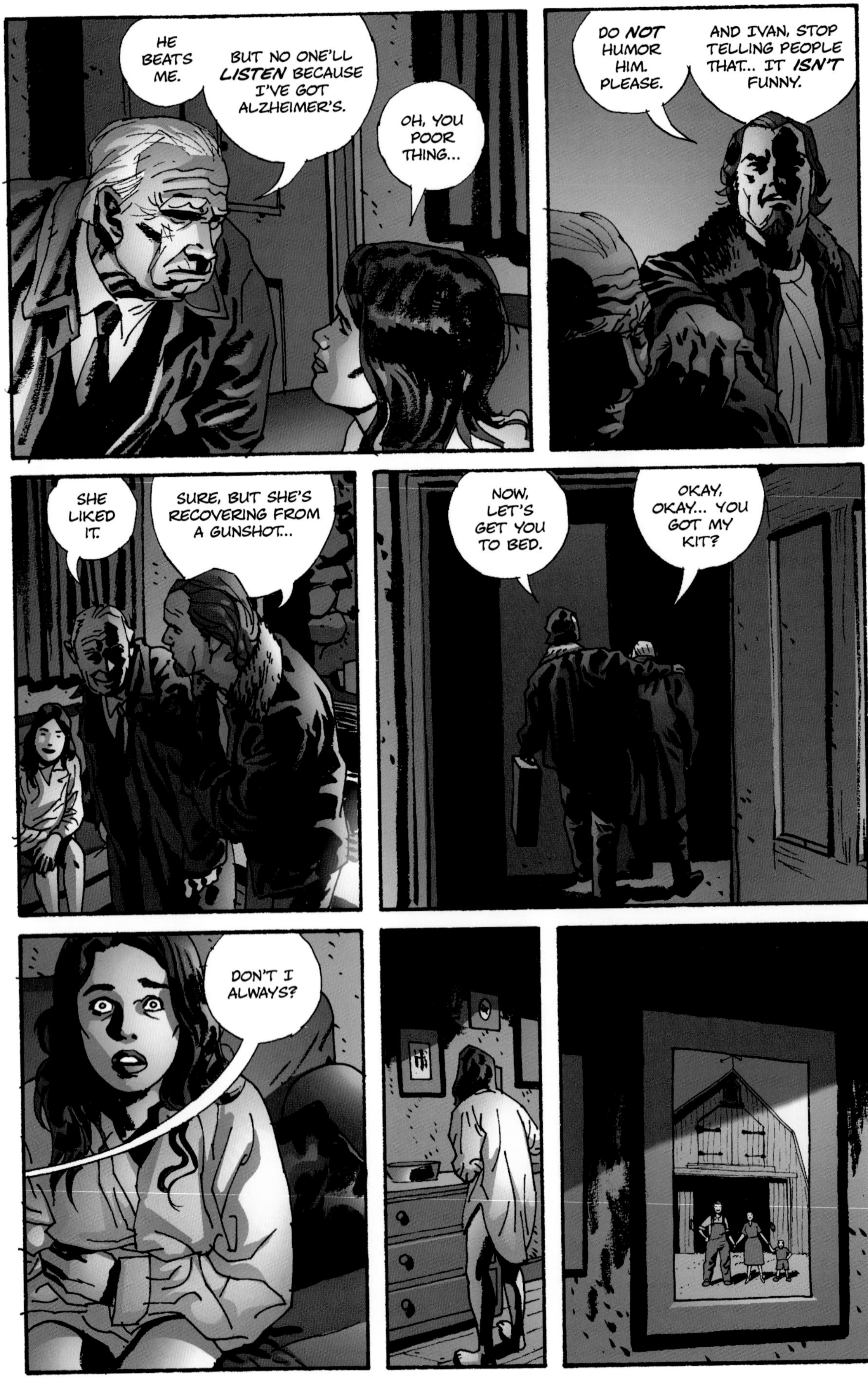
HE BEATS ME.
BUT NO ONE'LL LISTEN BECAUSE I'VE GOT ALZHEIMER'S.
OH, YOU POOR THING...
DO NOT HUMOR HIM. PLEASE.
AND IVAN, STOP TELLING PEOPLE THAT... IT ISN'T FUNNY.
SHE LIKED IT.
SURE, BUT SHE'S RECOVERING FROM A GUNSHOT...
NOW, LET'S GET YOU TO BED.
OKAY, OKAY... YOU GOT MY KIT?
DON'T I ALWAYS?

 HERE.

OH... THANKS.

 IS THAT YOUR PARENTS?

 YEAH, THIS WAS MY GRANDFATHER'S FARM... HE PUT IT INTO A TRUST FOR MY MOM, CAUSE HE DIDN'T WANT MY DAD'S NAME ON IT.

SO IT'S MY HOME AWAY, WHEN I NEED ONE.

 HOW OFTEN IS THAT?

I HAVEN'T BEEN HERE SINCE RIGHT AFTER THE SALT BAY JOB.

 RIGHT...

 SO, IVAN... YOU JUST SHOT HIM UP, RIGHT?

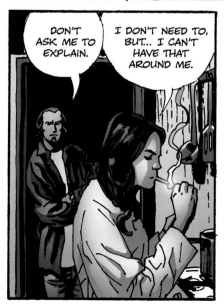 DON'T ASK ME TO EXPLAIN.

I DON'T NEED TO, BUT... I CAN'T HAVE THAT AROUND ME.

 NOT *HIS* STUFF, OR THE SHIT THAT WAS IN THAT BRIEFCASE...

 JUST... HIDE THEM SOMEPLACE *GOOD*, PLEASE.

 SURE, GRETA...

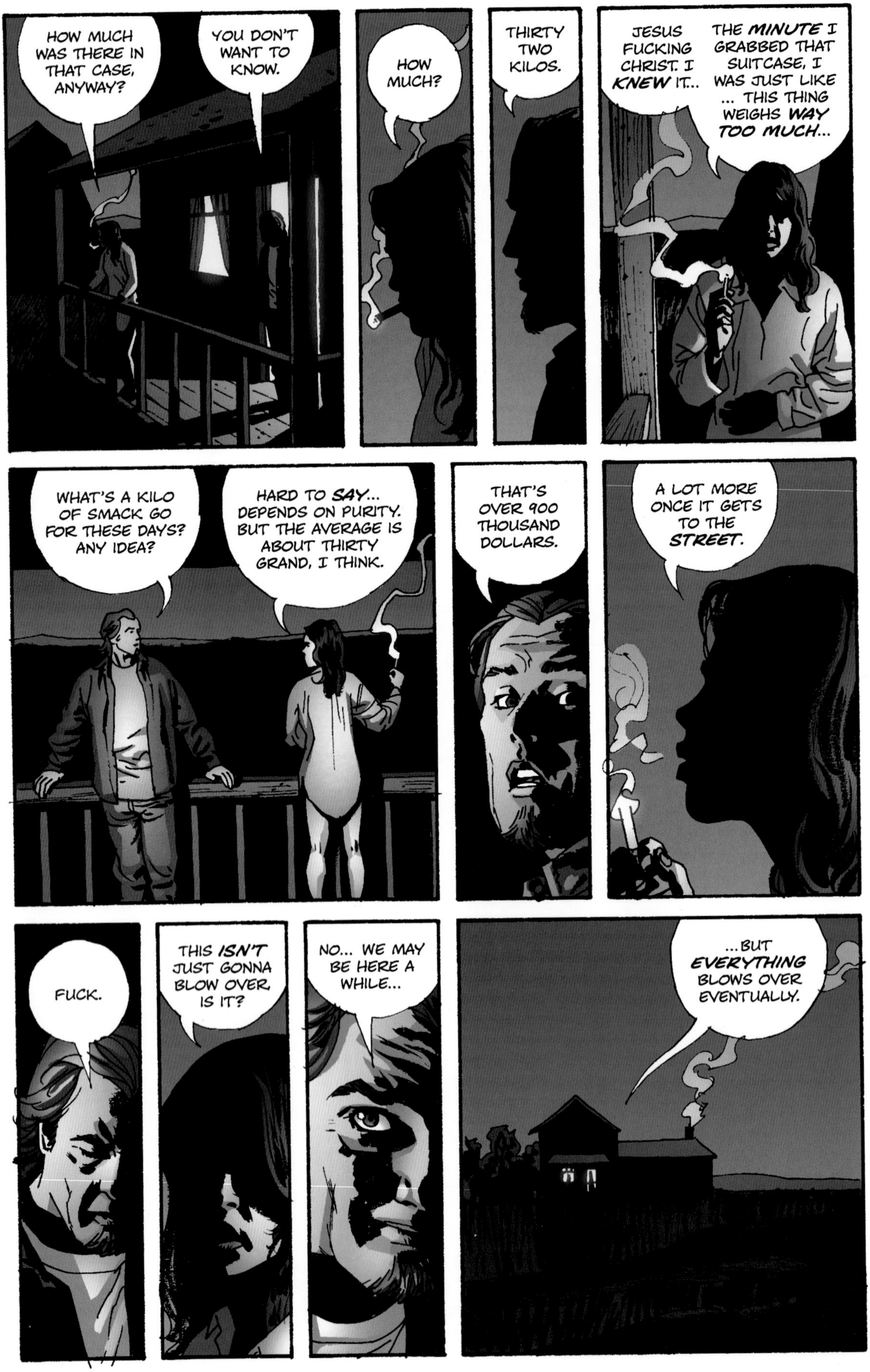

HOW MUCH WAS THERE IN THAT CASE, ANYWAY?
YOU DON'T WANT TO KNOW.
HOW MUCH?
THIRTY TWO KILOS.
JESUS FUCKING CHRIST. I KNEW IT...
THE MINUTE I GRABBED THAT SUITCASE, I WAS JUST LIKE ... THIS THING WEIGHS WAY TOO MUCH...
WHAT'S A KILO OF SMACK GO FOR THESE DAYS? ANY IDEA?
HARD TO SAY... DEPENDS ON PURITY. BUT THE AVERAGE IS ABOUT THIRTY GRAND, I THINK.
THAT'S OVER 900 THOUSAND DOLLARS.
A LOT MORE ONCE IT GETS TO THE STREET.
FUCK.
THIS ISN'T JUST GONNA BLOW OVER, IS IT?
NO... WE MAY BE HERE A WHILE...
...BUT EVERYTHING BLOWS OVER EVENTUALLY.

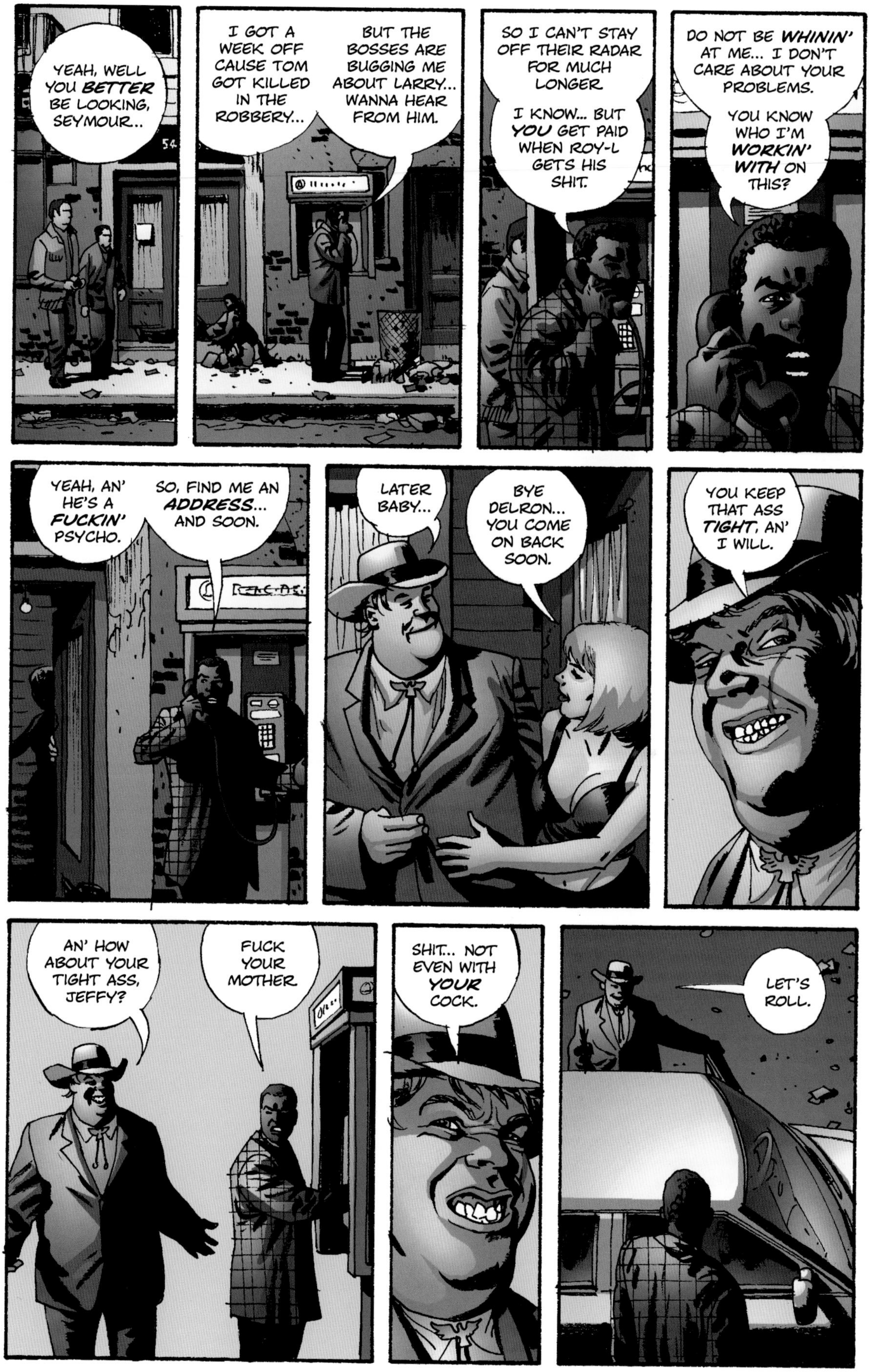
YEAH, WELL YOU BETTER BE LOOKING, SEYMOUR...
I GOT A WEEK OFF CAUSE TOM GOT KILLED IN THE ROBBERY...
BUT THE BOSSES ARE BUGGING ME ABOUT LARRY... WANNA HEAR FROM HIM.
SO I CAN'T STAY OFF THEIR RADAR FOR MUCH LONGER
I KNOW... BUT YOU GET PAID WHEN ROY-L GETS HIS SHIT.
DO NOT BE WHININ' AT ME... I DON'T CARE ABOUT YOUR PROBLEMS.
YOU KNOW WHO I'M WORKIN' WITH ON THIS?
YEAH, AN' HE'S A FUCKIN' PSYCHO.
SO, FIND ME AN ADDRESS... AND SOON.
LATER BABY...
BYE DELRON... YOU COME ON BACK SOON.
YOU KEEP THAT ASS TIGHT, AN' I WILL.
AN' HOW ABOUT YOUR TIGHT ASS, JEFFY?
FUCK YOUR MOTHER
SHIT.. NOT EVEN WITH YOUR COCK.
LET'S ROLL.

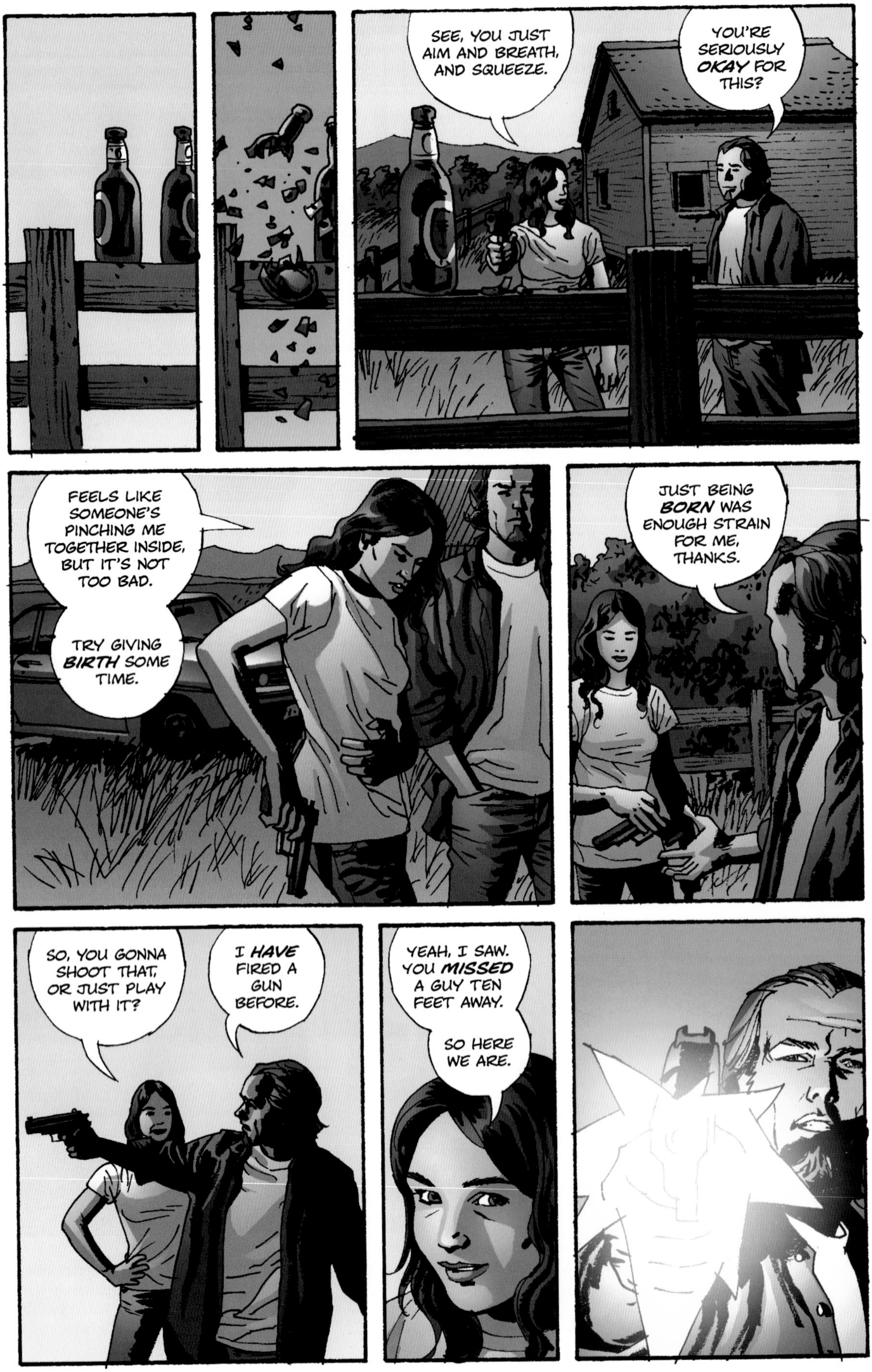
SEE, YOU JUST AIM AND BREATH, AND SQUEEZE.
YOU'RE SERIOUSLY OKAY FOR THIS?
FEELS LIKE SOMEONE'S PINCHING ME TOGETHER INSIDE, BUT IT'S NOT TOO BAD.
TRY GIVING BIRTH SOME TIME.
JUST BEING BORN WAS ENOUGH STRAIN FOR ME, THANKS.
SO, YOU GONNA SHOOT THAT, OR JUST PLAY WITH IT?
I HAVE FIRED A GUN BEFORE.
YEAH, I SAW. YOU MISSED A GUY TEN FEET AWAY.
SO HERE WE ARE.

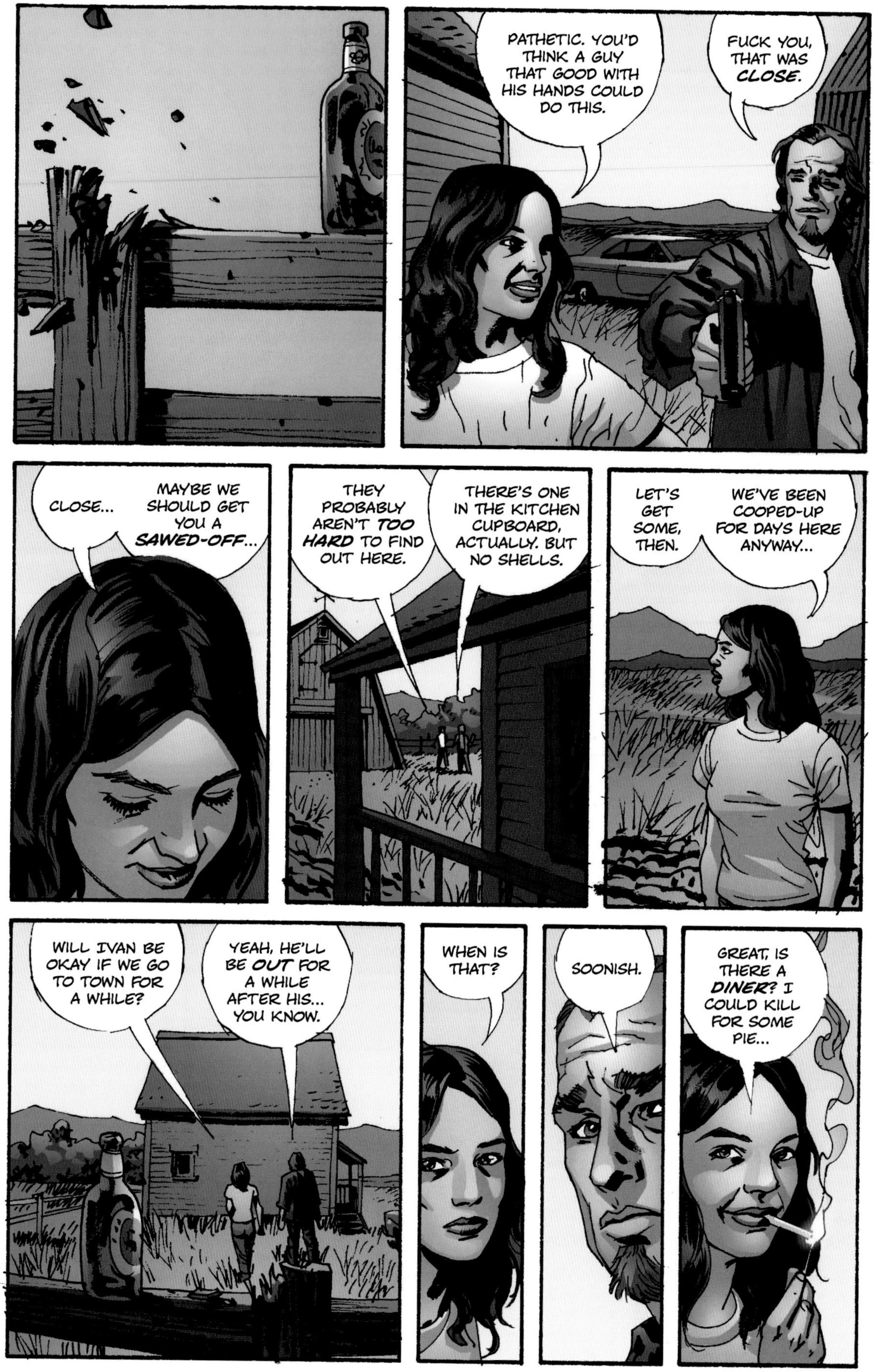
PATHETIC. YOU'D THINK A GUY THAT GOOD WITH HIS HANDS COULD DO THIS.
FUCK YOU, THAT WAS CLOSE.
CLOSE...
MAYBE WE SHOULD GET YOU A SAWED-OFF...
THEY PROBABLY AREN'T TOO HARD TO FIND OUT HERE.
THERE'S ONE IN THE KITCHEN CUPBOARD, ACTUALLY. BUT NO SHELLS.
LET'S GET SOME, THEN.
WE'VE BEEN COOPED-UP FOR DAYS HERE ANYWAY...
WILL IVAN BE OKAY IF WE GO TO TOWN FOR A WHILE?
YEAH, HE'LL BE OUT FOR A WHILE AFTER HIS... YOU KNOW.
WHEN IS THAT?
SOONISH.
GREAT, IS THERE A DINER? I COULD KILL FOR SOME PIE...

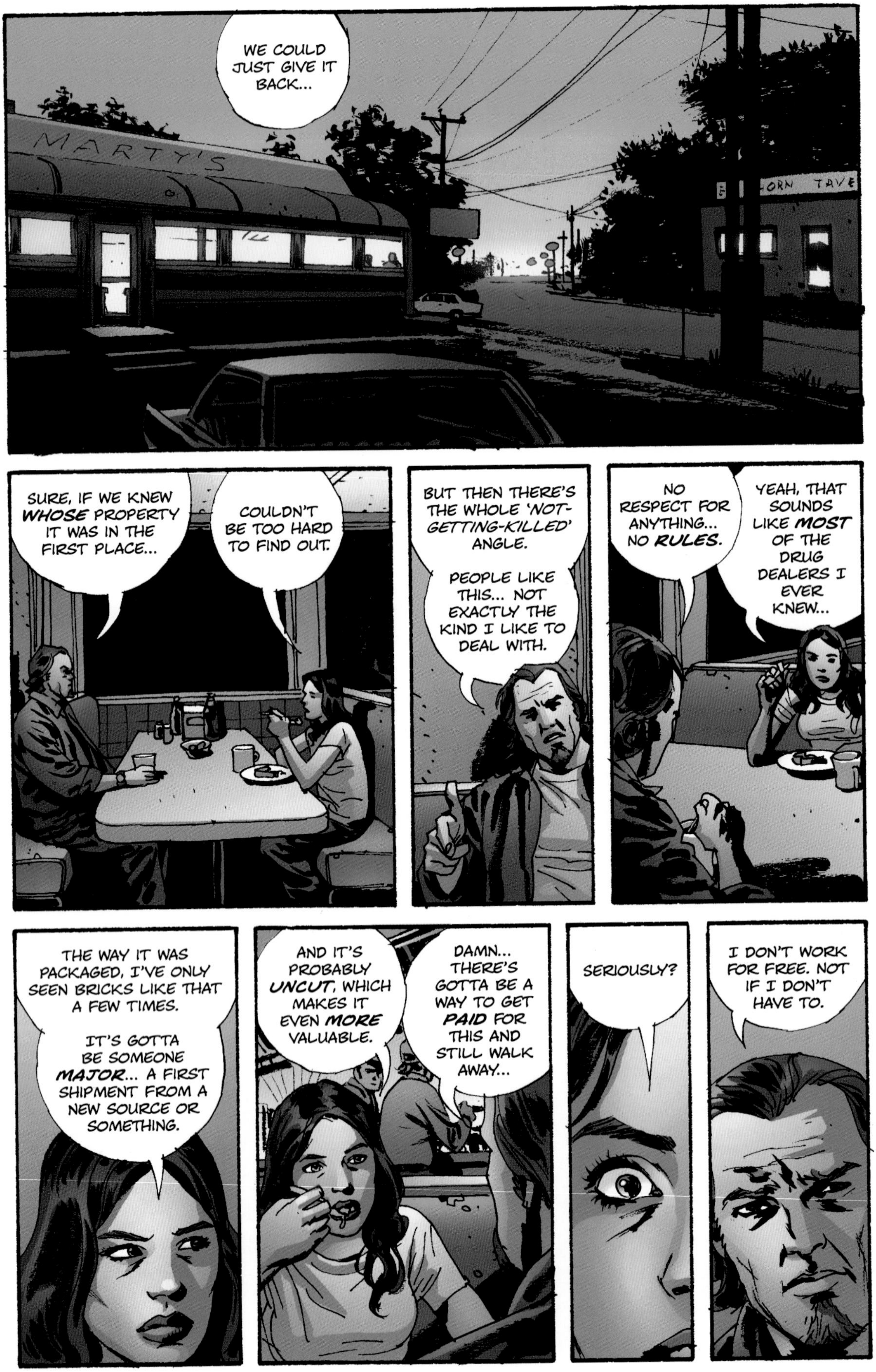
MARTY'S
WE COULD JUST GIVE IT BACK...
SURE, IF WE KNEW WHOSE PROPERTY IT WAS IN THE FIRST PLACE...
COULDN'T BE TOO HARD TO FIND OUT.
BUT THEN THERE'S THE WHOLE 'NOT-GETTING-KILLED' ANGLE.
PEOPLE LIKE THIS... NOT EXACTLY THE KIND I LIKE TO DEAL WITH.
NO RESPECT FOR ANYTHING... NO RULES.
YEAH, THAT SOUNDS LIKE MOST OF THE DRUG DEALERS I EVER KNEW...
THE WAY IT WAS PACKAGED, I'VE ONLY SEEN BRICKS LIKE THAT A FEW TIMES.
IT'S GOTTA BE SOMEONE MAJOR... A FIRST SHIPMENT FROM A NEW SOURCE OR SOMETHING.
AND IT'S PROBABLY UNCUT, WHICH MAKES IT EVEN MORE VALUABLE.
DAMN... THERE'S GOTTA BE A WAY TO GET PAID FOR THIS AND STILL WALK AWAY...
SERIOUSLY?
I DON'T WORK FOR FREE. NOT IF I DON'T HAVE TO.

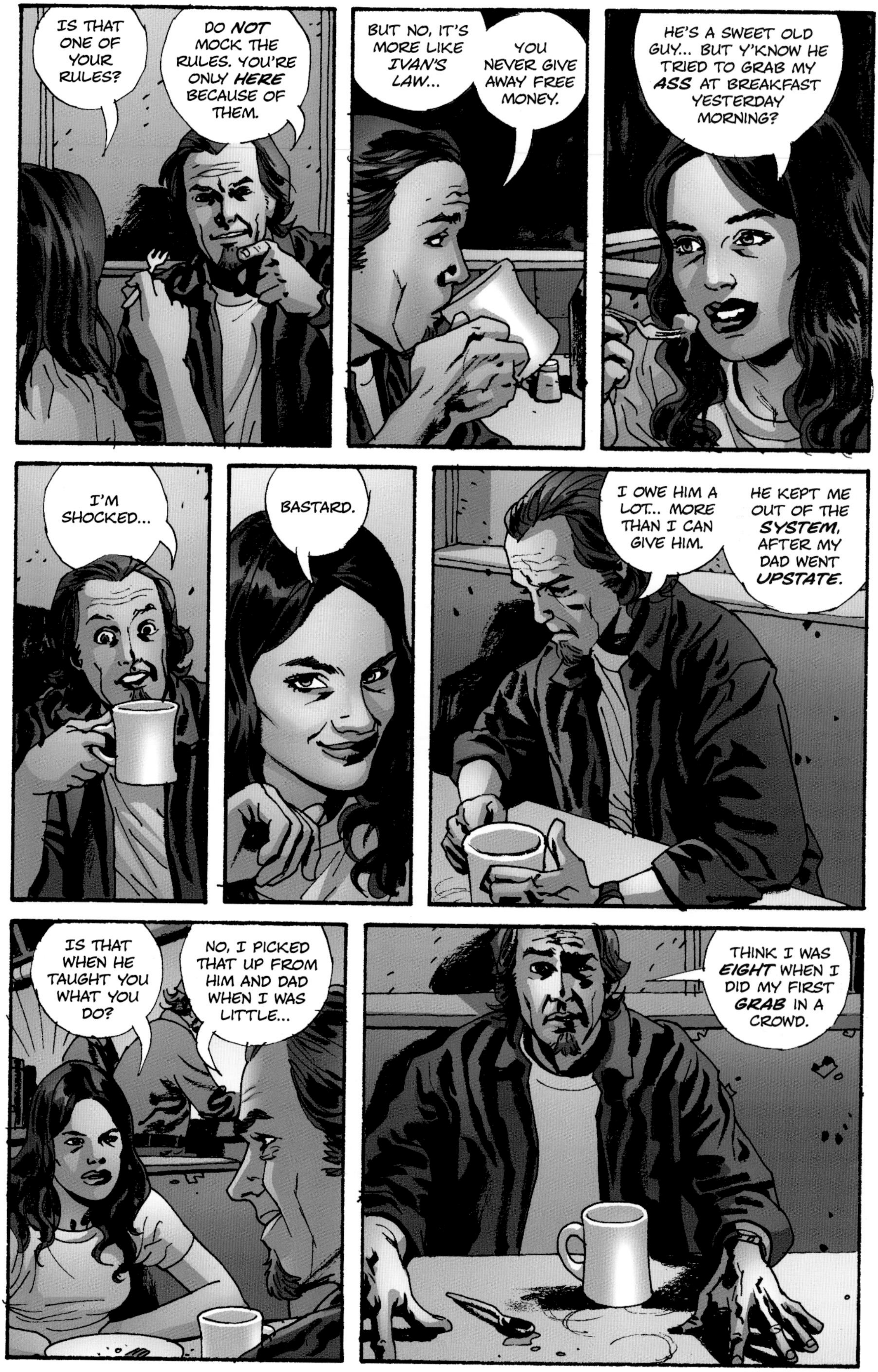
IS THAT ONE OF YOUR RULES?
DO NOT MOCK THE RULES. YOU'RE ONLY HERE BECAUSE OF THEM.
BUT NO, IT'S MORE LIKE IVAN'S LAW...
YOU NEVER GIVE AWAY FREE MONEY.
HE'S A SWEET OLD GUY... BUT Y'KNOW HE TRIED TO GRAB MY ASS AT BREAKFAST YESTERDAY MORNING?
I'M SHOCKED...
BASTARD.
I OWE HIM A LOT... MORE THAN I CAN GIVE HIM.
HE KEPT ME OUT OF THE SYSTEM, AFTER MY DAD WENT UPSTATE.
IS THAT WHEN HE TAUGHT YOU WHAT YOU DO?
NO, I PICKED THAT UP FROM HIM AND DAD WHEN I WAS LITTLE...
THINK I WAS EIGHT WHEN I DID MY FIRST GRAB IN A CROWD.

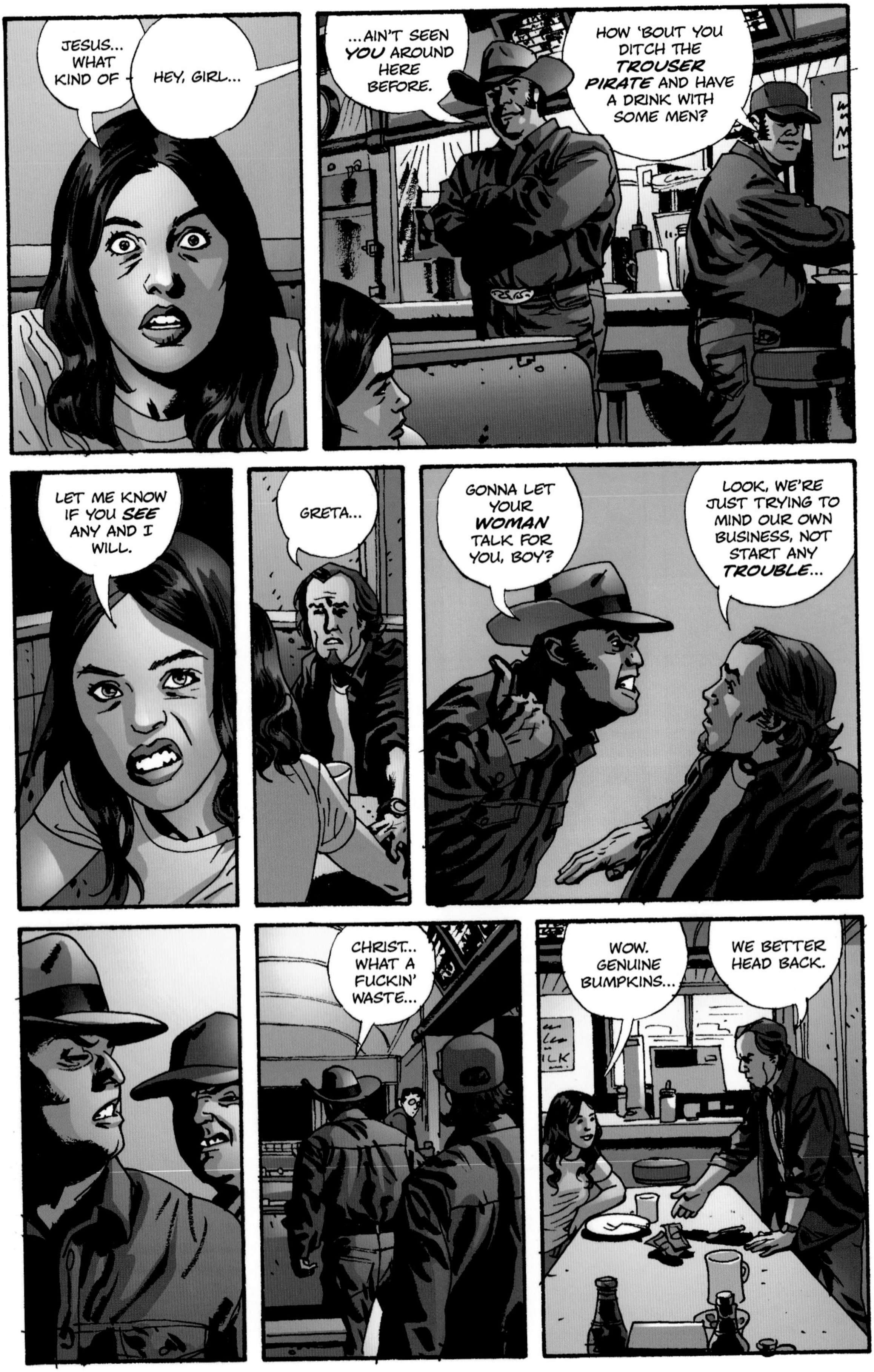
JESUS... WHAT KIND OF --
HEY, GIRL...
...AIN'T SEEN YOU AROUND HERE BEFORE.
HOW 'BOUT YOU DITCH THE TROUSER PIRATE AND HAVE A DRINK WITH SOME MEN?
LET ME KNOW IF YOU SEE ANY AND I WILL.
GRETA...
GONNA LET YOUR WOMAN TALK FOR YOU, BOY?
LOOK, WE'RE JUST TRYING TO MIND OUR OWN BUSINESS, NOT START ANY TROUBLE...
CHRIST... WHAT A FUCKIN' WASTE...
WOW. GENUINE BUMPKINS...
WE BETTER HEAD BACK.

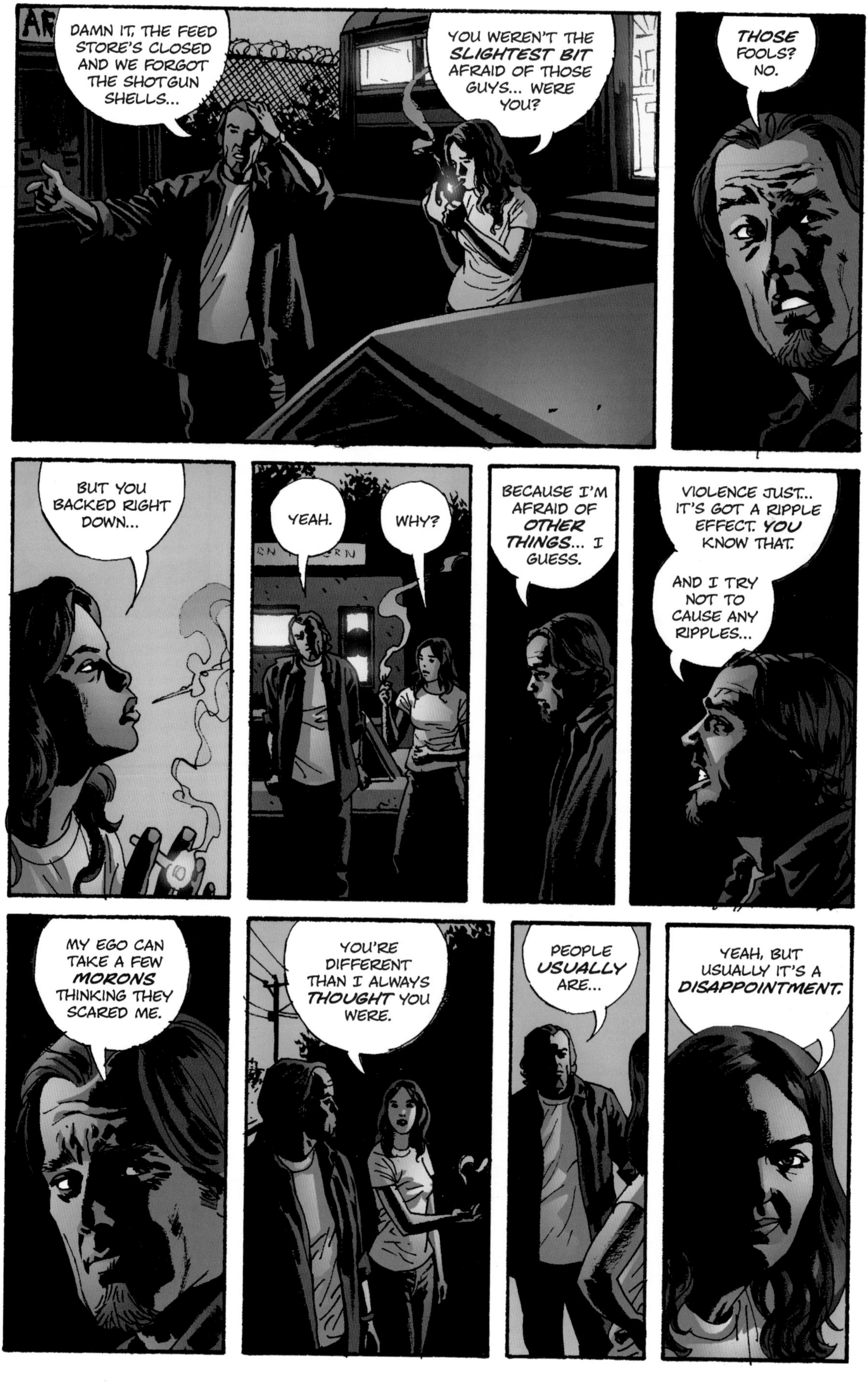
DAMN IT, THE FEED STORE'S CLOSED AND WE FORGOT THE SHOTGUN SHELLS...
YOU WEREN'T THE SLIGHTEST BIT AFRAID OF THOSE GUYS... WERE YOU?
THOSE FOOLS? NO.
BUT YOU BACKED RIGHT DOWN...
YEAH.
WHY?
BECAUSE I'M AFRAID OF OTHER THINGS... I GUESS.
VIOLENCE JUST... IT'S GOT A RIPPLE EFFECT. YOU KNOW THAT.
AND I TRY NOT TO CAUSE ANY RIPPLES...
MY EGO CAN TAKE A FEW MORONS THINKING THEY SCARED ME.
YOU'RE DIFFERENT THAN I ALWAYS THOUGHT YOU WERE.
PEOPLE USUALLY ARE...
YEAH, BUT USUALLY IT'S A DISAPPOINTMENT.

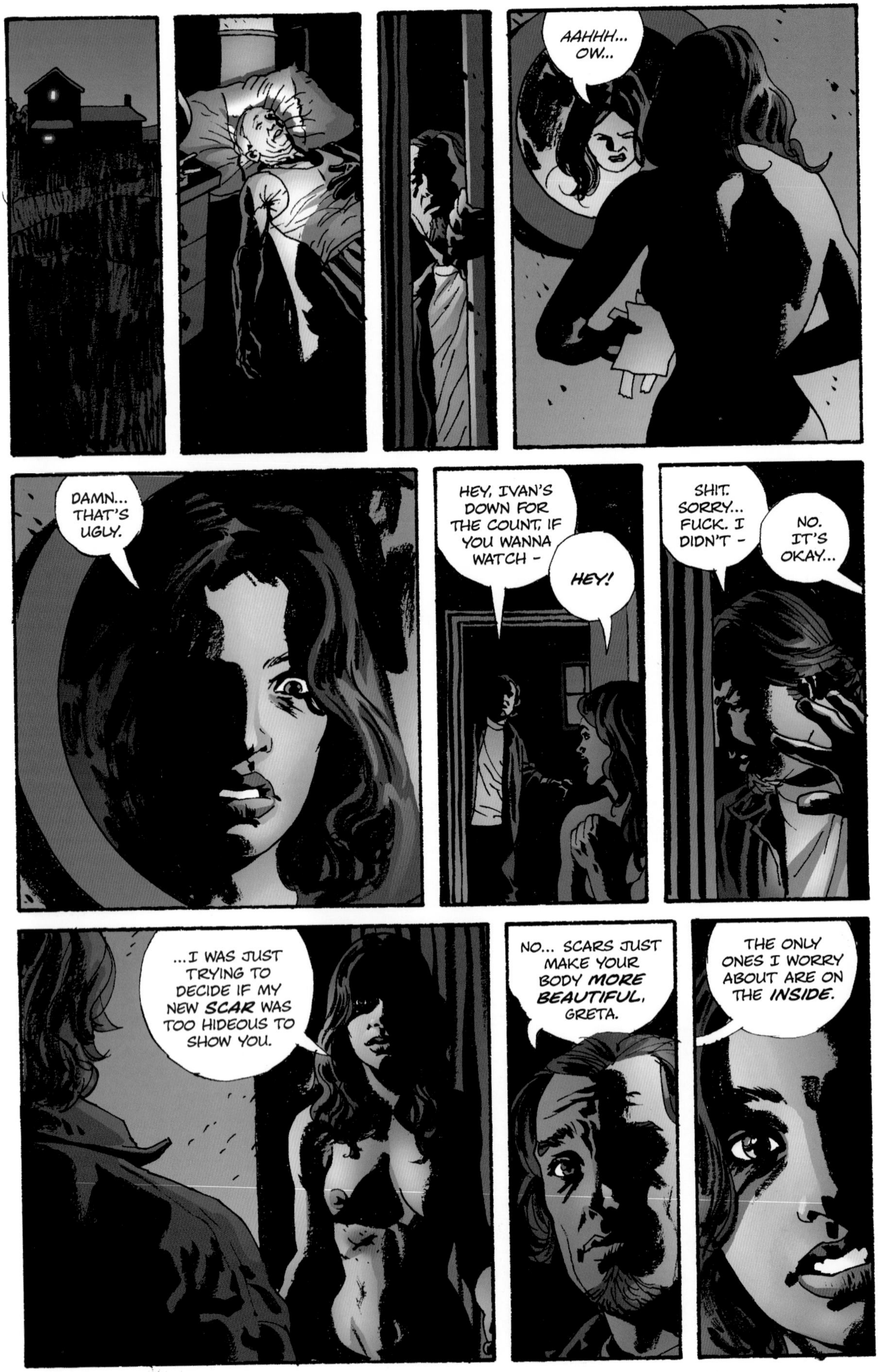
AAHHH... OW...
DAMN... THAT'S UGLY.
HEY, IVAN'S DOWN FOR THE COUNT, IF YOU WANNA WATCH -
HEY!
SHIT. SORRY... FUCK. I DIDN'T -
NO. IT'S OKAY...
...I WAS JUST TRYING TO DECIDE IF MY NEW SCAR WAS TOO HIDEOUS TO SHOW YOU.
NO... SCARS JUST MAKE YOUR BODY MORE BEAUTIFUL, GRETA.
THE ONLY ONES I WORRY ABOUT ARE ON THE INSIDE.

YOU'RE DIFFERENT.

SHE'S DIFFERENT, NOT ME... FRAGILE AND TOUGH ALL AT ONCE.

BUT HER TOUCH IS SO SOFT, I ALMOST MELT...

...AND THOUGHTS OF OUR PROBLEMS MELT WITH ME.

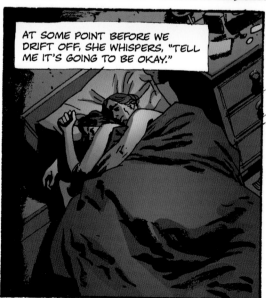

AT SOME POINT BEFORE WE DRIFT OFF, SHE WHISPERS, "TELL ME IT'S GOING TO BE OKAY."

AND I PROMISE HER IT WILL BE.

I PROMISE TO FIND US A WAY OUT.

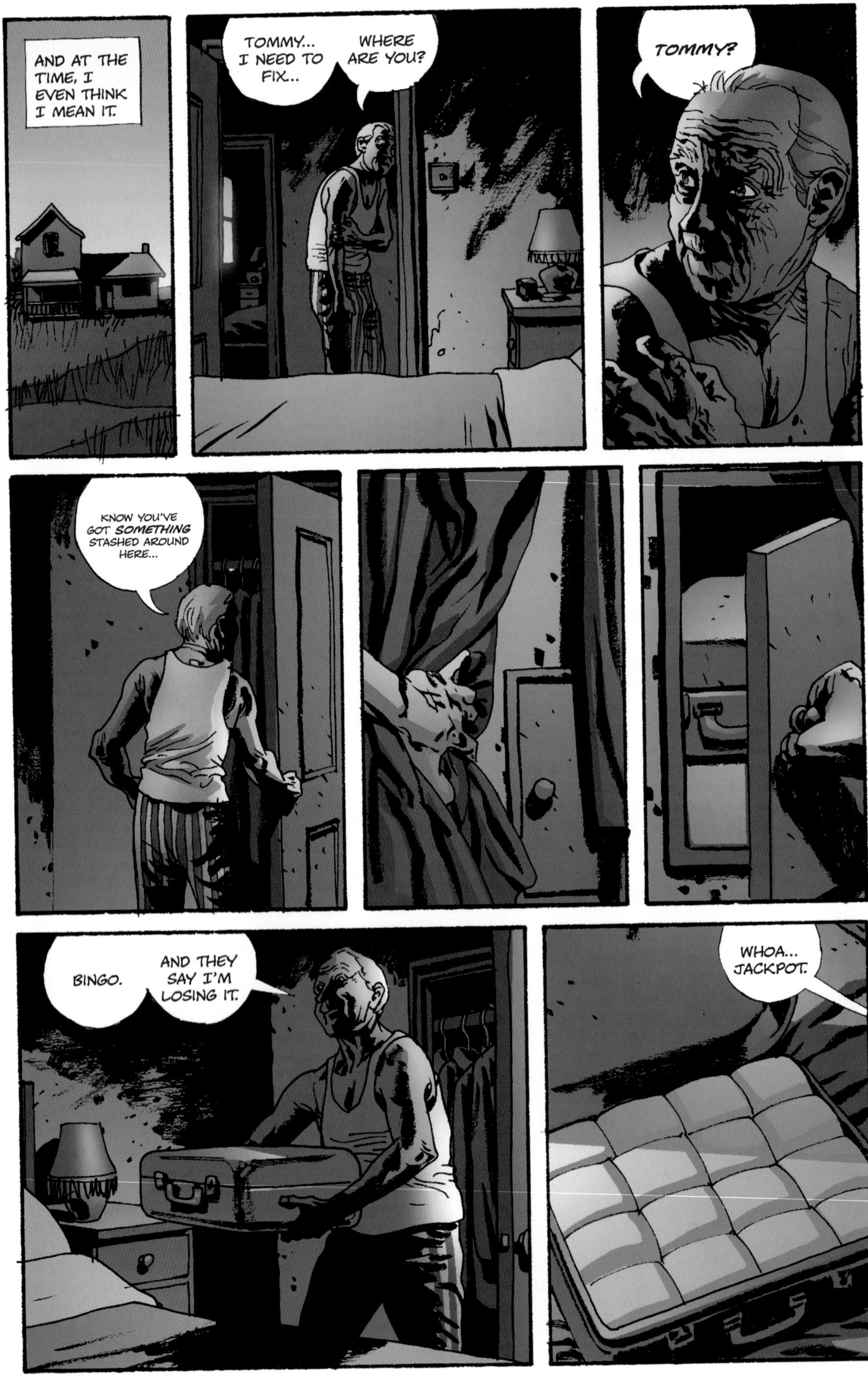
AND AT THE TIME, I EVEN THINK I MEAN IT.
TOMMY... I NEED TO FIX...
WHERE ARE YOU?
TOMMY?
KNOW YOU'VE GOT SOMETHING STASHED AROUND HERE...
BINGO.
AND THEY SAY I'M LOSING IT.
WHOA... JACKPOT.

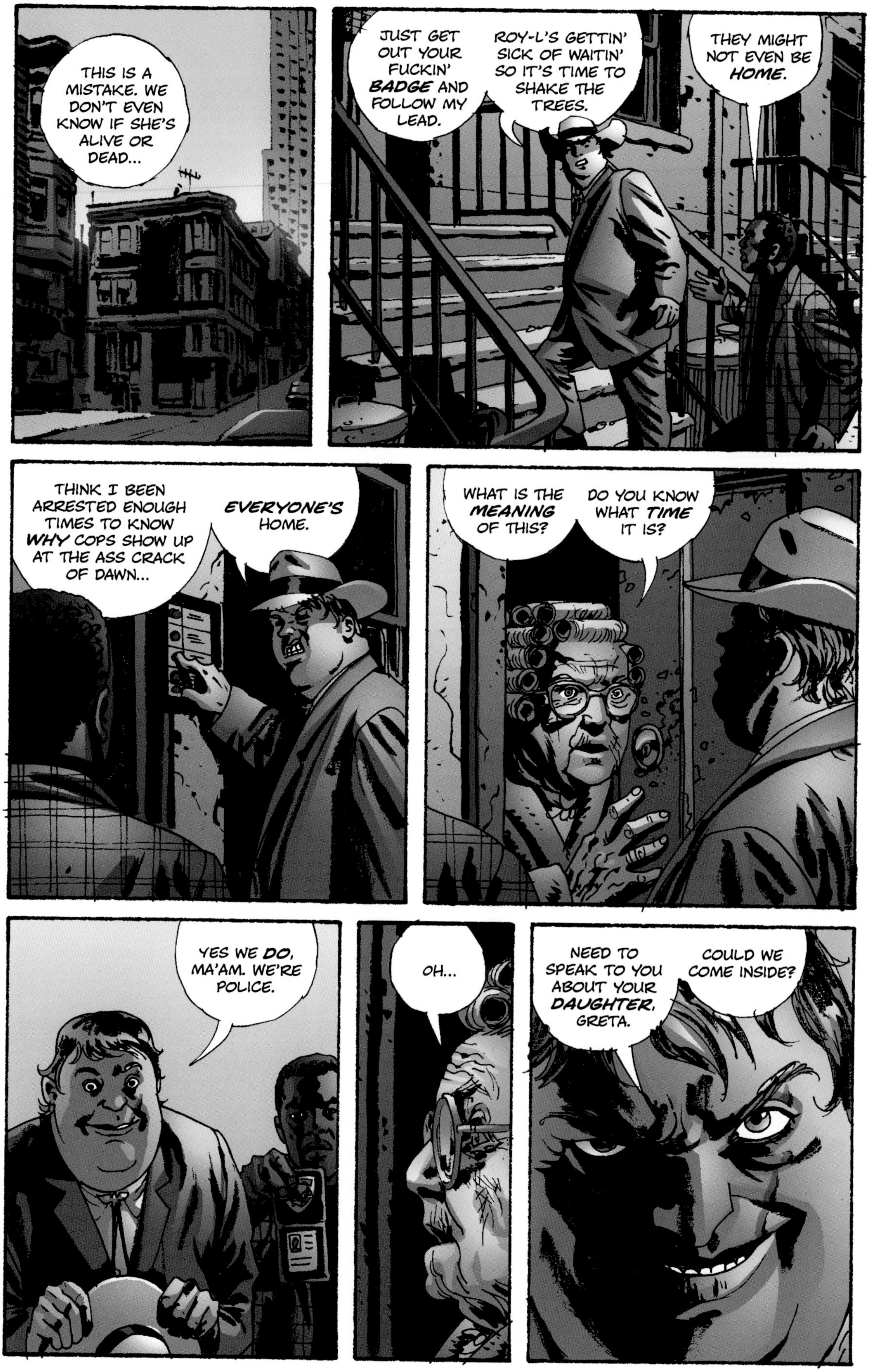
THIS IS A MISTAKE. WE DON'T EVEN KNOW IF SHE'S ALIVE OR DEAD...
JUST GET OUT YOUR FUCKIN' BADGE AND FOLLOW MY LEAD.
ROY-L'S GETTIN' SICK OF WAITIN' SO IT'S TIME TO SHAKE THE TREES.
THEY MIGHT NOT EVEN BE HOME.
THINK I BEEN ARRESTED ENOUGH TIMES TO KNOW WHY COPS SHOW UP AT THE ASS CRACK OF DAWN...
EVERYONE'S HOME.
WHAT IS THE MEANING OF THIS?
DO YOU KNOW WHAT TIME IT IS?
YES WE DO, MA'AM. WE'RE POLICE.
OH...
NEED TO SPEAK TO YOU ABOUT YOUR DAUGHTER, GRETA.
COULD WE COME INSIDE?

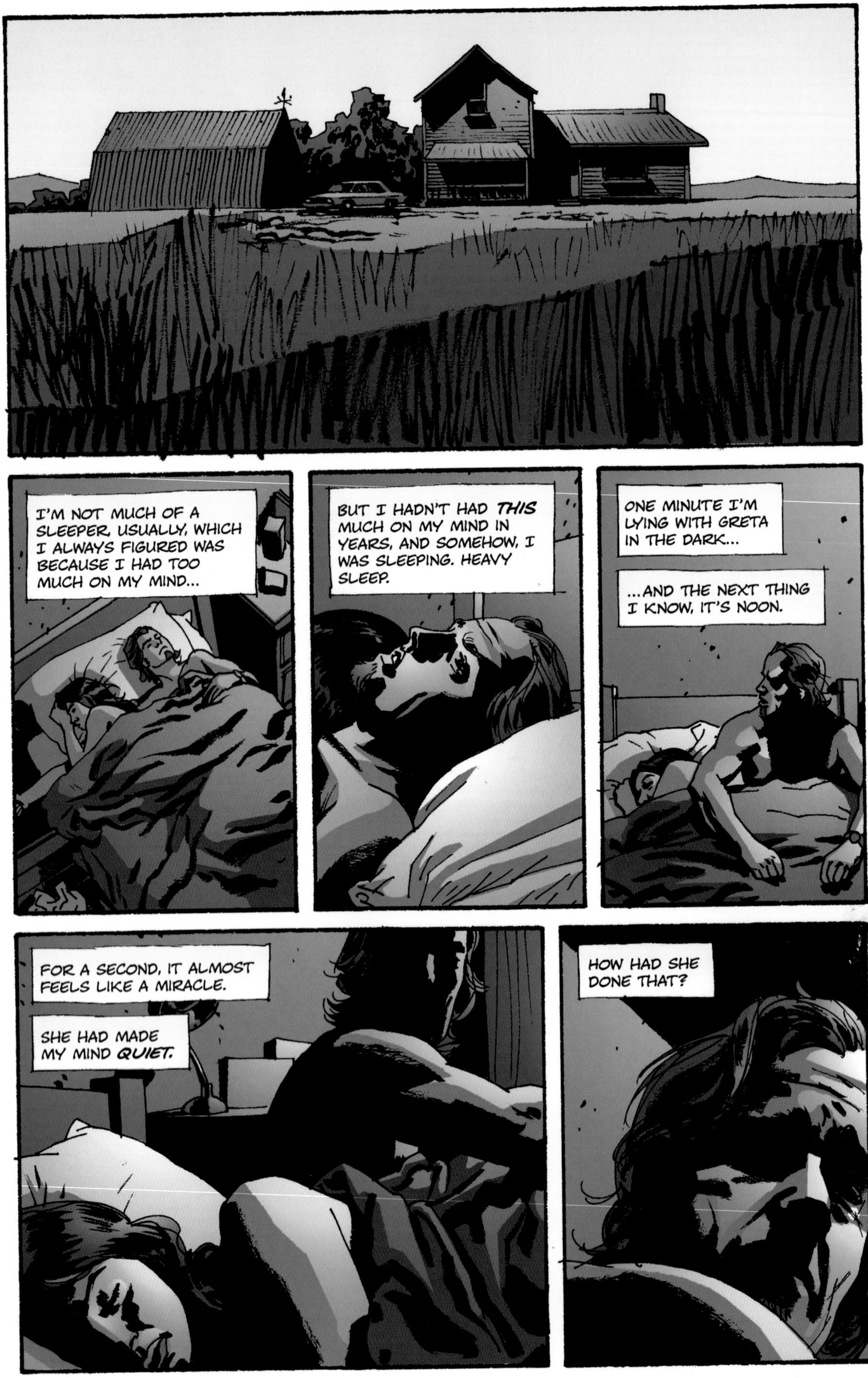

I'M NOT MUCH OF A SLEEPER, USUALLY, WHICH I ALWAYS FIGURED WAS BECAUSE I HAD TOO MUCH ON MY MIND...
BUT I HADN'T HAD THIS MUCH ON MY MIND IN YEARS, AND SOMEHOW, I WAS SLEEPING. HEAVY SLEEP.
ONE MINUTE I'M LYING WITH GRETA IN THE DARK...
...AND THE NEXT THING I KNOW, IT'S NOON.
FOR A SECOND, IT ALMOST FEELS LIKE A MIRACLE.
SHE HAD MADE MY MIND QUIET.
HOW HAD SHE DONE THAT?

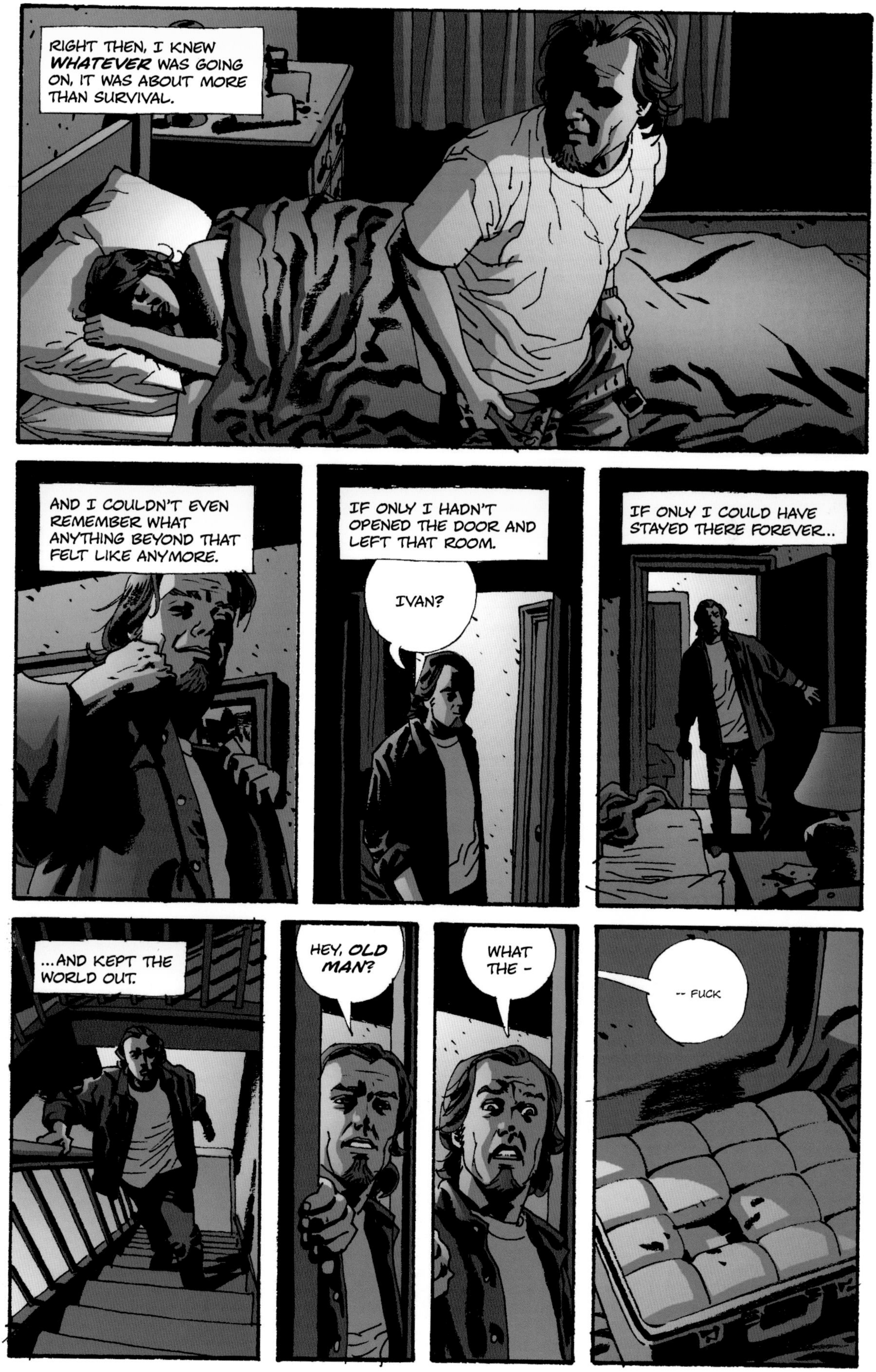
RIGHT THEN, I KNEW *WHATEVER* WAS GOING ON, IT WAS ABOUT MORE THAN SURVIVAL.
AND I COULDN'T EVEN REMEMBER WHAT ANYTHING BEYOND THAT FELT LIKE ANYMORE.
IF ONLY I HADN'T OPENED THE DOOR AND LEFT THAT ROOM.
IVAN?
IF ONLY I COULD HAVE STAYED THERE FOREVER..
...AND KEPT THE WORLD OUT.
HEY, *OLD MAN*?
WHAT THE -
-- FUCK

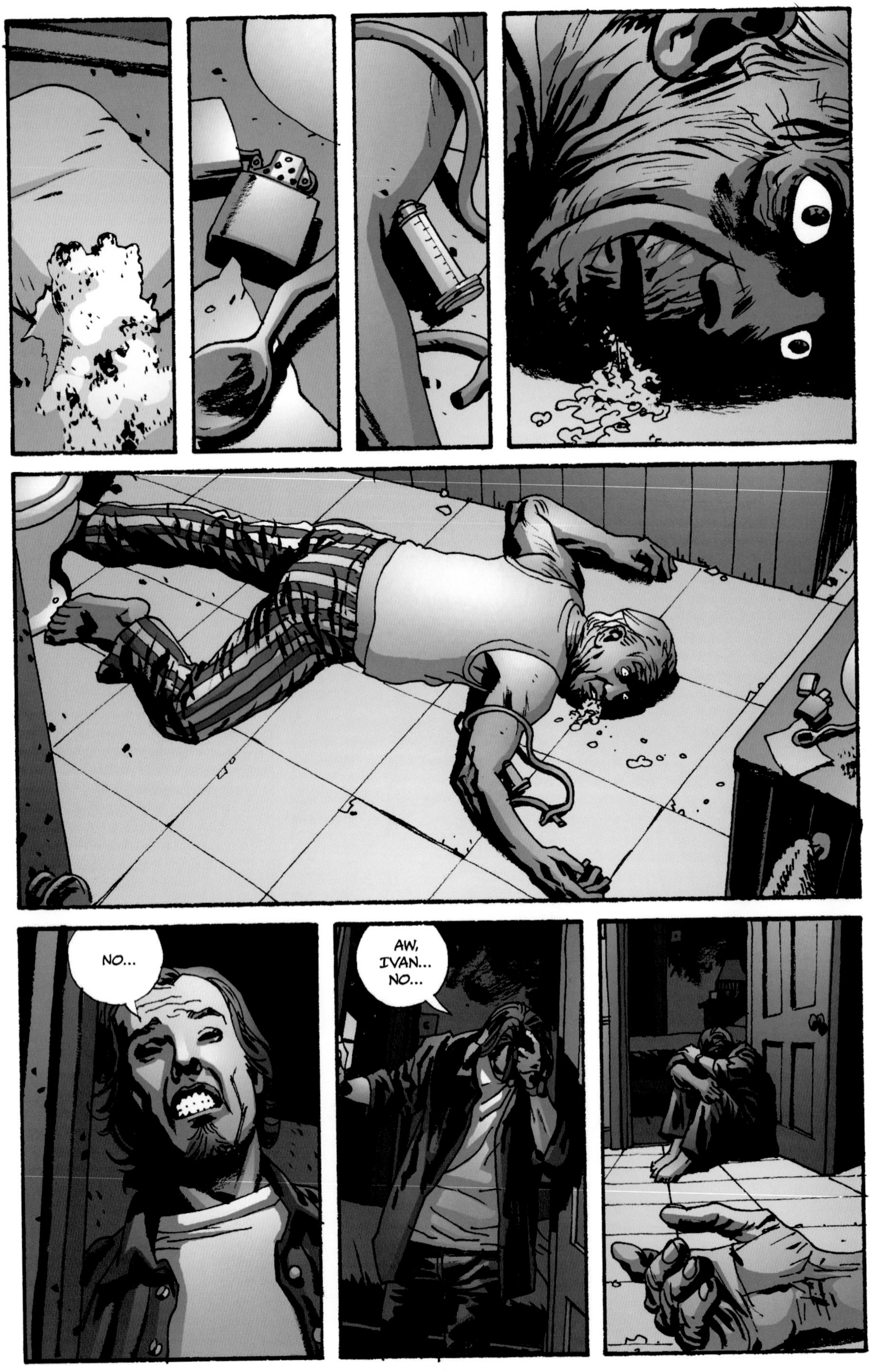
NO...
AW, IVAN... NO...

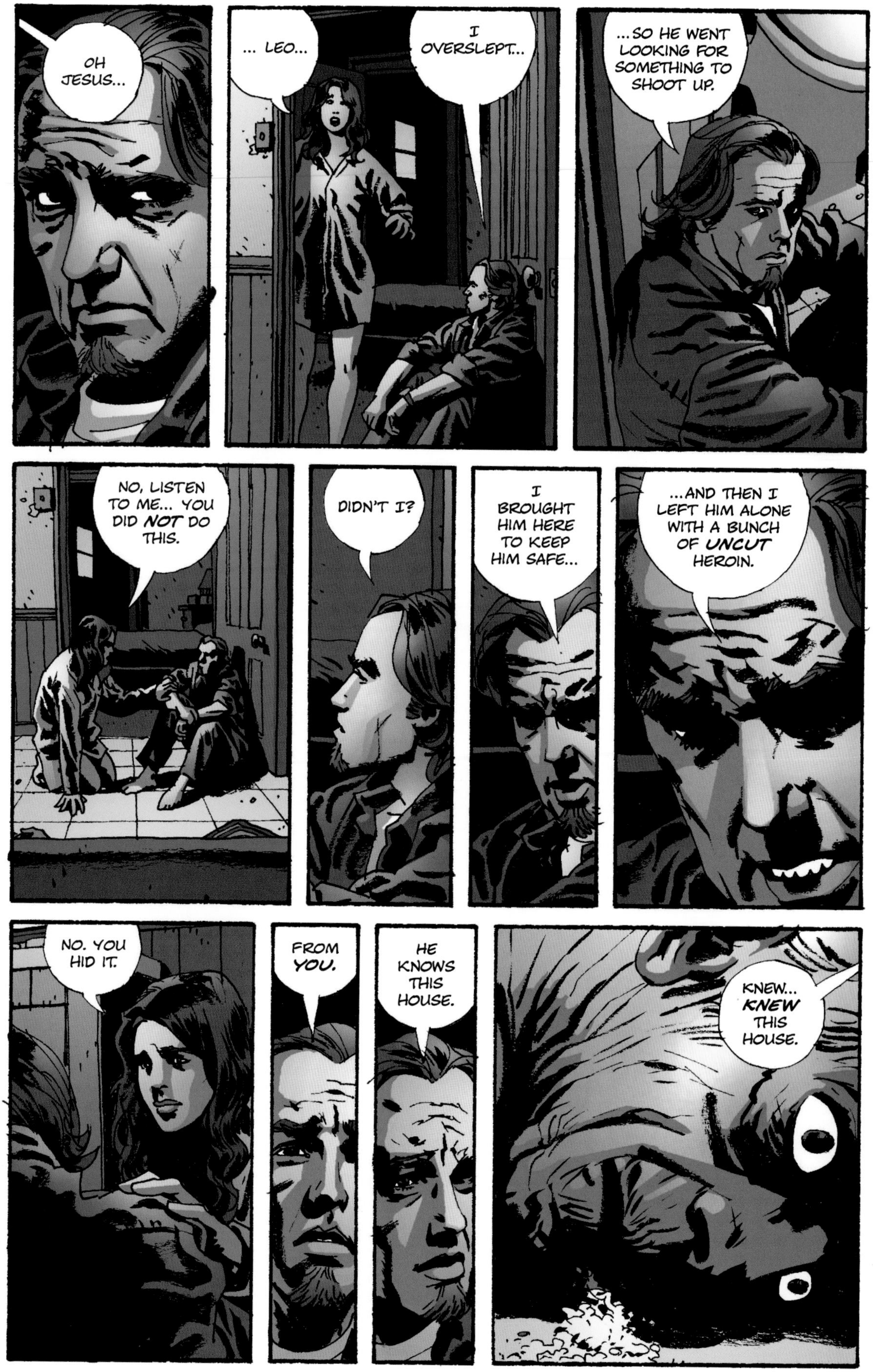
OH JESUS...
... LEO...
I OVERSLEPT...
...SO HE WENT LOOKING FOR SOMETHING TO SHOOT UP.
NO, LISTEN TO ME... YOU DID NOT DO THIS.
DIDN'T I?
I BROUGHT HIM HERE TO KEEP HIM SAFE...
...AND THEN I LEFT HIM ALONE WITH A BUNCH OF UNCUT HEROIN.
NO. YOU HID IT.
FROM YOU.
HE KNOWS THIS HOUSE.
KNEW... KNEW THIS HOUSE.

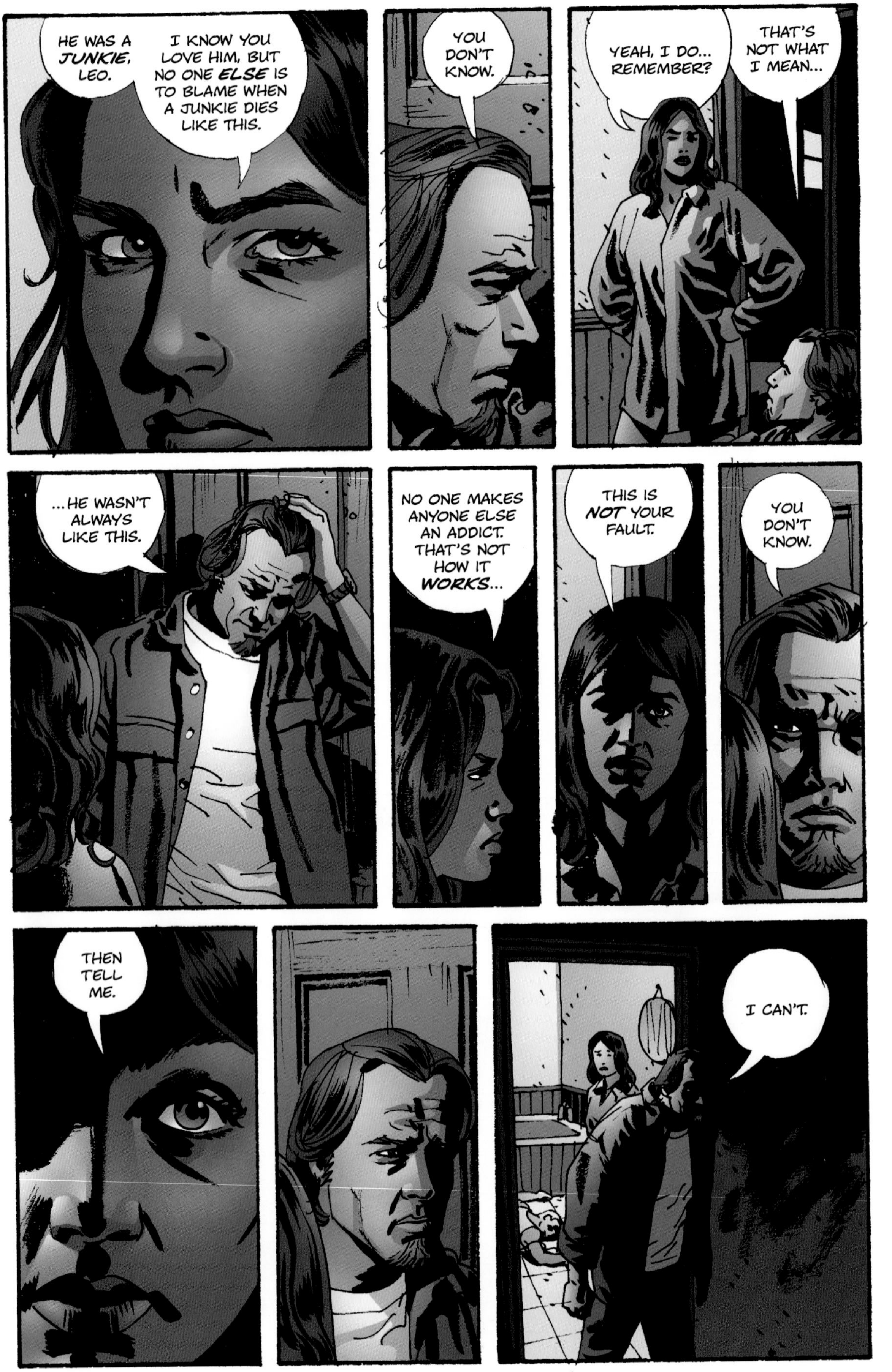
HE WAS A *JUNKIE*, LEO.
I KNOW YOU LOVE HIM, BUT NO ONE *ELSE* IS TO BLAME WHEN A JUNKIE DIES LIKE THIS.
YOU DON'T KNOW.
YEAH, I DO... REMEMBER?
THAT'S NOT WHAT I MEAN...
...HE WASN'T ALWAYS LIKE THIS.
NO ONE MAKES ANYONE ELSE AN ADDICT. THAT'S NOT HOW IT *WORKS*...
THIS IS *NOT* YOUR FAULT.
YOU DON'T KNOW.
THEN TELL ME.
I CAN'T.

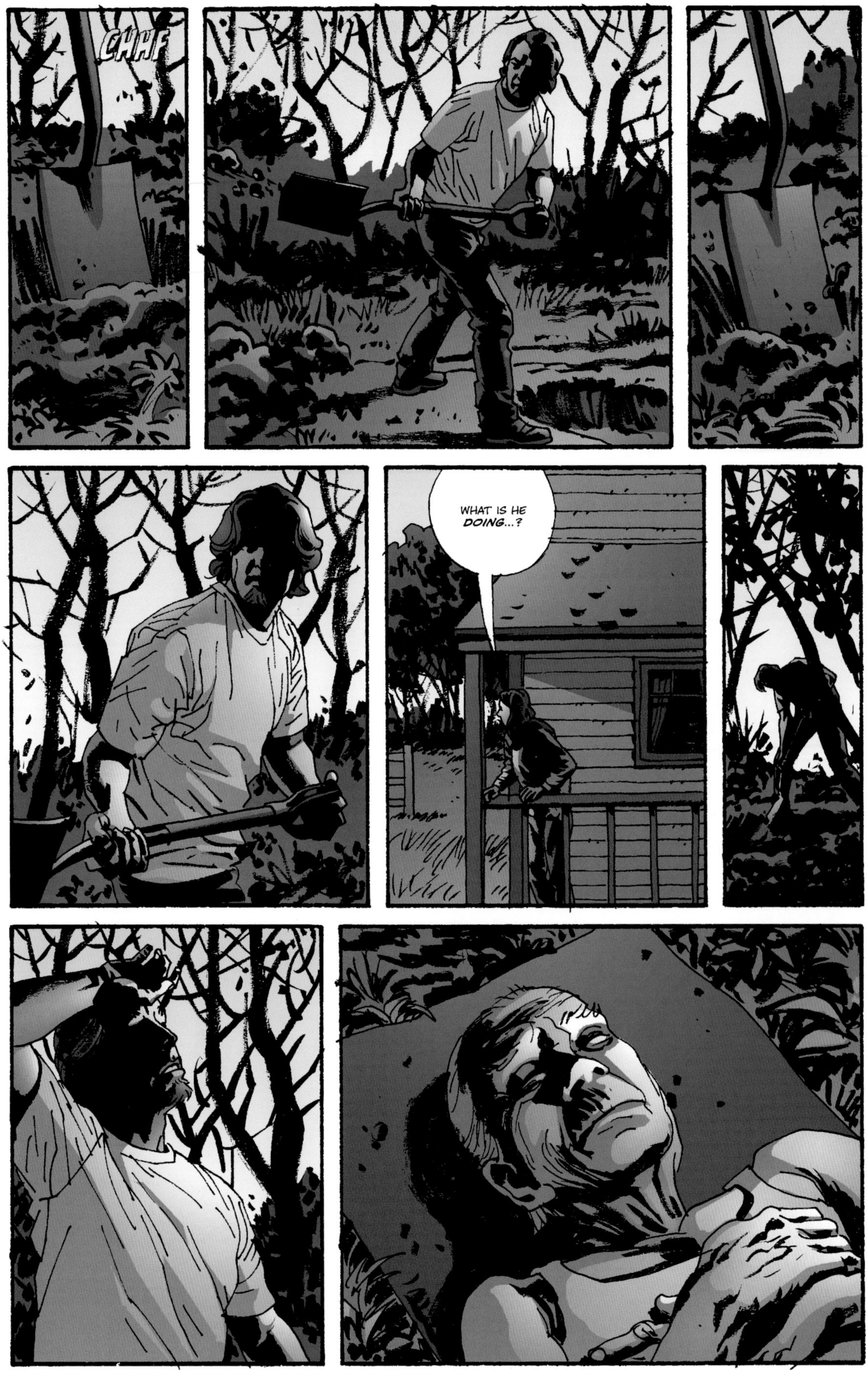
CHHF
WHAT IS HE DOING...?

NO... YOU DON'T BUMP UNLESS YOU *HAVE TO*.

THE *BUMP* IS FOR *AMATEURS*.

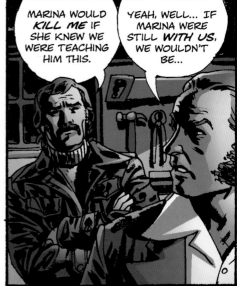

MARINA WOULD *KILL ME* IF SHE KNEW WE WERE TEACHING HIM THIS.

YEAH, WELL... IF MARINA WERE STILL *WITH US*, WE WOULDN'T BE...

BUT THE WAY I SEE IT, TOMMY, YOU'VE GOT TWO CHOICES...

FIND A NEW CAREER...OR TEACH *LEOPOLD* HERE WHAT WE DO.

THE KID'S *LIVING* IN THIS WORLD, MIGHT AS WELL KNOW HOW TO *SURVIVE* IN IT.

HEY UNCLE IVAN... *LOOK!*

OH MY GOD... THE KID'S A *NATURAL*.

BUT YOU *FELT IT*, DIDN'T YOU?

JUST A LITTLE, LEO, JUST A BIT... BUT YOU'VE GOT THE TOUCH.

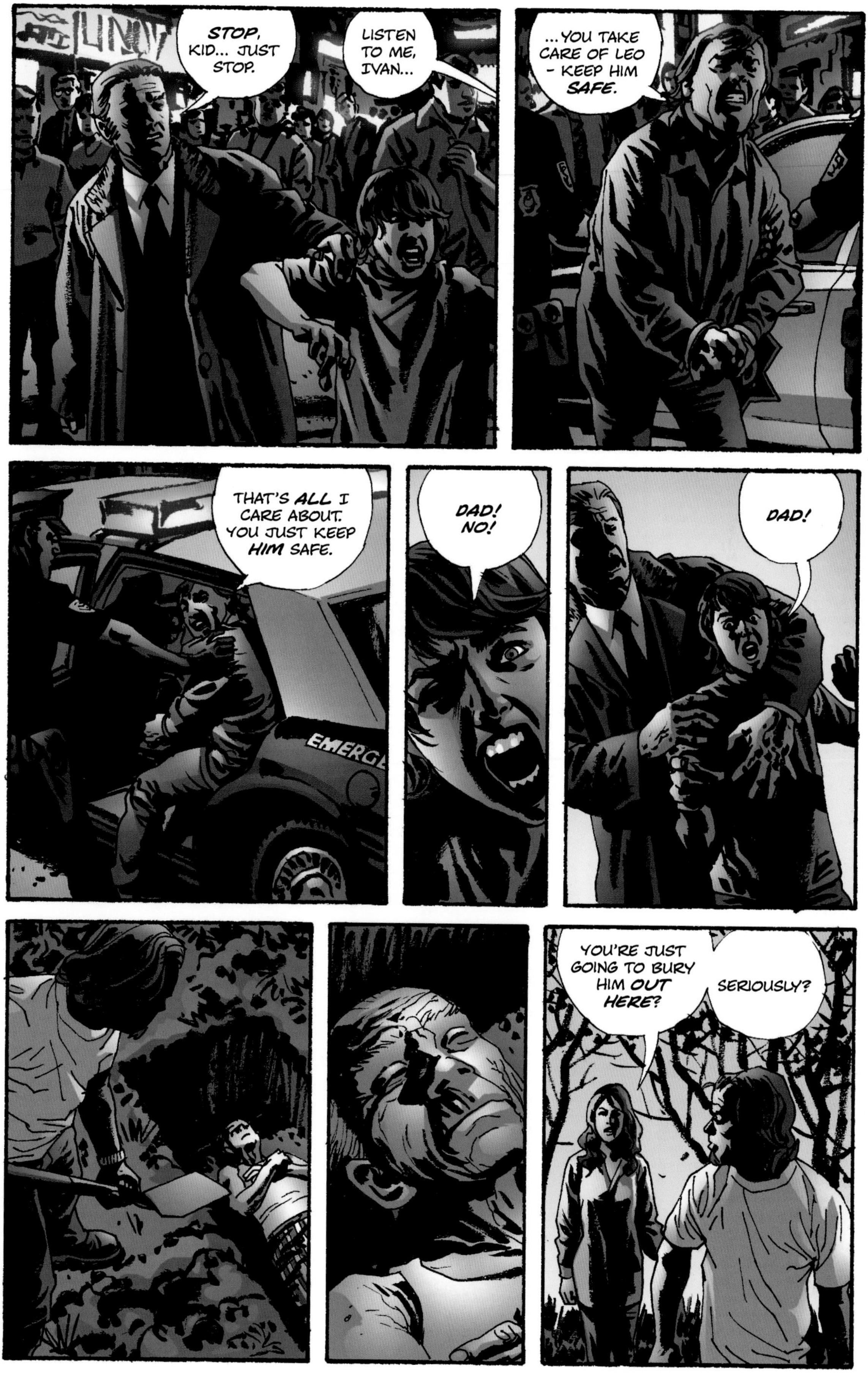
STOP, KID... JUST STOP.
LISTEN TO ME, IVAN...
...YOU TAKE CARE OF LEO - KEEP HIM SAFE.
THAT'S ALL I CARE ABOUT. YOU JUST KEEP HIM SAFE.
EMERGE
DAD! NO!
DAD!
YOU'RE JUST GOING TO BURY HIM OUT HERE?
SERIOUSLY?

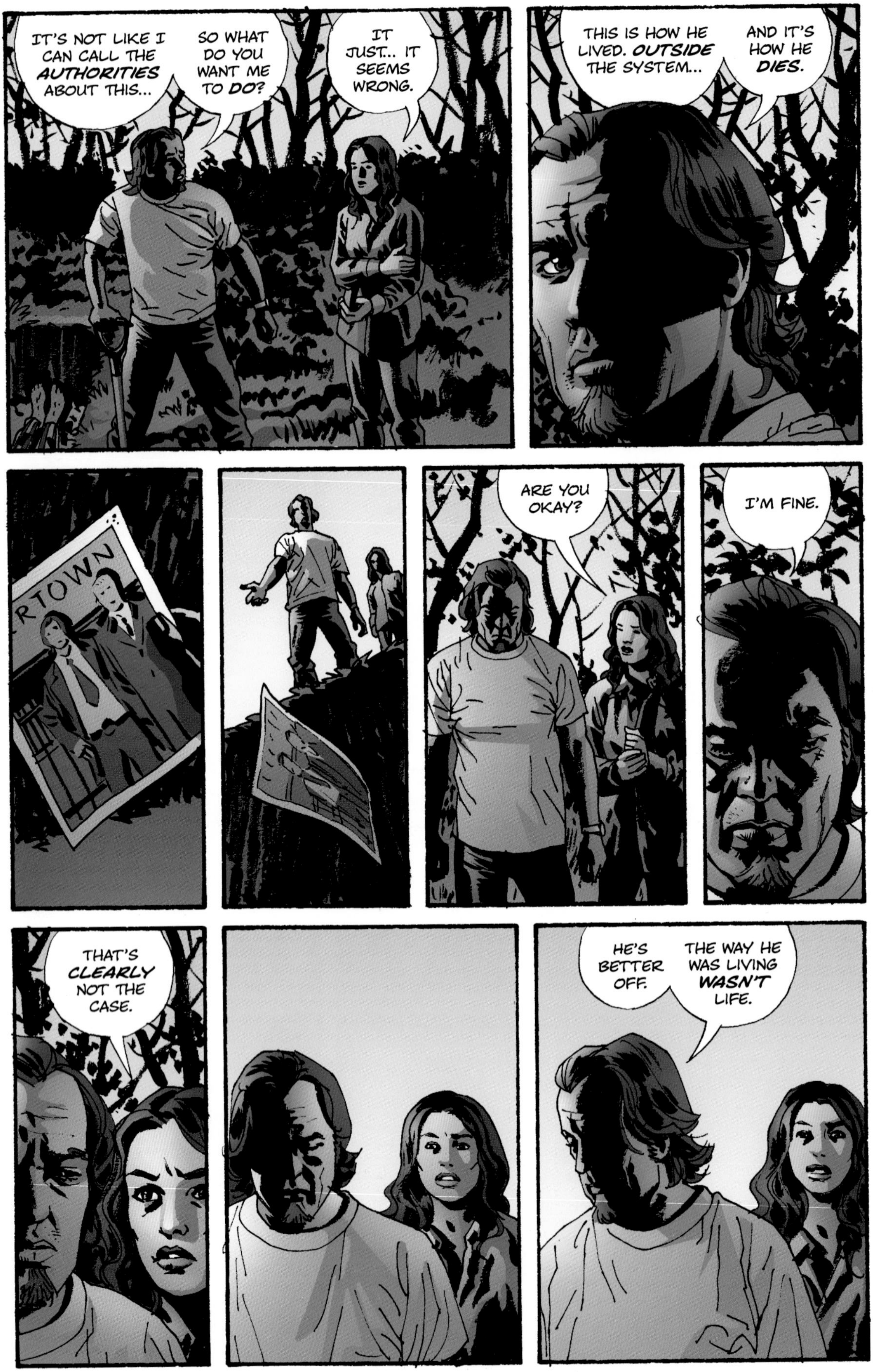
IT'S NOT LIKE I CAN CALL THE *AUTHORITIES* ABOUT THIS...
SO WHAT DO YOU WANT ME TO *DO?*
IT JUST... IT SEEMS WRONG.
THIS IS HOW HE LIVED. *OUTSIDE* THE SYSTEM...
AND IT'S HOW HE *DIES.*
RTOWN
ARE YOU OKAY?
I'M FINE.
THAT'S *CLEARLY* NOT THE CASE.
HE'S BETTER OFF.
THE WAY HE WAS LIVING *WASN'T* LIFE.

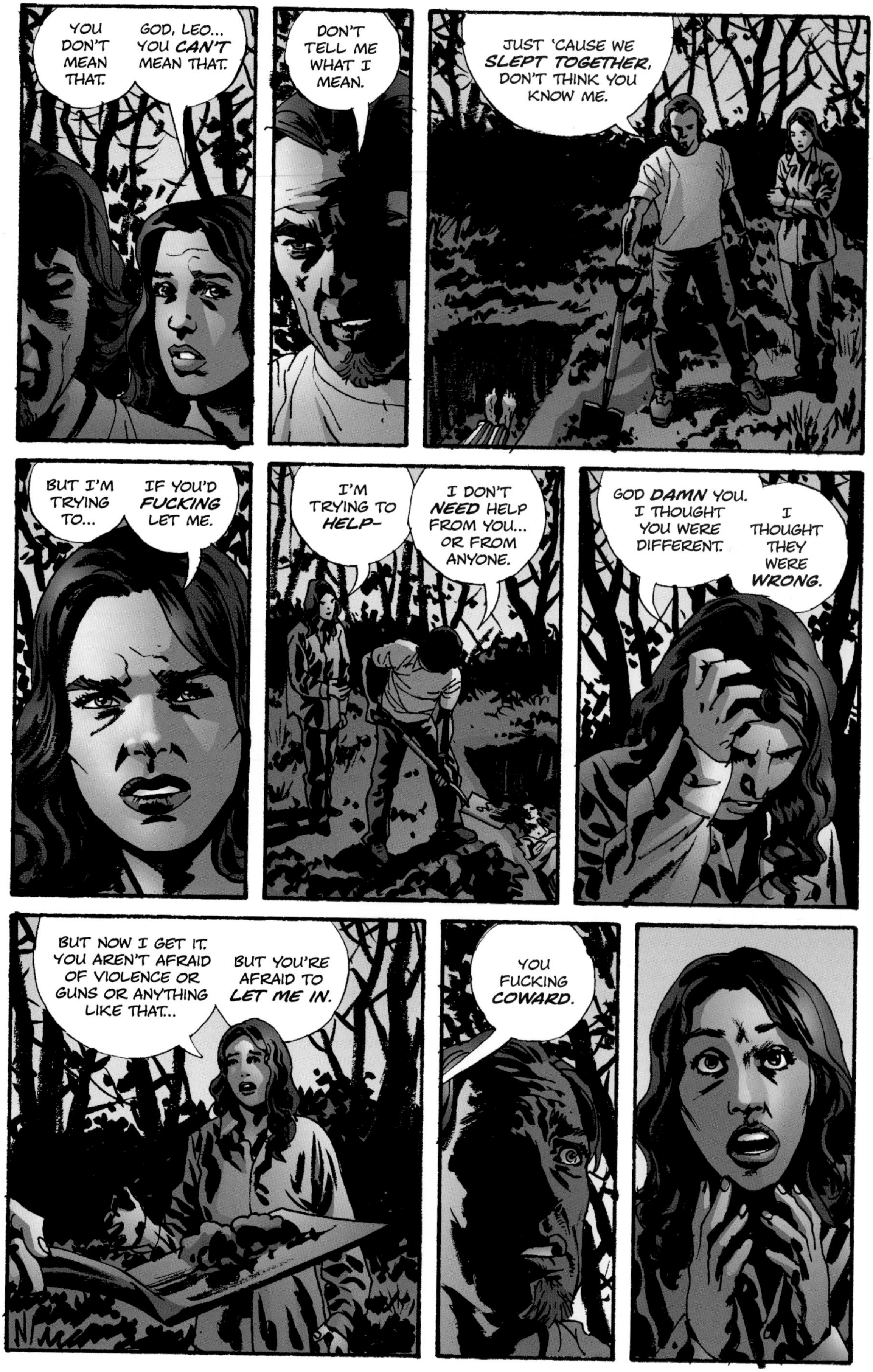
YOU DON'T MEAN THAT.
GOD, LEO... YOU CAN'T MEAN THAT.
DON'T TELL ME WHAT I MEAN.
JUST 'CAUSE WE SLEPT TOGETHER, DON'T THINK YOU KNOW ME.
BUT I'M TRYING TO...
IF YOU'D FUCKING LET ME.
I'M TRYING TO HELP-
I DON'T NEED HELP FROM YOU... OR FROM ANYONE.
GOD DAMN YOU. I THOUGHT YOU WERE DIFFERENT.
I THOUGHT THEY WERE WRONG.
BUT NOW I GET IT. YOU AREN'T AFRAID OF VIOLENCE OR GUNS OR ANYTHING LIKE THAT...
BUT YOU'RE AFRAID TO LET ME IN.
YOU FUCKING COWARD.

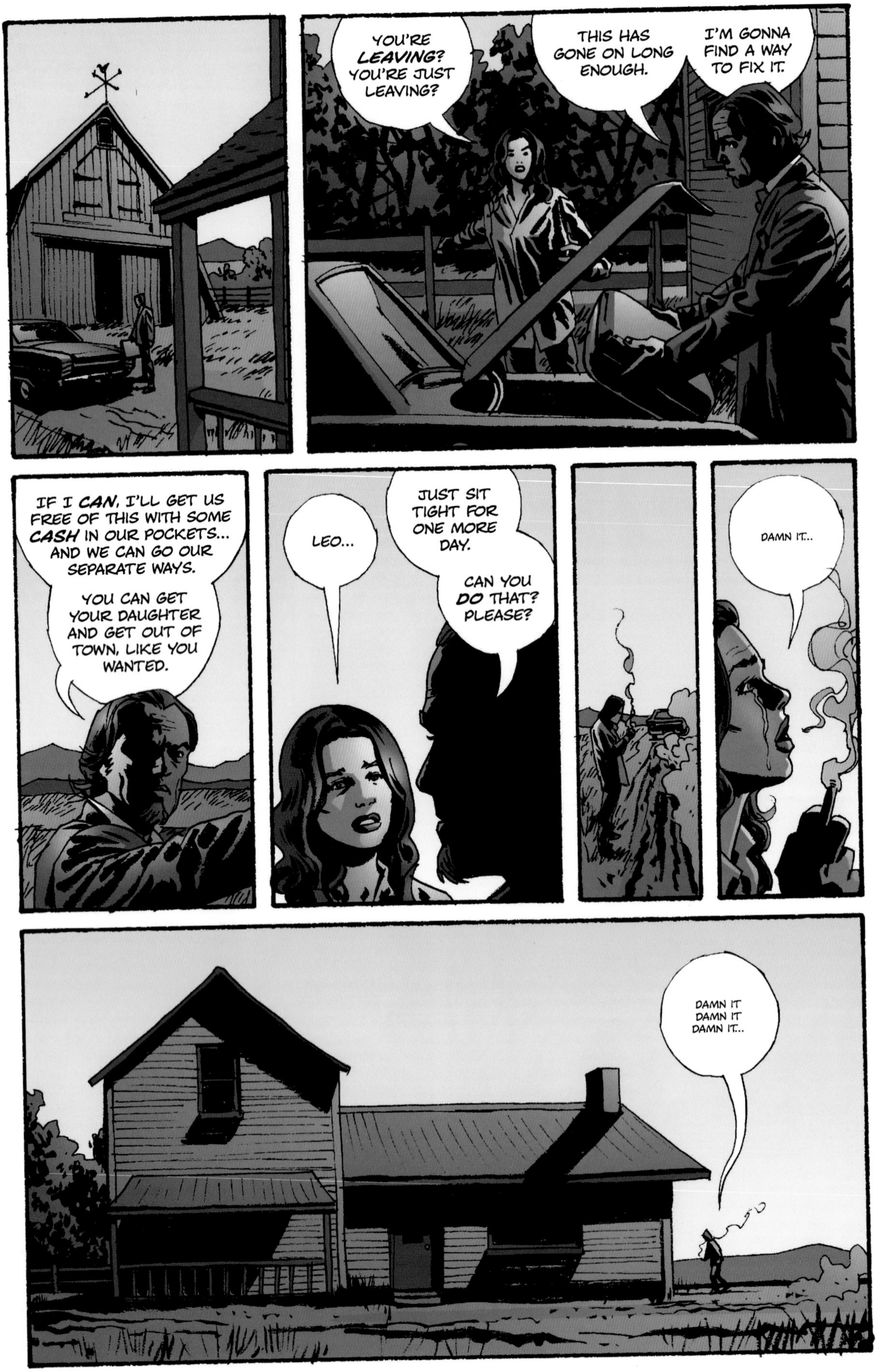
YOU'RE LEAVING? YOU'RE JUST LEAVING?
THIS HAS GONE ON LONG ENOUGH.
I'M GONNA FIND A WAY TO FIX IT.
IF I CAN, I'LL GET US FREE OF THIS WITH SOME CASH IN OUR POCKETS... AND WE CAN GO OUR SEPARATE WAYS.
YOU CAN GET YOUR DAUGHTER AND GET OUT OF TOWN, LIKE YOU WANTED.
LEO...
JUST SIT TIGHT FOR ONE MORE DAY.
CAN YOU DO THAT? PLEASE?
DAMN IT...
DAMN IT
DAMN IT
DAMN IT...

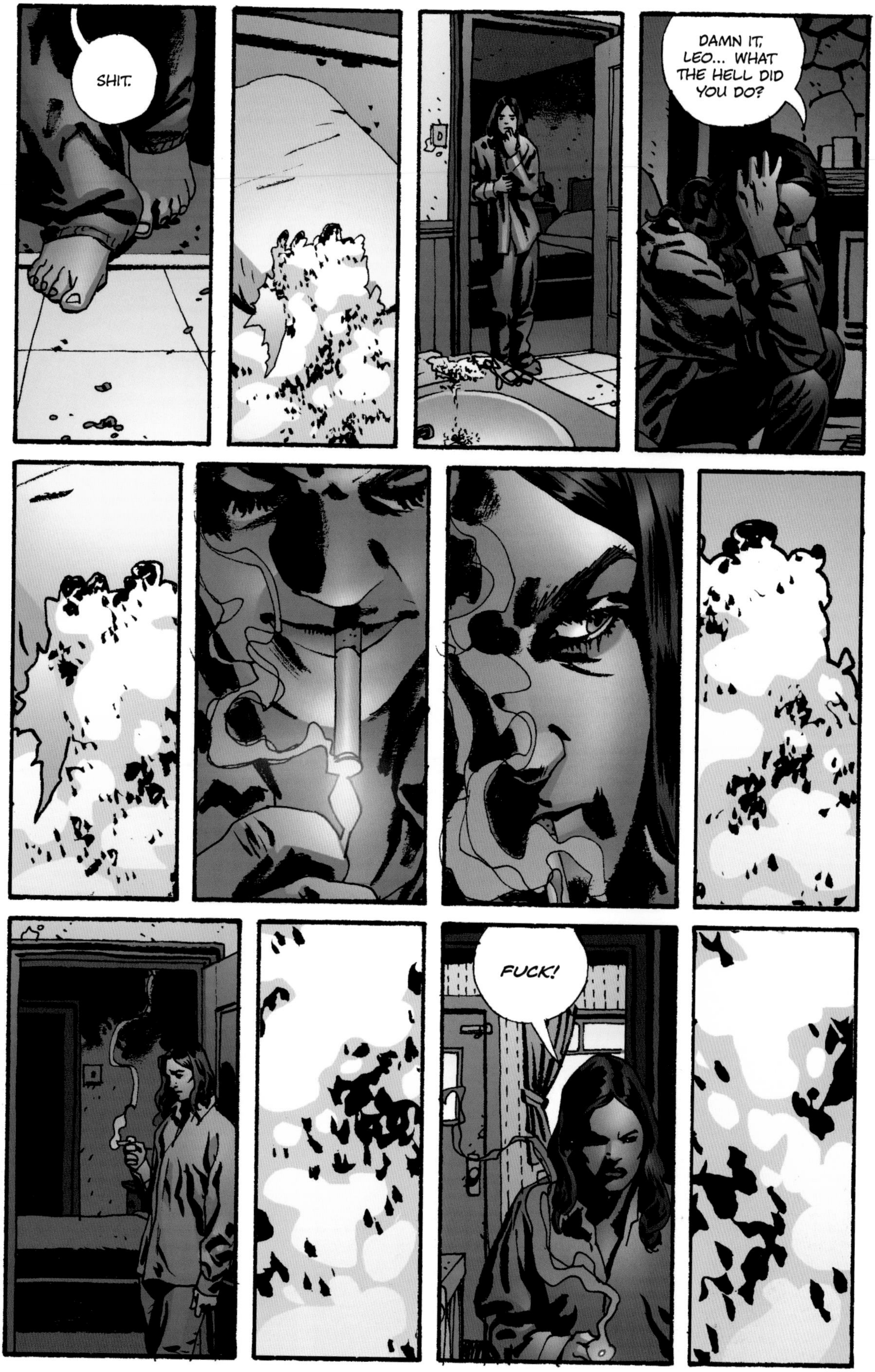
SHIT.
DAMN IT, LEO... WHAT THE HELL DID YOU DO?
FUCK!

FRANK KAFKA, PRIVATE EYE

by Jacob K.

G-MEN HAD SPENT ALL MORNING RUNNING ME THROUGH THE WRINGER...

I'M TELLIN' YA, I DON'T KNOW *NOTHIN'* ABOUT THAT DAME BEIN' *ICED*.

I WAS HIRED TO *FIND* HER!

OKAY, FRANK, THEN GIVE US THE NAME 'A YER CLIENT AND WE'LL *VERIFY*. THAT AIN'T A *PROBLEM*, IS IT?

MY CLIENT...? THAT'S -- THAT'S... *EASY*.

WHY COULDN'T I REMEMBER WHO HIRED ME? WHAT THE HELL WAS HAPPENING?

RINNNGG
BRRIING

BRRINNG RINNG
CLIK

I'M AFRAID WE CAN'T GET TO THE PHONE JUST NOW, BUT WE DO APPRECIATE YOUR CALL...

LEAVE A MESSAGE AND WE'LL GET RIGHT BACK TO YOU...

BEEP

MOM? ARE YOU THERE? HELLO?

LOOK, JUST - IF YOU'RE THERE, PICK UP, REALLY... PICK UP THE PHONE, MOM. I KNOW YOU'RE PROBABLY MAD, OR WORRIED... BUT JUST...

I NEED TO TALK TO YOU. I'M GOIN' A LITTLE NUTS HERE... GOIN' OUT OF MY SKIN...

I MEAN, GOD... I REALLY SCREWED UP, MOM. I'M SUCH AN IDIOT SOMETIMES.

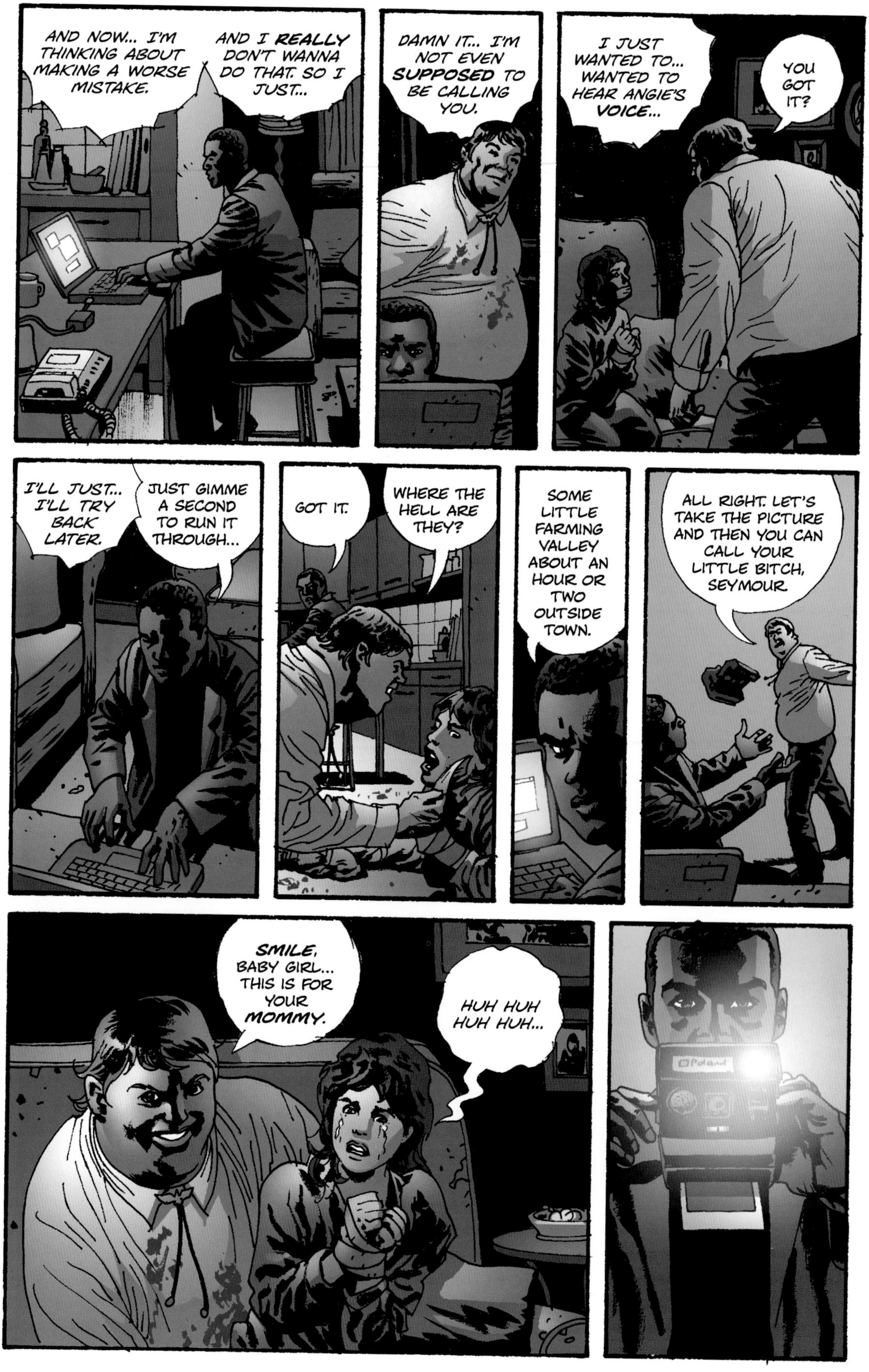
AND NOW... I'M THINKING ABOUT MAKING A WORSE MISTAKE.
AND I REALLY DON'T WANNA DO THAT. SO I JUST...
DAMN IT... I'M NOT EVEN SUPPOSED TO BE CALLING YOU.
I JUST WANTED TO... WANTED TO HEAR ANGIE'S VOICE...
YOU GOT IT?
I'LL JUST... I'LL TRY BACK LATER.
JUST GIMME A SECOND TO RUN IT THROUGH...
GOT IT.
WHERE THE HELL ARE THEY?
SOME LITTLE FARMING VALLEY ABOUT AN HOUR OR TWO OUTSIDE TOWN.
ALL RIGHT. LET'S TAKE THE PICTURE AND THEN YOU CAN CALL YOUR LITTLE BITCH, SEYMOUR.
SMILE, BABY GIRL... THIS IS FOR YOUR MOMMY.
HUH HUH HUH HUH...

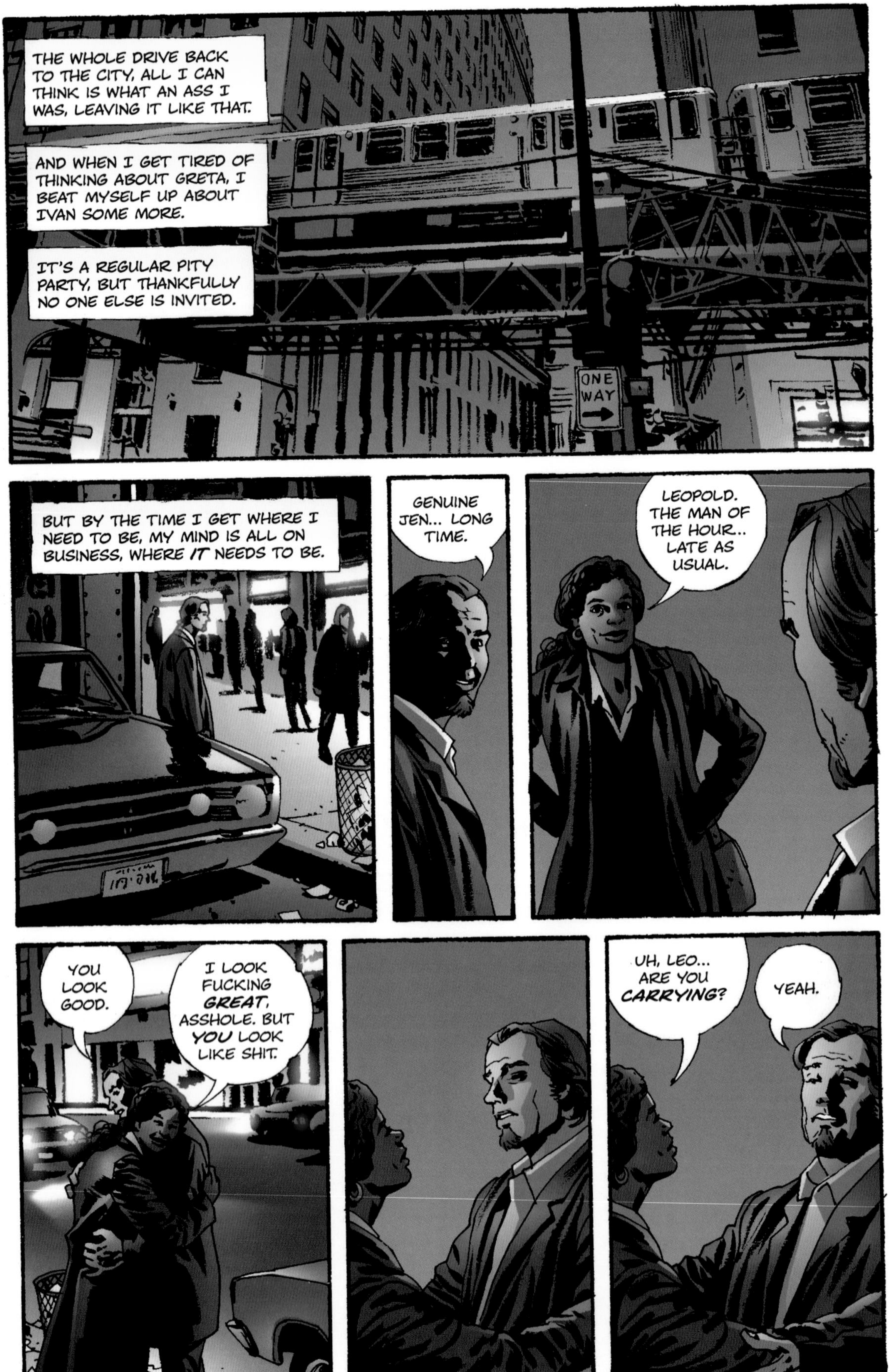
THE WHOLE DRIVE BACK TO THE CITY, ALL I CAN THINK IS WHAT AN ASS I WAS, LEAVING IT LIKE THAT.
AND WHEN I GET TIRED OF THINKING ABOUT GRETA, I BEAT MYSELF UP ABOUT IVAN SOME MORE.
IT'S A REGULAR PITY PARTY, BUT THANKFULLY NO ONE ELSE IS INVITED.
ONE WAY
BUT BY THE TIME I GET WHERE I NEED TO BE, MY MIND IS ALL ON BUSINESS, WHERE *IT* NEEDS TO BE.
GENUINE JEN... LONG TIME.
LEOPOLD. THE MAN OF THE HOUR... LATE AS USUAL.
YOU LOOK GOOD.
I LOOK FUCKING ***GREAT***, ASSHOLE. BUT ***YOU*** LOOK LIKE SHIT.
UH, LEO... ARE YOU ***CARRYING?***
YEAH.

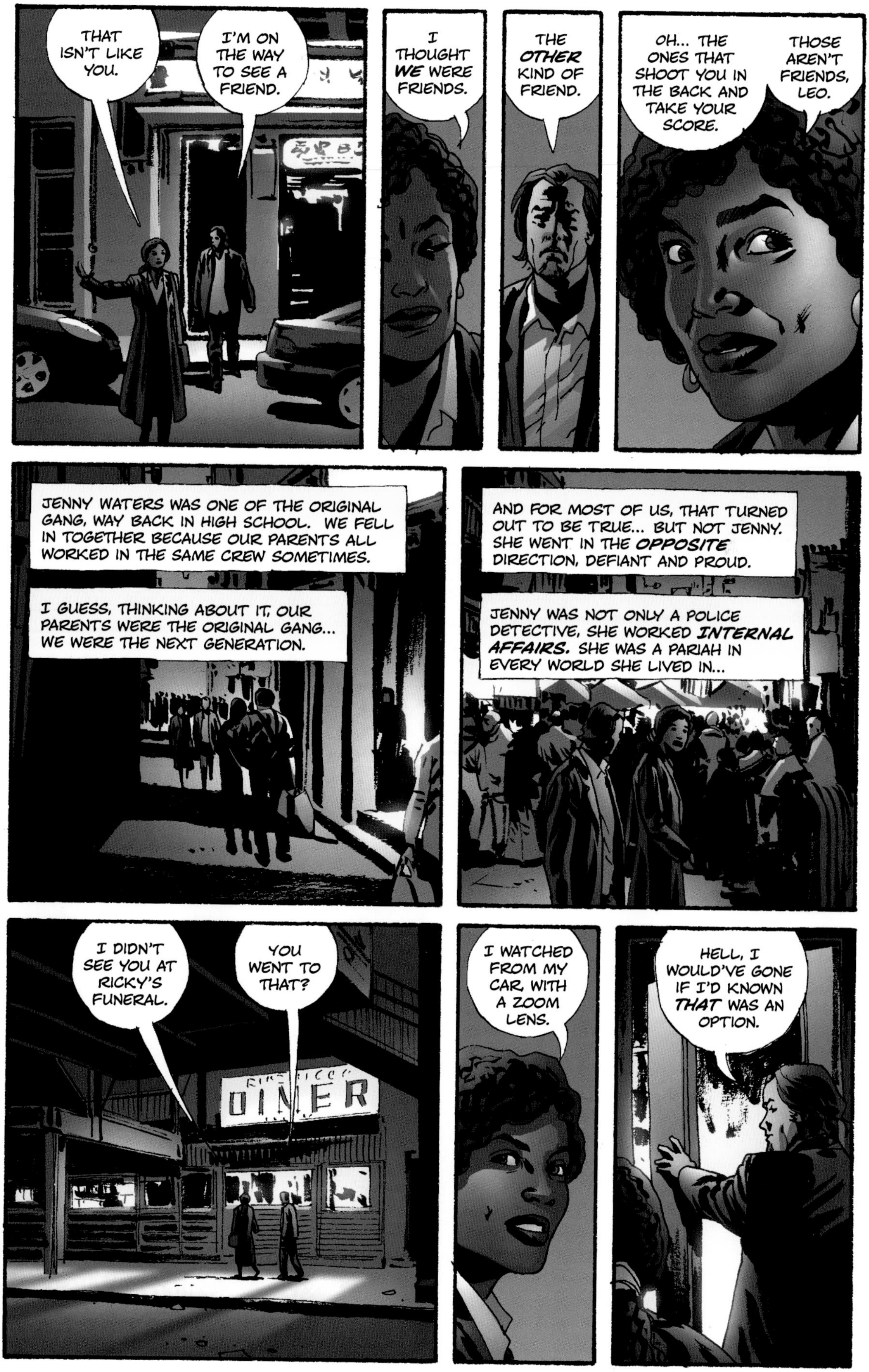
THAT ISN'T LIKE YOU.
I'M ON THE WAY TO SEE A FRIEND.
I THOUGHT WE WERE FRIENDS.
THE OTHER KIND OF FRIEND.
OH... THE ONES THAT SHOOT YOU IN THE BACK AND TAKE YOUR SCORE.
THOSE AREN'T FRIENDS, LEO.
JENNY WATERS WAS ONE OF THE ORIGINAL GANG, WAY BACK IN HIGH SCHOOL. WE FELL IN TOGETHER BECAUSE OUR PARENTS ALL WORKED IN THE SAME CREW SOMETIMES.
I GUESS, THINKING ABOUT IT, OUR PARENTS WERE THE ORIGINAL GANG... WE WERE THE NEXT GENERATION.
AND FOR MOST OF US, THAT TURNED OUT TO BE TRUE... BUT NOT JENNY. SHE WENT IN THE OPPOSITE DIRECTION, DEFIANT AND PROUD.
JENNY WAS NOT ONLY A POLICE DETECTIVE, SHE WORKED INTERNAL AFFAIRS. SHE WAS A PARIAH IN EVERY WORLD SHE LIVED IN...
I DIDN'T SEE YOU AT RICKY'S FUNERAL.
YOU WENT TO THAT?
DINER
I WATCHED FROM MY CAR, WITH A ZOOM LENS.
HELL, I WOULD'VE GONE IF I'D KNOWN THAT WAS AN OPTION.

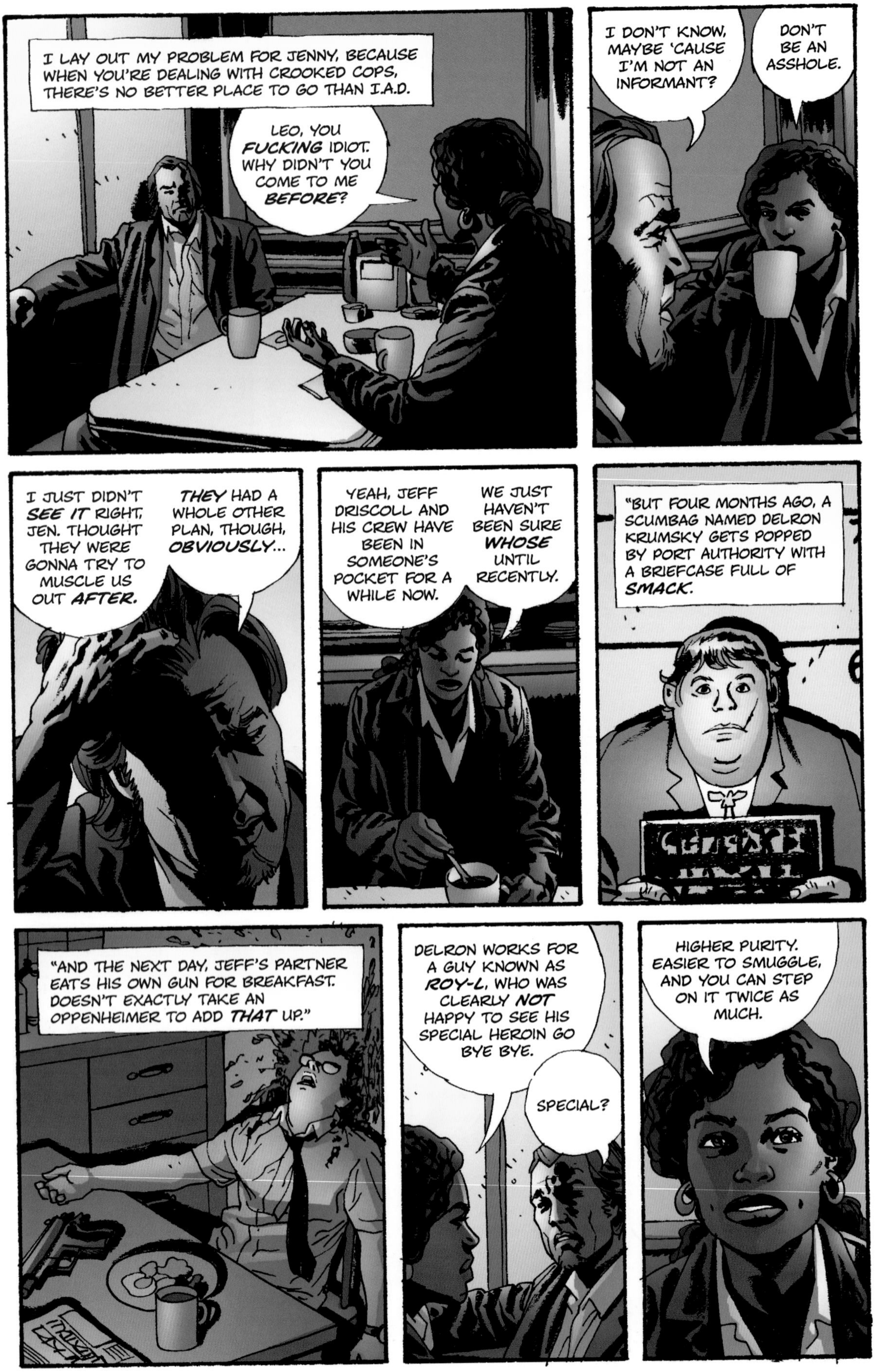
I LAY OUT MY PROBLEM FOR JENNY, BECAUSE WHEN YOU'RE DEALING WITH CROOKED COPS, THERE'S NO BETTER PLACE TO GO THAN I.A.D.
LEO, YOU FUCKING IDIOT. WHY DIDN'T YOU COME TO ME BEFORE?
I DON'T KNOW, MAYBE 'CAUSE I'M NOT AN INFORMANT?
DON'T BE AN ASSHOLE.
I JUST DIDN'T SEE IT RIGHT, JEN. THOUGHT THEY WERE GONNA TRY TO MUSCLE US OUT AFTER.
THEY HAD A WHOLE OTHER PLAN, THOUGH, OBVIOUSLY...
YEAH, JEFF DRISCOLL AND HIS CREW HAVE BEEN IN SOMEONE'S POCKET FOR A WHILE NOW.
WE JUST HAVEN'T BEEN SURE WHOSE UNTIL RECENTLY.
"BUT FOUR MONTHS AGO, A SCUMBAG NAMED DELRON KRUMSKY GETS POPPED BY PORT AUTHORITY WITH A BRIEFCASE FULL OF SMACK.
"AND THE NEXT DAY, JEFF'S PARTNER EATS HIS OWN GUN FOR BREAKFAST. DOESN'T EXACTLY TAKE AN OPPENHEIMER TO ADD THAT UP."
DELRON WORKS FOR A GUY KNOWN AS ROY-L, WHO WAS CLEARLY NOT HAPPY TO SEE HIS SPECIAL HEROIN GO BYE BYE.
SPECIAL?
HIGHER PURITY. EASIER TO SMUGGLE, AND YOU CAN STEP ON IT TWICE AS MUCH.

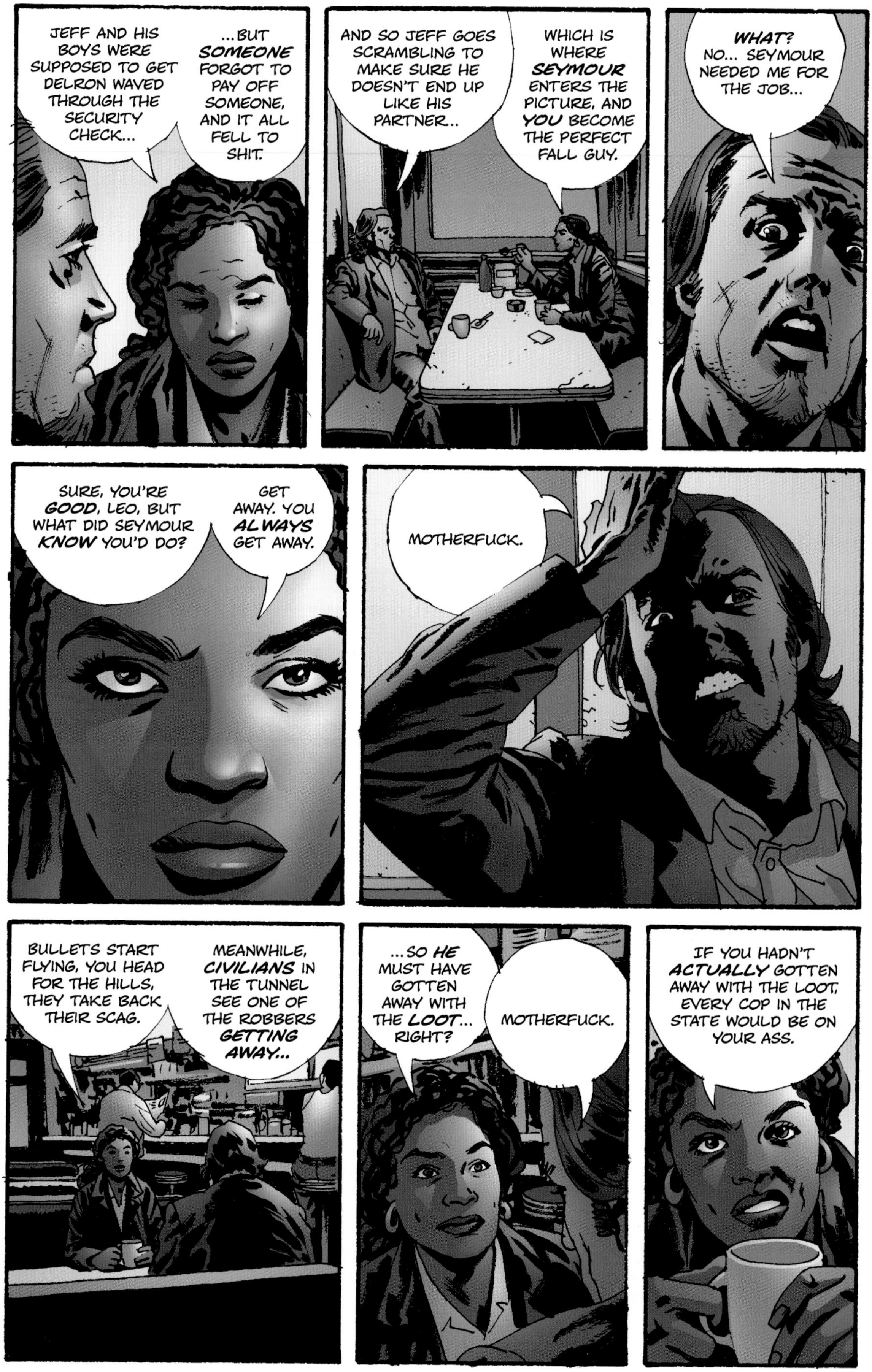
JEFF AND HIS BOYS WERE SUPPOSED TO GET DELRON WAVED THROUGH THE SECURITY CHECK...
...BUT SOMEONE FORGOT TO PAY OFF SOMEONE, AND IT ALL FELL TO SHIT.
AND SO JEFF GOES SCRAMBLING TO MAKE SURE HE DOESN'T END UP LIKE HIS PARTNER...
WHICH IS WHERE SEYMOUR ENTERS THE PICTURE, AND YOU BECOME THE PERFECT FALL GUY.
WHAT? NO... SEYMOUR NEEDED ME FOR THE JOB...
SURE, YOU'RE GOOD, LEO, BUT WHAT DID SEYMOUR KNOW YOU'D DO?
GET AWAY. YOU ALWAYS GET AWAY.
MOTHERFUCK.
BULLETS START FLYING, YOU HEAD FOR THE HILLS, THEY TAKE BACK THEIR SCAG.
MEANWHILE, CIVILIANS IN THE TUNNEL SEE ONE OF THE ROBBERS GETTING AWAY...
...SO HE MUST HAVE GOTTEN AWAY WITH THE LOOT... RIGHT?
MOTHERFUCK.
IF YOU HADN'T ACTUALLY GOTTEN AWAY WITH THE LOOT, EVERY COP IN THE STATE WOULD BE ON YOUR ASS.

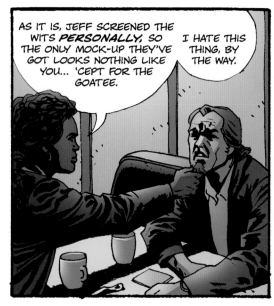

AS IT IS, JEFF SCREENED THE WITS *PERSONALLY*, SO THE ONLY MOCK-UP THEY'VE GOT LOOKS NOTHING LIKE YOU... 'CEPT FOR THE GOATEE.

I HATE THIS THING, BY THE WAY.

SO, ARE YOU PLANNING TO SWOOP ALL THESE BAD PEOPLE UP AND MAKE MY LIFE EASIER?

I WISH.

NO, THE LIEUTENANT WANTS US *WATCHING*, SEEING WHERE ELSE THIS ALL *LEADS*.

HE'S *STILL* HOPING FOR SOME WAY INTO HYDE'S BUSINESS.

DAMN.

SO, WHAT ARE YOU GONNA DO, LEOPOLD?

I HAVE NO IDEA... BUT AT LEAST NOW I KNOW WHERE THE SHIT I'M IN *CAME FROM*. THAT'S SOMETHING...

BE CAREFUL WITH THIS ROY-L AND HIS PEOPLE. THEY'LL KILL YOU JUST FOR *HAVING* THAT SUITCASE.

YOU KNOW DRUG DEALERS AND PIMPS, THEY'RE ALL *PARANOID*.

DON'T WORRY ABOUT ME. I'LL SURVIVE.

I KNOW *THAT*. THAT'S THE *OTHER* THING YOU ALWAYS DO.

BUT HOW EXACTLY WAS I GOING TO GO ABOUT DOING THAT *THIS TIME*? I FIGURED I HAD ONE ANGLE - *SEYMOUR.*

MUCH AS I HATED HANDING A MILLION DOLLAR SCORE TO THE GUY WHO DOUBLE-CROSSED ME... HE WAS THE ONE WHO'D STARTED THIS, AND HE'D HAVE TO END IT.

HE'D HAVE TO TAKE THE SMACK TO HIS PEOPLE AND GET THEM OFF MY BACK.

AND IF HE GOT PAID, THEN MAYBE I'D JUST COME BACK AND ROB HIM.

THAT WAS WHY I BROUGHT THE GUN GRETA HAD GRABBED DURING THE HEIST.

THE MOOD I WAS IN, I WASN'T PLANNING TO TAKE NO FOR AN ANSWER.

BUT HIS APARTMENT IS DARK... AND I DON'T NEED MORE DEAD TIME. MORE TIME TO THINK.

SO I WEIGHT MY OPTIONS... DO I GO TOSS THE PLACE AND THEN WAIT FOR SEYMOUR TO COME HOME?

OR DO I CALL IT A NIGHT AND HEAD BACK TO THE FARM? TRY TO TALK TO GRETA...

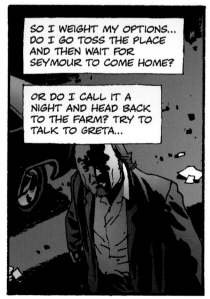

...TRY TO EXPLAIN TO HER WHY I'M SO FUCKED UP...

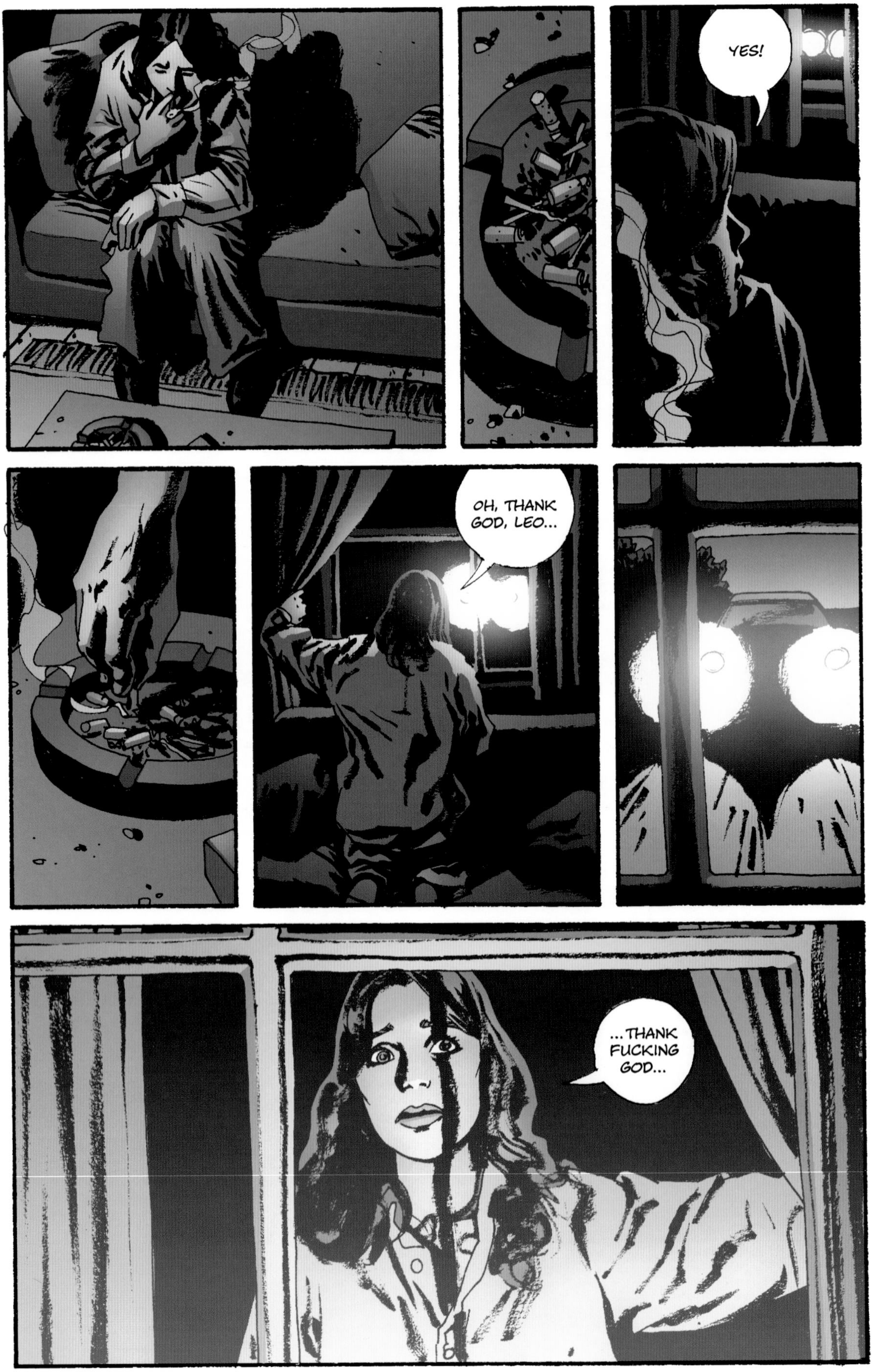
YES!
OH, THANK GOD, LEO...
...THANK FUCKING GOD...

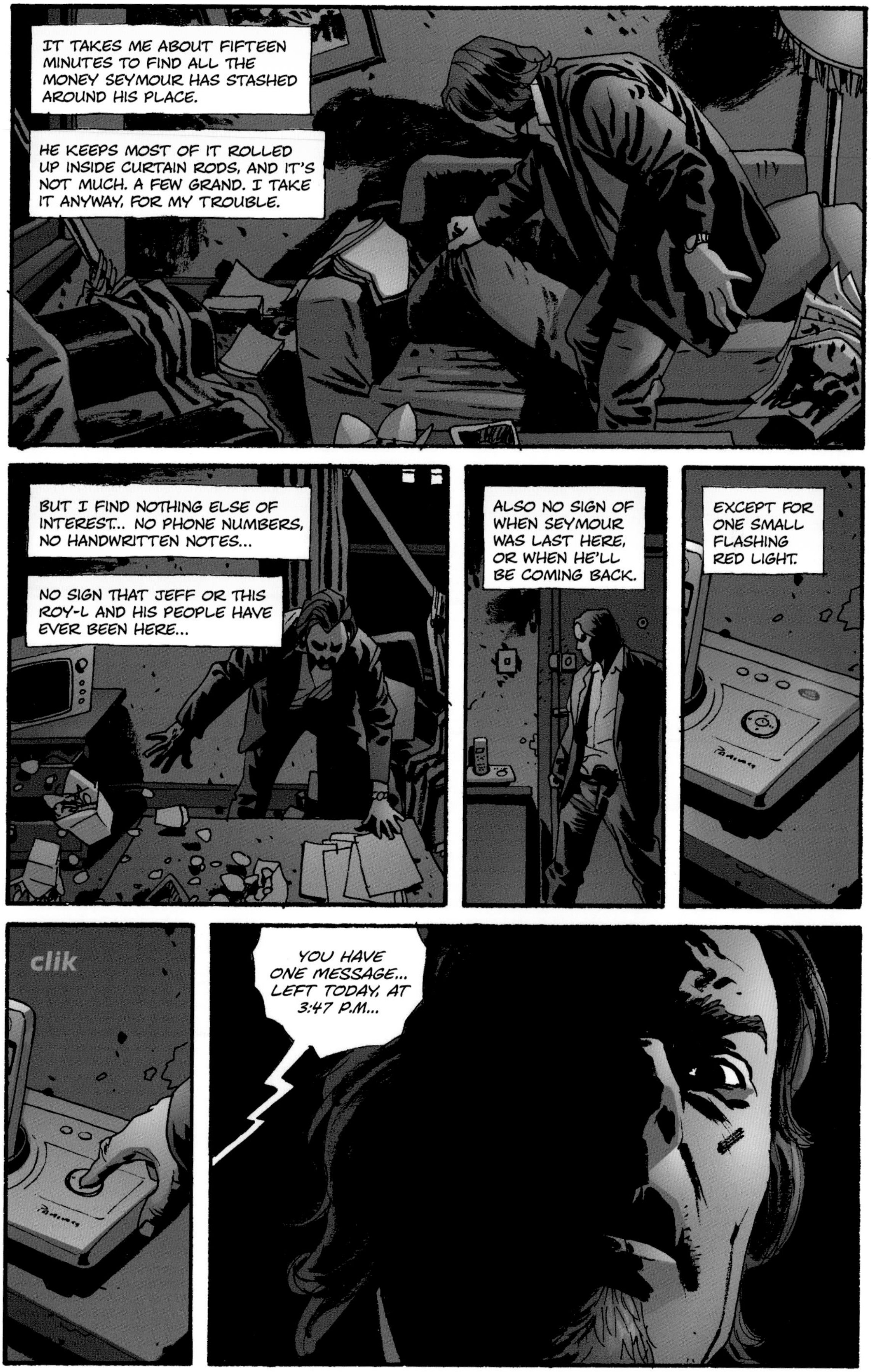
IT TAKES ME ABOUT FIFTEEN MINUTES TO FIND ALL THE MONEY SEYMOUR HAS STASHED AROUND HIS PLACE.
HE KEEPS MOST OF IT ROLLED UP INSIDE CURTAIN RODS, AND IT'S NOT MUCH. A FEW GRAND. I TAKE IT ANYWAY, FOR MY TROUBLE.
BUT I FIND NOTHING ELSE OF INTEREST... NO PHONE NUMBERS, NO HANDWRITTEN NOTES...
NO SIGN THAT JEFF OR THIS ROY-L AND HIS PEOPLE HAVE EVER BEEN HERE...
ALSO NO SIGN OF WHEN SEYMOUR WAS LAST HERE, OR WHEN HE'LL BE COMING BACK.
EXCEPT FOR ONE SMALL FLASHING RED LIGHT.
clik
YOU HAVE ONE MESSAGE... LEFT TODAY, AT 3:47 P.M...

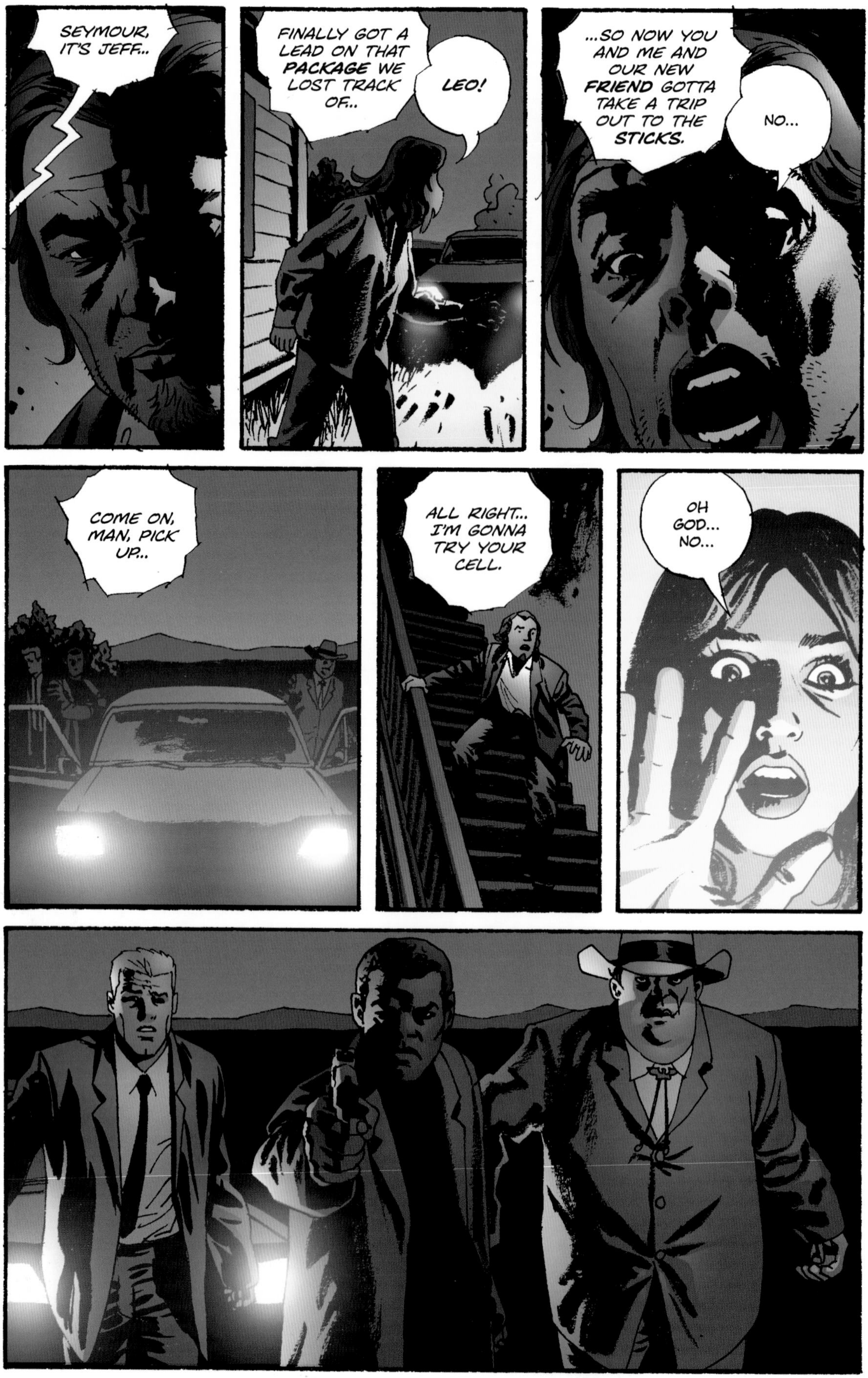
SEYMOUR, IT'S JEFF...
FINALLY GOT A LEAD ON THAT PACKAGE WE LOST TRACK OF...
LEO!
...SO NOW YOU AND ME AND OUR NEW FRIEND GOTTA TAKE A TRIP OUT TO THE STICKS.
NO...
COME ON, MAN, PICK UP...
ALL RIGHT... I'M GONNA TRY YOUR CELL.
OH GOD... NO...

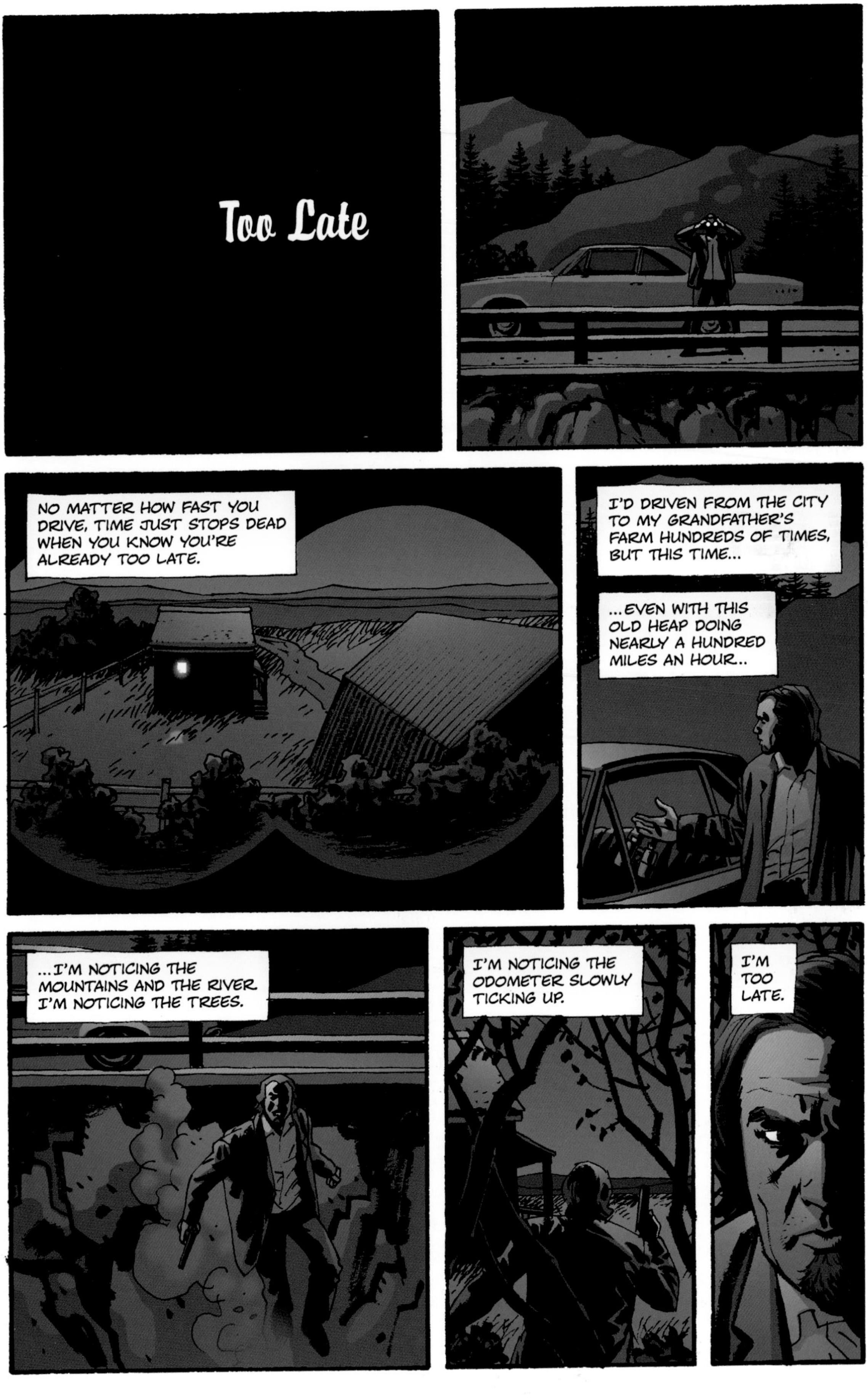
Too Late
NO MATTER HOW FAST YOU DRIVE, TIME JUST STOPS DEAD WHEN YOU KNOW YOU'RE ALREADY TOO LATE.
I'D DRIVEN FROM THE CITY TO MY GRANDFATHER'S FARM HUNDREDS OF TIMES, BUT THIS TIME...
...EVEN WITH THIS OLD HEAP DOING NEARLY A HUNDRED MILES AN HOUR..
...I'M NOTICING THE MOUNTAINS AND THE RIVER I'M NOTICING THE TREES.
I'M NOTICING THE ODOMETER SLOWLY TICKING UP.
I'M TOO LATE.

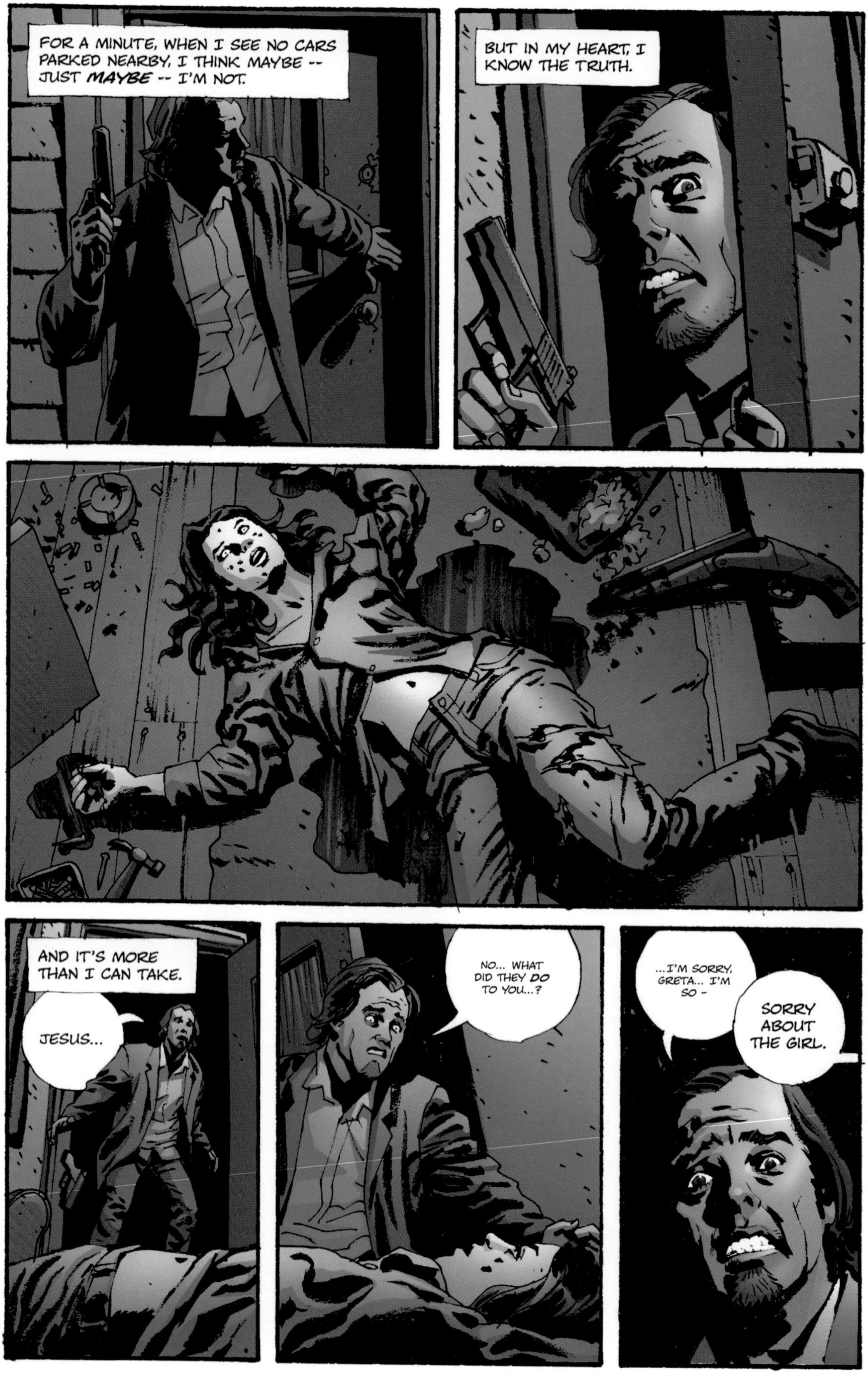
FOR A MINUTE, WHEN I SEE NO CARS PARKED NEARBY, I THINK MAYBE -- JUST *MAYBE* -- I'M NOT.
BUT IN MY HEART, I KNOW THE TRUTH.
AND IT'S MORE THAN I CAN TAKE.
JESUS...
NO... WHAT DID THEY *DO* TO YOU...?
...I'M SORRY, GRETA... I'M SO -
SORRY ABOUT THE GIRL.

DELRON WASN'T **EASY** TO CONVINCE THE ONLY DOPE **HERE** WAS THAT **ONE BRICK** IN THE UPSTAIRS BATHROOM.

YOU FUCKING BASTARD... YOU DIDN'T HAVE TO DO THIS. ANY OF IT...

HEY. I TRIED TO **SAVE HER**, LEO, I SWEAR

EVEN THOUGH SHE PRACTICALLY **BROKE MY NOSE** WITH THAT SHOTGUN.

BUT THESE GUYS, THEY JUST... YOU DON'T **KNOW** THESE TYPES OF GUYS.

YEAH, I **DO**, SEYMOUR

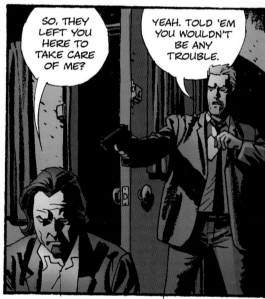

SO, THEY LEFT YOU HERE TO TAKE CARE OF ME?

YEAH. TOLD 'EM YOU WOULDN'T BE ANY TROUBLE.

NOT ONCE I SHOWED YOU **THIS.**

IS THIS --?

GRETA'S DAUGHTER **ANGIE.** DELRON'S HOLDING ONTO HER, AS AN INSURANCE POLICY.

I GUARANTEED HIM YOU'D GIVE A SHIT, JUST LIKE HER MOM DID...

THE DIFFERENCE BEING *YOU* CAN HAND OVER THE *BRIEFCASE* IN EXCHANGE FOR THE KID.

HELL, HE'S SO FUCKIN' *EXHAUSTED* WITH THIS SHIT, I EVEN CONVINCED HIM TO LET YOU *WALK AWAY.*

WHAT A *FRIEND* YOU ARE...

DON'T.

JUST GET ME THE REST OF THE FUCKING HEROIN.

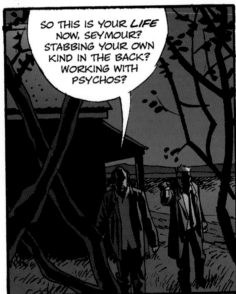

SO THIS IS YOUR *LIFE* NOW, SEYMOUR? STABBING YOUR OWN KIND IN THE BACK? WORKING WITH PSYCHOS?

THIS IS JUST *ONE* JOB... THAT GOT TOO MESSY FOR ITS OWN GOOD.

YOU DIDN'T HAVE TO LIE TO ME ABOUT THE SCORE.

YOU'D HAVE TAKEN A JOB STEALING A MILLION IN UNCUT *SMACK* FOR A DRUG DEALER?

SEE? I KNOW YOU.

114   CRIMINAL The Deluxe Edition

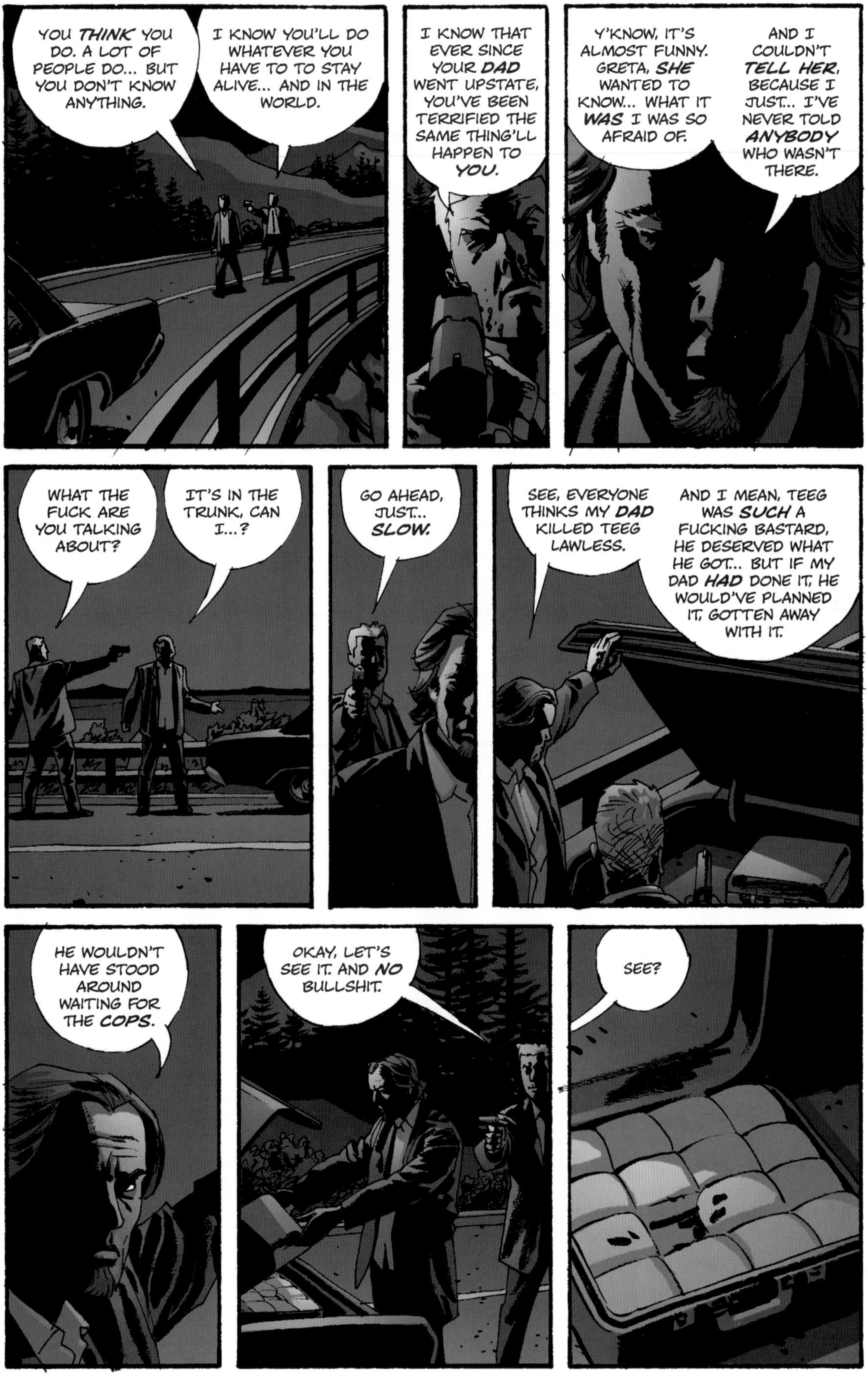
YOU THINK YOU DO. A LOT OF PEOPLE DO... BUT YOU DON'T KNOW ANYTHING.
I KNOW YOU'LL DO WHATEVER YOU HAVE TO TO STAY ALIVE... AND IN THE WORLD.
I KNOW THAT EVER SINCE YOUR DAD WENT UPSTATE, YOU'VE BEEN TERRIFIED THE SAME THING'LL HAPPEN TO YOU.
Y'KNOW, IT'S ALMOST FUNNY. GRETA, SHE WANTED TO KNOW... WHAT IT WAS I WAS SO AFRAID OF.
AND I COULDN'T TELL HER, BECAUSE I JUST... I'VE NEVER TOLD ANYBODY WHO WASN'T THERE.
WHAT THE FUCK ARE YOU TALKING ABOUT?
IT'S IN THE TRUNK, CAN I...?
GO AHEAD, JUST... SLOW.
SEE, EVERYONE THINKS MY DAD KILLED TEEG LAWLESS.
AND I MEAN, TEEG WAS SUCH A FUCKING BASTARD, HE DESERVED WHAT HE GOT... BUT IF MY DAD HAD DONE IT, HE WOULD'VE PLANNED IT, GOTTEN AWAY WITH IT.
HE WOULDN'T HAVE STOOD AROUND WAITING FOR THE COPS.
OKAY, LET'S SEE IT. AND NO BULLSHIT.
SEE?

SO, WAIT, WHAT ARE YOU *SAYING*? THAT *YOU* KILLED TEEG LAWLESS?

NO WAY.

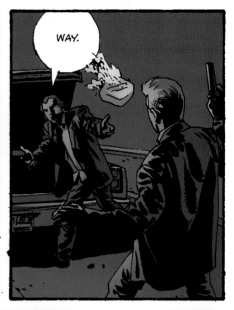

WAY.

HUTT—

FUCK! FUCK! FUCK!

THAT'S WHAT I'VE ALWAYS BEEN AFRAID OF, YOU STUPID PIECE OF SHIT...

...OF WHAT'S *INSIDE* OF ME.

RAGE IS BLIND, AND I'M AN IDIOT. THE MOMENT SEYMOUR'S *A CORPSE*, ALL I CAN THINK ABOUT IS THE GIRL. GRETA'S *KID*.

NO... DAMN IT...

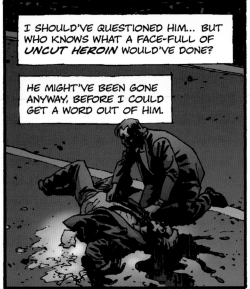

I SHOULD'VE QUESTIONED HIM... BUT WHO KNOWS WHAT A FACE-FULL OF *UNCUT HEROIN* WOULD'VE DONE?

HE MIGHT'VE BEEN GONE ANYWAY, BEFORE I COULD GET A WORD OUT OF HIM.

AS IT IS, I GET LUCKY.

LUCK. *RIGHT.*

EXCEPT, MY LUCK HAS NEVER BEEN ANYTHING BUT A CURSE.

DAMN IT...

THE *VOLUNTEER FIRE DEPARTMENT* AND THE COUNTY'S TWO POLICE CARS PASS ME ON THEIR WAY OUT TO THE FARM.

THE FIRE AND THE BODIES SHOULD KEEP THEM BUSY FOR A WHILE...

...AND GIVE ME TIME TO DO WHAT I HAVE TO IN TOWN.

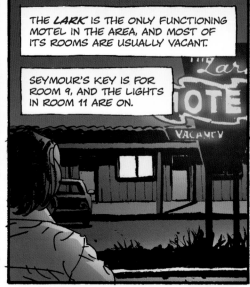

THE *LARK* IS THE ONLY FUNCTIONING MOTEL IN THE AREA, AND MOST OF ITS ROOMS ARE USUALLY VACANT.

SEYMOUR'S KEY IS FOR ROOM 9, AND THE LIGHTS IN ROOM 11 ARE ON.

MY HOPE IS THAT JEFF AND DELRON ARE WAITING HERE, WITH THE GIRL.

I JUST NEED TO MAKE *SURE* BEFORE –

JUST STOP YOUR FUCKIN' MOANIN' YOU LITTLE SHIT!

CHRIST... I CAN'T *WAIT* TO SELL THAT FUCKIN' BRAT...

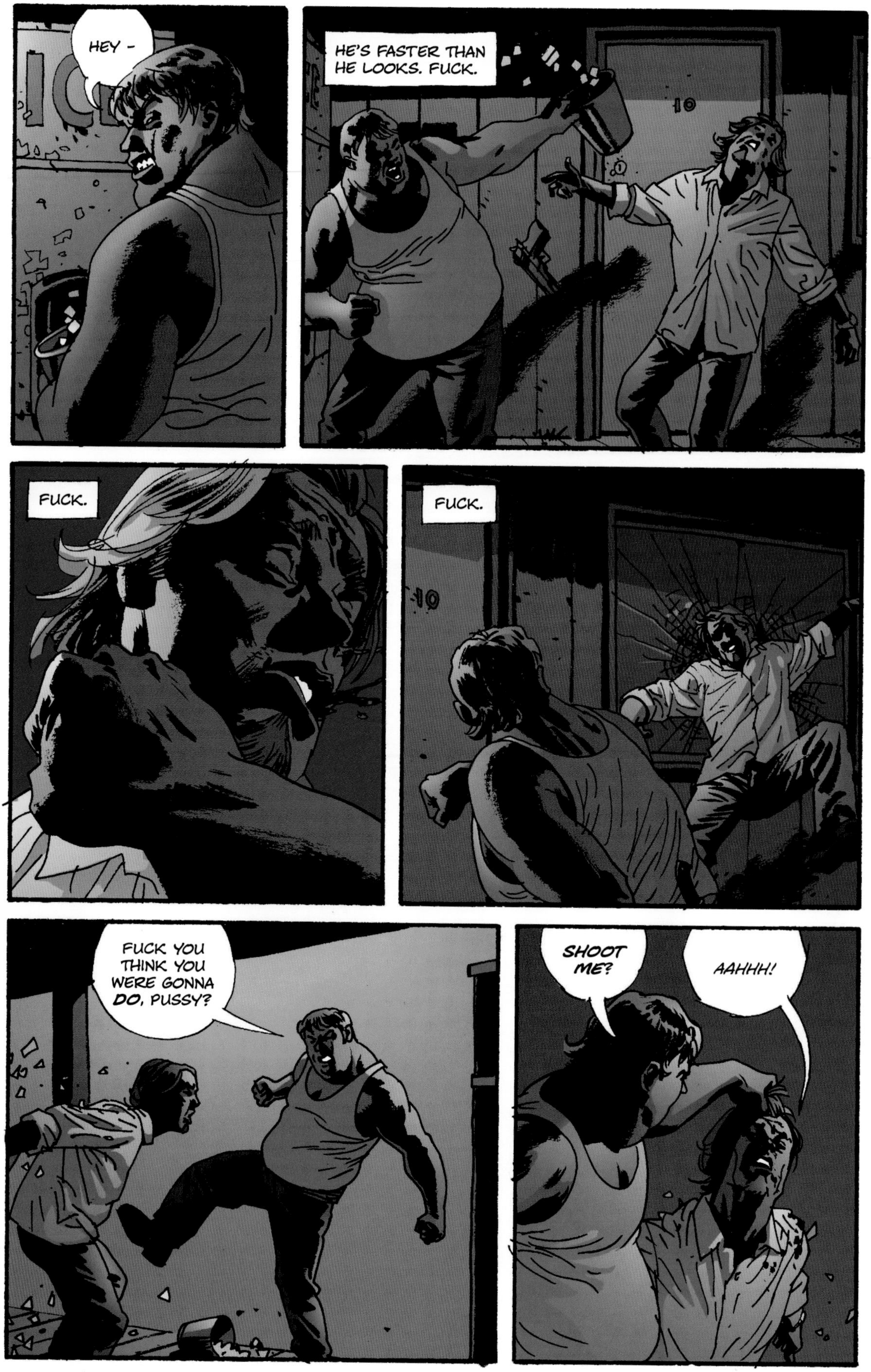
HEY -
HE'S FASTER THAN HE LOOKS. FUCK.
FUCK.
FUCK.
FUCK YOU THINK YOU WERE GONNA DO, PUSSY?
SHOOT ME?
AAHHH!

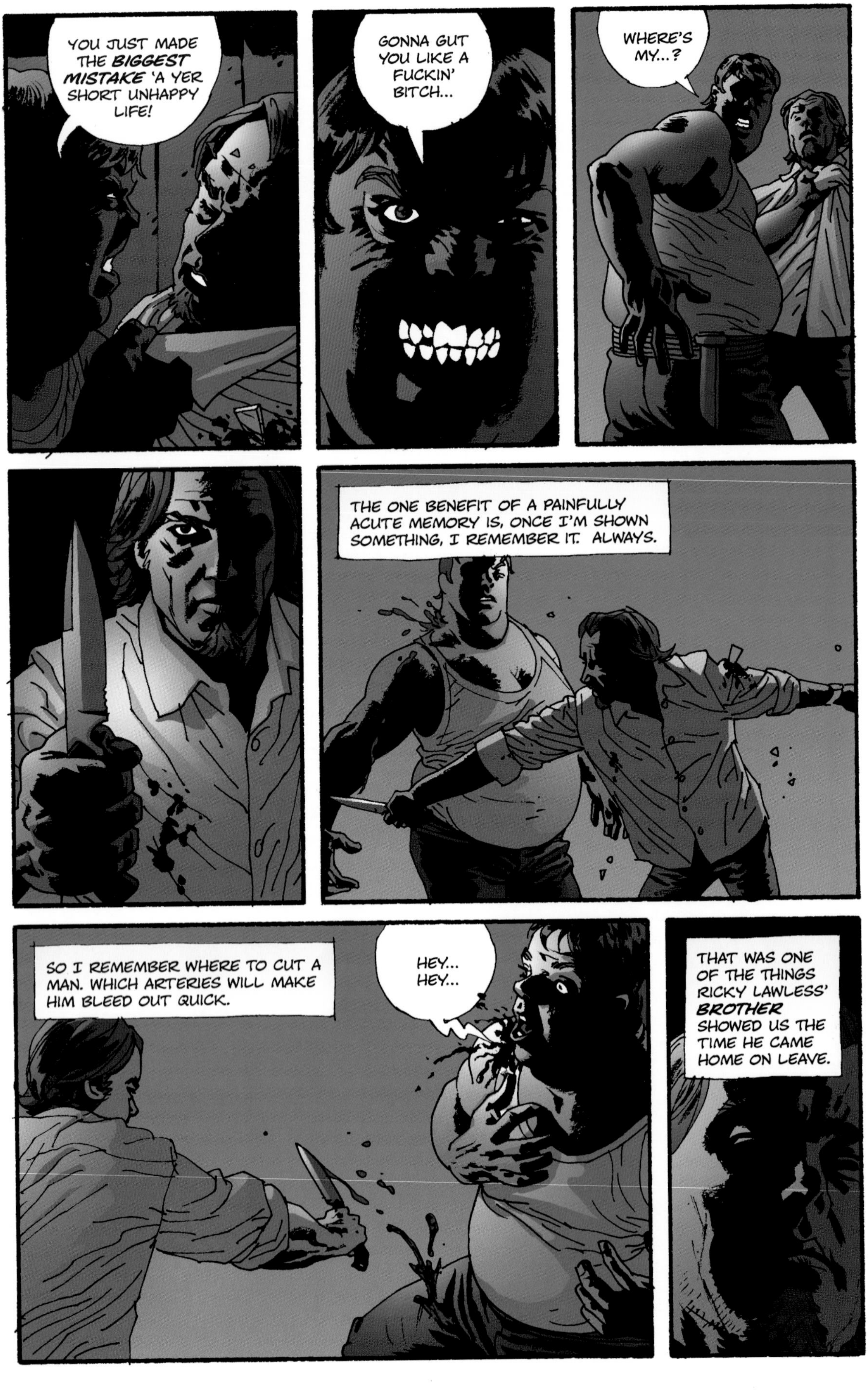

YOU JUST MADE THE BIGGEST MISTAKE 'A YER SHORT UNHAPPY LIFE!
GONNA GUT YOU LIKE A FUCKIN' BITCH...
WHERE'S MY...?
THE ONE BENEFIT OF A PAINFULLY ACUTE MEMORY IS, ONCE I'M SHOWN SOMETHING, I REMEMBER IT. ALWAYS.
SO I REMEMBER WHERE TO CUT A MAN. WHICH ARTERIES WILL MAKE HIM BLEED OUT QUICK.
HEY... HEY...
THAT WAS ONE OF THE THINGS RICKY LAWLESS' BROTHER SHOWED US THE TIME HE CAME HOME ON LEAVE.

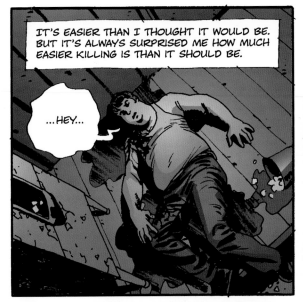

IT'S EASIER THAN I THOUGHT IT WOULD BE. BUT IT'S ALWAYS SURPRISED ME HOW MUCH EASIER KILLING IS THAN IT SHOULD BE.

...HEY...

ANOTHER REASON I HATE IT SO MUCH.

AHH... SHIT.

ANGIE?

IT'S OKAY... DON'T SCREAM... I'M NOT HERE TO HURT YOU.

BUH - BUH - WHAT -

EASY, EASY... WHERE'S THE *OTHER* MAN? THE BLACK MAN?

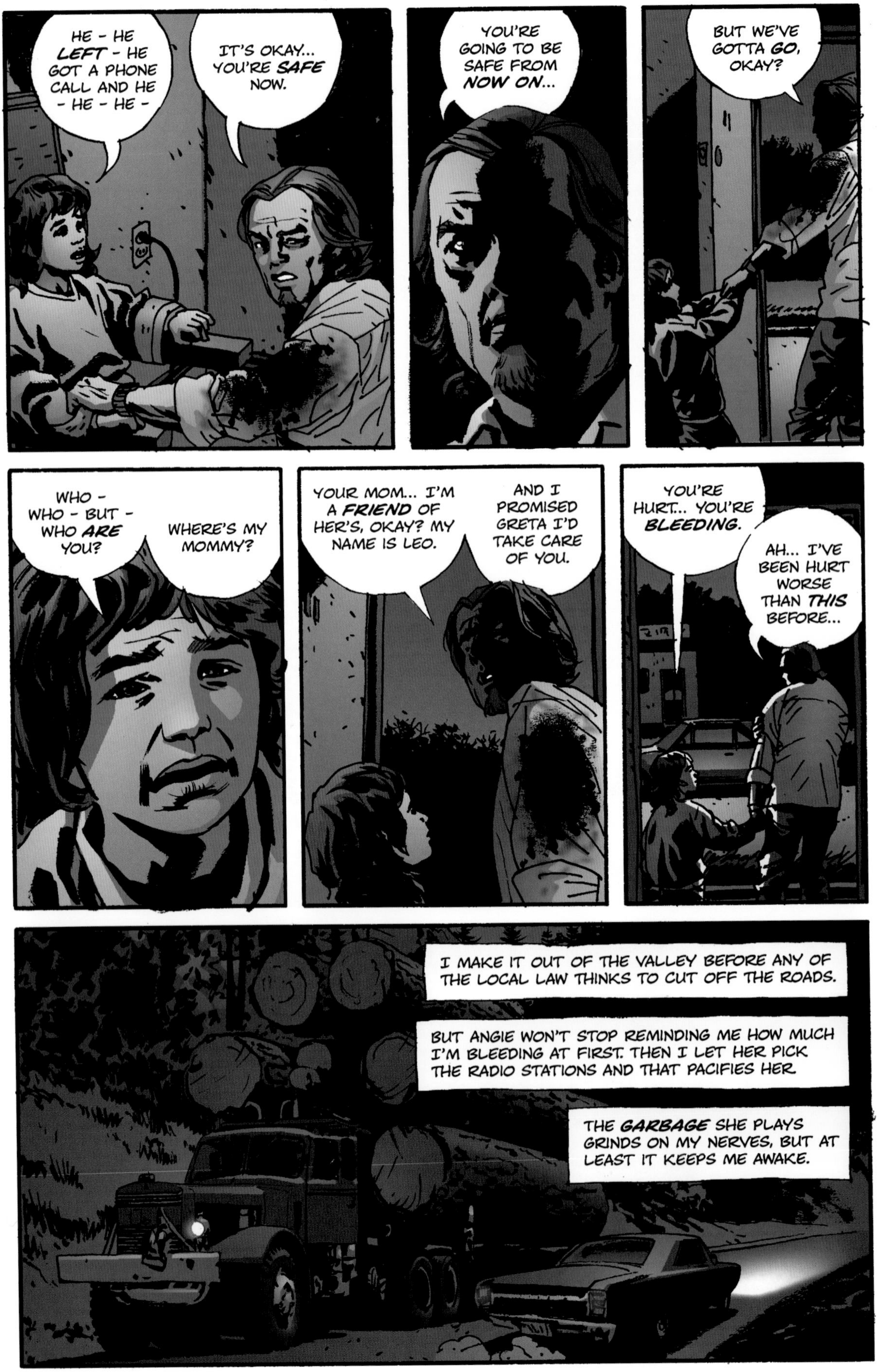
HE - HE LEFT - HE GOT A PHONE CALL AND HE - HE - HE -
IT'S OKAY... YOU'RE SAFE NOW.
YOU'RE GOING TO BE SAFE FROM NOW ON...
BUT WE'VE GOTTA GO, OKAY?
WHO - WHO - BUT - WHO ARE YOU?
WHERE'S MY MOMMY?
YOUR MOM... I'M A FRIEND OF HER'S, OKAY? MY NAME IS LEO.
AND I PROMISED GRETA I'D TAKE CARE OF YOU.
YOU'RE HURT... YOU'RE BLEEDING.
AH... I'VE BEEN HURT WORSE THAN THIS BEFORE...
I MAKE IT OUT OF THE VALLEY BEFORE ANY OF THE LOCAL LAW THINKS TO CUT OFF THE ROADS.
BUT ANGIE WON'T STOP REMINDING ME HOW MUCH I'M BLEEDING AT FIRST. THEN I LET HER PICK THE RADIO STATIONS AND THAT PACIFIES HER.
THE GARBAGE SHE PLAYS GRINDS ON MY NERVES, BUT AT LEAST IT KEEPS ME AWAKE.

I MANAGE TO HANG ON UNTIL I GET TO THE *UNDERTOW*, JUST BARELY...

...AND THANKFULLY I KNOW GNARLY CLEANS UP FOR AN HOUR OR TWO AFTER CLOSING.

HE CALLS IT HIS QUIET TIME.

I ALMOST FEEL BAD BARGING IN ON IT.

KID!

TELL ME YOU STILL HAVE THAT *AWESOME* FIRST AID KIT... PLEASE...

JESUS FUCKING CHRIST, LEO... WHAT'D YOU DO?

...NOT ENOUGH... YET...

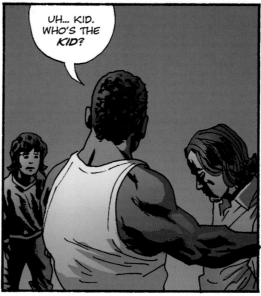

UH... KID. WHO'S THE *KID*?

I'M *ANGIE*. WHO ARE *YOU*?

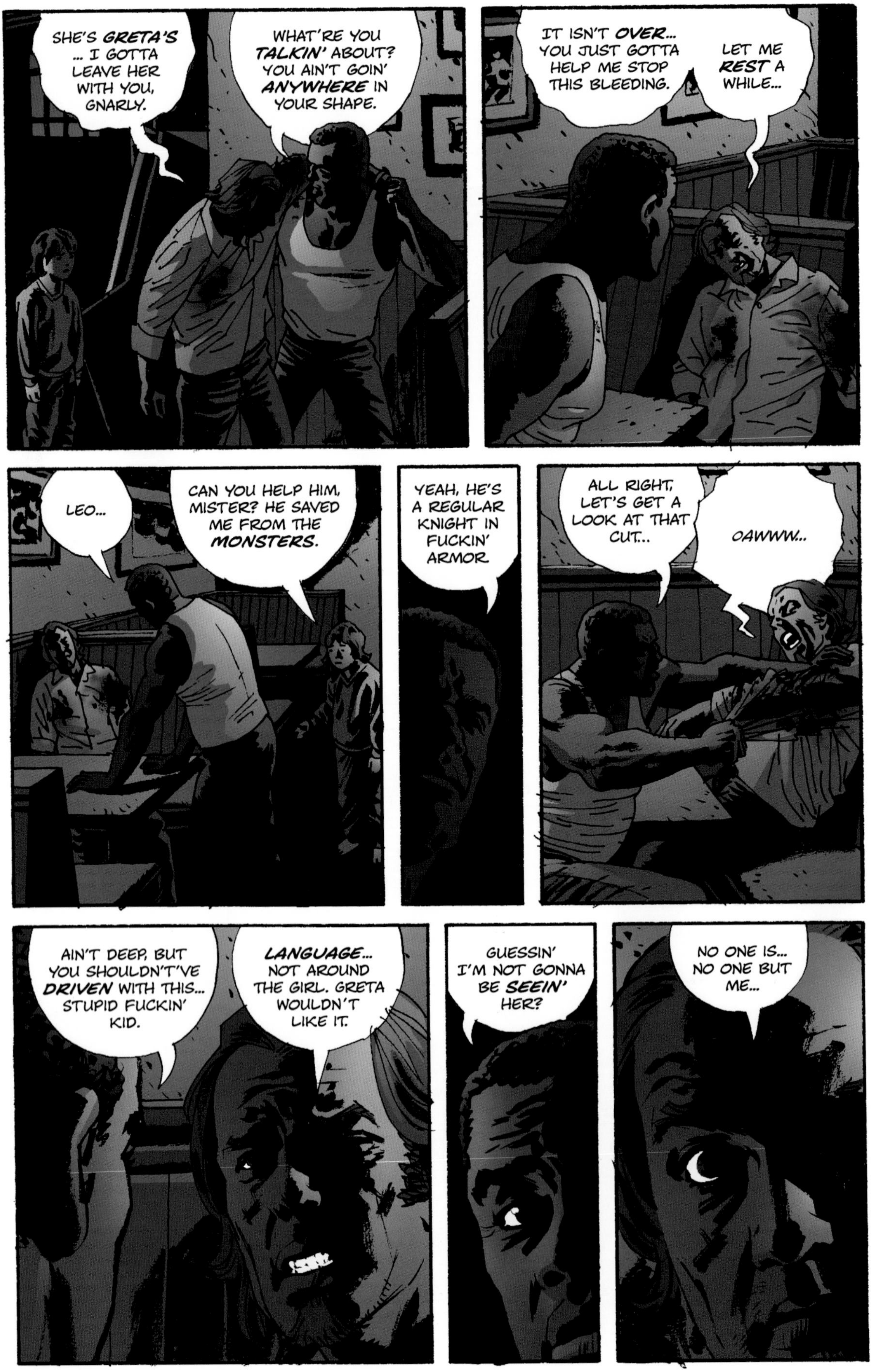

SHE'S GRETA'S ... I GOTTA LEAVE HER WITH YOU, GNARLY.
WHAT'RE YOU TALKIN' ABOUT? YOU AIN'T GOIN' ANYWHERE IN YOUR SHAPE.
IT ISN'T OVER... YOU JUST GOTTA HELP ME STOP THIS BLEEDING.
LET ME REST A WHILE...
LEO...
CAN YOU HELP HIM, MISTER? HE SAVED ME FROM THE MONSTERS.
YEAH, HE'S A REGULAR KNIGHT IN FUCKIN' ARMOR
ALL RIGHT, LET'S GET A LOOK AT THAT CUT...
OAWWW...
AIN'T DEEP, BUT YOU SHOULDN'T'VE DRIVEN WITH THIS... STUPID FUCKIN' KID.
LANGUAGE... NOT AROUND THE GIRL. GRETA WOULDN'T LIKE IT.
GUESSIN' I'M NOT GONNA BE SEEIN' HER?
NO ONE IS... NO ONE BUT ME...

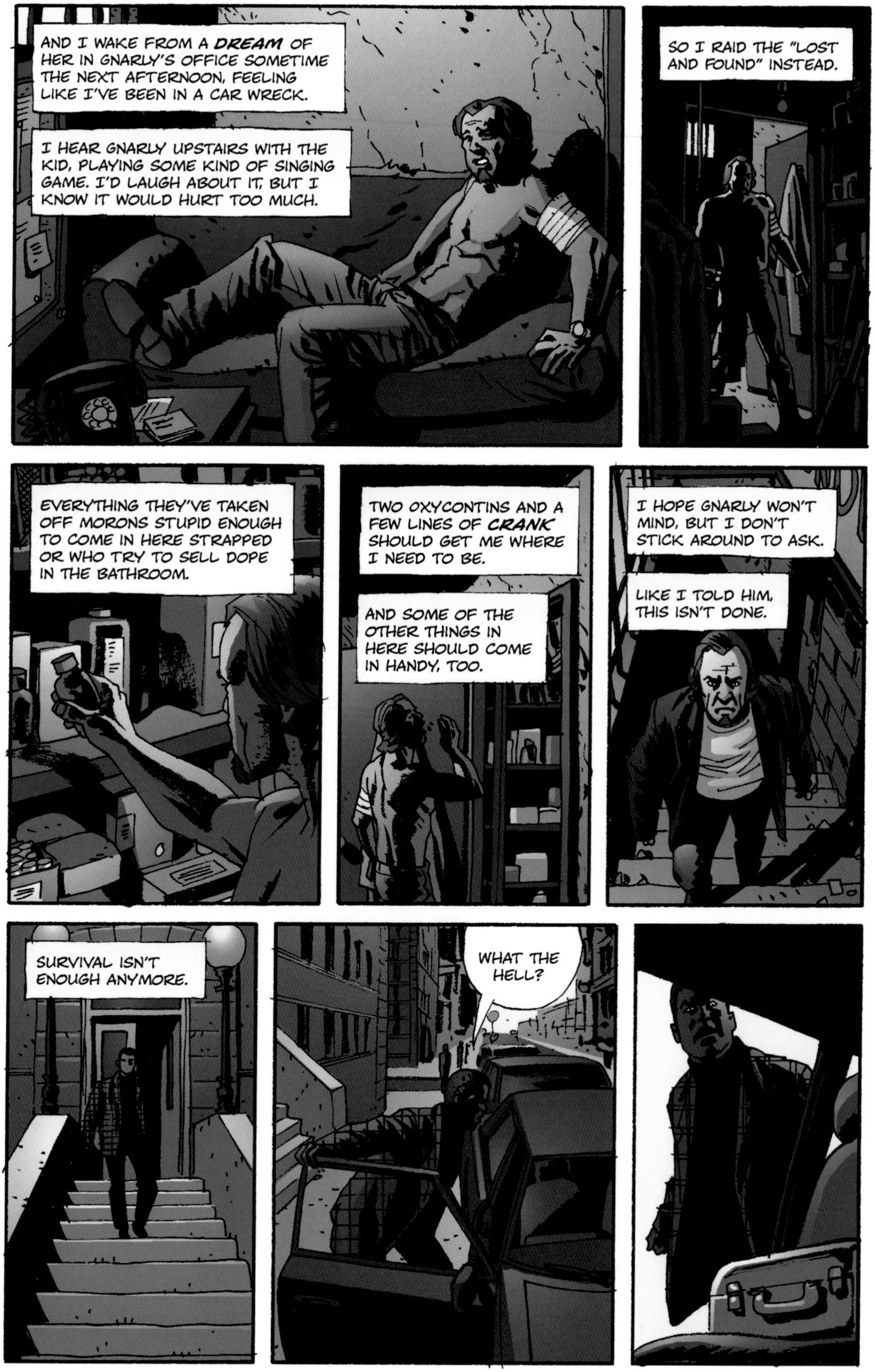
AND I WAKE FROM A *DREAM* OF HER IN GNARLY'S OFFICE SOMETIME THE NEXT AFTERNOON, FEELING LIKE I'VE BEEN IN A CAR WRECK.
I HEAR GNARLY UPSTAIRS WITH THE KID, PLAYING SOME KIND OF SINGING GAME. I'D LAUGH ABOUT IT, BUT I KNOW IT WOULD HURT TOO MUCH.
SO I RAID THE "LOST AND FOUND" INSTEAD.
EVERYTHING THEY'VE TAKEN OFF MORONS STUPID ENOUGH TO COME IN HERE STRAPPED OR WHO TRY TO SELL DOPE IN THE BATHROOM.
TWO OXYCONTINS AND A FEW LINES OF *CRANK* SHOULD GET ME WHERE I NEED TO BE.
AND SOME OF THE OTHER THINGS IN HERE SHOULD COME IN HANDY, TOO.
I HOPE GNARLY WON'T MIND, BUT I DON'T STICK AROUND TO ASK.
LIKE I TOLD HIM, THIS ISN'T DONE.
SURVIVAL ISN'T ENOUGH ANYMORE.
WHAT THE HELL?

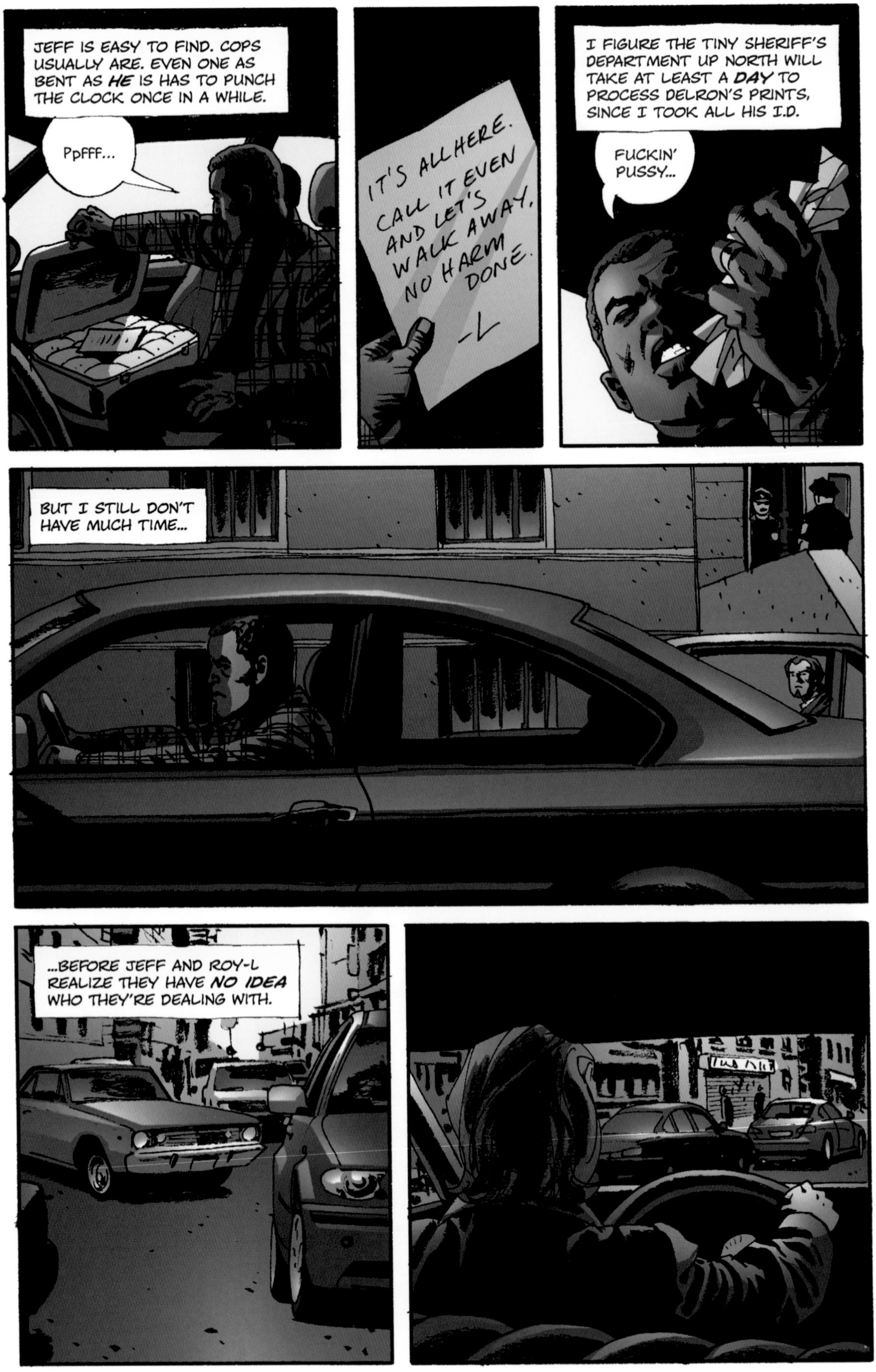
JEFF IS EASY TO FIND. COPS USUALLY ARE. EVEN ONE AS BENT AS HE IS HAS TO PUNCH THE CLOCK ONCE IN A WHILE.
PpFFF...
IT'S ALL HERE. CALL IT EVEN AND LET'S WALK AWAY, NO HARM DONE.
-L
I FIGURE THE TINY SHERIFF'S DEPARTMENT UP NORTH WILL TAKE AT LEAST A DAY TO PROCESS DELRON'S PRINTS, SINCE I TOOK ALL HIS I.D.
FUCKIN' PUSSY...
BUT I STILL DON'T HAVE MUCH TIME...
...BEFORE JEFF AND ROY-L REALIZE THEY HAVE NO IDEA WHO THEY'RE DEALING WITH.

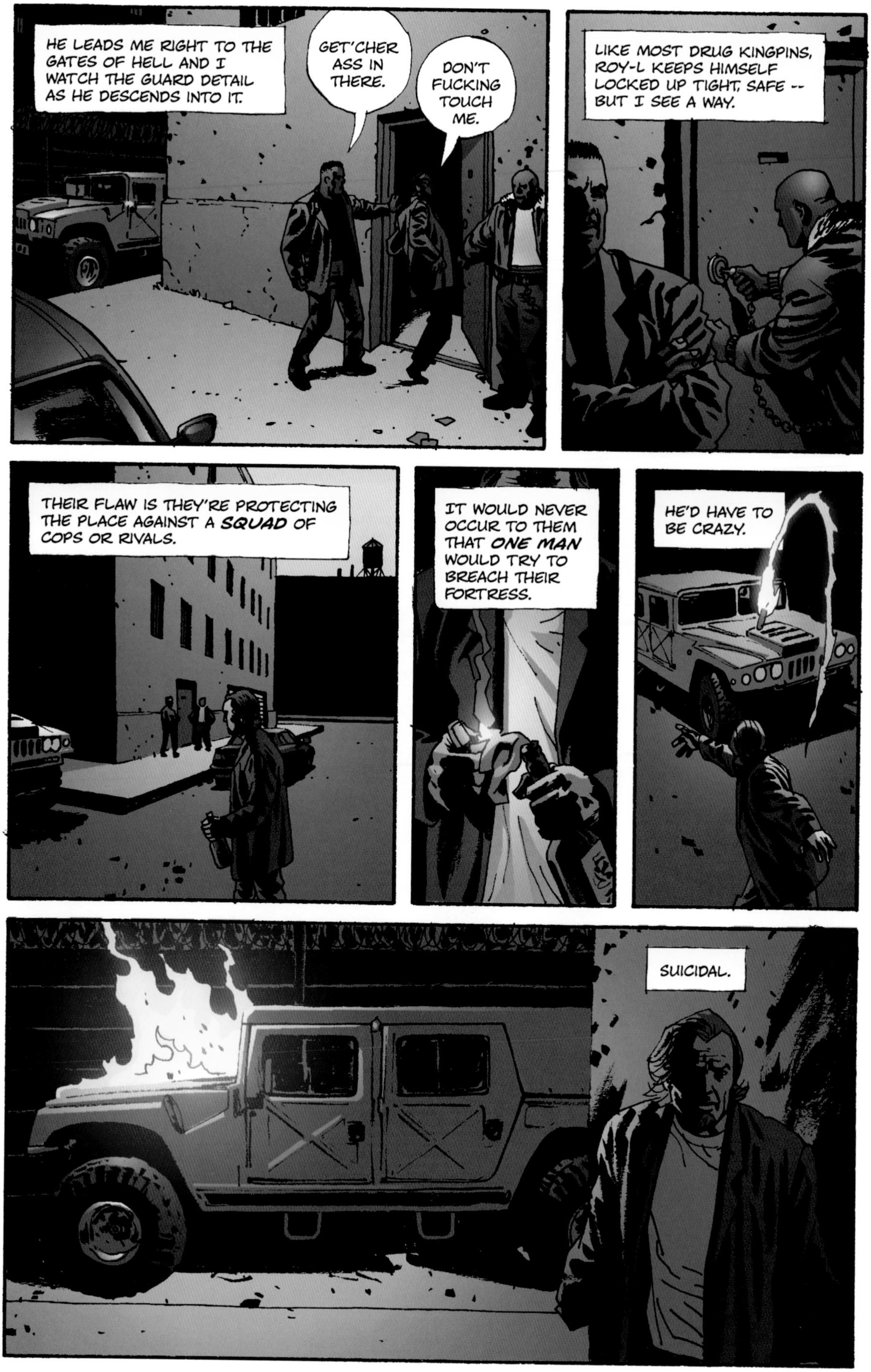
HE LEADS ME RIGHT TO THE GATES OF HELL AND I WATCH THE GUARD DETAIL AS HE DESCENDS INTO IT.
GET'CHER ASS IN THERE.
DON'T FUCKING TOUCH ME.
LIKE MOST DRUG KINGPINS, ROY-L KEEPS HIMSELF LOCKED UP TIGHT, SAFE -- BUT I SEE A WAY.
THEIR FLAW IS THEY'RE PROTECTING THE PLACE AGAINST A SQUAD OF COPS OR RIVALS.
IT WOULD NEVER OCCUR TO THEM THAT ONE MAN WOULD TRY TO BREACH THEIR FORTRESS.
HE'D HAVE TO BE CRAZY.
SUICIDAL.

HEY – THAT CAR'S ON *FIRE.* THAT *YOUR* CAR?

AW... SHIT!

ROY-L'S VEE!

OUTTA THE FUCKIN' WAY, WHITE BOY!

SHIT!

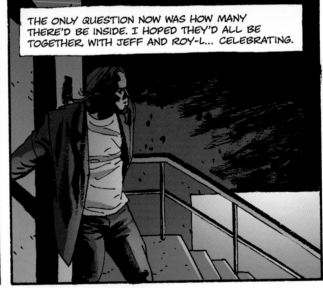

THE ONLY QUESTION NOW WAS HOW MANY THERE'D BE INSIDE. I HOPED THEY'D ALL BE TOGETHER, WITH JEFF AND ROY-L... CELEBRATING.

MOTHERFUCK ME IN THE ASS... YOU CAME THROUGH.

JUST A MATTER OF *TIME,* ROY-L. ALWAYS WAS JUST A MATTER OF TIME.

WHERE OL' DELRON AT?

PROBABLY HANDIN' OFF THAT LITTLE GIRL TO THE *IVANS* OR BEING A COMPLETE PERVERT...

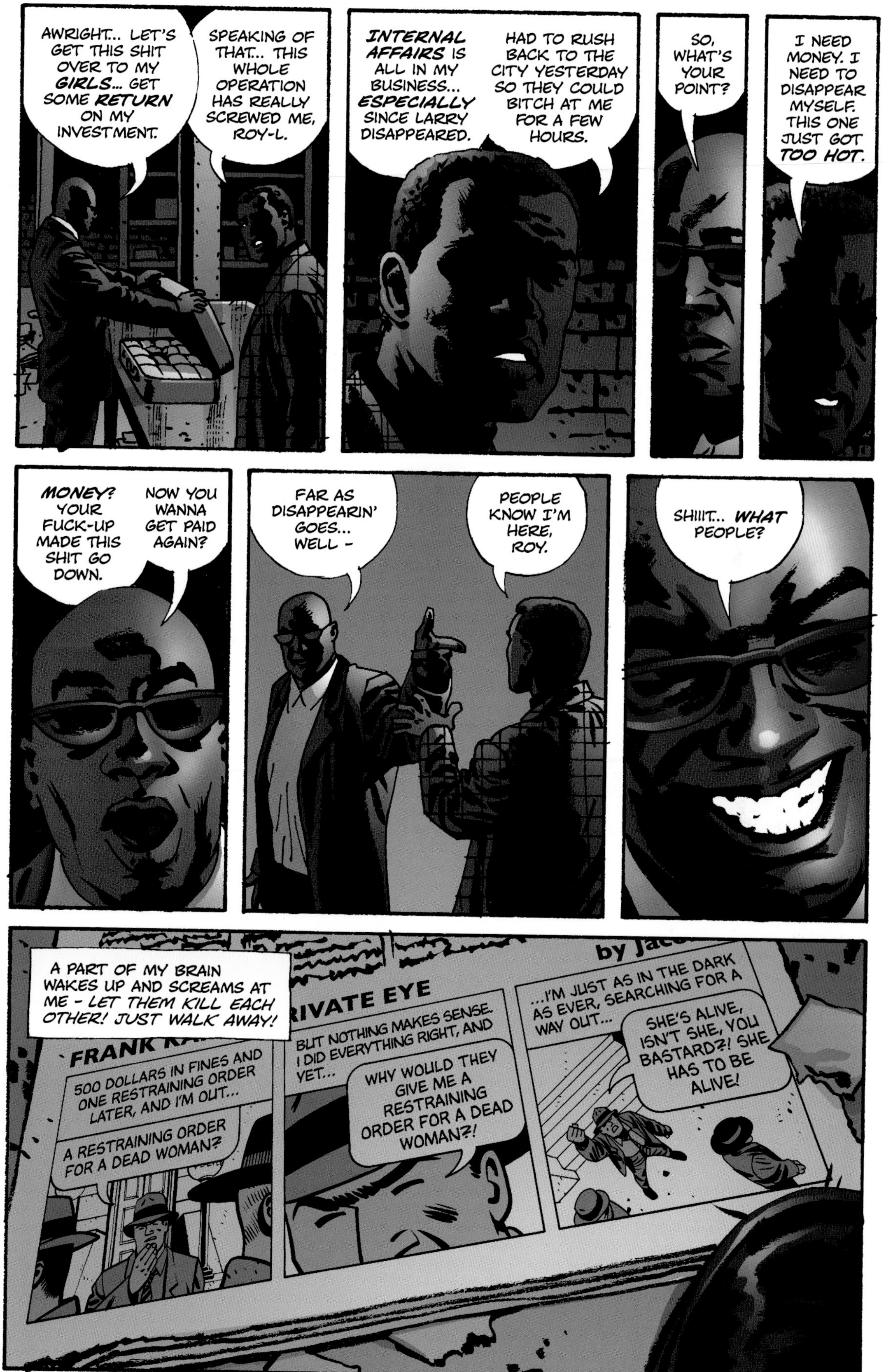

AWRIGHT... LET'S GET THIS SHIT OVER TO MY GIRLS... GET SOME RETURN ON MY INVESTMENT.
SPEAKING OF THAT... THIS WHOLE OPERATION HAS REALLY SCREWED ME, ROY-L.
INTERNAL AFFAIRS IS ALL IN MY BUSINESS... ESPECIALLY SINCE LARRY DISAPPEARED.
HAD TO RUSH BACK TO THE CITY YESTERDAY SO THEY COULD BITCH AT ME FOR A FEW HOURS.
SO, WHAT'S YOUR POINT?
I NEED MONEY. I NEED TO DISAPPEAR MYSELF. THIS ONE JUST GOT TOO HOT.
MONEY? YOUR FUCK-UP MADE THIS SHIT GO DOWN.
NOW YOU WANNA GET PAID AGAIN?
FAR AS DISAPPEARIN' GOES... WELL -
PEOPLE KNOW I'M HERE, ROY.
SHIIIT... WHAT PEOPLE?
A PART OF MY BRAIN WAKES UP AND SCREAMS AT ME - LET THEM KILL EACH OTHER! JUST WALK AWAY!
500 DOLLARS IN FINES AND ONE RESTRAINING ORDER LATER, AND I'M OUT...
A RESTRAINING ORDER FOR A DEAD WOMAN?
BUT NOTHING MAKES SENSE. I DID EVERYTHING RIGHT, AND YET...
WHY WOULD THEY GIVE ME A RESTRAINING ORDER FOR A DEAD WOMAN?!
...I'M JUST AS IN THE DARK AS EVER, SEARCHING FOR A WAY OUT...
SHE'S ALIVE, ISN'T SHE, YOU BASTARD?! SHE HAS TO BE ALIVE!

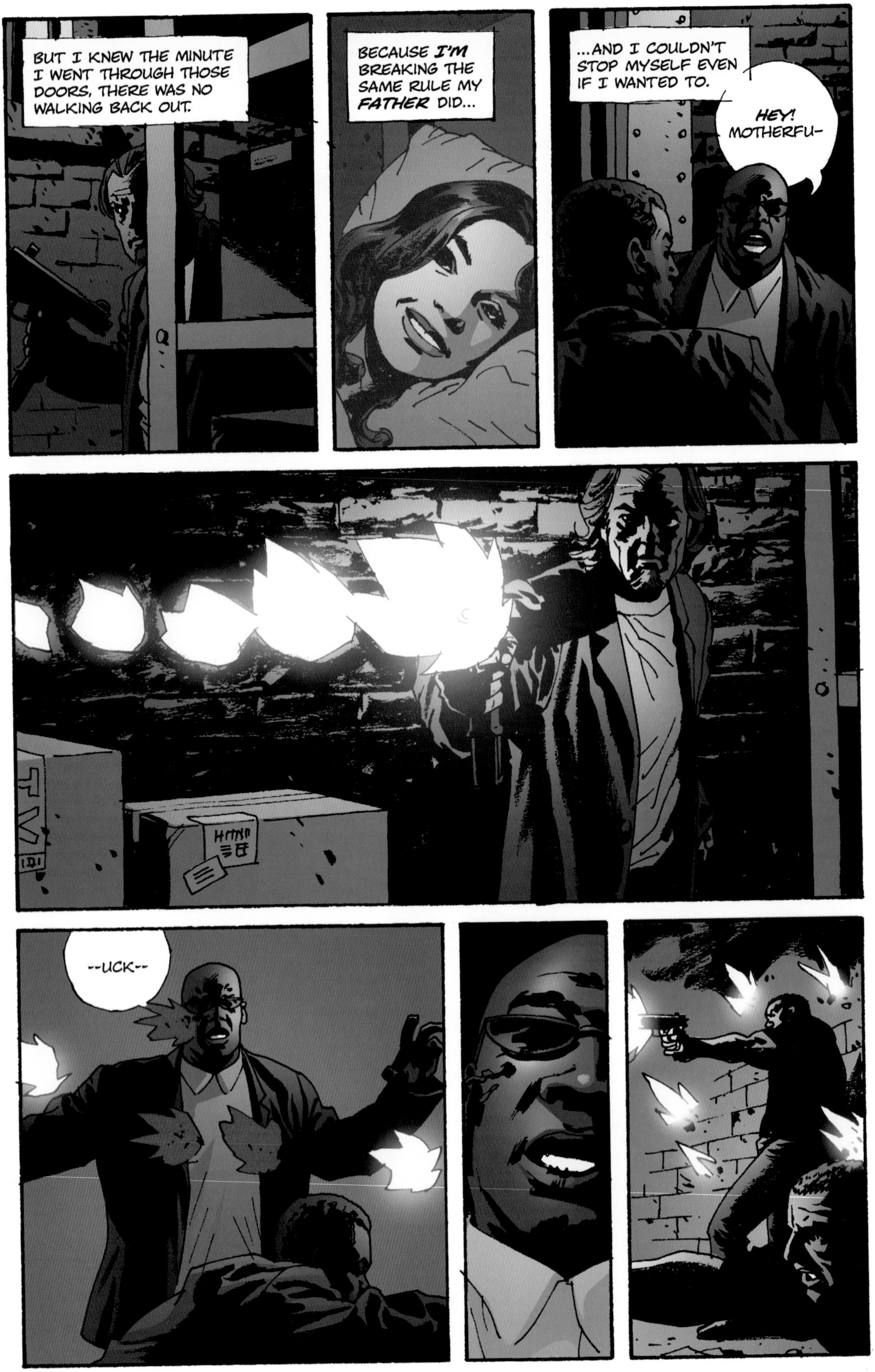
BUT I KNEW THE MINUTE I WENT THROUGH THOSE DOORS, THERE WAS NO WALKING BACK OUT.
BECAUSE *I'M* BREAKING THE SAME RULE MY *FATHER* DID...
...AND I COULDN'T STOP MYSELF EVEN IF I WANTED TO.
HEY! MOTHERFU-
TV
--UCK--

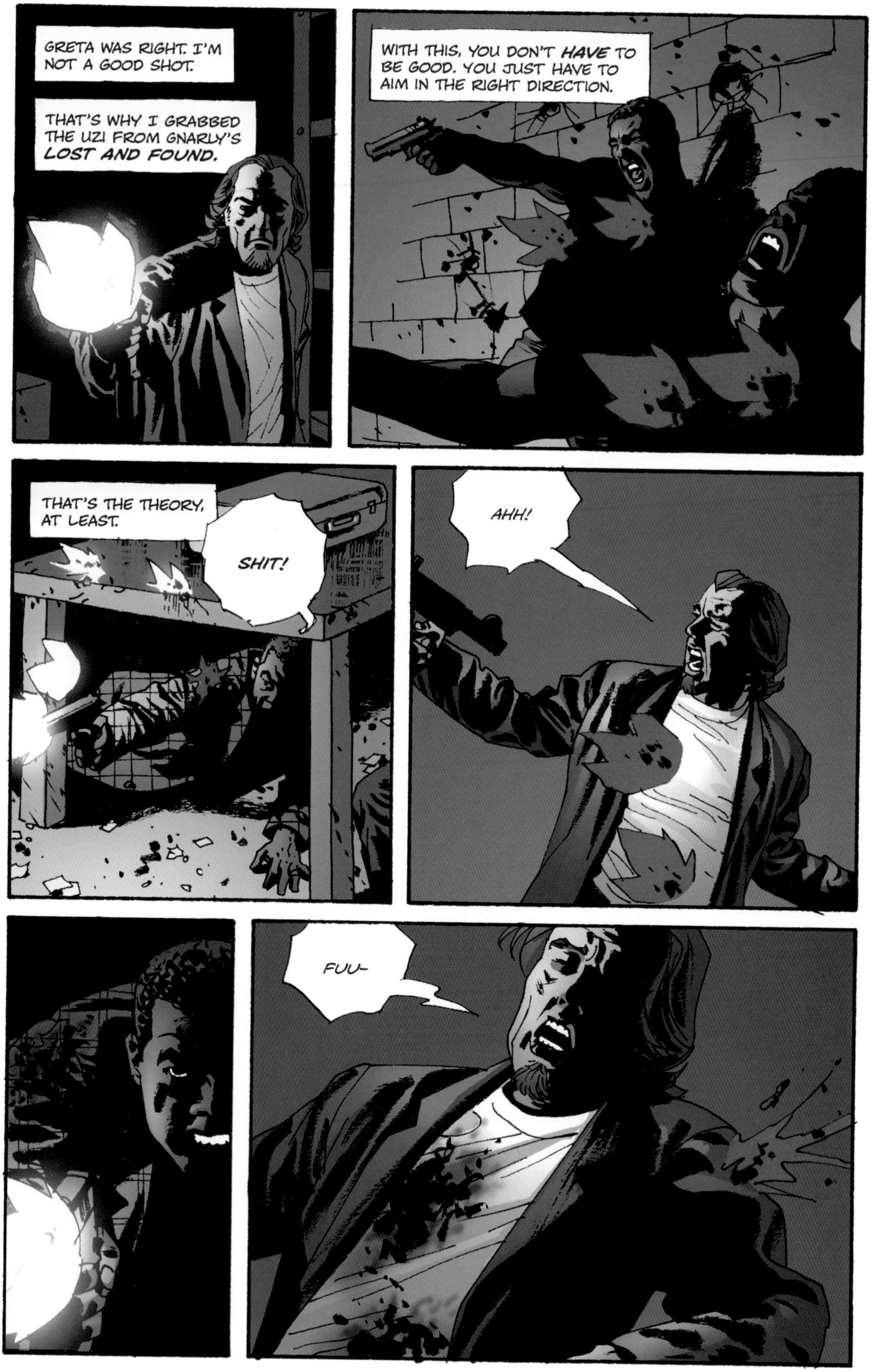
GRETA WAS RIGHT. I'M NOT A GOOD SHOT.
THAT'S WHY I GRABBED THE UZI FROM GNARLY'S LOST AND FOUND.
WITH THIS, YOU DON'T HAVE TO BE GOOD. YOU JUST HAVE TO AIM IN THE RIGHT DIRECTION.
THAT'S THE THEORY, AT LEAST.
SHIT!
AHH!
FUU-

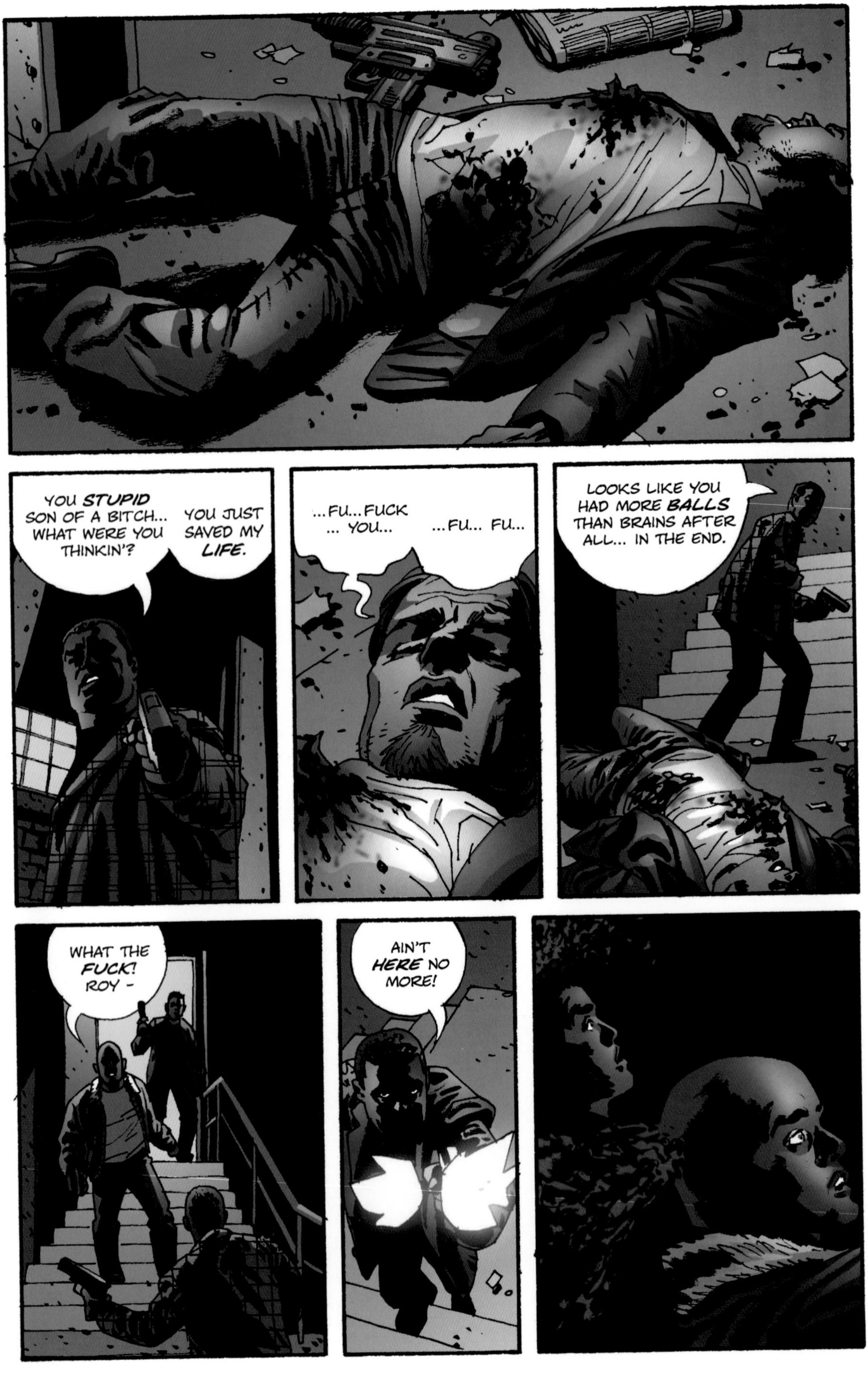
YOU STUPID SON OF A BITCH... WHAT WERE YOU THINKIN'?
YOU JUST SAVED MY LIFE.
...FU...FUCK ... YOU...
...FU... FU...
LOOKS LIKE YOU HAD MORE BALLS THAN BRAINS AFTER ALL... IN THE END.
WHAT THE FUCK! ROY -
AIN'T HERE NO MORE!

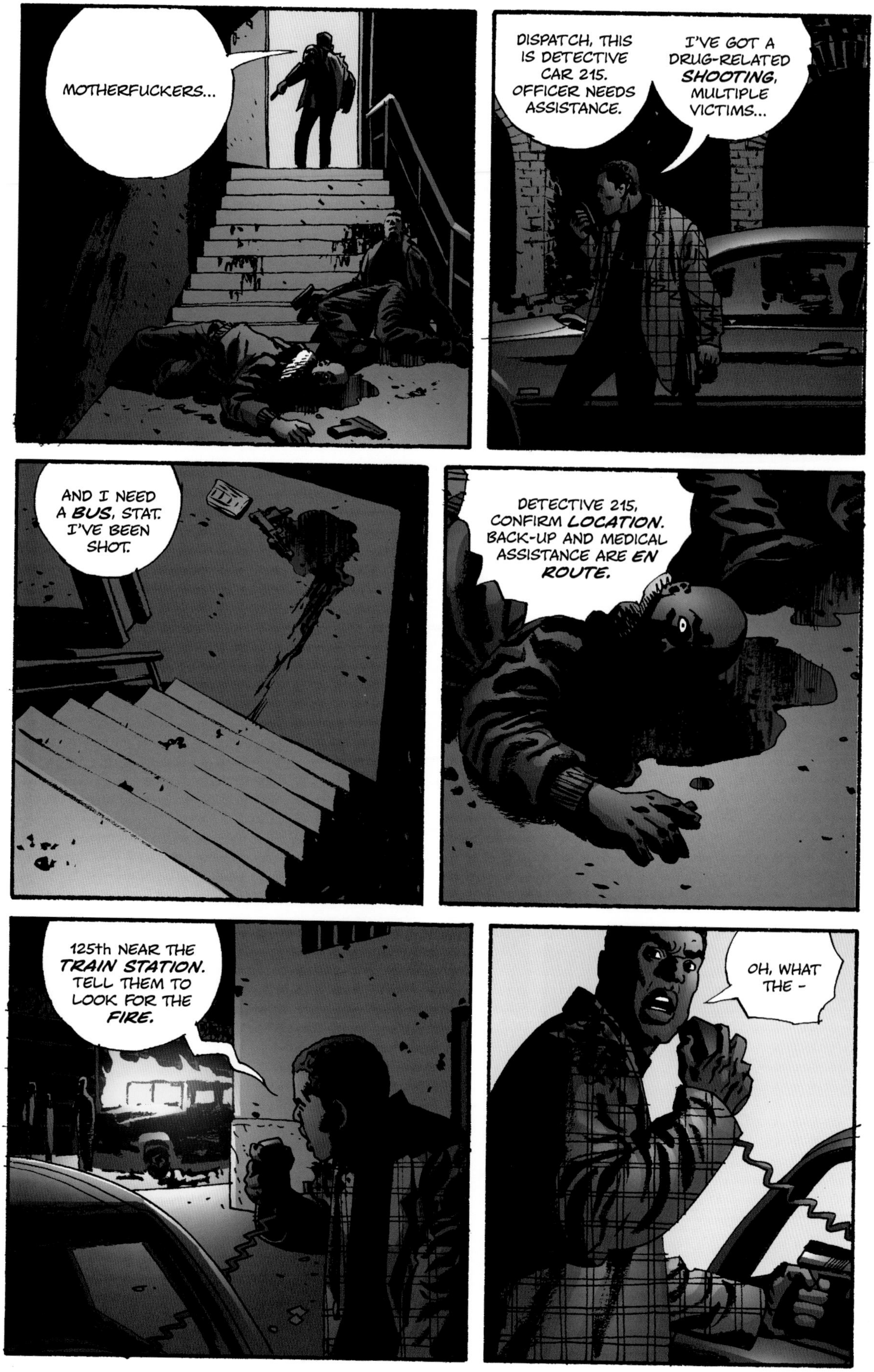
MOTHERFUCKERS...
DISPATCH, THIS IS DETECTIVE CAR 215. OFFICER NEEDS ASSISTANCE.
I'VE GOT A DRUG-RELATED *SHOOTING*, MULTIPLE VICTIMS...
AND I NEED A *BUS*, STAT. I'VE BEEN SHOT.
DETECTIVE 215, CONFIRM *LOCATION*. BACK-UP AND MEDICAL ASSISTANCE ARE *EN ROUTE*.
125th NEAR THE *TRAIN STATION*. TELL THEM TO LOOK FOR THE *FIRE*.
OH, WHAT THE -

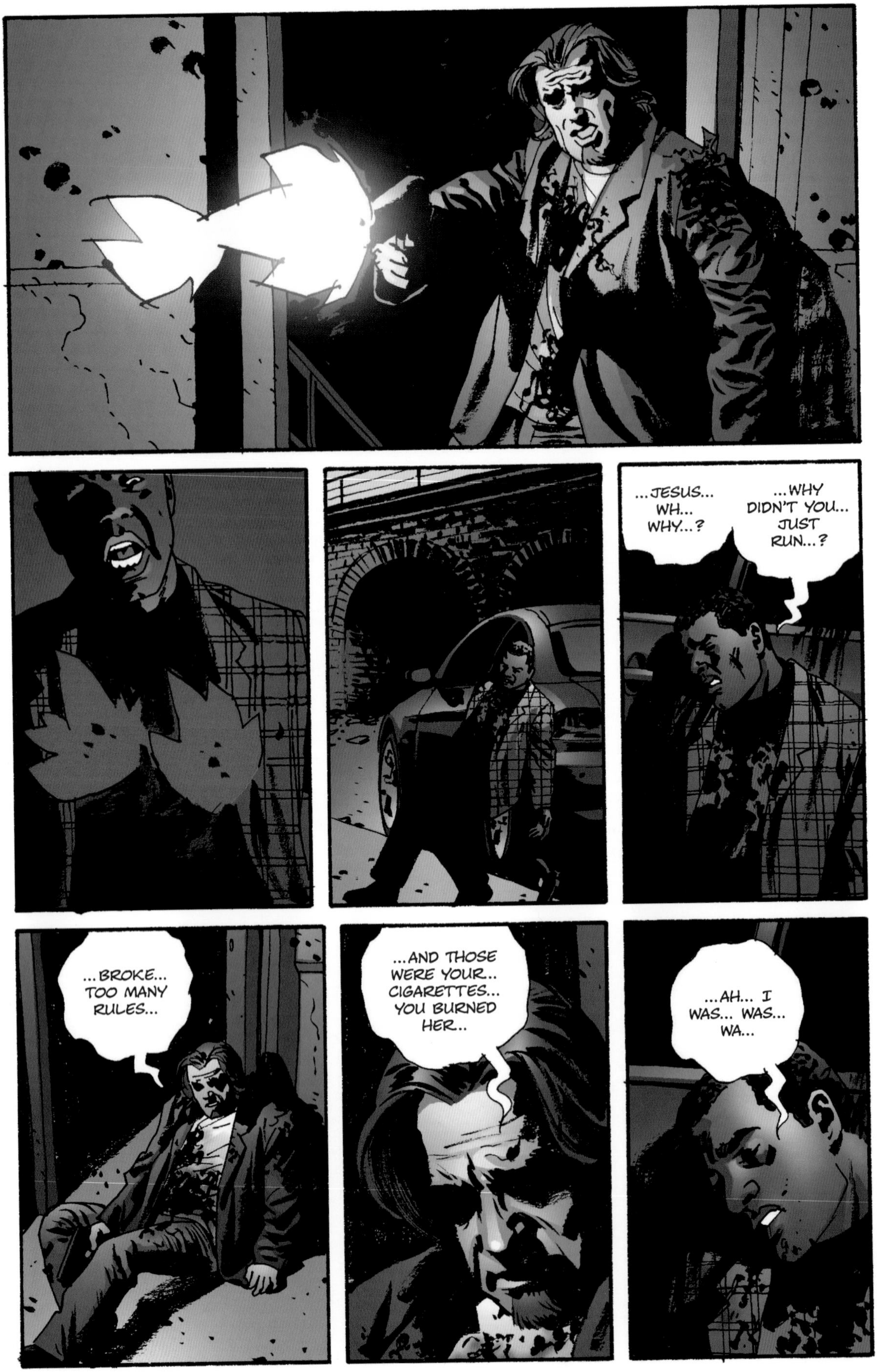
...JESUS... WH... WHY...?
...WHY DIDN'T YOU... JUST RUN...?
...BROKE... TOO MANY RULES...
...AND THOSE WERE YOUR.. CIGARETTES... YOU BURNED HER..
...AH... I WAS... WAS... WA...

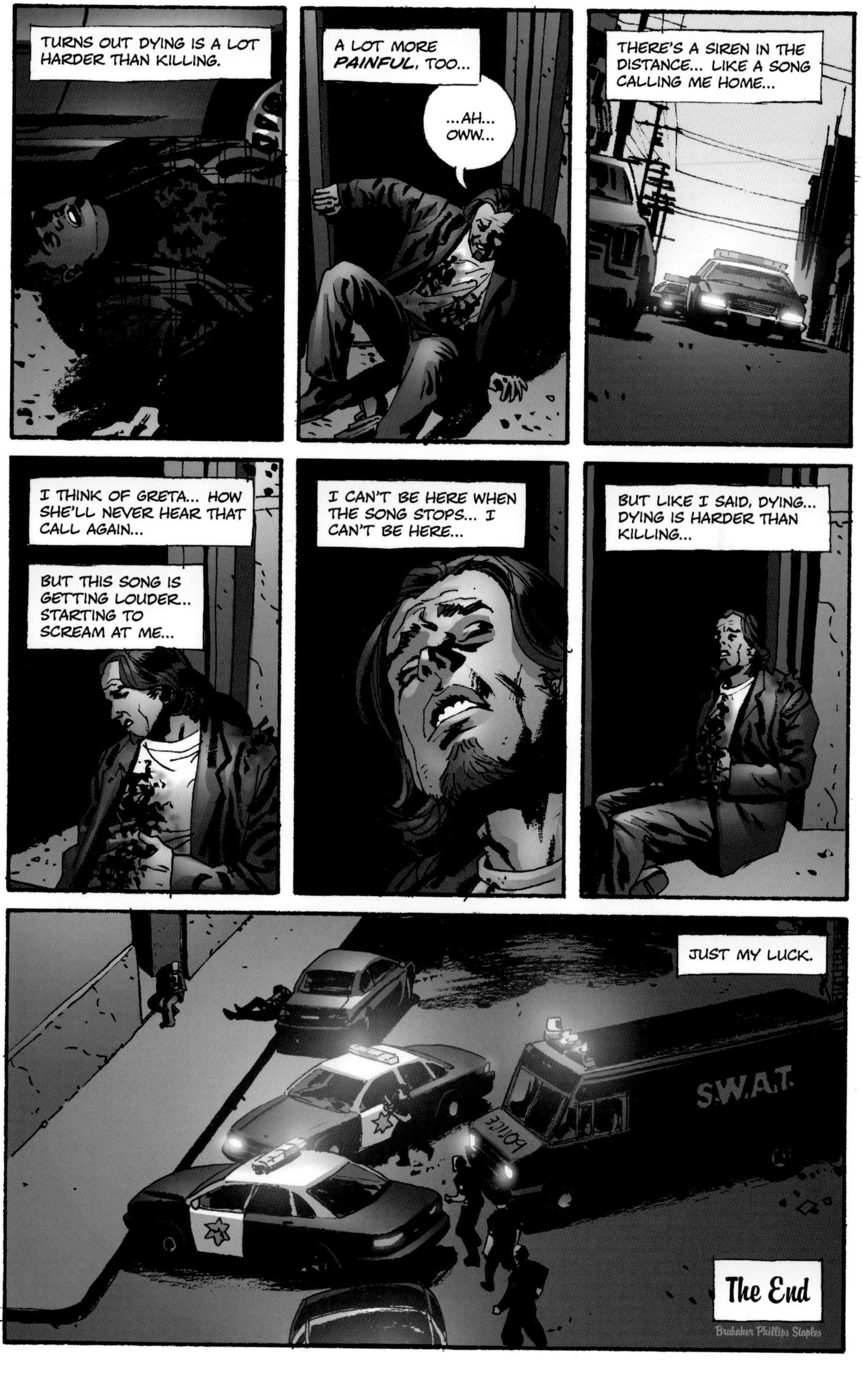
TURNS OUT DYING IS A LOT HARDER THAN KILLING.
A LOT MORE PAINFUL, TOO...
...AH... OWW...
THERE'S A SIREN IN THE DISTANCE... LIKE A SONG CALLING ME HOME...
I THINK OF GRETA... HOW SHE'LL NEVER HEAR THAT CALL AGAIN...
BUT THIS SONG IS GETTING LOUDER.. STARTING TO SCREAM AT ME...
I CAN'T BE HERE WHEN THE SONG STOPS... I CAN'T BE HERE...
BUT LIKE I SAID, DYING... DYING IS HARDER THAN KILLING...
JUST MY LUCK.
S.W.A.T.
POLICE
The End
Brubaker Phillips Staples

Lawless

CRIMINAL: Lawless

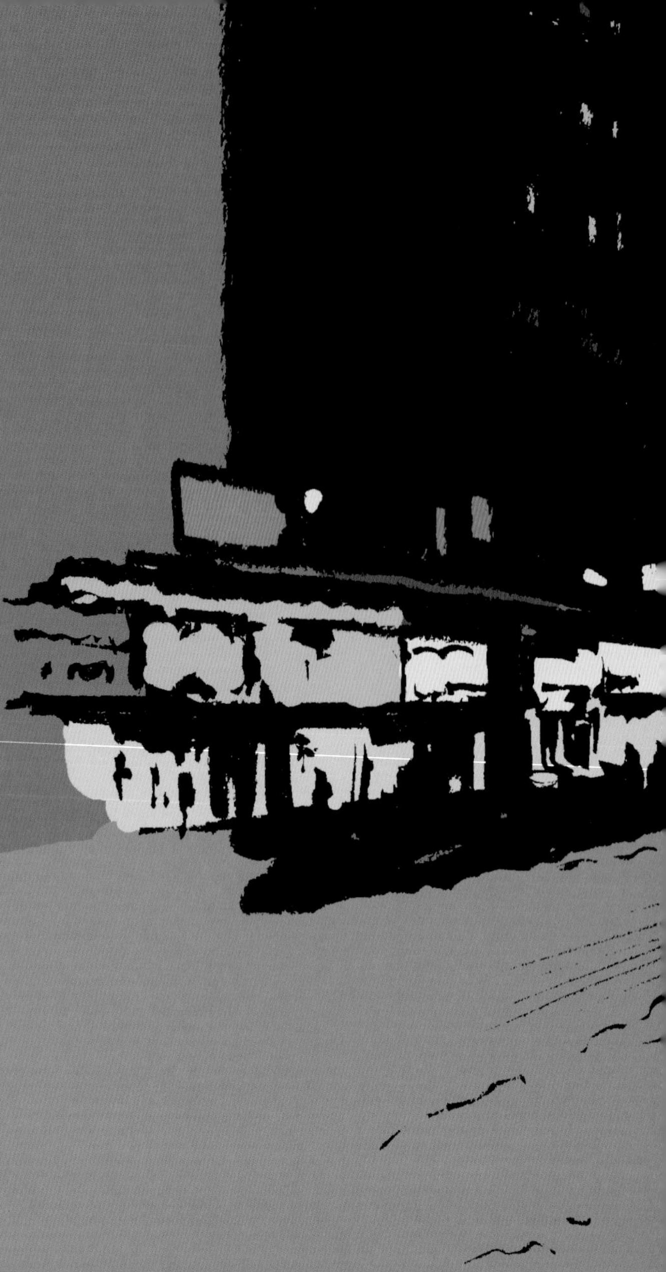

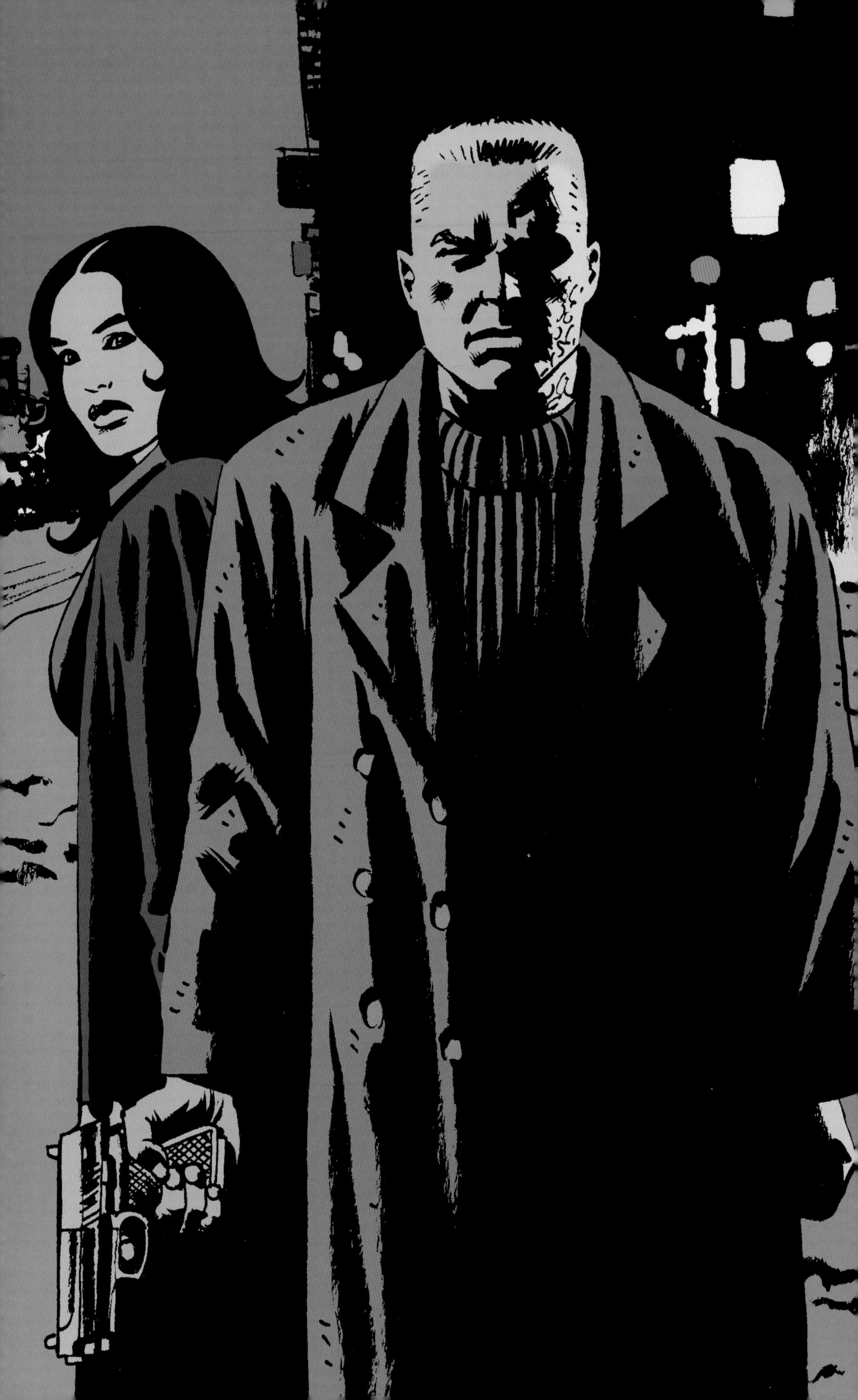

Part One

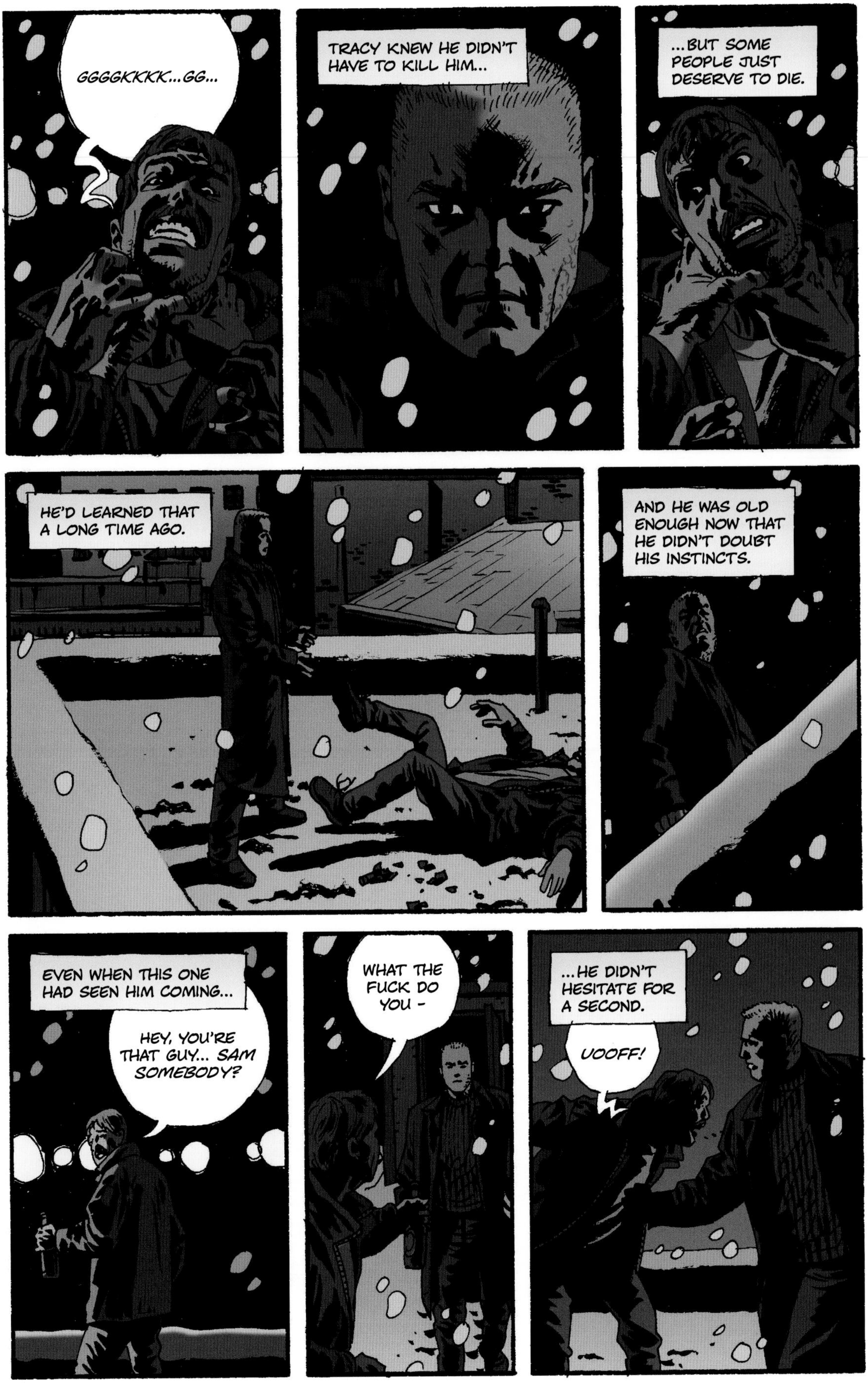
GGGGKKKK...GG...
TRACY KNEW HE DIDN'T HAVE TO KILL HIM...
...BUT SOME PEOPLE JUST DESERVE TO DIE.
HE'D LEARNED THAT A LONG TIME AGO.
AND HE WAS OLD ENOUGH NOW THAT HE DIDN'T DOUBT HIS INSTINCTS.
EVEN WHEN THIS ONE HAD SEEN HIM COMING...
HEY, YOU'RE THAT GUY... SAM SOMEBODY?
WHAT THE FUCK DO YOU -
...HE DIDN'T HESITATE FOR A SECOND.
UOOFF!

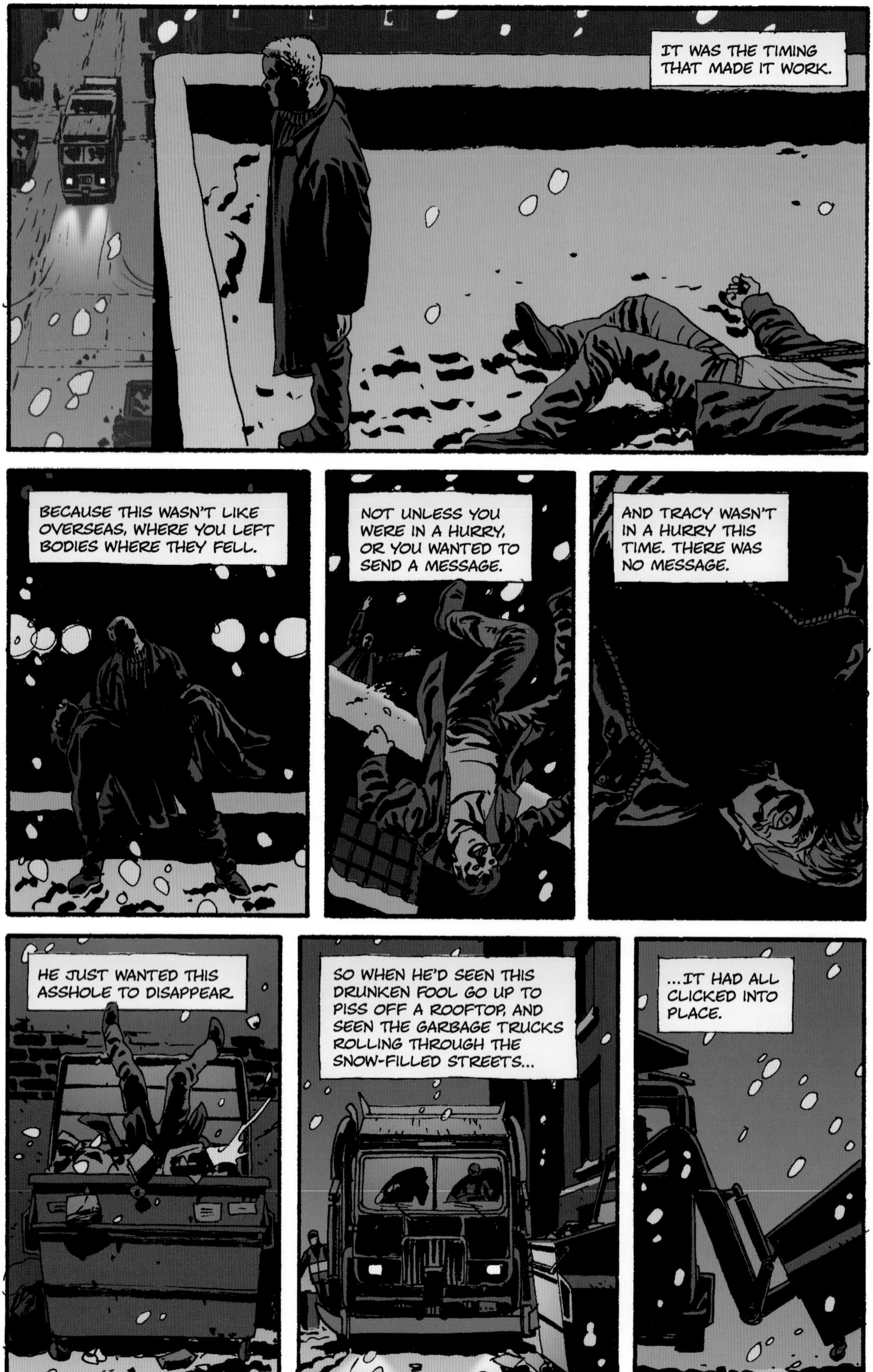
IT WAS THE TIMING THAT MADE IT WORK.
BECAUSE THIS WASN'T LIKE OVERSEAS, WHERE YOU LEFT BODIES WHERE THEY FELL.
NOT UNLESS YOU WERE IN A HURRY, OR YOU WANTED TO SEND A MESSAGE.
AND TRACY WASN'T IN A HURRY THIS TIME. THERE WAS NO MESSAGE.
HE JUST WANTED THIS ASSHOLE TO DISAPPEAR.
SO WHEN HE'D SEEN THIS DRUNKEN FOOL GO UP TO PISS OFF A ROOFTOP, AND SEEN THE GARBAGE TRUCKS ROLLING THROUGH THE SNOW-FILLED STREETS...
...IT HAD ALL CLICKED INTO PLACE.

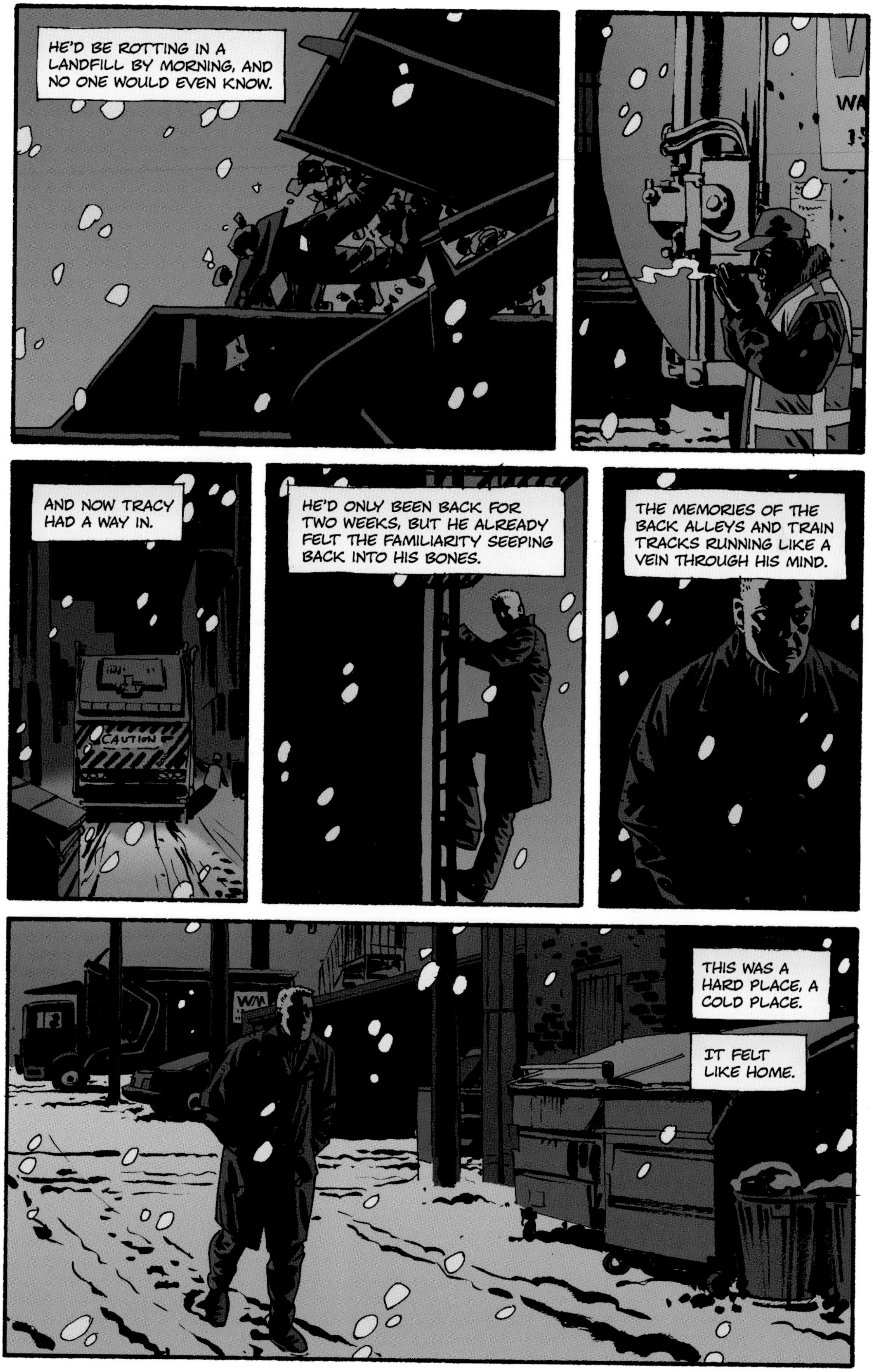
HE'D BE ROTTING IN A LANDFILL BY MORNING, AND NO ONE WOULD EVEN KNOW.
AND NOW TRACY HAD A WAY IN.
CAUTION
HE'D ONLY BEEN BACK FOR TWO WEEKS, BUT HE ALREADY FELT THE FAMILIARITY SEEPING BACK INTO HIS BONES.
THE MEMORIES OF THE BACK ALLEYS AND TRAIN TRACKS RUNNING LIKE A VEIN THROUGH HIS MIND.
WM
THIS WAS A HARD PLACE, A COLD PLACE.
IT FELT LIKE HOME.

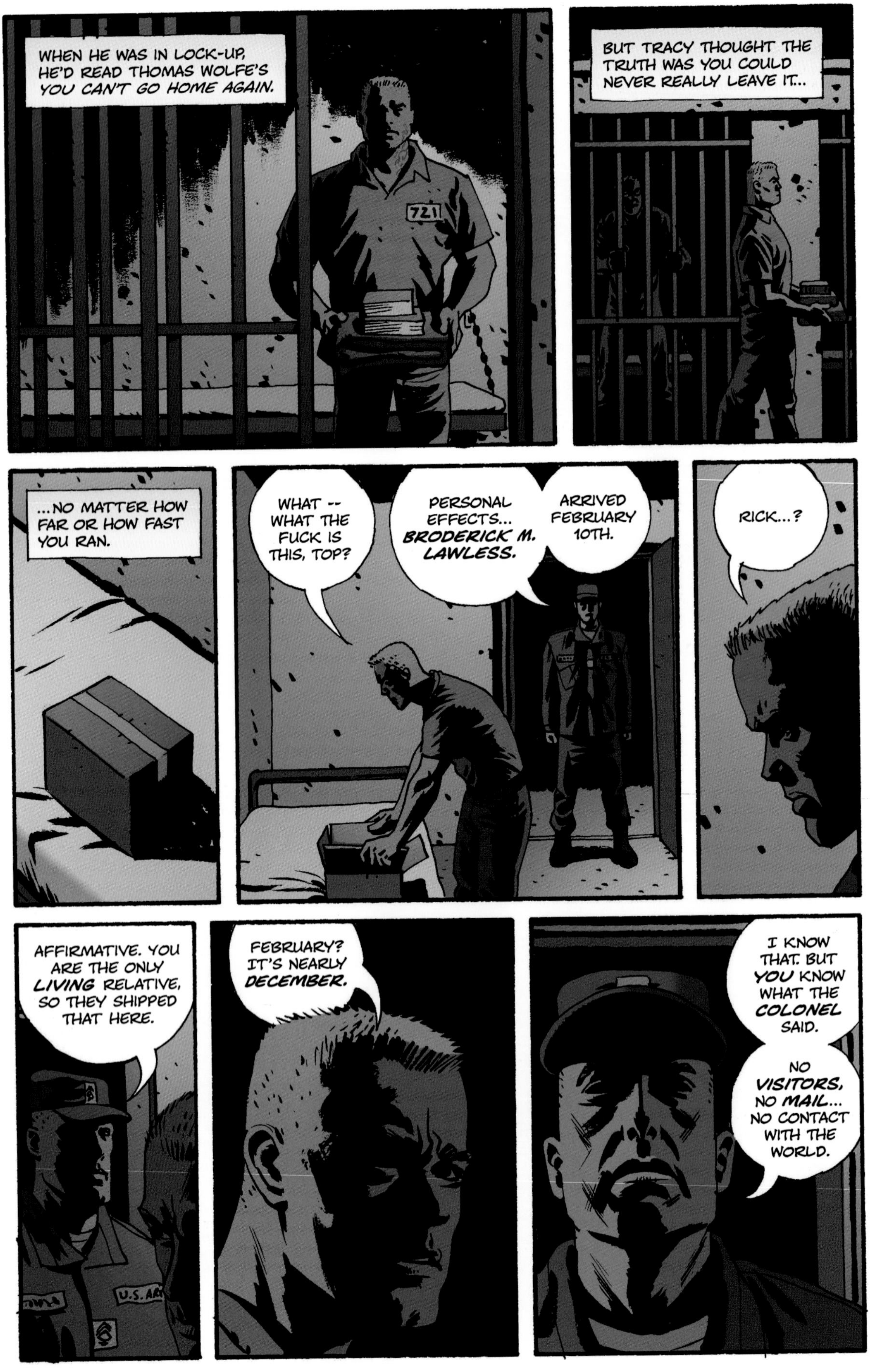
WHEN HE WAS IN LOCK-UP, HE'D READ THOMAS WOLFE'S *YOU CAN'T GO HOME AGAIN.*
BUT TRACY THOUGHT THE TRUTH WAS YOU COULD NEVER REALLY LEAVE IT...
...NO MATTER HOW FAR OR HOW FAST YOU RAN.
WHAT -- WHAT THE FUCK IS THIS, TOP?
PERSONAL EFFECTS... ***BRODERICK M. LAWLESS.***
ARRIVED FEBRUARY 10TH.
RICK...?
AFFIRMATIVE. YOU ARE THE ONLY ***LIVING*** RELATIVE, SO THEY SHIPPED THAT HERE.
U.S. AR
FEBRUARY? IT'S NEARLY ***DECEMBER.***
I KNOW THAT. BUT ***YOU*** KNOW WHAT THE ***COLONEL*** SAID.
NO ***VISITORS,*** NO ***MAIL***... NO CONTACT WITH THE WORLD.

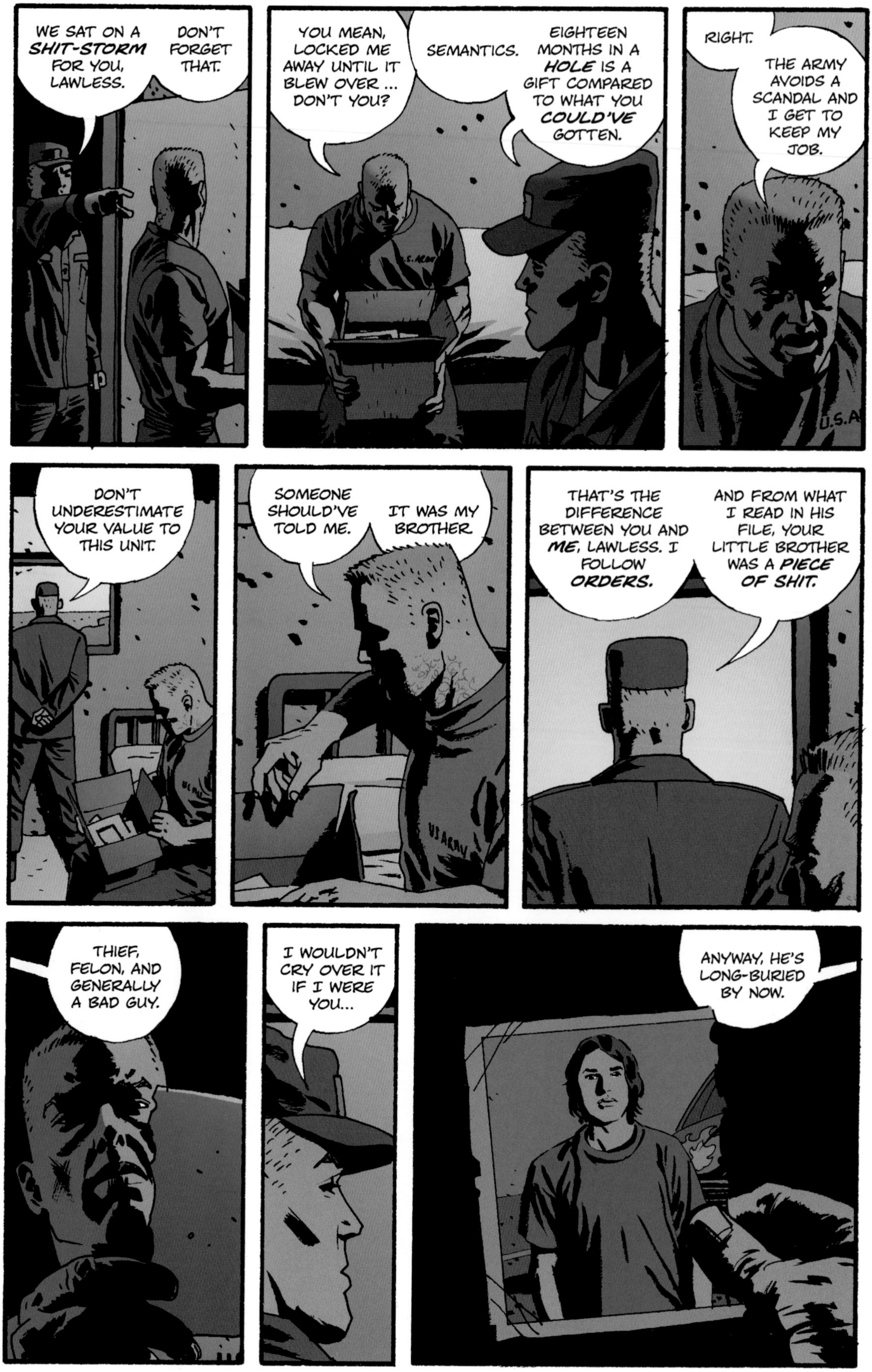
WE SAT ON A SHIT-STORM FOR YOU, LAWLESS.
DON'T FORGET THAT.
YOU MEAN, LOCKED ME AWAY UNTIL IT BLEW OVER ... DON'T YOU?
SEMANTICS.
EIGHTEEN MONTHS IN A HOLE IS A GIFT COMPARED TO WHAT YOU COULD'VE GOTTEN.
RIGHT.
THE ARMY AVOIDS A SCANDAL AND I GET TO KEEP MY JOB.
DON'T UNDERESTIMATE YOUR VALUE TO THIS UNIT.
SOMEONE SHOULD'VE TOLD ME.
IT WAS MY BROTHER
THAT'S THE DIFFERENCE BETWEEN YOU AND ME, LAWLESS. I FOLLOW ORDERS.
AND FROM WHAT I READ IN HIS FILE, YOUR LITTLE BROTHER WAS A PIECE OF SHIT.
THIEF, FELON, AND GENERALLY A BAD GUY.
I WOULDN'T CRY OVER IT IF I WERE YOU...
ANYWAY, HE'S LONG-BURIED BY NOW.

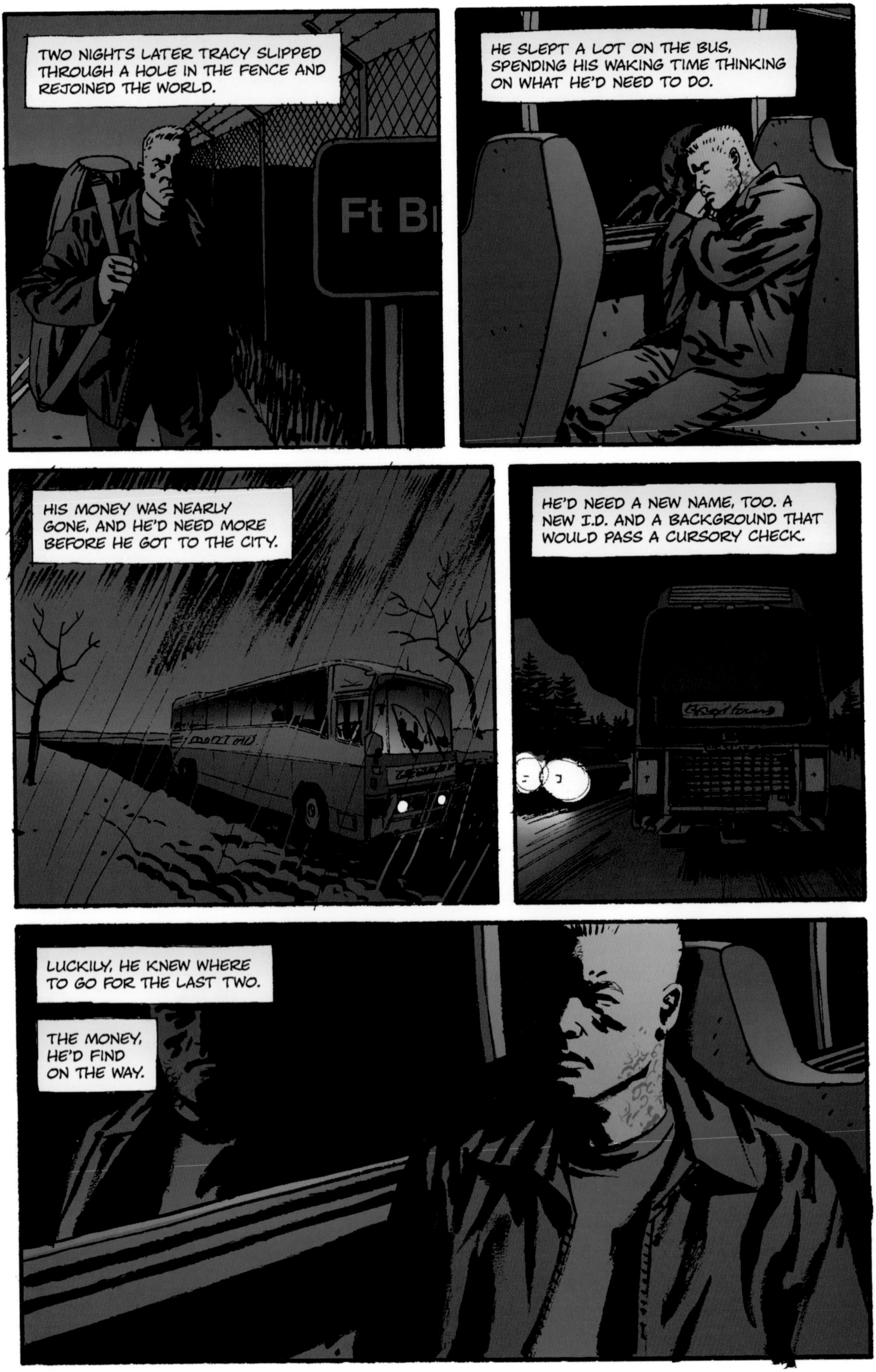
TWO NIGHTS LATER TRACY SLIPPED THROUGH A HOLE IN THE FENCE AND REJOINED THE WORLD.
HE SLEPT A LOT ON THE BUS, SPENDING HIS WAKING TIME THINKING ON WHAT HE'D NEED TO DO.
HIS MONEY WAS NEARLY GONE, AND HE'D NEED MORE BEFORE HE GOT TO THE CITY.
HE'D NEED A NEW NAME, TOO. A NEW I.D. AND A BACKGROUND THAT WOULD PASS A CURSORY CHECK.
LUCKILY, HE KNEW WHERE TO GO FOR THE LAST TWO.
THE MONEY, HE'D FIND ON THE WAY.

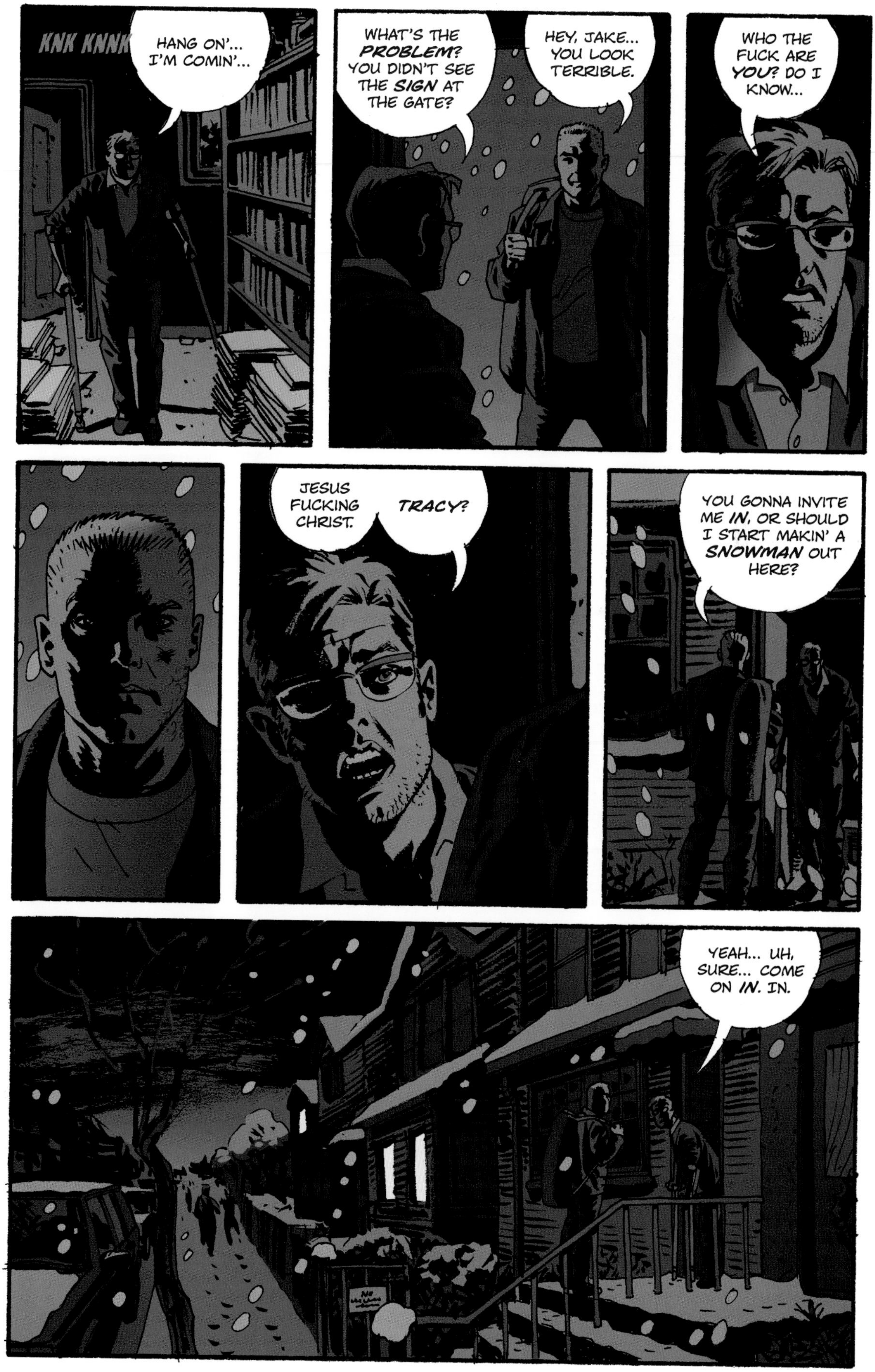
KNK KNNK
HANG ON'... I'M COMIN'...
WHAT'S THE PROBLEM? YOU DIDN'T SEE THE SIGN AT THE GATE?
HEY, JAKE... YOU LOOK TERRIBLE.
WHO THE FUCK ARE YOU? DO I KNOW...
JESUS FUCKING CHRIST.
TRACY?
YOU GONNA INVITE ME IN, OR SHOULD I START MAKIN' A SNOWMAN OUT HERE?
YEAH... UH, SURE... COME ON IN. IN.

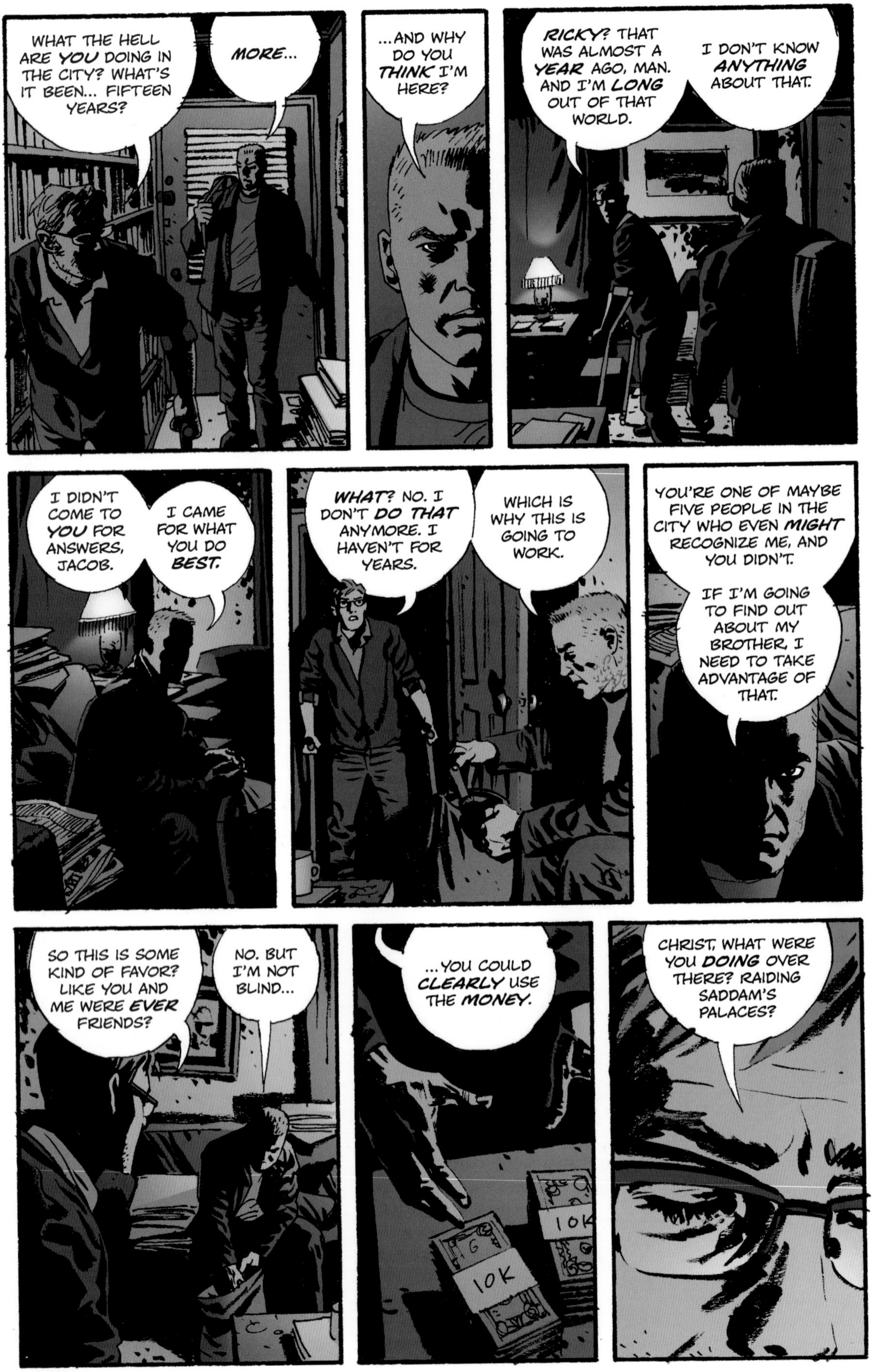
WHAT THE HELL ARE YOU DOING IN THE CITY? WHAT'S IT BEEN... FIFTEEN YEARS?
MORE...
...AND WHY DO YOU THINK I'M HERE?
RICKY? THAT WAS ALMOST A YEAR AGO, MAN. AND I'M LONG OUT OF THAT WORLD.
I DON'T KNOW ANYTHING ABOUT THAT.
I DIDN'T COME TO YOU FOR ANSWERS, JACOB.
I CAME FOR WHAT YOU DO BEST.
WHAT? NO. I DON'T DO THAT ANYMORE. I HAVEN'T FOR YEARS.
WHICH IS WHY THIS IS GOING TO WORK.
YOU'RE ONE OF MAYBE FIVE PEOPLE IN THE CITY WHO EVEN MIGHT RECOGNIZE ME, AND YOU DIDN'T.
IF I'M GOING TO FIND OUT ABOUT MY BROTHER, I NEED TO TAKE ADVANTAGE OF THAT.
SO THIS IS SOME KIND OF FAVOR? LIKE YOU AND ME WERE EVER FRIENDS?
NO. BUT I'M NOT BLIND...
...YOU COULD CLEARLY USE THE MONEY.
10K
10K
CHRIST, WHAT WERE YOU DOING OVER THERE? RAIDING SADDAM'S PALACES?

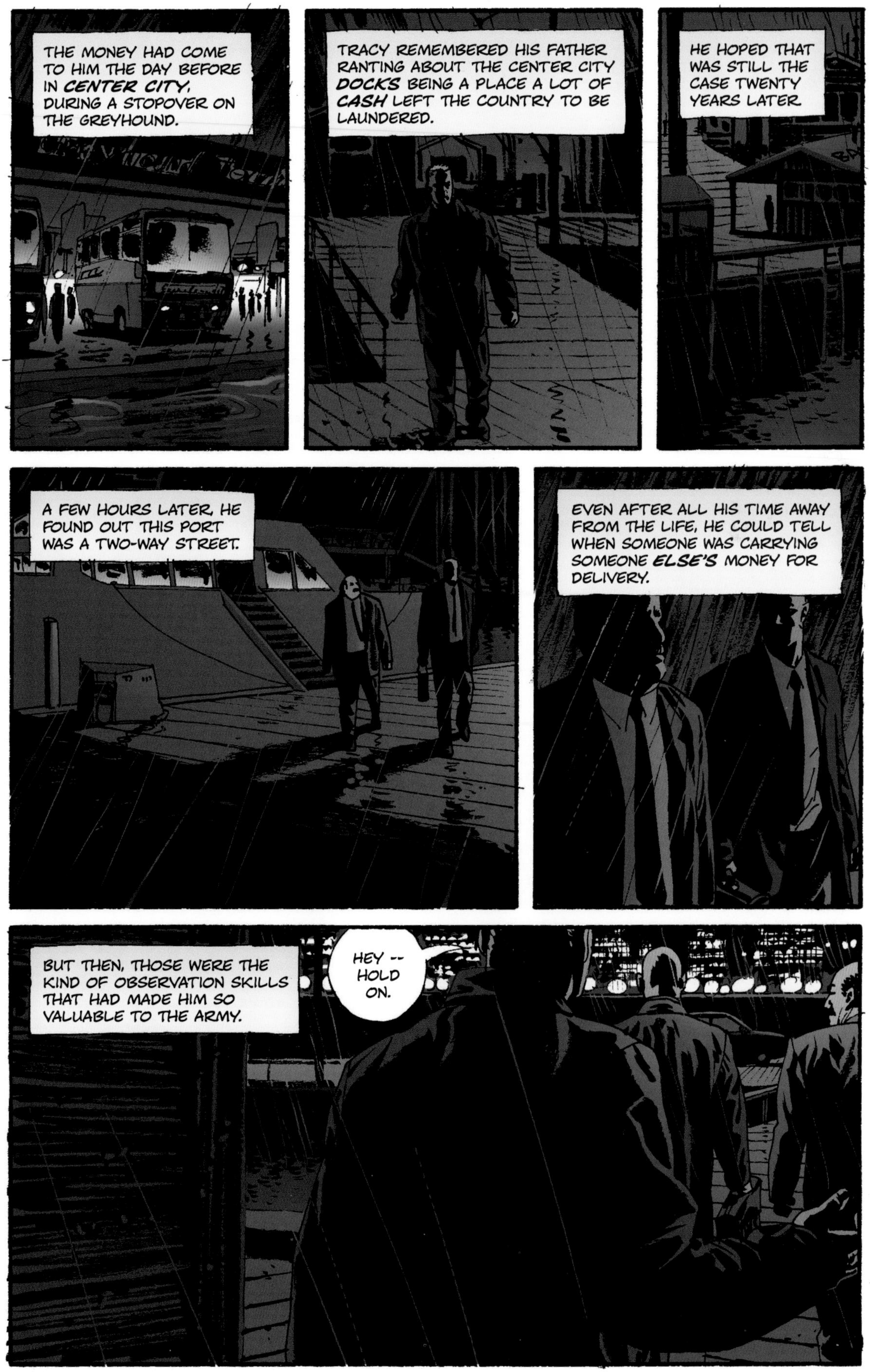
THE MONEY HAD COME TO HIM THE DAY BEFORE IN CENTER CITY, DURING A STOPOVER ON THE GREYHOUND.
TRACY REMEMBERED HIS FATHER RANTING ABOUT THE CENTER CITY DOCKS BEING A PLACE A LOT OF CASH LEFT THE COUNTRY TO BE LAUNDERED.
HE HOPED THAT WAS STILL THE CASE TWENTY YEARS LATER.
A FEW HOURS LATER, HE FOUND OUT THIS PORT WAS A TWO-WAY STREET.
EVEN AFTER ALL HIS TIME AWAY FROM THE LIFE, HE COULD TELL WHEN SOMEONE WAS CARRYING SOMEONE ELSE'S MONEY FOR DELIVERY.
BUT THEN, THOSE WERE THE KIND OF OBSERVATION SKILLS THAT HAD MADE HIM SO VALUABLE TO THE ARMY.
HEY -- HOLD ON.

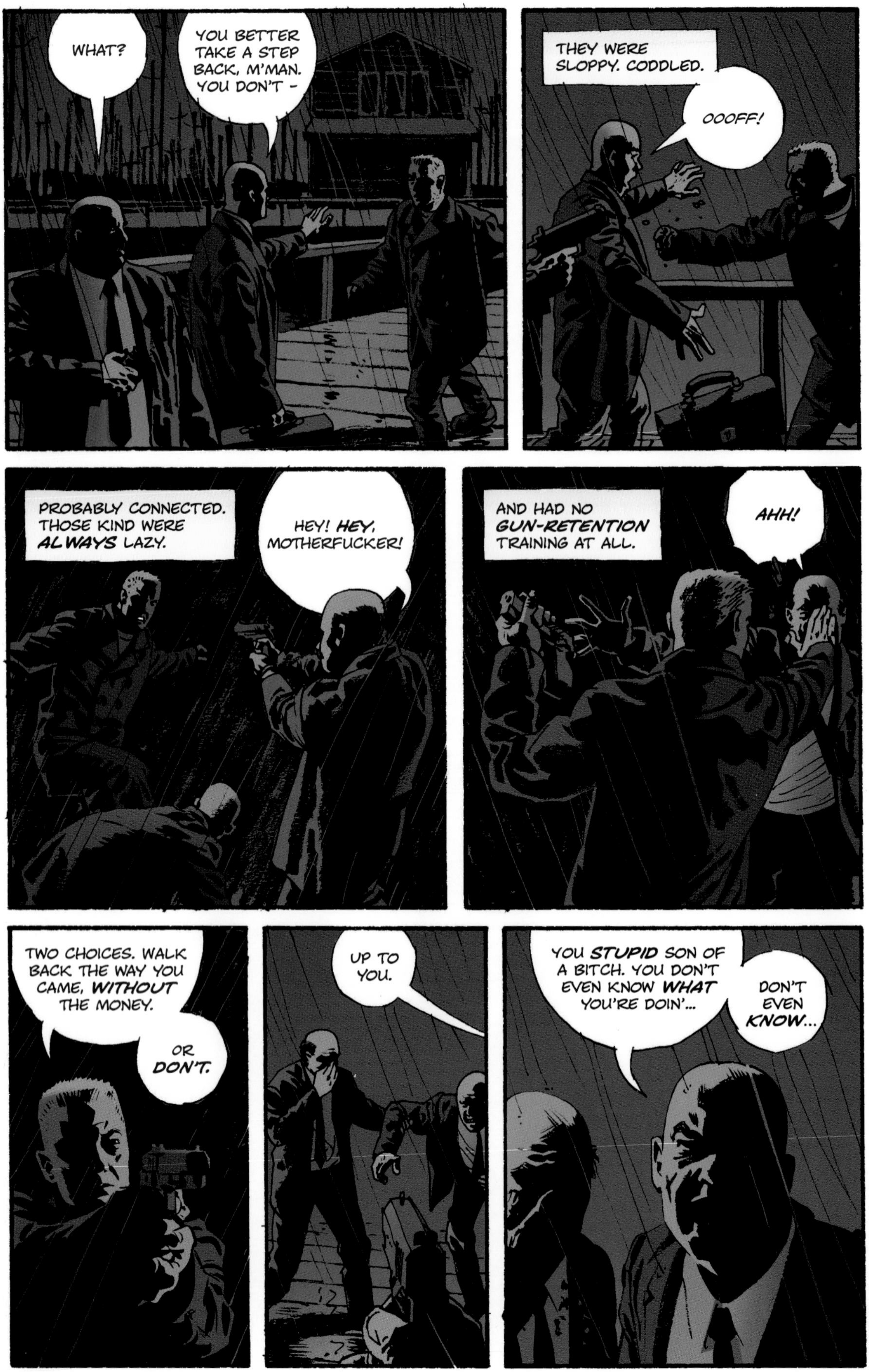
WHAT?
YOU BETTER TAKE A STEP BACK, M'MAN. YOU DON'T -
THEY WERE SLOPPY. CODDLED.
OOOFF!
PROBABLY CONNECTED. THOSE KIND WERE ALWAYS LAZY.
HEY! HEY, MOTHERFUCKER!
AND HAD NO GUN-RETENTION TRAINING AT ALL.
AHH!
TWO CHOICES. WALK BACK THE WAY YOU CAME, WITHOUT THE MONEY.
OR DON'T.
UP TO YOU.
YOU STUPID SON OF A BITCH. YOU DON'T EVEN KNOW WHAT YOU'RE DOIN'...
DON'T EVEN KNOW...

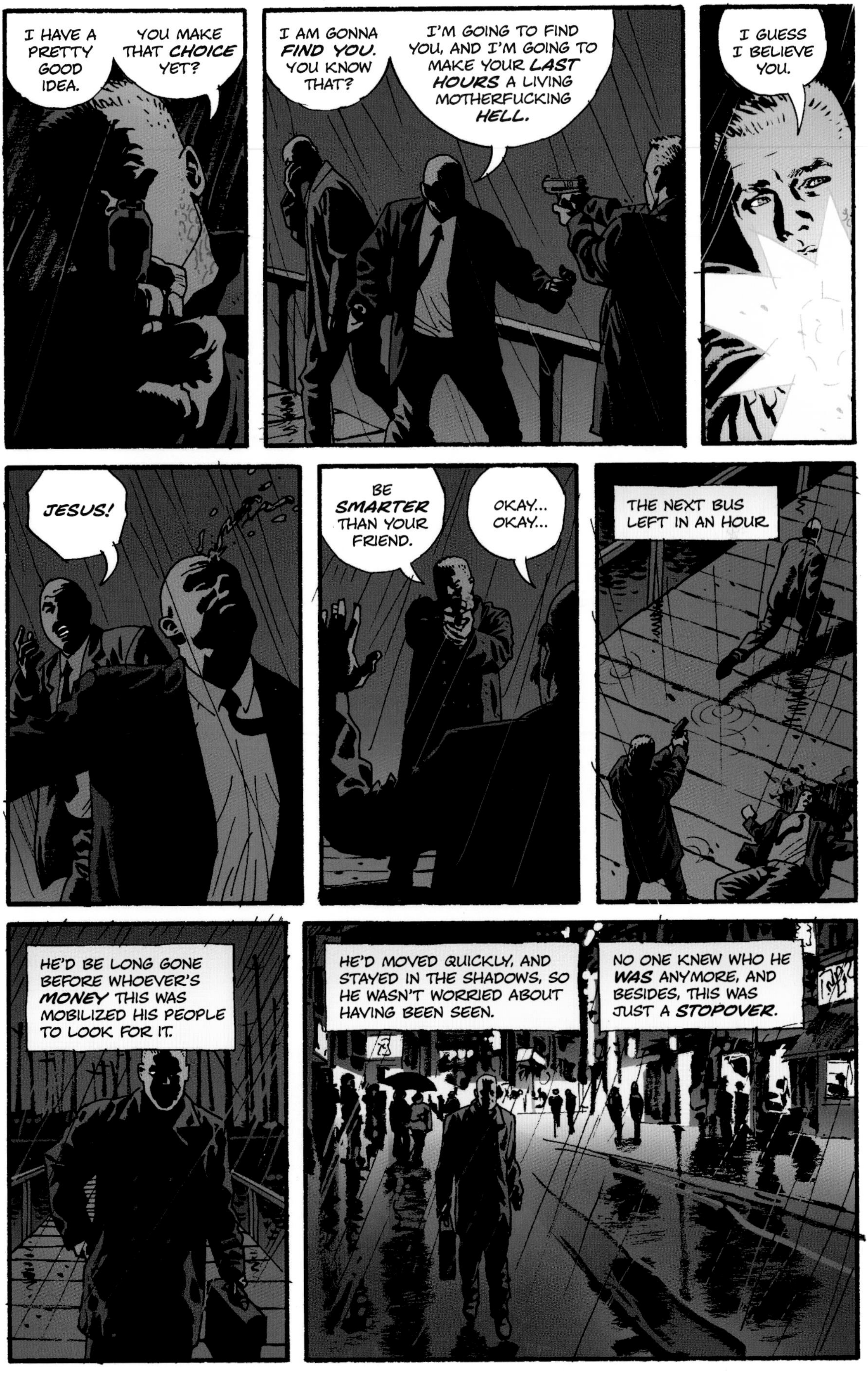
I HAVE A PRETTY GOOD IDEA.
YOU MAKE THAT CHOICE YET?
I AM GONNA FIND YOU. YOU KNOW THAT?
I'M GOING TO FIND YOU, AND I'M GOING TO MAKE YOUR LAST HOURS A LIVING MOTHERFUCKING HELL.
I GUESS I BELIEVE YOU.
JESUS!
BE SMARTER THAN YOUR FRIEND.
OKAY... OKAY...
THE NEXT BUS LEFT IN AN HOUR.
HE'D BE LONG GONE BEFORE WHOEVER'S MONEY THIS WAS MOBILIZED HIS PEOPLE TO LOOK FOR IT.
HE'D MOVED QUICKLY, AND STAYED IN THE SHADOWS, SO HE WASN'T WORRIED ABOUT HAVING BEEN SEEN.
NO ONE KNEW WHO HE WAS ANYMORE, AND BESIDES, THIS WAS JUST A STOPOVER.

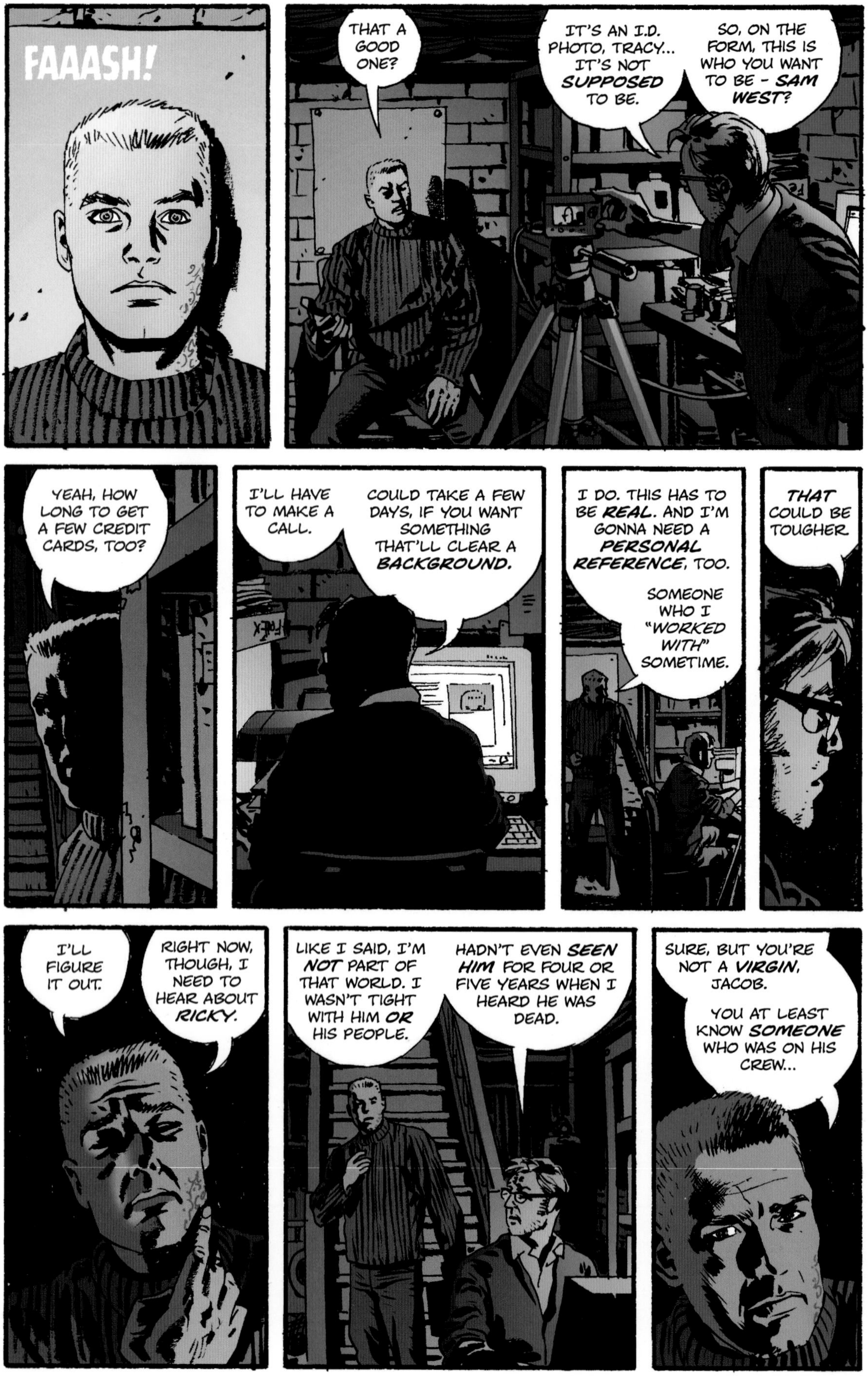
FAAASH!
THAT A GOOD ONE?
IT'S AN I.D. PHOTO, TRACY... IT'S NOT SUPPOSED TO BE.
SO, ON THE FORM, THIS IS WHO YOU WANT TO BE - SAM WEST?
YEAH, HOW LONG TO GET A FEW CREDIT CARDS, TOO?
I'LL HAVE TO MAKE A CALL.
COULD TAKE A FEW DAYS, IF YOU WANT SOMETHING THAT'LL CLEAR A BACKGROUND.
I DO. THIS HAS TO BE REAL. AND I'M GONNA NEED A PERSONAL REFERENCE, TOO.
SOMEONE WHO I "WORKED WITH" SOMETIME.
THAT COULD BE TOUGHER.
I'LL FIGURE IT OUT.
RIGHT NOW, THOUGH, I NEED TO HEAR ABOUT RICKY.
LIKE I SAID, I'M NOT PART OF THAT WORLD. I WASN'T TIGHT WITH HIM OR HIS PEOPLE.
HADN'T EVEN SEEN HIM FOR FOUR OR FIVE YEARS WHEN I HEARD HE WAS DEAD.
SURE, BUT YOU'RE NOT A VIRGIN, JACOB.
YOU AT LEAST KNOW SOMEONE WHO WAS ON HIS CREW...

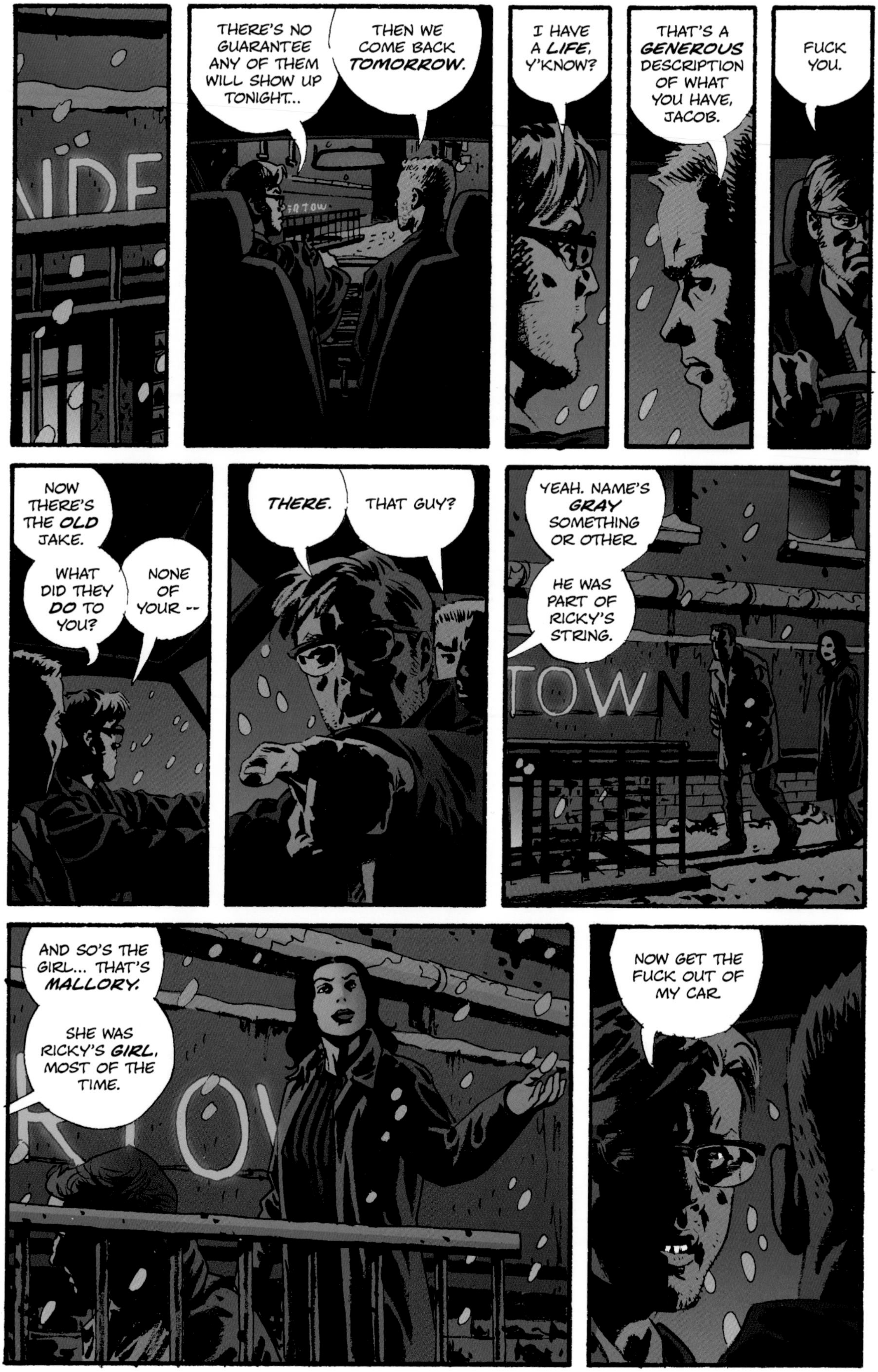

THERE'S NO GUARANTEE ANY OF THEM WILL SHOW UP TONIGHT...
THEN WE COME BACK *TOMORROW*.
I HAVE A *LIFE*, Y'KNOW?
THAT'S A *GENEROUS* DESCRIPTION OF WHAT YOU HAVE, JACOB.
FUCK YOU.
NOW THERE'S THE *OLD* JAKE.
WHAT DID THEY *DO* TO YOU?
NONE OF YOUR --
THERE.
THAT GUY?
YEAH. NAME'S *GRAY* SOMETHING OR OTHER.
HE WAS PART OF RICKY'S STRING.
TOWN
AND SO'S THE GIRL... THAT'S *MALLORY*.
SHE WAS RICKY'S *GIRL*, MOST OF THE TIME.
NOW GET THE FUCK OUT OF MY CAR

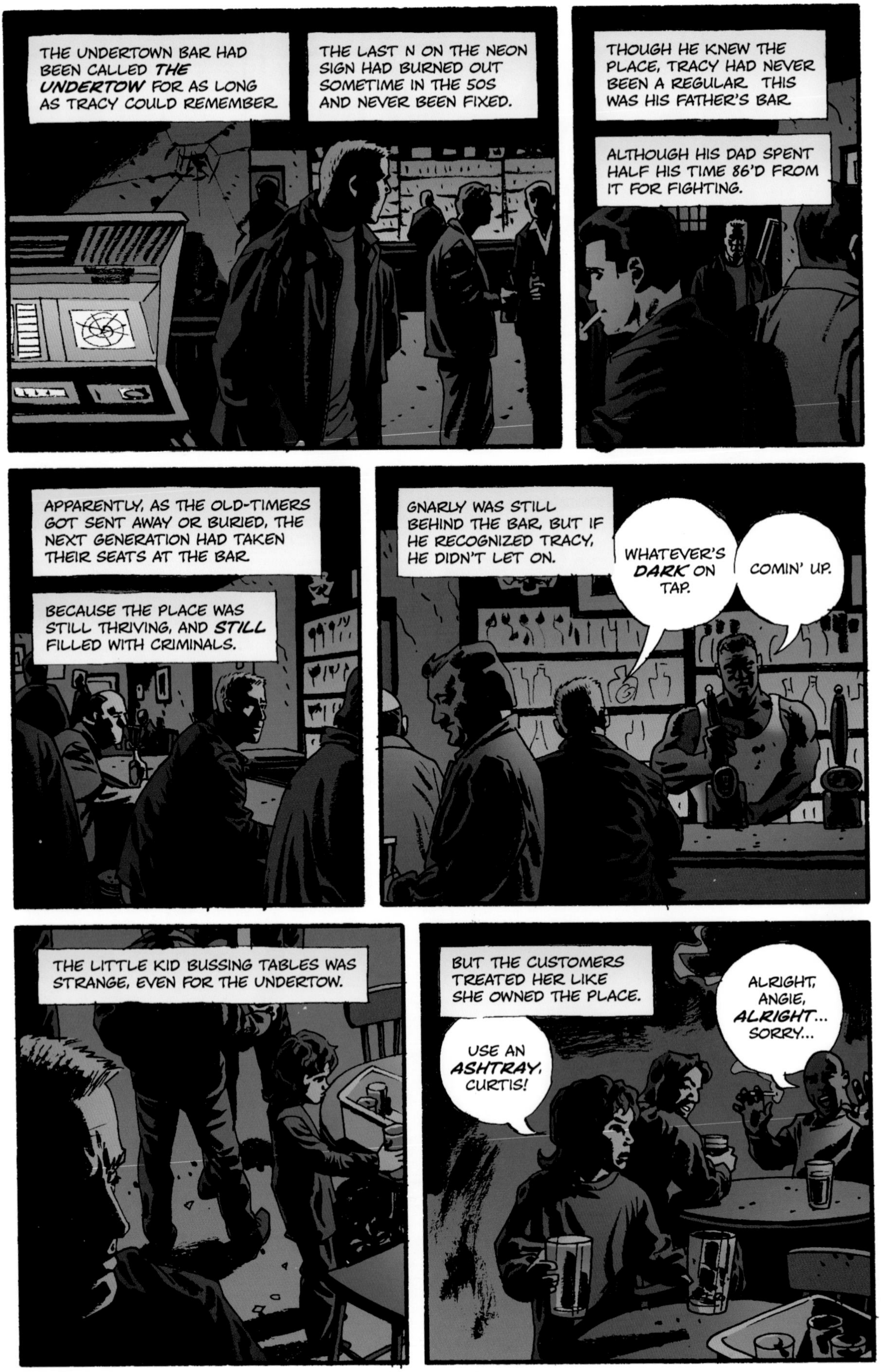
THE UNDERTOWN BAR HAD BEEN CALLED THE UNDERTOW FOR AS LONG AS TRACY COULD REMEMBER.
THE LAST N ON THE NEON SIGN HAD BURNED OUT SOMETIME IN THE 50S AND NEVER BEEN FIXED.
THOUGH HE KNEW THE PLACE, TRACY HAD NEVER BEEN A REGULAR. THIS WAS HIS FATHER'S BAR.
ALTHOUGH HIS DAD SPENT HALF HIS TIME 86'D FROM IT FOR FIGHTING.
APPARENTLY, AS THE OLD-TIMERS GOT SENT AWAY OR BURIED, THE NEXT GENERATION HAD TAKEN THEIR SEATS AT THE BAR.
BECAUSE THE PLACE WAS STILL THRIVING, AND STILL FILLED WITH CRIMINALS.
GNARLY WAS STILL BEHIND THE BAR, BUT IF HE RECOGNIZED TRACY, HE DIDN'T LET ON.
WHATEVER'S DARK ON TAP.
COMIN' UP.
THE LITTLE KID BUSSING TABLES WAS STRANGE, EVEN FOR THE UNDERTOW.
BUT THE CUSTOMERS TREATED HER LIKE SHE OWNED THE PLACE.
USE AN ASHTRAY, CURTIS!
ALRIGHT, ANGIE, ALRIGHT... SORRY...

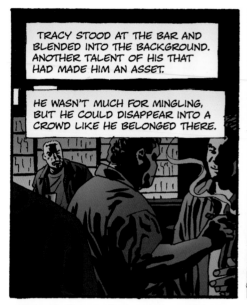

TRACY STOOD AT THE BAR AND BLENDED INTO THE BACKGROUND. ANOTHER TALENT OF HIS THAT HAD MADE HIM AN ASSET.

HE WASN'T MUCH FOR MINGLING, BUT HE COULD DISAPPEAR INTO A CROWD LIKE HE BELONGED THERE.

AFTER A FEW DRINKS MALLORY AND GRAY WERE JOINED BY TWO OTHER MEN...

DAVEY... WHAT THE **FUCK?** YOU'RE LATE.

WE ON A **CLOCK** ALL OF A SUDDEN?

THE WAY THEY HUDDLED TOGETHER IN THE BOOTH, IT WAS CLEAR THIS WAS THE CREW...

RICKY'S OLD CREW.

AS UNCOMFORTABLE TOGETHER AS ANY OTHER DYSFUNCTIONAL FAMILY, WHICH IS WHAT ANY TIGHT CREW OF THIEVES ULTIMATELY BECOMES.

DEPENDANT ON EACH OTHER FOR SURVIVAL AND FOR SECURITY, WHETHER THEY LIKE IT OR NOT.

THE THOUGHT THAT SOMEONE IN THIS CREW, ONE OF HIS **FAMILY**, HAD LEFT RICK FACE-DOWN IN AN ALLEY FLIPPED A SWITCH IN TRACY'S MIND.

HE STOPPED SEEING THEM AS PEOPLE, BUT AS TARGETS, INSTEAD.

STILL, THERE WERE ANSWERS THAT HAD TO COME BEFORE THAT... PATIENCE.

THE THING THE ARMY TEACHES BEST. THE ART OF WAITING.

SO HE WAITED AND WATCHED...

...AND THOUGHT ABOUT THE LAST TIME HE'D BEEN IN A BAR, NEARLY TWO YEARS BEFORE.

IN BAGHDAD, THE GREEN ZONE.

THE ENLISTED CLUB HAD ONCE BEEN A RESTAURANT, BUT IT DIDN'T SERVE ANYTHING BUT BOOZE AND STALE CHIPS ANYMORE.

STILL, IT WAS A PLACE TO BLOW OFF STEAM, AWAY FROM THE HOSTILES.

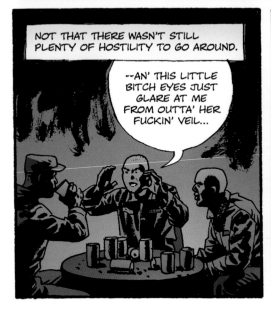

NOT THAT THERE WASN'T STILL PLENTY OF HOSTILITY TO GO AROUND.

--AN' THIS LITTLE BITCH EYES JUST GLARE AT ME FROM OUTTA' HER FUCKIN' VEIL...

SO I GRAB THAT SHIT. I PULL IT BACK AND SHOW THE WORLD HER FUCKIN' FACE.

EXPOSED.

SHOULDA' SEEN IT. HER FATHER GOES BA-FUCKIN'-LISTIC.

STARTS SCREAMIN' IN SAND-NIGGER... TOTAL CRACK-UP.

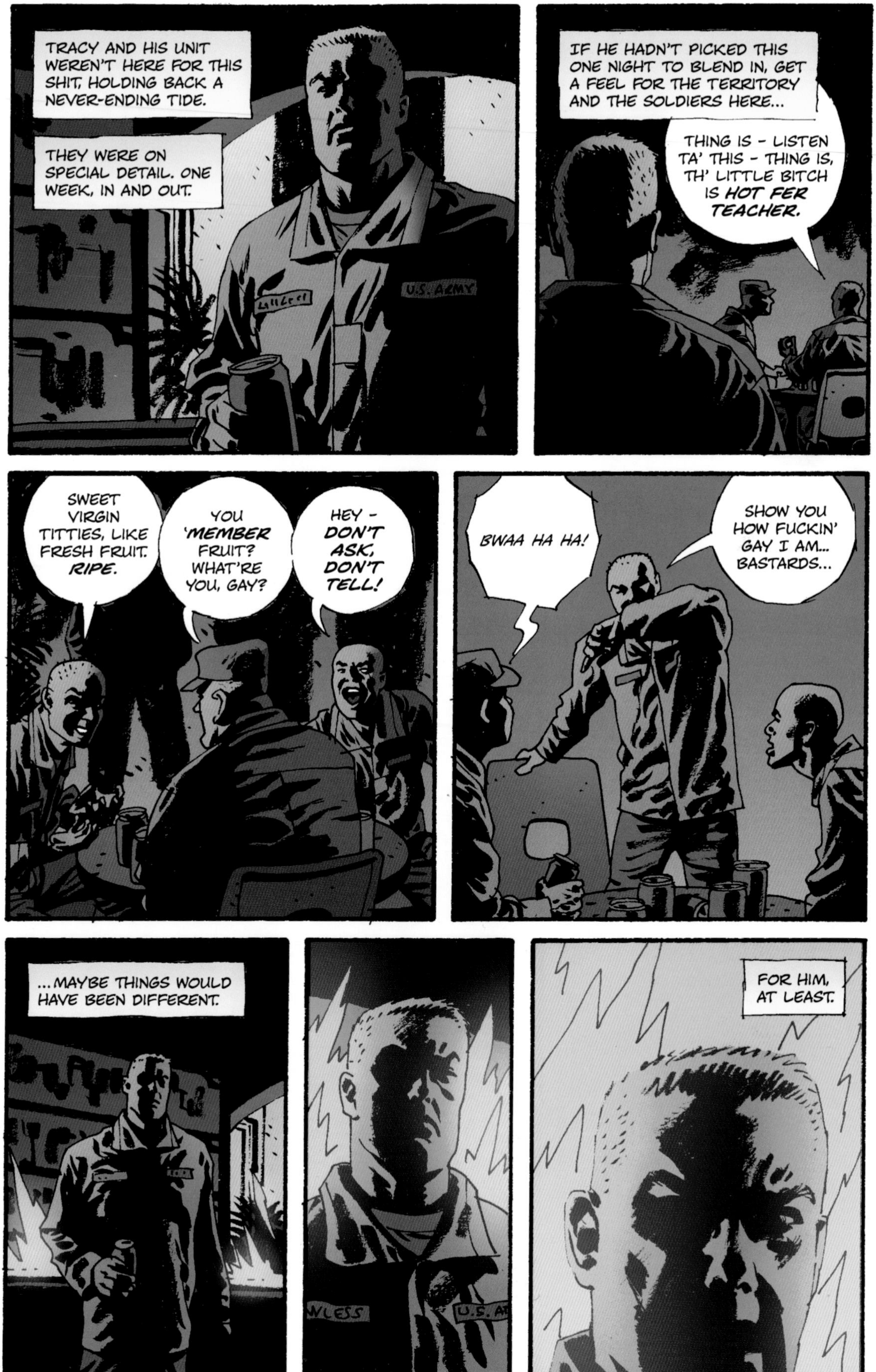
TRACY AND HIS UNIT WEREN'T HERE FOR THIS SHIT, HOLDING BACK A NEVER-ENDING TIDE.
THEY WERE ON SPECIAL DETAIL. ONE WEEK, IN AND OUT.
U.S. ARMY
IF HE HADN'T PICKED THIS ONE NIGHT TO BLEND IN, GET A FEEL FOR THE TERRITORY AND THE SOLDIERS HERE...
THING IS - LISTEN TA' THIS - THING IS, TH' LITTLE BITCH IS *HOT FER TEACHER.*
SWEET VIRGIN TITTIES, LIKE FRESH FRUIT. *RIPE.*
YOU '*MEMBER* FRUIT? WHAT'RE YOU, GAY?
HEY - *DON'T ASK, DON'T TELL!*
BWAA HA HA!
SHOW YOU HOW FUCKIN' GAY I AM... BASTARDS...
...MAYBE THINGS WOULD HAVE BEEN DIFFERENT.
FOR HIM, AT LEAST.

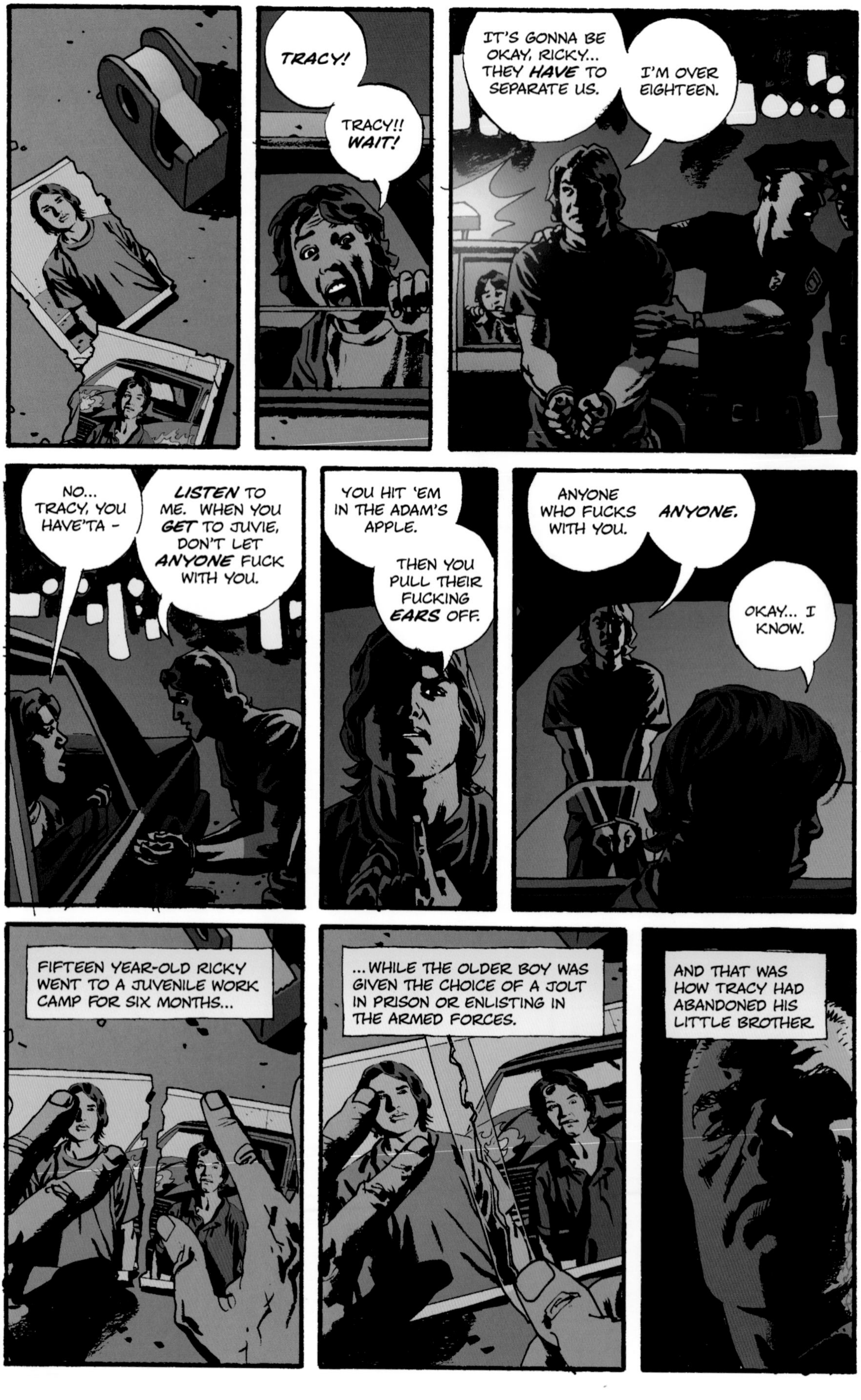
TRACY!
TRACY!! WAIT!
IT'S GONNA BE OKAY, RICKY... THEY HAVE TO SEPARATE US.
I'M OVER EIGHTEEN.
NO... TRACY, YOU HAVE'TA -
LISTEN TO ME. WHEN YOU GET TO JUVIE, DON'T LET ANYONE FUCK WITH YOU.
YOU HIT 'EM IN THE ADAM'S APPLE.
THEN YOU PULL THEIR FUCKING EARS OFF.
ANYONE WHO FUCKS WITH YOU.
ANYONE.
OKAY... I KNOW.
FIFTEEN YEAR-OLD RICKY WENT TO A JUVENILE WORK CAMP FOR SIX MONTHS...
...WHILE THE OLDER BOY WAS GIVEN THE CHOICE OF A JOLT IN PRISON OR ENLISTING IN THE ARMED FORCES.
AND THAT WAS HOW TRACY HAD ABANDONED HIS LITTLE BROTHER.

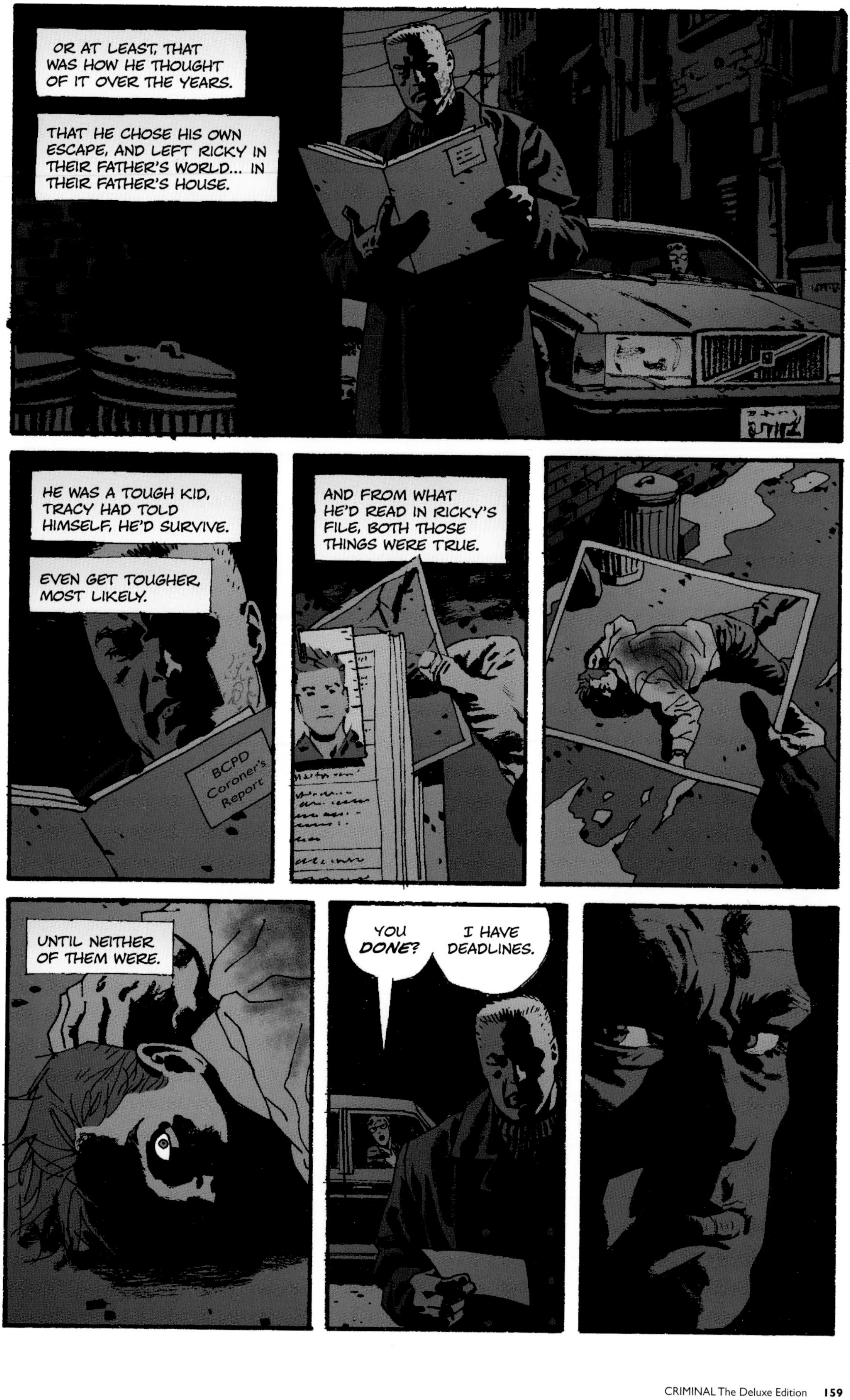
OR AT LEAST, THAT WAS HOW HE THOUGHT OF IT OVER THE YEARS.
THAT HE CHOSE HIS OWN ESCAPE, AND LEFT RICKY IN THEIR FATHER'S WORLD... IN THEIR FATHER'S HOUSE.
HE WAS A TOUGH KID, TRACY HAD TOLD HIMSELF, HE'D SURVIVE.
EVEN GET TOUGHER, MOST LIKELY.
BCPD Coroner's Report
AND FROM WHAT HE'D READ IN RICKY'S FILE, BOTH THOSE THINGS WERE TRUE.
UNTIL NEITHER OF THEM WERE.
YOU *DONE*?
I HAVE DEADLINES.

HE SPENT THE NEXT WEEK AND A HALF CREATING A LIFE FOR HIS NEW NAME.

HE USED **MOST** OF THE MONEY HE HAD LEFT TO BUY A FAST CAR

AND HE CASHED IN A LONG-OVERDUE FAVOR TO PAD OUT HIS REPUTATION.

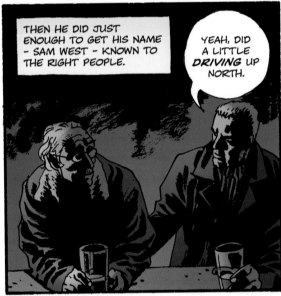

THEN HE DID JUST ENOUGH TO GET HIS NAME – SAM WEST – KNOWN TO THE RIGHT PEOPLE.

YEAH, DID A LITTLE **DRIVING** UP NORTH.

I'LL LET YOU KNOW IF I HEAR ANYTHING.

DOESN'T **HAVE** TO BE SOMETHING HEAVY...

I'M JUST LOOKING FOR SOME **PICK-UP.**

RICKY'S OLD CREW WERE MEETING ALMOST EVERY NIGHT, AND THE WAY THEY ACTED REMINDED HIM OF HIS DAD'S GANG...

...WHENEVER THEY WERE ABOUT TO TAKE DOWN A SCORE.

SO, IF HIS PLAN WAS GOING TO WORK, HE HAD TO MOVE SOON.

LATER, DAVEY... AND GET SOME **SLEEP** FOR A CHANGE.

SLEEP IS FOR **PUSSIES!** HA HA HA...

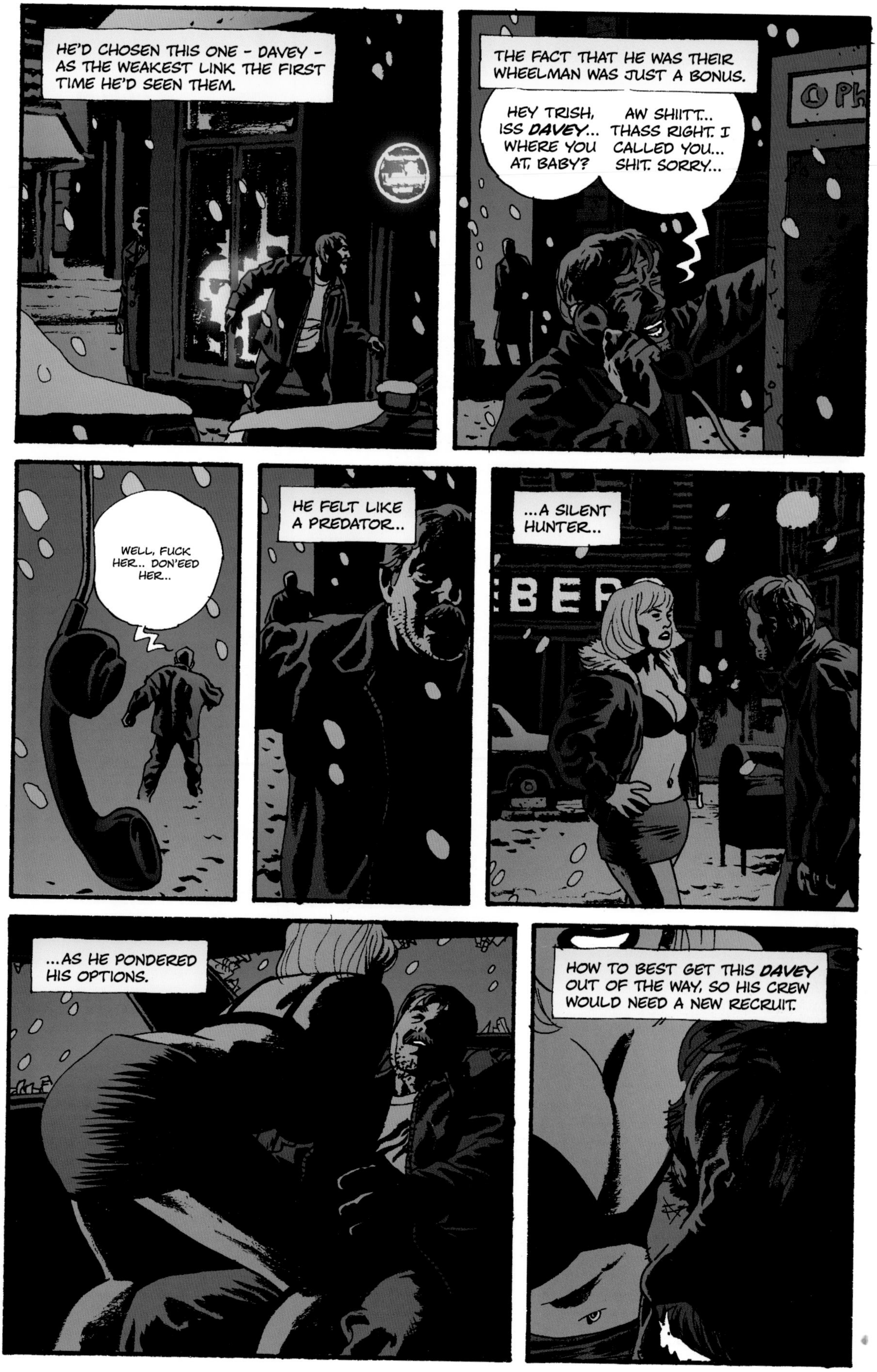

HE'D CHOSEN THIS ONE - DAVEY - AS THE WEAKEST LINK THE FIRST TIME HE'D SEEN THEM.
THE FACT THAT HE WAS THEIR WHEELMAN WAS JUST A BONUS.
HEY TRISH, ISS DAVEY... WHERE YOU AT, BABY?
AW SHIITT... THASS RIGHT. I CALLED YOU... SHIT. SORRY...
WELL, FUCK HER.. DON'EED HER..
HE FELT LIKE A PREDATOR..
...A SILENT HUNTER..
...AS HE PONDERED HIS OPTIONS.
HOW TO BEST GET THIS DAVEY OUT OF THE WAY, SO HIS CREW WOULD NEED A NEW RECRUIT.

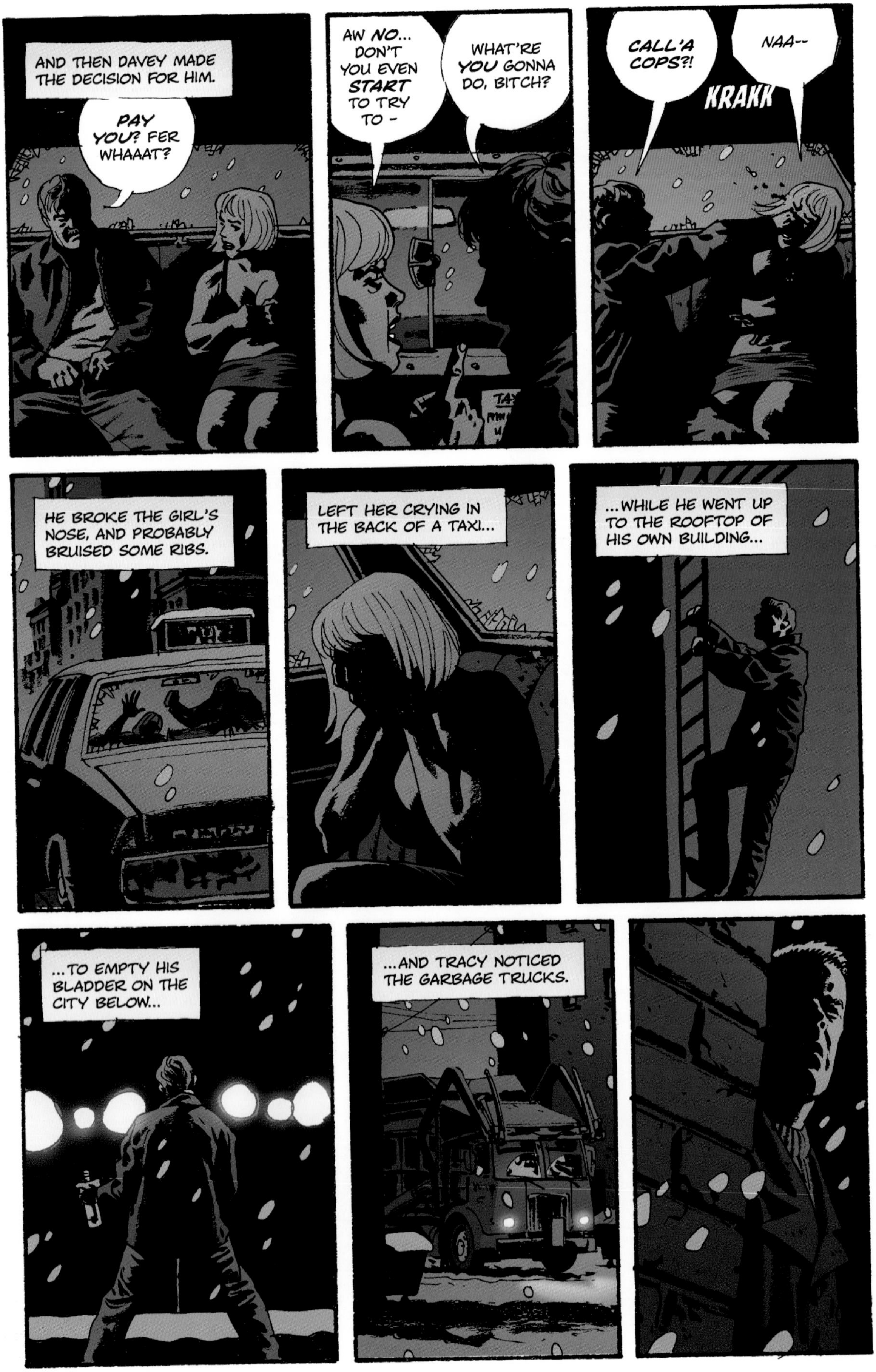
AND THEN DAVEY MADE THE DECISION FOR HIM.
PAY YOU? FER WHAAAT?
AW NO... DON'T YOU EVEN START TO TRY TO -
WHAT'RE YOU GONNA DO, BITCH?
CALL'A COPS?!
NAA--
KRAKK
HE BROKE THE GIRL'S NOSE, AND PROBABLY BRUISED SOME RIBS.
LEFT HER CRYING IN THE BACK OF A TAXI...
...WHILE HE WENT UP TO THE ROOFTOP OF HIS OWN BUILDING...
...TO EMPTY HIS BLADDER ON THE CITY BELOW...
...AND TRACY NOTICED THE GARBAGE TRUCKS.

AFTER THAT, HE WOULDN'T HAVE LONG TO WAIT.

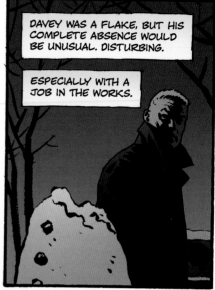

DAVEY WAS A FLAKE, BUT HIS COMPLETE ABSENCE WOULD BE UNUSUAL. DISTURBING.

ESPECIALLY WITH A JOB IN THE WORKS.

HE SAW THAT THE NEXT NIGHT, AS DAVEY'S PEOPLE QUICKLY WENT FROM ANNOYED TO ANGRY...

ASSHOLE PROBABLY FOUND SOMEWHERE TO GET HIS *DICK STINKY* AND FELL IN...

AND HE NOTICED GRAY CALCULATING WHAT THIS MEANT FOR THEIR PLANS.

CALL HIM AGAIN, NELSON.

HE AIN'T PICKIN' UP, MAN. GOES STRAIGHT TO MESSAGE.

I *WARNED YOU* ABOUT COUNTING ON HIM.

HE HASN'T BEEN RIGHT SINCE... SHIT, MAYBE *EVER.*

SHUT UP, MAL... ALL RIGHT?

JUST LET ME THINK.

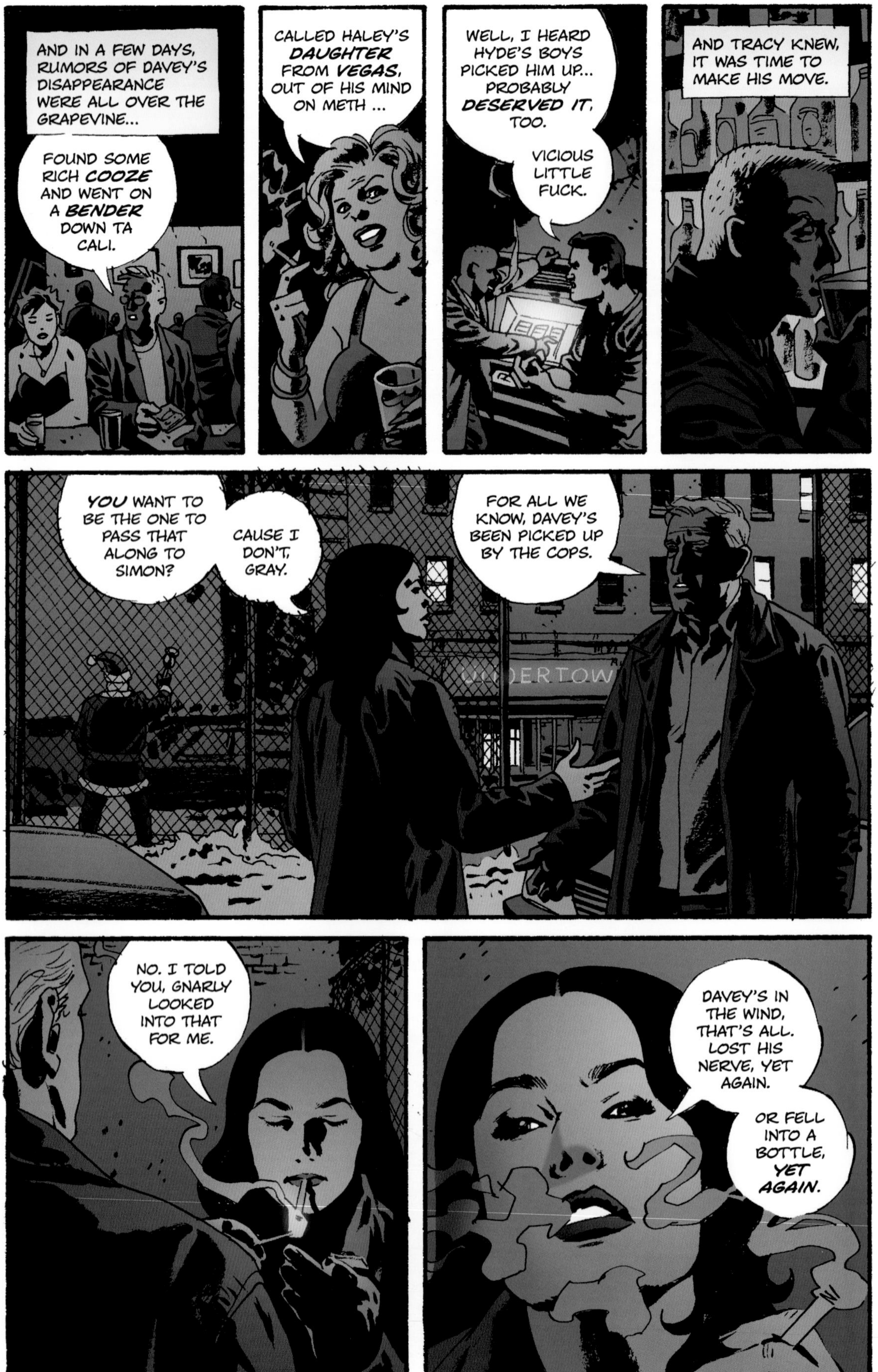
AND IN A FEW DAYS, RUMORS OF DAVEY'S DISAPPEARANCE WERE ALL OVER THE GRAPEVINE...
FOUND SOME RICH COOZE AND WENT ON A BENDER DOWN TA CALI.
CALLED HALEY'S DAUGHTER FROM VEGAS, OUT OF HIS MIND ON METH ...
WELL, I HEARD HYDE'S BOYS PICKED HIM UP... PROBABLY DESERVED IT, TOO.
VICIOUS LITTLE FUCK.
AND TRACY KNEW, IT WAS TIME TO MAKE HIS MOVE.
YOU WANT TO BE THE ONE TO PASS THAT ALONG TO SIMON?
CAUSE I DON'T, GRAY.
FOR ALL WE KNOW, DAVEY'S BEEN PICKED UP BY THE COPS.
NO. I TOLD YOU, GNARLY LOOKED INTO THAT FOR ME.
DAVEY'S IN THE WIND, THAT'S ALL. LOST HIS NERVE, YET AGAIN.
OR FELL INTO A BOTTLE, YET AGAIN.

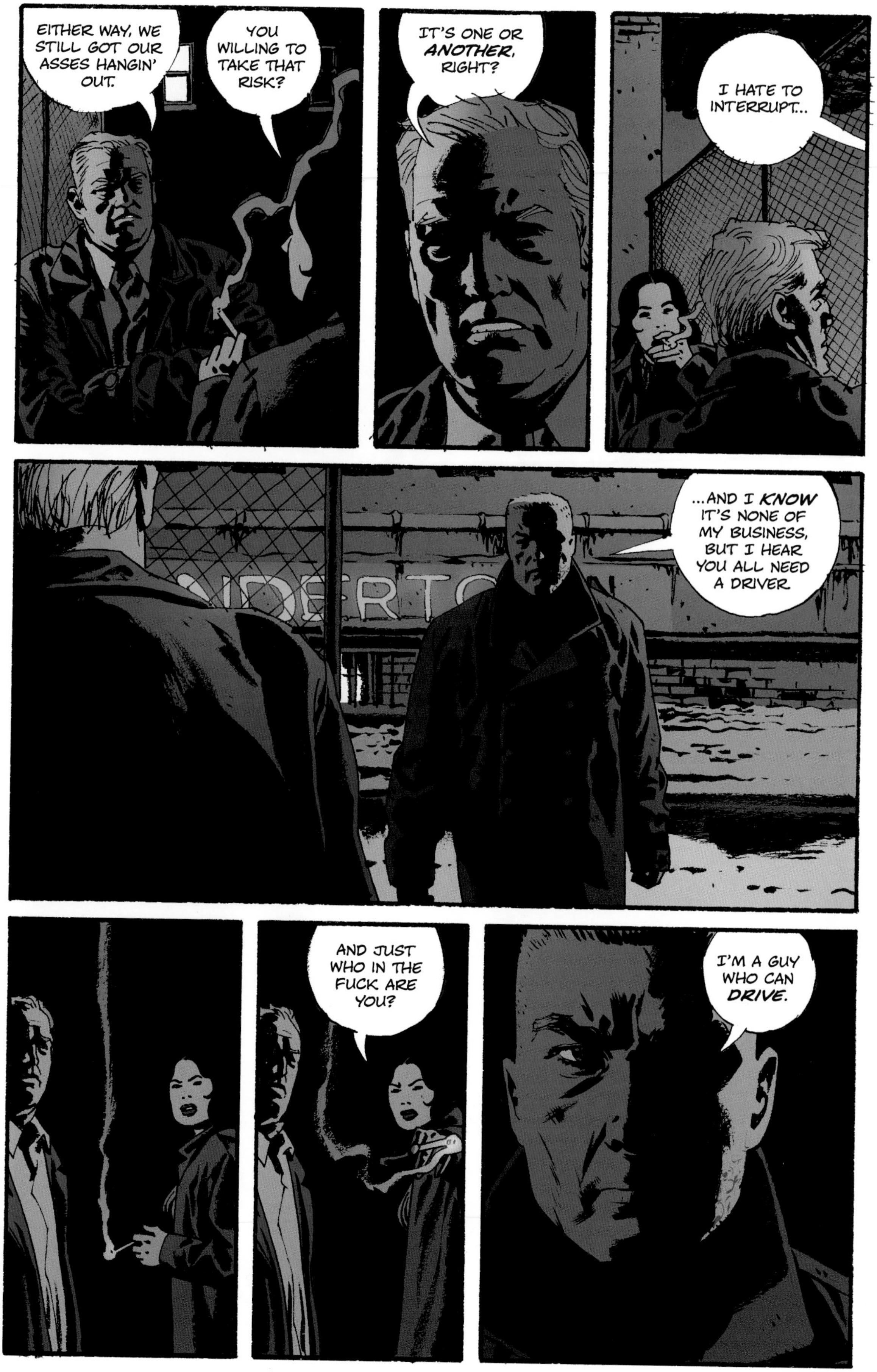
EITHER WAY, WE STILL GOT OUR ASSES HANGIN' OUT.
YOU WILLING TO TAKE THAT RISK?
IT'S ONE OR ANOTHER, RIGHT?
I HATE TO INTERRUPT...
...AND I KNOW IT'S NONE OF MY BUSINESS, BUT I HEAR YOU ALL NEED A DRIVER.
AND JUST WHO IN THE FUCK ARE YOU?
I'M A GUY WHO CAN DRIVE.

Part Two

Charger

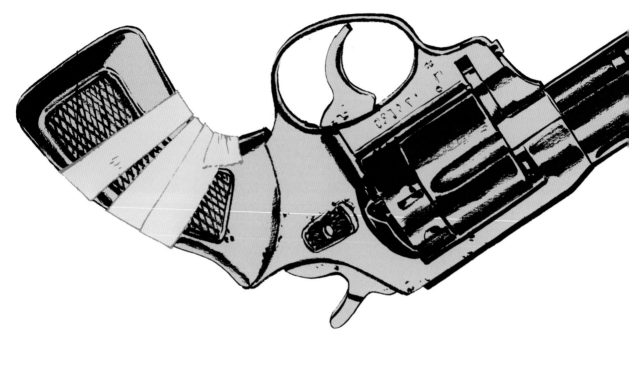

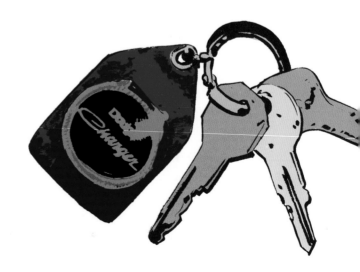

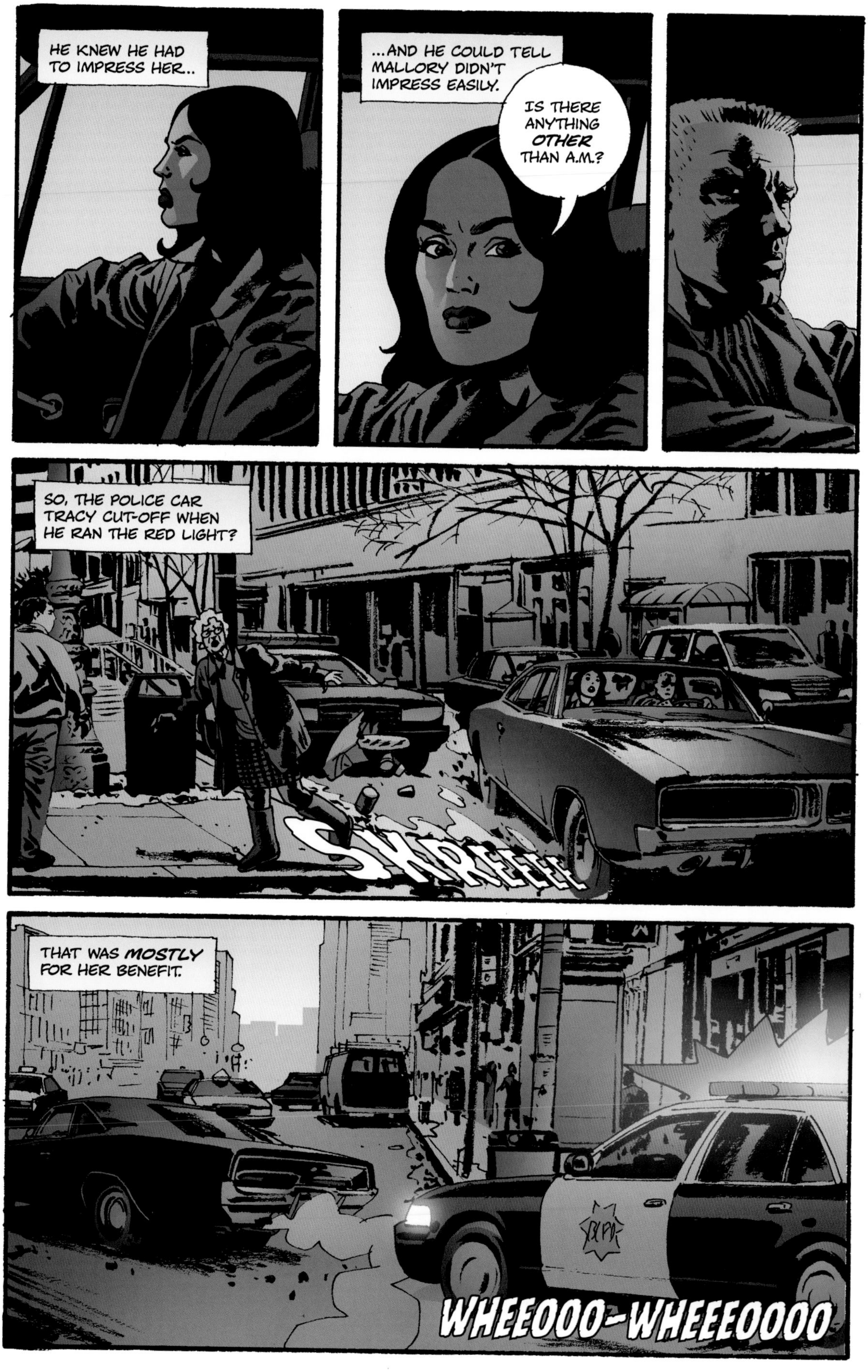
HE KNEW HE HAD TO IMPRESS HER...
...AND HE COULD TELL MALLORY DIDN'T IMPRESS EASILY.
IS THERE ANYTHING OTHER THAN A.M.?
SO, THE POLICE CAR TRACY CUT-OFF WHEN HE RAN THE RED LIGHT?
SKREEEE
THAT WAS MOSTLY FOR HER BENEFIT.
WHEEOOO-WHEEEOOOO

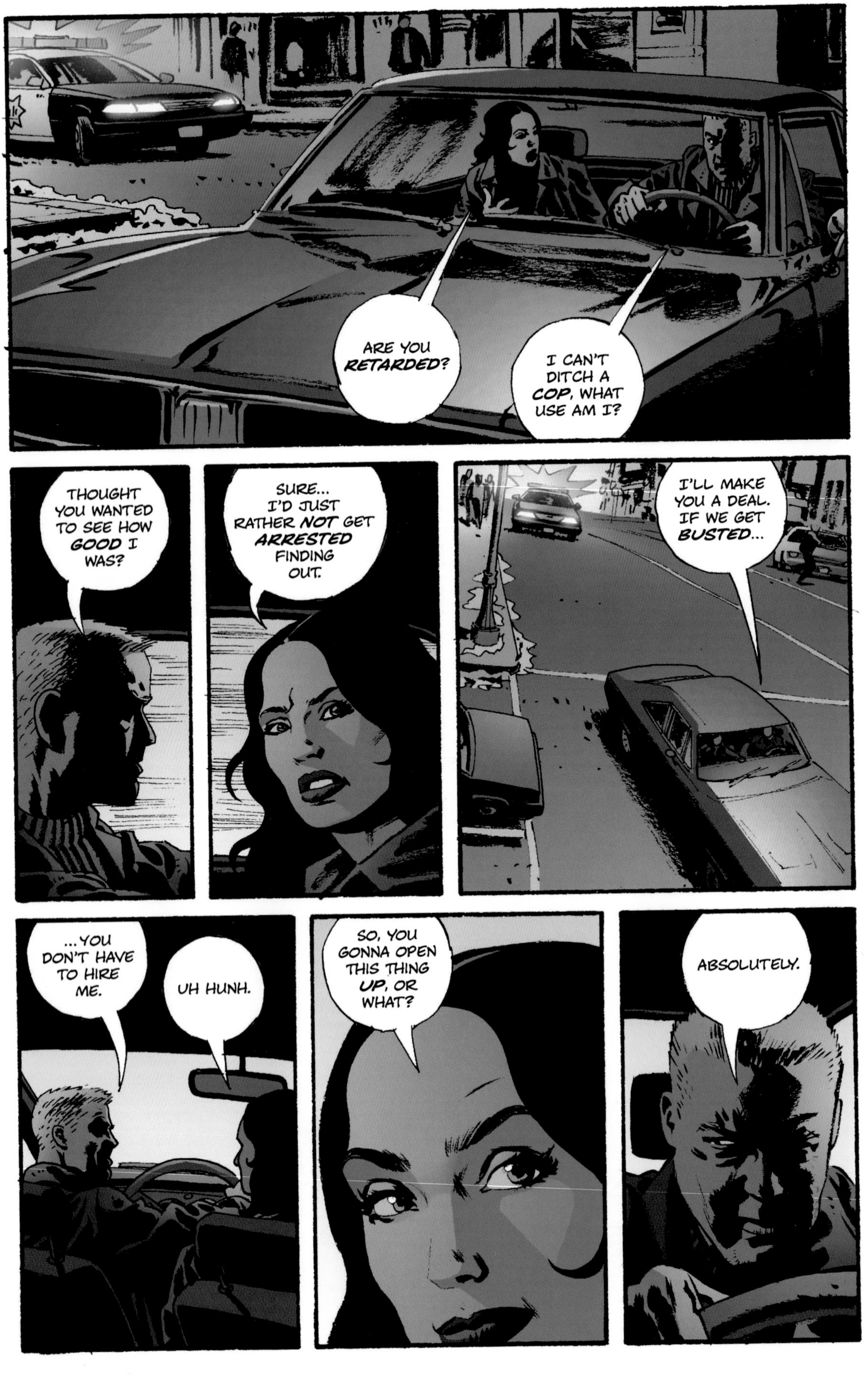
ARE YOU RETARDED?
I CAN'T DITCH A COP, WHAT USE AM I?
THOUGHT YOU WANTED TO SEE HOW GOOD I WAS?
SURE... I'D JUST RATHER NOT GET ARRESTED FINDING OUT.
I'LL MAKE YOU A DEAL. IF WE GET BUSTED...
...YOU DON'T HAVE TO HIRE ME.
UH HUNH.
SO, YOU GONNA OPEN THIS THING UP, OR WHAT?
ABSOLUTELY.

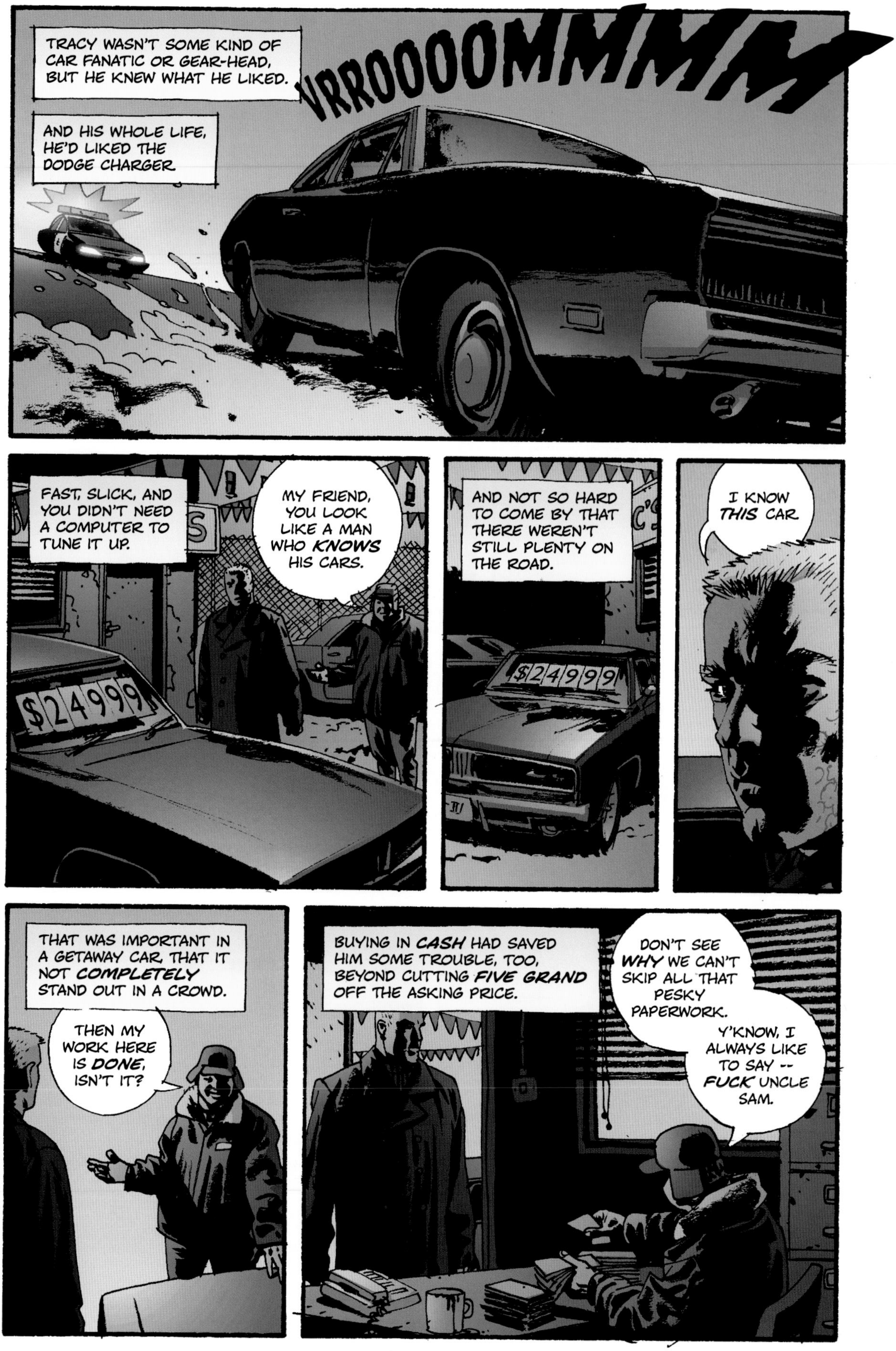

TRACY WASN'T SOME KIND OF CAR FANATIC OR GEAR-HEAD, BUT HE KNEW WHAT HE LIKED.
VRROOOOMMMMM
AND HIS WHOLE LIFE, HE'D LIKED THE DODGE CHARGER.
FAST, SLICK, AND YOU DIDN'T NEED A COMPUTER TO TUNE IT UP.
MY FRIEND, YOU LOOK LIKE A MAN WHO KNOWS HIS CARS.
$24999
AND NOT SO HARD TO COME BY THAT THERE WEREN'T STILL PLENTY ON THE ROAD.
$24999
I KNOW THIS CAR.
THAT WAS IMPORTANT IN A GETAWAY CAR, THAT IT NOT COMPLETELY STAND OUT IN A CROWD.
THEN MY WORK HERE IS DONE, ISN'T IT?
BUYING IN CASH HAD SAVED HIM SOME TROUBLE, TOO, BEYOND CUTTING FIVE GRAND OFF THE ASKING PRICE.
DON'T SEE WHY WE CAN'T SKIP ALL THAT PESKY PAPERWORK.
Y'KNOW, I ALWAYS LIKE TO SAY -- FUCK UNCLE SAM.

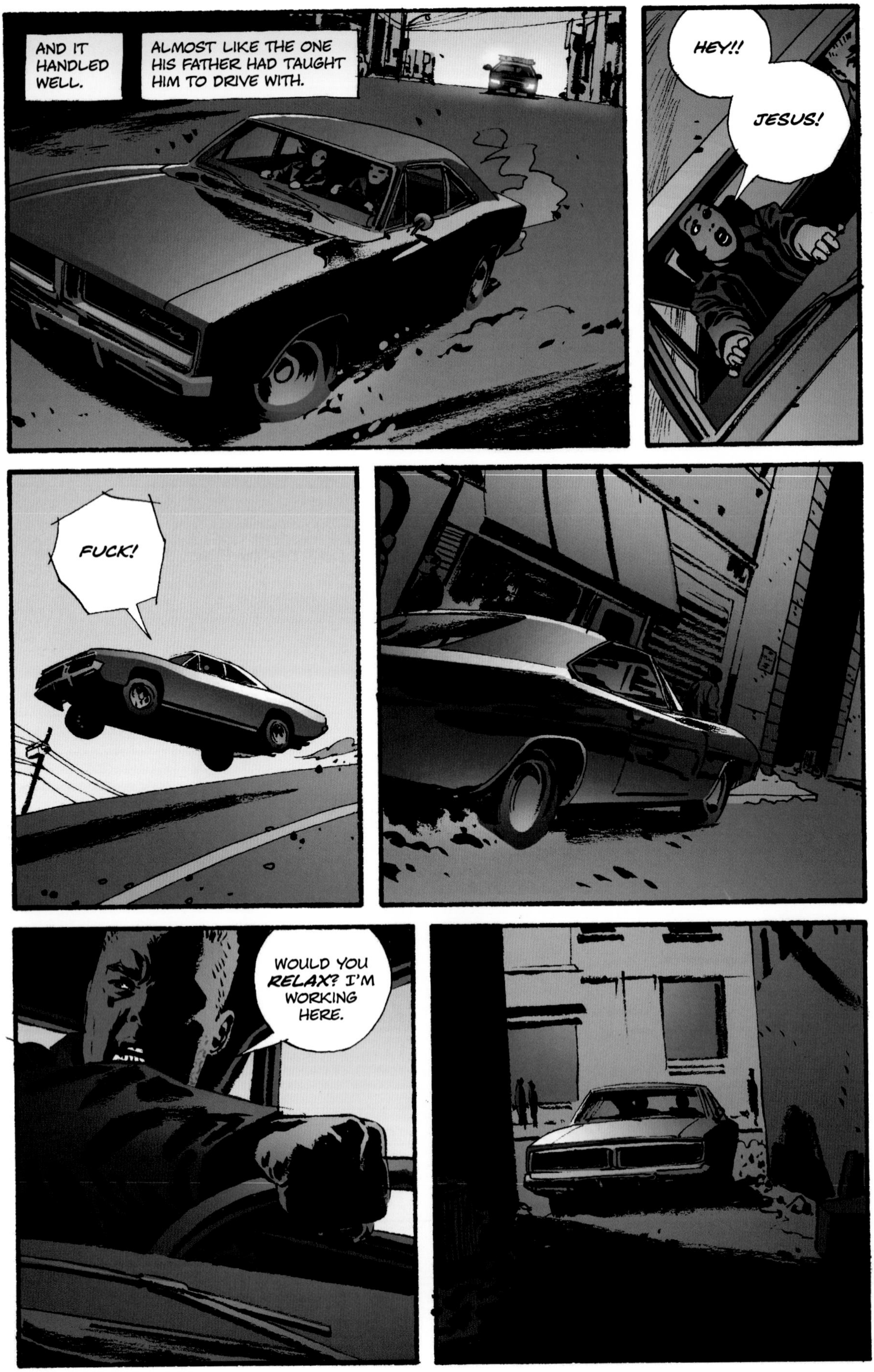
AND IT HANDLED WELL.
ALMOST LIKE THE ONE HIS FATHER HAD TAUGHT HIM TO DRIVE WITH.
HEY!!
JESUS!
FUCK!
WOULD YOU RELAX? I'M WORKING HERE.

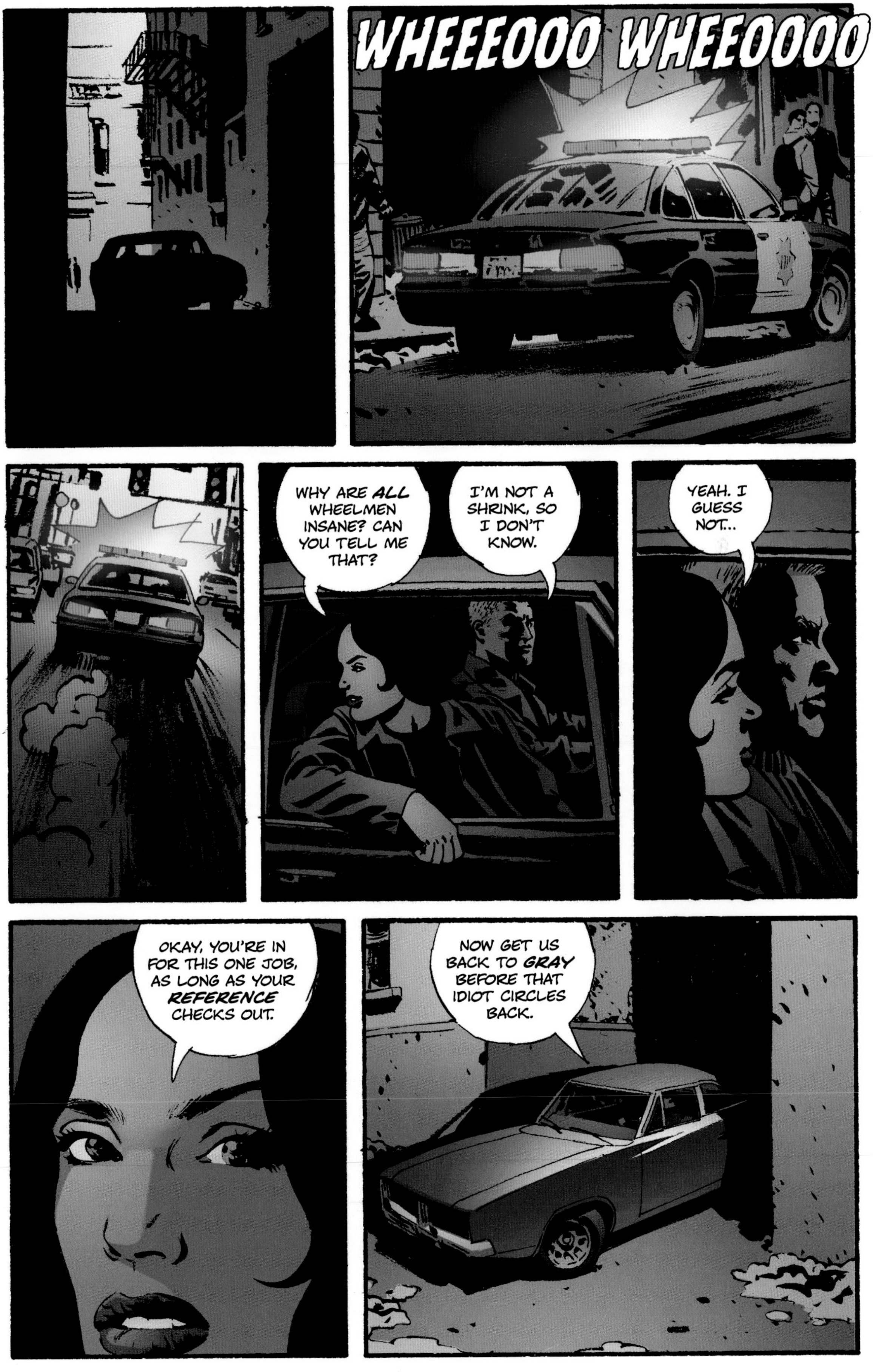
WHEEEOOO WHEEOOOO
WHY ARE ALL WHEELMEN INSANE? CAN YOU TELL ME THAT?
I'M NOT A SHRINK, SO I DON'T KNOW.
YEAH. I GUESS NOT...
OKAY, YOU'RE IN FOR THIS ONE JOB, AS LONG AS YOUR REFERENCE CHECKS OUT.
NOW GET US BACK TO GRAY BEFORE THAT IDIOT CIRCLES BACK.

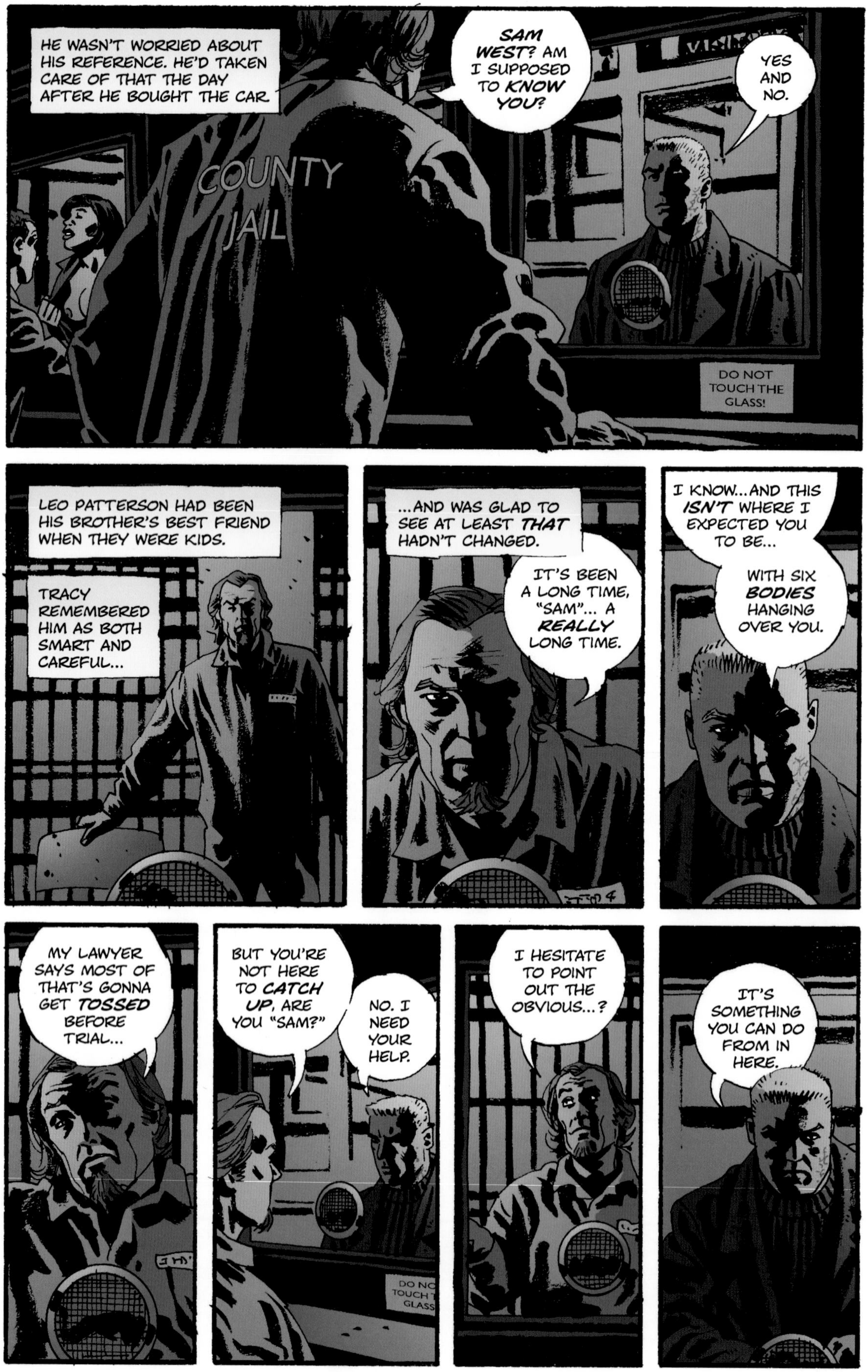
HE WASN'T WORRIED ABOUT HIS REFERENCE. HE'D TAKEN CARE OF THAT THE DAY AFTER HE BOUGHT THE CAR
SAM WEST? AM I SUPPOSED TO KNOW YOU?
YES AND NO.
COUNTY JAIL
DO NOT TOUCH THE GLASS!
LEO PATTERSON HAD BEEN HIS BROTHER'S BEST FRIEND WHEN THEY WERE KIDS.
TRACY REMEMBERED HIM AS BOTH SMART AND CAREFUL...
...AND WAS GLAD TO SEE AT LEAST THAT HADN'T CHANGED.
IT'S BEEN A LONG TIME, "SAM"... A REALLY LONG TIME.
I KNOW...AND THIS ISN'T WHERE I EXPECTED YOU TO BE...
WITH SIX BODIES HANGING OVER YOU.
MY LAWYER SAYS MOST OF THAT'S GONNA GET TOSSED BEFORE TRIAL...
BUT YOU'RE NOT HERE TO CATCH UP, ARE YOU "SAM?"
NO. I NEED YOUR HELP.
I HESITATE TO POINT OUT THE OBVIOUS...?
IT'S SOMETHING YOU CAN DO FROM IN HERE.

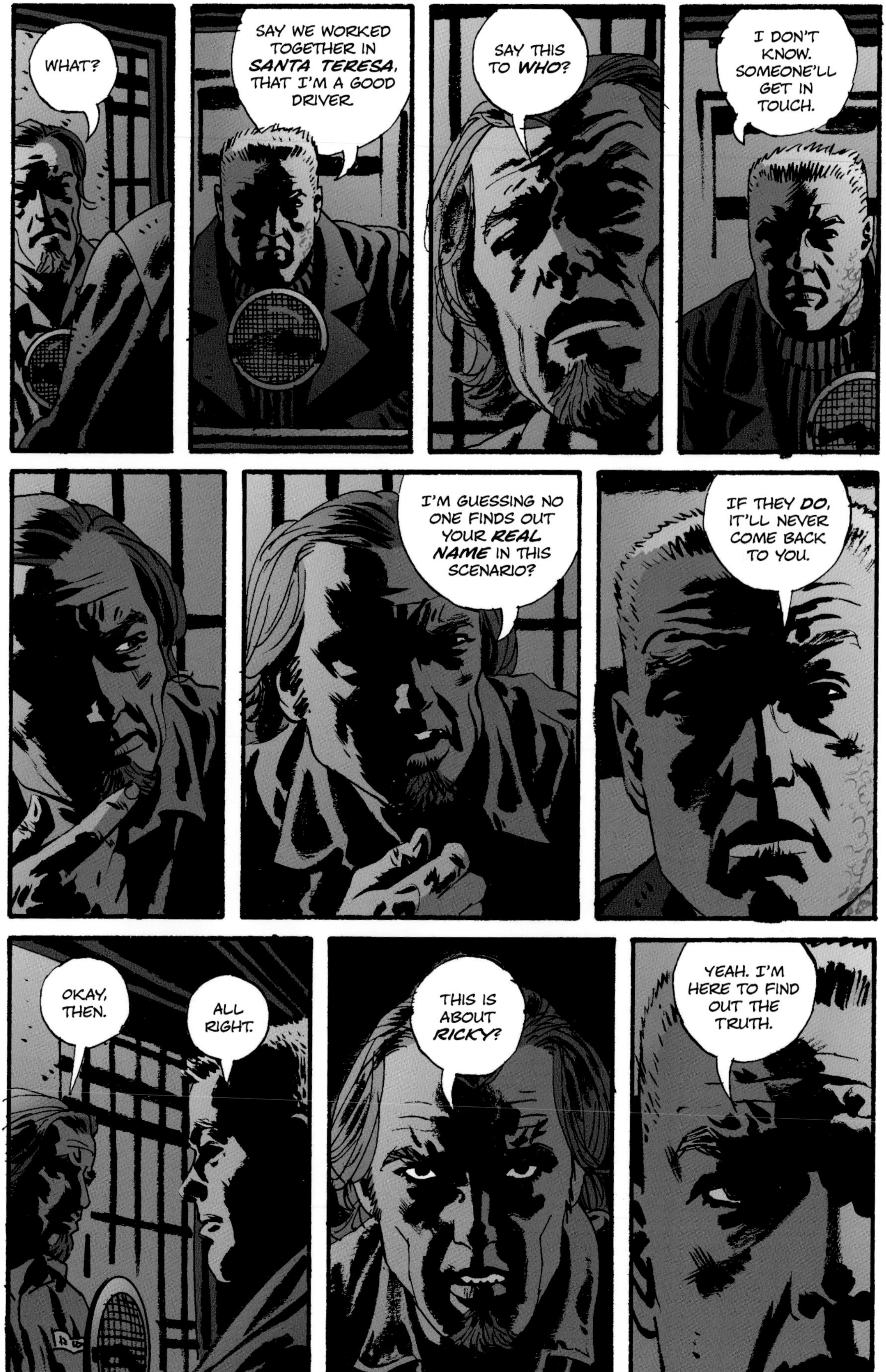

WHAT?
SAY WE WORKED TOGETHER IN *SANTA TERESA*, THAT I'M A GOOD DRIVER.
SAY THIS TO *WHO*?
I DON'T KNOW. SOMEONE'LL GET IN TOUCH.
I'M GUESSING NO ONE FINDS OUT YOUR *REAL NAME* IN THIS SCENARIO?
IF THEY *DO*, IT'LL NEVER COME BACK TO YOU.
OKAY, THEN.
ALL RIGHT.
THIS IS ABOUT *RICKY*?
YEAH. I'M HERE TO FIND OUT THE TRUTH.

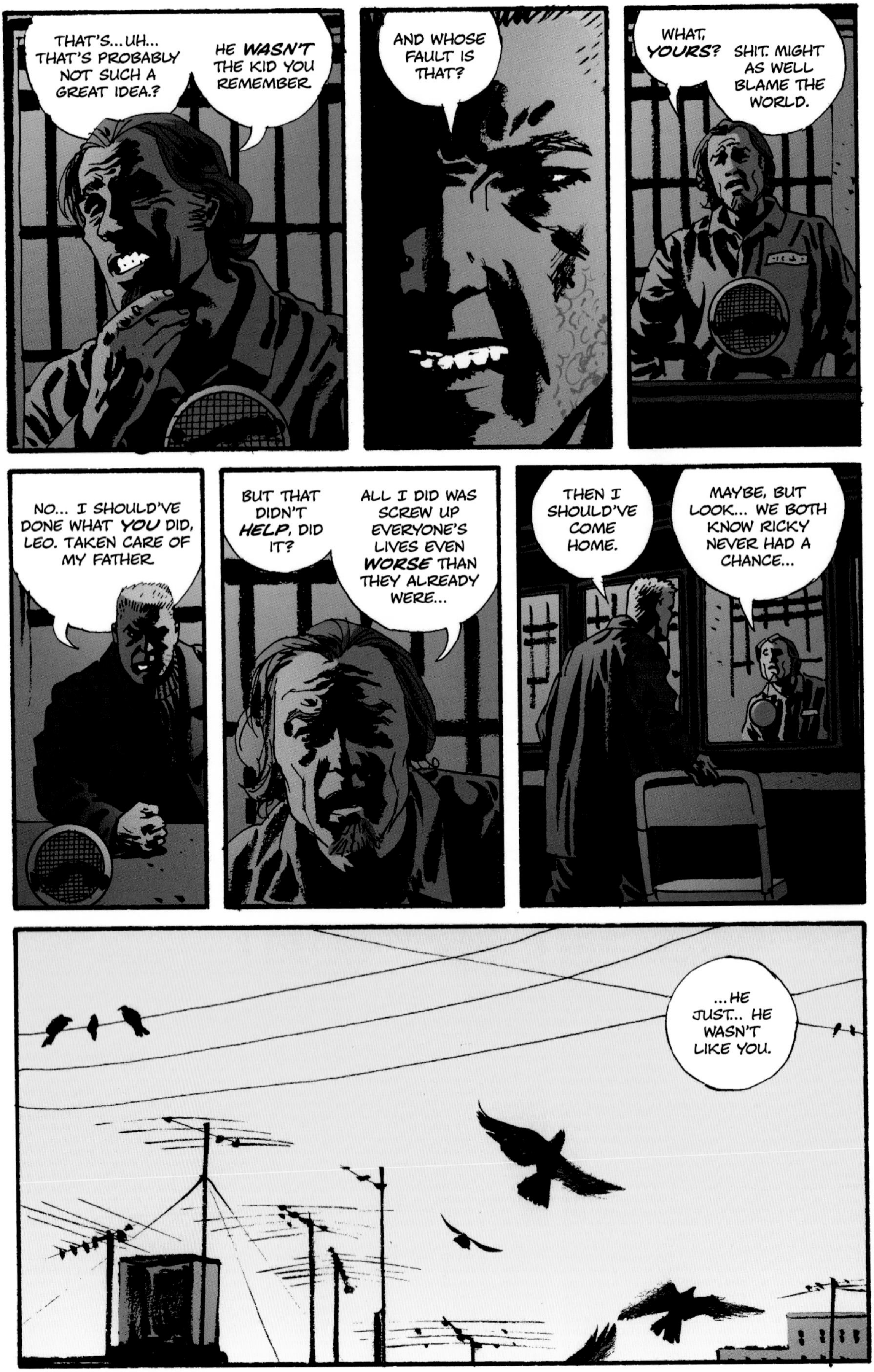
THAT'S...UH... THAT'S PROBABLY NOT SUCH A GREAT IDEA.?
HE WASN'T THE KID YOU REMEMBER
AND WHOSE FAULT IS THAT?
WHAT, YOURS?
SHIT. MIGHT AS WELL BLAME THE WORLD.
NO... I SHOULD'VE DONE WHAT YOU DID, LEO. TAKEN CARE OF MY FATHER
BUT THAT DIDN'T HELP, DID IT?
ALL I DID WAS SCREW UP EVERYONE'S LIVES EVEN WORSE THAN THEY ALREADY WERE...
THEN I SHOULD'VE COME HOME.
MAYBE, BUT LOOK... WE BOTH KNOW RICKY NEVER HAD A CHANCE...
...HE JUST... HE WASN'T LIKE YOU.

POP

WELL, ALL RIGHT, LITTLE RICKY...

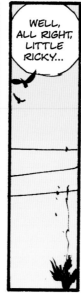

...LOOKS LIKE WE'RE GONNA MAKE A *MAN* OUTTA YOU, AFTER ALL.

IT'S DEAD... OH... OH.

I DON'T *FEEL GOOD,* DADDY... I WANNA GO HOME.

WHAT?! ARE YOU – *GOD DAMN IT!*

YOU LITTLE FUCKIN' *CRYBABY!*

WAIT! WAIT! DADDY – NO, I –

HIS FATHER'S IDEA OF TARGET PRACTICE. SHOOTING BIRDS ON THE CITY'S ROOFTOPS.

TRACY WOULD NEVER FORGET THE TREMOR IN HIS LITTLE BROTHER'S VOICE THAT DAY, AFTER HIS FIRST KILL.

HIS HEART CLEARLY *BROKEN* BY THE SAD, LONESOME DEATH OF A PIGEON.

POP

FOR HIS PART, TRACY FELT NOTHING.

HE'D BEEN ON THESE ROOFTOPS WITH DAD BEFORE AND DEATH DIDN'T PHASE HIM.

CERTAINLY NOT THE DEATH OF A BIRD.

POP

SO HE KEPT SHOOTING... HOPING TO WIPE OUT THE SOUND OF HIS BROTHER'S CRYING.

POP

POP

POP

WHAT I STILL DON'T GET IS WHY YOU THINK *THEY* KILLED RICKY?

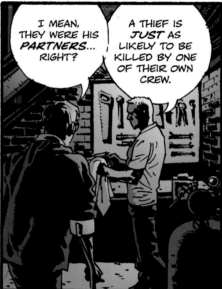

I MEAN, THEY WERE HIS *PARTNERS*... RIGHT?

A THIEF IS *JUST* AS LIKELY TO BE KILLED BY ONE OF THEIR OWN CREW.

YOU SHOULD KNOW *THAT*, JAKE.

OR WEREN'T YOU PAYING ATTENTION TO OUR PARENTS AT ALL?

SOMETIMES I FEEL LIKE THAT'S *ALL* I DID... PAY ATTENTION TO THOSE ASSHOLES.

THOUGHT THEY WERE SO COOL. I USED TO SIT ON THE BASEMENT STAIRS AND LISTEN TO THEM...

PLANNING THEIR JOBS, ARGUING, SMOKING... ALWAYS *SO* DANGEROUS, RIGHT?

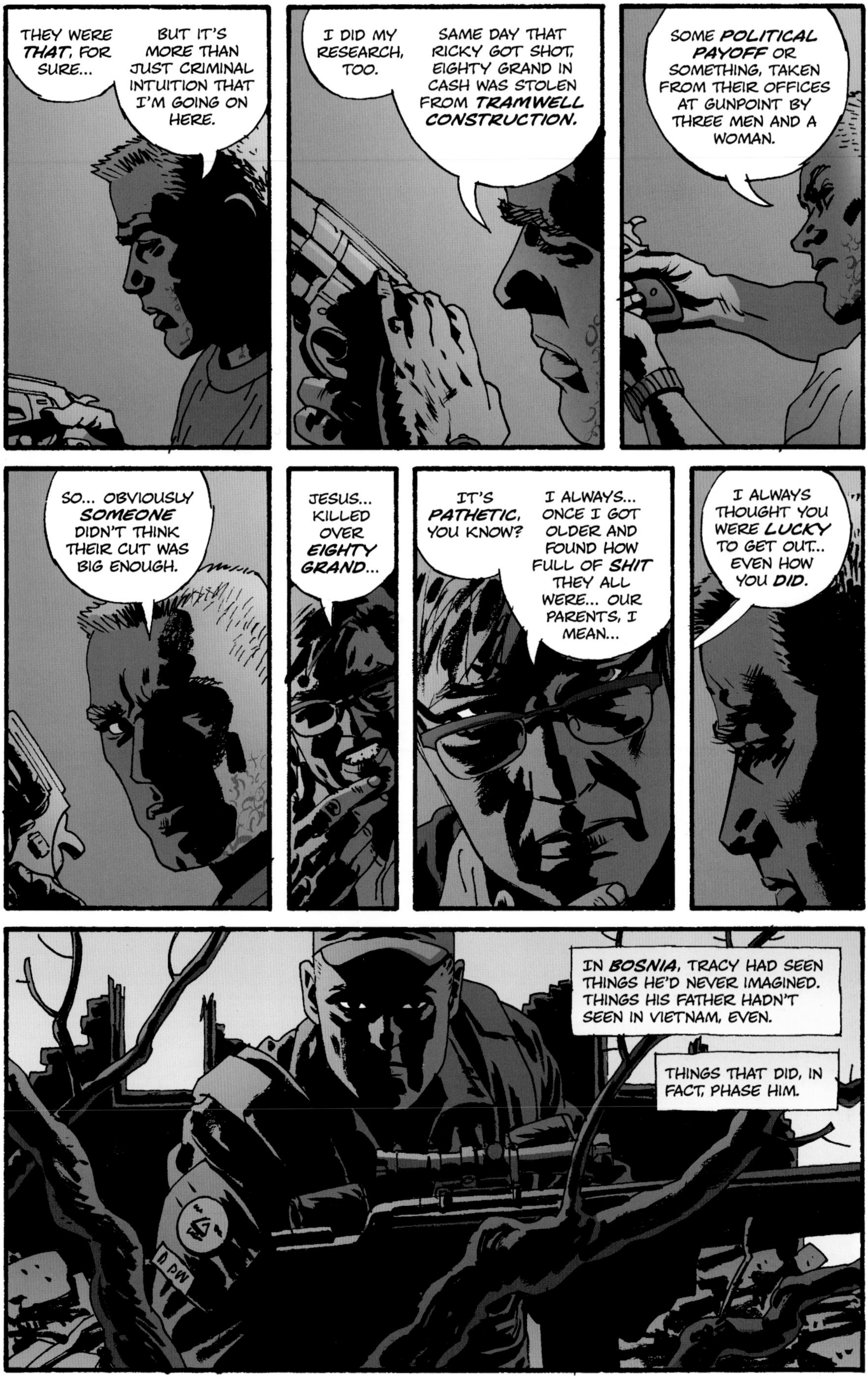

THEY WERE *THAT*, FOR SURE...
BUT IT'S MORE THAN JUST CRIMINAL INTUITION THAT I'M GOING ON HERE.
I DID MY RESEARCH, TOO.
SAME DAY THAT RICKY GOT SHOT, EIGHTY GRAND IN CASH WAS STOLEN FROM *TRAMWELL CONSTRUCTION.*
SOME *POLITICAL PAYOFF* OR SOMETHING, TAKEN FROM THEIR OFFICES AT GUNPOINT BY THREE MEN AND A WOMAN.
SO... OBVIOUSLY *SOMEONE* DIDN'T THINK THEIR CUT WAS BIG ENOUGH.
JESUS... KILLED OVER *EIGHTY GRAND*...
IT'S *PATHETIC*, YOU KNOW?
I ALWAYS... ONCE I GOT OLDER AND FOUND HOW FULL OF *SHIT* THEY ALL WERE... OUR PARENTS, I MEAN...
I ALWAYS THOUGHT YOU WERE *LUCKY* TO GET OUT... EVEN HOW YOU *DID*.
IN *BOSNIA*, TRACY HAD SEEN THINGS HE'D NEVER IMAGINED. THINGS HIS FATHER HADN'T SEEN IN VIETNAM, EVEN.
THINGS THAT DID, IN FACT, PHASE HIM.

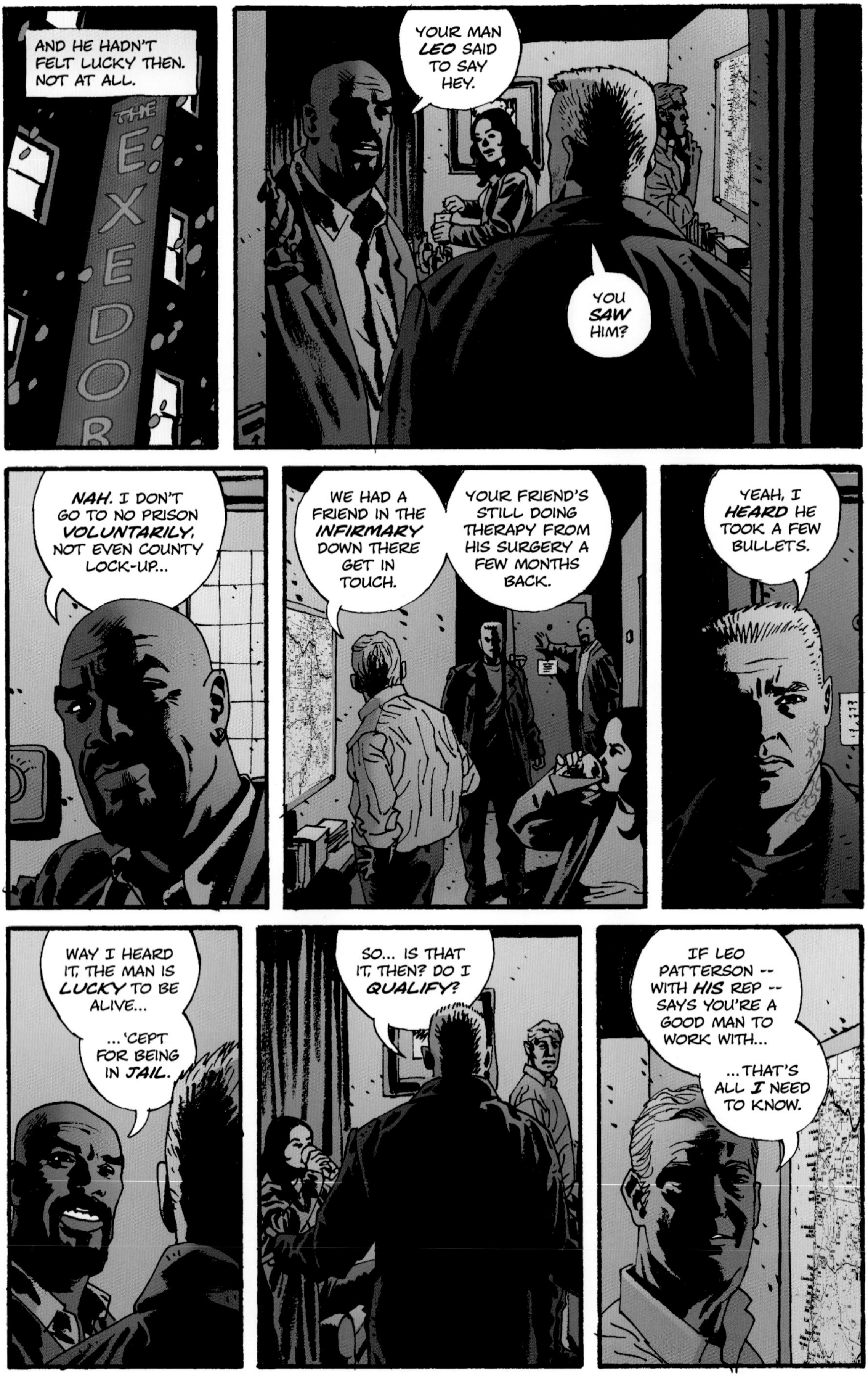
AND HE HADN'T FELT LUCKY THEN. NOT AT ALL.
THE EXEDOR
YOUR MAN LEO SAID TO SAY HEY.
YOU SAW HIM?
NAH. I DON'T GO TO NO PRISON VOLUNTARILY, NOT EVEN COUNTY LOCK-UP...
WE HAD A FRIEND IN THE INFIRMARY DOWN THERE GET IN TOUCH.
YOUR FRIEND'S STILL DOING THERAPY FROM HIS SURGERY A FEW MONTHS BACK.
YEAH, I HEARD HE TOOK A FEW BULLETS.
WAY I HEARD IT, THE MAN IS LUCKY TO BE ALIVE...
...'CEPT FOR BEING IN JAIL.
SO... IS THAT IT, THEN? DO I QUALIFY?
IF LEO PATTERSON -- WITH HIS REP -- SAYS YOU'RE A GOOD MAN TO WORK WITH...
...THAT'S ALL I NEED TO KNOW.

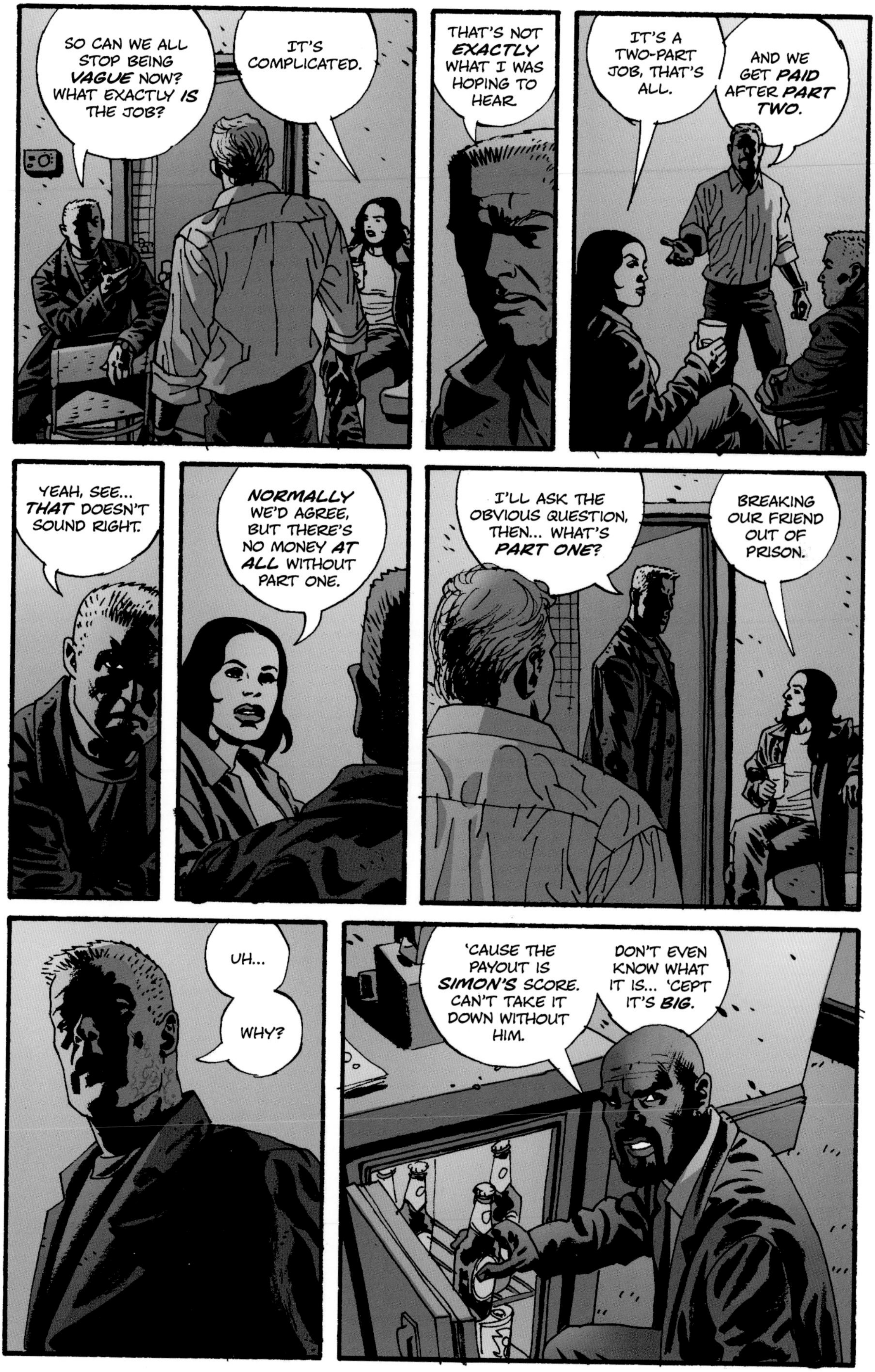
SO CAN WE ALL STOP BEING VAGUE NOW? WHAT EXACTLY IS THE JOB?
IT'S COMPLICATED.
THAT'S NOT EXACTLY WHAT I WAS HOPING TO HEAR.
IT'S A TWO-PART JOB, THAT'S ALL.
AND WE GET PAID AFTER PART TWO.
YEAH, SEE... THAT DOESN'T SOUND RIGHT.
NORMALLY WE'D AGREE, BUT THERE'S NO MONEY AT ALL WITHOUT PART ONE.
I'LL ASK THE OBVIOUS QUESTION, THEN... WHAT'S PART ONE?
BREAKING OUR FRIEND OUT OF PRISON.
UH...
WHY?
'CAUSE THE PAYOUT IS SIMON'S SCORE. CAN'T TAKE IT DOWN WITHOUT HIM.
DON'T EVEN KNOW WHAT IT IS... 'CEPT IT'S BIG.

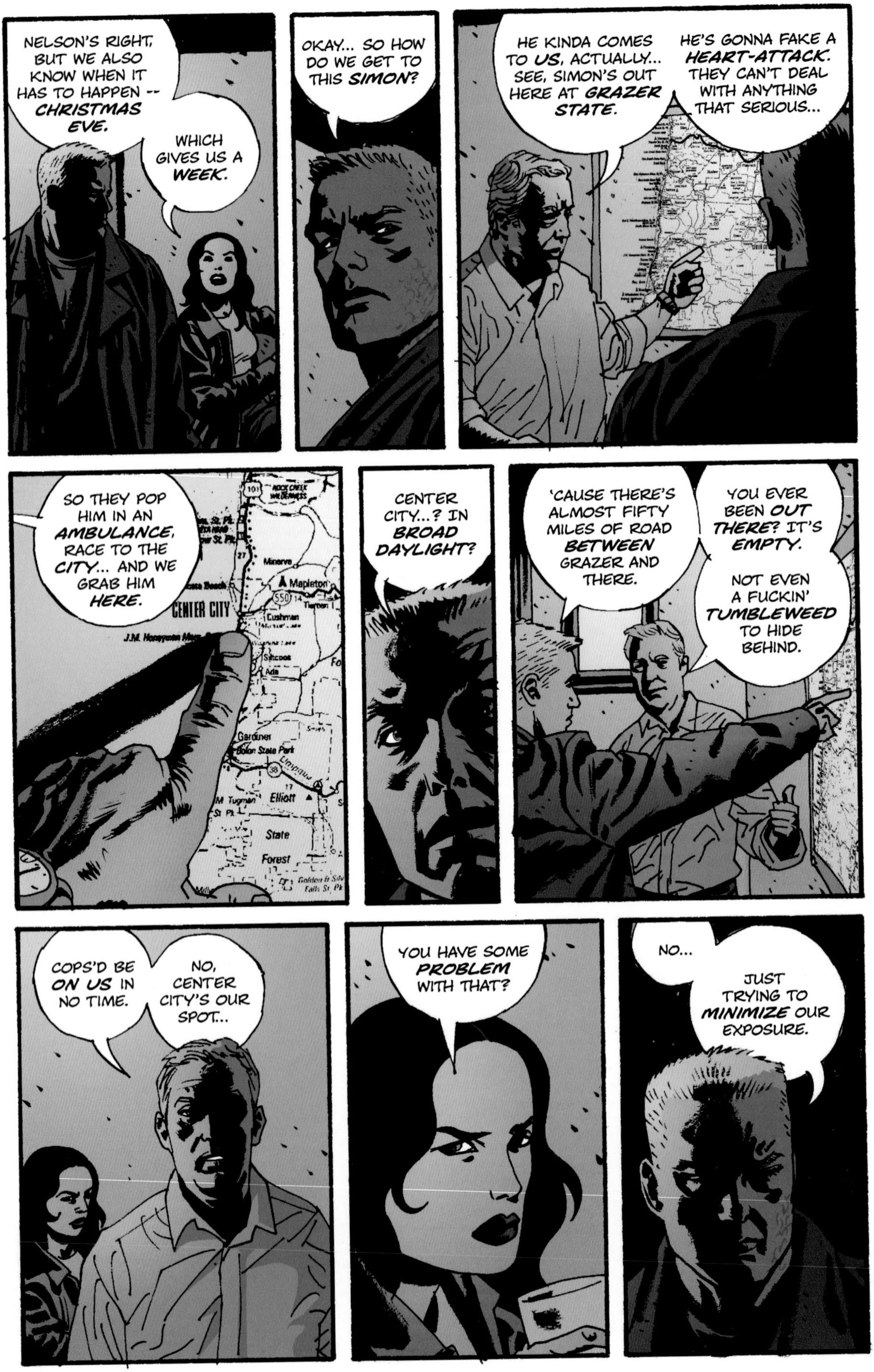
NELSON'S RIGHT, BUT WE ALSO KNOW WHEN IT HAS TO HAPPEN -- CHRISTMAS EVE.
WHICH GIVES US A WEEK.
OKAY... SO HOW DO WE GET TO THIS SIMON?
HE KINDA COMES TO US, ACTUALLY... SEE, SIMON'S OUT HERE AT GRAZER STATE.
HE'S GONNA FAKE A HEART-ATTACK. THEY CAN'T DEAL WITH ANYTHING THAT SERIOUS...
SO THEY POP HIM IN AN AMBULANCE, RACE TO THE CITY... AND WE GRAB HIM HERE.
Minerva
Mapleton
CENTER CITY
Cushman
Gardiner
Elliott
State
Forest
CENTER CITY...? IN BROAD DAYLIGHT?
'CAUSE THERE'S ALMOST FIFTY MILES OF ROAD BETWEEN GRAZER AND THERE.
YOU EVER BEEN OUT THERE? IT'S EMPTY.
NOT EVEN A FUCKIN' TUMBLEWEED TO HIDE BEHIND.
COPS'D BE ON US IN NO TIME.
NO, CENTER CITY'S OUR SPOT...
YOU HAVE SOME PROBLEM WITH THAT?
NO...
JUST TRYING TO MINIMIZE OUR EXPOSURE.

TRACY HADN'T PLANNED TO SEE CENTER CITY AGAIN ANYTIME SOON... BUT THE PLAN WAS DECENT.

THOUGH HE FOUND ONE PART TO IMPROVE ON, THAT WOULD HOPEFULLY MAKE THE TRIP SMOOTHER, AND SHORTER

SIMON WAS APPARENTLY THE PLANNER IN THE CREW, WHAT THEY USED TO CALL A JUGGER OR JUGMARKER, IN THE OLD DAYS.

THE ONE WHO FOUND THE SCORES AND MAPPED OUT HOW TO TAKE THEM DOWN.

A FEW MONTHS AGO, HE'D BEEN CAUGHT DRIVING DRUNK AND HIS PAROLE WAS REVOKED.

BUT EVEN LOCKED AWAY IN PRISON, SIMON WAS STILL FIGURING ANGLES.

MEDIC!

LIKE WHICH MIXTURE OF **CRYSTAL METH** AND **VALIUM** WOULD MIMIC THE MOST BASIC SYMPTOMS OF A HEART-ATTACK.

JESUS... HIS **HEART-RATE'S** GOING CRAZY.

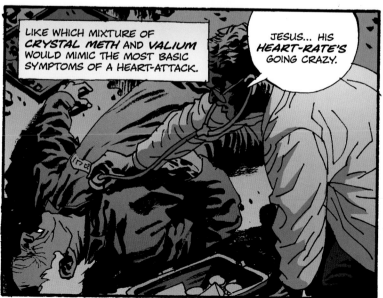

...MY ARM... FEELS **WRONG**...

WE GOTTA GET HIM TO AN E.R. - NOW.

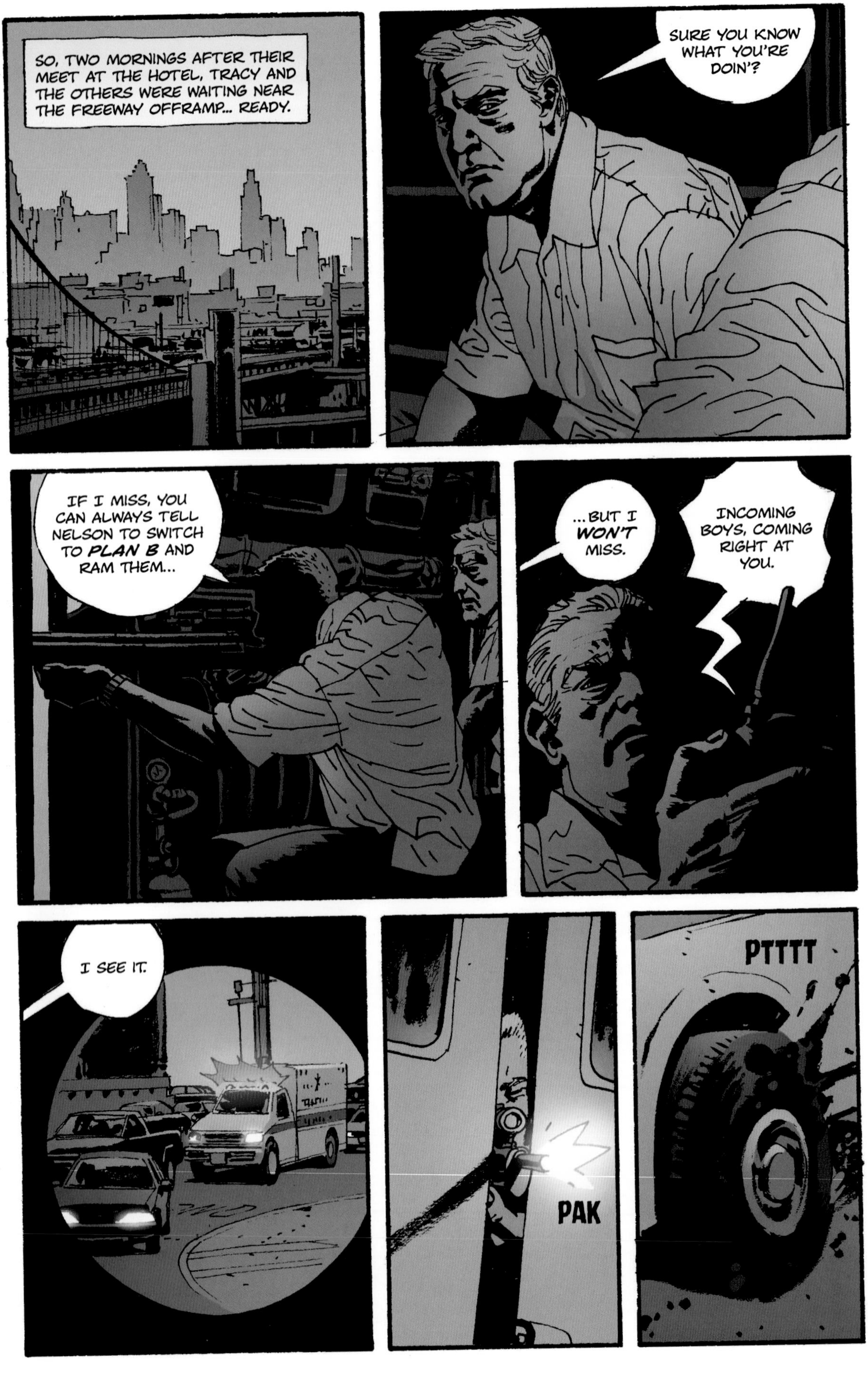
SO, TWO MORNINGS AFTER THEIR MEET AT THE HOTEL, TRACY AND THE OTHERS WERE WAITING NEAR THE FREEWAY OFFRAMP... READY.
SURE YOU KNOW WHAT YOU'RE DOIN'?
IF I MISS, YOU CAN ALWAYS TELL NELSON TO SWITCH TO *PLAN B* AND RAM THEM...
...BUT I *WON'T* MISS.
INCOMING BOYS, COMING RIGHT AT YOU.
I SEE IT.
PAK
PTTTT

DID YOU *HIT 'EM?*

SEE FOR YOURSELF, THEY'RE ALREADY PULLING OVER

WE GOTTA *MOVE.*

RIGHT. LET'S GO...

MAL – KEEP WATCH FOR THE PIGS AND FOLLOW OUR LEAD.

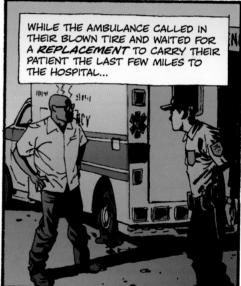

WHILE THE AMBULANCE CALLED IN THEIR BLOWN TIRE AND WAITED FOR A *REPLACEMENT* TO CARRY THEIR PATIENT THE LAST FEW MILES TO THE HOSPITAL...

...TRACY AND GRAY CIRCLED THE BLOCK IN A NEARLY IDENTICAL AMBULANCE STOLEN EARLIER THAT MORNING.

YOU *READY?*

I'M ONLY DRIVING FOR THIS PART... SO I'M *ALREADY* WORKING.

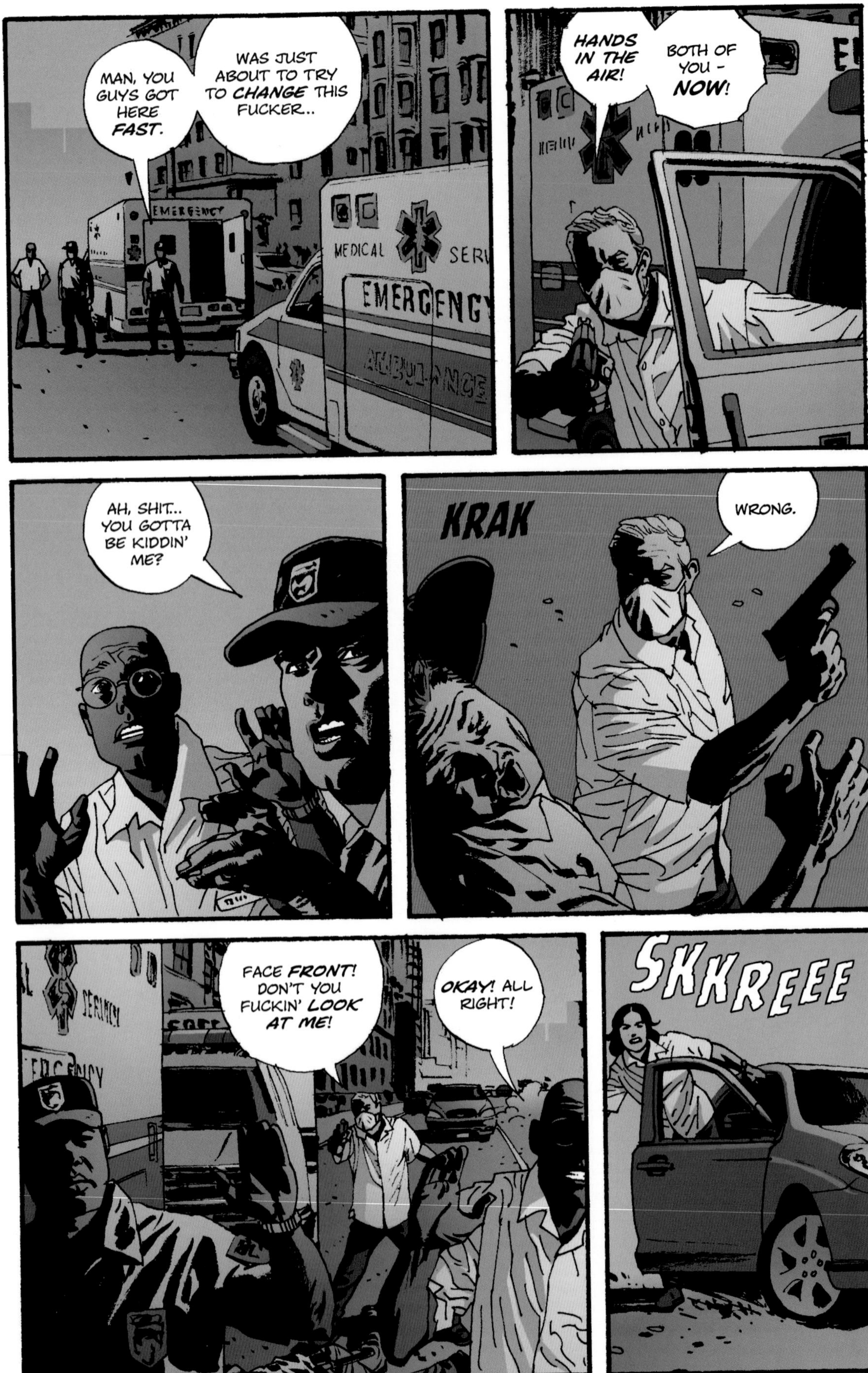
MAN, YOU GUYS GOT HERE **FAST**.
WAS JUST ABOUT TO TRY TO **CHANGE** THIS FUCKER..
EMERGENCY
MEDICAL SERV
EMERGENCY
HANDS IN THE AIR!
BOTH OF YOU - **NOW**!
AH, SHIT... YOU GOTTA BE KIDDIN' ME?
KRAK
WRONG.
FACE **FRONT**! DON'T YOU FUCKIN' **LOOK AT ME**!
OKAY! ALL RIGHT!
SKKREEE

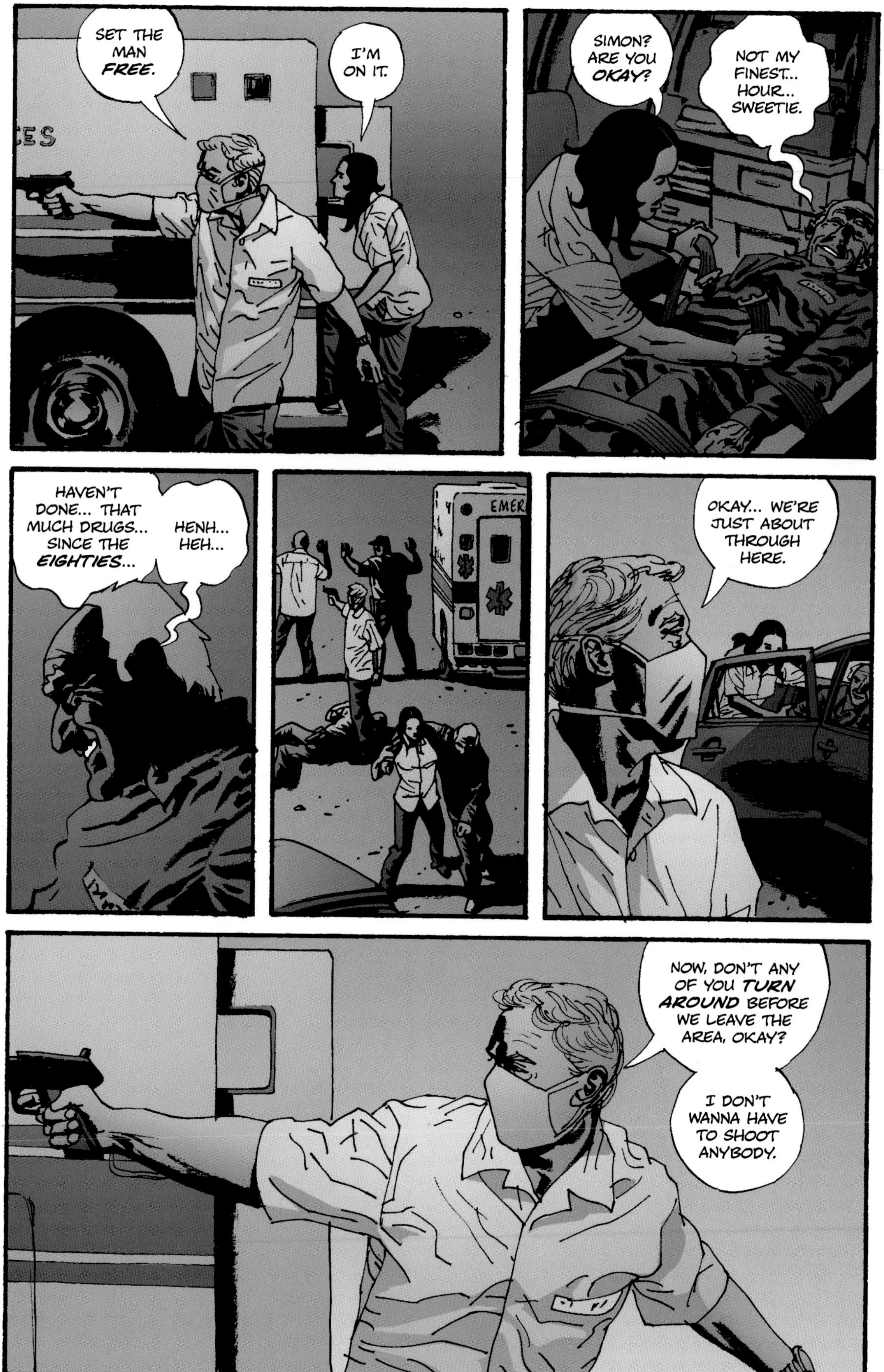
SET THE MAN FREE.
I'M ON IT.
SIMON? ARE YOU OKAY?
NOT MY FINEST... HOUR.. SWEETIE.
HAVEN'T DONE... THAT MUCH DRUGS... SINCE THE EIGHTIES...
HENH... HEH...
EMER
OKAY... WE'RE JUST ABOUT THROUGH HERE.
NOW, DON'T ANY OF YOU TURN AROUND BEFORE WE LEAVE THE AREA, OKAY?
I DON'T WANNA HAVE TO SHOOT ANYBODY.

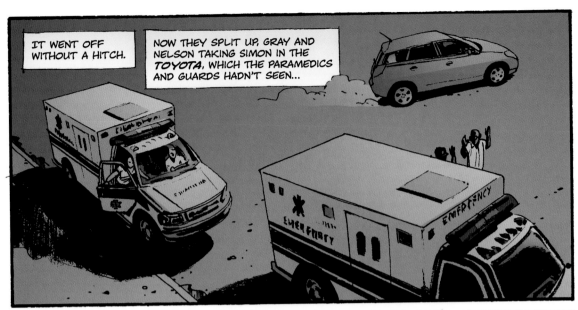

IT WENT OFF WITHOUT A HITCH.

NOW THEY SPLIT UP, GRAY AND NELSON TAKING SIMON IN THE *TOYOTA*, WHICH THE PARAMEDICS AND GUARDS HADN'T SEEN...

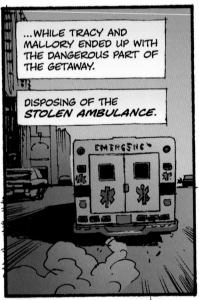

...WHILE TRACY AND MALLORY ENDED UP WITH THE DANGEROUS PART OF THE GETAWAY.

DISPOSING OF THE *STOLEN AMBULANCE.*

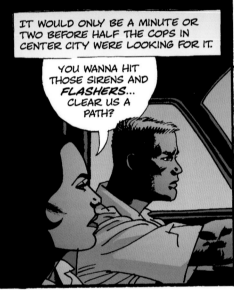

IT WOULD ONLY BE A MINUTE OR TWO BEFORE HALF THE COPS IN CENTER CITY WERE LOOKING FOR IT.

YOU WANNA HIT THOSE SIRENS AND *FLASHERS*... CLEAR US A PATH?

NAH... LET'S NOT DRAW ANY *MORE* ATTENTION THAN WE HAVE TO.

A COP JUST DROVE PAST BACK THERE.

YEAH, THE *OTHER* WAY... WE'RE GOOD.

TRUST ME. I KNOW HOW TO BLEND INTO THE BACKGROUND.

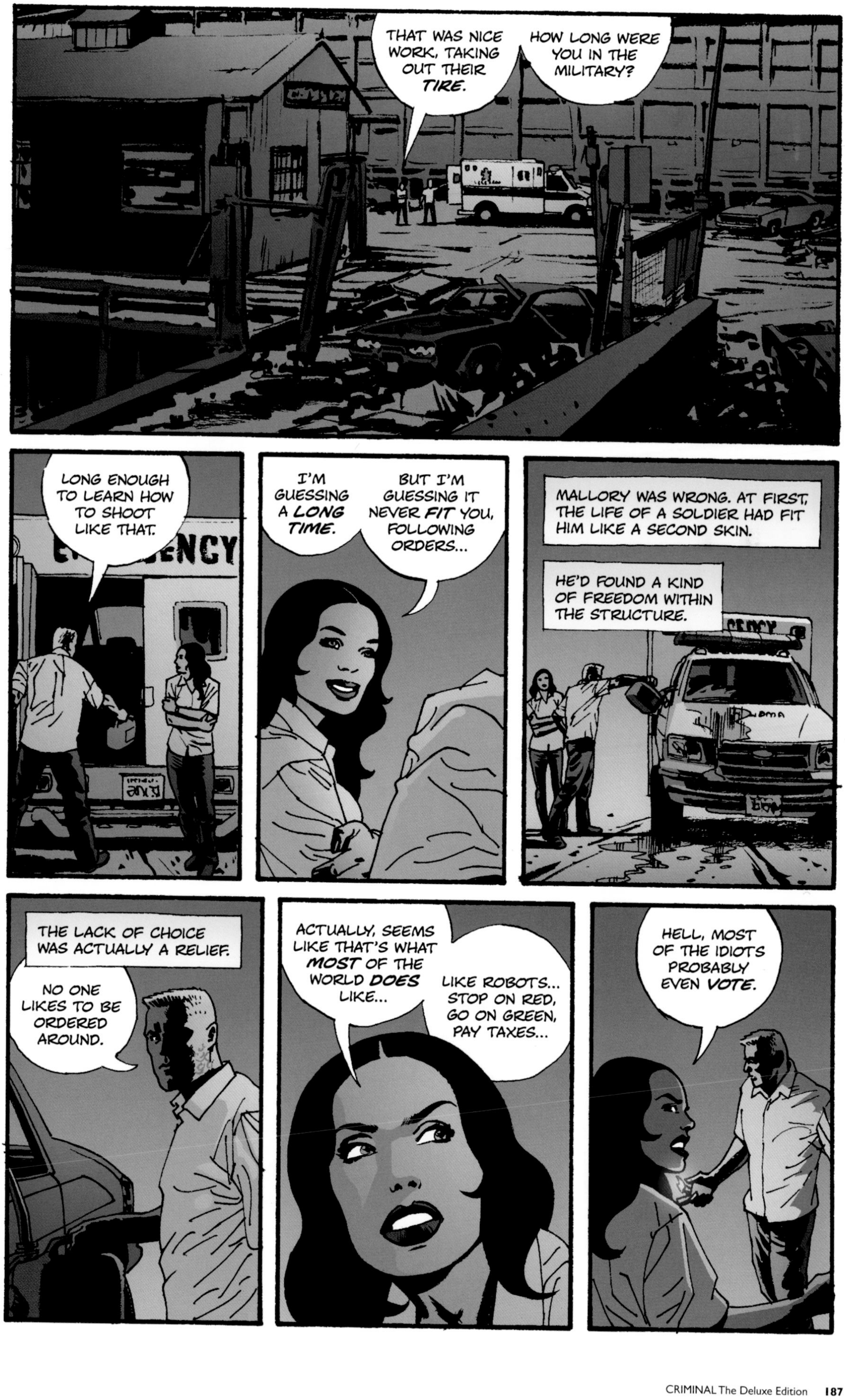
THAT WAS NICE WORK, TAKING OUT THEIR TIRE.
HOW LONG WERE YOU IN THE MILITARY?
LONG ENOUGH TO LEARN HOW TO SHOOT LIKE THAT.
I'M GUESSING A LONG TIME.
BUT I'M GUESSING IT NEVER FIT YOU, FOLLOWING ORDERS...
MALLORY WAS WRONG. AT FIRST, THE LIFE OF A SOLDIER HAD FIT HIM LIKE A SECOND SKIN.
HE'D FOUND A KIND OF FREEDOM WITHIN THE STRUCTURE.
THE LACK OF CHOICE WAS ACTUALLY A RELIEF.
NO ONE LIKES TO BE ORDERED AROUND.
ACTUALLY, SEEMS LIKE THAT'S WHAT MOST OF THE WORLD DOES LIKE...
LIKE ROBOTS... STOP ON RED, GO ON GREEN, PAY TAXES...
HELL, MOST OF THE IDIOTS PROBABLY EVEN VOTE.

CAN YOU **STOP** TALKING? I'M TRYING TO TORCH A VAN HERE...

OH, AM I RUINING YOUR BIG MOMENT?

YES.

FOR A MOMENT, WHEN SHE LAUGHED, HE KNEW WHAT RICK HAD SEEN IN HER

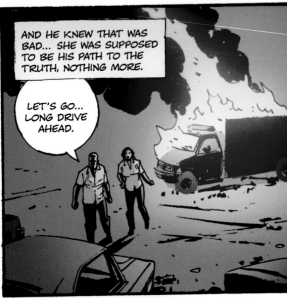

AND HE KNEW THAT WAS BAD... SHE WAS SUPPOSED TO BE HIS PATH TO THE TRUTH, NOTHING MORE.

LET'S GO... LONG DRIVE AHEAD.

ANYTHING ELSE WAS TROUBLE.

HEY, YEAH, THIS IS GUMBIE, AT THE JUNK-YARD...

YOU STILL LOOKIN' FOR A **MEAN-LOOKIN'** DUDE WITH A **BURN SCAR** ON HIS FACE ON ONE SIDE?

'CAUSE I THINK I JUST GOT HIS LICENSE PLATE FOR YA'...

Part Three

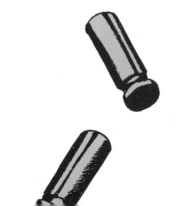

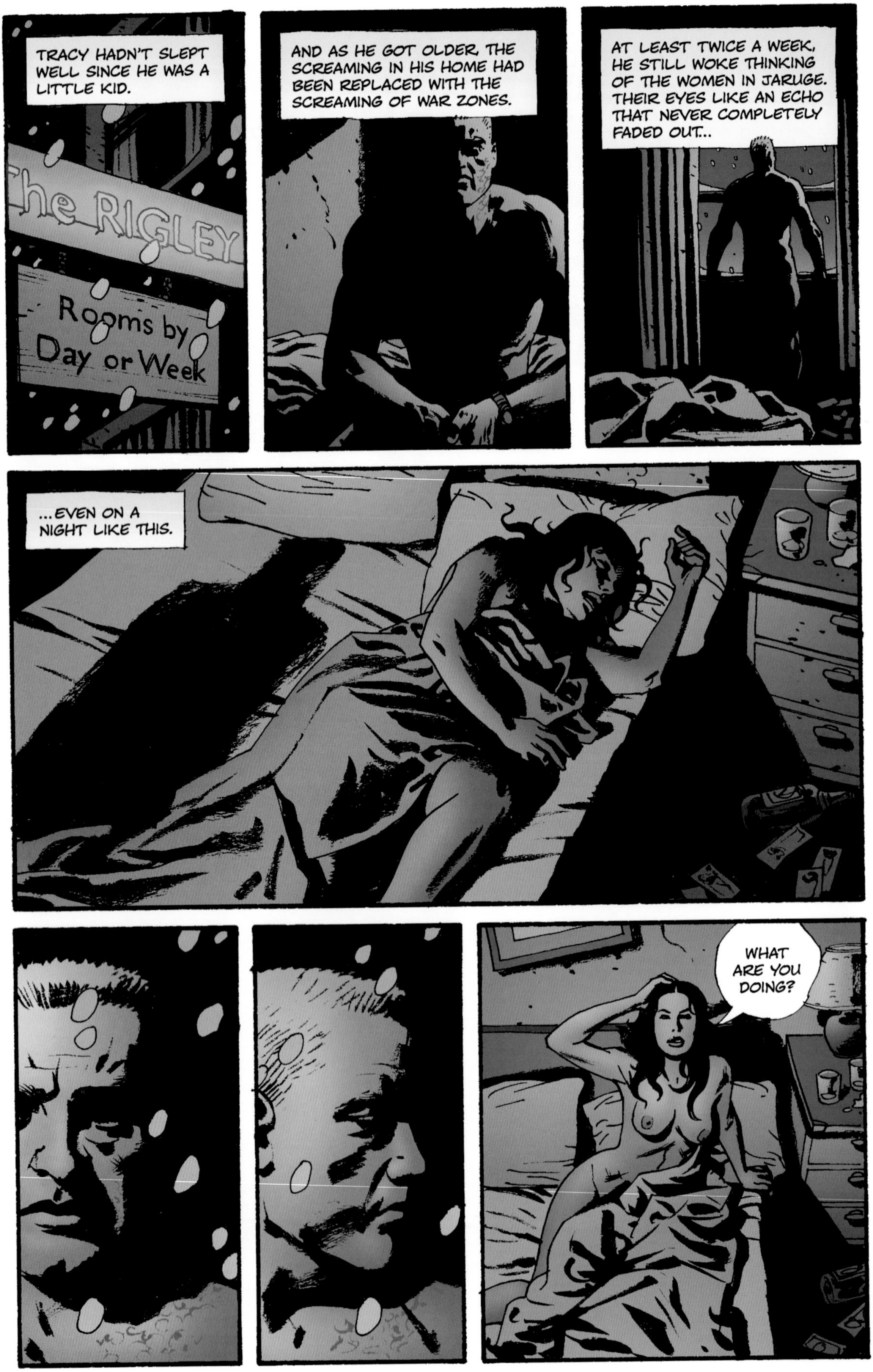
TRACY HADN'T SLEPT WELL SINCE HE WAS A LITTLE KID.
The RIGLEY
Rooms by Day or Week
AND AS HE GOT OLDER, THE SCREAMING IN HIS HOME HAD BEEN REPLACED WITH THE SCREAMING OF WAR ZONES.
AT LEAST TWICE A WEEK, HE STILL WOKE THINKING OF THE WOMEN IN JARUGE. THEIR EYES LIKE AN ECHO THAT NEVER COMPLETELY FADED OUT...
...EVEN ON A NIGHT LIKE THIS.
WHAT ARE YOU DOING?

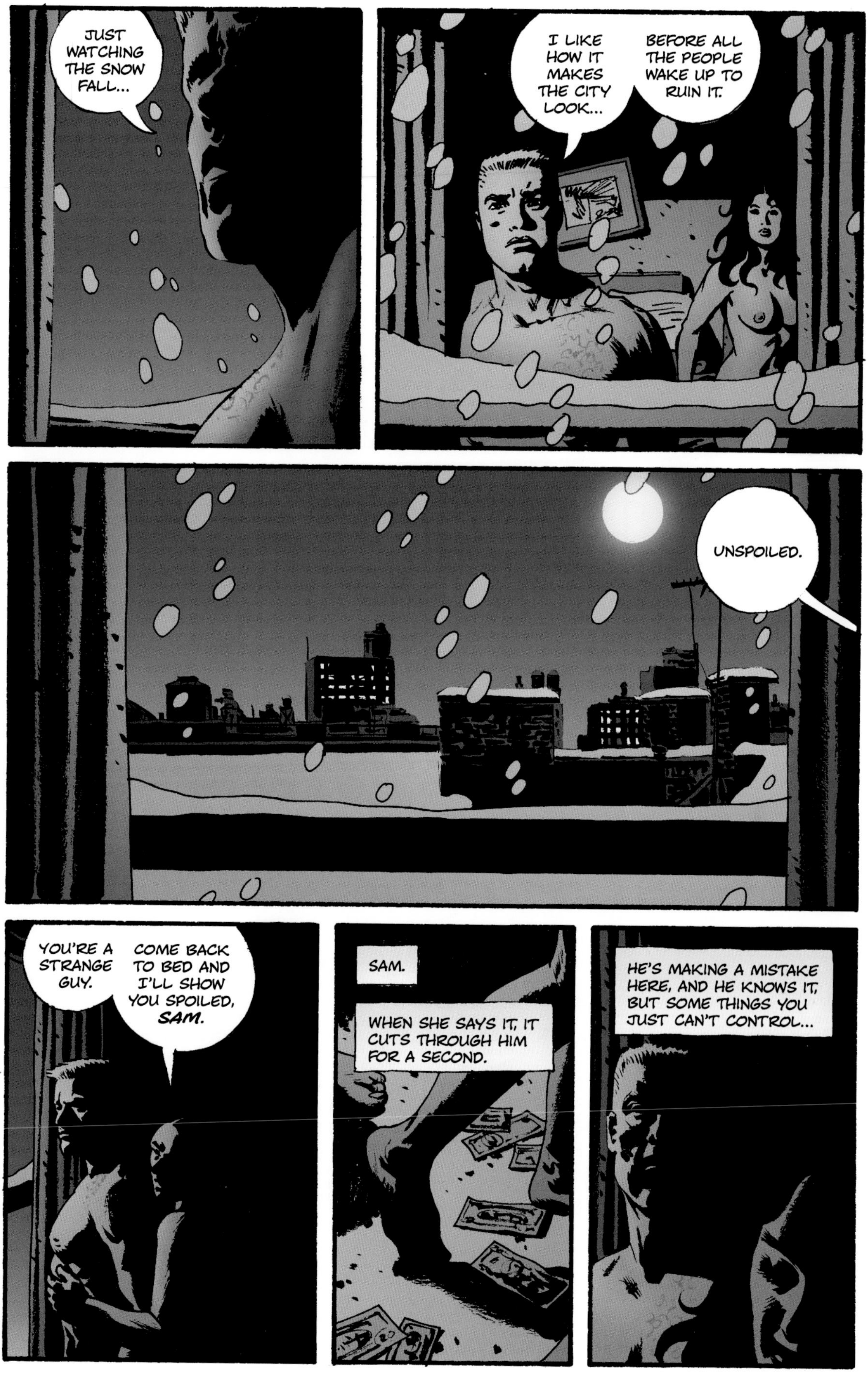
JUST WATCHING THE SNOW FALL...
I LIKE HOW IT MAKES THE CITY LOOK...
BEFORE ALL THE PEOPLE WAKE UP TO RUIN IT.
UNSPOILED.
YOU'RE A STRANGE GUY.
COME BACK TO BED AND I'LL SHOW YOU SPOILED, *SAM*.
SAM.
WHEN SHE SAYS IT, IT CUTS THROUGH HIM FOR A SECOND.
HE'S MAKING A MISTAKE HERE, AND HE KNOWS IT, BUT SOME THINGS YOU JUST CAN'T CONTROL...

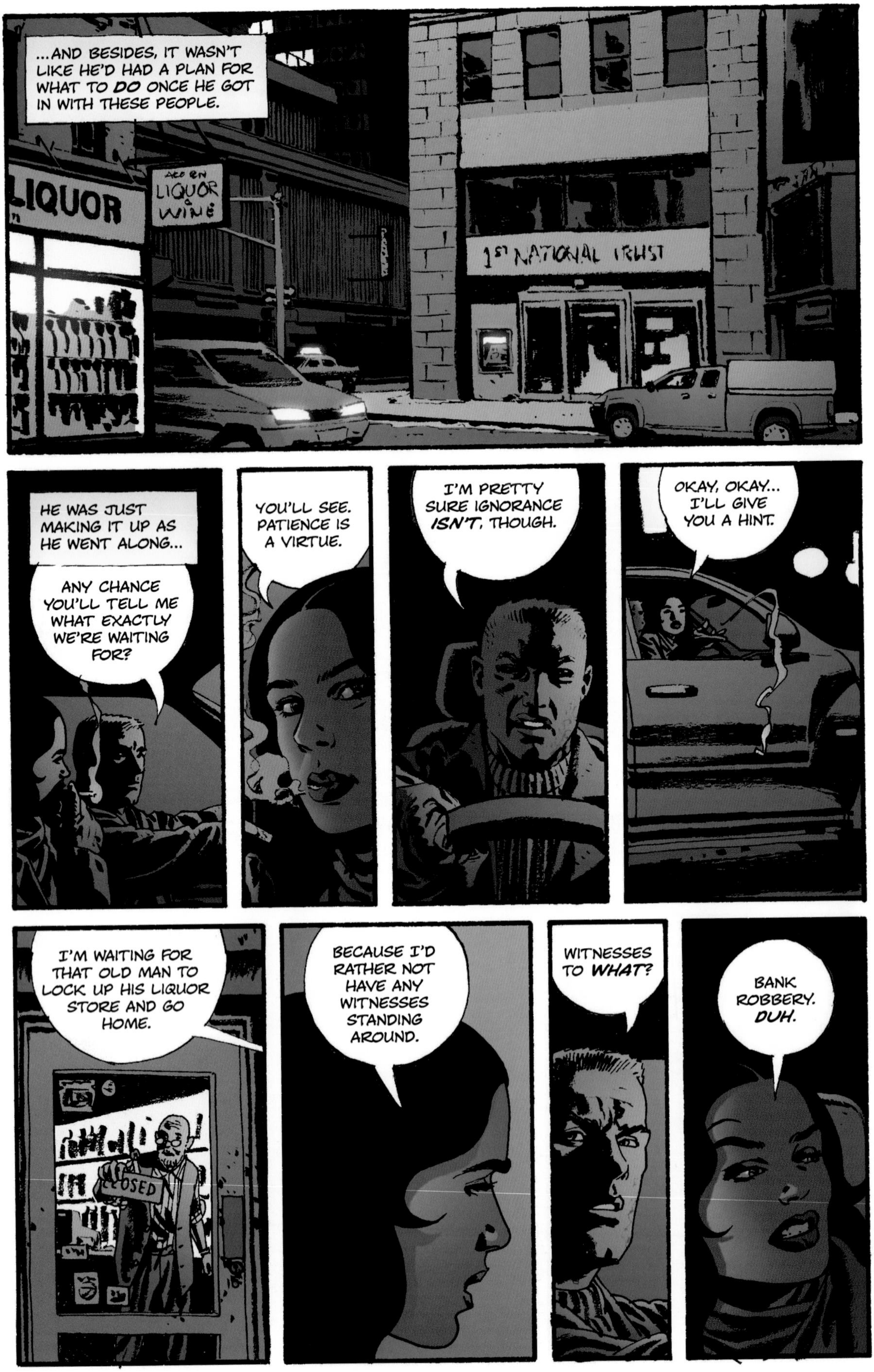
...AND BESIDES, IT WASN'T LIKE HE'D HAD A PLAN FOR WHAT TO ***DO*** ONCE HE GOT IN WITH THESE PEOPLE.
LIQUOR
LIQUOR & WINE
1ST NATIONAL TRUST
HE WAS JUST MAKING IT UP AS HE WENT ALONG...
ANY CHANCE YOU'LL TELL ME WHAT EXACTLY WE'RE WAITING FOR?
YOU'LL SEE. PATIENCE IS A VIRTUE.
I'M PRETTY SURE IGNORANCE ***ISN'T***, THOUGH.
OKAY, OKAY... I'LL GIVE YOU A HINT.
I'M WAITING FOR THAT OLD MAN TO LOCK UP HIS LIQUOR STORE AND GO HOME.
CLOSED
BECAUSE I'D RATHER NOT HAVE ANY WITNESSES STANDING AROUND.
WITNESSES TO ***WHAT?***
BANK ROBBERY. ***DUH.***

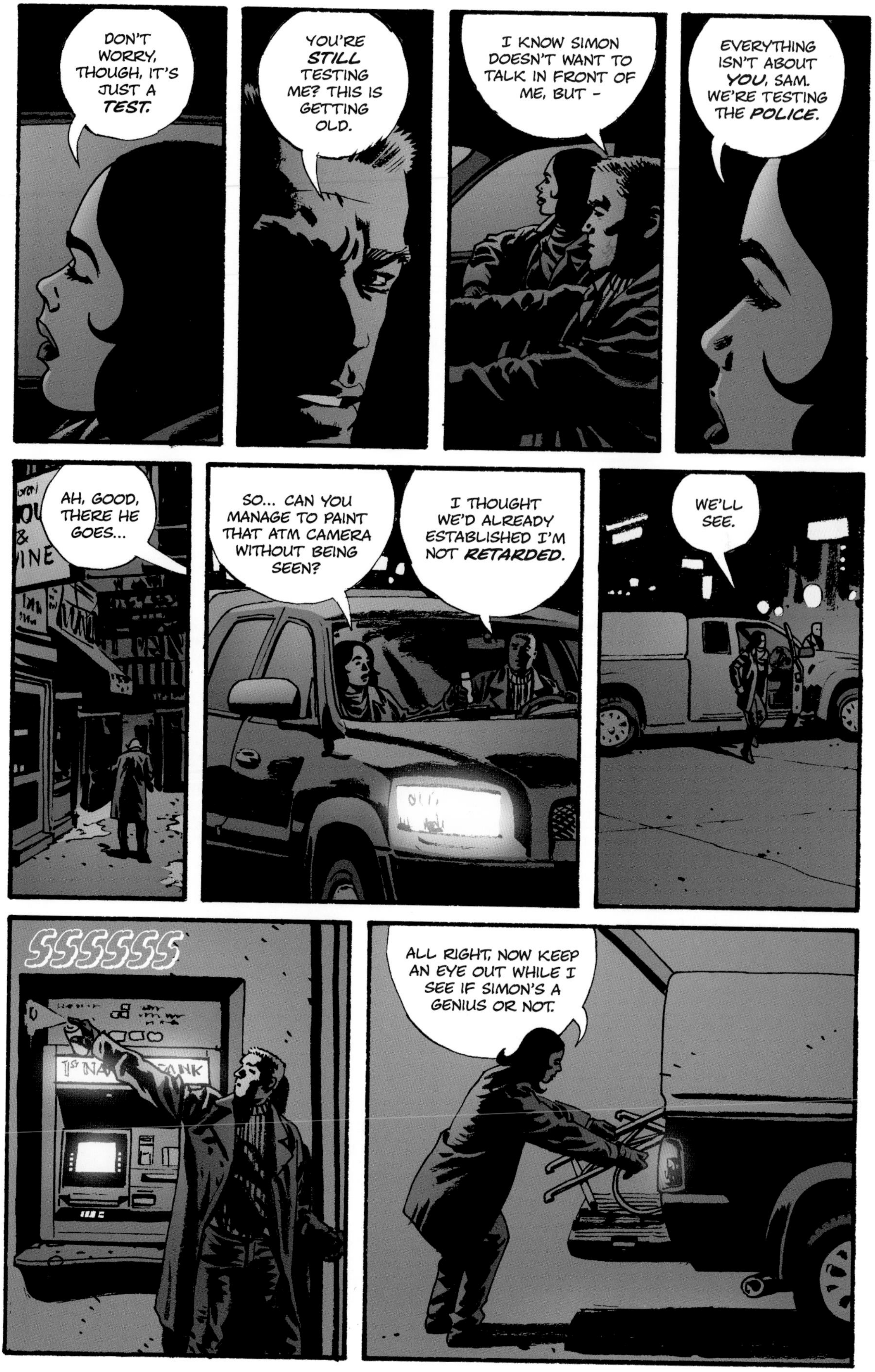
DON'T WORRY, THOUGH, IT'S JUST A TEST.
YOU'RE STILL TESTING ME? THIS IS GETTING OLD.
I KNOW SIMON DOESN'T WANT TO TALK IN FRONT OF ME, BUT -
EVERYTHING ISN'T ABOUT YOU, SAM. WE'RE TESTING THE POLICE.
AH, GOOD, THERE HE GOES...
SO... CAN YOU MANAGE TO PAINT THAT ATM CAMERA WITHOUT BEING SEEN?
I THOUGHT WE'D ALREADY ESTABLISHED I'M NOT RETARDED.
WE'LL SEE.
SSSSSS
ALL RIGHT, NOW KEEP AN EYE OUT WHILE I SEE IF SIMON'S A GENIUS OR NOT.

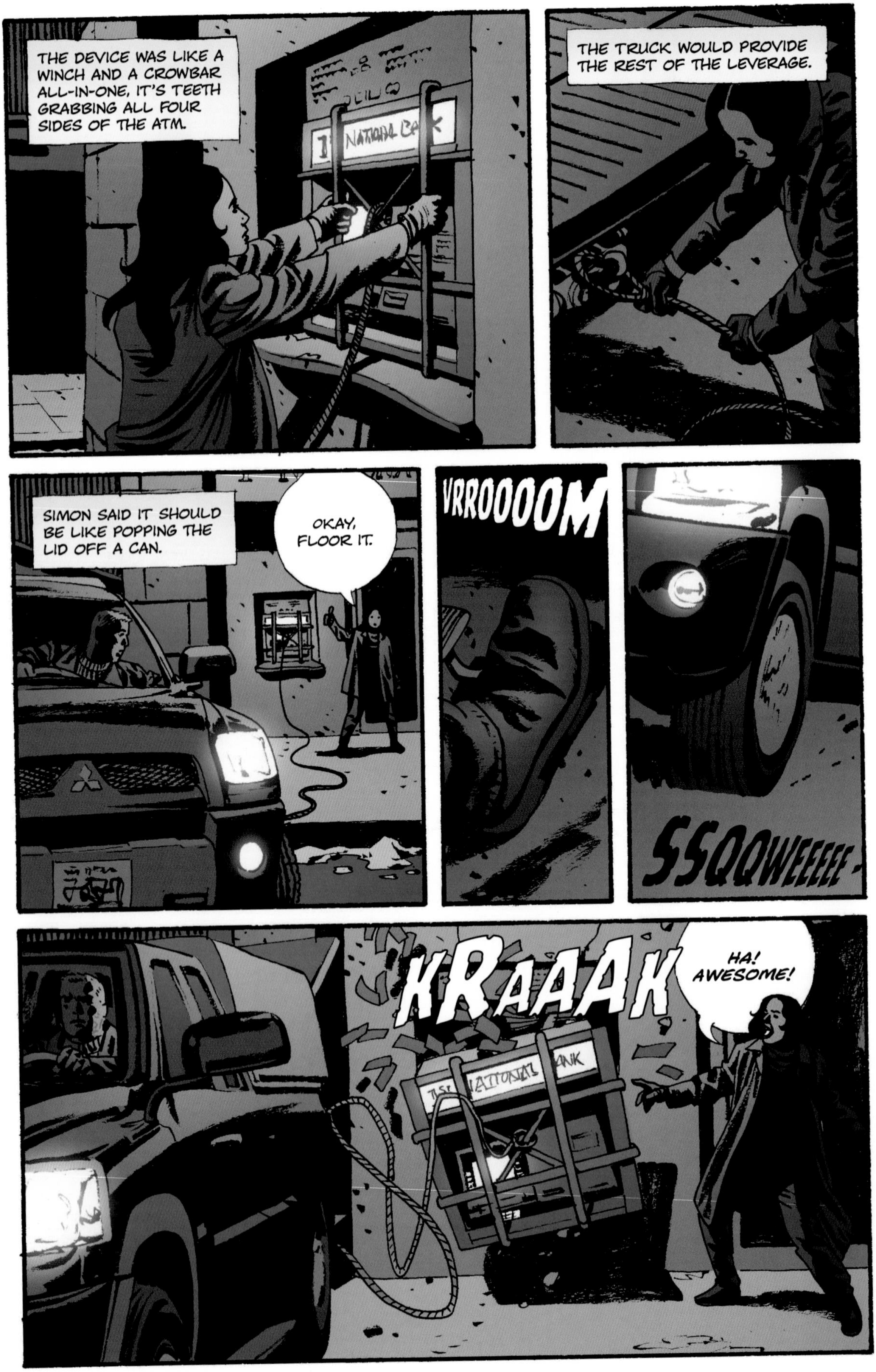
THE DEVICE WAS LIKE A WINCH AND A CROWBAR ALL-IN-ONE, IT'S TEETH GRABBING ALL FOUR SIDES OF THE ATM.
THE TRUCK WOULD PROVIDE THE REST OF THE LEVERAGE.
SIMON SAID IT SHOULD BE LIKE POPPING THE LID OFF A CAN.
OKAY, FLOOR IT.
VRROOOOM
SSQQWEEEEE-
KRAAAK
HA! AWESOME!

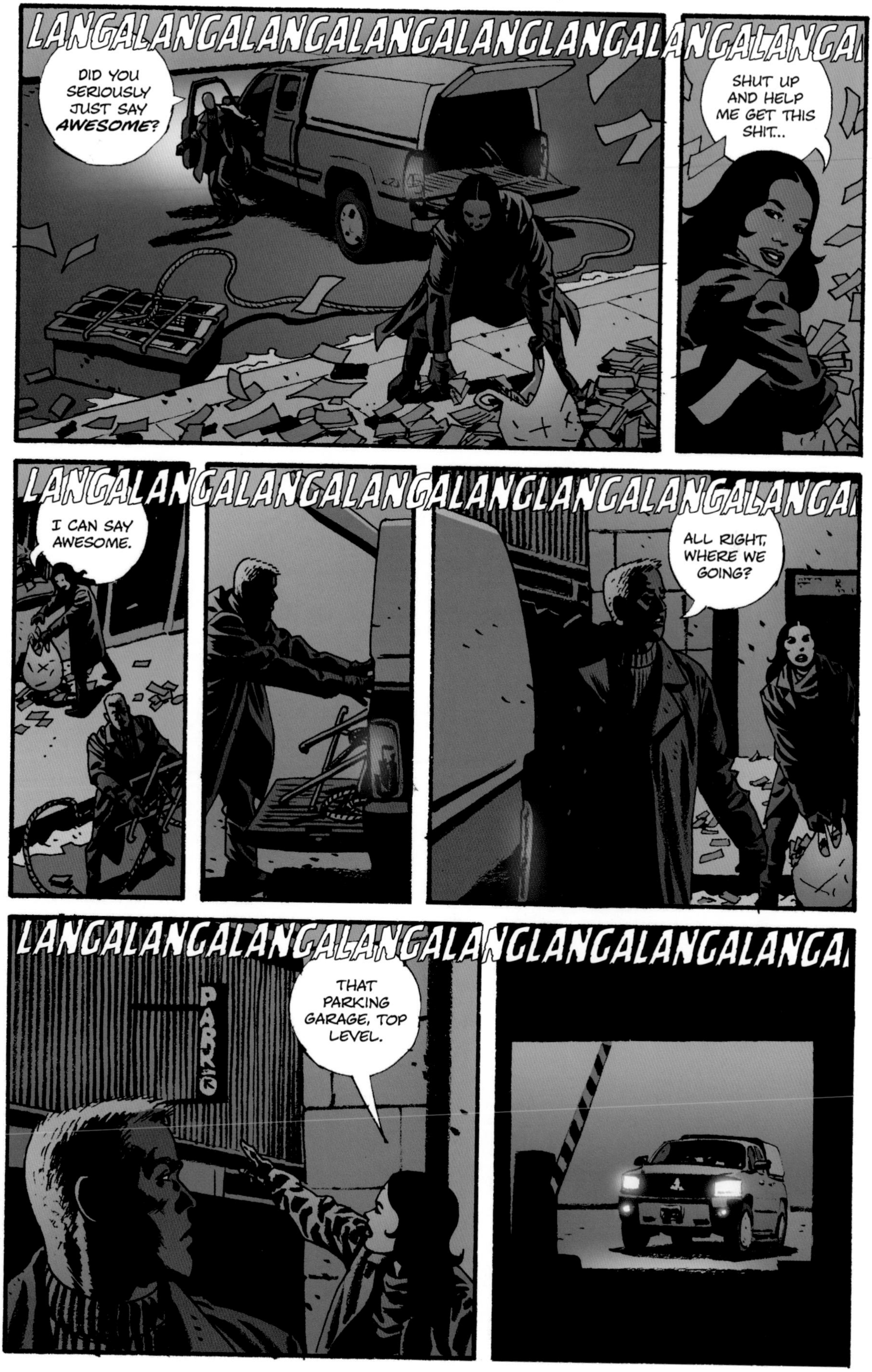
LANGALANGALANGALANGALANGLANGALANGALANGA
DID YOU SERIOUSLY JUST SAY AWESOME?
SHUT UP AND HELP ME GET THIS SHIT...
LANGALANGALANGALANGALANGLANGALANGALANGA
I CAN SAY AWESOME.
ALL RIGHT, WHERE WE GOING?
LANGALANGALANGALANGALANGLANGALANGALANGA
PARKER
THAT PARKING GARAGE, TOP LEVEL.

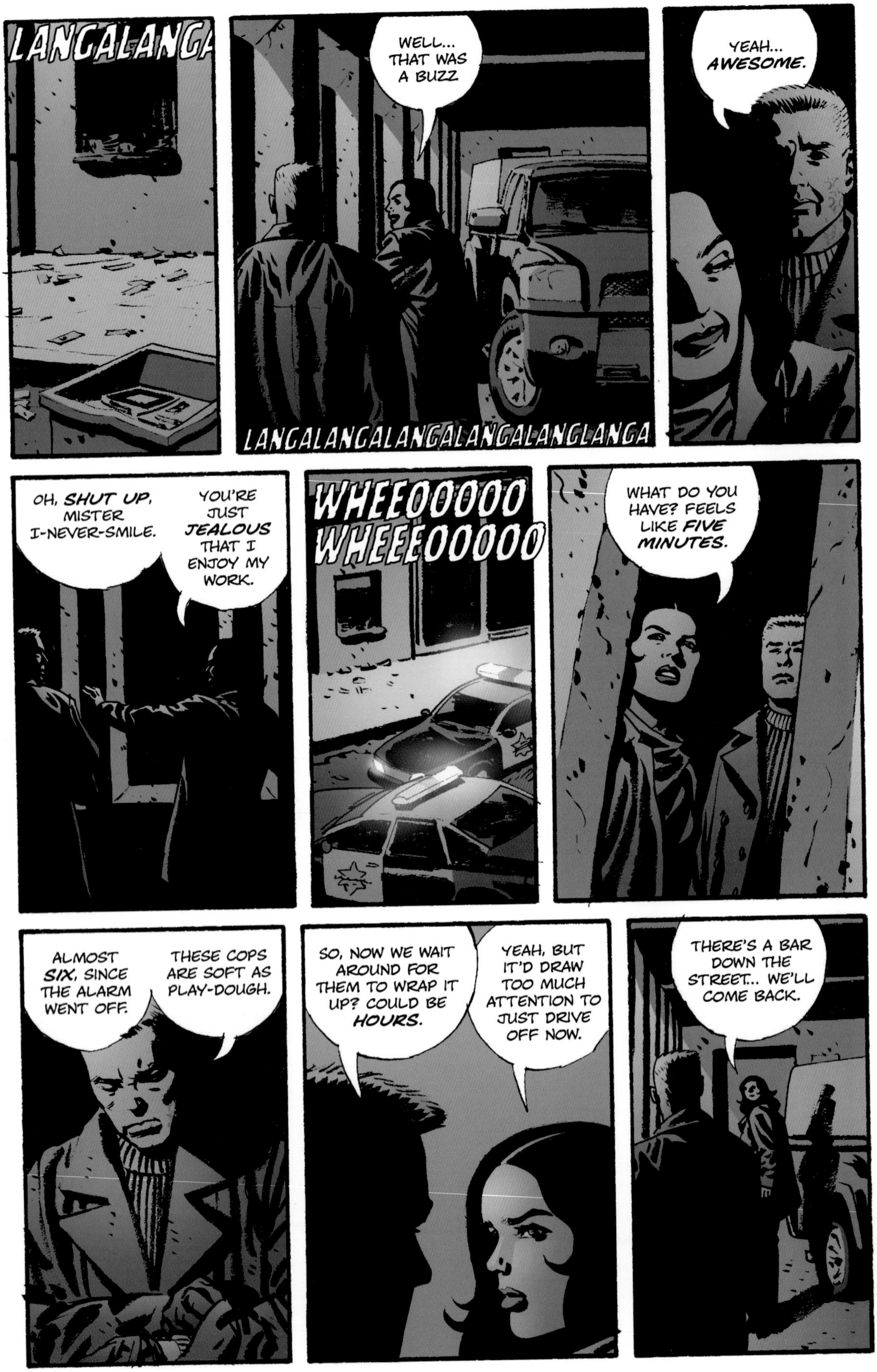
LANGALANGA
WELL... THAT WAS A BUZZ
LANGALANGALANGALANGALANGLANGA
YEAH... AWESOME.
OH, SHUT UP, MISTER I-NEVER-SMILE.
YOU'RE JUST JEALOUS THAT I ENJOY MY WORK.
WHEEOOOOO WHEEEOOOOO
WHAT DO YOU HAVE? FEELS LIKE FIVE MINUTES.
ALMOST SIX, SINCE THE ALARM WENT OFF.
THESE COPS ARE SOFT AS PLAY-DOUGH.
SO, NOW WE WAIT AROUND FOR THEM TO WRAP IT UP? COULD BE HOURS.
YEAH, BUT IT'D DRAW TOO MUCH ATTENTION TO JUST DRIVE OFF NOW.
THERE'S A BAR DOWN THE STREET... WE'LL COME BACK.

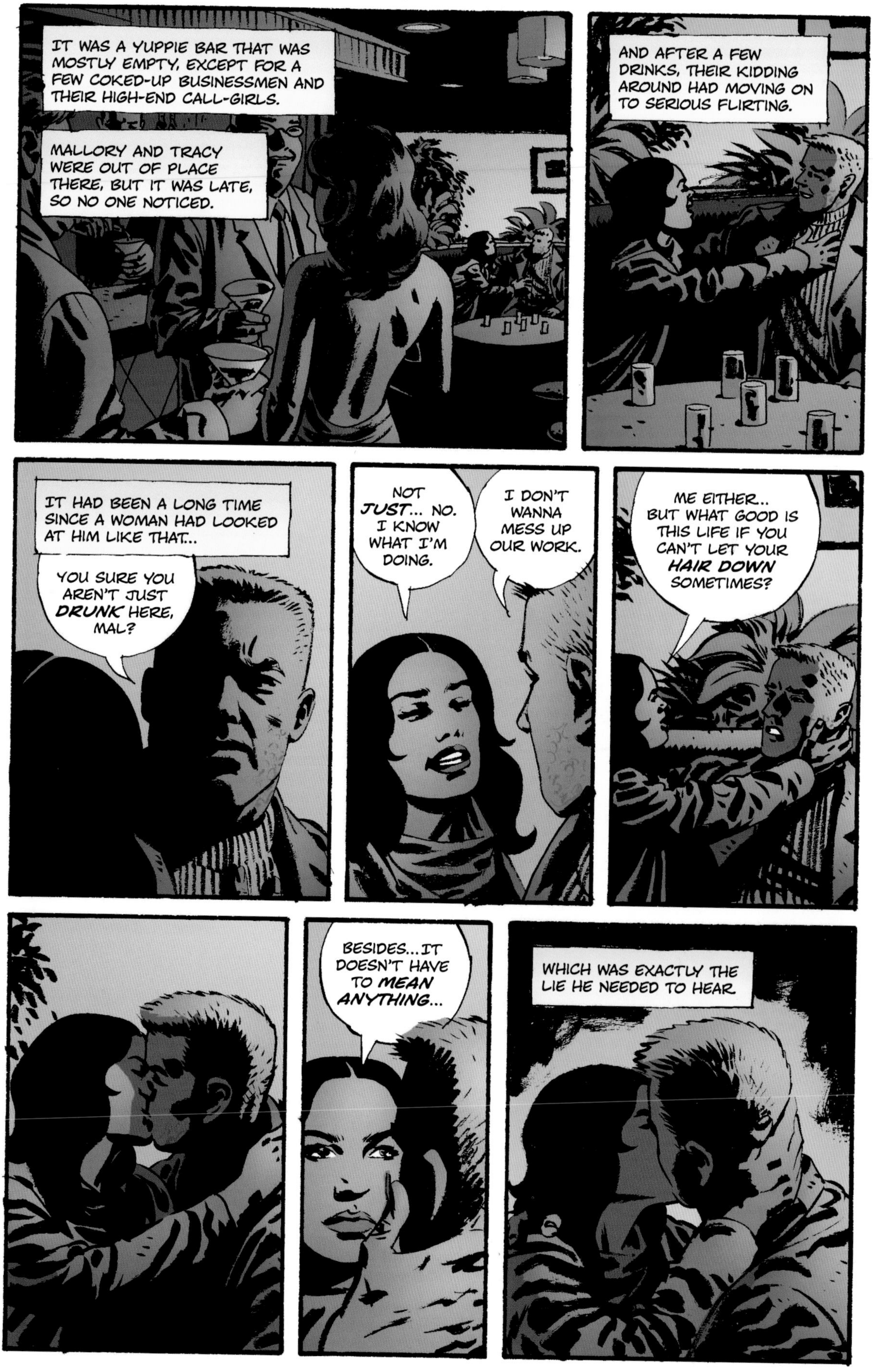

IT WAS A YUPPIE BAR THAT WAS MOSTLY EMPTY, EXCEPT FOR A FEW COKED-UP BUSINESSMEN AND THEIR HIGH-END CALL-GIRLS.
MALLORY AND TRACY WERE OUT OF PLACE THERE, BUT IT WAS LATE, SO NO ONE NOTICED.
AND AFTER A FEW DRINKS, THEIR KIDDING AROUND HAD MOVING ON TO SERIOUS FLIRTING.
IT HAD BEEN A LONG TIME SINCE A WOMAN HAD LOOKED AT HIM LIKE THAT...
YOU SURE YOU AREN'T JUST DRUNK HERE, MAL?
NOT JUST... NO. I KNOW WHAT I'M DOING.
I DON'T WANNA MESS UP OUR WORK.
ME EITHER.. BUT WHAT GOOD IS THIS LIFE IF YOU CAN'T LET YOUR HAIR DOWN SOMETIMES?
BESIDES...IT DOESN'T HAVE TO MEAN ANYTHING...
WHICH WAS EXACTLY THE LIE HE NEEDED TO HEAR.

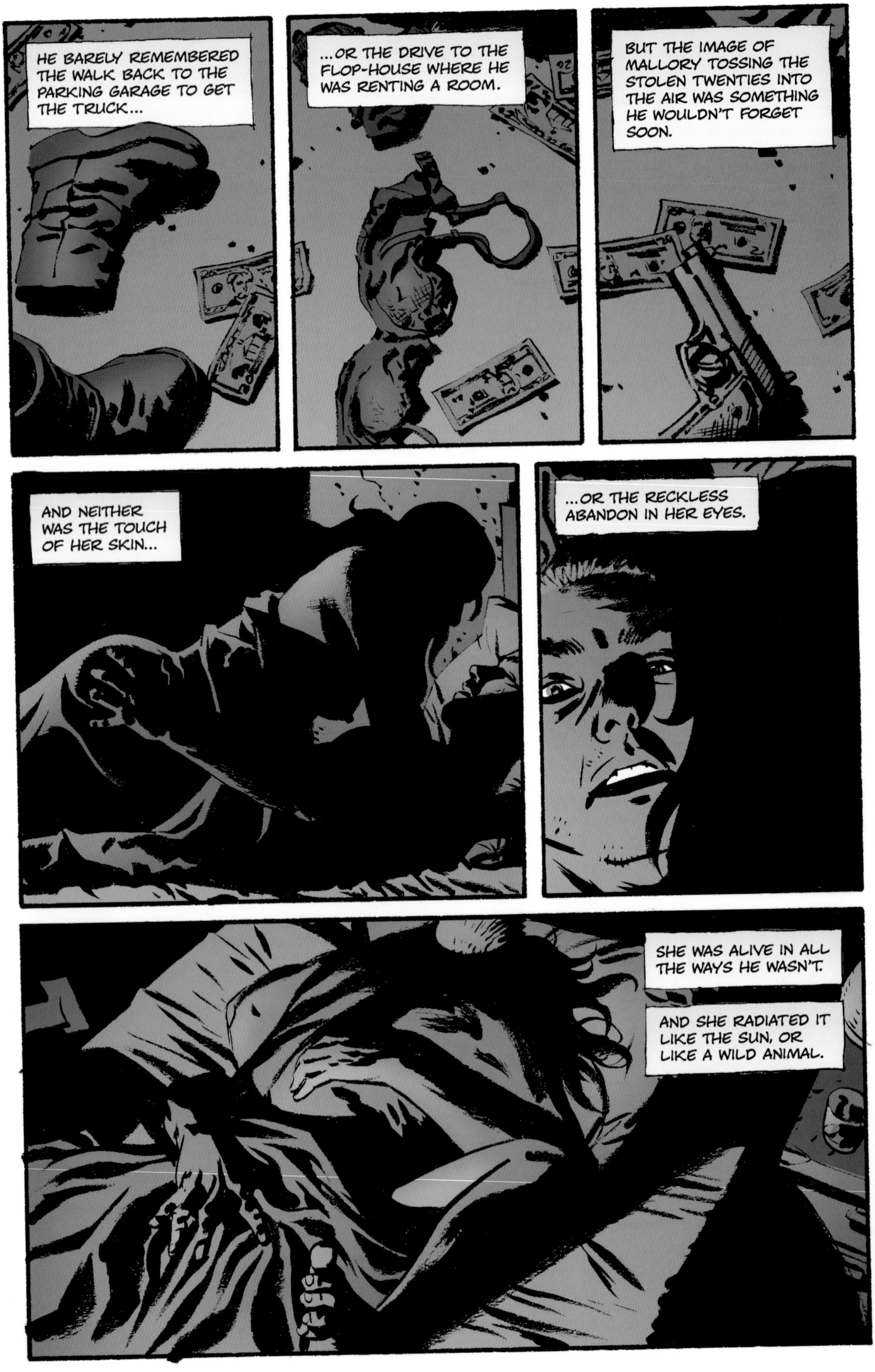
HE BARELY REMEMBERED THE WALK BACK TO THE PARKING GARAGE TO GET THE TRUCK...
...OR THE DRIVE TO THE FLOP-HOUSE WHERE HE WAS RENTING A ROOM.
BUT THE IMAGE OF MALLORY TOSSING THE STOLEN TWENTIES INTO THE AIR WAS SOMETHING HE WOULDN'T FORGET SOON.
AND NEITHER WAS THE TOUCH OF HER SKIN...
...OR THE RECKLESS ABANDON IN HER EYES.
SHE WAS ALIVE IN ALL THE WAYS HE WASN'T.
AND SHE RADIATED IT LIKE THE SUN, OR LIKE A WILD ANIMAL.

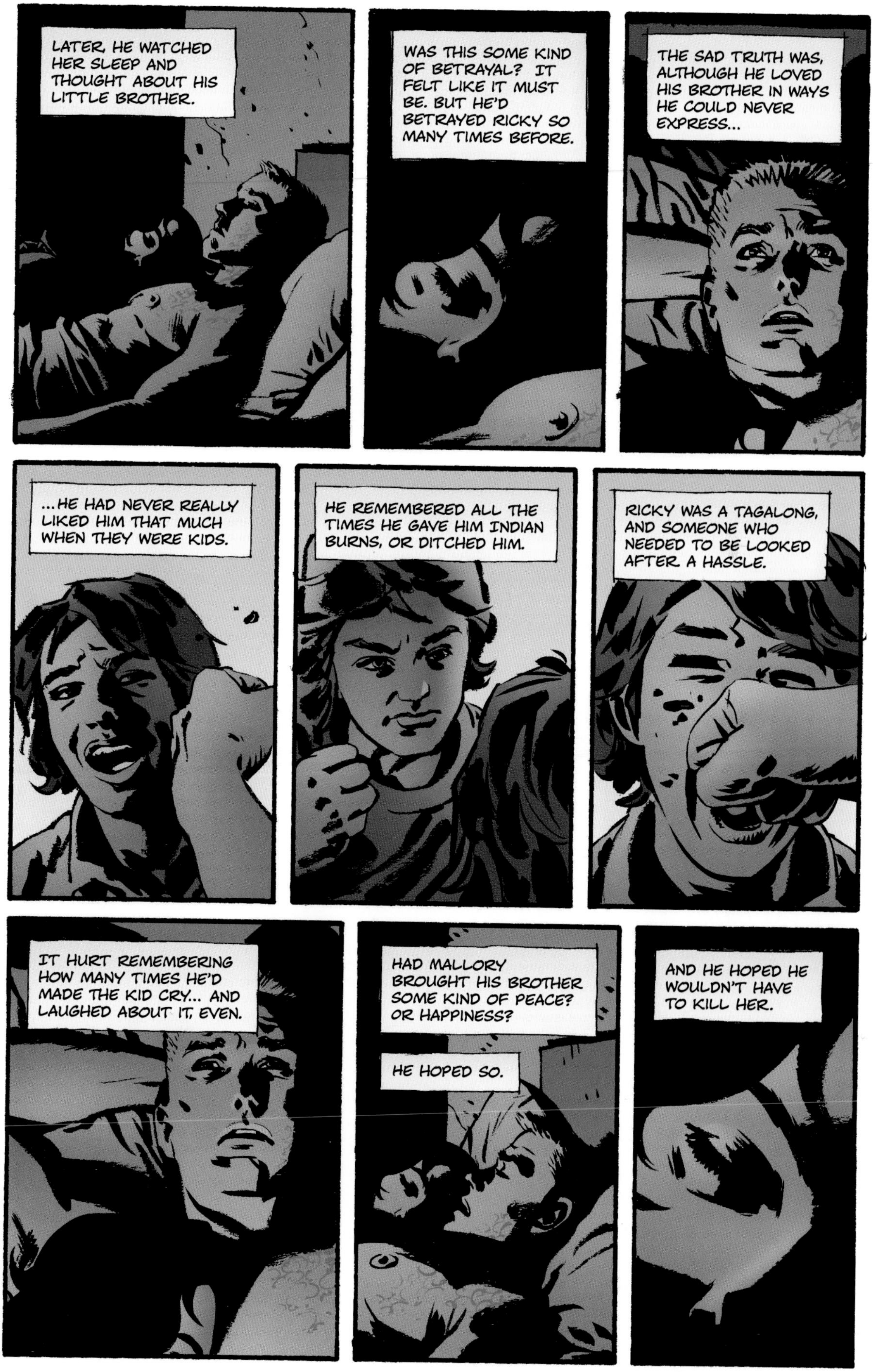
LATER, HE WATCHED HER SLEEP AND THOUGHT ABOUT HIS LITTLE BROTHER.
WAS THIS SOME KIND OF BETRAYAL? IT FELT LIKE IT MUST BE. BUT HE'D BETRAYED RICKY SO MANY TIMES BEFORE.
THE SAD TRUTH WAS, ALTHOUGH HE LOVED HIS BROTHER IN WAYS HE COULD NEVER EXPRESS...
...HE HAD NEVER REALLY LIKED HIM THAT MUCH WHEN THEY WERE KIDS.
HE REMEMBERED ALL THE TIMES HE GAVE HIM INDIAN BURNS, OR DITCHED HIM.
RICKY WAS A TAGALONG, AND SOMEONE WHO NEEDED TO BE LOOKED AFTER. A HASSLE.
IT HURT REMEMBERING HOW MANY TIMES HE'D MADE THE KID CRY... AND LAUGHED ABOUT IT, EVEN.
HAD MALLORY BROUGHT HIS BROTHER SOME KIND OF PEACE? OR HAPPINESS?
HE HOPED SO.
AND HE HOPED HE WOULDN'T HAVE TO KILL HER.

THE REST OF THE CREW, THOUGH, HE COULD GO EITHER WAY ON...

ARE YOU **SERIOUSLY** CHECKING ME FOR A **WIRE?**

GONE OUT O BUSINE

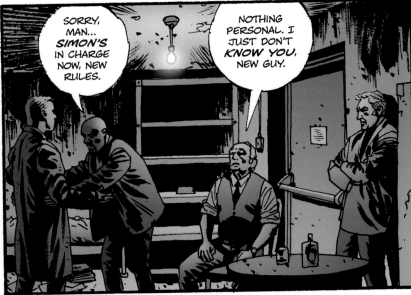

SORRY, MAN... **SIMON'S** IN CHARGE NOW, NEW RULES.

NOTHING PERSONAL. I JUST DON'T **KNOW YOU,** NEW GUY.

HELL, I ONLY **BARELY** TRUSTED THE GUY YOU'RE REPLACING.

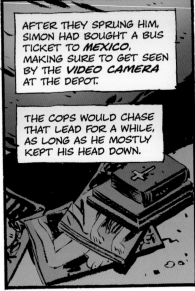

AFTER THEY SPRUNG HIM, SIMON HAD BOUGHT A BUS TICKET TO **MEXICO,** MAKING SURE TO GET SEEN BY THE **VIDEO CAMERA** AT THE DEPOT.

THE COPS WOULD CHASE THAT LEAD FOR A WHILE, AS LONG AS HE MOSTLY KEPT HIS HEAD DOWN.

I GOT YOU OUT OF **PRISON,** OLD MAN.

THAT'S THE **ONLY REASON** YOU'RE STILL AROUND AT ALL.

BUT DON'T THINK 'CAUSE MALLORY SPREADS HER LEGS FOR YOU, THE **REST OF US** ARE PLANNING TO BEND OVER

MAL'S GOT HER **PROBLEMS,** YOU'RE JUST ANOTHER ONE OF THEM NOW.

WHAT THE HELL DOES **THAT** MEAN?

THINK YOU'RE THE ONLY GUY IN THIS CREW SHE'S FUCKED?

JUST **DON'T** LET IT AFFECT THE JOB.

SHE WON'T.

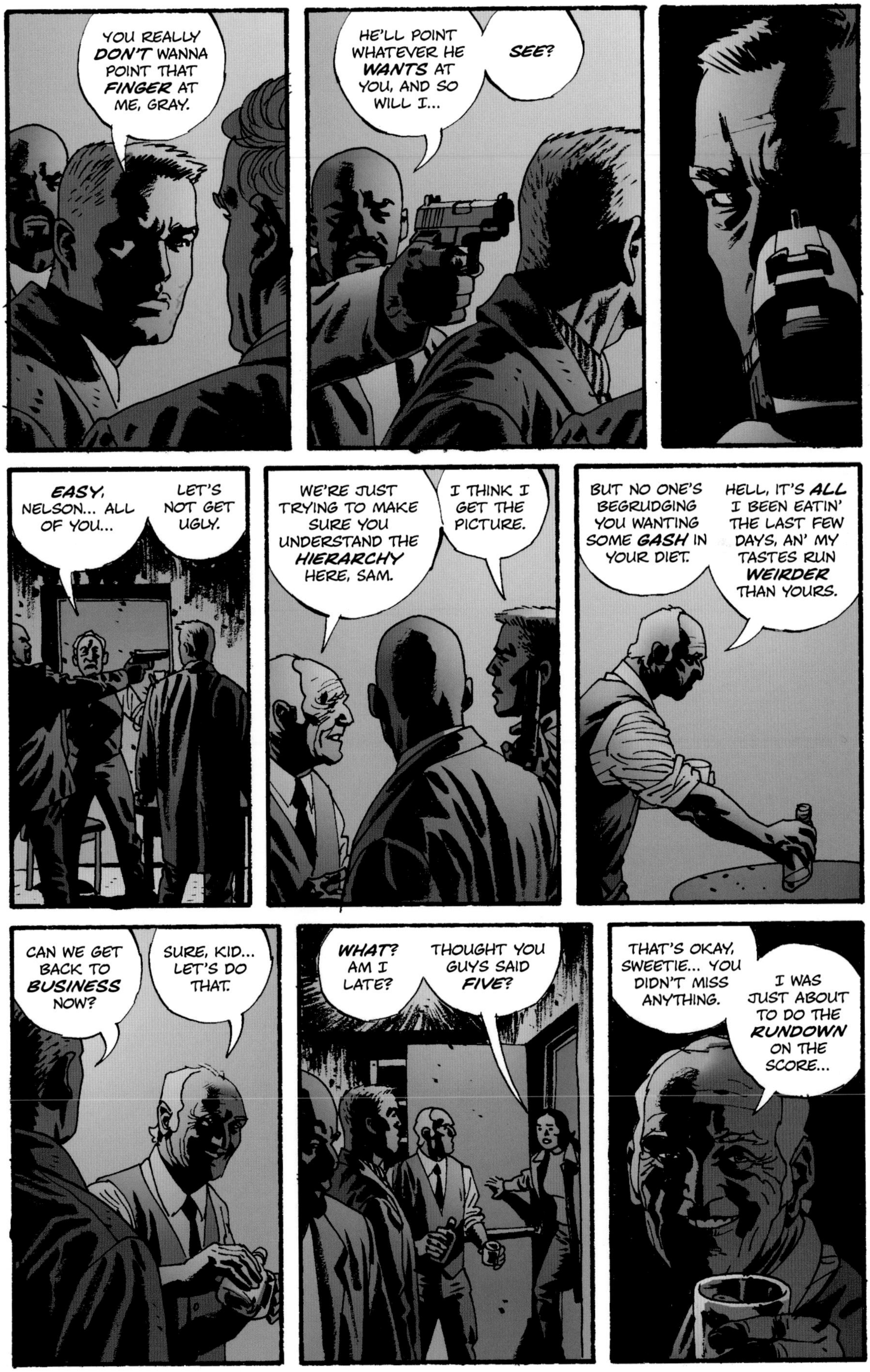
YOU REALLY DON'T WANNA POINT THAT FINGER AT ME, GRAY.
HE'LL POINT WHATEVER HE WANTS AT YOU, AND SO WILL I...
SEE?
EASY, NELSON... ALL OF YOU...
LET'S NOT GET UGLY.
WE'RE JUST TRYING TO MAKE SURE YOU UNDERSTAND THE HIERARCHY HERE, SAM.
I THINK I GET THE PICTURE.
BUT NO ONE'S BEGRUDGING YOU WANTING SOME GASH IN YOUR DIET.
HELL, IT'S ALL I BEEN EATIN' THE LAST FEW DAYS, AN' MY TASTES RUN WEIRDER THAN YOURS.
CAN WE GET BACK TO BUSINESS NOW?
SURE, KID... LET'S DO THAT.
WHAT? AM I LATE?
THOUGHT YOU GUYS SAID FIVE?
THAT'S OKAY, SWEETIE... YOU DIDN'T MISS ANYTHING.
I WAS JUST ABOUT TO DO THE RUNDOWN ON THE SCORE...

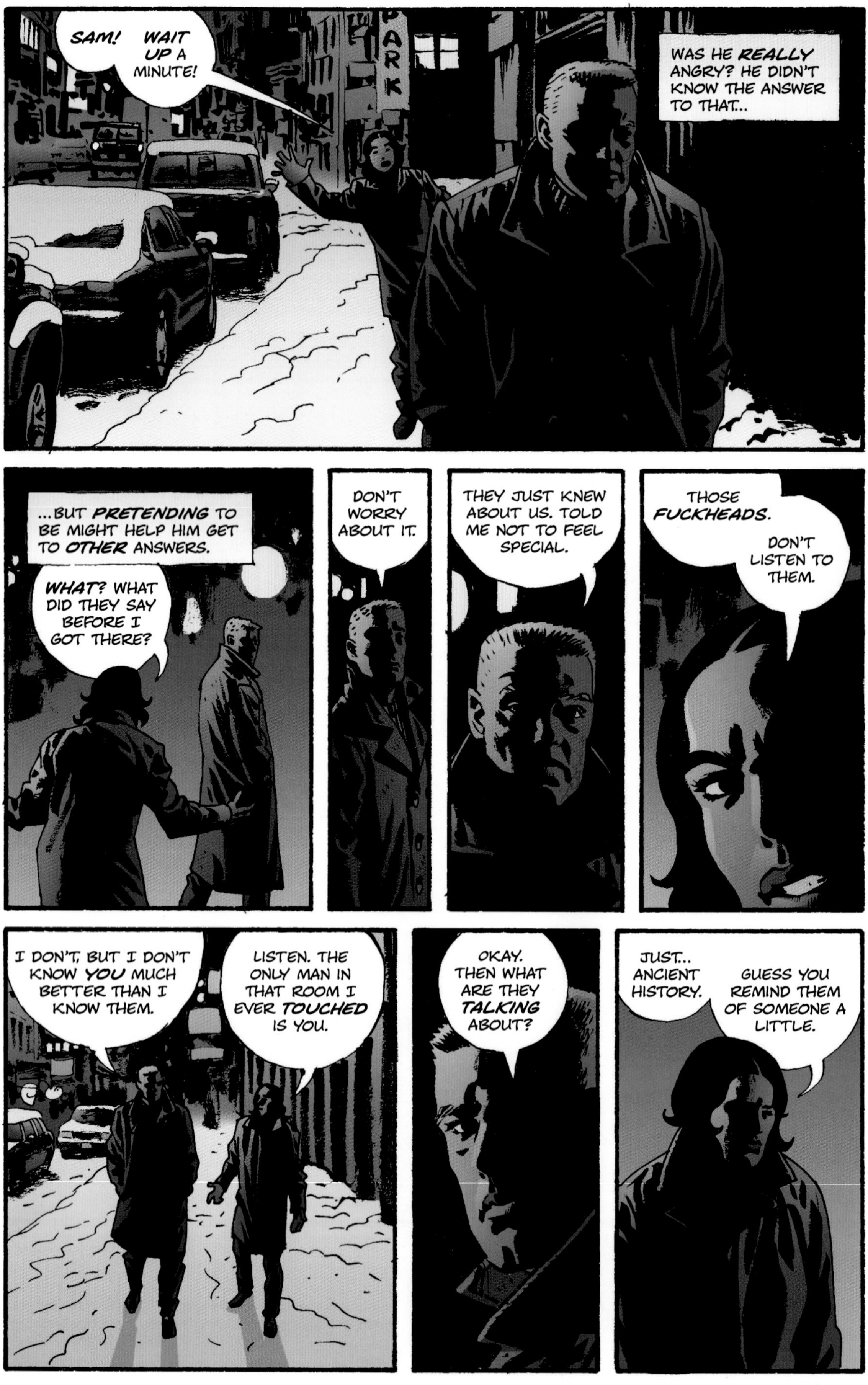
SAM! WAIT UP A MINUTE!
WAS HE REALLY ANGRY? HE DIDN'T KNOW THE ANSWER TO THAT...
...BUT PRETENDING TO BE MIGHT HELP HIM GET TO OTHER ANSWERS.
WHAT? WHAT DID THEY SAY BEFORE I GOT THERE?
DON'T WORRY ABOUT IT.
THEY JUST KNEW ABOUT US. TOLD ME NOT TO FEEL SPECIAL.
THOSE FUCKHEADS.
DON'T LISTEN TO THEM.
I DON'T, BUT I DON'T KNOW YOU MUCH BETTER THAN I KNOW THEM.
LISTEN. THE ONLY MAN IN THAT ROOM I EVER TOUCHED IS YOU.
OKAY. THEN WHAT ARE THEY TALKING ABOUT?
JUST... ANCIENT HISTORY.
GUESS YOU REMIND THEM OF SOMEONE A LITTLE.

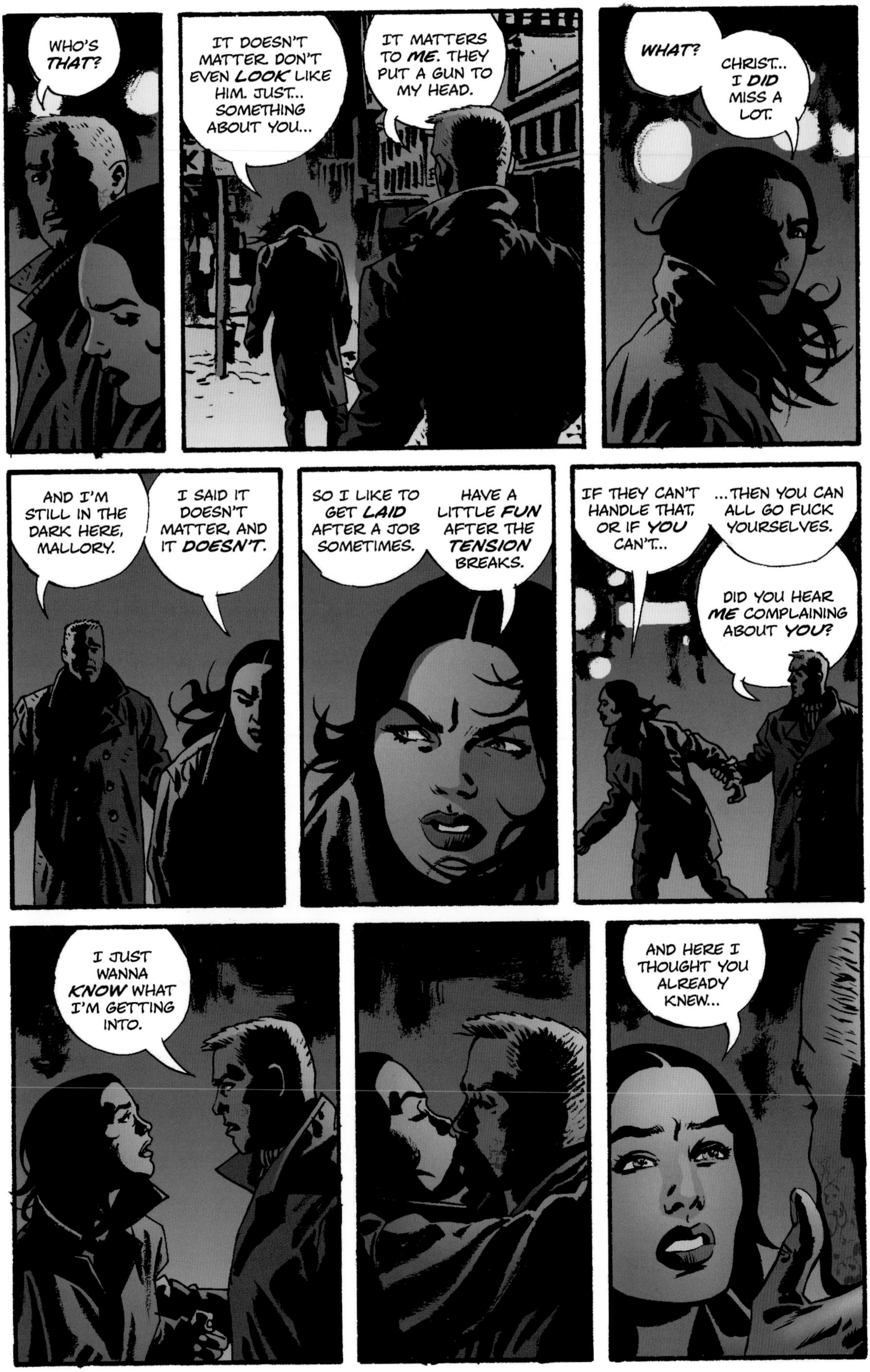
WHO'S THAT?
IT DOESN'T MATTER. DON'T EVEN LOOK LIKE HIM. JUST... SOMETHING ABOUT YOU...
IT MATTERS TO ME. THEY PUT A GUN TO MY HEAD.
WHAT?
CHRIST... I DID MISS A LOT.
AND I'M STILL IN THE DARK HERE, MALLORY.
I SAID IT DOESN'T MATTER, AND IT DOESN'T.
SO I LIKE TO GET LAID AFTER A JOB SOMETIMES.
HAVE A LITTLE FUN AFTER THE TENSION BREAKS.
IF THEY CAN'T HANDLE THAT, OR IF YOU CAN'T...
...THEN YOU CAN ALL GO FUCK YOURSELVES.
DID YOU HEAR ME COMPLAINING ABOUT YOU?
I JUST WANNA KNOW WHAT I'M GETTING INTO.
AND HERE I THOUGHT YOU ALREADY KNEW...

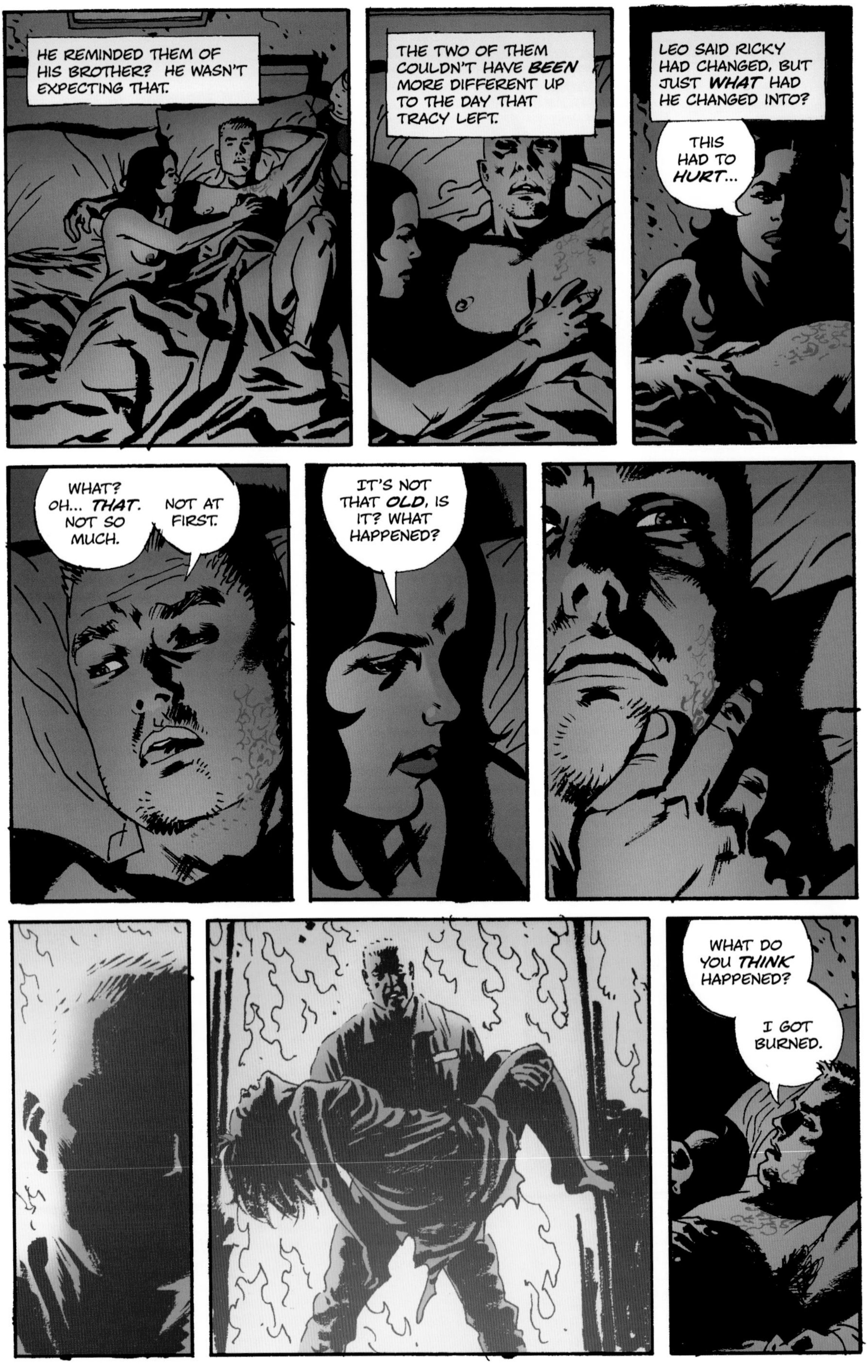
HE REMINDED THEM OF HIS BROTHER? HE WASN'T EXPECTING THAT.
THE TWO OF THEM COULDN'T HAVE BEEN MORE DIFFERENT UP TO THE DAY THAT TRACY LEFT.
LEO SAID RICKY HAD CHANGED, BUT JUST WHAT HAD HE CHANGED INTO?
THIS HAD TO HURT...
WHAT? OH... THAT. NOT SO MUCH.
NOT AT FIRST.
IT'S NOT THAT OLD, IS IT? WHAT HAPPENED?
WHAT DO YOU THINK HAPPENED?
I GOT BURNED.

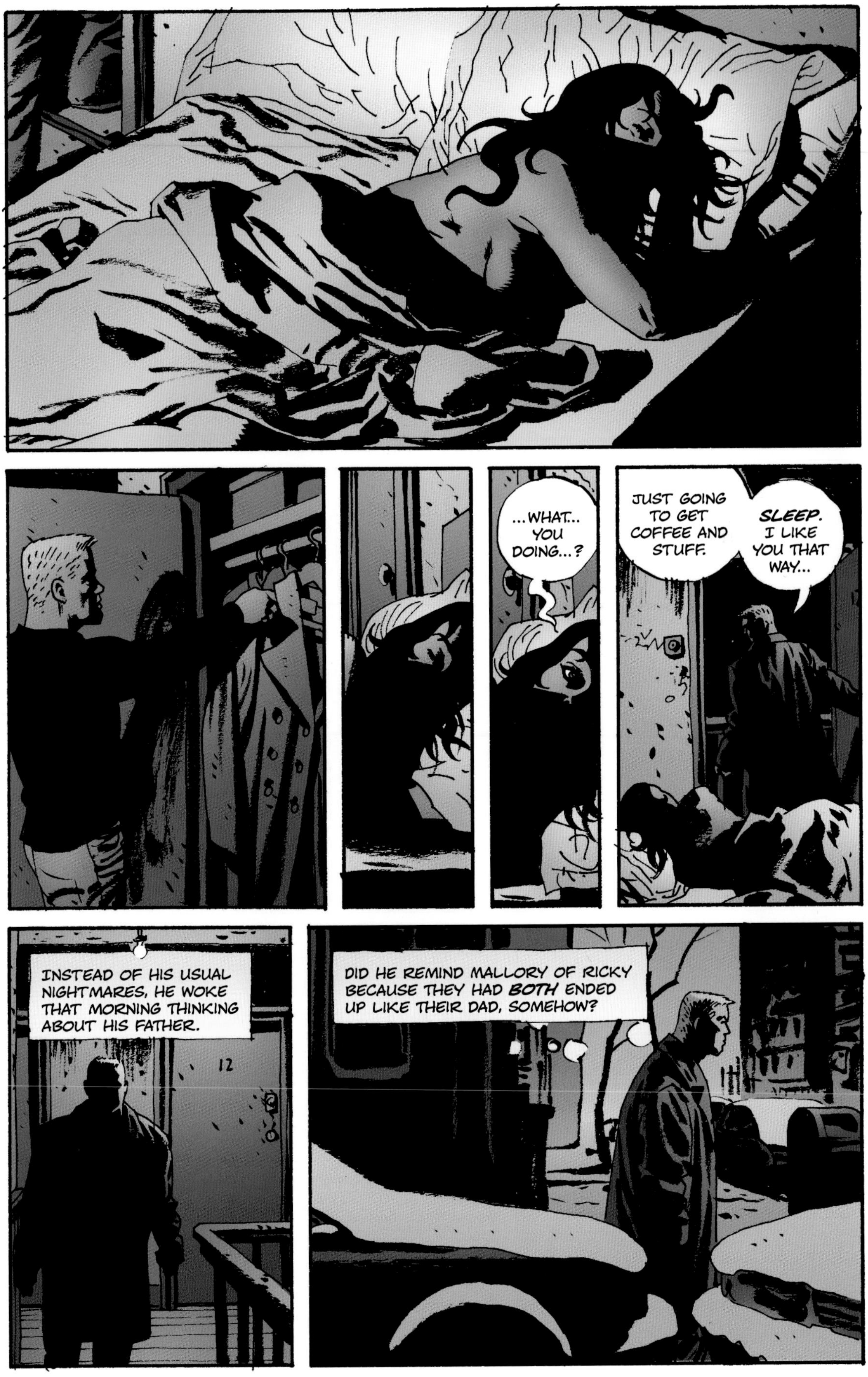
...WHAT... YOU DOING...?
JUST GOING TO GET COFFEE AND STUFF.
SLEEP. I LIKE YOU THAT WAY...
INSTEAD OF HIS USUAL NIGHTMARES, HE WOKE THAT MORNING THINKING ABOUT HIS FATHER.
12
DID HE REMIND MALLORY OF RICKY BECAUSE THEY HAD BOTH ENDED UP LIKE THEIR DAD, SOMEHOW?

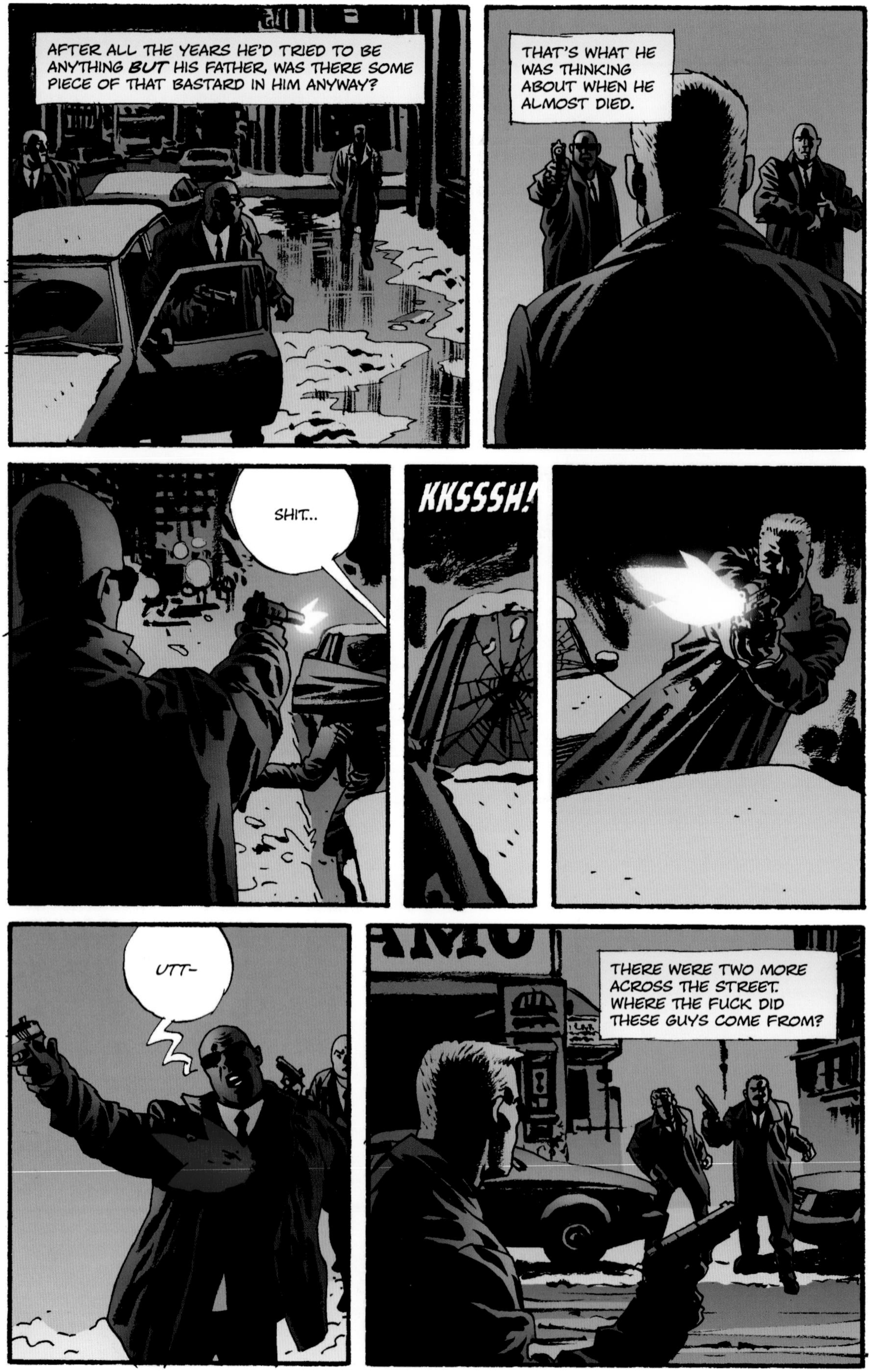
AFTER ALL THE YEARS HE'D TRIED TO BE ANYTHING BUT HIS FATHER, WAS THERE SOME PIECE OF THAT BASTARD IN HIM ANYWAY?
THAT'S WHAT HE WAS THINKING ABOUT WHEN HE ALMOST DIED.
SHIT...
KKSSSH!
UTT-
THERE WERE TWO MORE ACROSS THE STREET. WHERE THE FUCK DID THESE GUYS COME FROM?

AS IT TURNED OUT, THESE GUYS HAD BEEN LOOKING FOR HIM FOR THREE DAYS, EVER SINCE HE AND THE OTHERS HAD SPRUNG SIMON IN CENTER CITY.

HIS CAR HAD BEEN TRACED BACK TO THE DEALER, WHO TOLD THEM EVERYTHING HE KNEW.

--NAME'S *SAM WEST.* GOT A COPY OF HIS LICENSE HERE SOMEWHERE...

LET ME GUESS, HE PAID *CASH?*

UH...

HAND IT OVER

AW, COME ON.

I'LL BREAK YOUR KNEECAPS AN' TAKE IT ANYWAY.

DAMN IT... KNEW THAT ASSHOLE WAS *TROUBLE.*

MORE THAN YOU *KNOW,* MAN.

LUCKY YOU DIDN'T TRY TO *SPEND* ANY OF THIS...

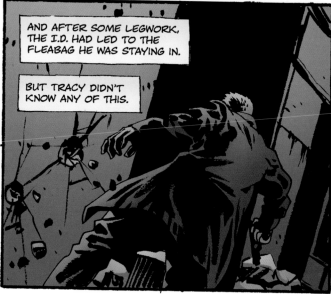

AND AFTER SOME LEGWORK, THE I.D. HAD LED TO THE FLEABAG HE WAS STAYING IN.

BUT TRACY DIDN'T KNOW ANY OF THIS.

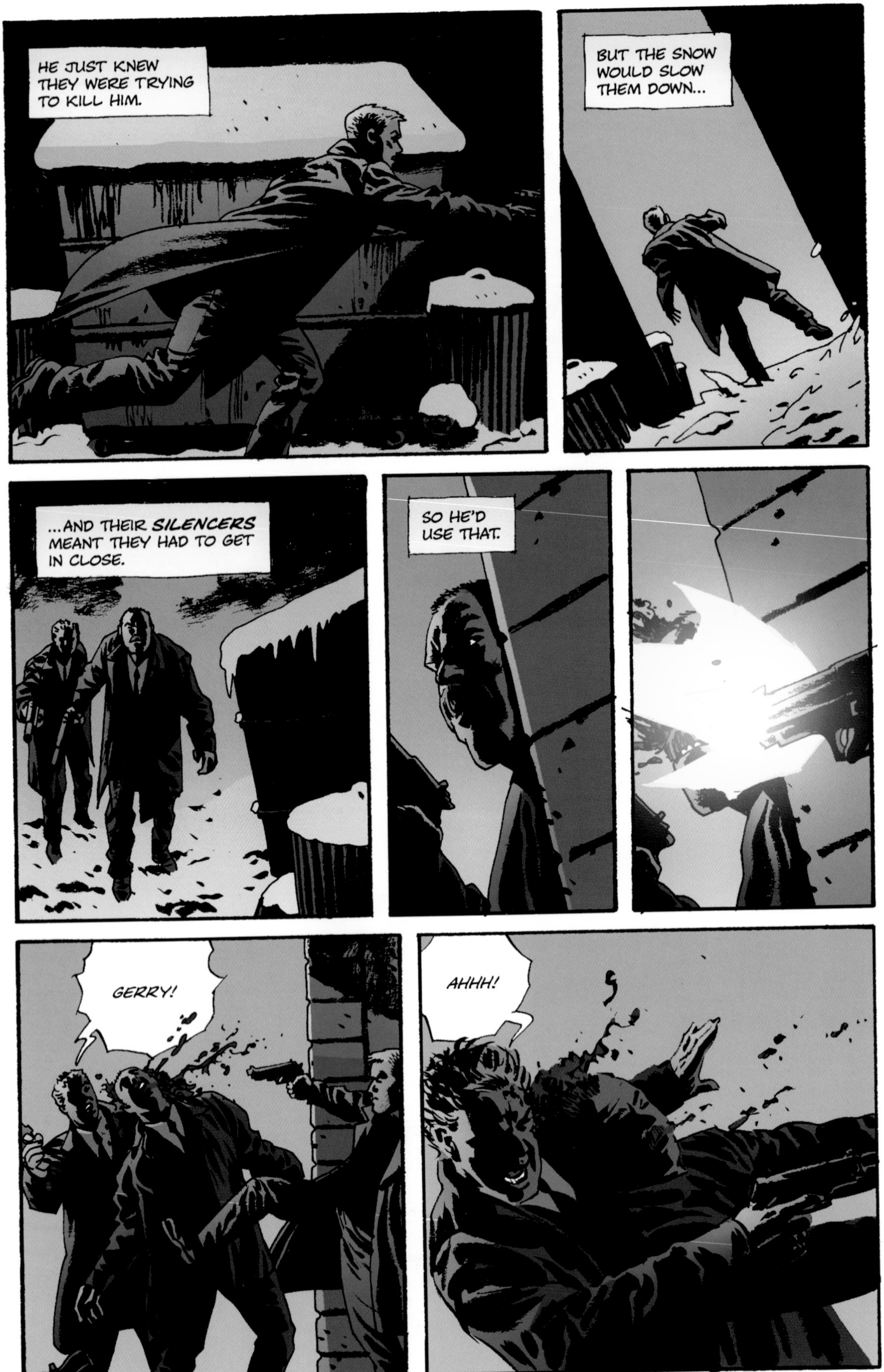
HE JUST KNEW THEY WERE TRYING TO KILL HIM.
BUT THE SNOW WOULD SLOW THEM DOWN...
...AND THEIR SILENCERS MEANT THEY HAD TO GET IN CLOSE.
SO HE'D USE THAT.
GERRY!
AHHH!

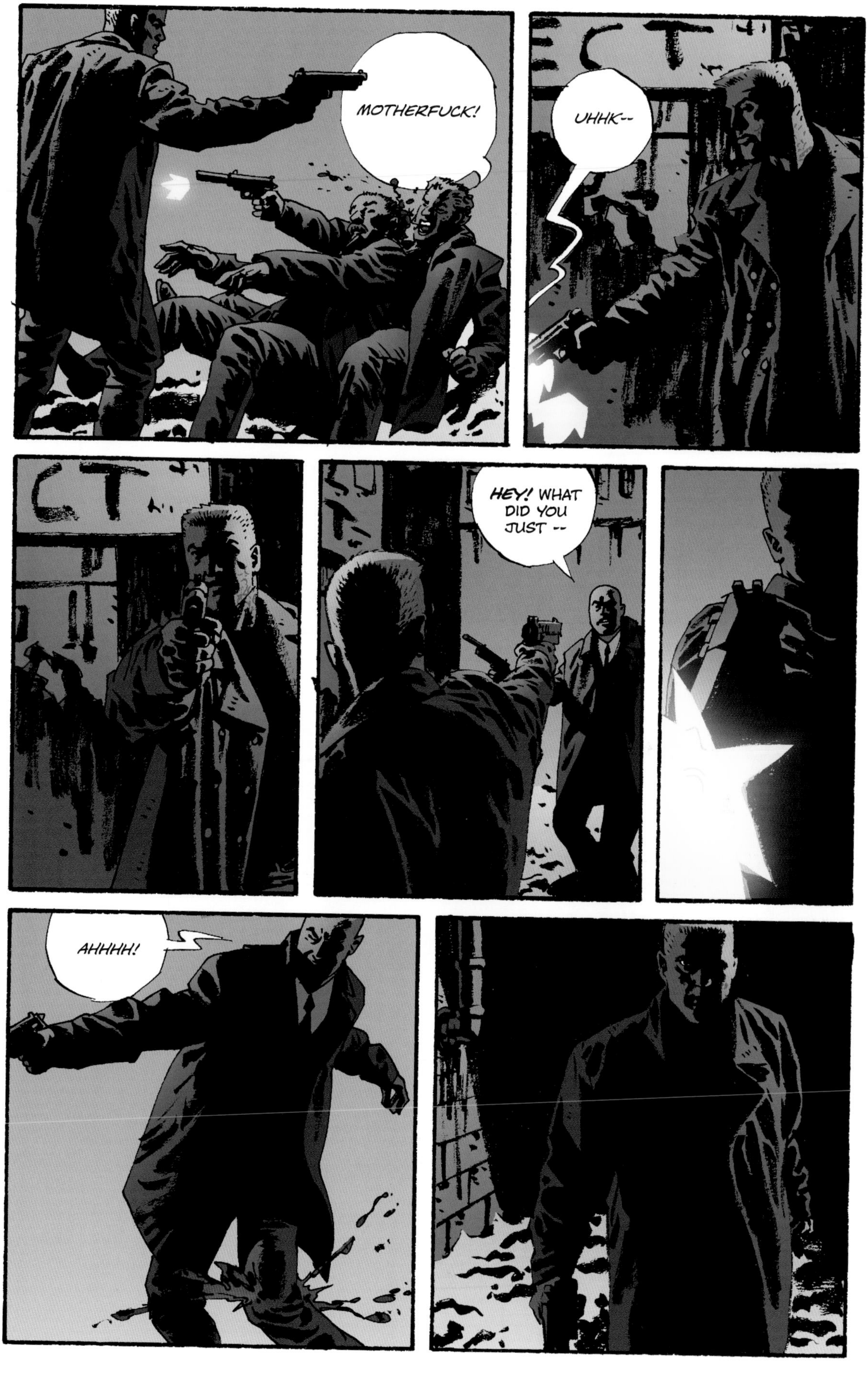
MOTHERFUCK!
UHHK--
HEY! WHAT DID YOU JUST --
AHHHH!

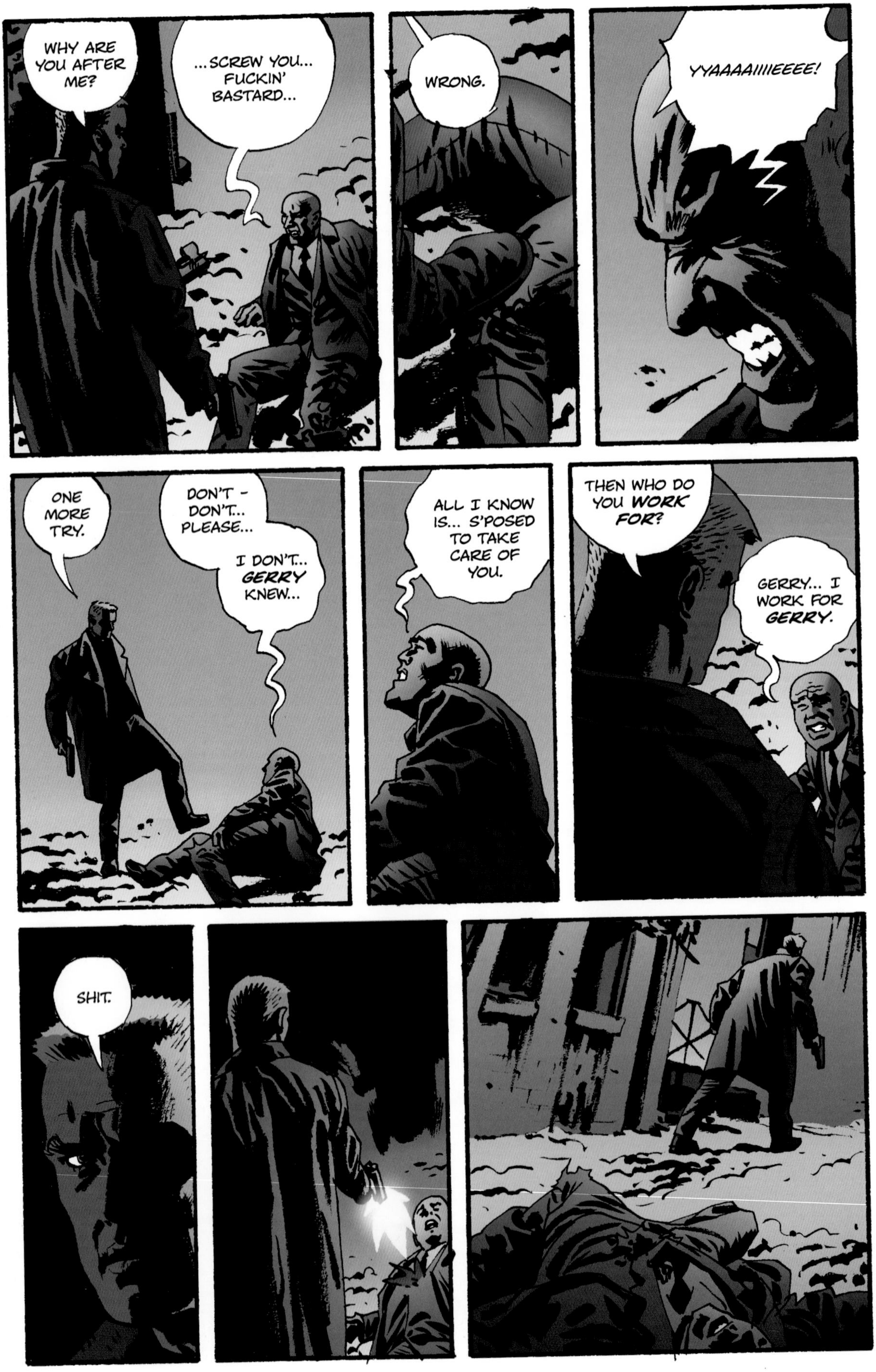
WHY ARE YOU AFTER ME?
...SCREW YOU... FUCKIN' BASTARD...
WRONG.
YYAAAAIIIIEEEE!
ONE MORE TRY.
DON'T - DON'T... PLEASE...
I DON'T... GERRY KNEW...
ALL I KNOW IS... S'POSED TO TAKE CARE OF YOU.
THEN WHO DO YOU WORK FOR?
GERRY... I WORK FOR GERRY.
SHIT.

THAT MANY SHOTS FIRED, SOMEONE HAD TO HAVE CALLED THE COPS BY NOW.

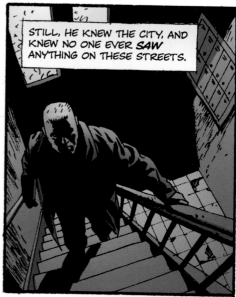

STILL, HE KNEW THE CITY, AND KNEW NO ONE EVER *SAW* ANYTHING ON THESE STREETS.

HE JUST HAD TO GET OUT OF THERE, AND FAST.

SOMEONE KNEW *WHERE* HE WAS, AT LEAST... IF NOT *WHO*.

THAT WAS QUICK... BARELY HAD TIME TO TAKE A SHOWER

WHERE'S THE COFFEE?

OH, *YEAH*... I WAS THINKING...

...LET'S GO *OUT* FOR BREAKFAST INSTEAD.

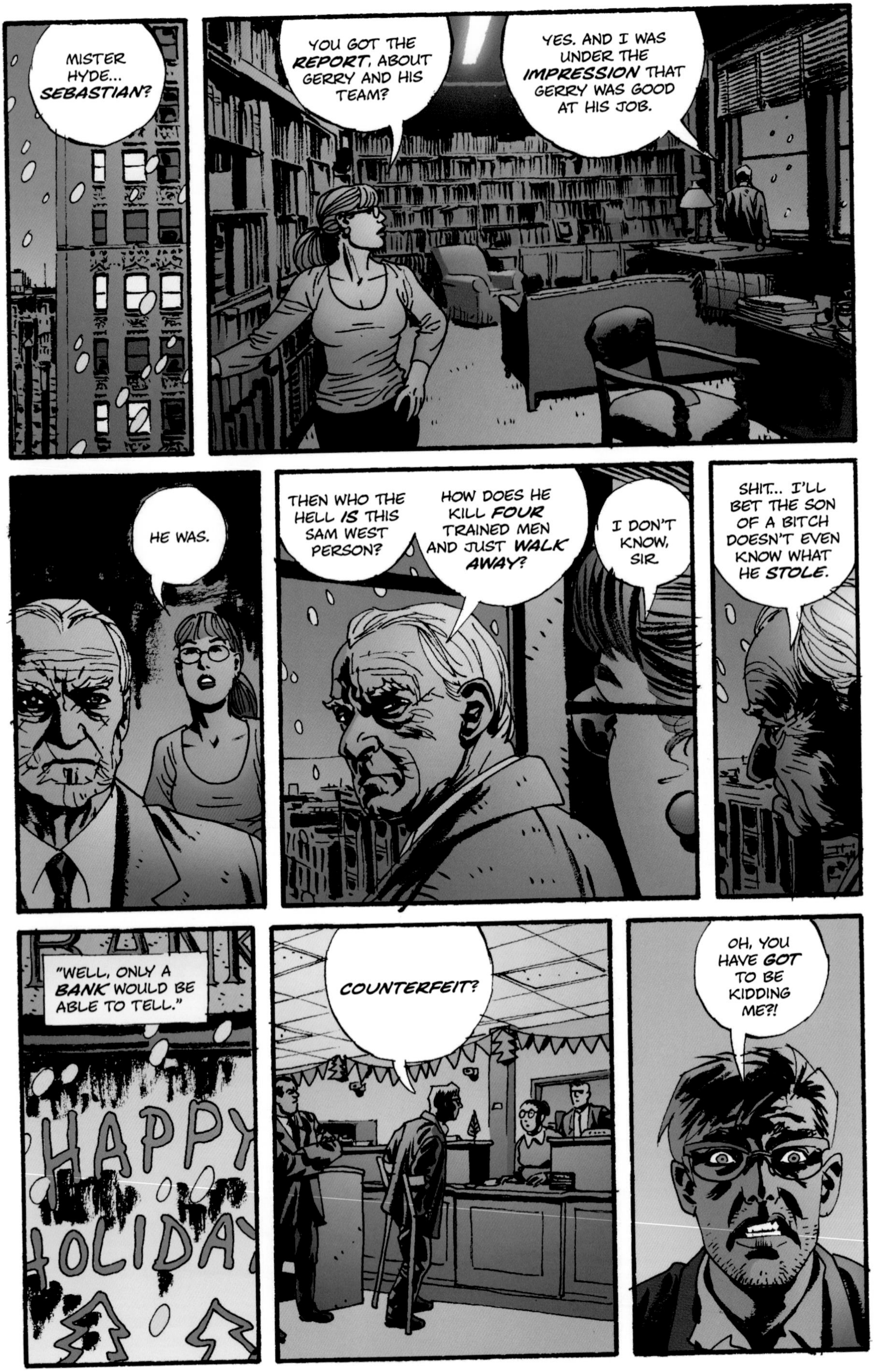
MISTER HYDE... SEBASTIAN?
YOU GOT THE REPORT, ABOUT GERRY AND HIS TEAM?
YES. AND I WAS UNDER THE IMPRESSION THAT GERRY WAS GOOD AT HIS JOB.
HE WAS.
THEN WHO THE HELL IS THIS SAM WEST PERSON?
HOW DOES HE KILL FOUR TRAINED MEN AND JUST WALK AWAY?
I DON'T KNOW, SIR.
SHIT... I'LL BET THE SON OF A BITCH DOESN'T EVEN KNOW WHAT HE STOLE.
"WELL, ONLY A BANK WOULD BE ABLE TO TELL."
HAPPY HOLIDAY
COUNTERFEIT?
OH, YOU HAVE GOT TO BE KIDDING ME?!

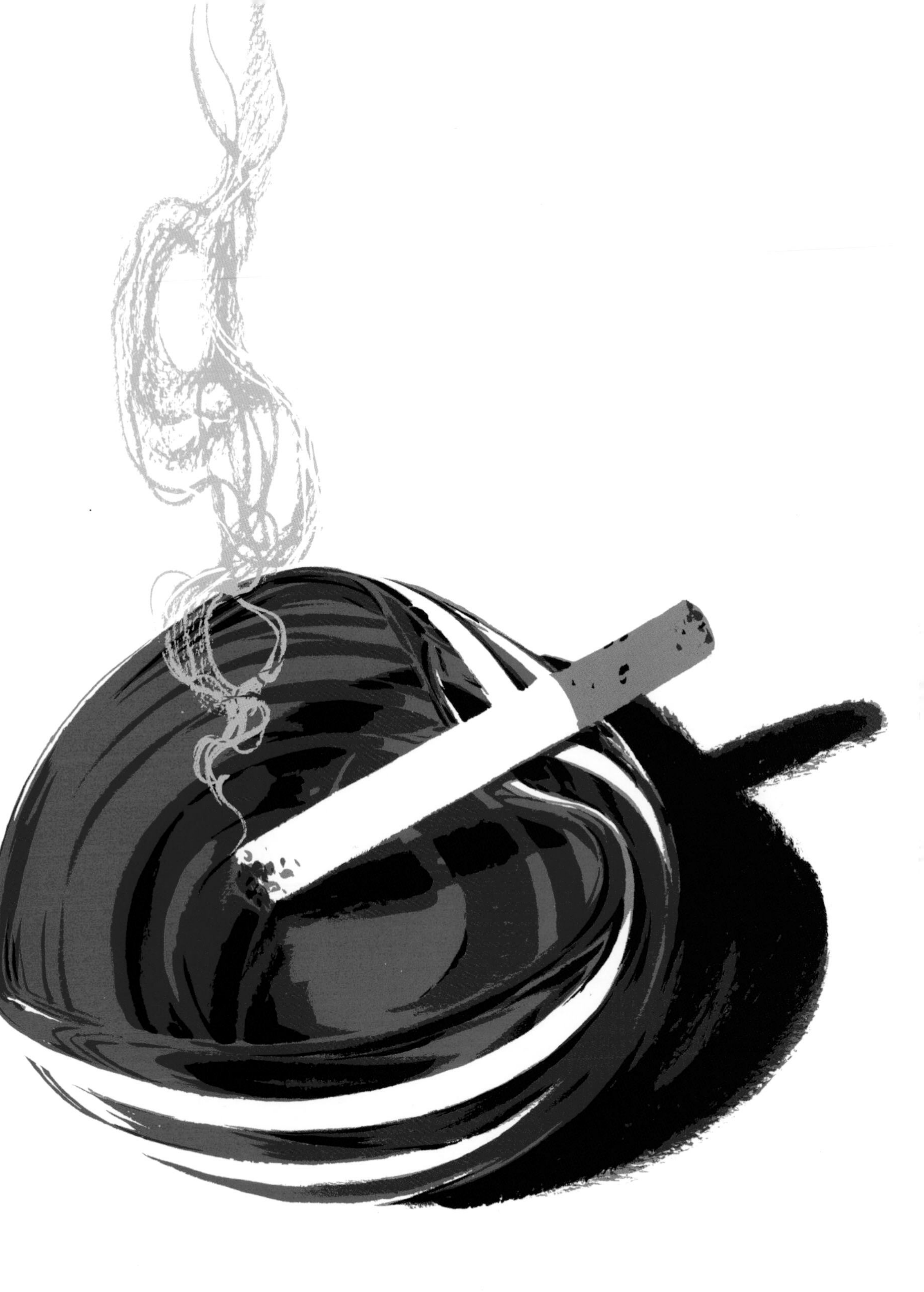

Part Four

THE ONLY PERSON THAT TRACY WAS EVER AFRAID OF WAS HIS FATHER.

HIS EARLIEST MEMORIES WERE VAGUE, HAZY IMAGES AT BEST... BUT HE REMEMBERED SCREAMING.

HE REMEMBERED HIS FATHER'S VOICE, YELLING.

AND HE REMEMBERED FEAR.

A FEAR SO TOTAL THAT HE WAS WRAPPED IN IT.

IN HIS LIFE, NO ONE SCARED HIM. NO ONE MADE HIM FLINCH.

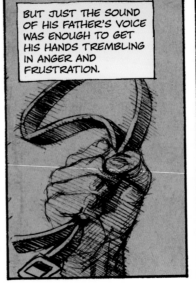

BUT JUST THE SOUND OF HIS FATHER'S VOICE WAS ENOUGH TO GET HIS HANDS TREMBLING IN ANGER AND FRUSTRATION.

AND HE HATED HIMSELF FOR THAT.

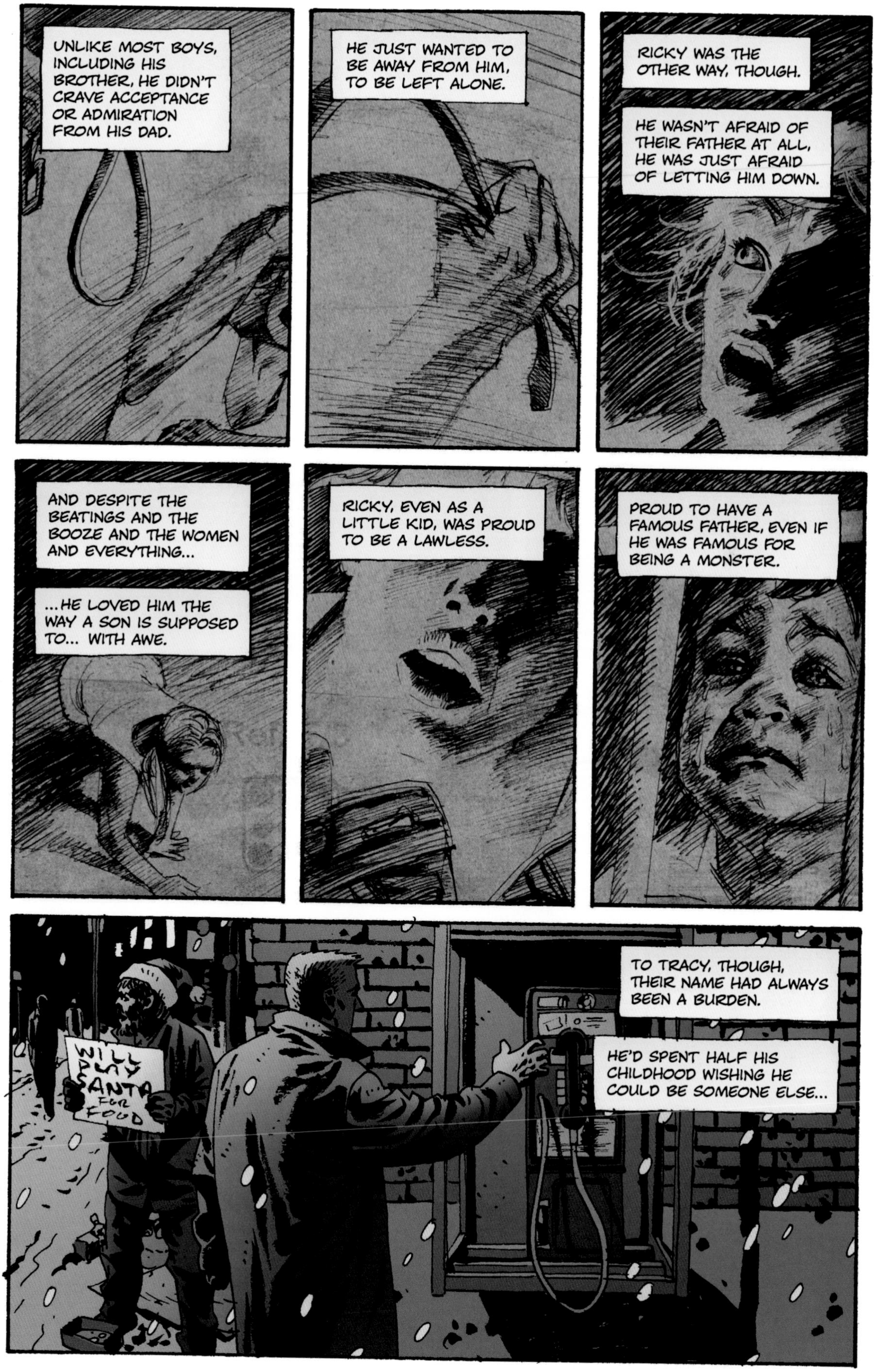
UNLIKE MOST BOYS, INCLUDING HIS BROTHER, HE DIDN'T CRAVE ACCEPTANCE OR ADMIRATION FROM HIS DAD.
HE JUST WANTED TO BE AWAY FROM HIM, TO BE LEFT ALONE.
RICKY WAS THE OTHER WAY, THOUGH.
HE WASN'T AFRAID OF THEIR FATHER AT ALL, HE WAS JUST AFRAID OF LETTING HIM DOWN.
AND DESPITE THE BEATINGS AND THE BOOZE AND THE WOMEN AND EVERYTHING...
...HE LOVED HIM THE WAY A SON IS SUPPOSED TO... WITH AWE.
RICKY, EVEN AS A LITTLE KID, WAS PROUD TO BE A LAWLESS.
PROUD TO HAVE A FAMOUS FATHER, EVEN IF HE WAS FAMOUS FOR BEING A MONSTER.
WILL PLAY SANTA FOR FOOD
TO TRACY, THOUGH, THEIR NAME HAD ALWAYS BEEN A BURDEN.
HE'D SPENT HALF HIS CHILDHOOD WISHING HE COULD BE SOMEONE ELSE...

...BUT NOW *THAT* WAS BECOMING A PROBLEM, TOO.

COME ON, YOU LAZY BASTARD... PICK UP THE PHONE...

HELLO?

JAKE, IT'S *ME*. LISTEN, I NEED A FAVOR...

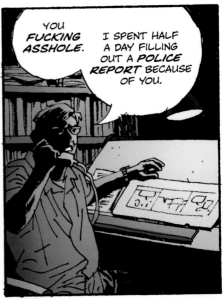

YOU *FUCKING ASSHOLE.*

I SPENT HALF A DAY FILLING OUT A *POLICE REPORT* BECAUSE OF YOU.

WHAT? WHAT THE FUCK ARE YOU TALKING ABOUT?

TRIED TO *DEPOSIT* SOME OF THE MONEY YOU GAVE ME, AND GUESS WHAT?

IT'S FUCKING *COUNTERFEIT!*

SHIT...

WAIT, WHEN WAS THIS?

YOU DIDN'T *TELL THEM* ABOUT ME, DID YOU?

IT WAS *TODAY,* ASSHOLE... AND NO, I DIDN'T *TELL THEM* ABOUT YOU.

SAID I FOUND IT IN THE *GUTTER,* DOWNTOWN.

I DON'T GENERALLY LIKE TO *ADMIT* TO TAKING PART IN *CRIMINAL ENTERPRISES.*

JACOB... RELAX... JUST RELAX...

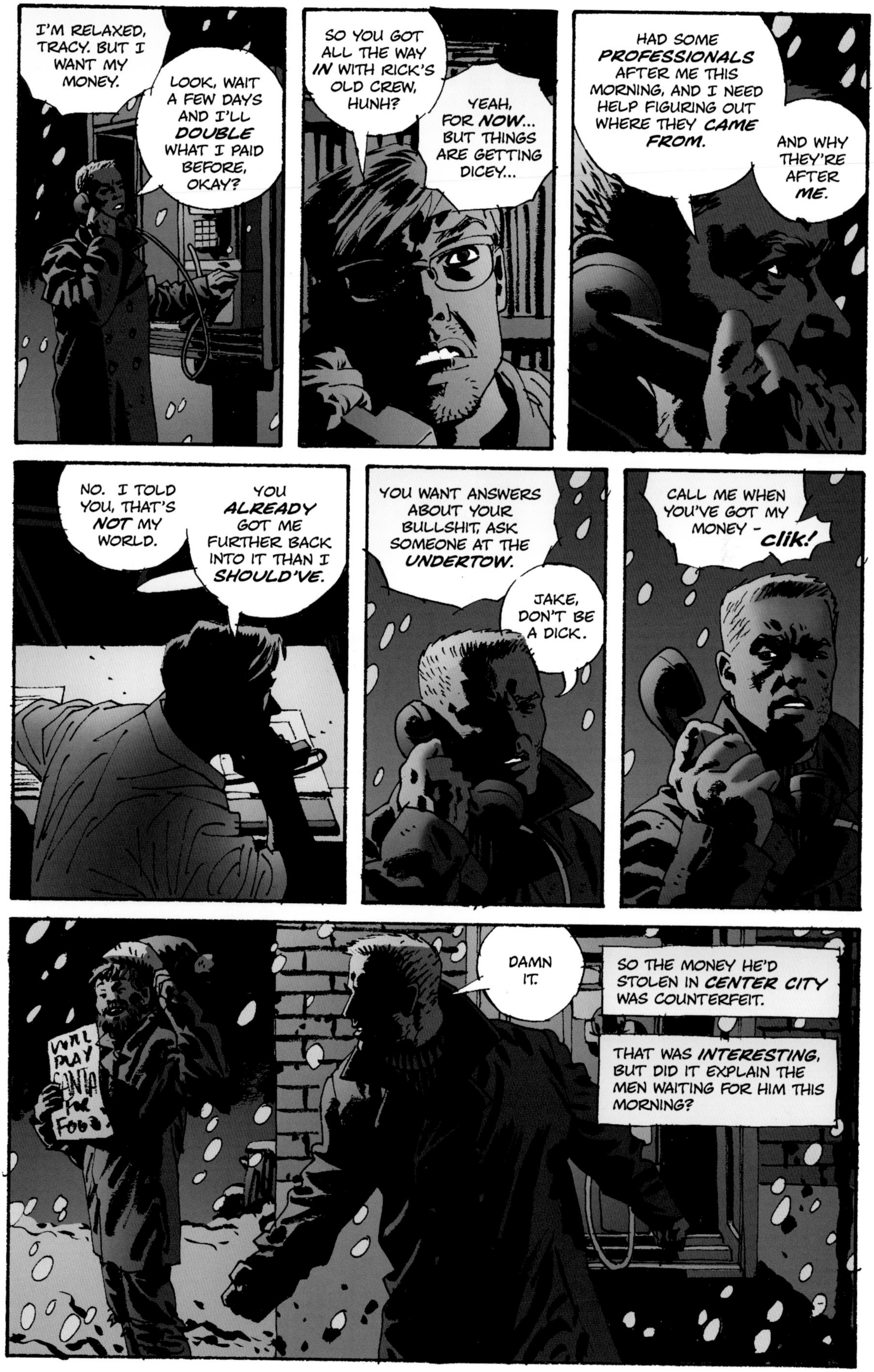

I'M RELAXED, TRACY. BUT I WANT MY MONEY.
LOOK, WAIT A FEW DAYS AND I'LL DOUBLE WHAT I PAID BEFORE, OKAY?
SO YOU GOT ALL THE WAY IN WITH RICK'S OLD CREW, HUNH?
YEAH, FOR NOW... BUT THINGS ARE GETTING DICEY...
HAD SOME PROFESSIONALS AFTER ME THIS MORNING, AND I NEED HELP FIGURING OUT WHERE THEY CAME FROM.
AND WHY THEY'RE AFTER ME.
NO. I TOLD YOU, THAT'S NOT MY WORLD.
YOU ALREADY GOT ME FURTHER BACK INTO IT THAN I SHOULD'VE.
YOU WANT ANSWERS ABOUT YOUR BULLSHIT, ASK SOMEONE AT THE UNDERTOW.
JAKE, DON'T BE A DICK.
CALL ME WHEN YOU'VE GOT MY MONEY -
clik!
DAMN IT.
SO THE MONEY HE'D STOLEN IN CENTER CITY WAS COUNTERFEIT.
THAT WAS INTERESTING, BUT DID IT EXPLAIN THE MEN WAITING FOR HIM THIS MORNING?

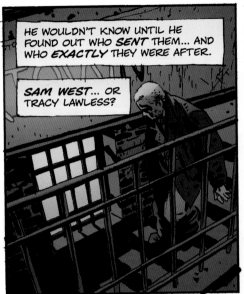

HE WOULDN'T KNOW UNTIL HE FOUND OUT WHO *SENT* THEM... AND WHO *EXACTLY* THEY WERE AFTER.

SAM WEST... OR *TRACY LAWLESS?*

HE'D DONE A LOT OF BAD THINGS IN THE PAST FEW WEEKS, AND TOLD A LOT OF LIES TO BAD PEOPLE.

ANY OF THAT COULD BE BLOWING BACK AT HIM NOW.

SORRY ABOUT PULLIN' MY PIECE ON YOU LAST NIGHT.

THAT LOOK IN YOUR EYE, THOUGH YOU WAS ABOUT TO *KILL* GREY.

DON'T SWEAT IT, NELSON...

YOU GUYS ARE A *TIGHT* CREW, I UNDERSTAND...

ME BEING THE NEWCOMER, AN' ALL.

GLAD TO HEAR IT.

DON'T BE NEEDIN' NO BULLSHIT BETWEEN US TOMORROW NIGHT...

SO, YOU THREE'VE BEEN TOGETHER A LONG TIME, HUNH?

SORTA.

USED TO BE A FEW OTHERS, TOO...

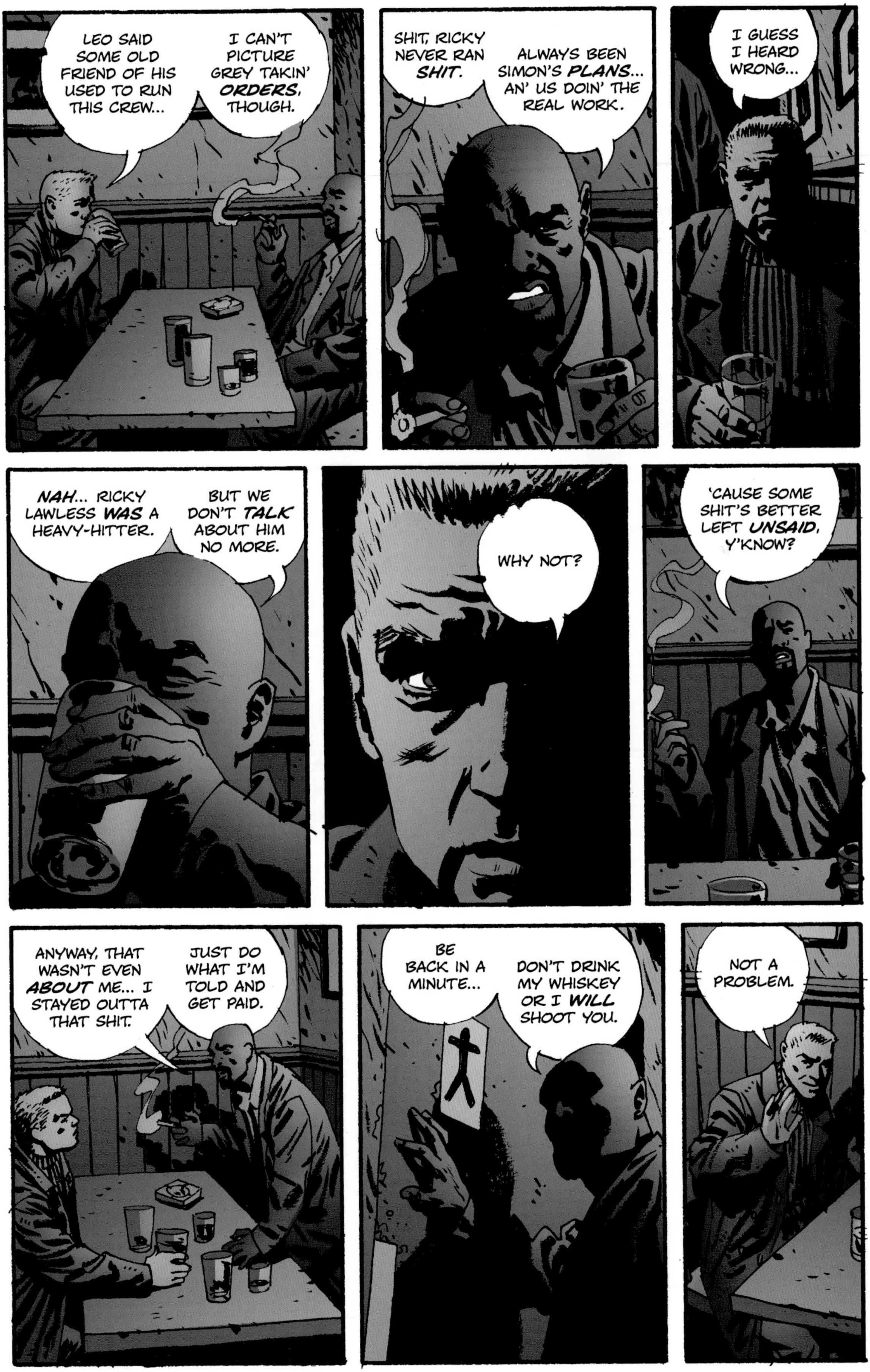
LEO SAID SOME OLD FRIEND OF HIS USED TO RUN THIS CREW...
I CAN'T PICTURE GREY TAKIN' ORDERS, THOUGH.
SHIT, RICKY NEVER RAN SHIT.
ALWAYS BEEN SIMON'S PLANS... AN' US DOIN' THE REAL WORK.
I GUESS I HEARD WRONG...
NAH... RICKY LAWLESS WAS A HEAVY-HITTER.
BUT WE DON'T TALK ABOUT HIM NO MORE.
WHY NOT?
'CAUSE SOME SHIT'S BETTER LEFT UNSAID, Y'KNOW?
ANYWAY, THAT WASN'T EVEN ABOUT ME... I STAYED OUTTA THAT SHIT.
JUST DO WHAT I'M TOLD AND GET PAID.
BE BACK IN A MINUTE...
DON'T DRINK MY WHISKEY OR I WILL SHOOT YOU.
NOT A PROBLEM.

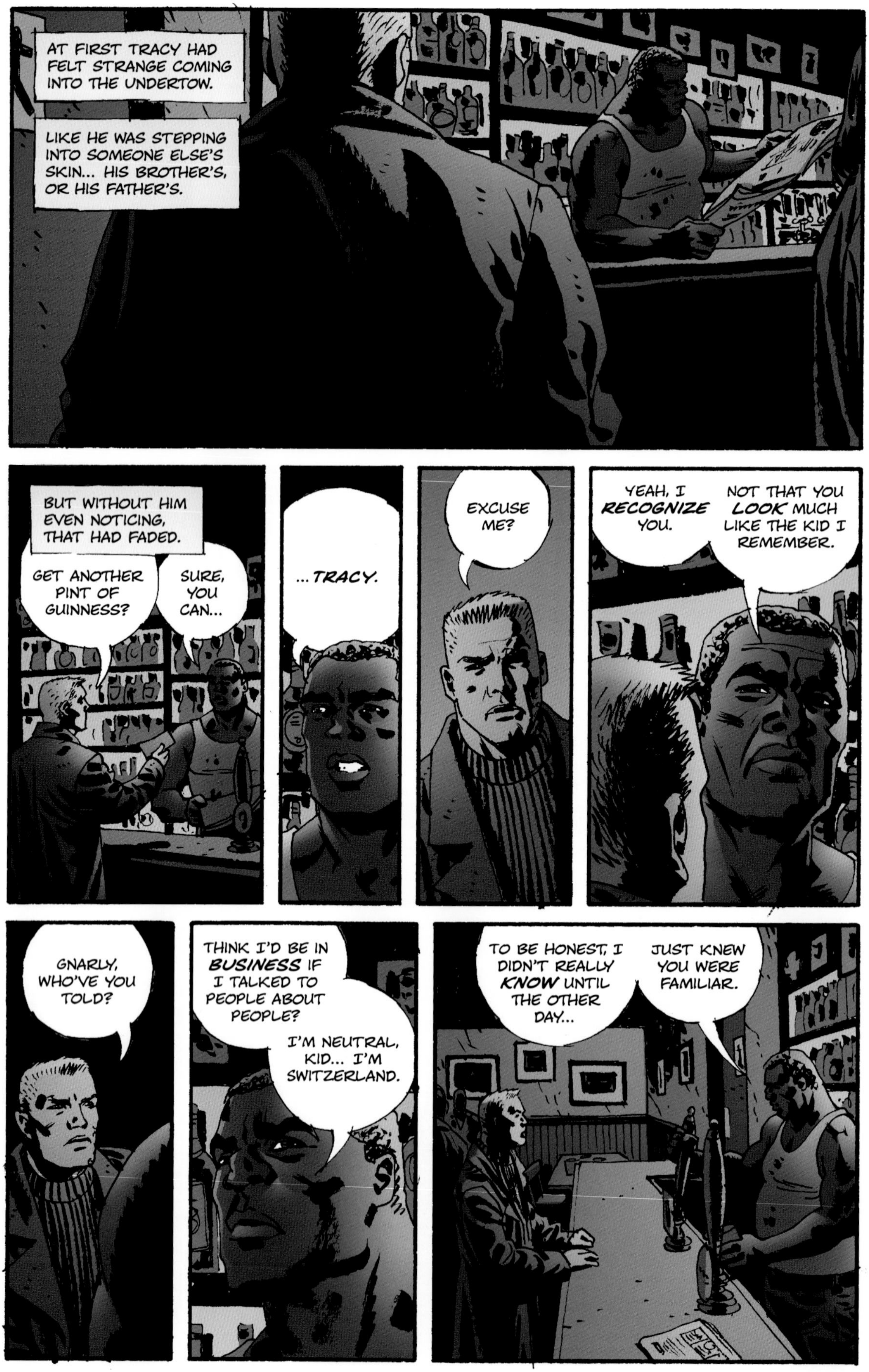
AT FIRST TRACY HAD FELT STRANGE COMING INTO THE UNDERTOW.
LIKE HE WAS STEPPING INTO SOMEONE ELSE'S SKIN... HIS BROTHER'S, OR HIS FATHER'S.
BUT WITHOUT HIM EVEN NOTICING, THAT HAD FADED.
GET ANOTHER PINT OF GUINNESS?
SURE, YOU CAN...
...TRACY.
EXCUSE ME?
YEAH, I RECOGNIZE YOU.
NOT THAT YOU LOOK MUCH LIKE THE KID I REMEMBER.
GNARLY, WHO'VE YOU TOLD?
THINK I'D BE IN BUSINESS IF I TALKED TO PEOPLE ABOUT PEOPLE?
I'M NEUTRAL, KID... I'M SWITZERLAND.
TO BE HONEST, I DIDN'T REALLY KNOW UNTIL THE OTHER DAY...
JUST KNEW YOU WERE FAMILIAR.

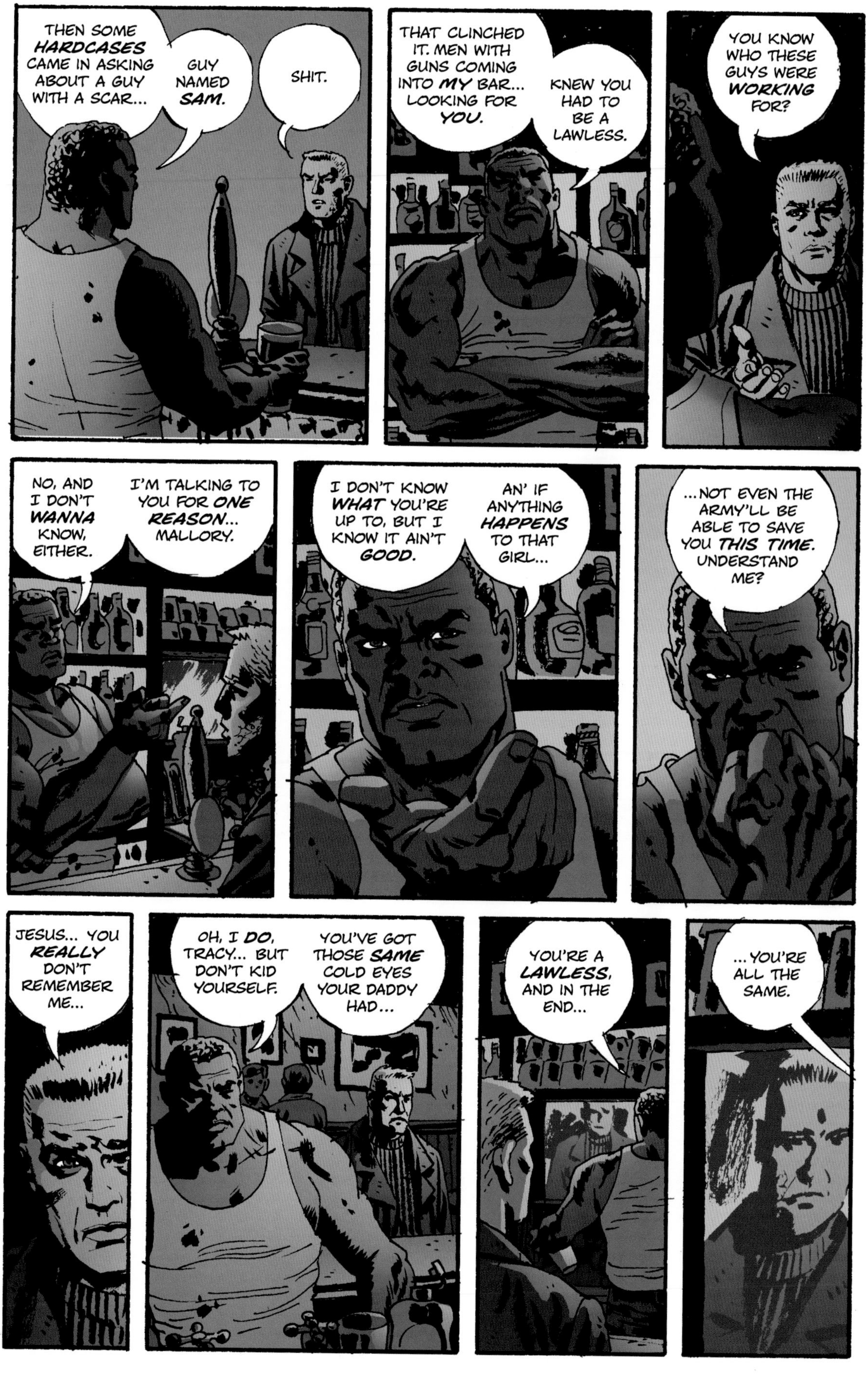
THEN SOME HARDCASES CAME IN ASKING ABOUT A GUY WITH A SCAR...
GUY NAMED SAM.
SHIT.
THAT CLINCHED IT. MEN WITH GUNS COMING INTO MY BAR... LOOKING FOR YOU.
KNEW YOU HAD TO BE A LAWLESS.
YOU KNOW WHO THESE GUYS WERE WORKING FOR?
NO, AND I DON'T WANNA KNOW, EITHER.
I'M TALKING TO YOU FOR ONE REASON... MALLORY.
I DON'T KNOW WHAT YOU'RE UP TO, BUT I KNOW IT AIN'T GOOD.
AN' IF ANYTHING HAPPENS TO THAT GIRL...
...NOT EVEN THE ARMY'LL BE ABLE TO SAVE YOU THIS TIME. UNDERSTAND ME?
JESUS... YOU REALLY DON'T REMEMBER ME...
OH, I DO, TRACY... BUT DON'T KID YOURSELF.
YOU'VE GOT THOSE SAME COLD EYES YOUR DADDY HAD...
YOU'RE A LAWLESS, AND IN THE END...
...YOU'RE ALL THE SAME.

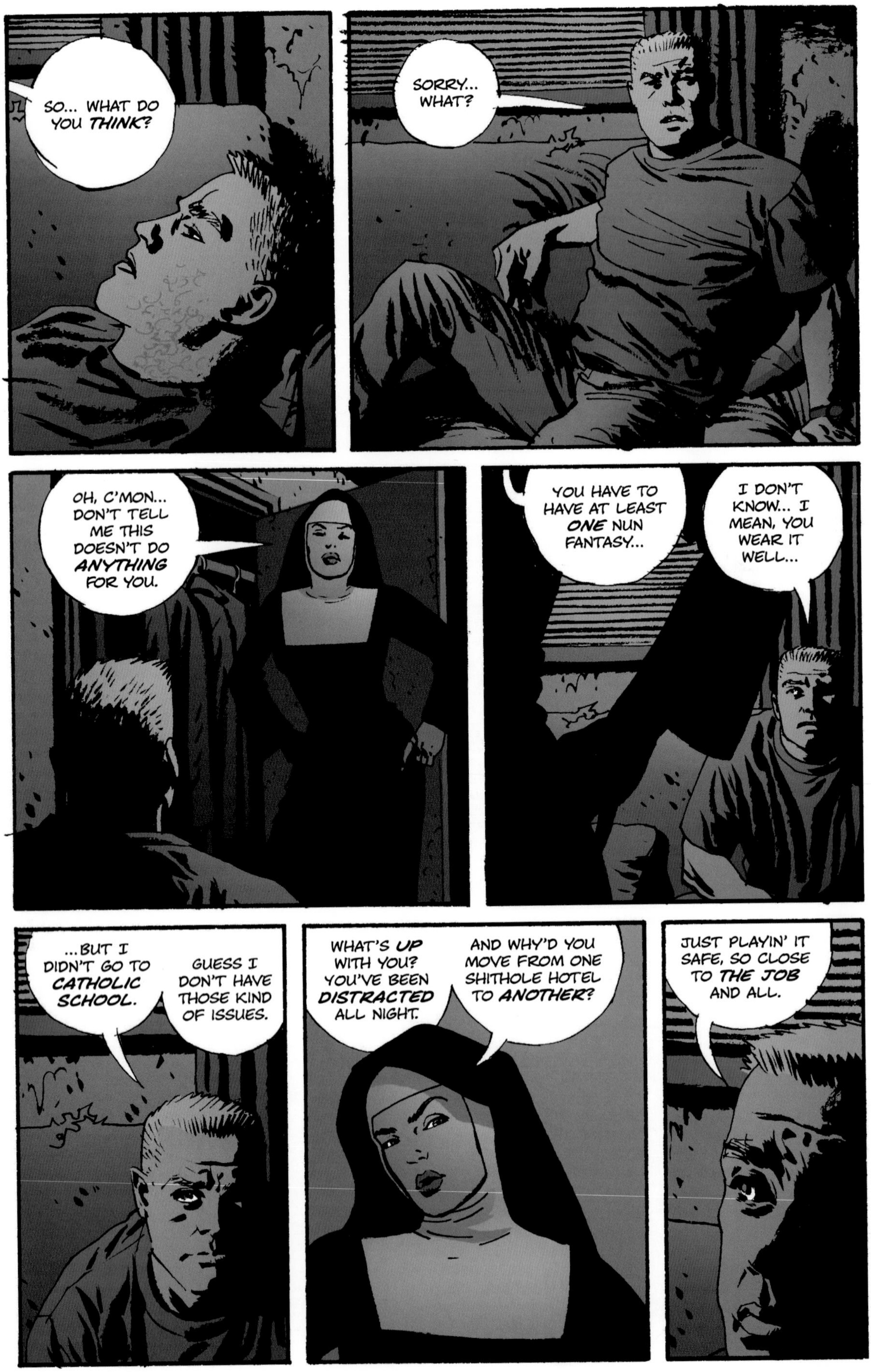
SO... WHAT DO YOU THINK?
SORRY... WHAT?
OH, C'MON... DON'T TELL ME THIS DOESN'T DO ANYTHING FOR YOU.
YOU HAVE TO HAVE AT LEAST ONE NUN FANTASY...
I DON'T KNOW... I MEAN, YOU WEAR IT WELL...
...BUT I DIDN'T GO TO CATHOLIC SCHOOL.
GUESS I DON'T HAVE THOSE KIND OF ISSUES.
WHAT'S UP WITH YOU? YOU'VE BEEN DISTRACTED ALL NIGHT.
AND WHY'D YOU MOVE FROM ONE SHITHOLE HOTEL TO ANOTHER?
JUST PLAYIN' IT SAFE, SO CLOSE TO THE JOB AND ALL.

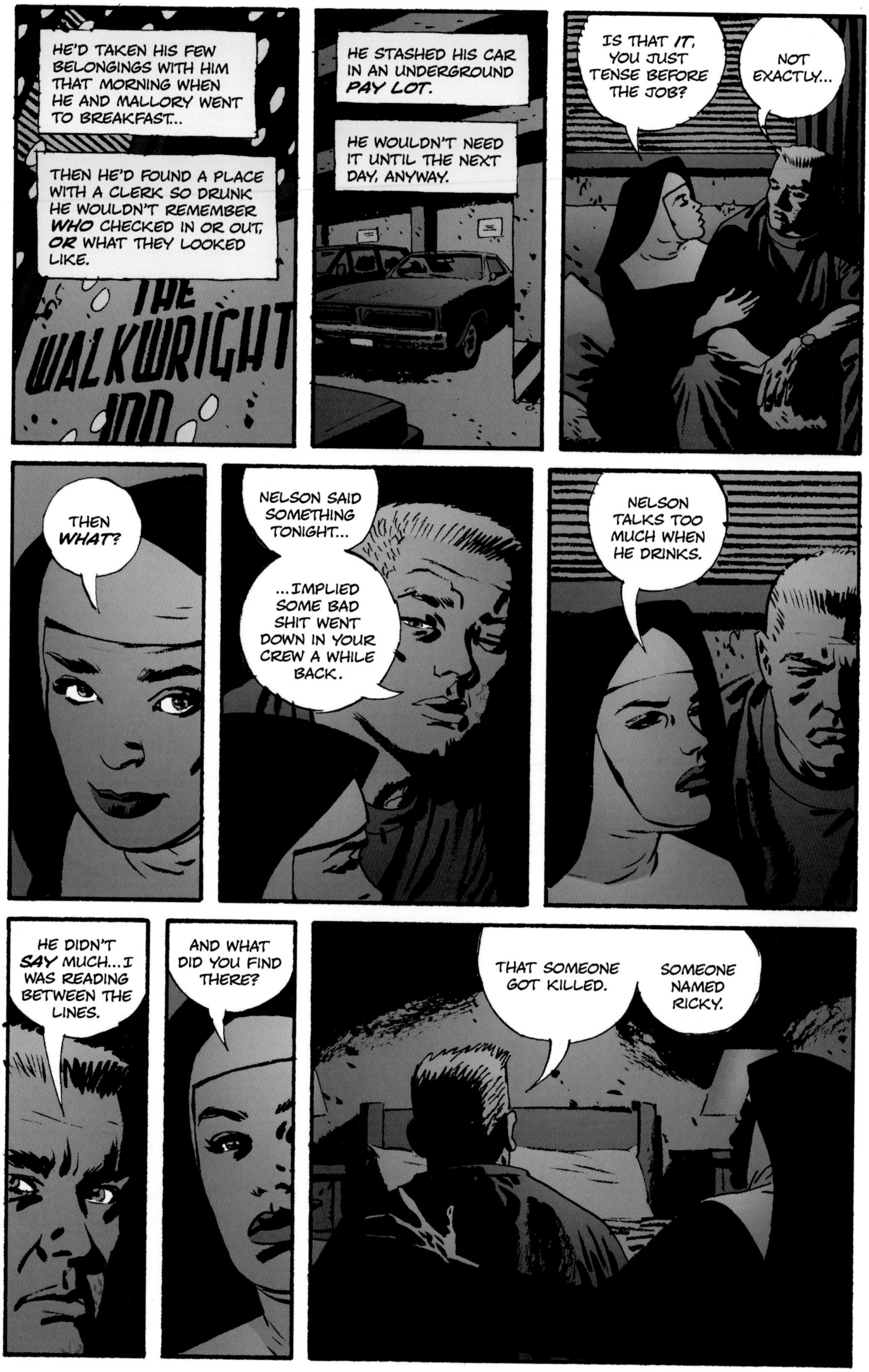
HE'D TAKEN HIS FEW BELONGINGS WITH HIM THAT MORNING WHEN HE AND MALLORY WENT TO BREAKFAST...
THEN HE'D FOUND A PLACE WITH A CLERK SO DRUNK HE WOULDN'T REMEMBER WHO CHECKED IN OR OUT, OR WHAT THEY LOOKED LIKE.
THE WALKWRIGHT INN
HE STASHED HIS CAR IN AN UNDERGROUND PAY LOT.
HE WOULDN'T NEED IT UNTIL THE NEXT DAY, ANYWAY.
IS THAT IT, YOU JUST TENSE BEFORE THE JOB?
NOT EXACTLY...
THEN WHAT?
NELSON SAID SOMETHING TONIGHT...
...IMPLIED SOME BAD SHIT WENT DOWN IN YOUR CREW A WHILE BACK.
NELSON TALKS TOO MUCH WHEN HE DRINKS.
HE DIDN'T SAY MUCH...I WAS READING BETWEEN THE LINES.
AND WHAT DID YOU FIND THERE?
THAT SOMEONE GOT KILLED.
SOMEONE NAMED RICKY.

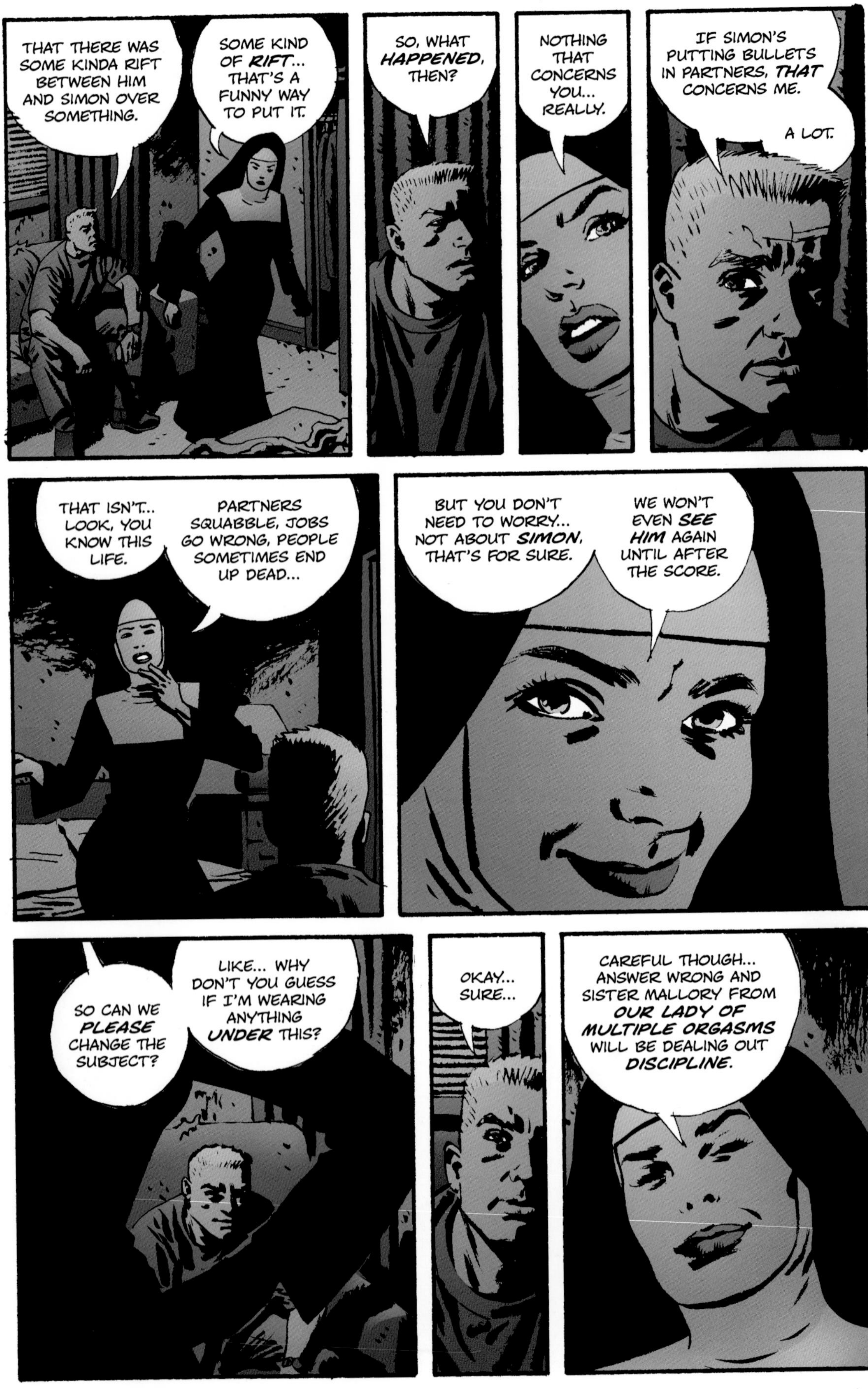
THAT THERE WAS SOME KINDA RIFT BETWEEN HIM AND SIMON OVER SOMETHING.
SOME KIND OF RIFT... THAT'S A FUNNY WAY TO PUT IT.
SO, WHAT HAPPENED, THEN?
NOTHING THAT CONCERNS YOU... REALLY.
IF SIMON'S PUTTING BULLETS IN PARTNERS, THAT CONCERNS ME.
A LOT.
THAT ISN'T... LOOK, YOU KNOW THIS LIFE.
PARTNERS SQUABBLE, JOBS GO WRONG, PEOPLE SOMETIMES END UP DEAD...
BUT YOU DON'T NEED TO WORRY... NOT ABOUT SIMON, THAT'S FOR SURE.
WE WON'T EVEN SEE HIM AGAIN UNTIL AFTER THE SCORE.
SO CAN WE PLEASE CHANGE THE SUBJECT?
LIKE... WHY DON'T YOU GUESS IF I'M WEARING ANYTHING UNDER THIS?
OKAY... SURE...
CAREFUL THOUGH... ANSWER WRONG AND SISTER MALLORY FROM OUR LADY OF MULTIPLE ORGASMS WILL BE DEALING OUT DISCIPLINE.

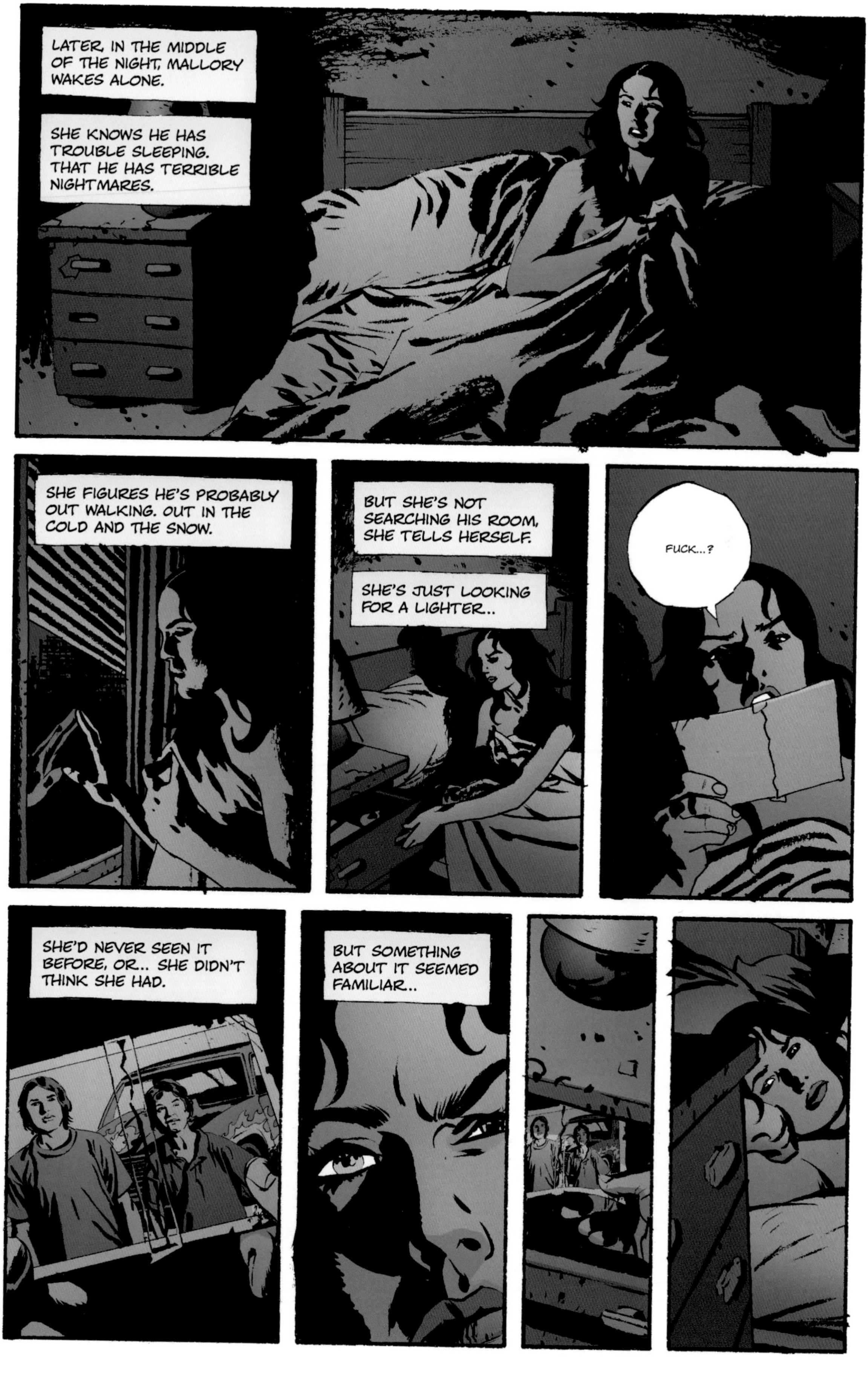
LATER, IN THE MIDDLE OF THE NIGHT, MALLORY WAKES ALONE.
SHE KNOWS HE HAS TROUBLE SLEEPING. THAT HE HAS TERRIBLE NIGHTMARES.
SHE FIGURES HE'S PROBABLY OUT WALKING. OUT IN THE COLD AND THE SNOW.
BUT SHE'S NOT SEARCHING HIS ROOM, SHE TELLS HERSELF.
SHE'S JUST LOOKING FOR A LIGHTER..
FUCK...?
SHE'D NEVER SEEN IT BEFORE, OR... SHE DIDN'T THINK SHE HAD.
BUT SOMETHING ABOUT IT SEEMED FAMILIAR..

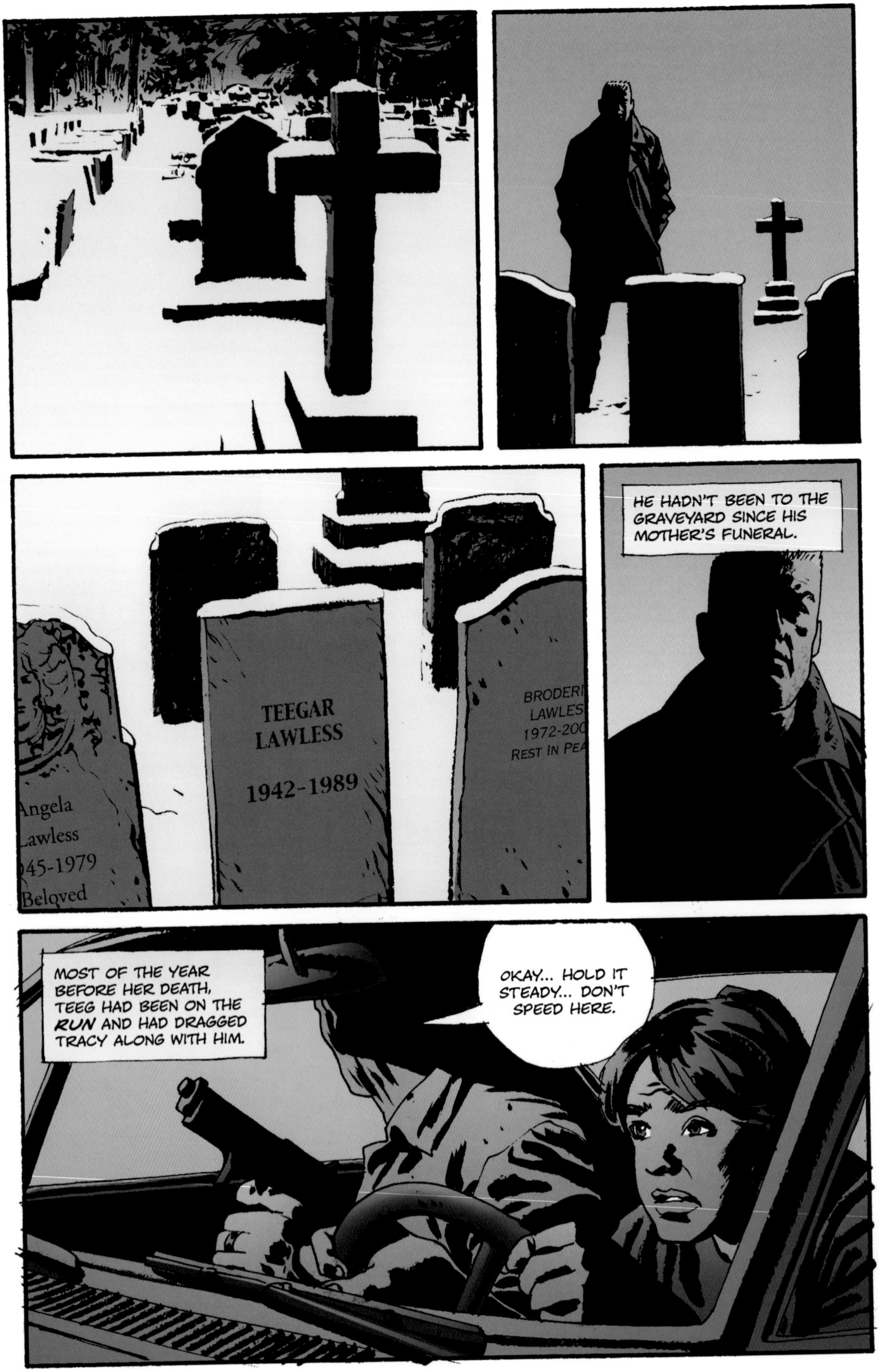
HE HADN'T BEEN TO THE GRAVEYARD SINCE HIS MOTHER'S FUNERAL.
ngela
awless
945-1979
Beloved
TEEGAR
LAWLESS
1942-1989
BRODERI
LAWLES
1972-200
REST IN PEA
MOST OF THE YEAR BEFORE HER DEATH, TEEG HAD BEEN ON THE *RUN* AND HAD DRAGGED TRACY ALONG WITH HIM.
OKAY... HOLD IT STEADY... DON'T SPEED HERE.

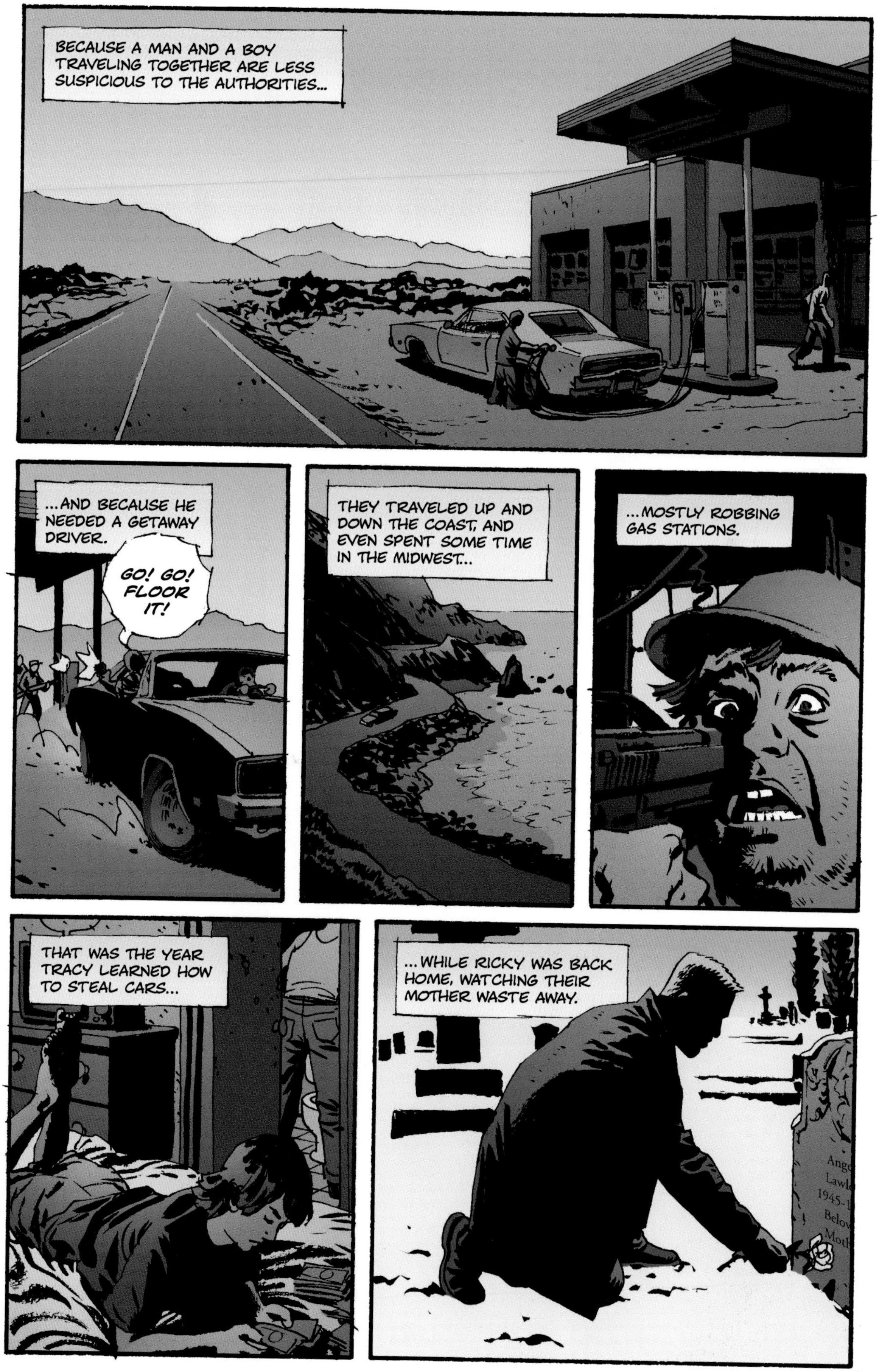
BECAUSE A MAN AND A BOY TRAVELING TOGETHER ARE LESS SUSPICIOUS TO THE AUTHORITIES...
...AND BECAUSE HE NEEDED A GETAWAY DRIVER.
GO! GO! FLOOR IT!
THEY TRAVELED UP AND DOWN THE COAST, AND EVEN SPENT SOME TIME IN THE MIDWEST...
...MOSTLY ROBBING GAS STATIONS.
THAT WAS THE YEAR TRACY LEARNED HOW TO STEAL CARS...
...WHILE RICKY WAS BACK HOME, WATCHING THEIR MOTHER WASTE AWAY.

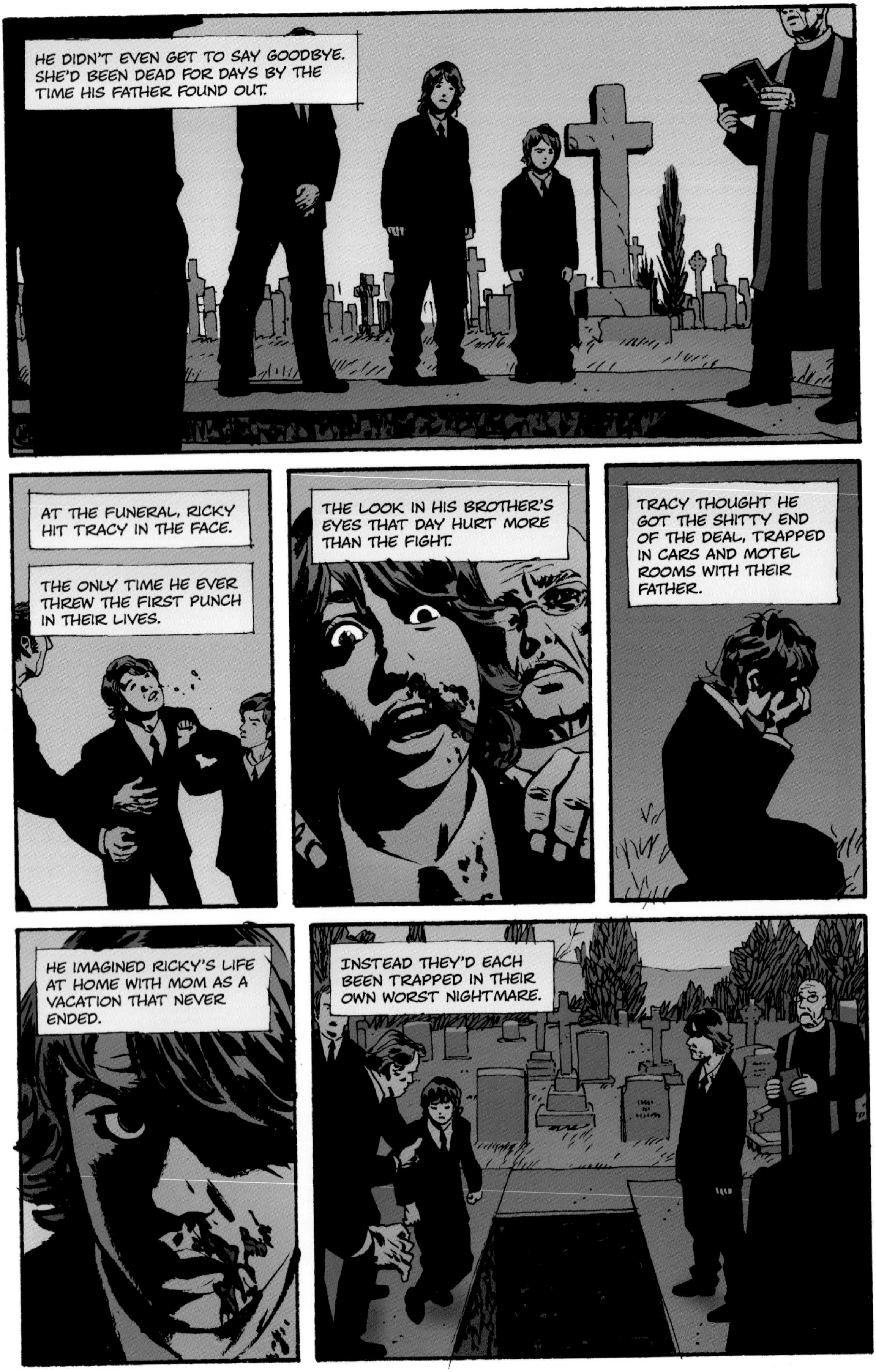
HE DIDN'T EVEN GET TO SAY GOODBYE. SHE'D BEEN DEAD FOR DAYS BY THE TIME HIS FATHER FOUND OUT.
AT THE FUNERAL, RICKY HIT TRACY IN THE FACE.
THE ONLY TIME HE EVER THREW THE FIRST PUNCH IN THEIR LIVES.
THE LOOK IN HIS BROTHER'S EYES THAT DAY HURT MORE THAN THE FIGHT.
TRACY THOUGHT HE GOT THE SHITTY END OF THE DEAL, TRAPPED IN CARS AND MOTEL ROOMS WITH THEIR FATHER.
HE IMAGINED RICKY'S LIFE AT HOME WITH MOM AS A VACATION THAT NEVER ENDED.
INSTEAD THEY'D EACH BEEN TRAPPED IN THEIR OWN WORST NIGHTMARE.

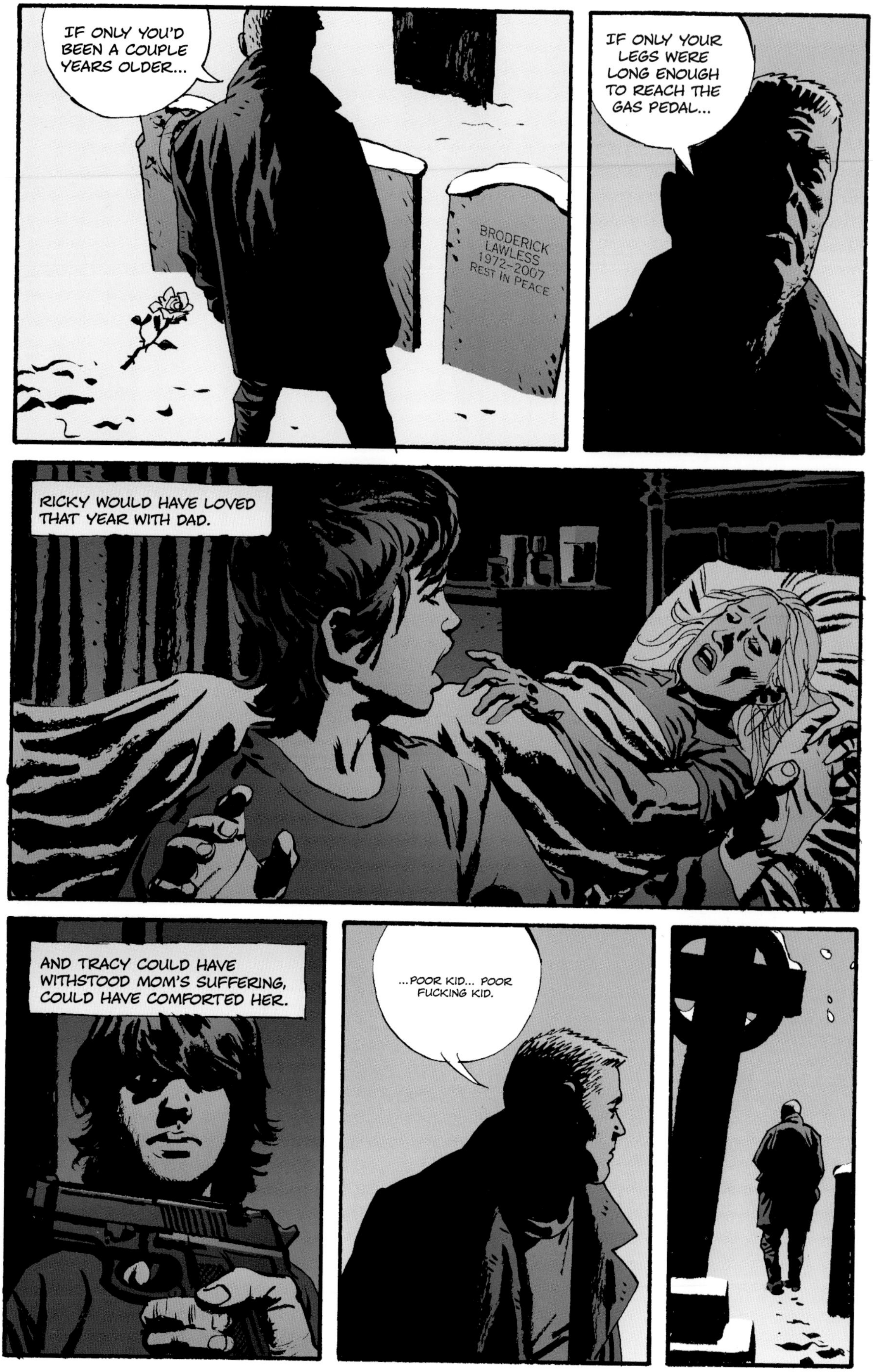
IF ONLY YOU'D BEEN A COUPLE YEARS OLDER...
BRODERICK LAWLESS 1972-2007 REST IN PEACE
IF ONLY YOUR LEGS WERE LONG ENOUGH TO REACH THE GAS PEDAL...
RICKY WOULD HAVE LOVED THAT YEAR WITH DAD.
AND TRACY COULD HAVE WITHSTOOD MOM'S SUFFERING, COULD HAVE COMFORTED HER.
...POOR KID... POOR FUCKING KID.

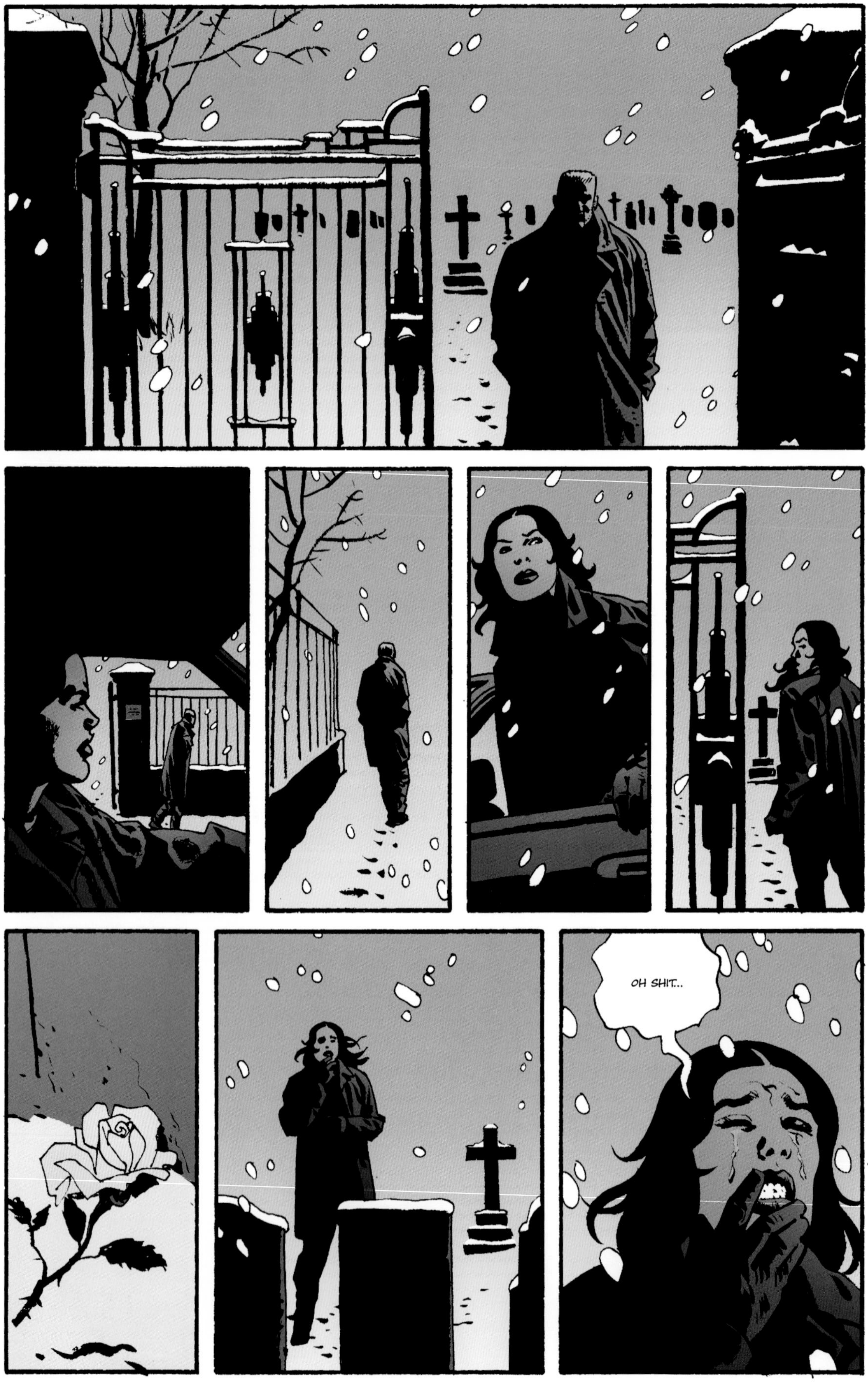
OH SHIT..

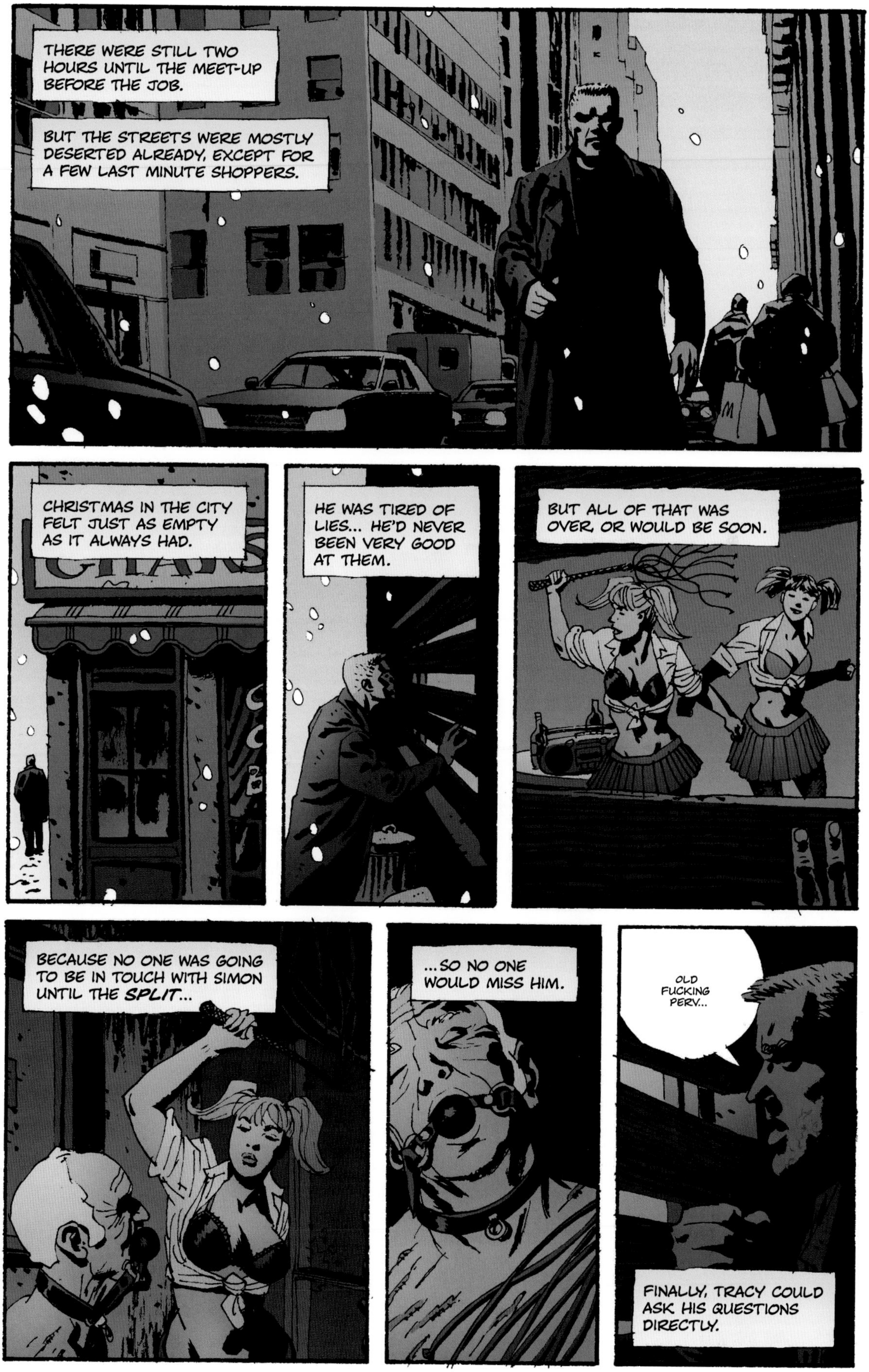
THERE WERE STILL TWO HOURS UNTIL THE MEET-UP BEFORE THE JOB.
BUT THE STREETS WERE MOSTLY DESERTED ALREADY, EXCEPT FOR A FEW LAST MINUTE SHOPPERS.
CHRISTMAS IN THE CITY FELT JUST AS EMPTY AS IT ALWAYS HAD.
HE WAS TIRED OF LIES... HE'D NEVER BEEN VERY GOOD AT THEM.
BUT ALL OF THAT WAS OVER, OR WOULD BE SOON.
BECAUSE NO ONE WAS GOING TO BE IN TOUCH WITH SIMON UNTIL THE *SPLIT*...
...SO NO ONE WOULD MISS HIM.
OLD FUCKING PERV...
FINALLY, TRACY COULD ASK HIS QUESTIONS DIRECTLY.

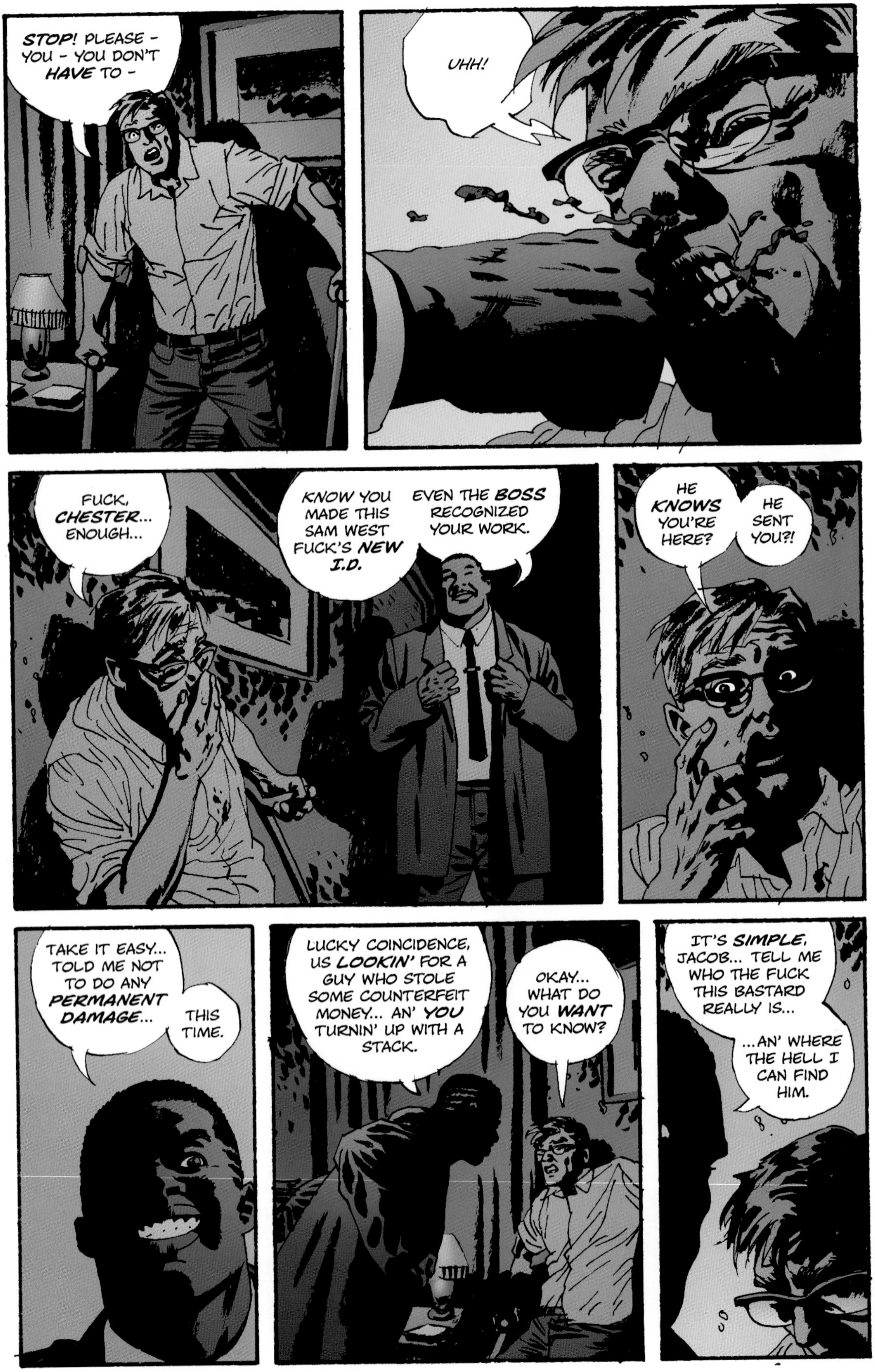
STOP! PLEASE - YOU - YOU DON'T HAVE TO -
UHH!
FUCK, CHESTER... ENOUGH...
KNOW YOU MADE THIS SAM WEST FUCK'S NEW I.D.
EVEN THE BOSS RECOGNIZED YOUR WORK.
HE KNOWS YOU'RE HERE?
HE SENT YOU?!
TAKE IT EASY... TOLD ME NOT TO DO ANY PERMANENT DAMAGE...
THIS TIME.
LUCKY COINCIDENCE, US LOOKIN' FOR A GUY WHO STOLE SOME COUNTERFEIT MONEY... AN' YOU TURNIN' UP WITH A STACK.
OKAY... WHAT DO YOU WANT TO KNOW?
IT'S SIMPLE, JACOB... TELL ME WHO THE FUCK THIS BASTARD REALLY IS...
...AN' WHERE THE HELL I CAN FIND HIM.

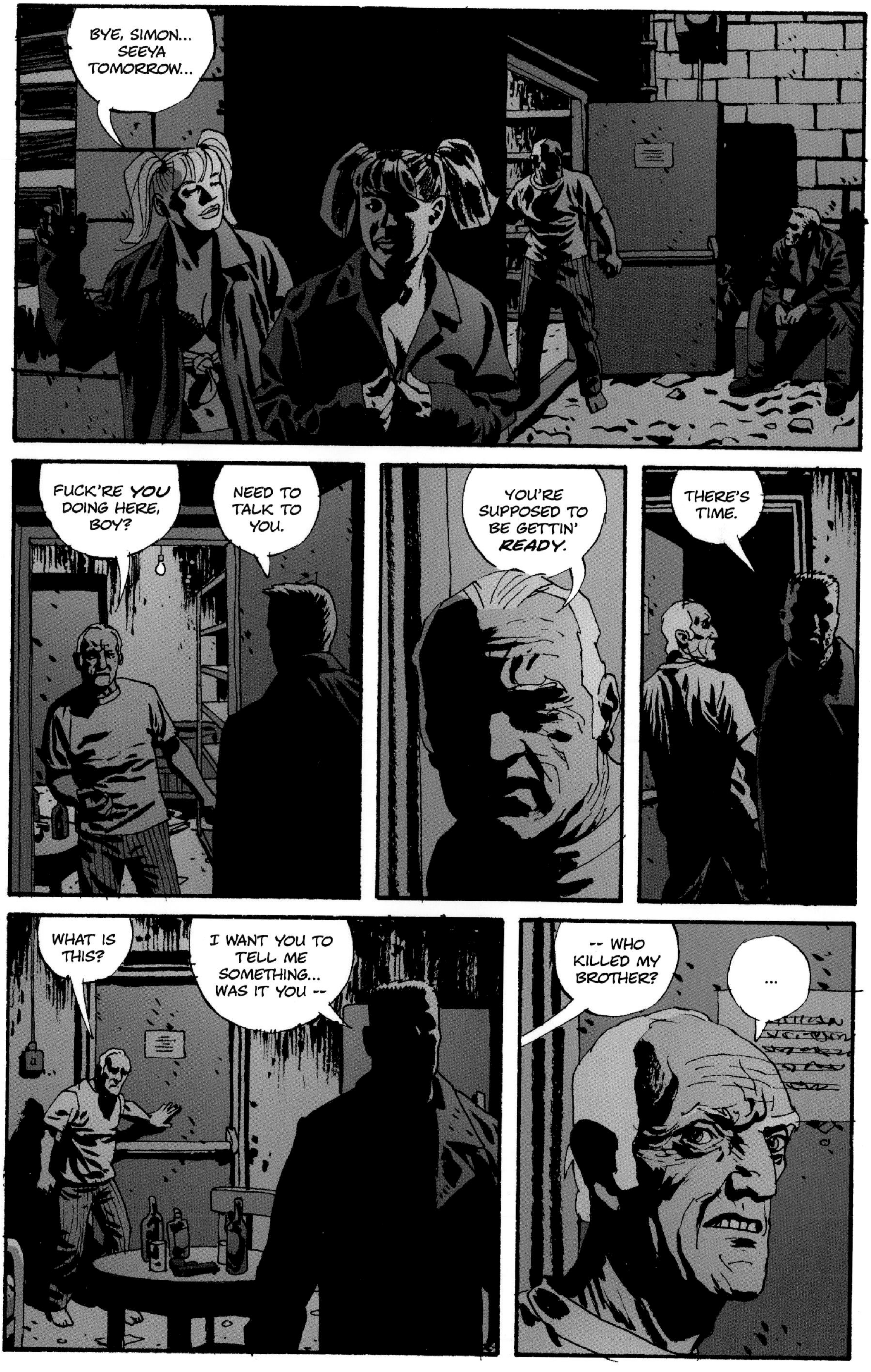
BYE, SIMON... SEEYA TOMORROW...
FUCK'RE *YOU* DOING HERE, BOY?
NEED TO TALK TO YOU.
YOU'RE SUPPOSED TO BE GETTIN' *READY*.
THERE'S TIME.
WHAT IS THIS?
I WANT YOU TO TELL ME SOMETHING... WAS IT YOU --
-- WHO KILLED MY BROTHER?
...

Y'KNOW, I *THOUGHT* I RECOGNIZED YOU, I JUST...

NO.

AHH!

UHN!

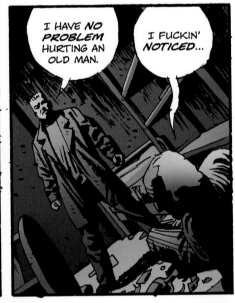

I HAVE *NO PROBLEM* HURTING AN OLD MAN.

I FUCKIN' *NOTICED*...

BUT THIS DOESN'T *HAVE* TO GET UGLY... NECESSARILY.

SHIT... IT'S AS UGLY AS THEY GET, KID...

WHAT *ELSE* WOULD'JA CALL IT, WHAT YOU'RE DOIN'?

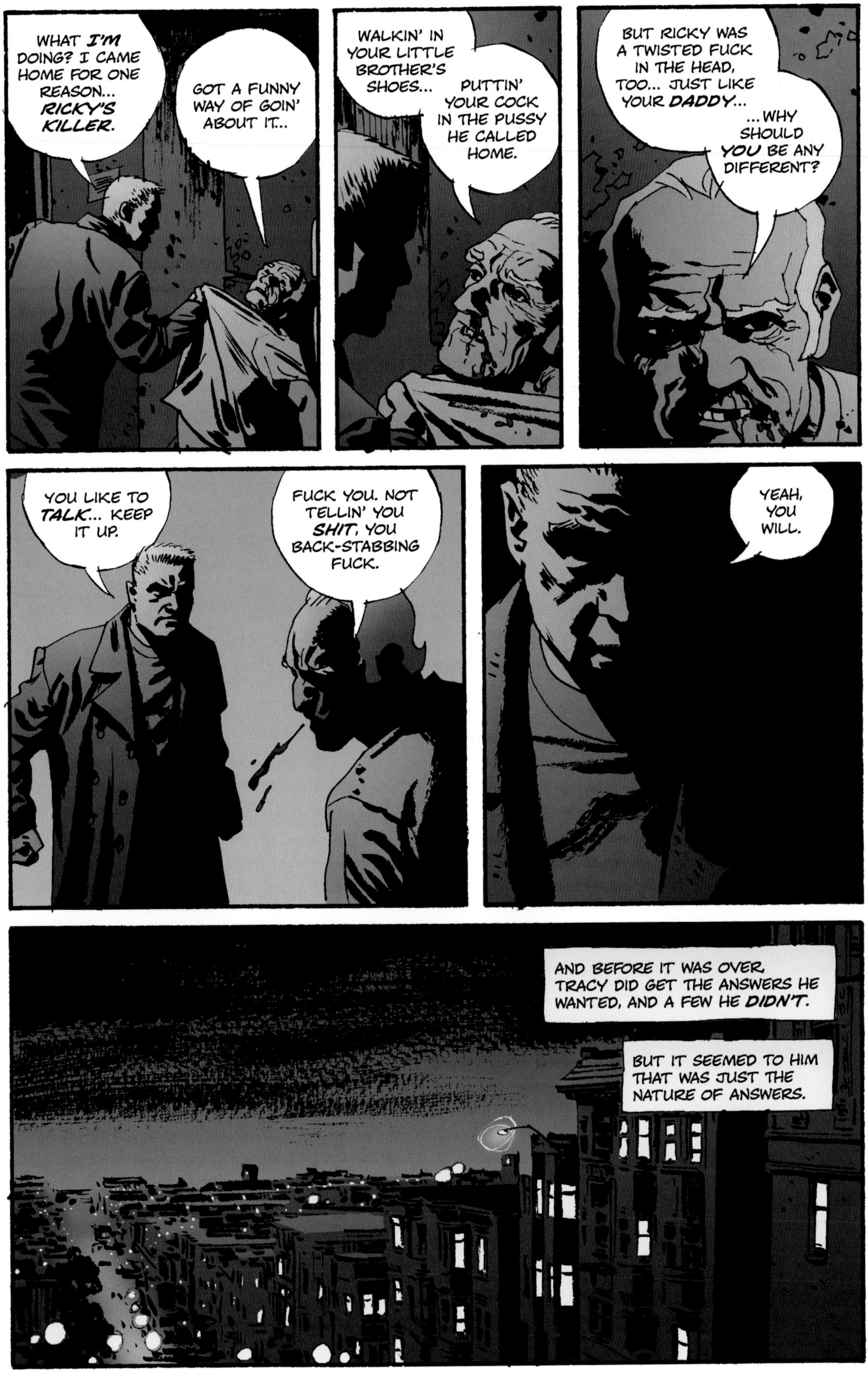
WHAT I'M DOING? I CAME HOME FOR ONE REASON... RICKY'S KILLER.
GOT A FUNNY WAY OF GOIN' ABOUT IT...
WALKIN' IN YOUR LITTLE BROTHER'S SHOES...
PUTTIN' YOUR COCK IN THE PUSSY HE CALLED HOME.
BUT RICKY WAS A TWISTED FUCK IN THE HEAD, TOO... JUST LIKE YOUR DADDY...
...WHY SHOULD YOU BE ANY DIFFERENT?
YOU LIKE TO TALK... KEEP IT UP.
FUCK YOU. NOT TELLIN' YOU SHIT, YOU BACK-STABBING FUCK.
YEAH, YOU WILL.
AND BEFORE IT WAS OVER, TRACY DID GET THE ANSWERS HE WANTED, AND A FEW HE DIDN'T.
BUT IT SEEMED TO HIM THAT WAS JUST THE NATURE OF ANSWERS.

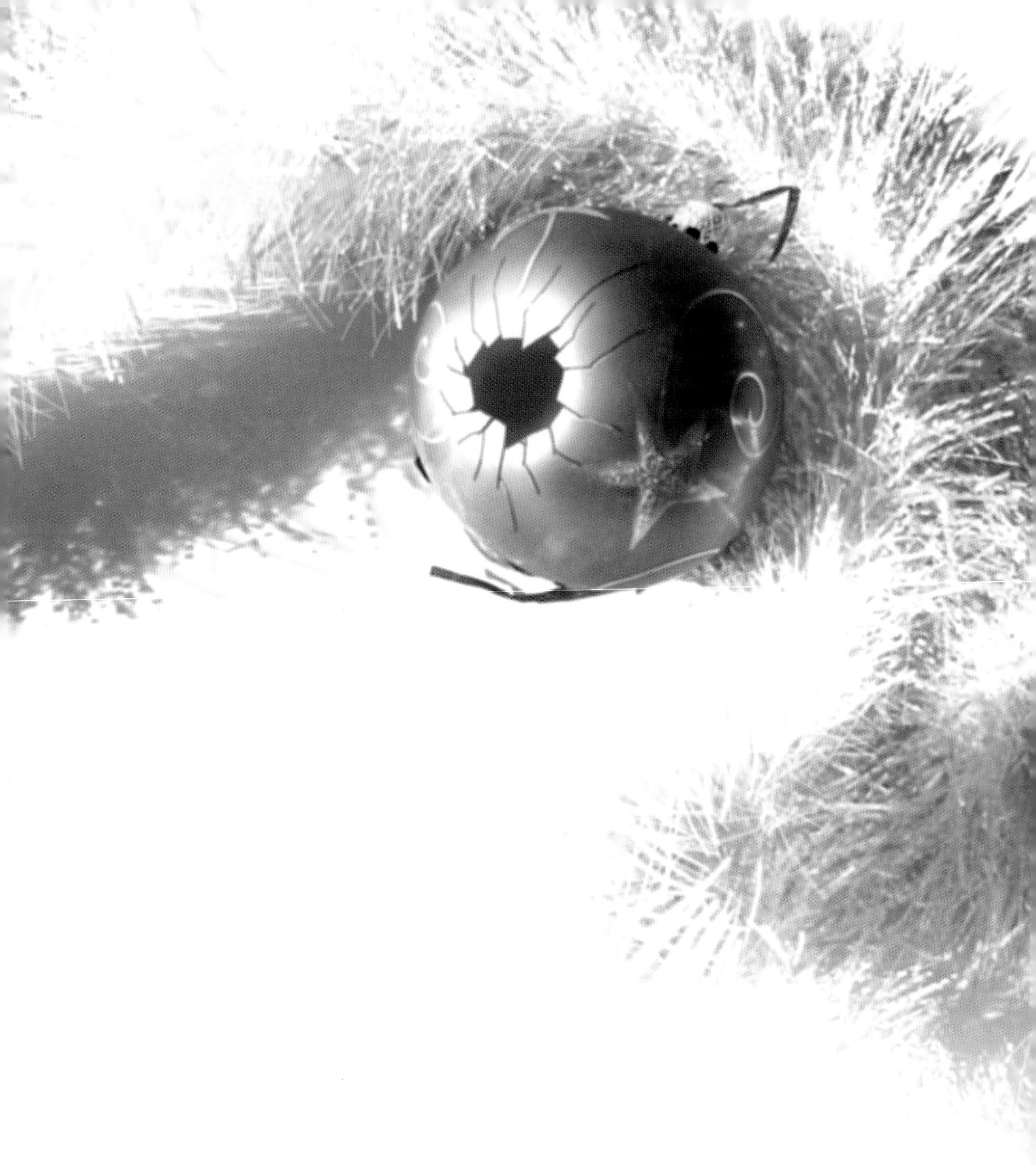

Part Five

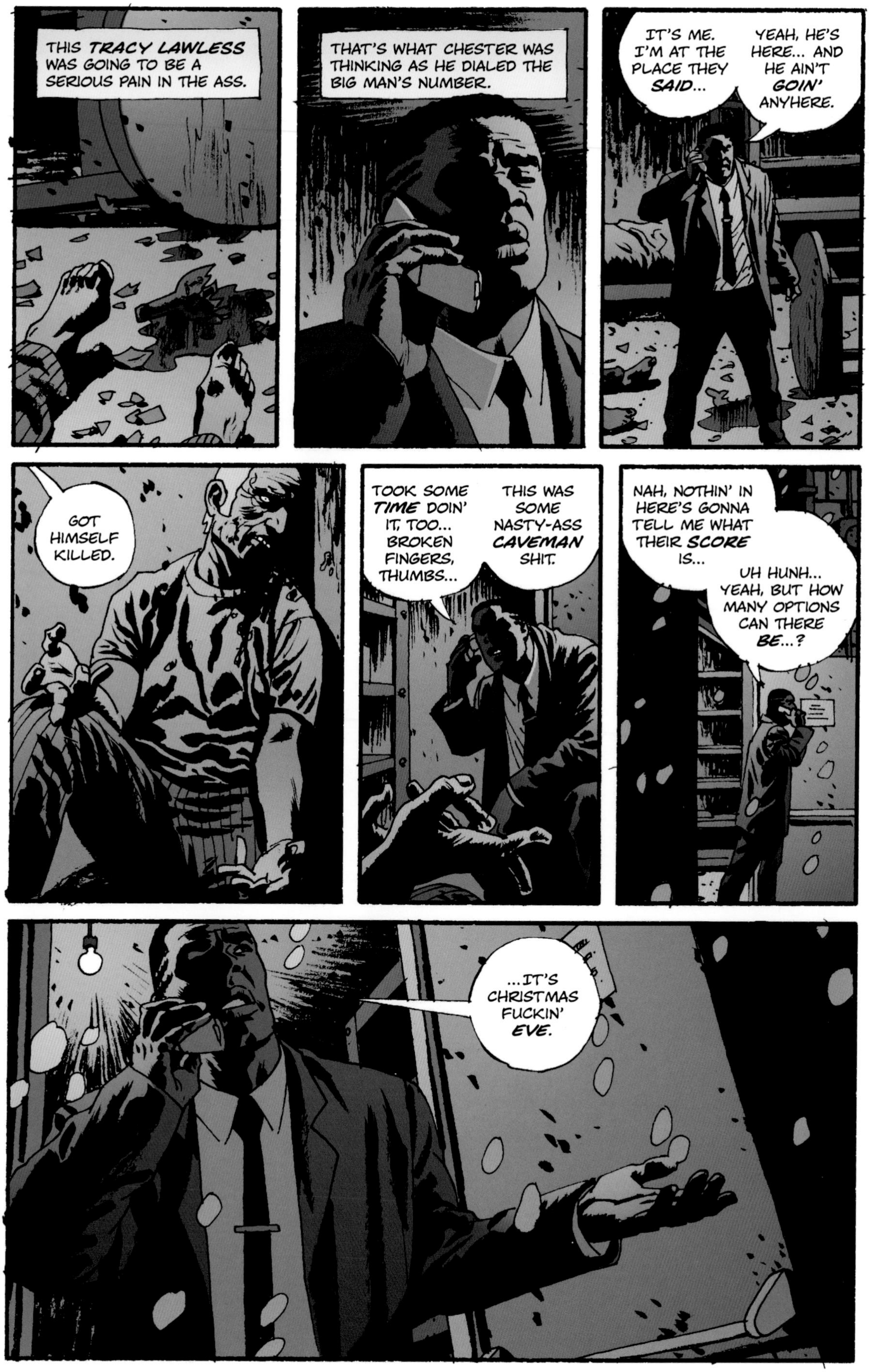

THIS TRACY LAWLESS WAS GOING TO BE A SERIOUS PAIN IN THE ASS.
THAT'S WHAT CHESTER WAS THINKING AS HE DIALED THE BIG MAN'S NUMBER.
IT'S ME. I'M AT THE PLACE THEY SAID...
YEAH, HE'S HERE... AND HE AIN'T GOIN' ANYHERE.
GOT HIMSELF KILLED.
TOOK SOME TIME DOIN' IT, TOO... BROKEN FINGERS, THUMBS...
THIS WAS SOME NASTY-ASS CAVEMAN SHIT.
NAH, NOTHIN' IN HERE'S GONNA TELL ME WHAT THEIR SCORE IS...
UH HUNH... YEAH, BUT HOW MANY OPTIONS CAN THERE BE...?
...IT'S CHRISTMAS FUCKIN' EVE.

SIMON HAD BEEN PLANNING THIS HEIST FOR YEARS.

EVER SINCE HE'D FOUND OUT HOW MUCH CASH THE *SAINT DOMINIC'S CATHEDRAL* BLACK TIE *BENEFIT* USUALLY TOOK IN.

THIS *THOUSAND DOLLAR* PER PERSON EVENT HAD BECOME A FIXTURE AMONG THE CITY'S UPPER CLASS.

ALL DONATIONS WERE MADE *IN CASH*, WITH PROCEEDS SUPPOSEDLY GOING TO CAUSES IN AFRICA.

SO, THE IDLE RICH GOT THEIR PICTURE IN THE *SOCIETY PAGES* ON CHRISTMAS MORNING...

...*AND* GOT TO FEEL LIKE THEY WERE SAVING THE WORLD A LITTLE BIT.

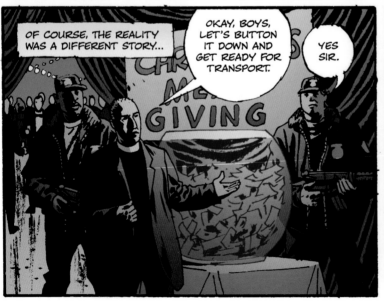

OF COURSE, THE REALITY WAS A DIFFERENT STORY...

OKAY, BOYS, LET'S BUTTON IT DOWN AND GET READY FOR TRANSPORT.

YES SIR.

...BECAUSE *FATHER BRIAN GRANT*, WHO RAN SAINT DOMINIC'S, WAS CROOKED AS HELL.

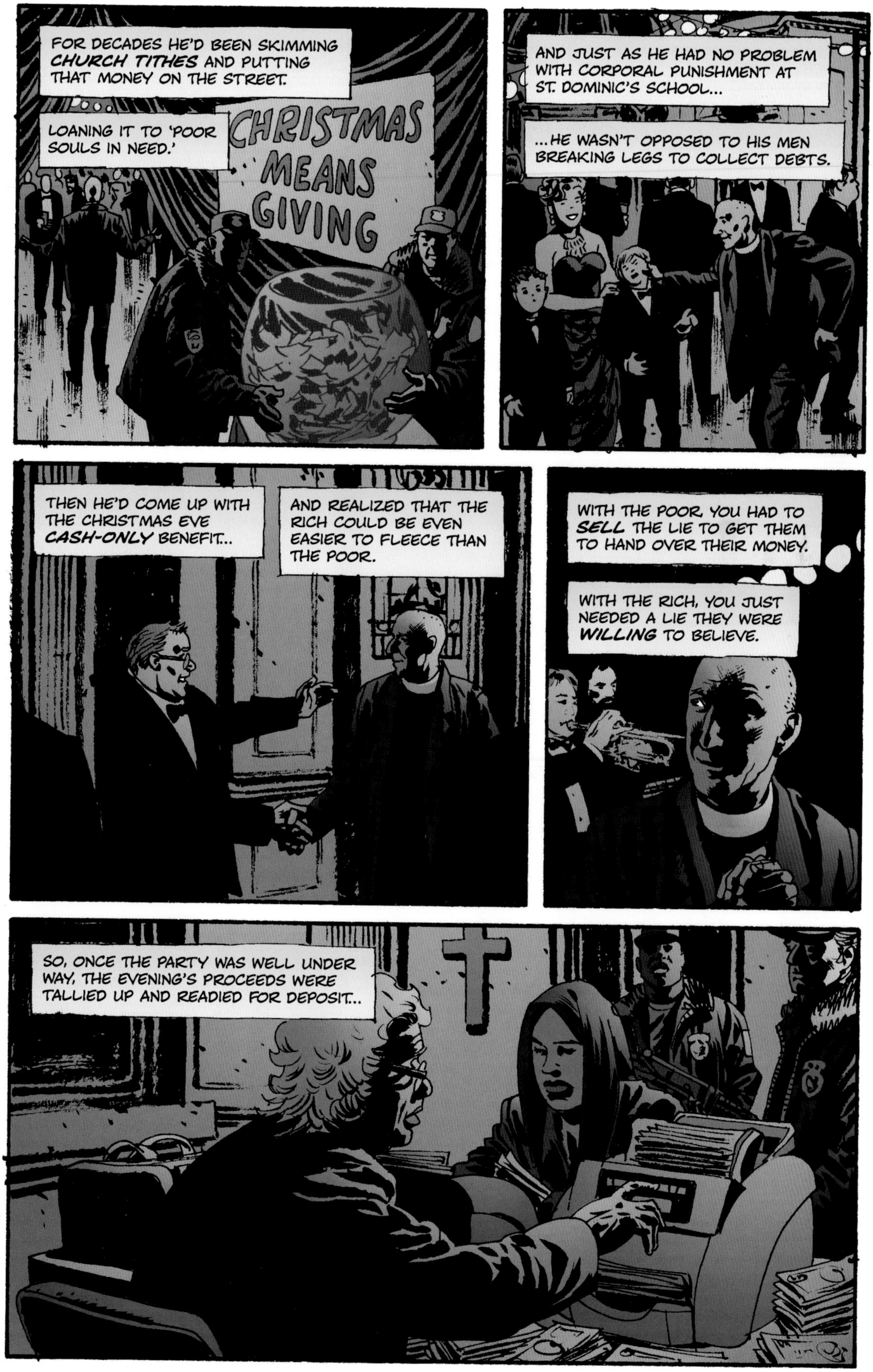
FOR DECADES HE'D BEEN SKIMMING ***CHURCH TITHES*** AND PUTTING THAT MONEY ON THE STREET.
LOANING IT TO 'POOR SOULS IN NEED.'
CHRISTMAS MEANS GIVING
AND JUST AS HE HAD NO PROBLEM WITH CORPORAL PUNISHMENT AT ST. DOMINIC'S SCHOOL...
...HE WASN'T OPPOSED TO HIS MEN BREAKING LEGS TO COLLECT DEBTS.
THEN HE'D COME UP WITH THE CHRISTMAS EVE ***CASH-ONLY*** BENEFIT...
AND REALIZED THAT THE RICH COULD BE EVEN EASIER TO FLEECE THAN THE POOR.
WITH THE POOR, YOU HAD TO ***SELL*** THE LIE TO GET THEM TO HAND OVER THEIR MONEY.
WITH THE RICH, YOU JUST NEEDED A LIE THEY WERE ***WILLING*** TO BELIEVE.
SO, ONCE THE PARTY WAS WELL UNDER WAY, THE EVENING'S PROCEEDS WERE TALLIED UP AND READIED FOR DEPOSIT...

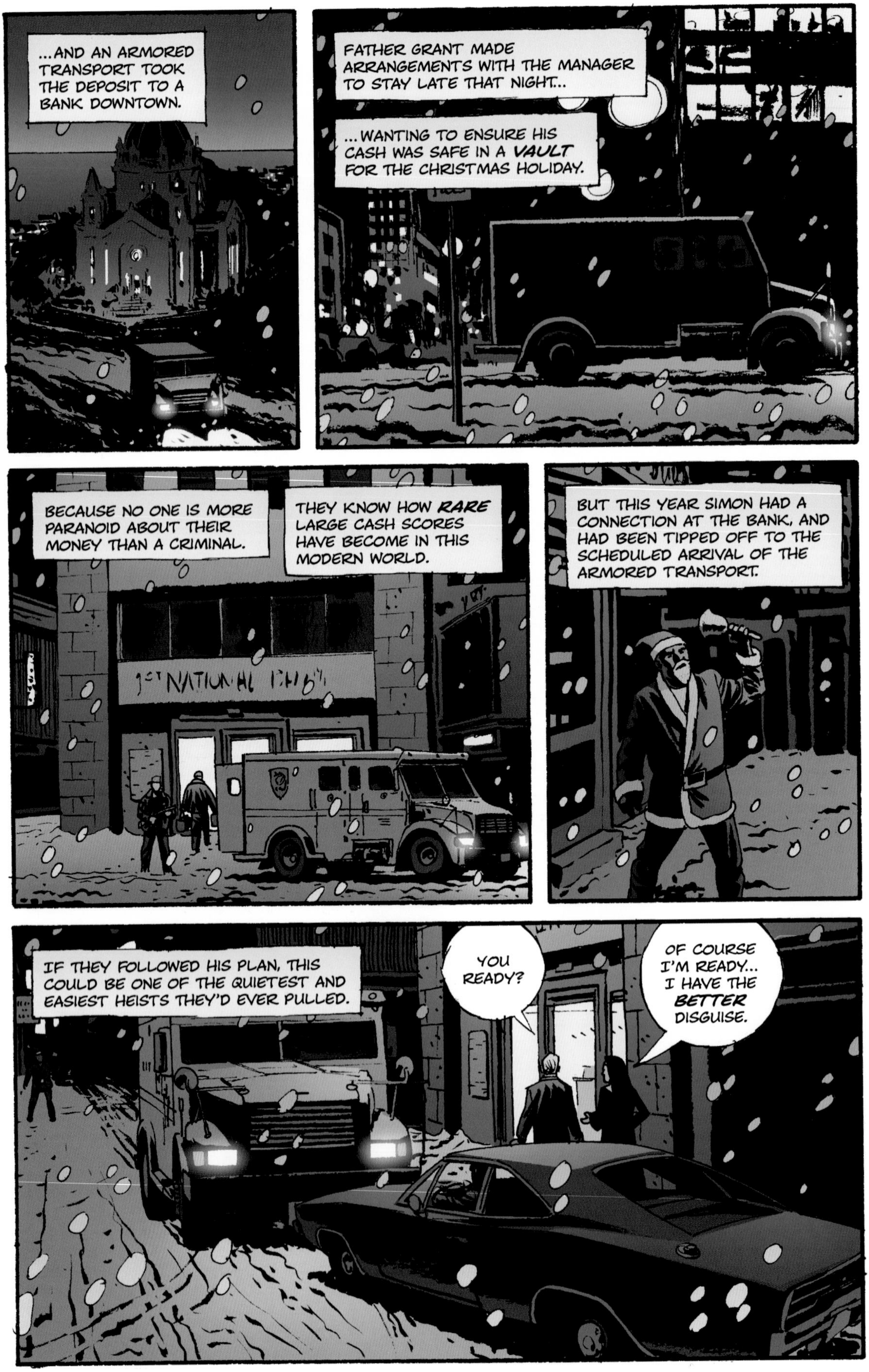
...AND AN ARMORED TRANSPORT TOOK THE DEPOSIT TO A BANK DOWNTOWN.
FATHER GRANT MADE ARRANGEMENTS WITH THE MANAGER TO STAY LATE THAT NIGHT...
...WANTING TO ENSURE HIS CASH WAS SAFE IN A VAULT FOR THE CHRISTMAS HOLIDAY.
BECAUSE NO ONE IS MORE PARANOID ABOUT THEIR MONEY THAN A CRIMINAL.
THEY KNOW HOW RARE LARGE CASH SCORES HAVE BECOME IN THIS MODERN WORLD.
BUT THIS YEAR SIMON HAD A CONNECTION AT THE BANK, AND HAD BEEN TIPPED OFF TO THE SCHEDULED ARRIVAL OF THE ARMORED TRANSPORT.
IF THEY FOLLOWED HIS PLAN, THIS COULD BE ONE OF THE QUIETEST AND EASIEST HEISTS THEY'D EVER PULLED.
YOU READY?
OF COURSE I'M READY... I HAVE THE BETTER DISGUISE.

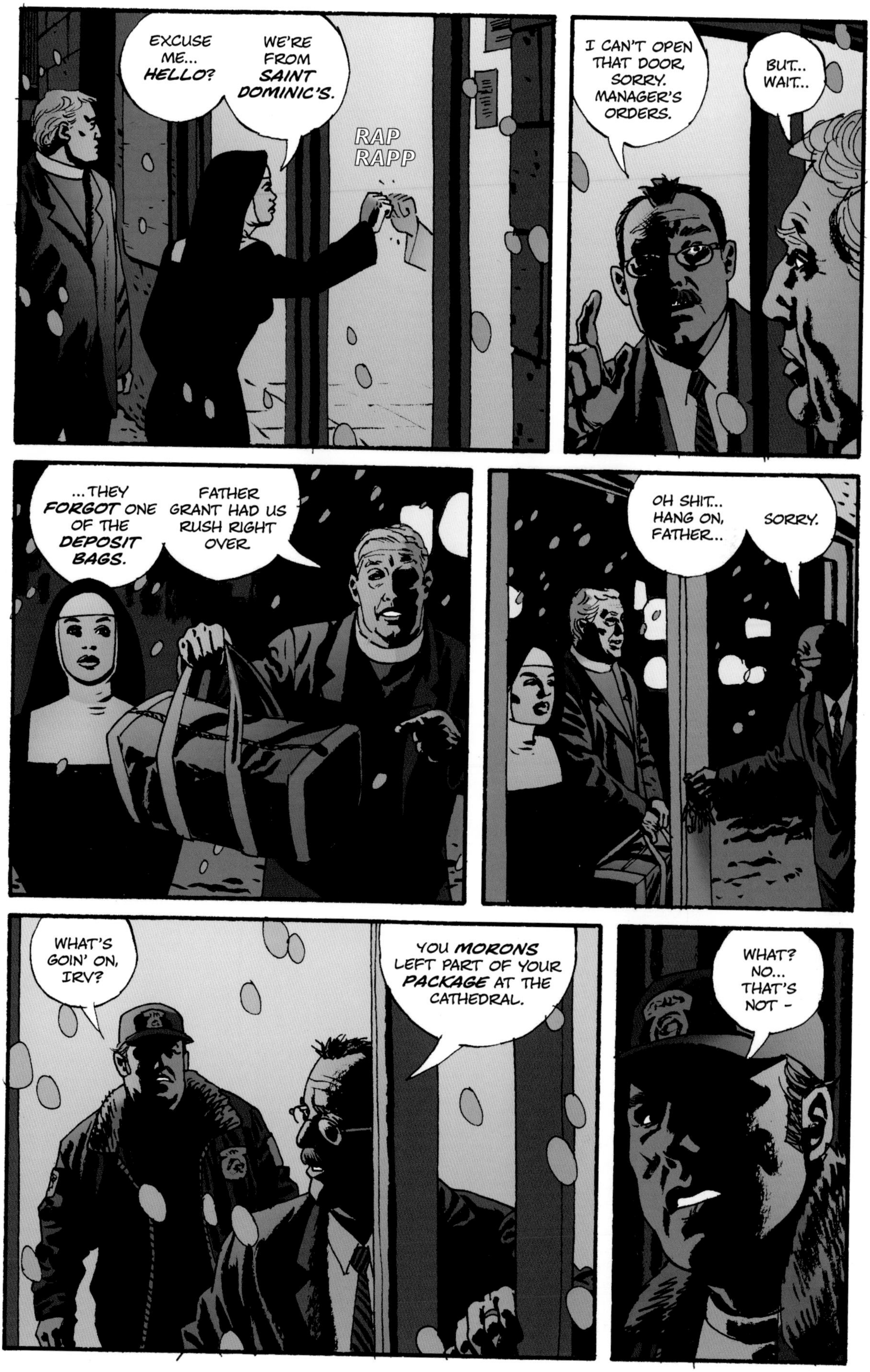
EXCUSE ME... HELLO?
WE'RE FROM SAINT DOMINIC'S.
RAP RAPP
I CAN'T OPEN THAT DOOR, SORRY. MANAGER'S ORDERS.
BUT... WAIT...
...THEY FORGOT ONE OF THE DEPOSIT BAGS.
FATHER GRANT HAD US RUSH RIGHT OVER
OH SHIT... HANG ON, FATHER...
SORRY.
WHAT'S GOIN' ON, IRV?
YOU MORONS LEFT PART OF YOUR PACKAGE AT THE CATHEDRAL.
WHAT? NO... THAT'S NOT -

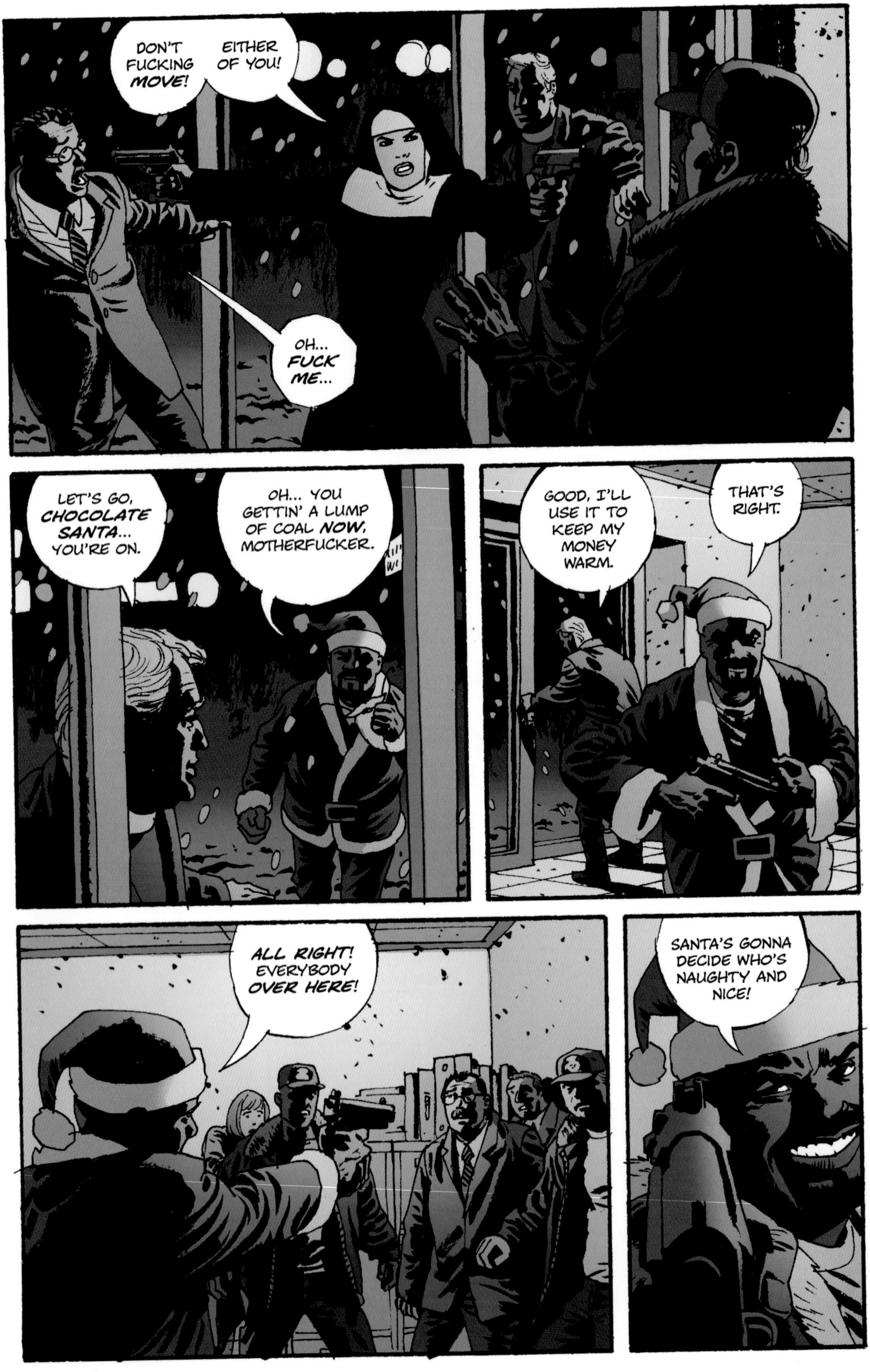
DON'T FUCKING MOVE!
EITHER OF YOU!
OH... FUCK ME...
LET'S GO, CHOCOLATE SANTA... YOU'RE ON.
OH... YOU GETTIN' A LUMP OF COAL NOW, MOTHERFUCKER.
GOOD, I'LL USE IT TO KEEP MY MONEY WARM.
THAT'S RIGHT.
ALL RIGHT! EVERYBODY OVER HERE!
SANTA'S GONNA DECIDE WHO'S NAUGHTY AND NICE!

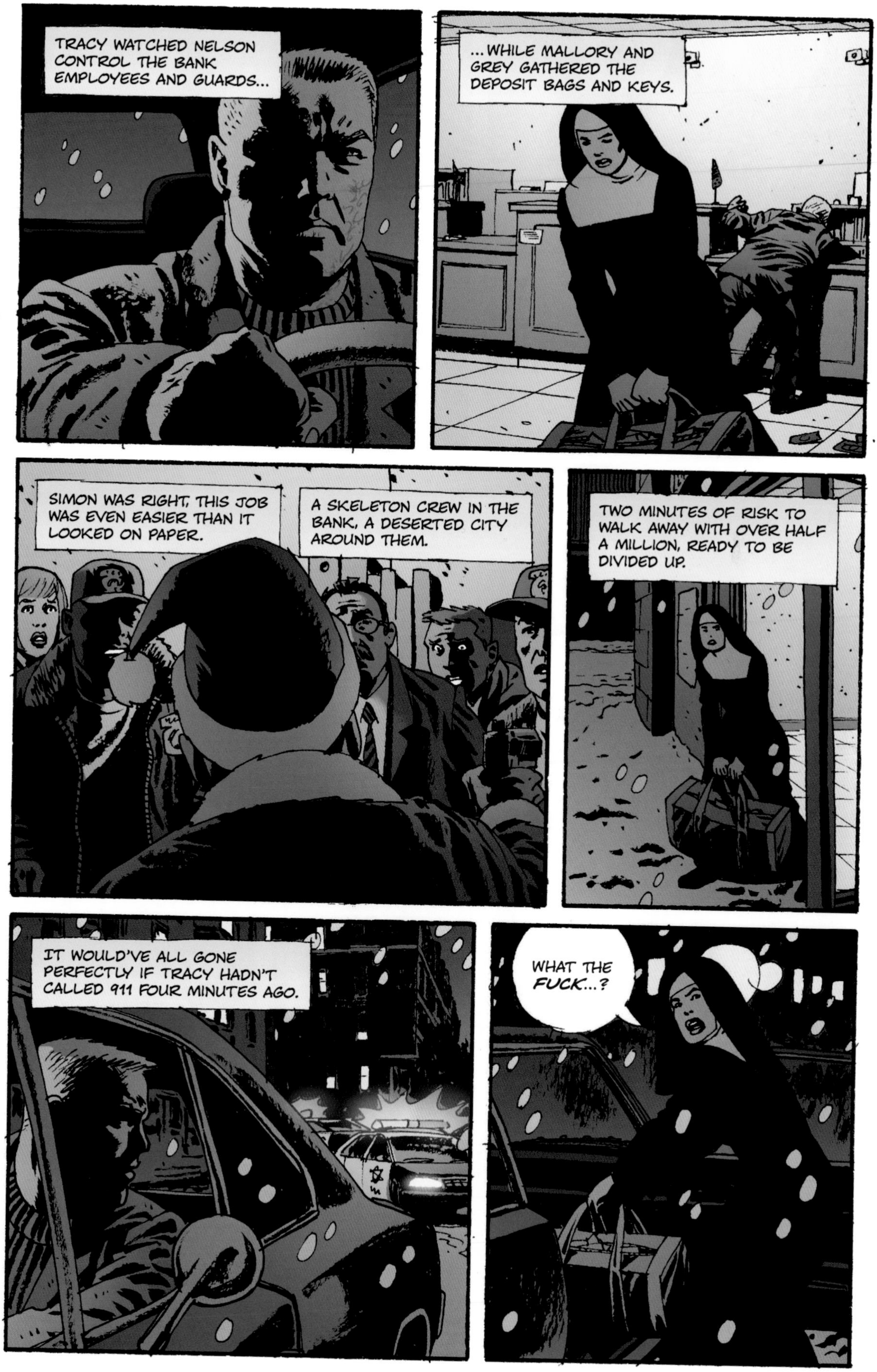
TRACY WATCHED NELSON CONTROL THE BANK EMPLOYEES AND GUARDS...
...WHILE MALLORY AND GREY GATHERED THE DEPOSIT BAGS AND KEYS.
SIMON WAS RIGHT; THIS JOB WAS EVEN EASIER THAN IT LOOKED ON PAPER.
A SKELETON CREW IN THE BANK, A DESERTED CITY AROUND THEM.
TWO MINUTES OF RISK TO WALK AWAY WITH OVER HALF A MILLION, READY TO BE DIVIDED UP.
IT WOULD'VE ALL GONE PERFECTLY IF TRACY HADN'T CALLED 911 FOUR MINUTES AGO.
WHAT THE *FUCK*...?

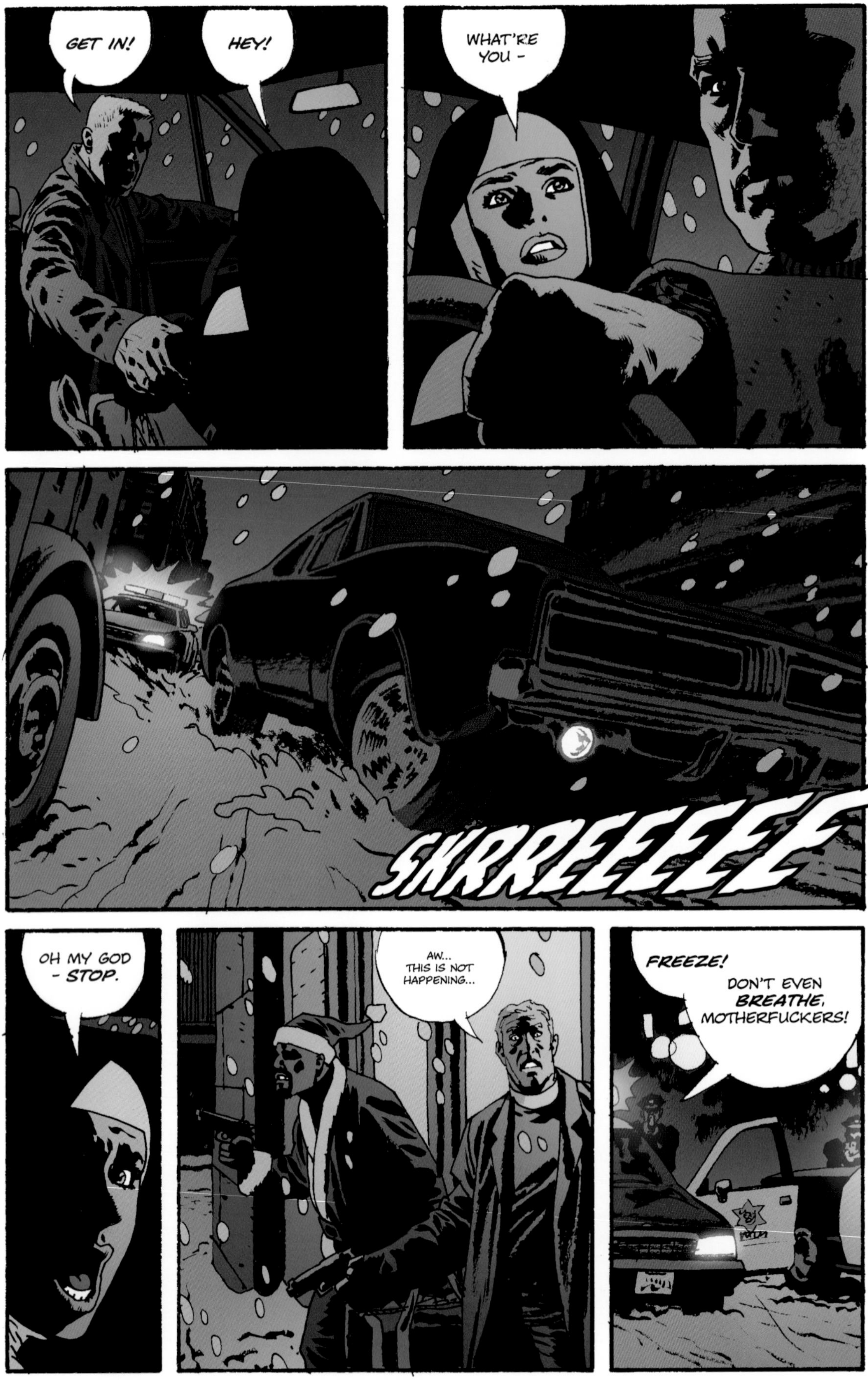
GET IN!
HEY!
WHAT'RE YOU -
SKRREEEEEE
OH MY GOD - STOP.
AW... THIS IS NOT HAPPENING...
FREEZE!
DON'T EVEN BREATHE, MOTHERFUCKERS!

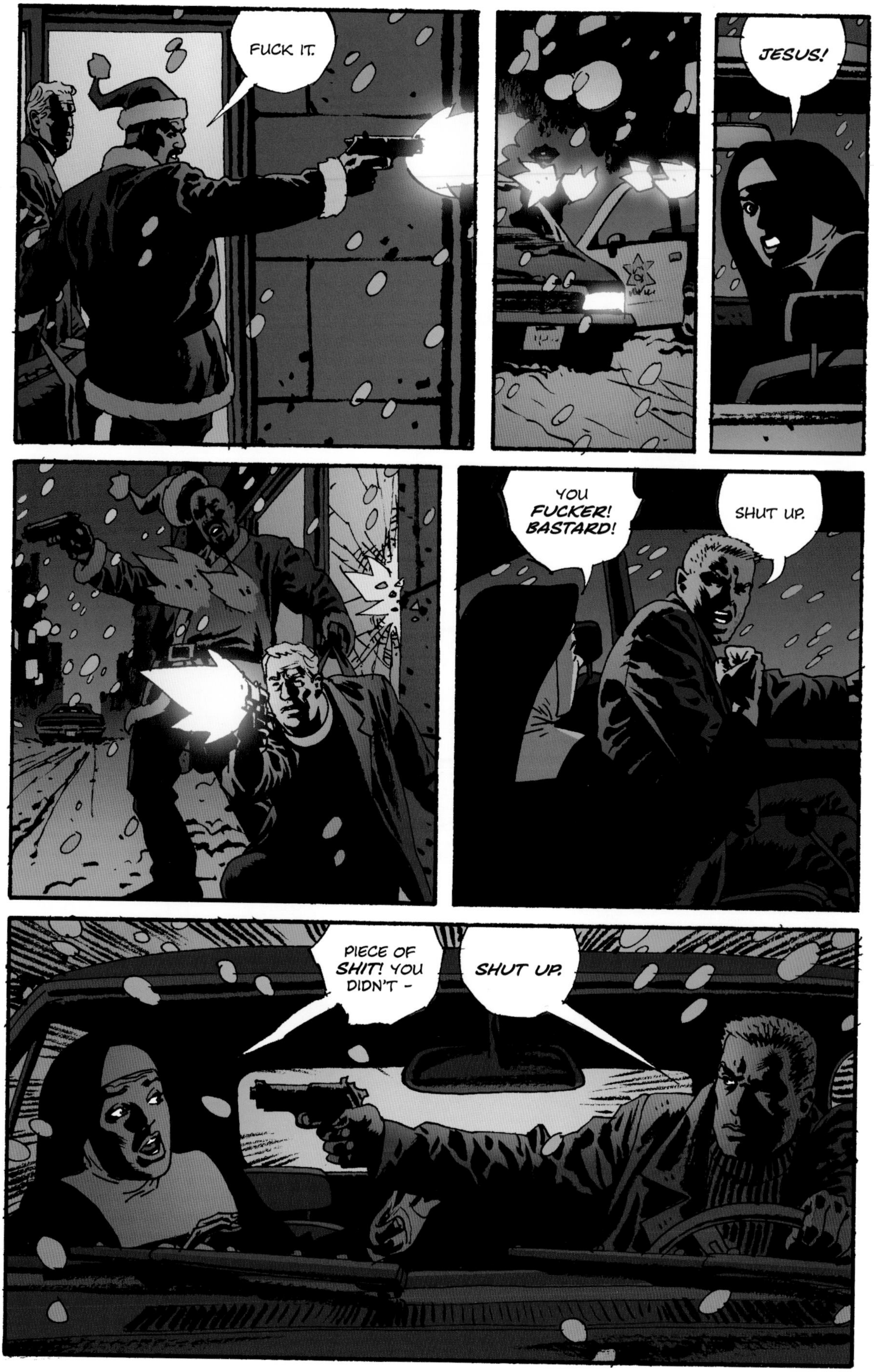
FUCK IT.
JESUS!
YOU FUCKER! BASTARD!
SHUT UP.
PIECE OF SHIT! YOU DIDN'T -
SHUT UP.

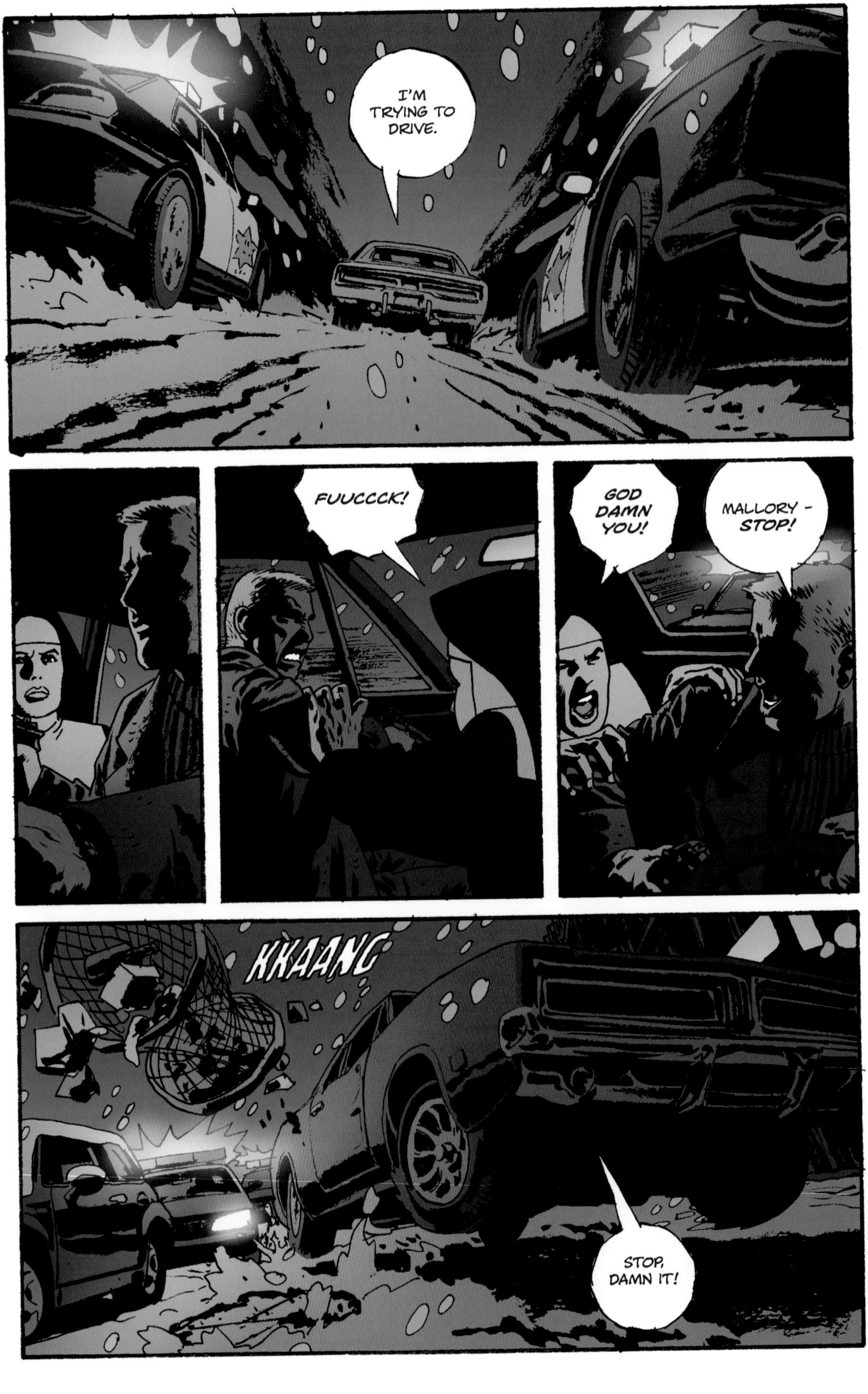
I'M TRYING TO DRIVE.
FUUCCCK!
GOD DAMN YOU!
MALLORY - STOP!
KKAANG
STOP, DAMN IT!

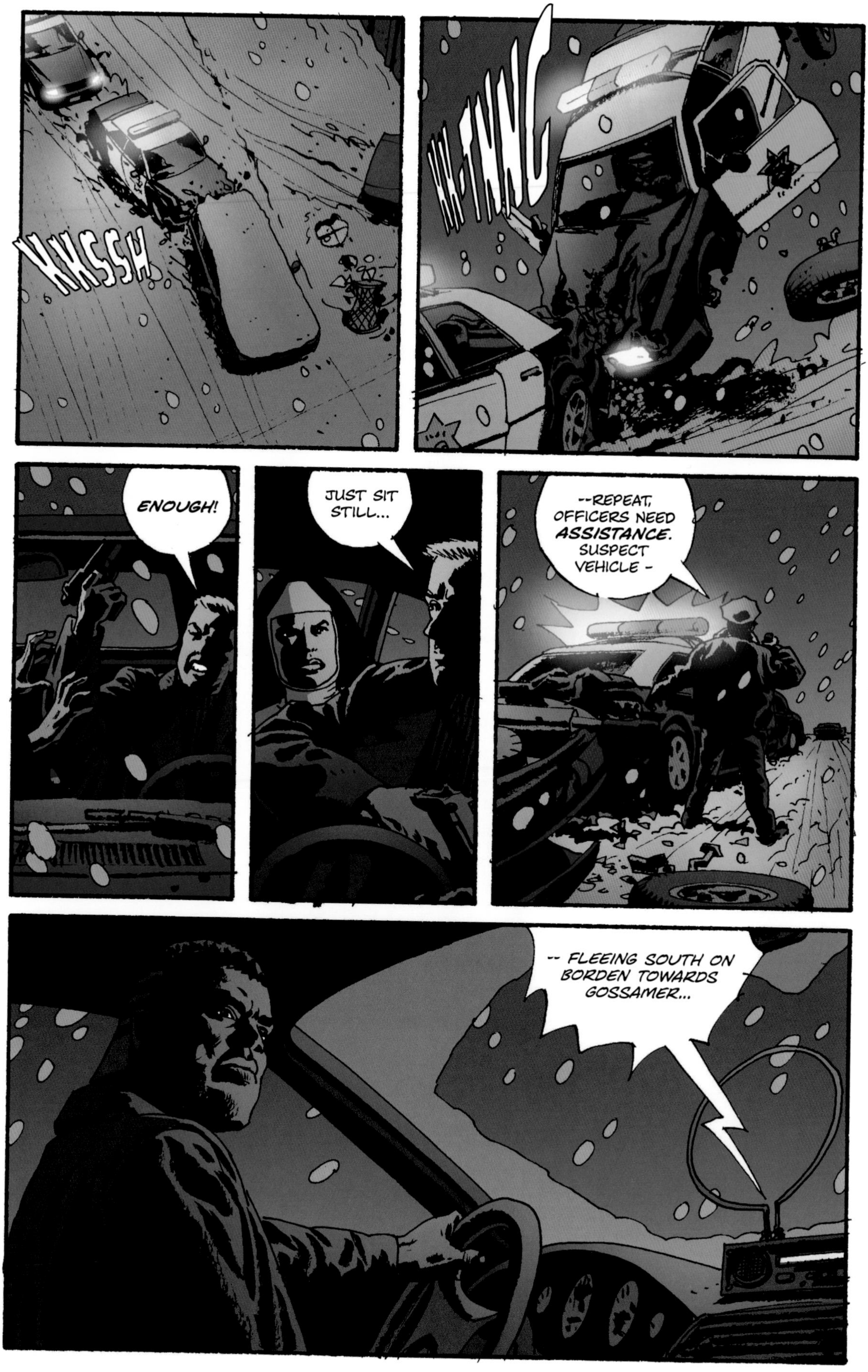
KKSSH
KK-TNNG
ENOUGH!
JUST SIT STILL...
--REPEAT, OFFICERS NEED ASSISTANCE. SUSPECT VEHICLE -
-- FLEEING SOUTH ON BORDEN TOWARDS GOSSAMER...

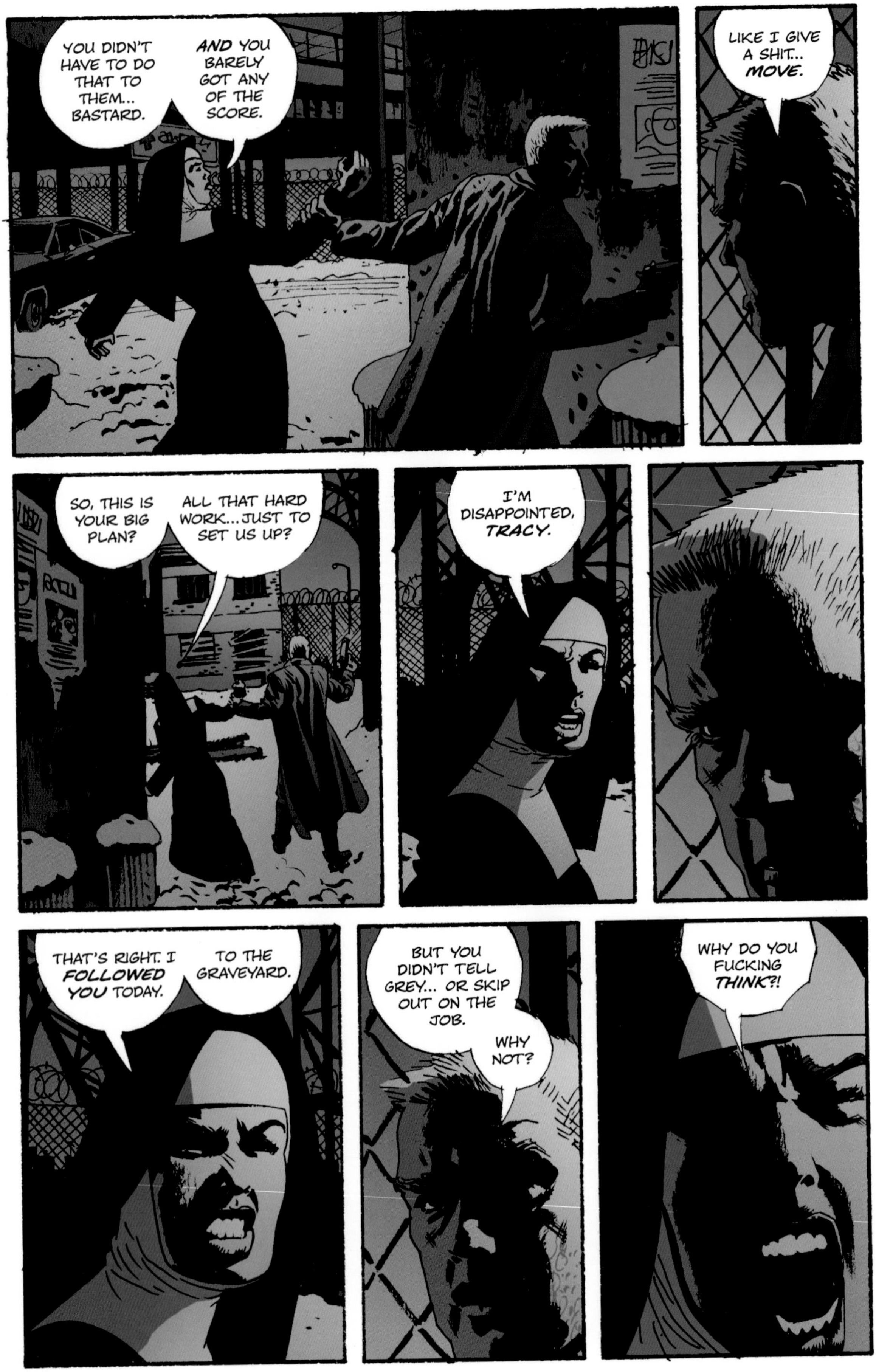
YOU DIDN'T HAVE TO DO THAT TO THEM... BASTARD.
AND YOU BARELY GOT ANY OF THE SCORE.
LIKE I GIVE A SHIT... MOVE.
SO, THIS IS YOUR BIG PLAN?
ALL THAT HARD WORK... JUST TO SET US UP?
I'M DISAPPOINTED, TRACY.
THAT'S RIGHT. I FOLLOWED YOU TODAY.
TO THE GRAVEYARD.
BUT YOU DIDN'T TELL GREY... OR SKIP OUT ON THE JOB.
WHY NOT?
WHY DO YOU FUCKING THINK?!

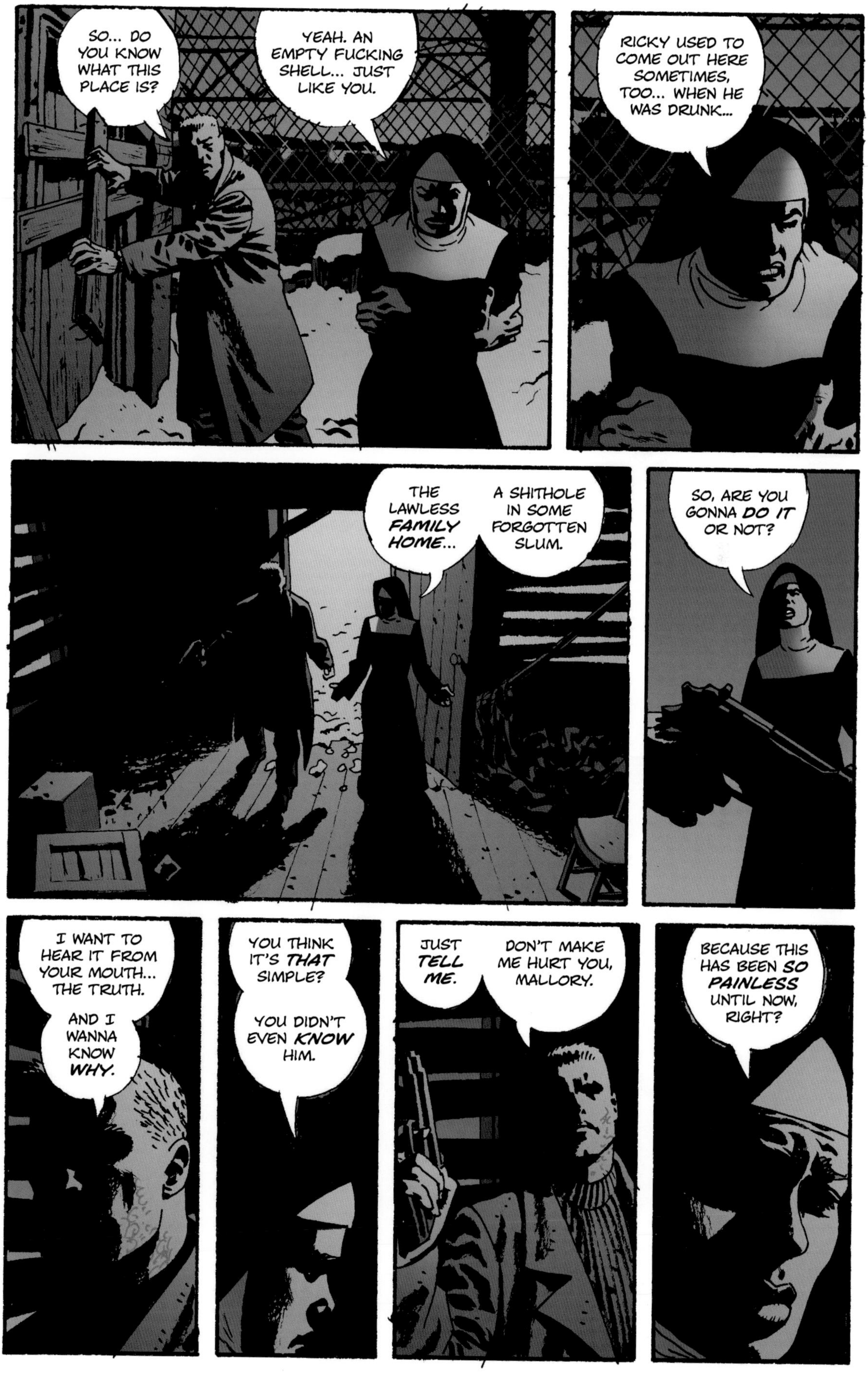
SO... DO YOU KNOW WHAT THIS PLACE IS?
YEAH. AN EMPTY FUCKING SHELL... JUST LIKE YOU.
RICKY USED TO COME OUT HERE SOMETIMES, TOO... WHEN HE WAS DRUNK...
THE LAWLESS FAMILY HOME...
A SHITHOLE IN SOME FORGOTTEN SLUM.
SO, ARE YOU GONNA DO IT OR NOT?
I WANT TO HEAR IT FROM YOUR MOUTH... THE TRUTH.
AND I WANNA KNOW WHY.
YOU THINK IT'S THAT SIMPLE?
YOU DIDN'T EVEN KNOW HIM.
JUST TELL ME.
DON'T MAKE ME HURT YOU, MALLORY.
BECAUSE THIS HAS BEEN SO PAINLESS UNTIL NOW, RIGHT?

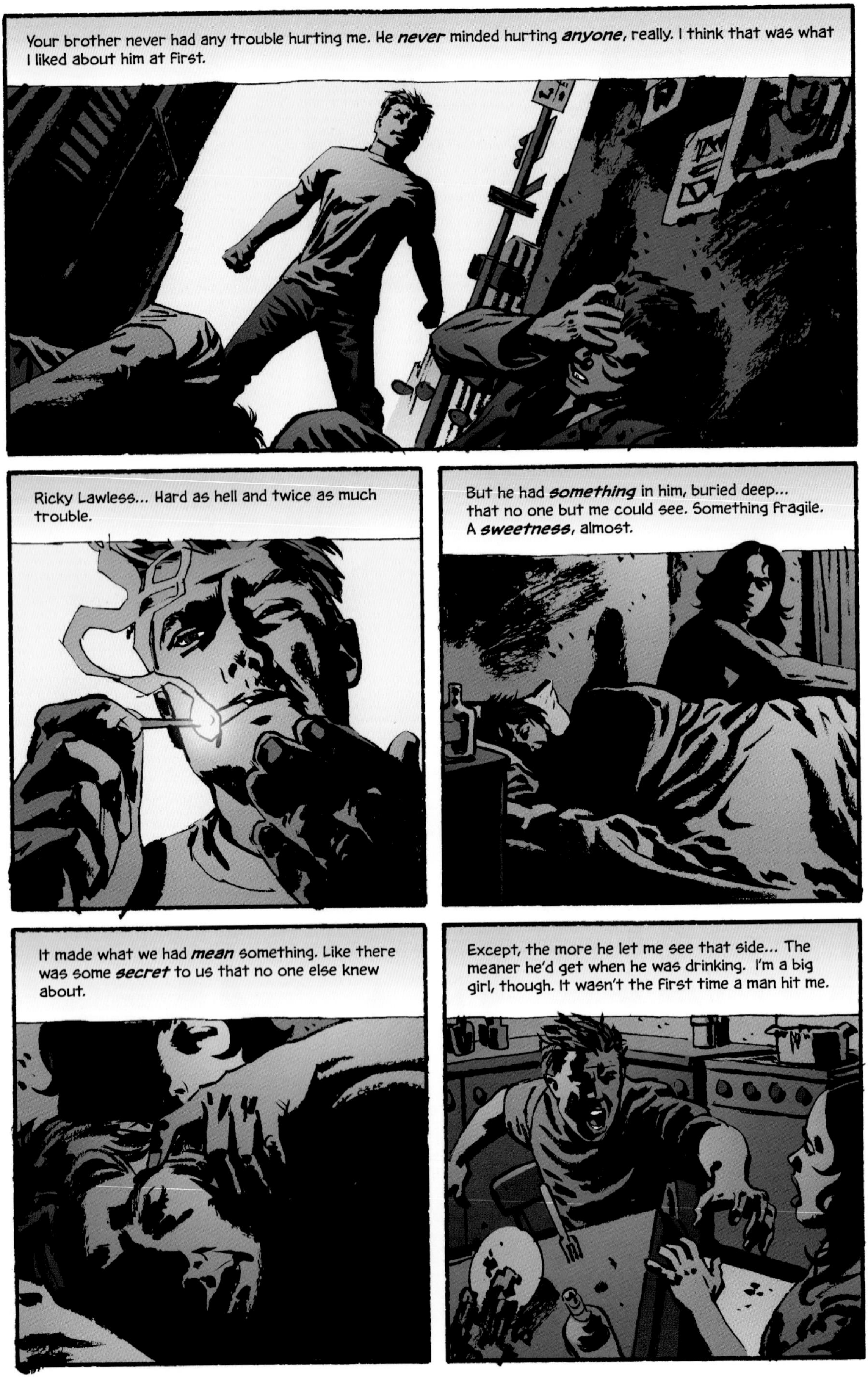
Your brother never had any trouble hurting me. He never minded hurting anyone, really. I think that was what I liked about him at first.
Ricky Lawless... Hard as hell and twice as much trouble.
But he had something in him, buried deep... that no one but me could see. Something fragile. A sweetness, almost.
It made what we had mean something. Like there was some secret to us that no one else knew about.
Except, the more he let me see that side... The meaner he'd get when he was drinking. I'm a big girl, though. It wasn't the first time a man hit me.

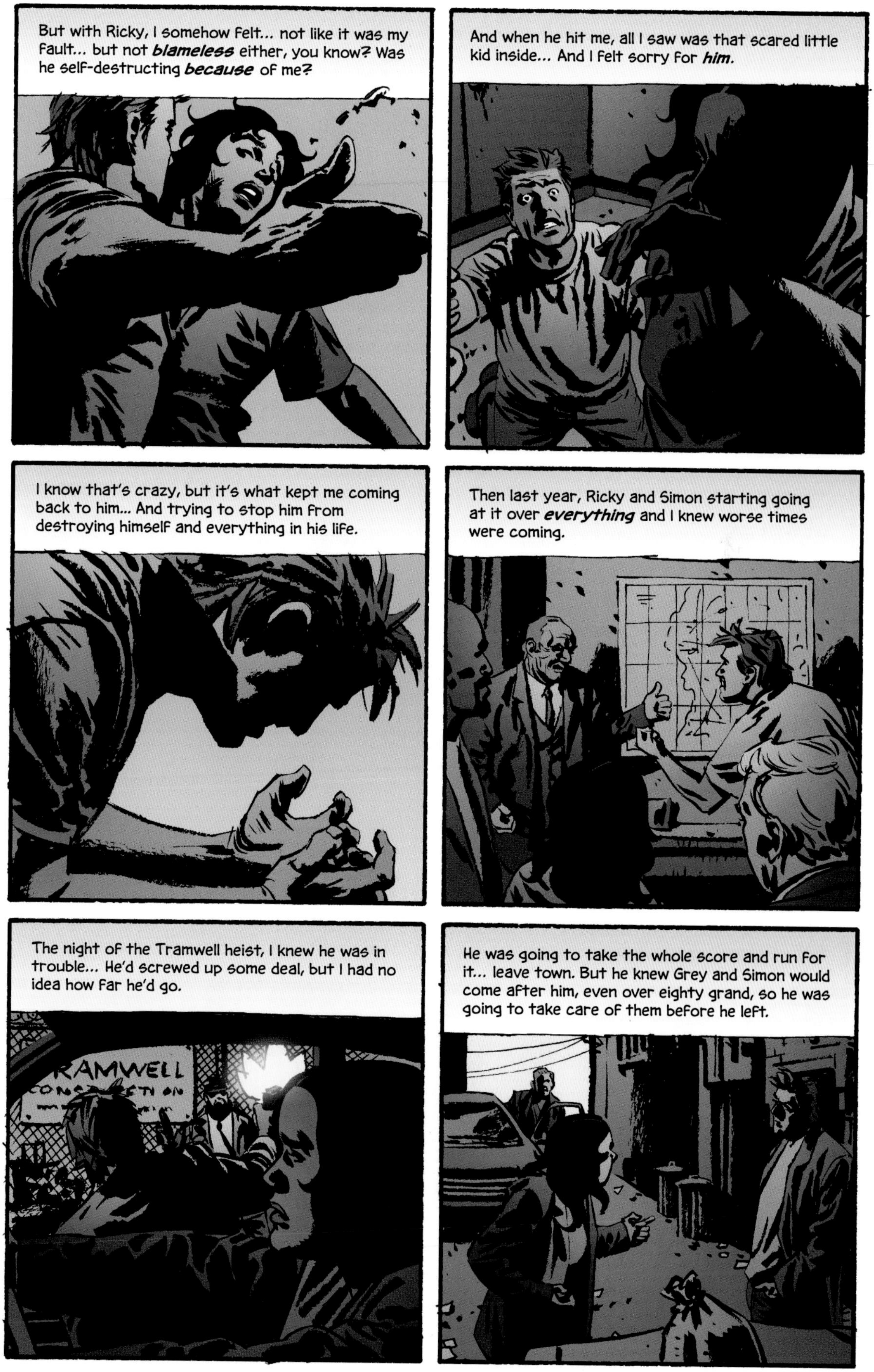
But with Ricky, I somehow felt... not like it was my fault... but not *blameless* either, you know? Was he self-destructing *because* of me?
And when he hit me, all I saw was that scared little kid inside... And I felt sorry for *him.*
I know that's crazy, but it's what kept me coming back to him... And trying to stop him from destroying himself and everything in his life.
Then last year, Ricky and Simon starting going at it over *everything* and I knew worse times were coming.
The night of the Tramwell heist, I knew he was in trouble... He'd screwed up some deal, but I had no idea how far he'd go.
RAMWELL
He was going to take the whole score and run for it... leave town. But he knew Grey and Simon would come after him, even over eighty grand, so he was going to take care of them before he left.

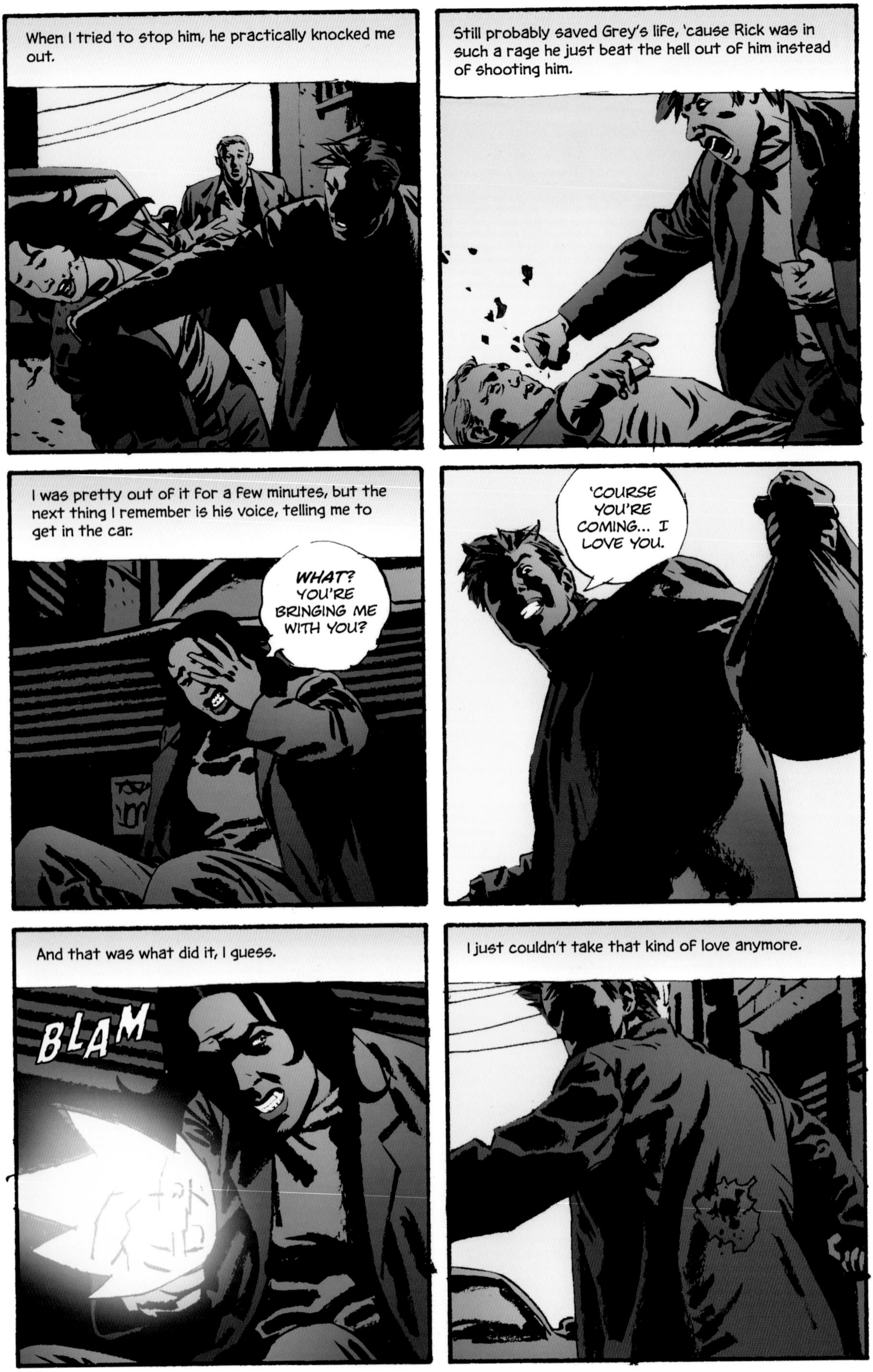
When I tried to stop him, he practically knocked me out.
Still probably saved Grey's life, 'cause Rick was in such a rage he just beat the hell out of him instead of shooting him.
I was pretty out of it for a few minutes, but the next thing I remember is his voice, telling me to get in the car.
WHAT? YOU'RE BRINGING ME WITH YOU?
'COURSE YOU'RE COMING... I LOVE YOU.
And that was what did it, I guess.
BLAM
I just couldn't take that kind of love anymore.

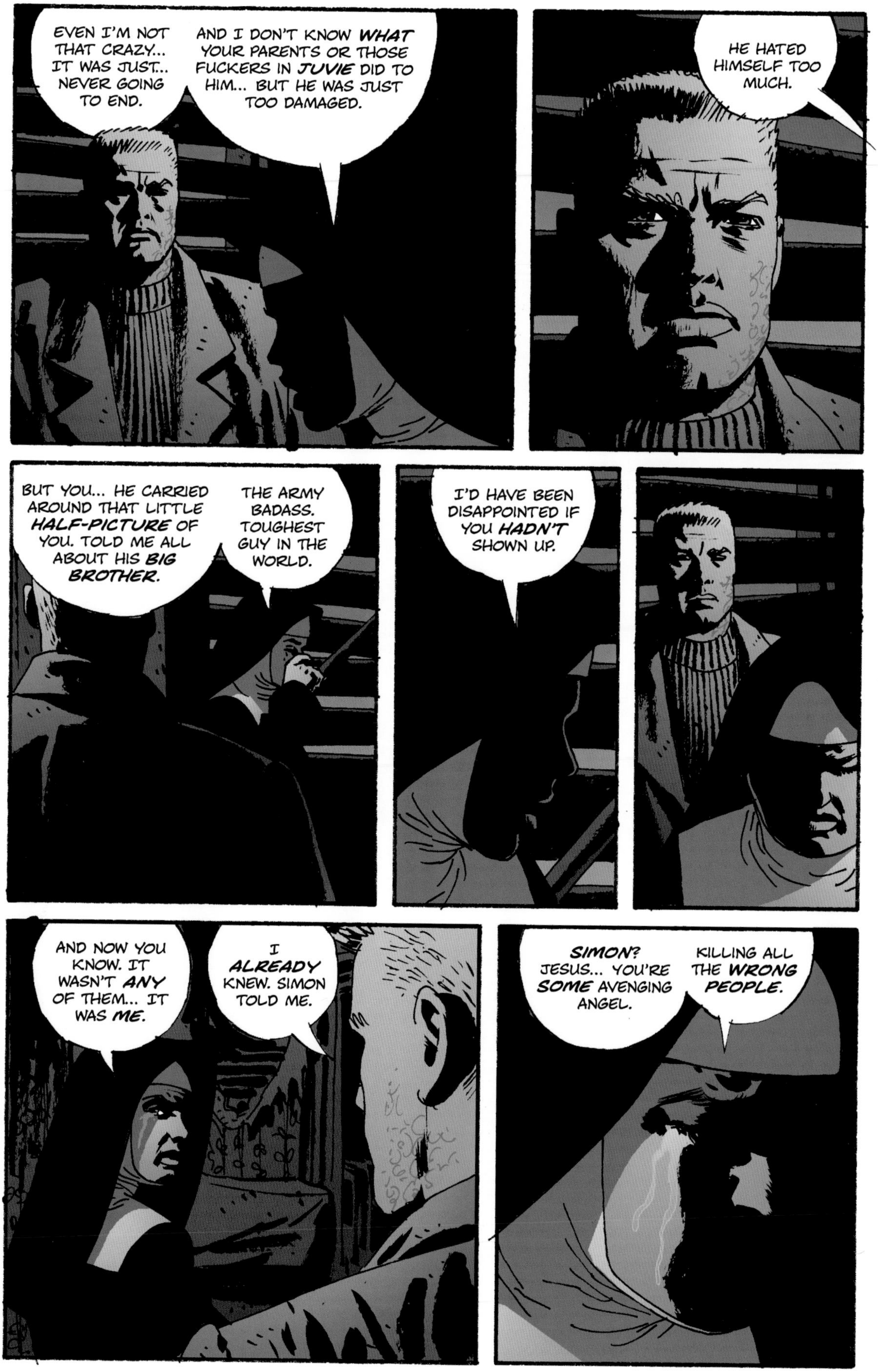
EVEN I'M NOT THAT CRAZY... IT WAS JUST... NEVER GOING TO END.
AND I DON'T KNOW WHAT YOUR PARENTS OR THOSE FUCKERS IN JUVIE DID TO HIM... BUT HE WAS JUST TOO DAMAGED.
HE HATED HIMSELF TOO MUCH.
BUT YOU... HE CARRIED AROUND THAT LITTLE HALF-PICTURE OF YOU. TOLD ME ALL ABOUT HIS BIG BROTHER.
THE ARMY BADASS. TOUGHEST GUY IN THE WORLD.
I'D HAVE BEEN DISAPPOINTED IF YOU HADN'T SHOWN UP.
AND NOW YOU KNOW. IT WASN'T ANY OF THEM... IT WAS ME.
I ALREADY KNEW. SIMON TOLD ME.
SIMON? JESUS... YOU'RE SOME AVENGING ANGEL.
KILLING ALL THE WRONG PEOPLE.

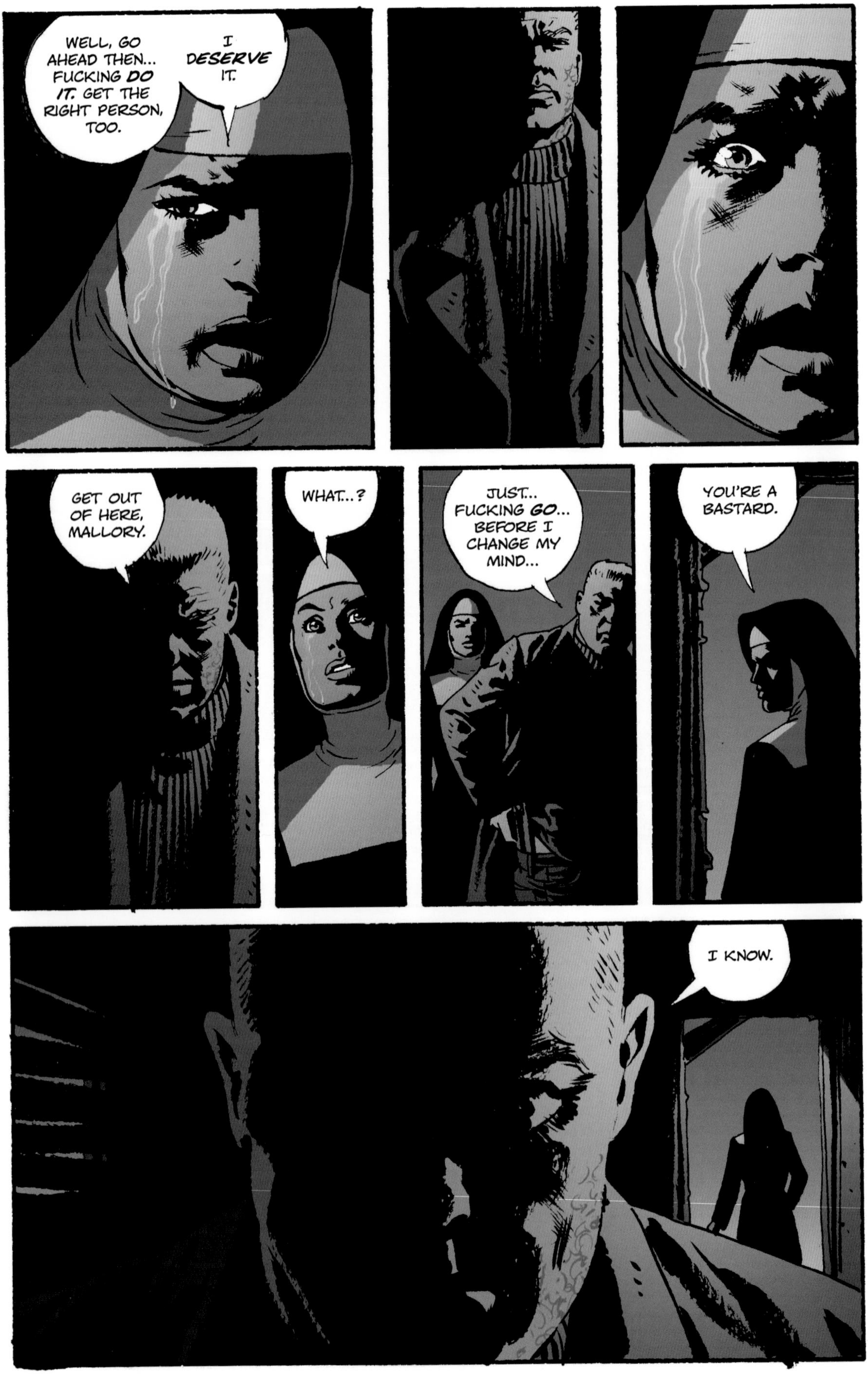
WELL, GO AHEAD THEN... FUCKING DO IT. GET THE RIGHT PERSON, TOO.
I DESERVE IT.
GET OUT OF HERE, MALLORY.
WHAT...?
JUST... FUCKING GO... BEFORE I CHANGE MY MIND...
YOU'RE A BASTARD.
I KNOW.

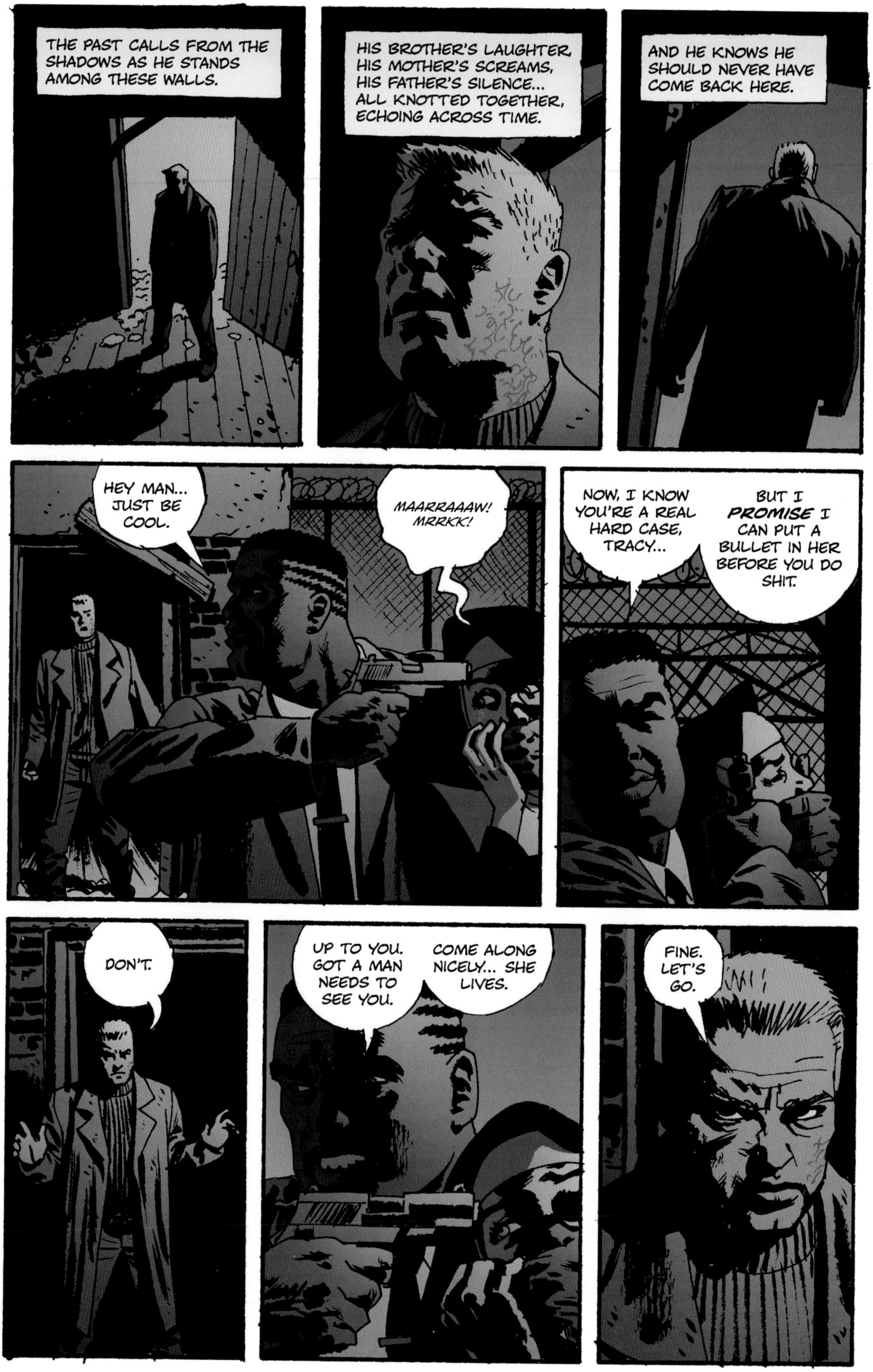
THE PAST CALLS FROM THE SHADOWS AS HE STANDS AMONG THESE WALLS.
HIS BROTHER'S LAUGHTER, HIS MOTHER'S SCREAMS, HIS FATHER'S SILENCE... ALL KNOTTED TOGETHER, ECHOING ACROSS TIME.
AND HE KNOWS HE SHOULD NEVER HAVE COME BACK HERE.
HEY MAN... JUST BE COOL.
MAARRAAAW! MRRKK!
NOW, I KNOW YOU'RE A REAL HARD CASE, TRACY...
BUT I PROMISE I CAN PUT A BULLET IN HER BEFORE YOU DO SHIT.
DON'T.
UP TO YOU. GOT A MAN NEEDS TO SEE YOU.
COME ALONG NICELY... SHE LIVES.
FINE. LET'S GO.

THIS GUY IS GOOD, TRACY THINKS. KEEPS A COOL HEAD. KNOWS HOW TO CONTROL A SITUATION.

HE TAKES MALLORY, AND MAKES TRACY FOLLOW IN HIS CAR KNOWS TRACY WON'T MAKE A FALSE MOVE WHILE SHE'S AT RISK.

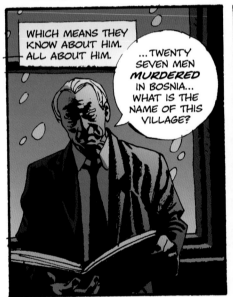

WHICH MEANS THEY KNOW ABOUT HIM. ALL ABOUT HIM.

...TWENTY SEVEN MEN *MURDERED* IN BOSNIA... WHAT IS THE NAME OF THIS VILLAGE?

JARUGE.

THOSE MEN WERE RUNNING A *CAMP.*

SO IT *SAYS* IN YOUR FILE. BUT WHAT ABOUT THE THREE *U.S. SOLDIERS* KILLED IN BAGHDAD?

THAT PART HAS BEEN *REDACTED* HERE.

HE'D BEEN TOO LATE. THAT WAS THE TRAGEDY. TOO LATE TO DO ANYTHING BUT KILL.

THE GIRL HAD BEEN SAVED, OF COURSE... BUT JUST FROM THE FIRE.

HER FAMILY LAY DEAD IN THE DIRT, HER LIFE IN RUINS.

...I'M SORRY...

TRACY WAS THROWN IN A HOLE WHILE THE HIGHER-UPS TRIED TO BURY YET ANOTHER DISASTER IN IRAQ.

IT WAS ONE THING TO LOOK THE OTHER WAY ON WHAT HE'D DONE IN BOSNIA... BUT WHEN *U.S. SOLDIERS* WERE INVOLVED...

...THEN IT WAS ABOUT MORE THAN RIGHT AND WRONG. THEN IT WAS ABOUT PERCEPTION.

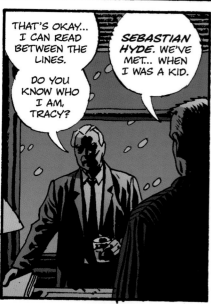

THAT'S OKAY... I CAN READ BETWEEN THE LINES.

DO YOU KNOW WHO I AM, TRACY?

SEBASTIAN HYDE. WE'VE MET... WHEN I WAS A KID.

GOOD MEMORY.

YOU *COST ME* THESE PAST WEEKS, KID. *PRESTIGE* MOSTLY, BUT STILL...

THAT MONEY YOU TOOK WAS A *SAMPLE DELIVERY* FROM A NEW SUPPLIER.

IMAGINE HOW I *LOOK* TO THEM NOW... IT'S EMBARRASSING.

HOW DID YOU FIND ME?

WHEN YOU'RE DRIVING A GETAWAY CAR, DON'T TAKE IT *HOME*. EVEN TO AN *OLD* HOME.

'CAUSE THERE'S ALWAYS A CHANCE SOMEONE'S GONNA KNOW WHO YOU *REALLY* ARE.

SOMEONE LIKE CHESTER, MY FRIEND WHO'S WATCHING YOUR LADY.

YOU CAN LET HER GO NOW.

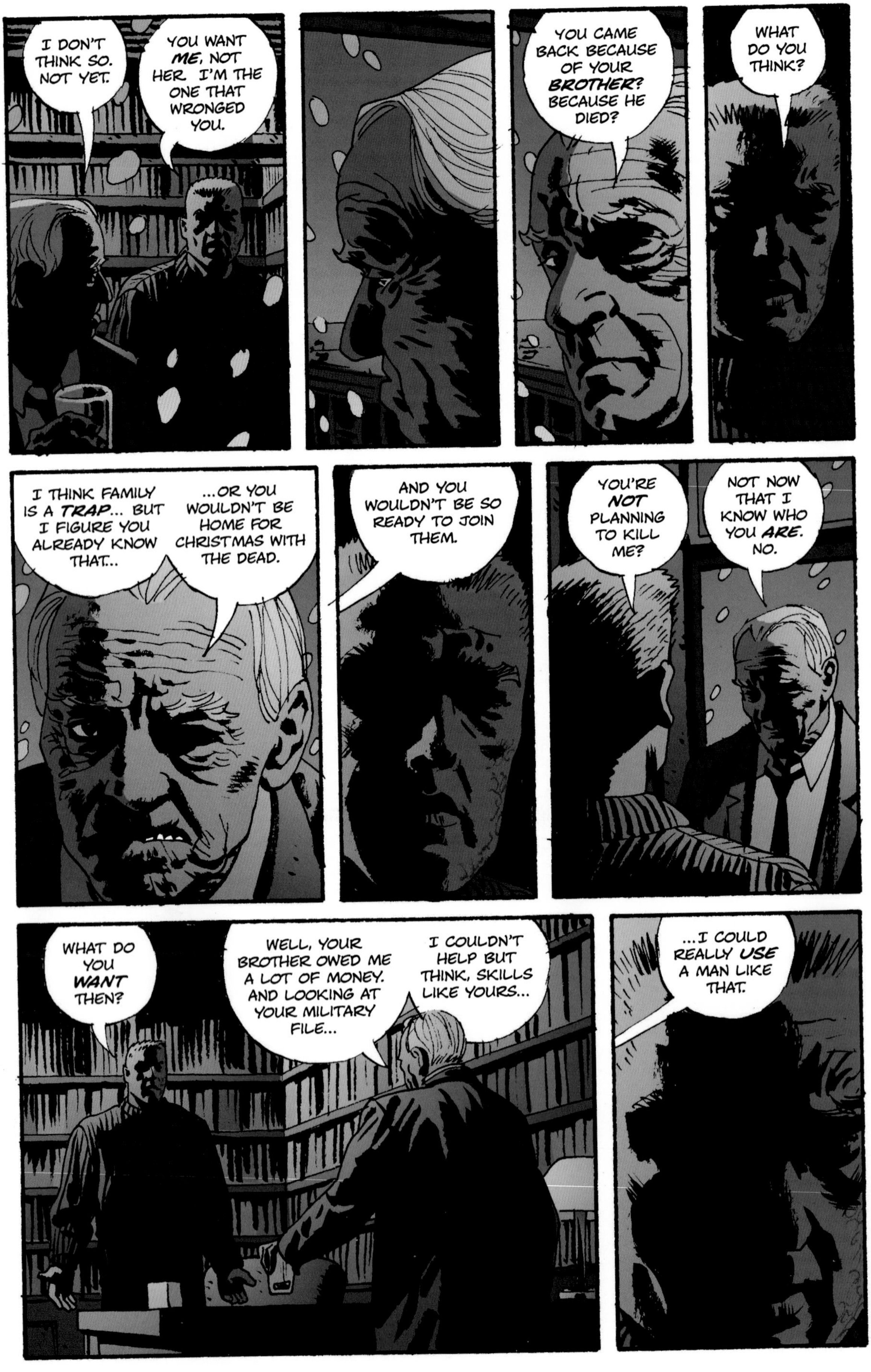
I DON'T THINK SO. NOT YET.
YOU WANT ME, NOT HER. I'M THE ONE THAT WRONGED YOU.
YOU CAME BACK BECAUSE OF YOUR BROTHER? BECAUSE HE DIED?
WHAT DO YOU THINK?
I THINK FAMILY IS A TRAP... BUT I FIGURE YOU ALREADY KNOW THAT...
...OR YOU WOULDN'T BE HOME FOR CHRISTMAS WITH THE DEAD.
AND YOU WOULDN'T BE SO READY TO JOIN THEM.
YOU'RE NOT PLANNING TO KILL ME?
NOT NOW THAT I KNOW WHO YOU ARE. NO.
WHAT DO YOU WANT THEN?
WELL, YOUR BROTHER OWED ME A LOT OF MONEY. AND LOOKING AT YOUR MILITARY FILE...
I COULDN'T HELP BUT THINK, SKILLS LIKE YOURS...
...I COULD REALLY USE A MAN LIKE THAT.

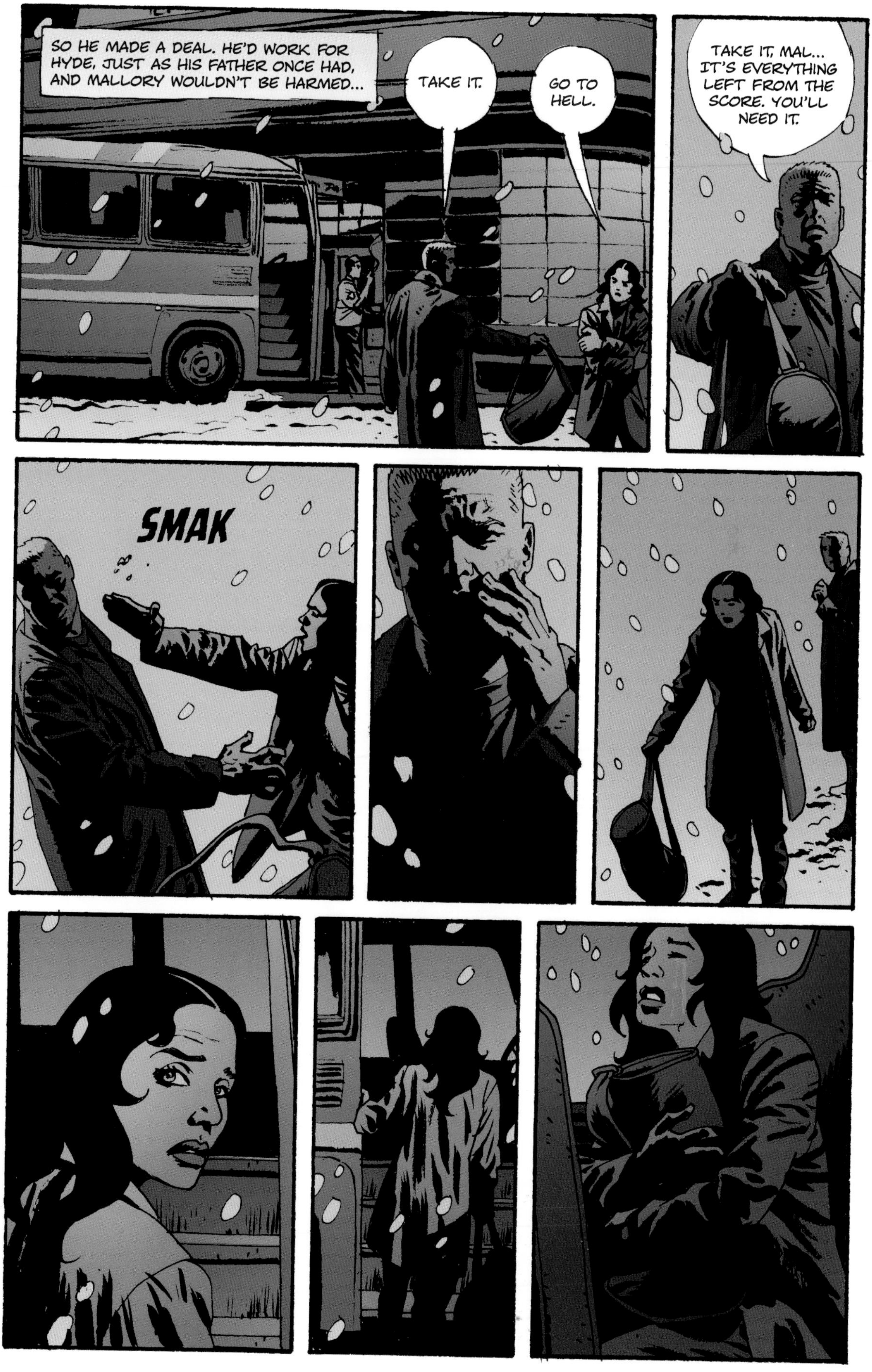
SO HE MADE A DEAL. HE'D WORK FOR HYDE, JUST AS HIS FATHER ONCE HAD, AND MALLORY WOULDN'T BE HARMED...
TAKE IT.
GO TO HELL.
TAKE IT, MAL... IT'S EVERYTHING LEFT FROM THE SCORE. YOU'LL NEED IT.
SMAK

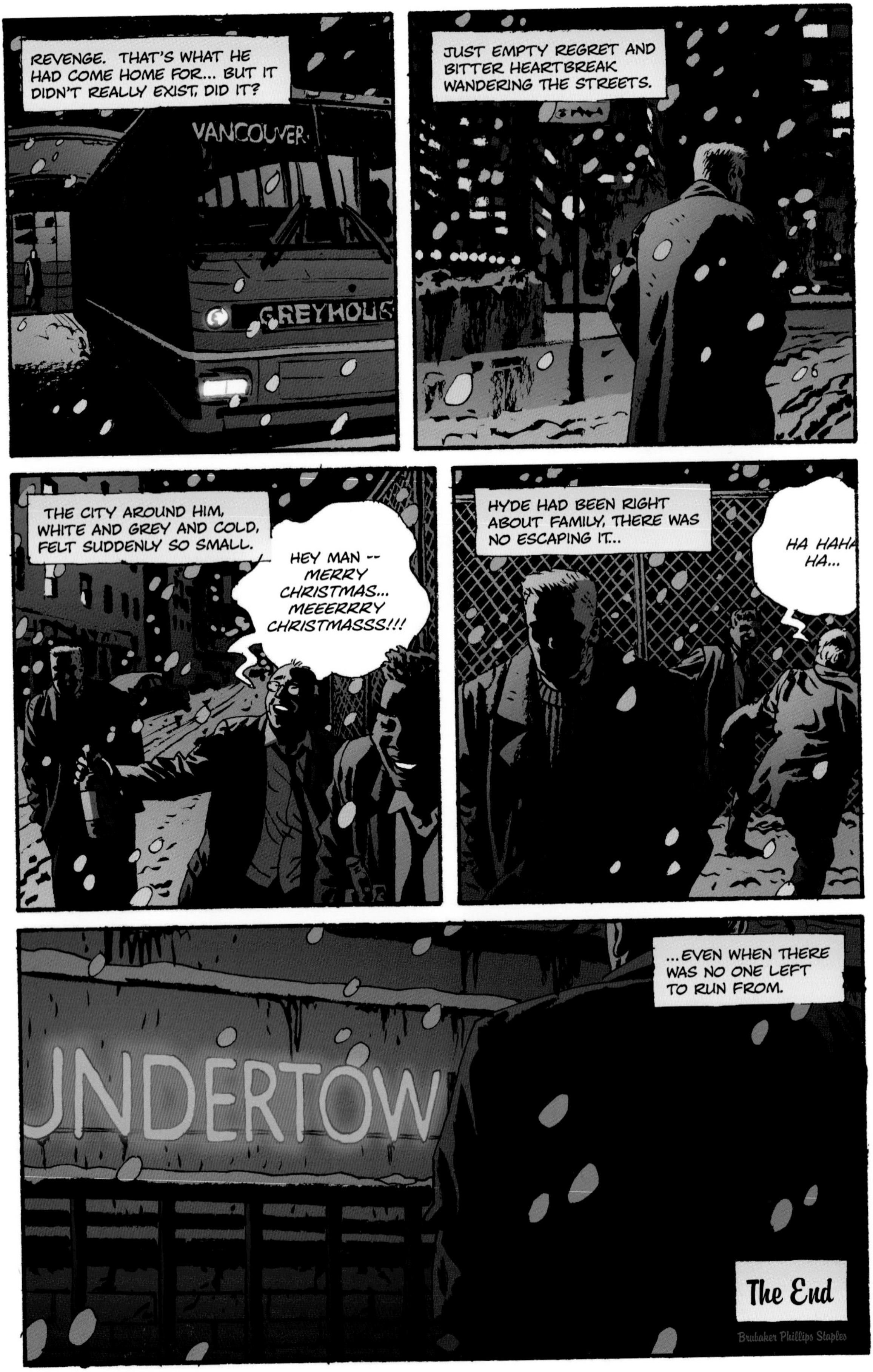
REVENGE. THAT'S WHAT HE HAD COME HOME FOR... BUT IT DIDN'T REALLY EXIST, DID IT?
VANCOUVER
GREYHOUS
JUST EMPTY REGRET AND BITTER HEARTBREAK WANDERING THE STREETS.
THE CITY AROUND HIM, WHITE AND GREY AND COLD, FELT SUDDENLY SO SMALL.
HEY MAN -- MERRY CHRISTMAS... MEEERRRY CHRISTMASSS!!!
HYDE HAD BEEN RIGHT ABOUT FAMILY, THERE WAS NO ESCAPING IT...
HA HAHA HA...
...EVEN WHEN THERE WAS NO ONE LEFT TO RUN FROM.
UNDERTOW
The End
Brubaker Phillips Staples

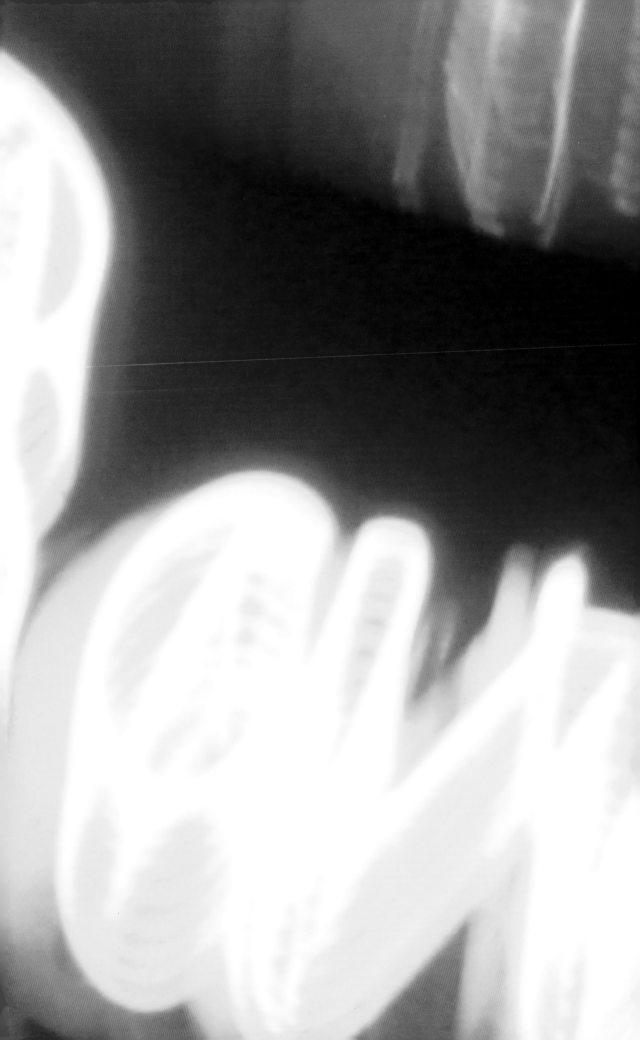

The Dead and the Dying

CRIMINAL: The Dead and the Dying

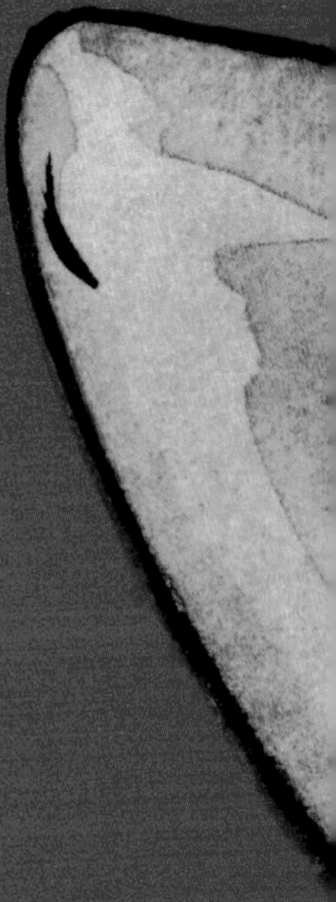

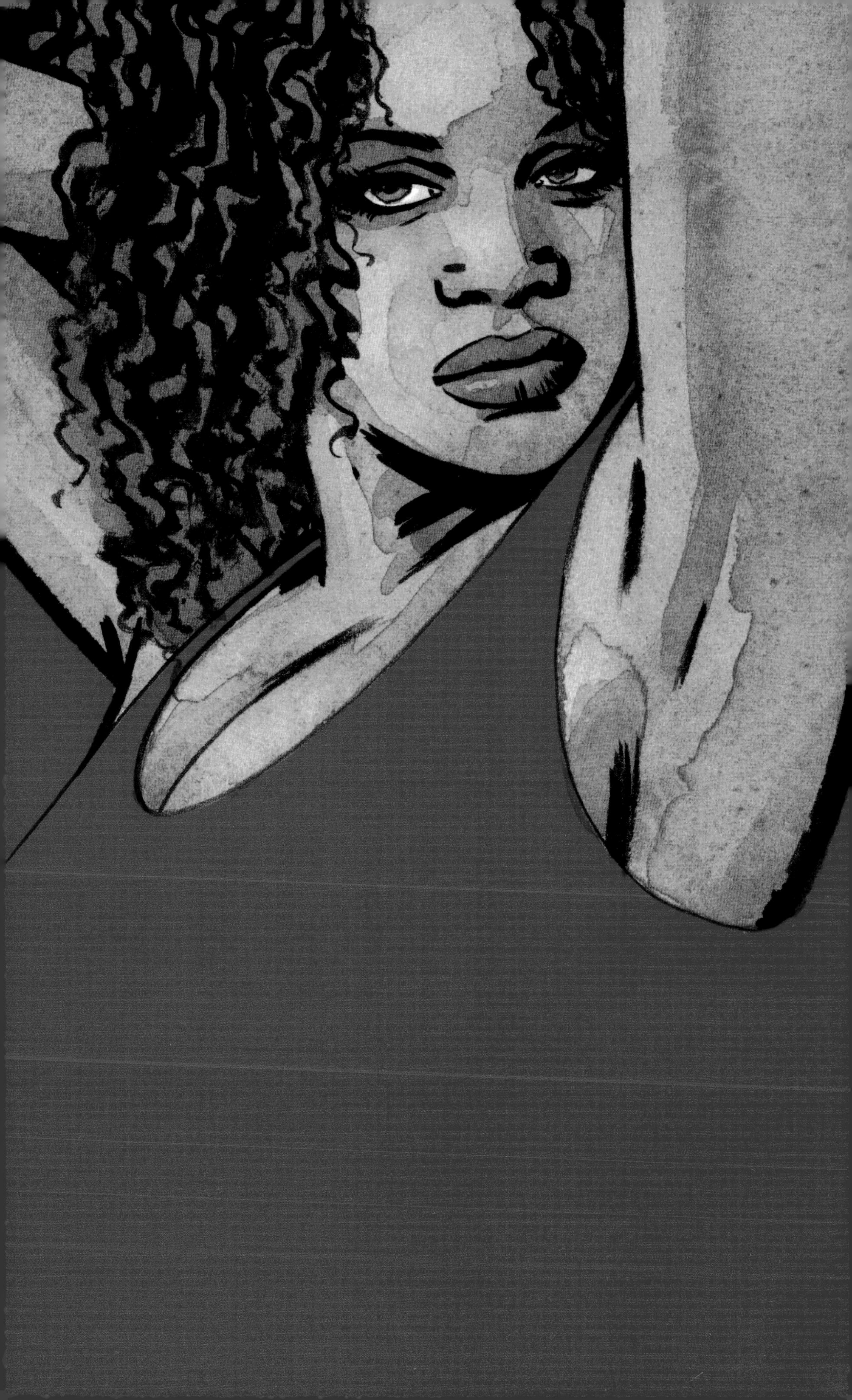

SECOND CHANCE IN HELL

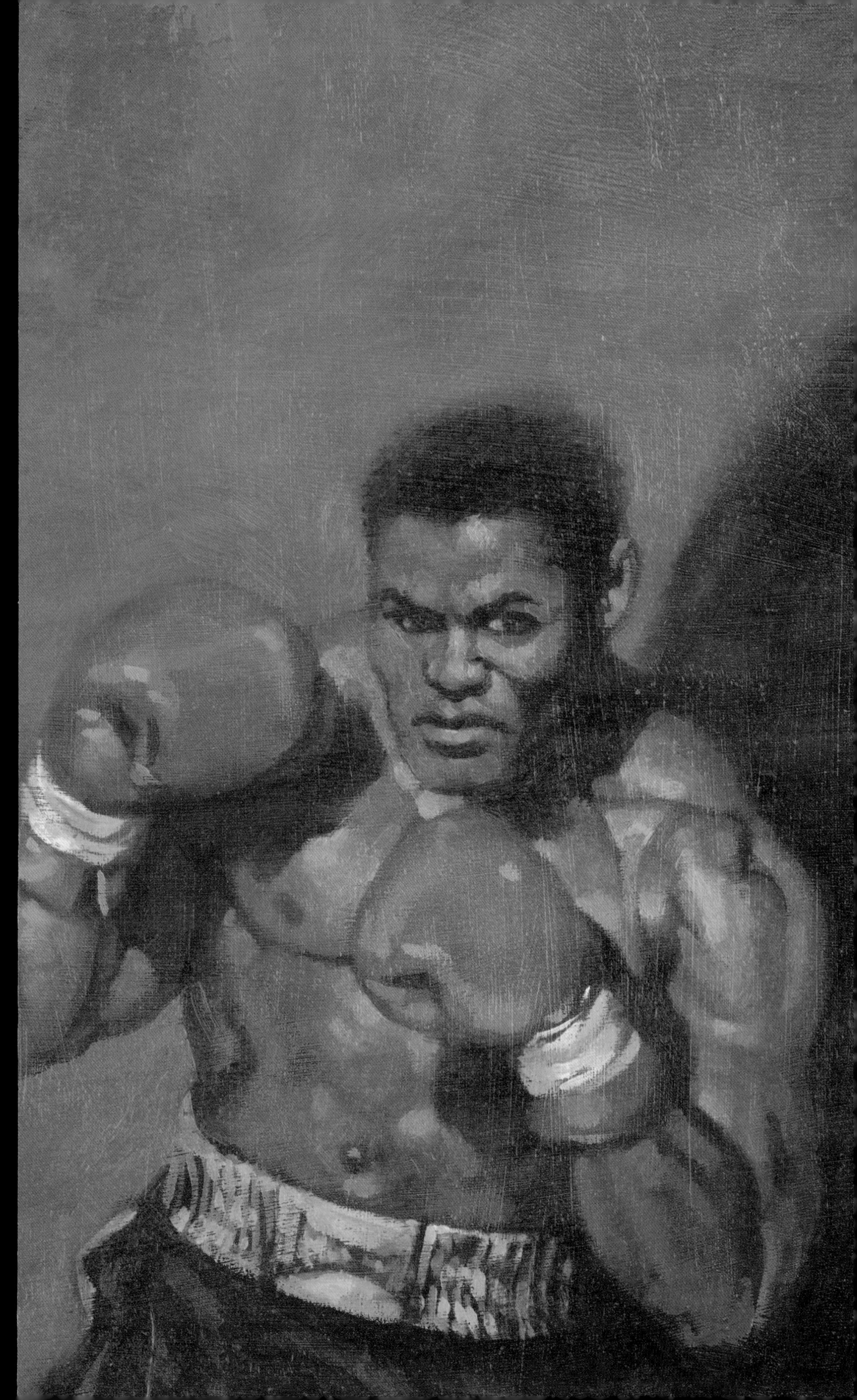

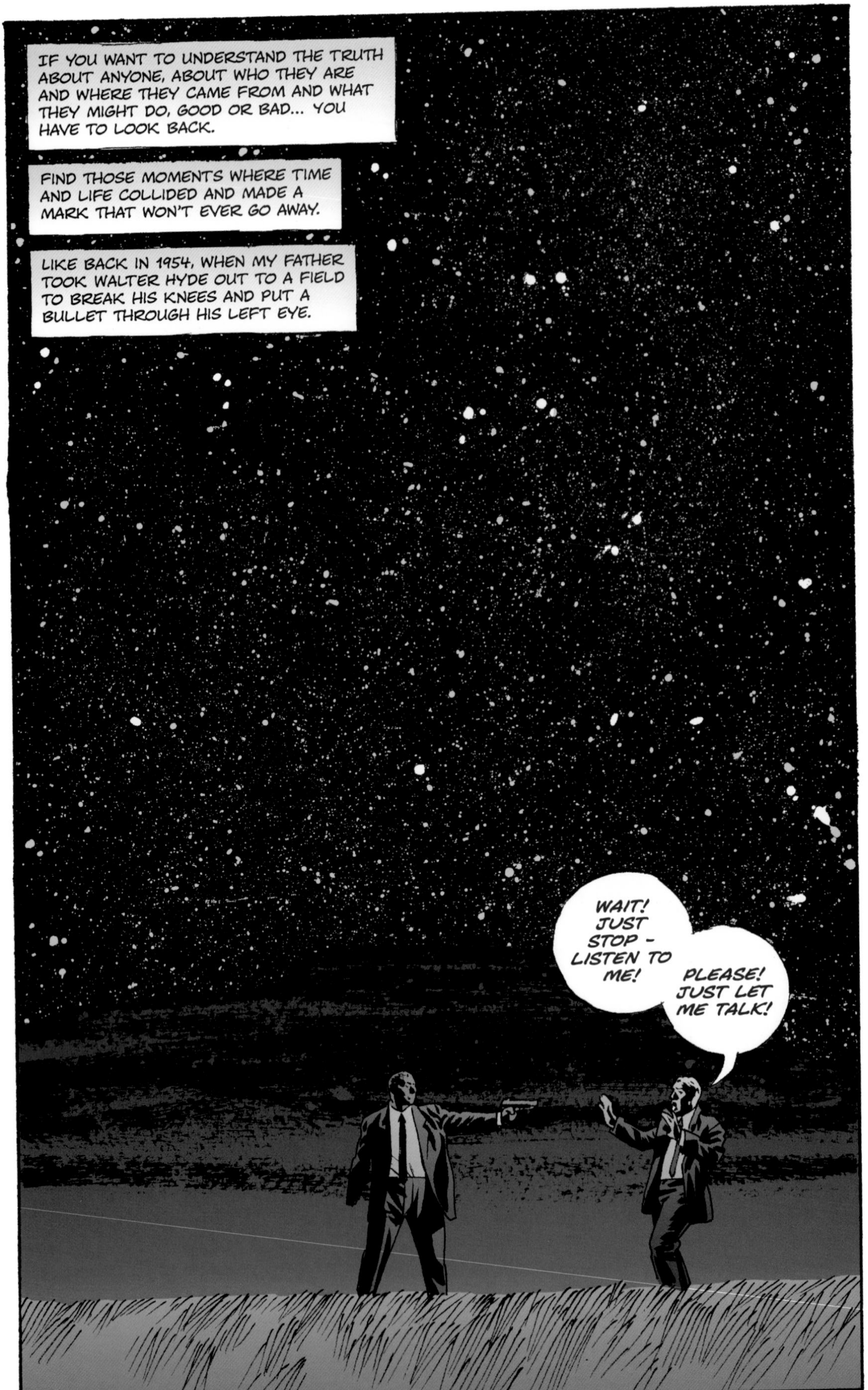
IF YOU WANT TO UNDERSTAND THE TRUTH ABOUT ANYONE, ABOUT WHO THEY ARE AND WHERE THEY CAME FROM AND WHAT THEY MIGHT DO, GOOD OR BAD... YOU HAVE TO LOOK BACK.
FIND THOSE MOMENTS WHERE TIME AND LIFE COLLIDED AND MADE A MARK THAT WON'T EVER GO AWAY.
LIKE BACK IN 1954, WHEN MY FATHER TOOK WALTER HYDE OUT TO A FIELD TO BREAK HIS KNEES AND PUT A BULLET THROUGH HIS LEFT EYE.
WAIT! JUST STOP - LISTEN TO ME!
PLEASE! JUST LET ME TALK!

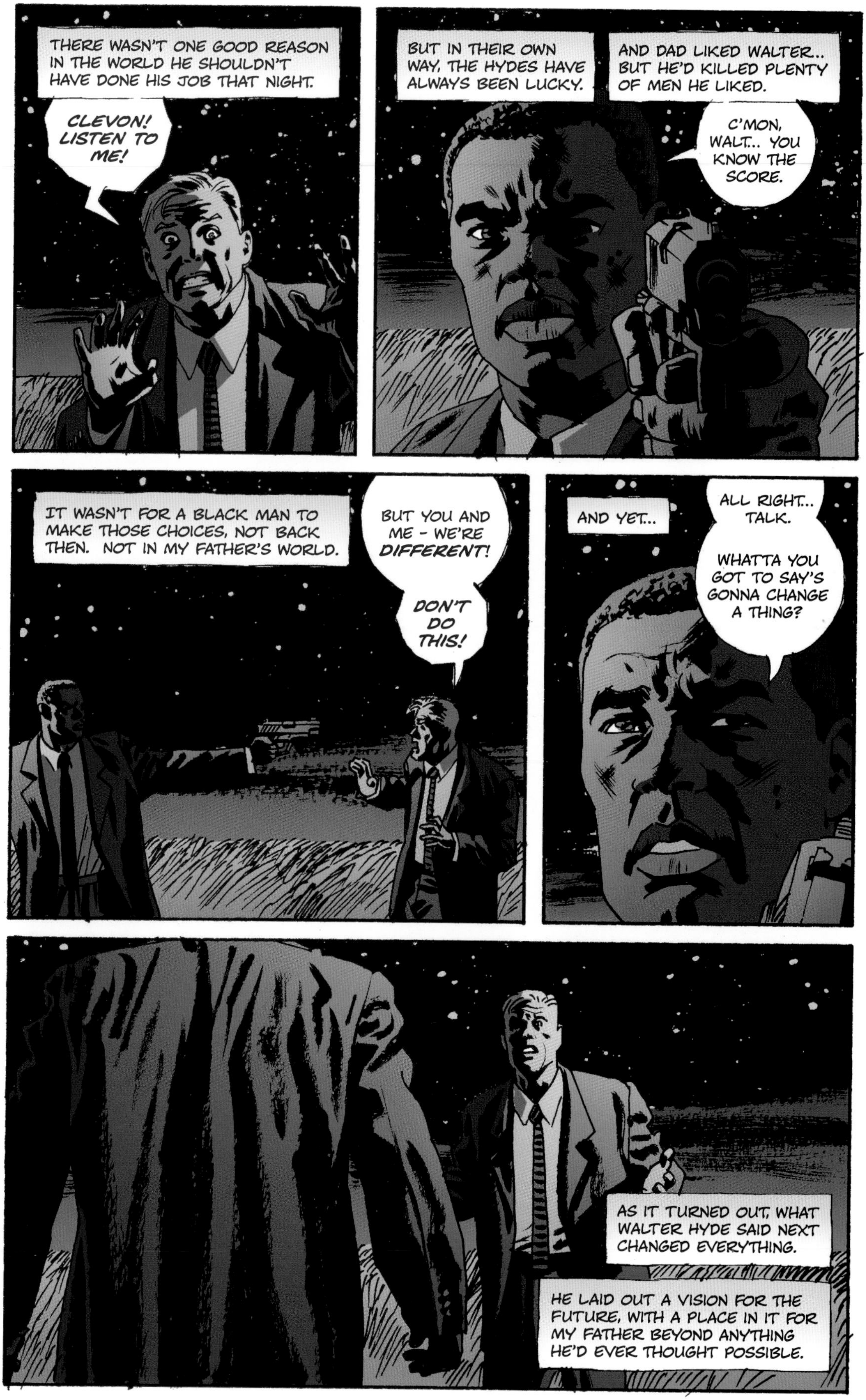
THERE WASN'T ONE GOOD REASON IN THE WORLD HE SHOULDN'T HAVE DONE HIS JOB THAT NIGHT.
CLEVON! LISTEN TO ME!
BUT IN THEIR OWN WAY, THE HYDES HAVE ALWAYS BEEN LUCKY.
AND DAD LIKED WALTER.. BUT HE'D KILLED PLENTY OF MEN HE LIKED.
C'MON, WALT... YOU KNOW THE SCORE.
IT WASN'T FOR A BLACK MAN TO MAKE THOSE CHOICES, NOT BACK THEN. NOT IN MY FATHER'S WORLD.
BUT YOU AND ME - WE'RE DIFFERENT!
DON'T DO THIS!
AND YET...
ALL RIGHT... TALK.
WHATTA YOU GOT TO SAY'S GONNA CHANGE A THING?
AS IT TURNED OUT, WHAT WALTER HYDE SAID NEXT CHANGED EVERYTHING.
HE LAID OUT A VISION FOR THE FUTURE, WITH A PLACE IN IT FOR MY FATHER BEYOND ANYTHING HE'D EVER THOUGHT POSSIBLE.

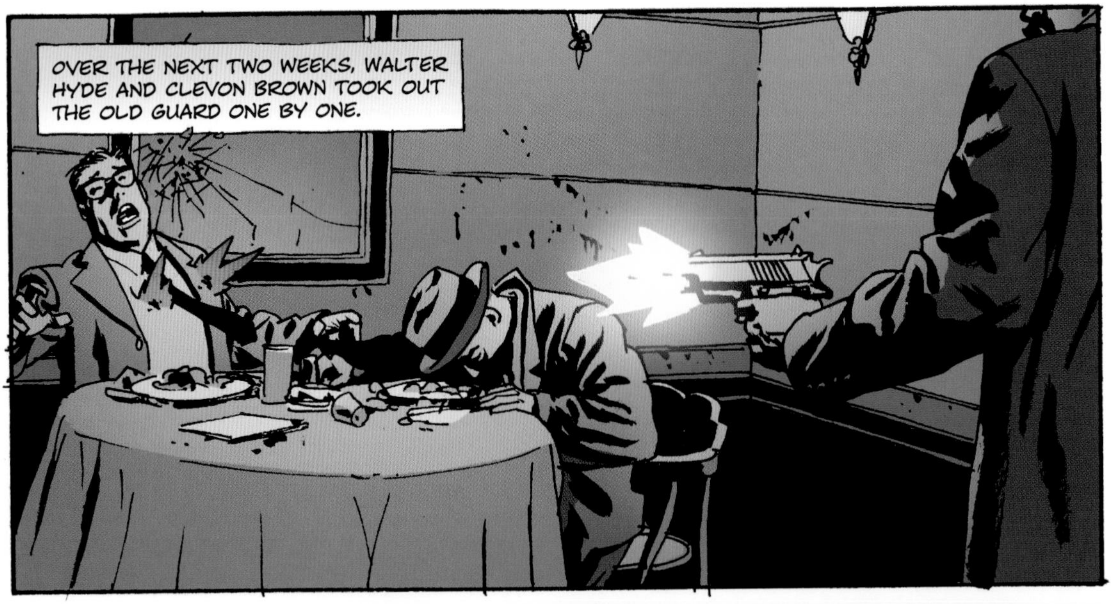
OVER THE NEXT TWO WEEKS, WALTER HYDE AND CLEVON BROWN TOOK OUT THE OLD GUARD ONE BY ONE.

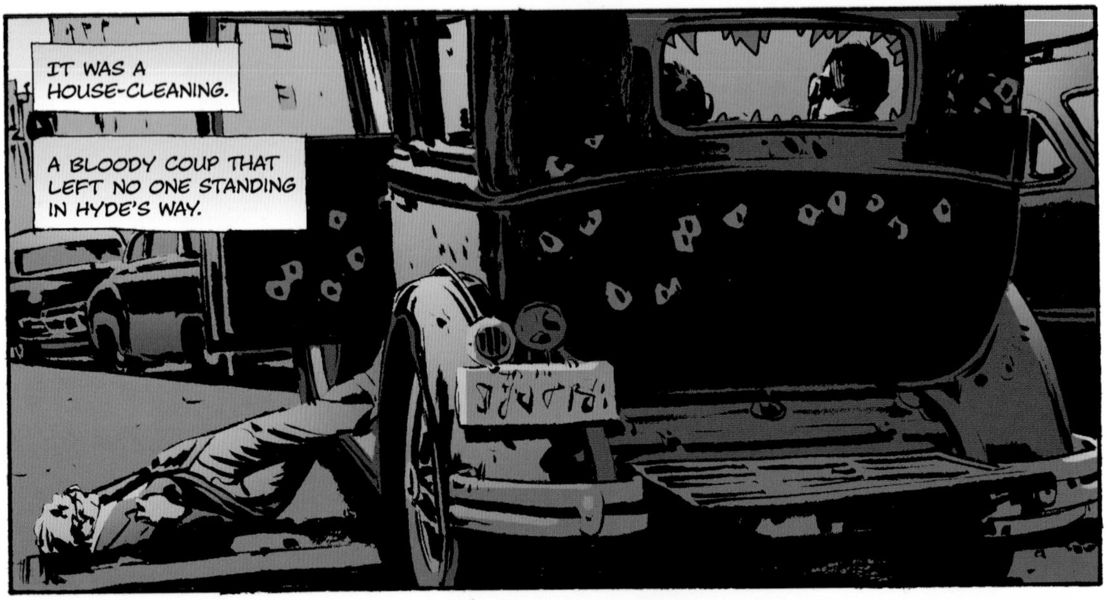
IT WAS A HOUSE-CLEANING.
A BLOODY COUP THAT LEFT NO ONE STANDING IN HYDE'S WAY.

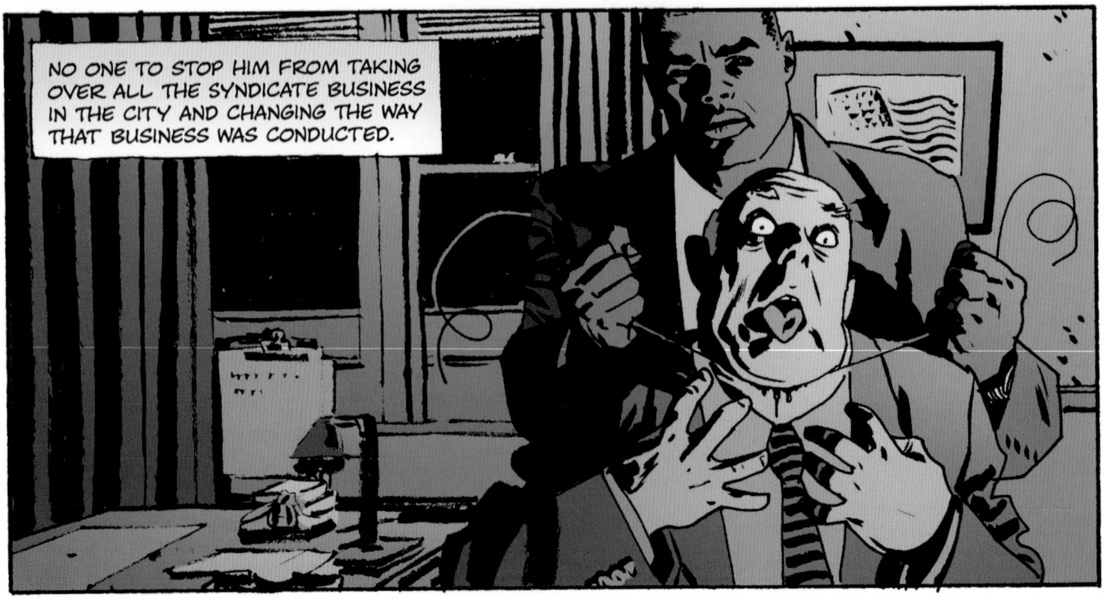
NO ONE TO STOP HIM FROM TAKING OVER ALL THE SYNDICATE BUSINESS IN THE CITY AND CHANGING THE WAY THAT BUSINESS WAS CONDUCTED.

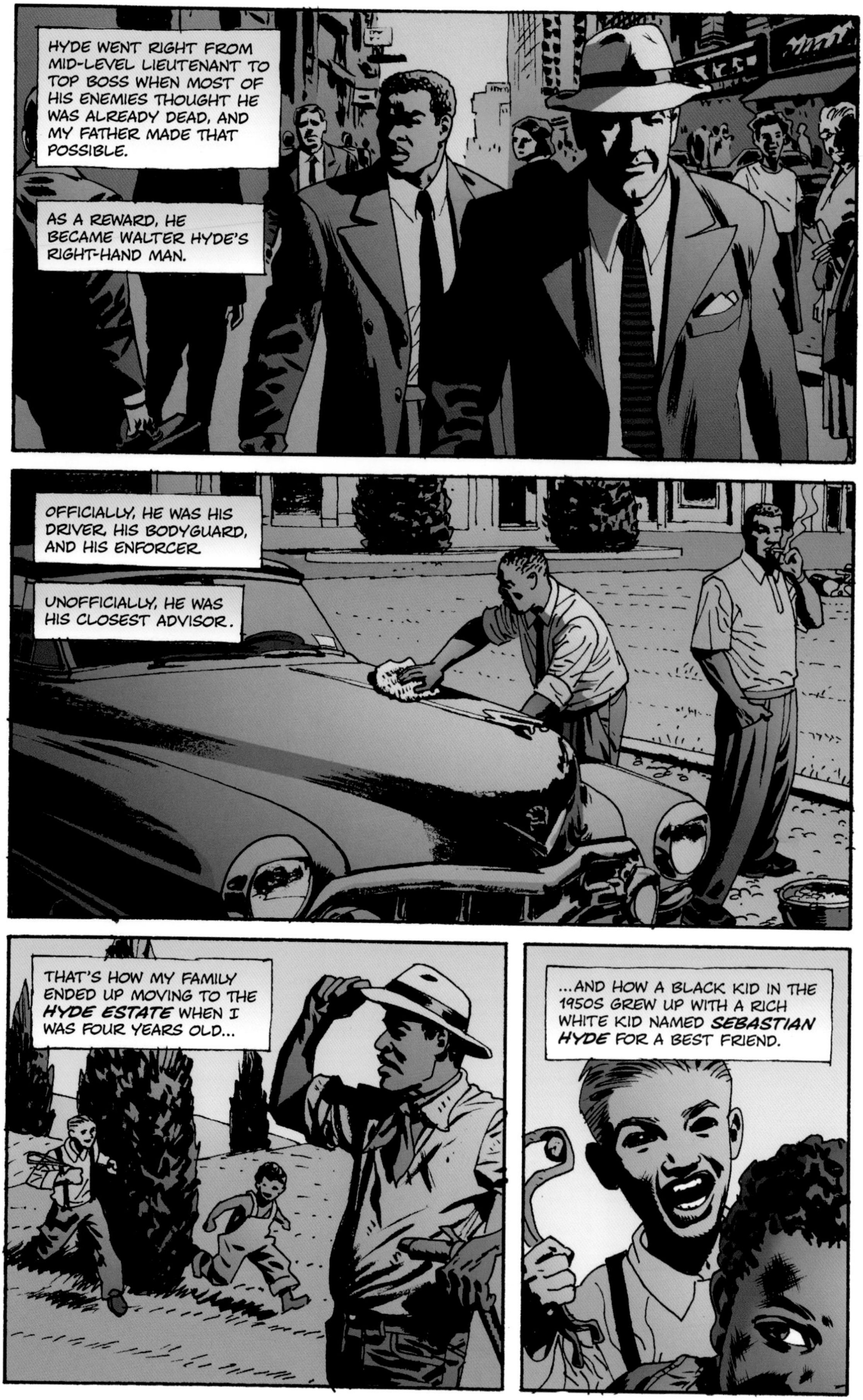
HYDE WENT RIGHT FROM MID-LEVEL LIEUTENANT TO TOP BOSS WHEN MOST OF HIS ENEMIES THOUGHT HE WAS ALREADY DEAD, AND MY FATHER MADE THAT POSSIBLE.
AS A REWARD, HE BECAME WALTER HYDE'S RIGHT-HAND MAN.
OFFICIALLY, HE WAS HIS DRIVER, HIS BODYGUARD, AND HIS ENFORCER.
UNOFFICIALLY, HE WAS HIS CLOSEST ADVISOR.
THAT'S HOW MY FAMILY ENDED UP MOVING TO THE ***HYDE ESTATE*** WHEN I WAS FOUR YEARS OLD...
...AND HOW A BLACK KID IN THE 1950S GREW UP WITH A RICH WHITE KID NAMED ***SEBASTIAN HYDE*** FOR A BEST FRIEND.

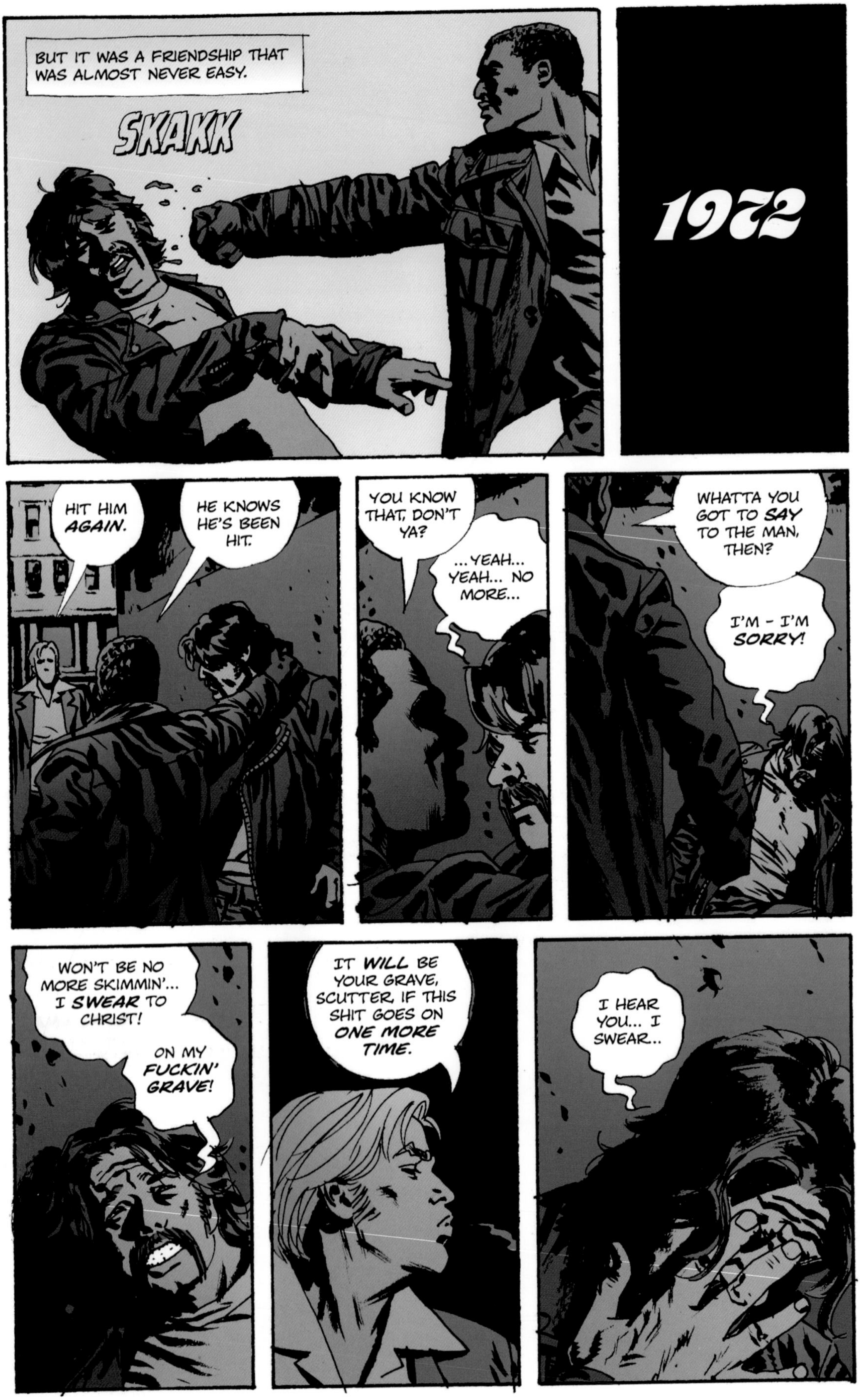
BUT IT WAS A FRIENDSHIP THAT WAS ALMOST NEVER EASY.
SKAKK
1972
HIT HIM AGAIN.
HE KNOWS HE'S BEEN HIT.
YOU KNOW THAT, DON'T YA?
...YEAH... YEAH... NO MORE...
WHATTA YOU GOT TO SAY TO THE MAN, THEN?
I'M - I'M SORRY!
WON'T BE NO MORE SKIMMIN'... I SWEAR TO CHRIST!
ON MY FUCKIN' GRAVE!
IT WILL BE YOUR GRAVE, SCUTTER, IF THIS SHIT GOES ON ONE MORE TIME.
I HEAR YOU... I SWEAR..

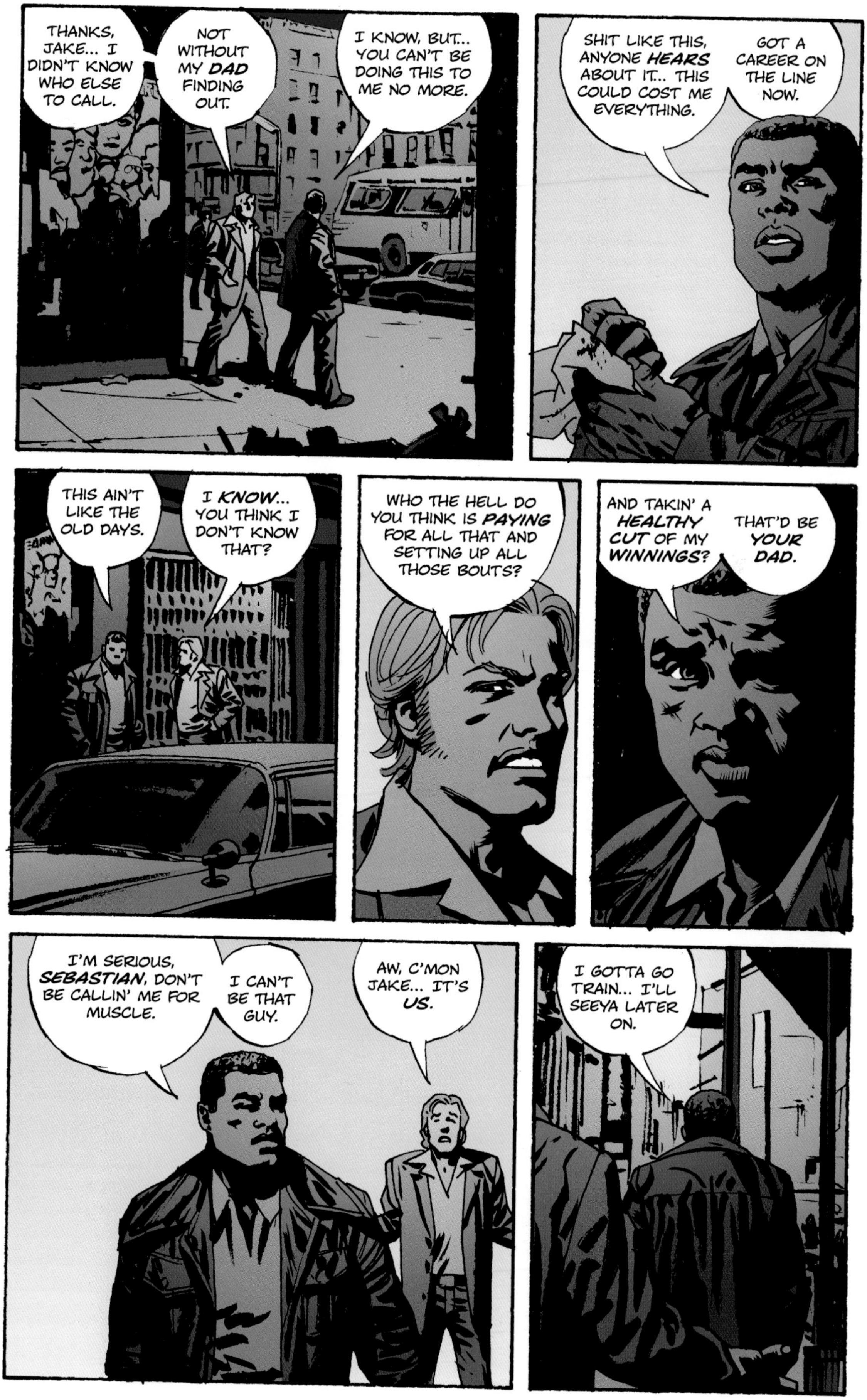
THANKS, JAKE... I DIDN'T KNOW WHO ELSE TO CALL.
NOT WITHOUT MY DAD FINDING OUT.
I KNOW, BUT... YOU CAN'T BE DOING THIS TO ME NO MORE.
SHIT LIKE THIS, ANYONE HEARS ABOUT IT... THIS COULD COST ME EVERYTHING.
GOT A CAREER ON THE LINE NOW.
THIS AIN'T LIKE THE OLD DAYS.
I KNOW... YOU THINK I DON'T KNOW THAT?
WHO THE HELL DO YOU THINK IS PAYING FOR ALL THAT AND SETTING UP ALL THOSE BOUTS?
AND TAKIN' A HEALTHY CUT OF MY WINNINGS?
THAT'D BE YOUR DAD.
I'M SERIOUS, SEBASTIAN, DON'T BE CALLIN' ME FOR MUSCLE.
I CAN'T BE THAT GUY.
AW, C'MON JAKE... IT'S US.
I GOTTA GO TRAIN... I'LL SEEYA LATER ON.

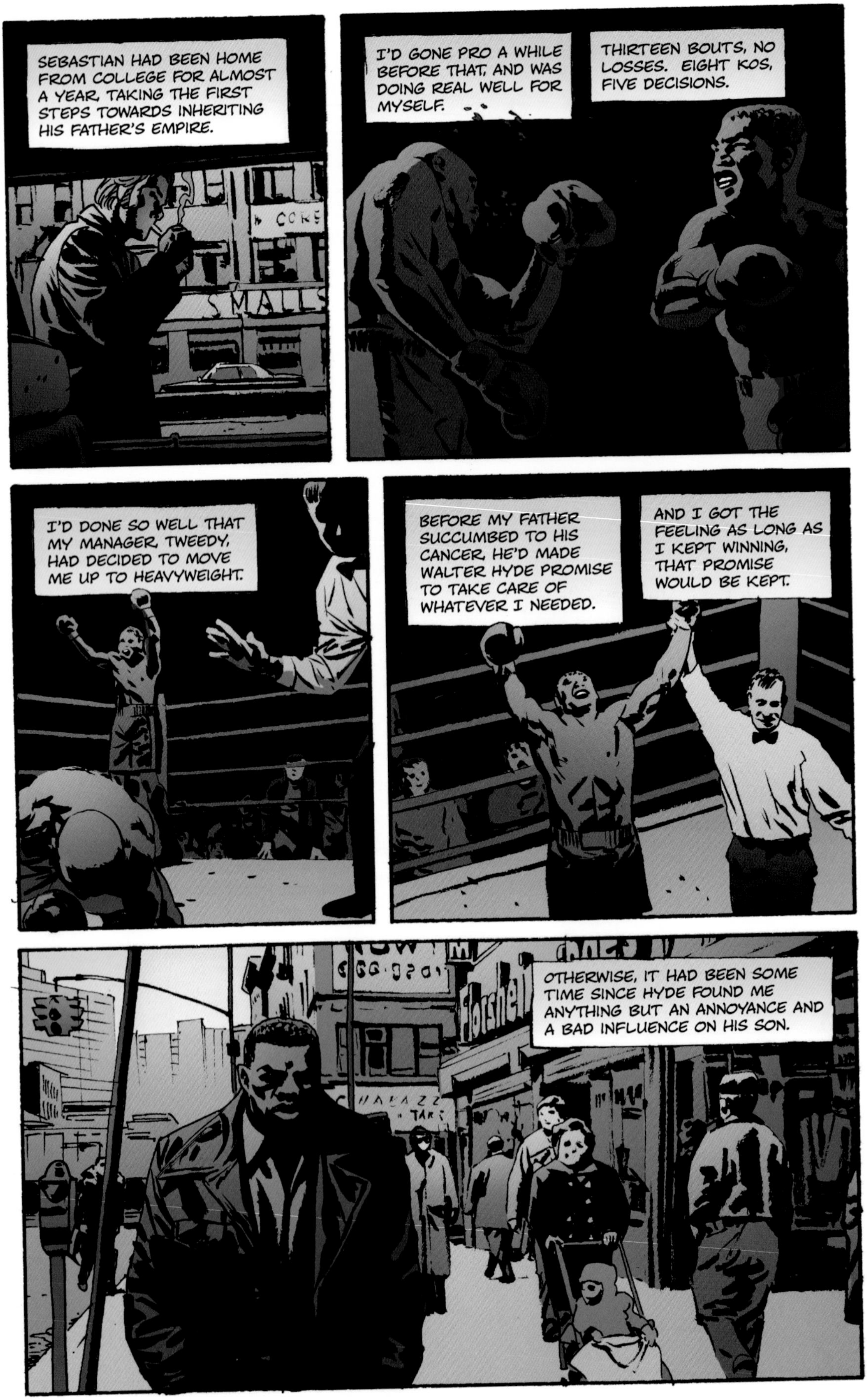
SEBASTIAN HAD BEEN HOME FROM COLLEGE FOR ALMOST A YEAR, TAKING THE FIRST STEPS TOWARDS INHERITING HIS FATHER'S EMPIRE.
I'D GONE PRO A WHILE BEFORE THAT, AND WAS DOING REAL WELL FOR MYSELF.
THIRTEEN BOUTS, NO LOSSES. EIGHT KOS, FIVE DECISIONS.
I'D DONE SO WELL THAT MY MANAGER, TWEEDY, HAD DECIDED TO MOVE ME UP TO HEAVYWEIGHT.
BEFORE MY FATHER SUCCUMBED TO HIS CANCER, HE'D MADE WALTER HYDE PROMISE TO TAKE CARE OF WHATEVER I NEEDED.
AND I GOT THE FEELING AS LONG AS I KEPT WINNING, THAT PROMISE WOULD BE KEPT.
OTHERWISE, IT HAD BEEN SOME TIME SINCE HYDE FOUND ME ANYTHING BUT AN ANNOYANCE AND A BAD INFLUENCE ON HIS SON.

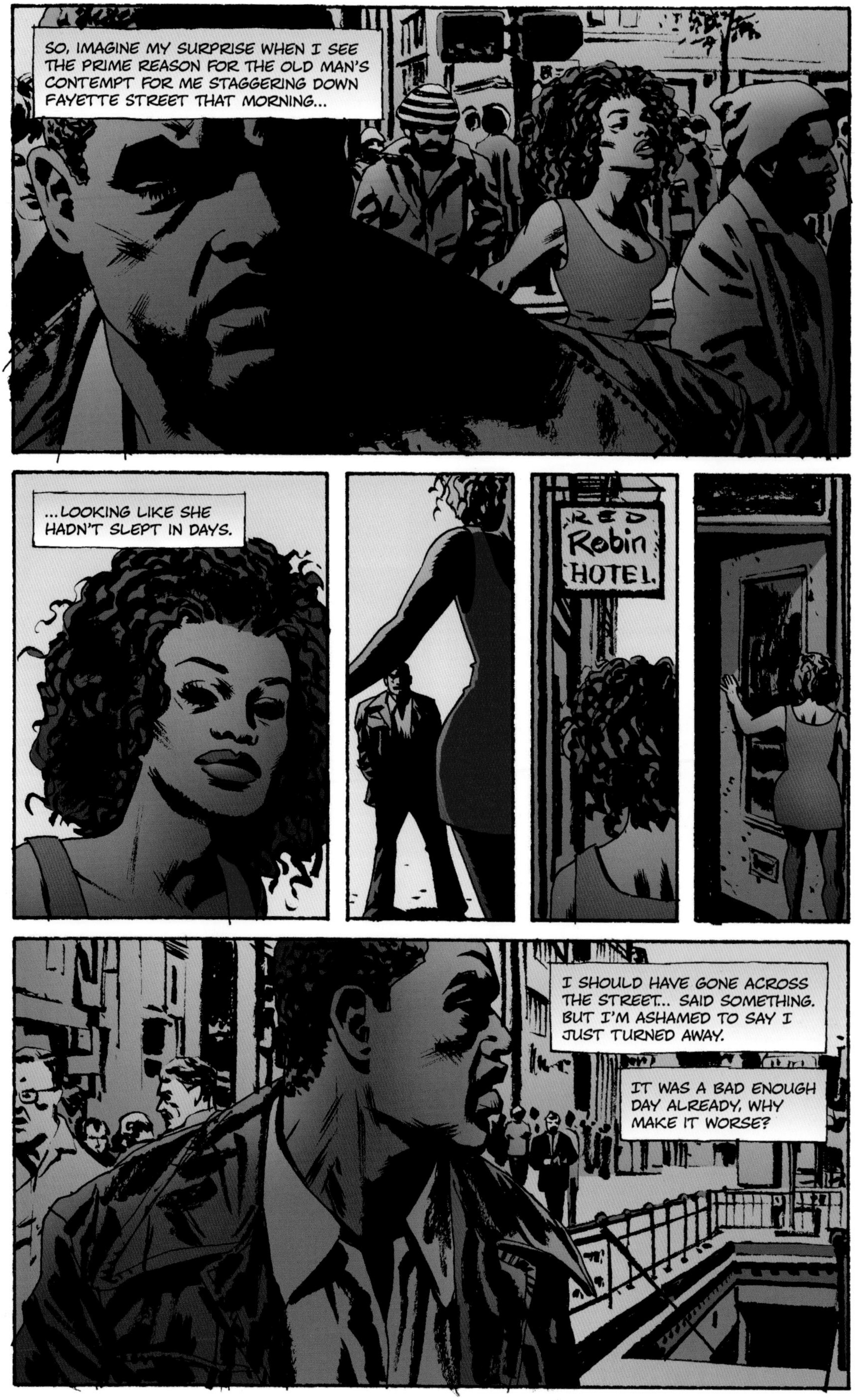
SO, IMAGINE MY SURPRISE WHEN I SEE THE PRIME REASON FOR THE OLD MAN'S CONTEMPT FOR ME STAGGERING DOWN FAYETTE STREET THAT MORNING...
...LOOKING LIKE SHE HADN'T SLEPT IN DAYS.
RED Robin HOTEL
I SHOULD HAVE GONE ACROSS THE STREET... SAID SOMETHING. BUT I'M ASHAMED TO SAY I JUST TURNED AWAY.
IT WAS A BAD ENOUGH DAY ALREADY, WHY MAKE IT WORSE?

BUT IT GOT WORSE ANYWAY. SOME THINGS ARE JUST LIKE THAT.

AND DANICA BRIGGS WAS ONE OF THOSE THINGS.

SHE GOT RIGHT IN MY HEAD AND GNAWED AT ME ALL THROUGH MY WORK-OUT.

NO! NO NO NO!

THE HELL'RE YOU *DOIN'*, GNARLY?

WE DON'T PAY MELVIN TO WHALE ON YER BLACK ASS.

YER S'POSED TO WHALE ON *HIS*!

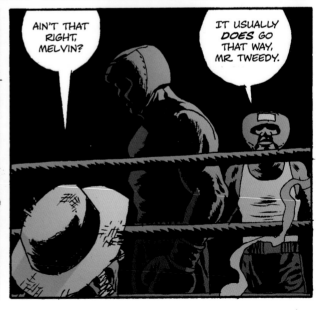

AIN'T THAT RIGHT, MELVIN?

IT USUALLY *DOES* GO THAT WAY, MR TWEEDY.

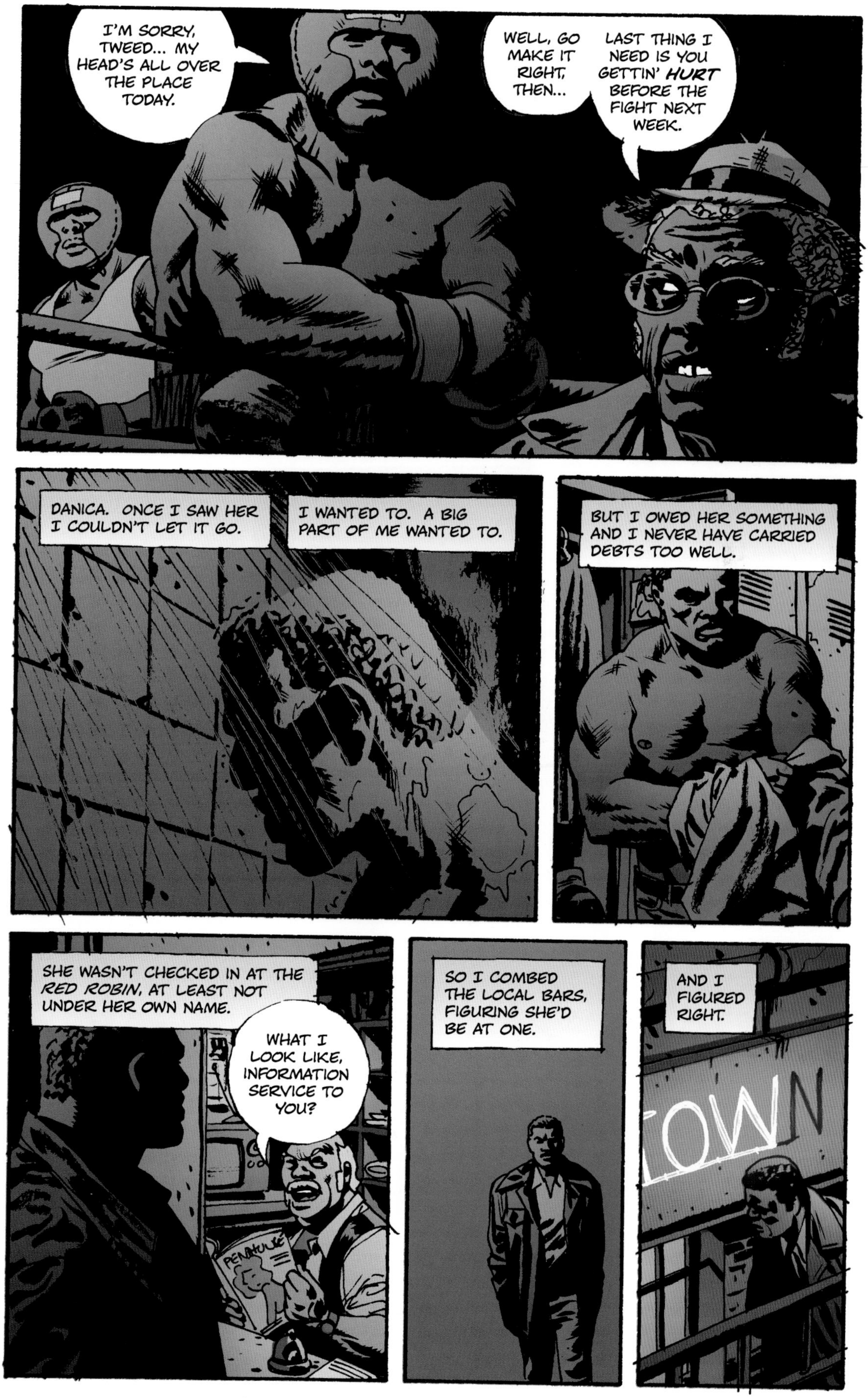
I'M SORRY, TWEED... MY HEAD'S ALL OVER THE PLACE TODAY.
WELL, GO MAKE IT RIGHT, THEN...
LAST THING I NEED IS YOU GETTIN' *HURT* BEFORE THE FIGHT NEXT WEEK.
DANICA. ONCE I SAW HER I COULDN'T LET IT GO.
I WANTED TO. A BIG PART OF ME WANTED TO.
BUT I OWED HER SOMETHING AND I NEVER HAVE CARRIED DEBTS TOO WELL.
SHE WASN'T CHECKED IN AT THE *RED ROBIN*, AT LEAST NOT UNDER HER OWN NAME.
WHAT I LOOK LIKE, INFORMATION SERVICE TO YOU?
SO I COMBED THE LOCAL BARS, FIGURING SHE'D BE AT ONE.
AND I FIGURED RIGHT.
OWN

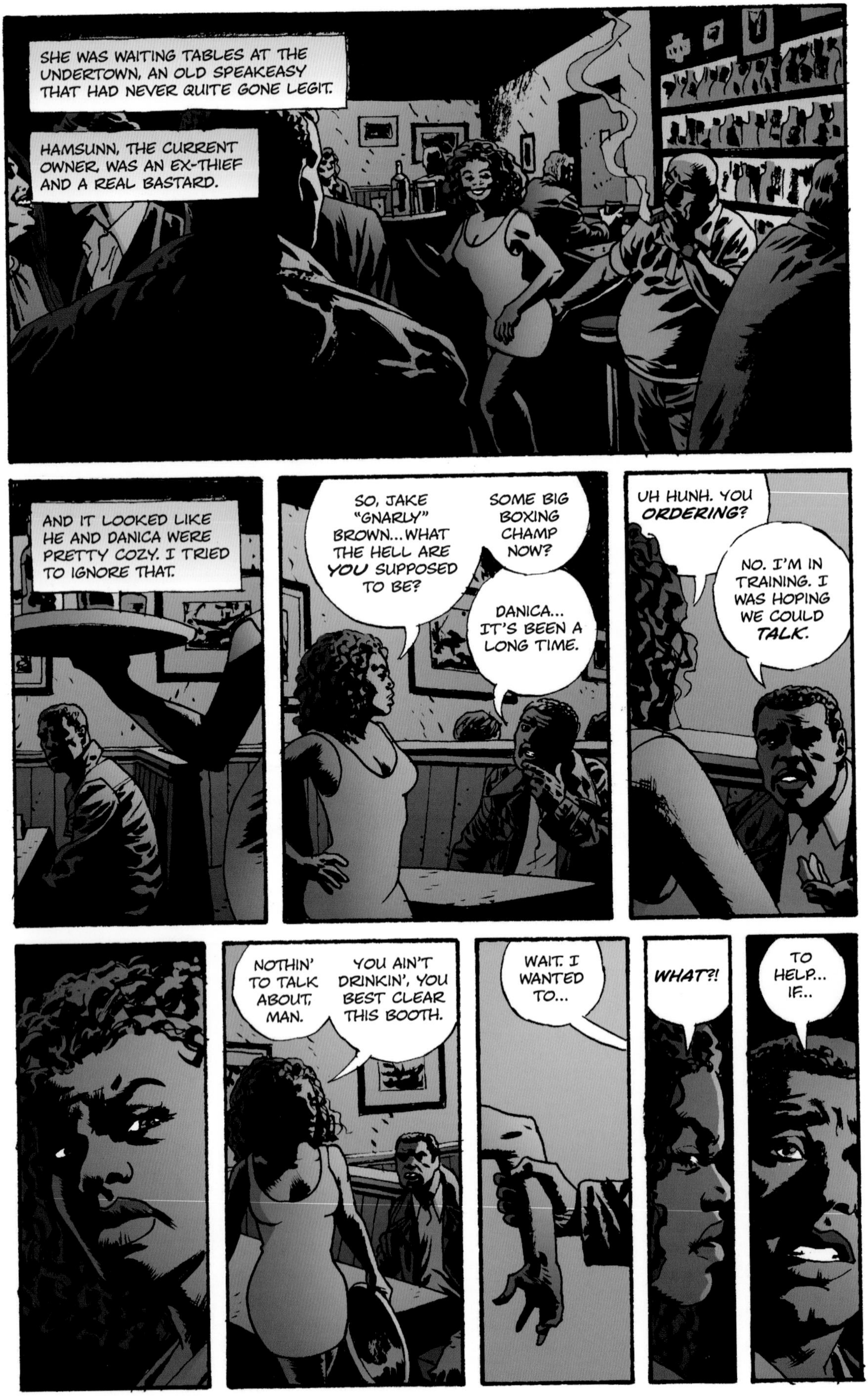
SHE WAS WAITING TABLES AT THE UNDERTOWN, AN OLD SPEAKEASY THAT HAD NEVER QUITE GONE LEGIT.
HAMSUNN, THE CURRENT OWNER, WAS AN EX-THIEF AND A REAL BASTARD.
AND IT LOOKED LIKE HE AND DANICA WERE PRETTY COZY. I TRIED TO IGNORE THAT.
SO, JAKE "GNARLY" BROWN...WHAT THE HELL ARE YOU SUPPOSED TO BE?
SOME BIG BOXING CHAMP NOW?
DANICA... IT'S BEEN A LONG TIME.
UH HUNH. YOU ORDERING?
NO. I'M IN TRAINING. I WAS HOPING WE COULD TALK.
NOTHIN' TO TALK ABOUT, MAN.
YOU AIN'T DRINKIN', YOU BEST CLEAR THIS BOOTH.
WAIT. I WANTED TO...
WHAT?!
TO HELP... IF...

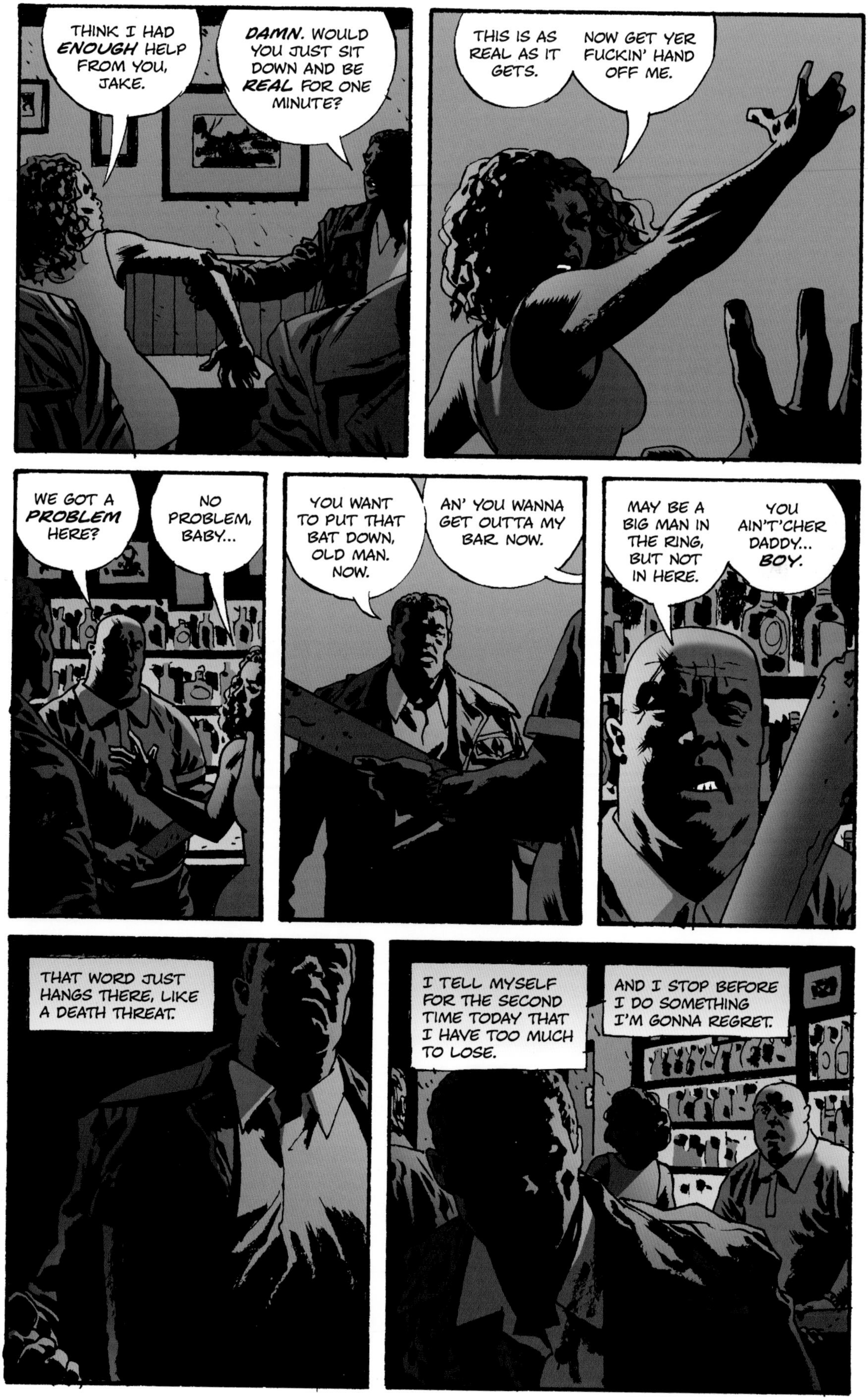
THINK I HAD ENOUGH HELP FROM YOU, JAKE.
DAMN. WOULD YOU JUST SIT DOWN AND BE REAL FOR ONE MINUTE?
THIS IS AS REAL AS IT GETS.
NOW GET YER FUCKIN' HAND OFF ME.
WE GOT A PROBLEM HERE?
NO PROBLEM, BABY...
YOU WANT TO PUT THAT BAT DOWN, OLD MAN. NOW.
AN' YOU WANNA GET OUTTA MY BAR NOW.
MAY BE A BIG MAN IN THE RING, BUT NOT IN HERE.
YOU AIN'T'CHER DADDY... BOY.
THAT WORD JUST HANGS THERE, LIKE A DEATH THREAT.
I TELL MYSELF FOR THE SECOND TIME TODAY THAT I HAVE TOO MUCH TO LOSE.
AND I STOP BEFORE I DO SOMETHING I'M GONNA REGRET.

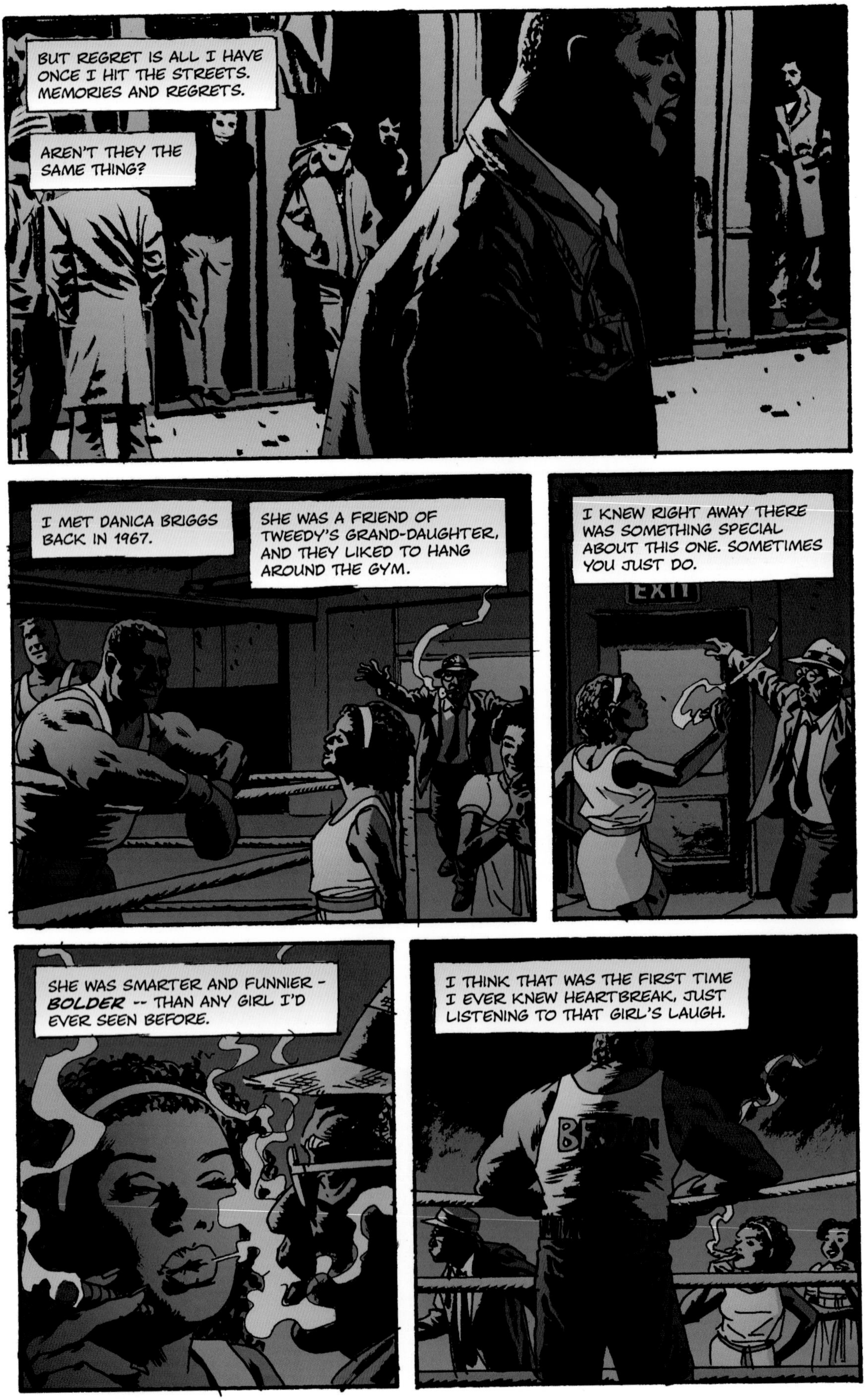
BUT REGRET IS ALL I HAVE ONCE I HIT THE STREETS. MEMORIES AND REGRETS.
AREN'T THEY THE SAME THING?
I MET DANICA BRIGGS BACK IN 1967.
SHE WAS A FRIEND OF TWEEDY'S GRAND-DAUGHTER, AND THEY LIKED TO HANG AROUND THE GYM.
I KNEW RIGHT AWAY THERE WAS SOMETHING SPECIAL ABOUT THIS ONE. SOMETIMES YOU JUST DO.
EXIT
SHE WAS SMARTER AND FUNNIER -- *BOLDER* -- THAN ANY GIRL I'D EVER SEEN BEFORE.
I THINK THAT WAS THE FIRST TIME I EVER KNEW HEARTBREAK, JUST LISTENING TO THAT GIRL'S LAUGH.

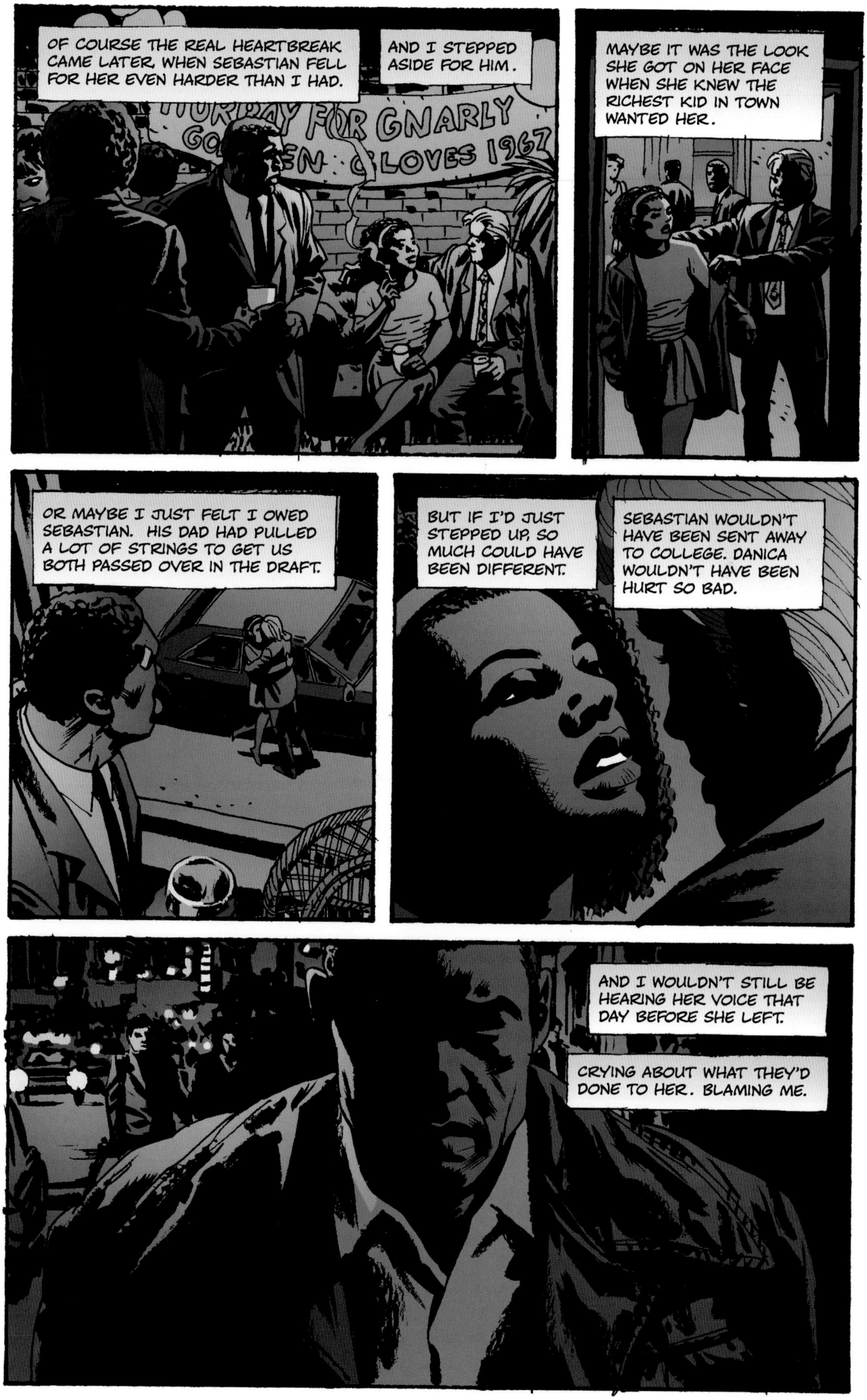
OF COURSE THE REAL HEARTBREAK CAME LATER, WHEN SEBASTIAN FELL FOR HER EVEN HARDER THAN I HAD.
AND I STEPPED ASIDE FOR HIM.
MAYBE IT WAS THE LOOK SHE GOT ON HER FACE WHEN SHE KNEW THE RICHEST KID IN TOWN WANTED HER.
OR MAYBE I JUST FELT I OWED SEBASTIAN. HIS DAD HAD PULLED A LOT OF STRINGS TO GET US BOTH PASSED OVER IN THE DRAFT.
BUT IF I'D JUST STEPPED UP, SO MUCH COULD HAVE BEEN DIFFERENT.
SEBASTIAN WOULDN'T HAVE BEEN SENT AWAY TO COLLEGE. DANICA WOULDN'T HAVE BEEN HURT SO BAD.
AND I WOULDN'T STILL BE HEARING HER VOICE THAT DAY BEFORE SHE LEFT.
CRYING ABOUT WHAT THEY'D DONE TO HER. BLAMING ME.

DID YOU HEAR ABOUT *SCUTTER*?

NO... WHAT IS IT *THIS* TIME?

HE GOT KILLED.

THEY FOUND HIM LATE LAST NIGHT... SHOT IN THE BACK, ALL HIS FINGERS CUT OFF.

JESUS.

YEAH. DAD HAS PEOPLE REPORTING BACK TO HIM ABOUT MY BUSINESS.

PEOPLE WHO *SUPPOSEDLY* WORK FOR *ME*.

WELL, YOU *WANTED* THAT WORLD, MAN...

IS *THAT* HOW I GOT HERE? 'CAUSE I FORGET SOMETIMES *WHO* WANTED *WHAT*.

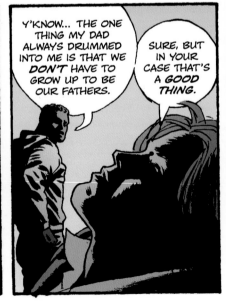

Y'KNOW... THE ONE THING MY DAD ALWAYS DRUMMED INTO ME IS THAT WE *DON'T* HAVE TO GROW UP TO BE OUR FATHERS.

SURE, BUT IN YOUR CASE THAT'S A *GOOD* THING.

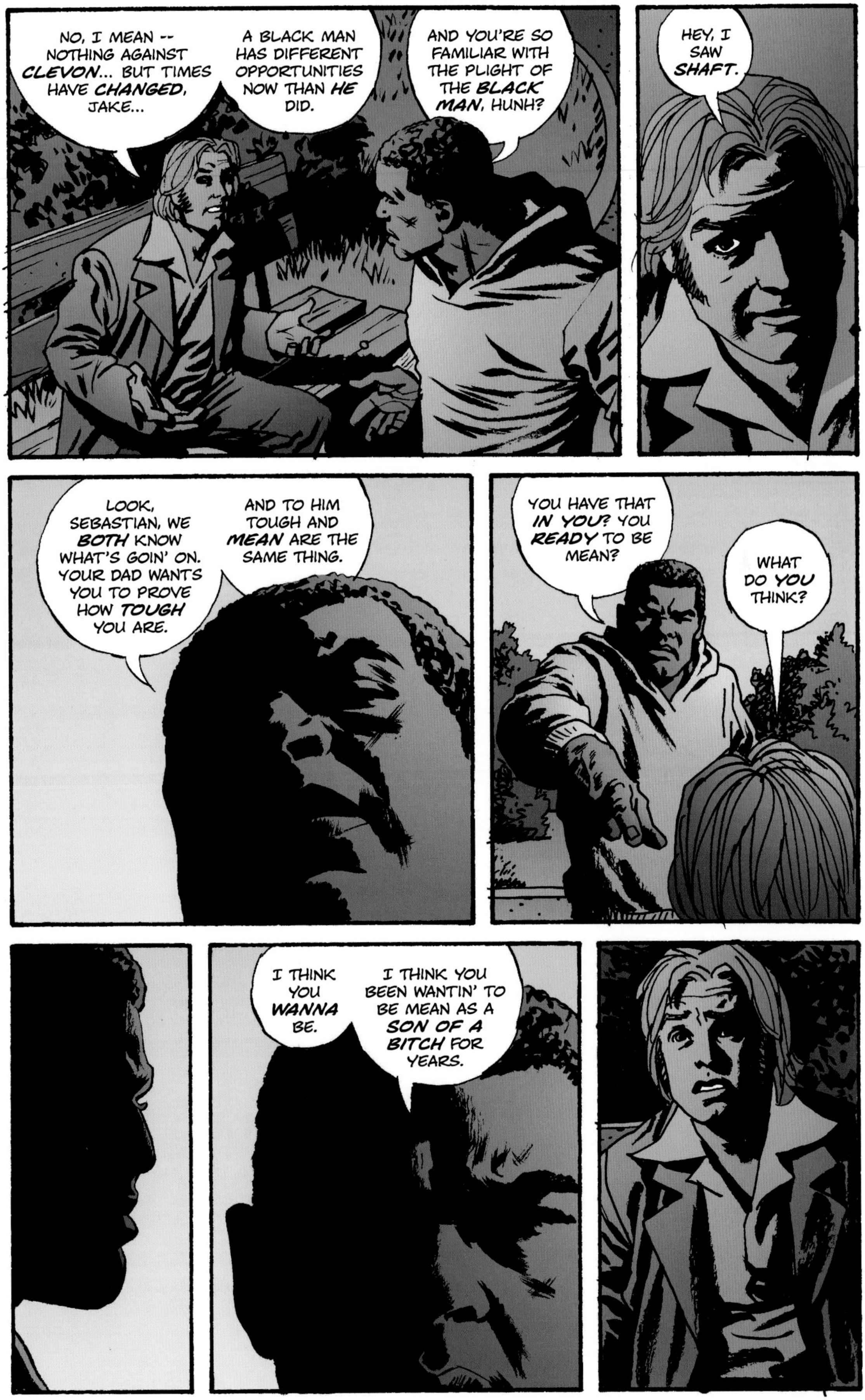
NO, I MEAN -- NOTHING AGAINST CLEVON... BUT TIMES HAVE CHANGED, JAKE...
A BLACK MAN HAS DIFFERENT OPPORTUNITIES NOW THAN HE DID.
AND YOU'RE SO FAMILIAR WITH THE PLIGHT OF THE BLACK MAN, HUNH?
HEY, I SAW SHAFT.
LOOK, SEBASTIAN, WE BOTH KNOW WHAT'S GOIN' ON. YOUR DAD WANTS YOU TO PROVE HOW TOUGH YOU ARE.
AND TO HIM TOUGH AND MEAN ARE THE SAME THING.
YOU HAVE THAT IN YOU? YOU READY TO BE MEAN?
WHAT DO YOU THINK?
I THINK YOU WANNA BE.
I THINK YOU BEEN WANTIN' TO BE MEAN AS A SON OF A BITCH FOR YEARS.

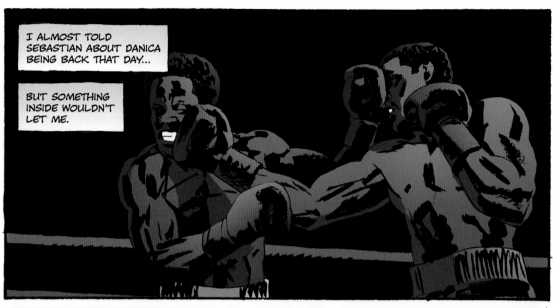

I ALMOST TOLD SEBASTIAN ABOUT DANICA BEING BACK THAT DAY...

BUT SOMETHING INSIDE WOULDN'T LET ME.

SHE WAS SOMETHING WE HADN'T TALKED ABOUT FOR YEARS.

NOT SINCE THE NIGHT WHEN I FIRST SAW REAL HATE IN SEBASTIAN'S EYES.

BEFORE THAT, WE'D BEEN BROTHERS, OF A STRANGE SORT.

EACH OUT OF PLACE IN THE OTHER'S WORLD, BUT FEARLESS ABOUT IT.

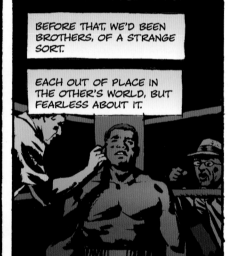

SO I HAD THOUGHT.

BUT I DIDN'T TRUST HIM ANYMORE. NOT LIKE I WANTED TO.

I JUST TRUSTED HE'D DO THE WRONG THING.

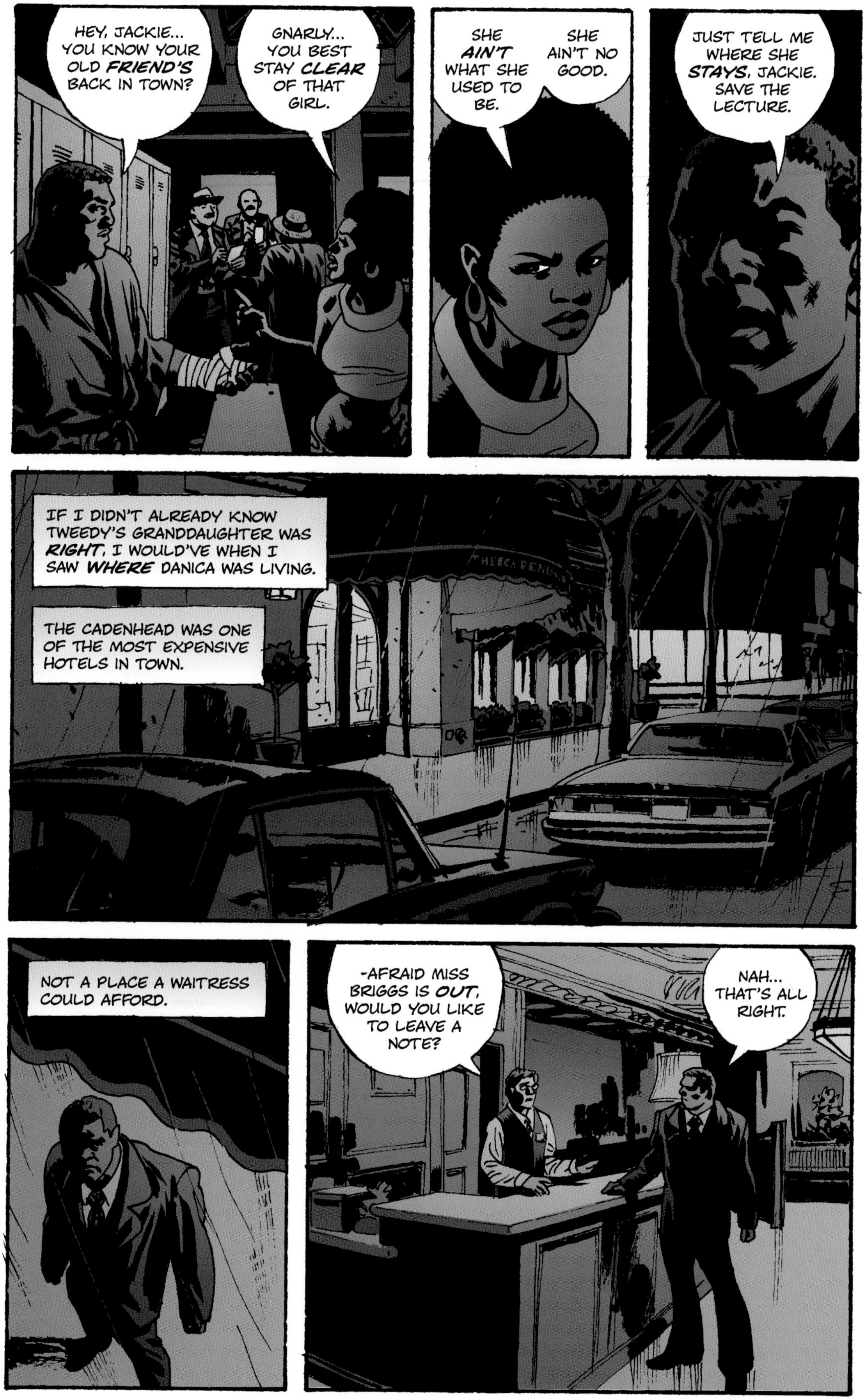
HEY, JACKIE... YOU KNOW YOUR OLD FRIEND'S BACK IN TOWN?
GNARLY... YOU BEST STAY CLEAR OF THAT GIRL.
SHE AIN'T WHAT SHE USED TO BE.
SHE AIN'T NO GOOD.
JUST TELL ME WHERE SHE STAYS, JACKIE. SAVE THE LECTURE.
IF I DIDN'T ALREADY KNOW TWEEDY'S GRANDDAUGHTER WAS RIGHT, I WOULD'VE WHEN I SAW WHERE DANICA WAS LIVING.
THE CADENHEAD WAS ONE OF THE MOST EXPENSIVE HOTELS IN TOWN.
NOT A PLACE A WAITRESS COULD AFFORD.
-AFRAID MISS BRIGGS IS OUT, WOULD YOU LIKE TO LEAVE A NOTE?
NAH... THAT'S ALL RIGHT.

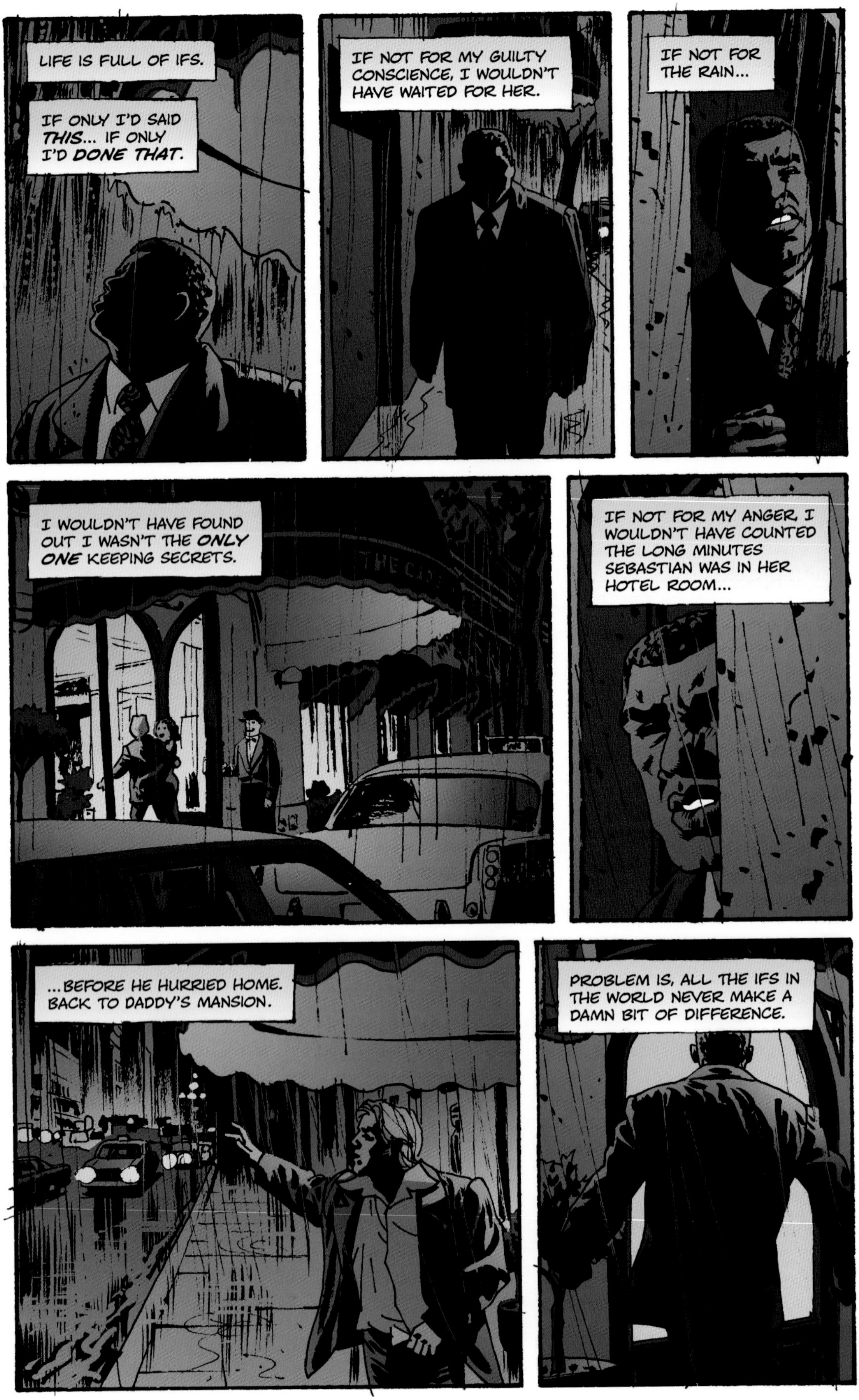
LIFE IS FULL OF IFS.
IF ONLY I'D SAID *THIS*... IF ONLY I'D *DONE THAT*.
IF NOT FOR MY GUILTY CONSCIENCE, I WOULDN'T HAVE WAITED FOR HER.
IF NOT FOR THE RAIN...
I WOULDN'T HAVE FOUND OUT I WASN'T THE *ONLY ONE* KEEPING SECRETS.
IF NOT FOR MY ANGER, I WOULDN'T HAVE COUNTED THE LONG MINUTES SEBASTIAN WAS IN HER HOTEL ROOM...
...BEFORE HE HURRIED HOME. BACK TO DADDY'S MANSION.
PROBLEM IS, ALL THE IFS IN THE WORLD NEVER MAKE A DAMN BIT OF DIFFERENCE.

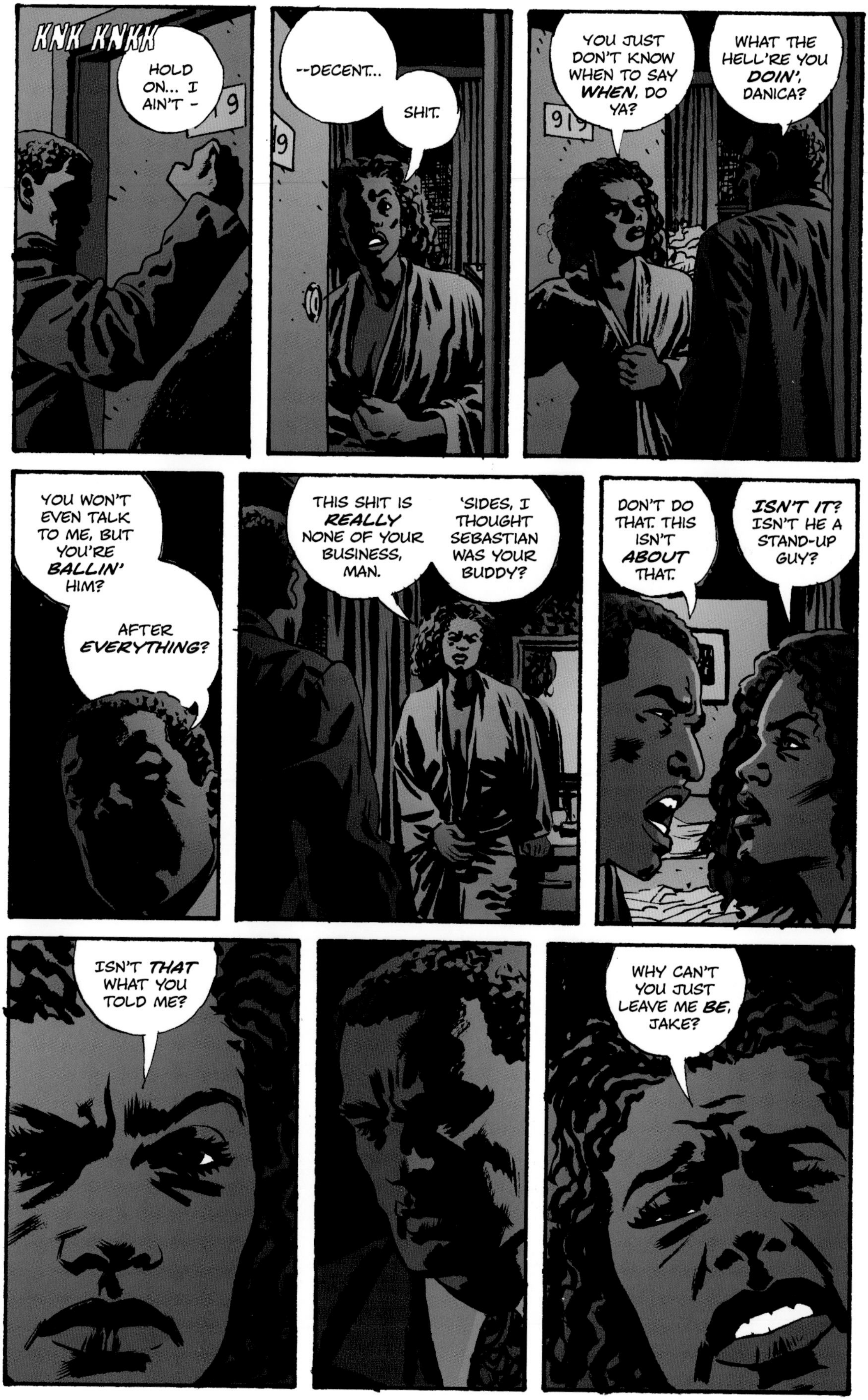
KNK KNKK
HOLD ON... I AIN'T -
--DECENT...
SHIT.
YOU JUST DON'T KNOW WHEN TO SAY WHEN, DO YA?
WHAT THE HELL'RE YOU DOIN', DANICA?
YOU WON'T EVEN TALK TO ME, BUT YOU'RE BALLIN' HIM?
AFTER EVERYTHING?
THIS SHIT IS REALLY NONE OF YOUR BUSINESS, MAN.
'SIDES, I THOUGHT SEBASTIAN WAS YOUR BUDDY?
DON'T DO THAT. THIS ISN'T ABOUT THAT.
ISN'T IT? ISN'T HE A STAND-UP GUY?
ISN'T THAT WHAT YOU TOLD ME?
WHY CAN'T YOU JUST LEAVE ME BE, JAKE?

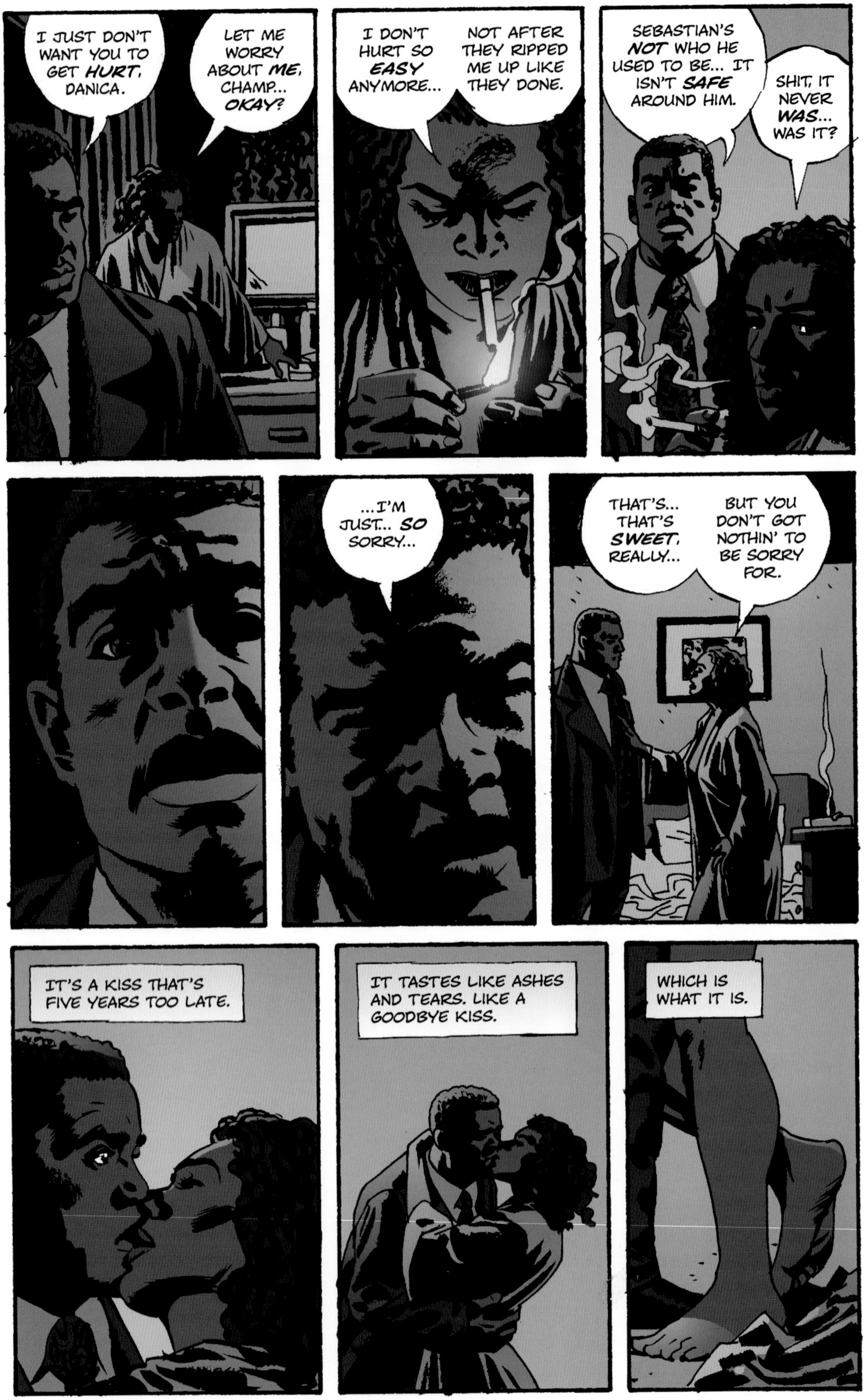
I JUST DON'T WANT YOU TO GET HURT, DANICA.
LET ME WORRY ABOUT ME, CHAMP... OKAY?
I DON'T HURT SO EASY ANYMORE...
NOT AFTER THEY RIPPED ME UP LIKE THEY DONE.
SEBASTIAN'S NOT WHO HE USED TO BE... IT ISN'T SAFE AROUND HIM.
SHIT, IT NEVER WAS... WAS IT?
...I'M JUST... SO SORRY...
THAT'S... THAT'S SWEET, REALLY...
BUT YOU DON'T GOT NOTHIN' TO BE SORRY FOR.
IT'S A KISS THAT'S FIVE YEARS TOO LATE.
IT TASTES LIKE ASHES AND TEARS. LIKE A GOODBYE KISS.
WHICH IS WHAT IT IS.

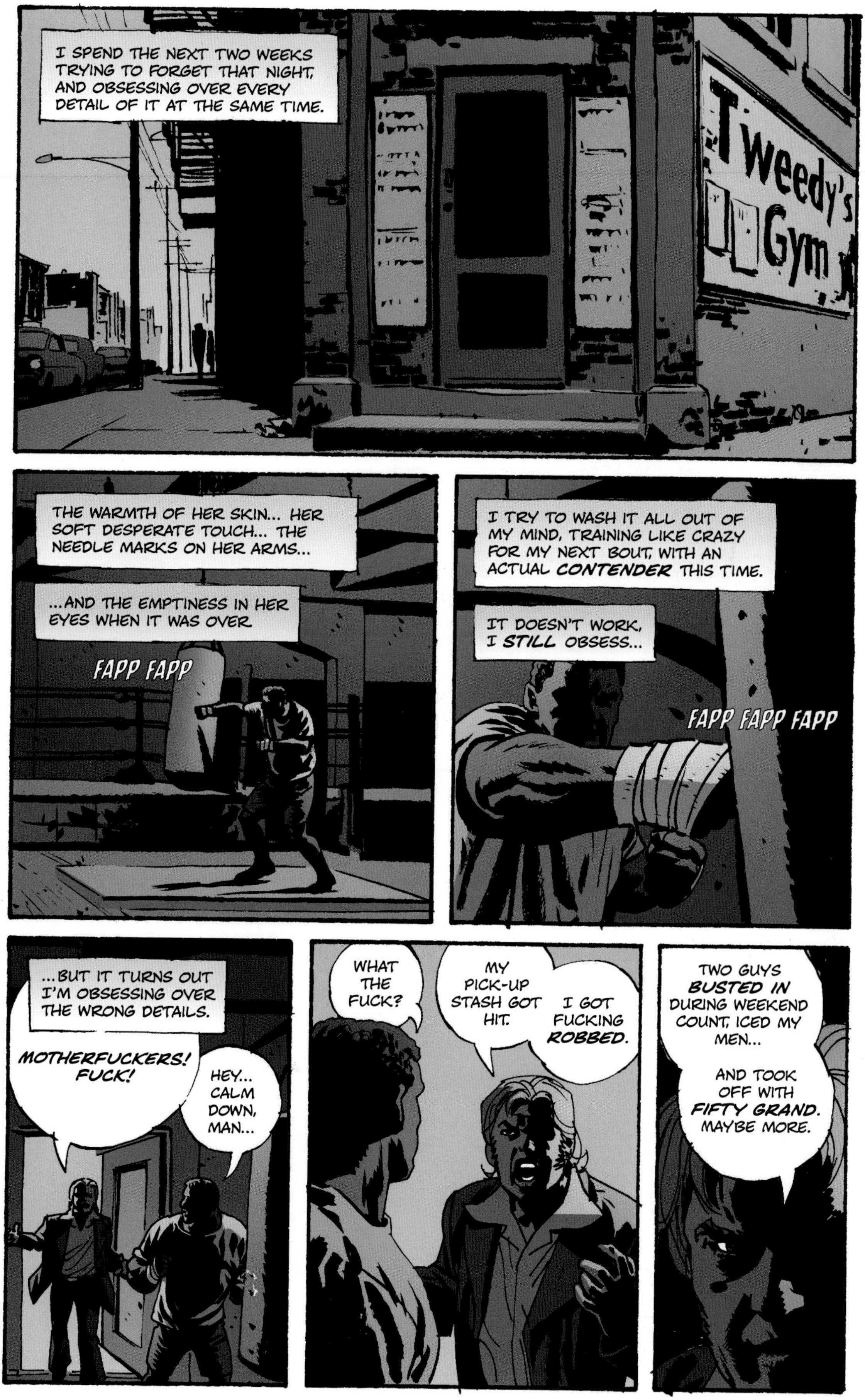
I SPEND THE NEXT TWO WEEKS TRYING TO FORGET THAT NIGHT, AND OBSESSING OVER EVERY DETAIL OF IT AT THE SAME TIME.
Tweedy's Gym
THE WARMTH OF HER SKIN... HER SOFT DESPERATE TOUCH... THE NEEDLE MARKS ON HER ARMS...
...AND THE EMPTINESS IN HER EYES WHEN IT WAS OVER.
FAPP FAPP
I TRY TO WASH IT ALL OUT OF MY MIND, TRAINING LIKE CRAZY FOR MY NEXT BOUT, WITH AN ACTUAL CONTENDER THIS TIME.
IT DOESN'T WORK, I STILL OBSESS...
FAPP FAPP FAPP
...BUT IT TURNS OUT I'M OBSESSING OVER THE WRONG DETAILS.
MOTHERFUCKERS! FUCK!
HEY... CALM DOWN, MAN...
WHAT THE FUCK?
MY PICK-UP STASH GOT HIT.
I GOT FUCKING ROBBED.
TWO GUYS BUSTED IN DURING WEEKEND COUNT, ICED MY MEN...
AND TOOK OFF WITH FIFTY GRAND. MAYBE MORE.

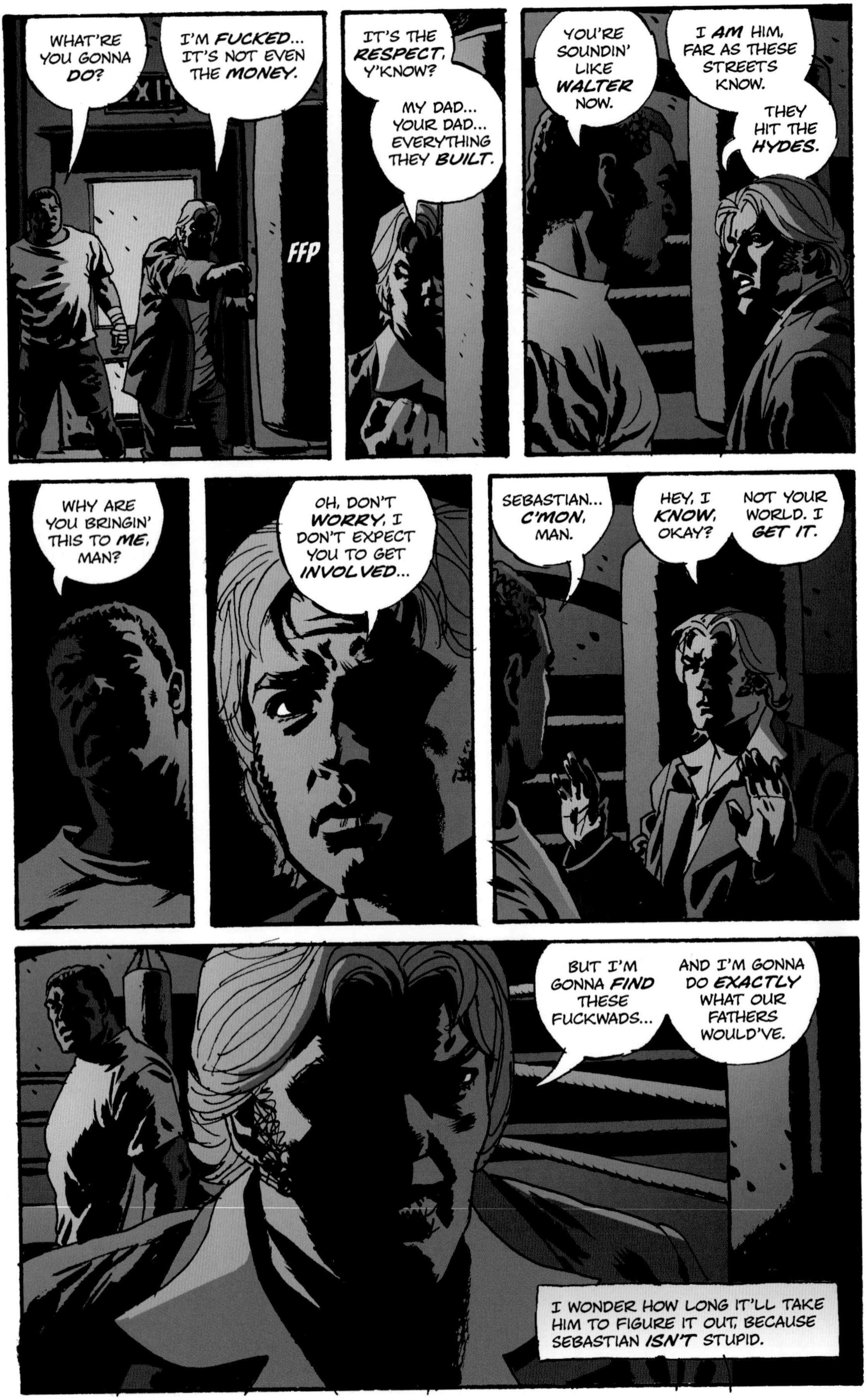
WHAT'RE YOU GONNA DO?
I'M FUCKED... IT'S NOT EVEN THE MONEY.
EXIT
FFP
IT'S THE RESPECT, Y'KNOW?
MY DAD... YOUR DAD... EVERYTHING THEY BUILT.
YOU'RE SOUNDIN' LIKE WALTER NOW.
I AM HIM, FAR AS THESE STREETS KNOW.
THEY HIT THE HYDES.
WHY ARE YOU BRINGIN' THIS TO ME, MAN?
OH, DON'T WORRY, I DON'T EXPECT YOU TO GET INVOLVED...
SEBASTIAN... C'MON, MAN.
HEY, I KNOW, OKAY?
NOT YOUR WORLD. I GET IT.
BUT I'M GONNA FIND THESE FUCKWADS...
AND I'M GONNA DO EXACTLY WHAT OUR FATHERS WOULD'VE.
I WONDER HOW LONG IT'LL TAKE HIM TO FIGURE IT OUT, BECAUSE SEBASTIAN ISN'T STUPID.

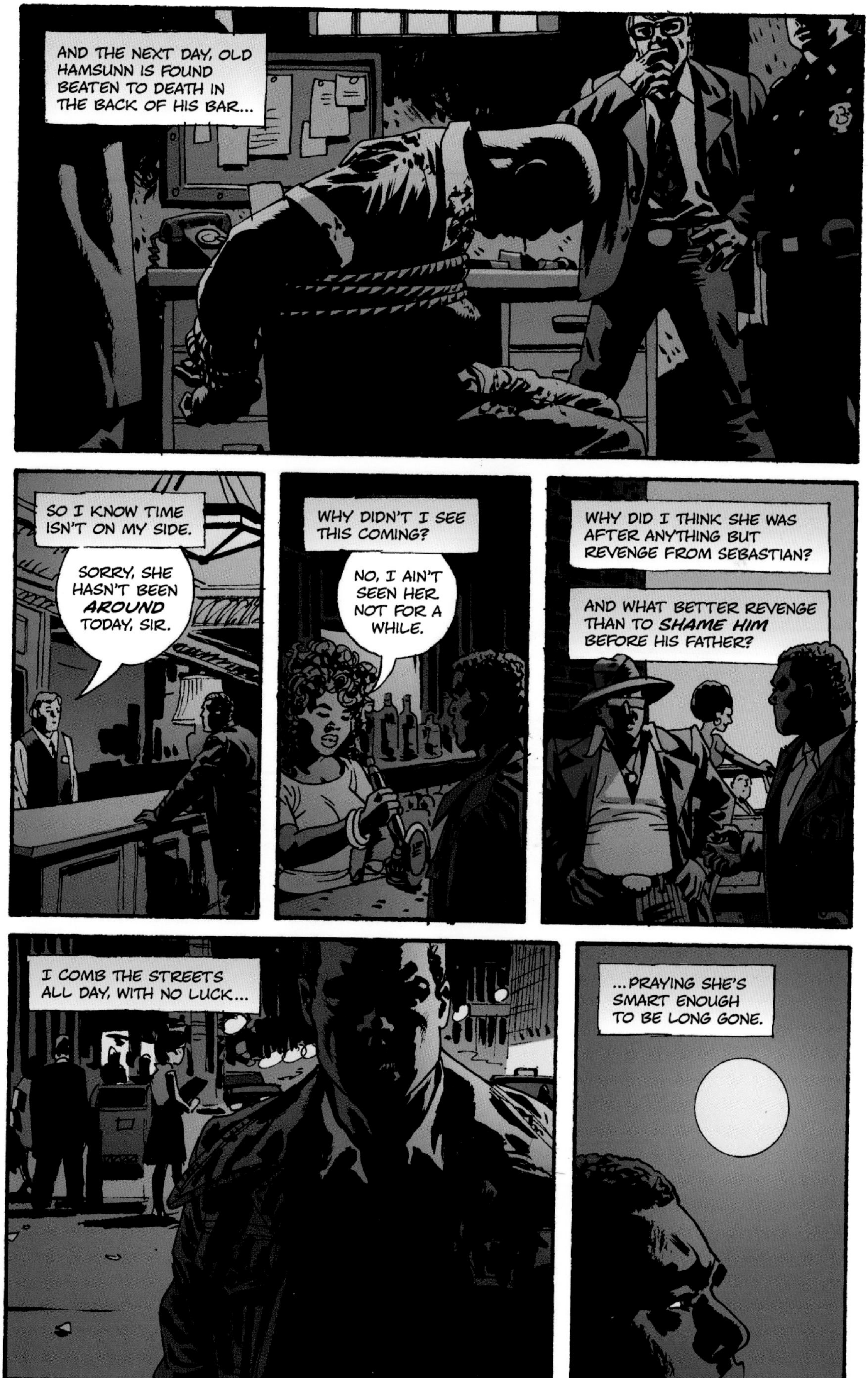
AND THE NEXT DAY, OLD HAMSUNN IS FOUND BEATEN TO DEATH IN THE BACK OF HIS BAR...
SO I KNOW TIME ISN'T ON MY SIDE.
SORRY, SHE HASN'T BEEN AROUND TODAY, SIR.
WHY DIDN'T I SEE THIS COMING?
NO, I AIN'T SEEN HER NOT FOR A WHILE.
WHY DID I THINK SHE WAS AFTER ANYTHING BUT REVENGE FROM SEBASTIAN?
AND WHAT BETTER REVENGE THAN TO SHAME HIM BEFORE HIS FATHER?
I COMB THE STREETS ALL DAY, WITH NO LUCK...
...PRAYING SHE'S SMART ENOUGH TO BE LONG GONE.

AND SHE IS, JUST NOT HOW I MEANT.

YEAH, THAT'S HER

ANY *REASON* YOU WERE ALL OVER TOWN ASKIN' FOR HER YESTERDAY?

AM I A *SUSPECT*?

NAH... SHE WAS IN HERE THE WHOLE TIME YOU WERE LOOKIN'.

BEEN DEAD SINCE YESTERDAY *MORNIN'*.

NO... SHE WAS DEAD A *LONG TIME* BEFORE THAT.

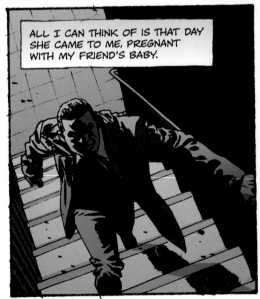

ALL I CAN THINK OF IS THAT DAY SHE CAME TO ME, PREGNANT WITH MY FRIEND'S BABY.

AND HOW I SENT HER TO THE WOLVES.

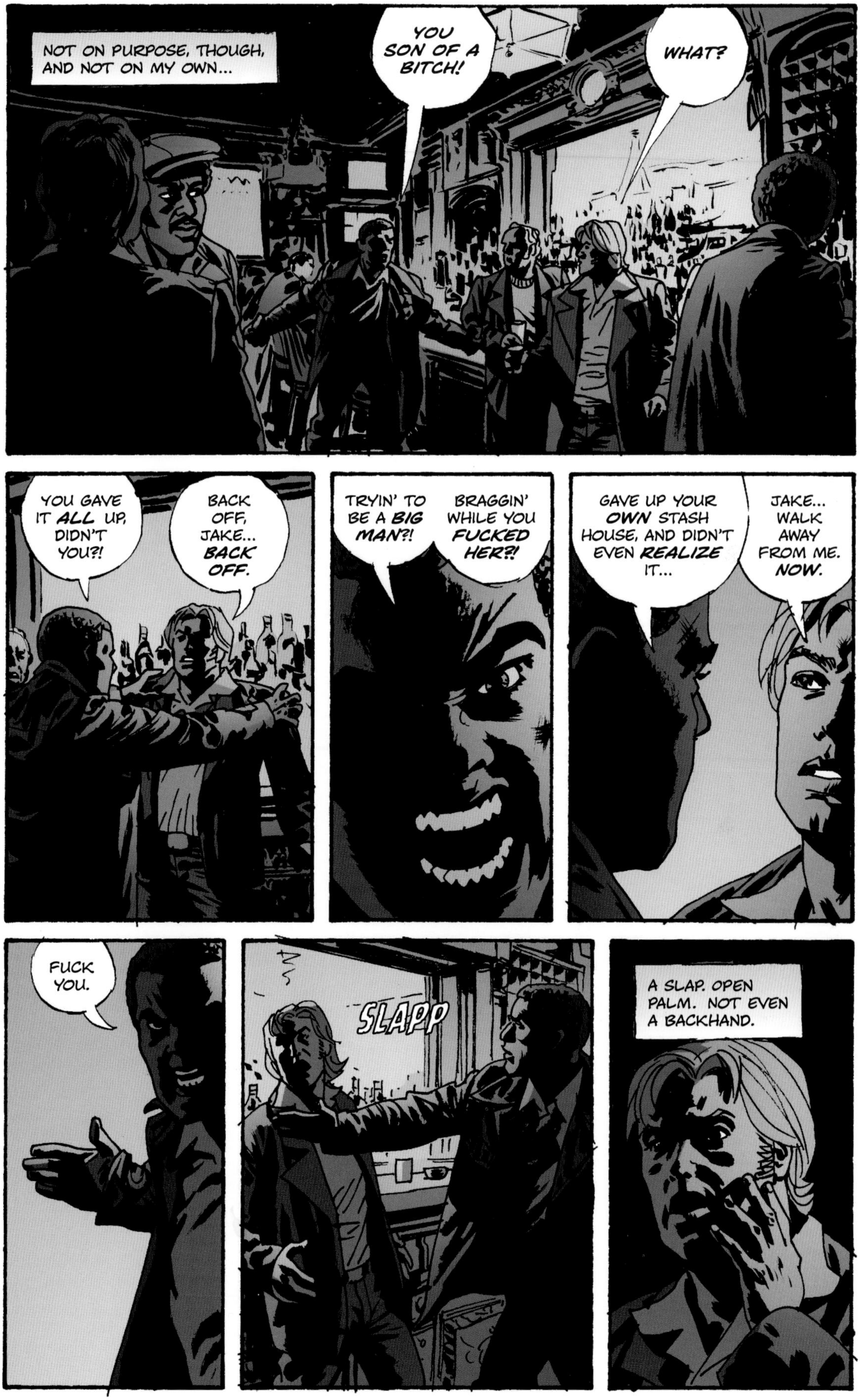
NOT ON PURPOSE, THOUGH, AND NOT ON MY OWN...
YOU SON OF A BITCH!
WHAT?
YOU GAVE IT ALL UP, DIDN'T YOU?!
BACK OFF, JAKE... BACK OFF.
TRYIN' TO BE A BIG MAN?!
BRAGGIN' WHILE YOU FUCKED HER?!
GAVE UP YOUR OWN STASH HOUSE, AND DIDN'T EVEN REALIZE IT...
JAKE... WALK AWAY FROM ME. NOW.
FUCK YOU.
SLAPP
A SLAP. OPEN PALM. NOT EVEN A BACKHAND.

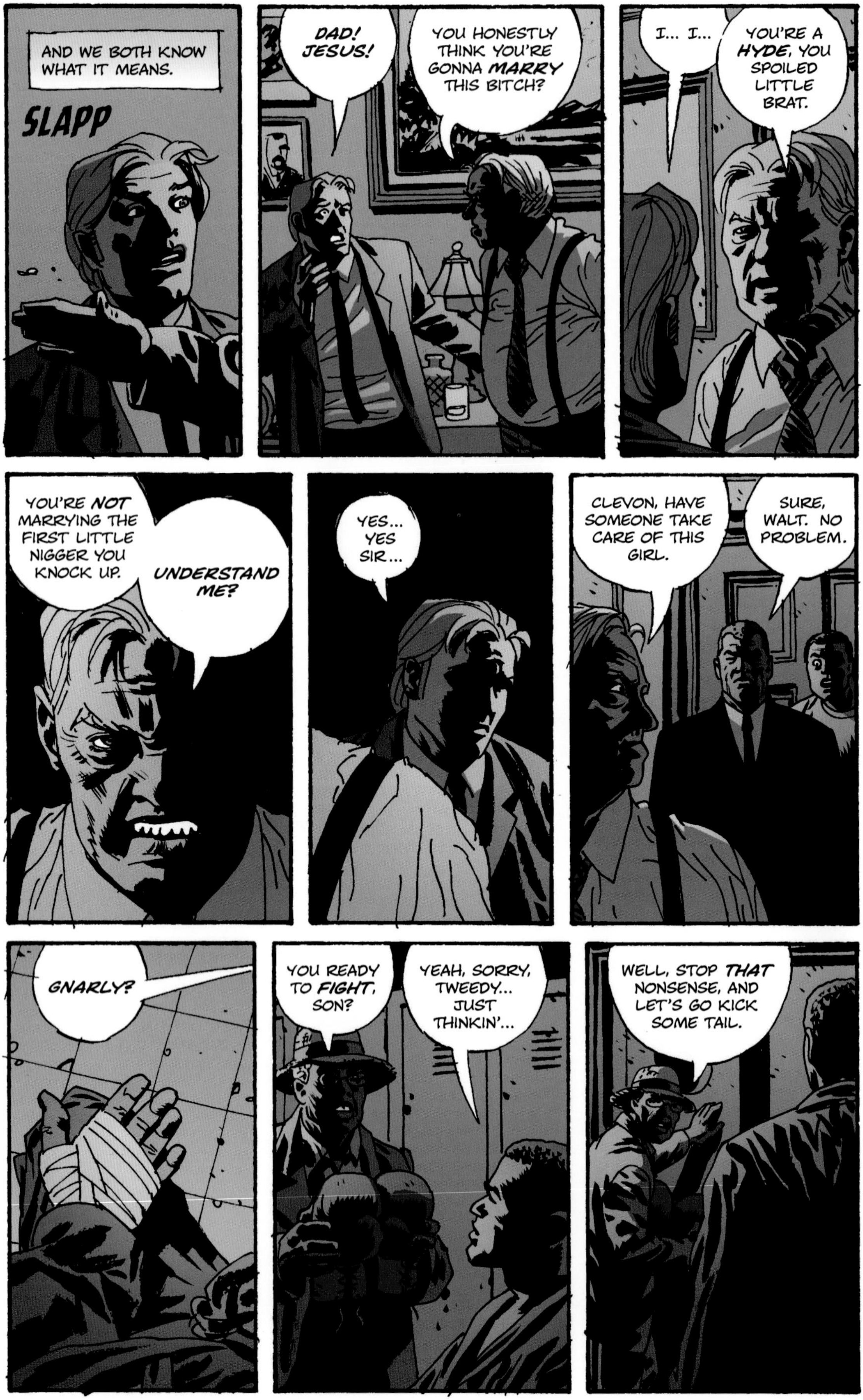
AND WE BOTH KNOW WHAT IT MEANS.
SLAPP
DAD! JESUS!
YOU HONESTLY THINK YOU'RE GONNA MARRY THIS BITCH?
I... I...
YOU'RE A HYDE, YOU SPOILED LITTLE BRAT.
YOU'RE NOT MARRYING THE FIRST LITTLE NIGGER YOU KNOCK UP.
UNDERSTAND ME?
YES... YES SIR...
CLEVON, HAVE SOMEONE TAKE CARE OF THIS GIRL.
SURE, WALT. NO PROBLEM.
GNARLY?
YOU READY TO FIGHT, SON?
YEAH, SORRY, TWEEDY... JUST THINKIN'...
WELL, STOP THAT NONSENSE, AND LET'S GO KICK SOME TAIL.

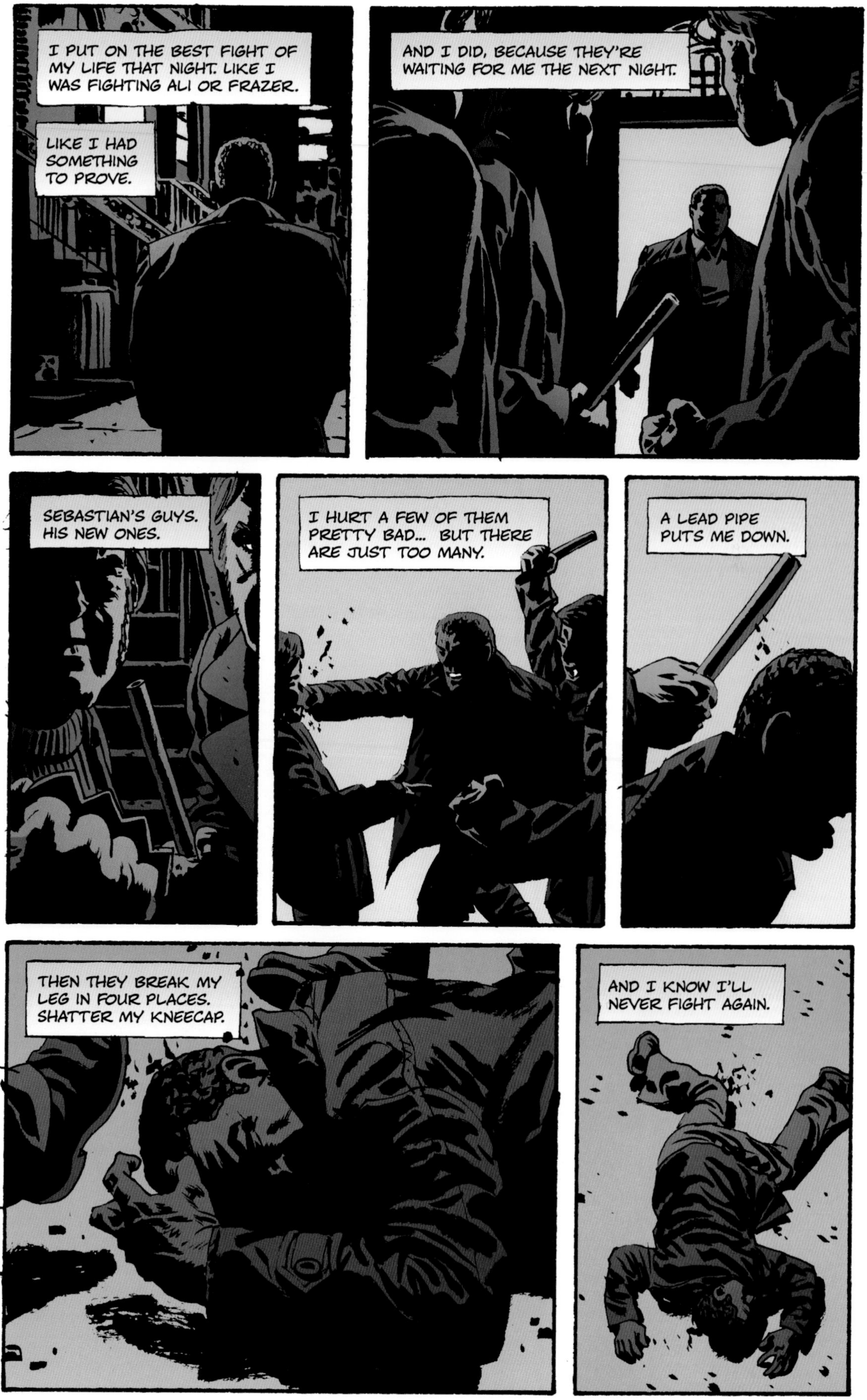
I PUT ON THE BEST FIGHT OF MY LIFE THAT NIGHT. LIKE I WAS FIGHTING ALI OR FRAZER.
LIKE I HAD SOMETHING TO PROVE.
AND I DID, BECAUSE THEY'RE WAITING FOR ME THE NEXT NIGHT.
SEBASTIAN'S GUYS. HIS NEW ONES.
I HURT A FEW OF THEM PRETTY BAD... BUT THERE ARE JUST TOO MANY.
A LEAD PIPE PUTS ME DOWN.
THEN THEY BREAK MY LEG IN FOUR PLACES. SHATTER MY KNEECAP.
AND I KNOW I'LL NEVER FIGHT AGAIN.

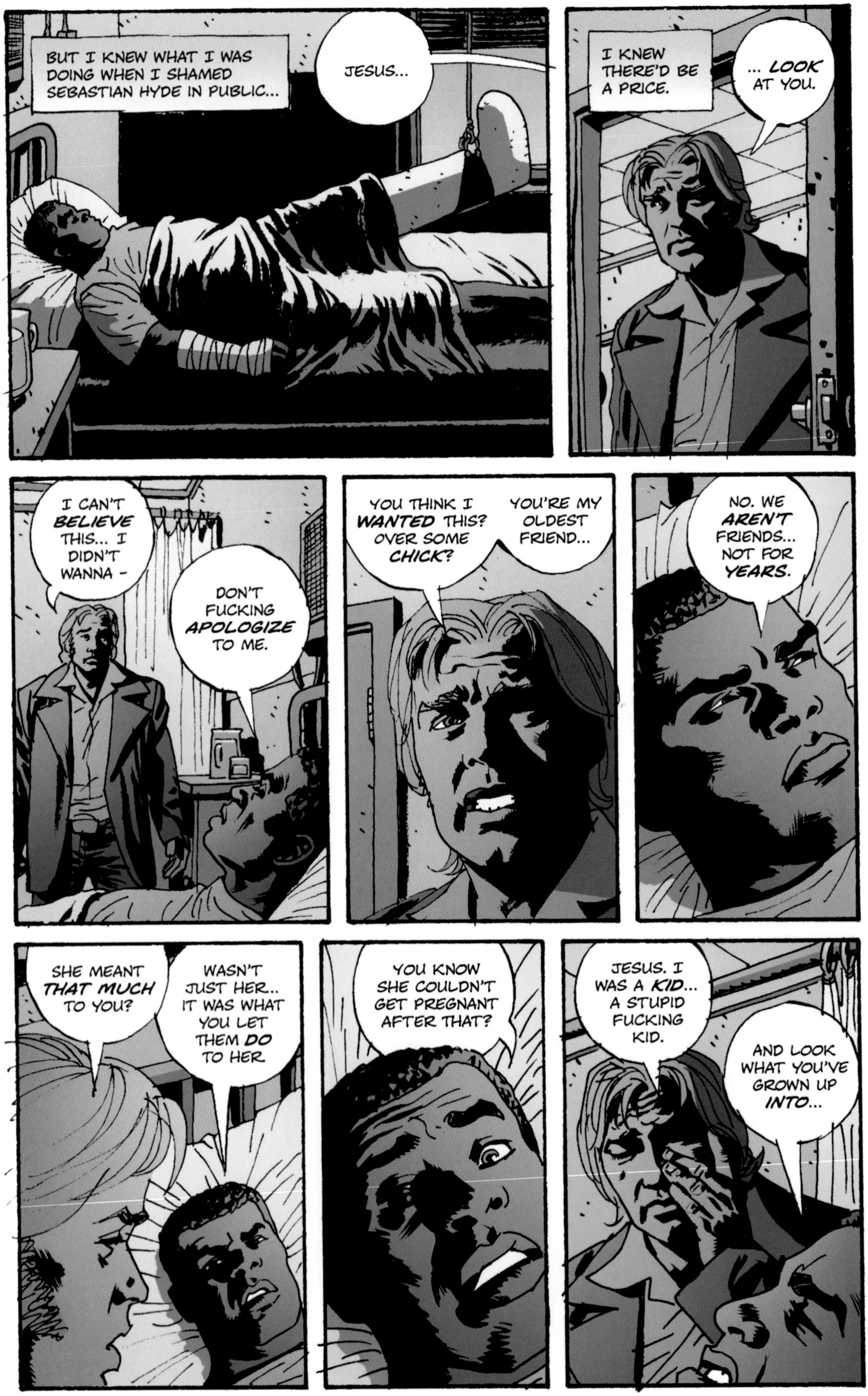
BUT I KNEW WHAT I WAS DOING WHEN I SHAMED SEBASTIAN HYDE IN PUBLIC...
JESUS...
I KNEW THERE'D BE A PRICE.
... LOOK AT YOU.
I CAN'T BELIEVE THIS... I DIDN'T WANNA -
DON'T FUCKING APOLOGIZE TO ME.
YOU THINK I WANTED THIS? OVER SOME CHICK?
YOU'RE MY OLDEST FRIEND...
NO. WE AREN'T FRIENDS... NOT FOR YEARS.
SHE MEANT THAT MUCH TO YOU?
WASN'T JUST HER.. IT WAS WHAT YOU LET THEM DO TO HER.
YOU KNOW SHE COULDN'T GET PREGNANT AFTER THAT?
JESUS. I WAS A KID... A STUPID FUCKING KID.
AND LOOK WHAT YOU'VE GROWN UP INTO...

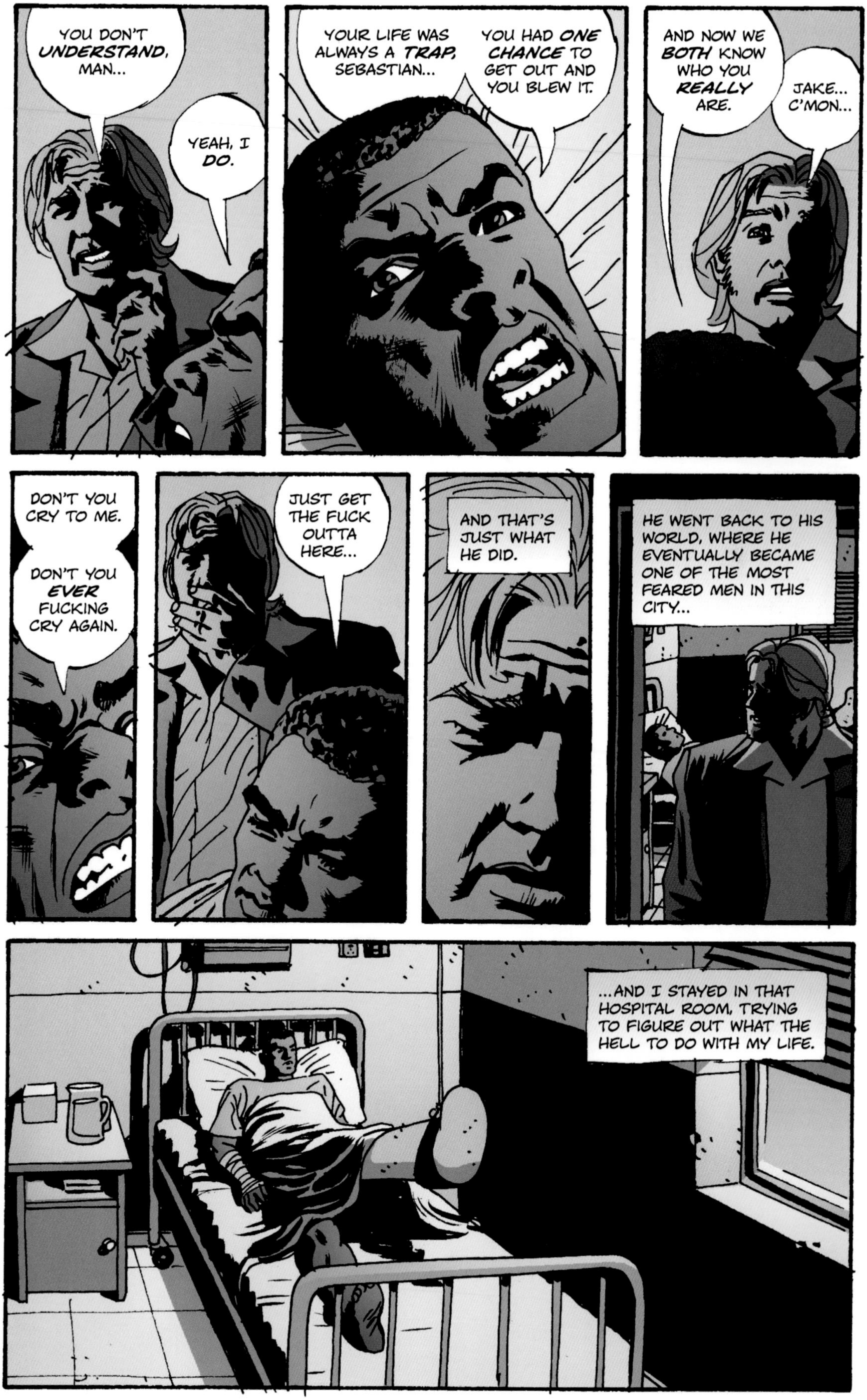
YOU DON'T UNDERSTAND, MAN...
YEAH, I DO.
YOUR LIFE WAS ALWAYS A TRAP, SEBASTIAN...
YOU HAD ONE CHANCE TO GET OUT AND YOU BLEW IT.
AND NOW WE BOTH KNOW WHO YOU REALLY ARE.
JAKE... C'MON...
DON'T YOU CRY TO ME.
DON'T YOU EVER FUCKING CRY AGAIN.
JUST GET THE FUCK OUTTA HERE...
AND THAT'S JUST WHAT HE DID.
HE WENT BACK TO HIS WORLD, WHERE HE EVENTUALLY BECAME ONE OF THE MOST FEARED MEN IN THIS CITY...
...AND I STAYED IN THAT HOSPITAL ROOM, TRYING TO FIGURE OUT WHAT THE HELL TO DO WITH MY LIFE.

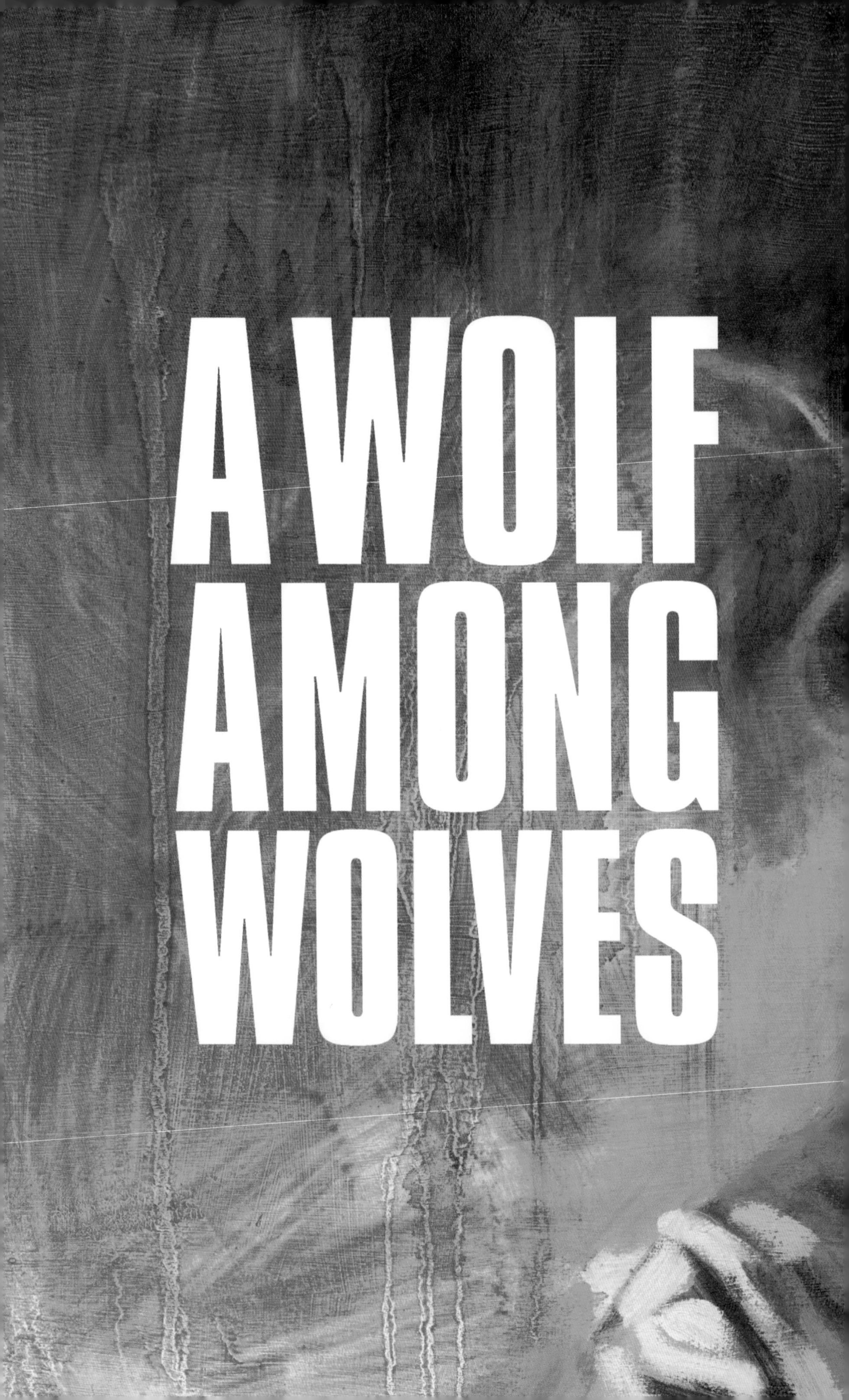
A WOLF
AMONG
WOLVES

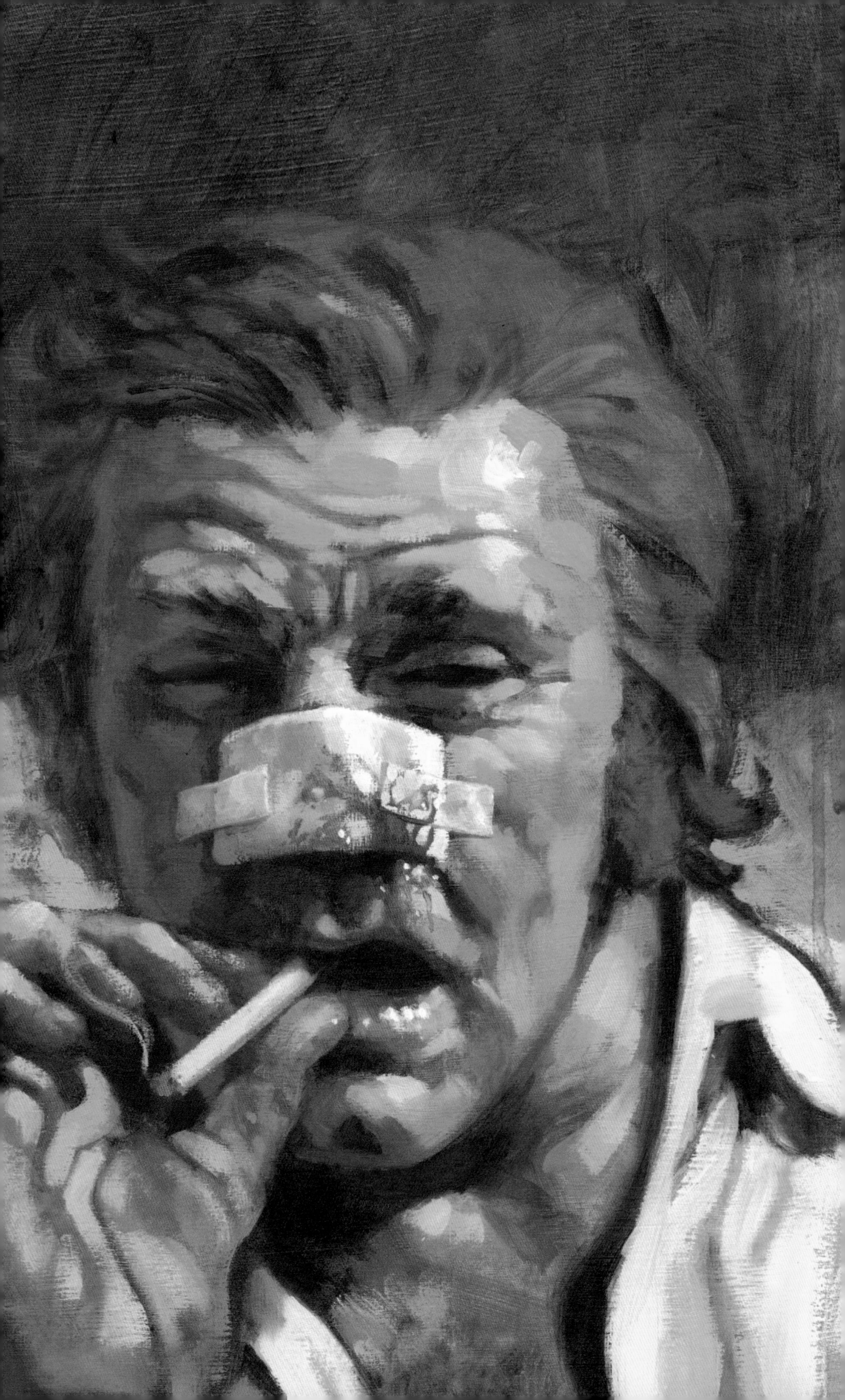

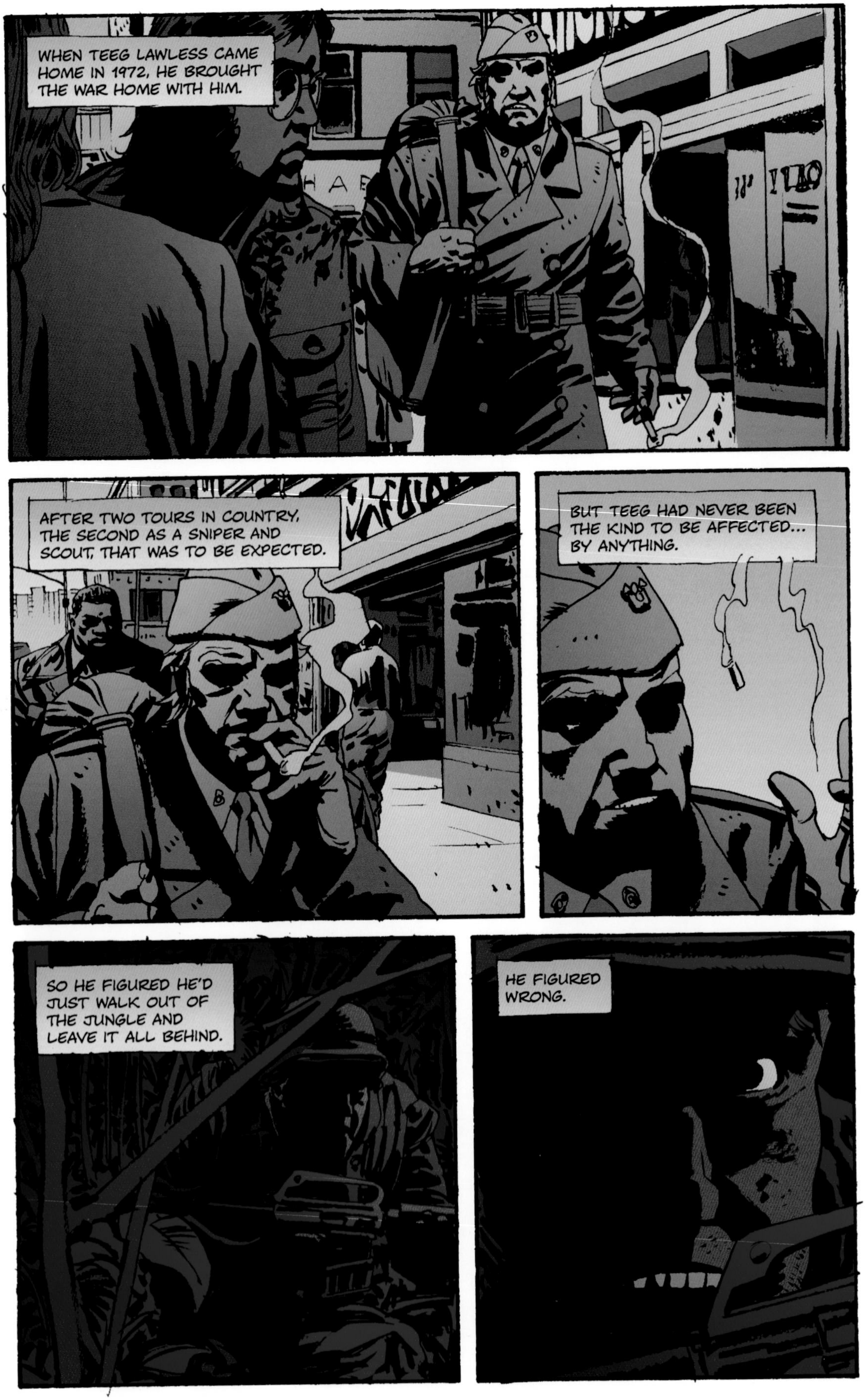
WHEN TEEG LAWLESS CAME HOME IN 1972, HE BROUGHT THE WAR HOME WITH HIM.
AFTER TWO TOURS IN COUNTRY, THE SECOND AS A SNIPER AND SCOUT, THAT WAS TO BE EXPECTED.
BUT TEEG HAD NEVER BEEN THE KIND TO BE AFFECTED... BY ANYTHING.
SO HE FIGURED HE'D JUST WALK OUT OF THE JUNGLE AND LEAVE IT ALL BEHIND.
HE FIGURED WRONG.

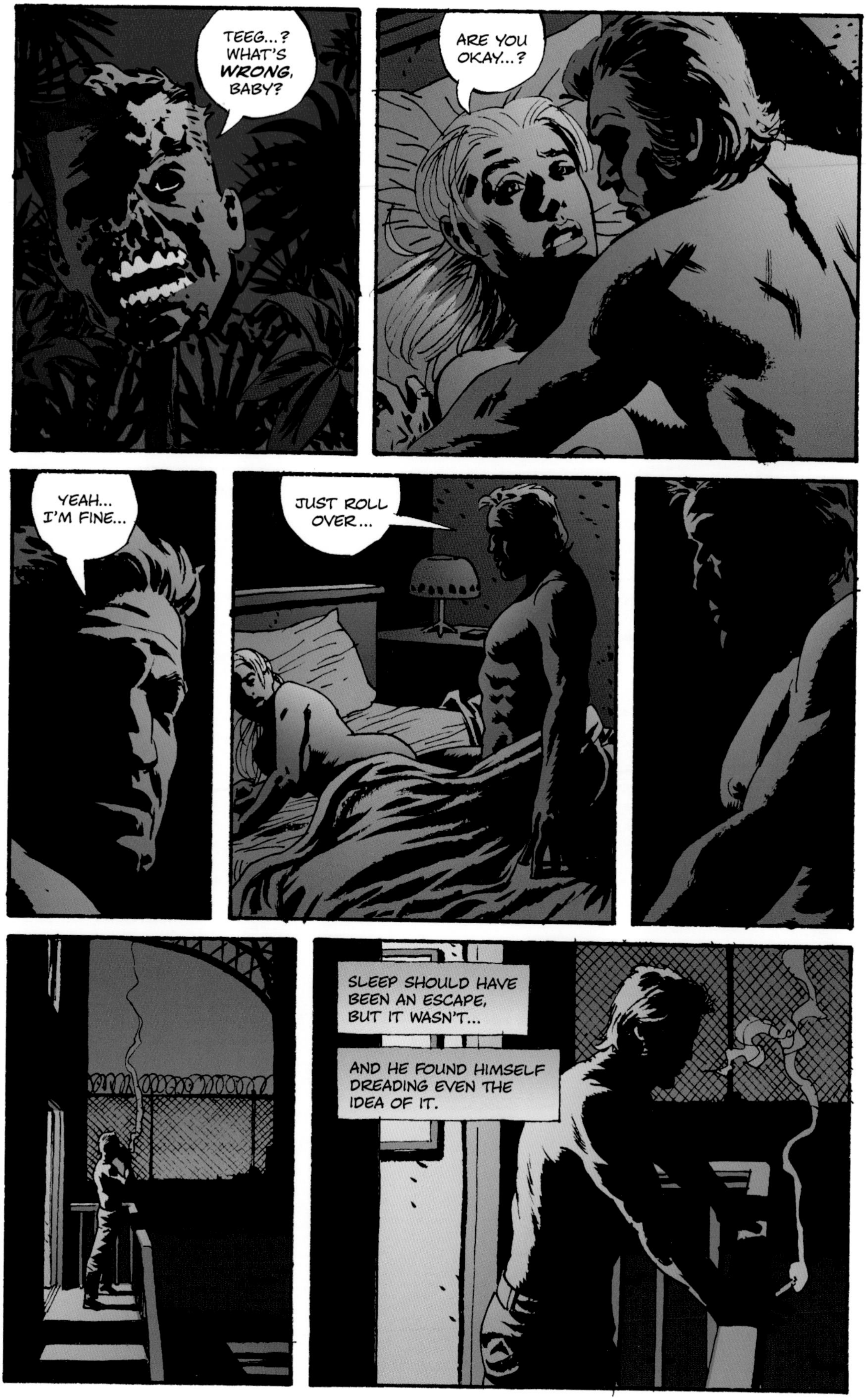
TEEG...? WHAT'S **WRONG**, BABY?
ARE YOU OKAY...?
YEAH... I'M FINE...
JUST ROLL OVER...
SLEEP SHOULD HAVE BEEN AN ESCAPE, BUT IT WASN'T...
AND HE FOUND HIMSELF DREADING EVEN THE IDEA OF IT.

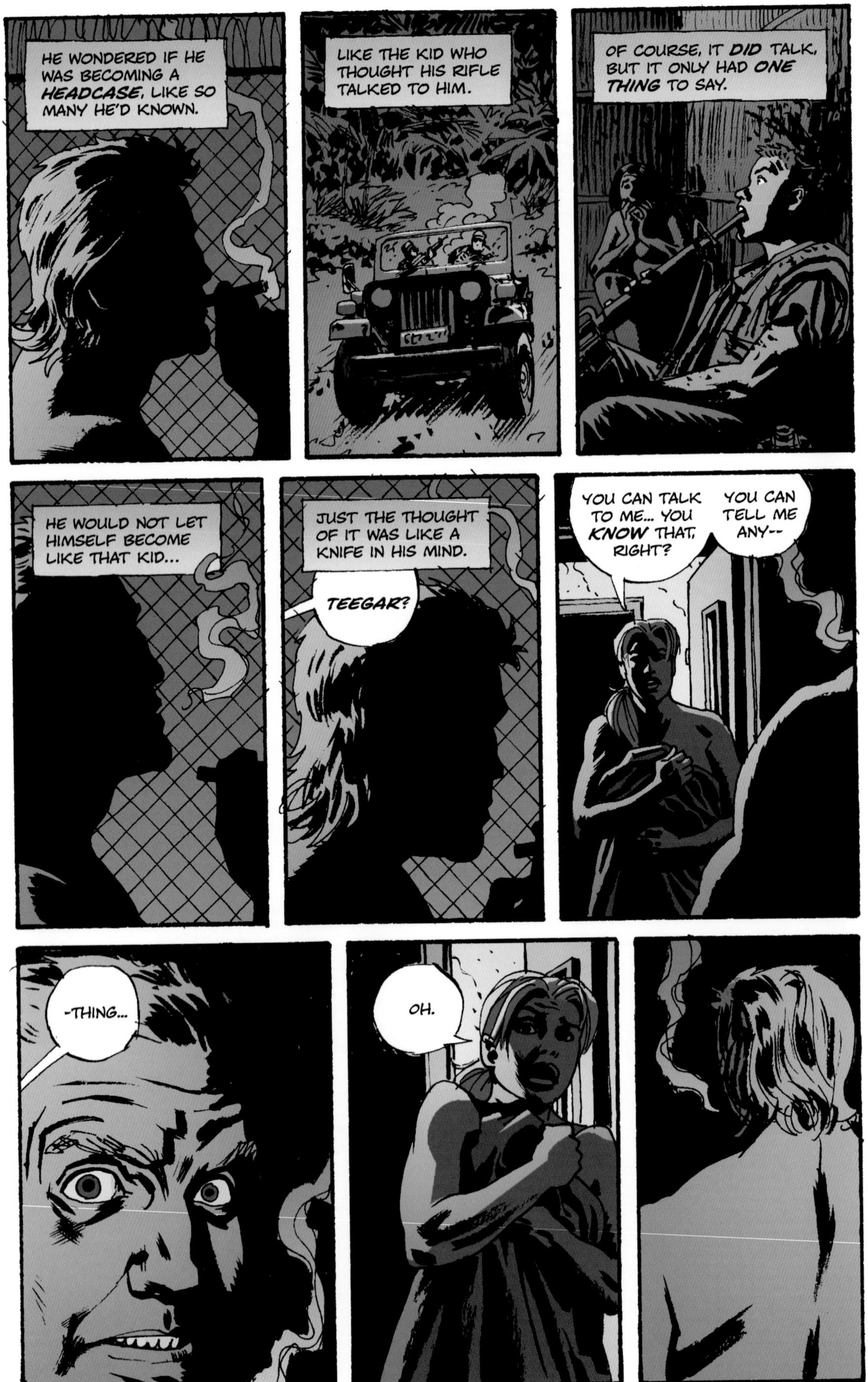
HE WONDERED IF HE WAS BECOMING A HEADCASE, LIKE SO MANY HE'D KNOWN.
LIKE THE KID WHO THOUGHT HIS RIFLE TALKED TO HIM.
OF COURSE, IT DID TALK, BUT IT ONLY HAD ONE THING TO SAY.
HE WOULD NOT LET HIMSELF BECOME LIKE THAT KID...
JUST THE THOUGHT OF IT WAS LIKE A KNIFE IN HIS MIND.
TEEGAR?
YOU CAN TALK TO ME... YOU KNOW THAT, RIGHT?
YOU CAN TELL ME ANY--
-THING...
OH.

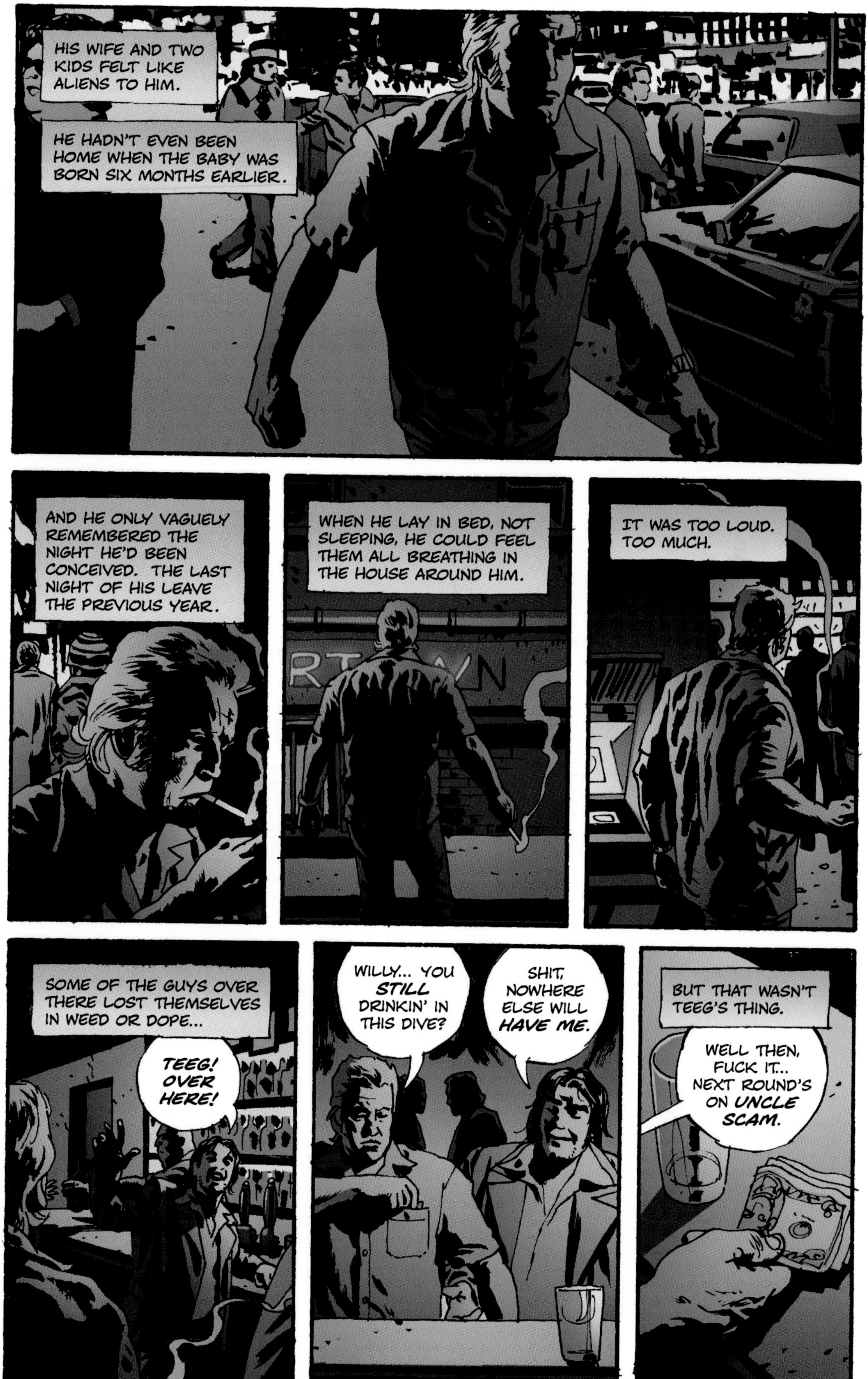
HIS WIFE AND TWO KIDS FELT LIKE ALIENS TO HIM.
HE HADN'T EVEN BEEN HOME WHEN THE BABY WAS BORN SIX MONTHS EARLIER.
AND HE ONLY VAGUELY REMEMBERED THE NIGHT HE'D BEEN CONCEIVED. THE LAST NIGHT OF HIS LEAVE THE PREVIOUS YEAR.
WHEN HE LAY IN BED, NOT SLEEPING, HE COULD FEEL THEM ALL BREATHING IN THE HOUSE AROUND HIM.
IT WAS TOO LOUD. TOO MUCH.
SOME OF THE GUYS OVER THERE LOST THEMSELVES IN WEED OR DOPE...
TEEG! OVER HERE!
WILLY... YOU STILL DRINKIN' IN THIS DIVE?
SHIT, NOWHERE ELSE WILL HAVE ME.
BUT THAT WASN'T TEEG'S THING.
WELL THEN, FUCK IT... NEXT ROUND'S ON UNCLE SCAM.

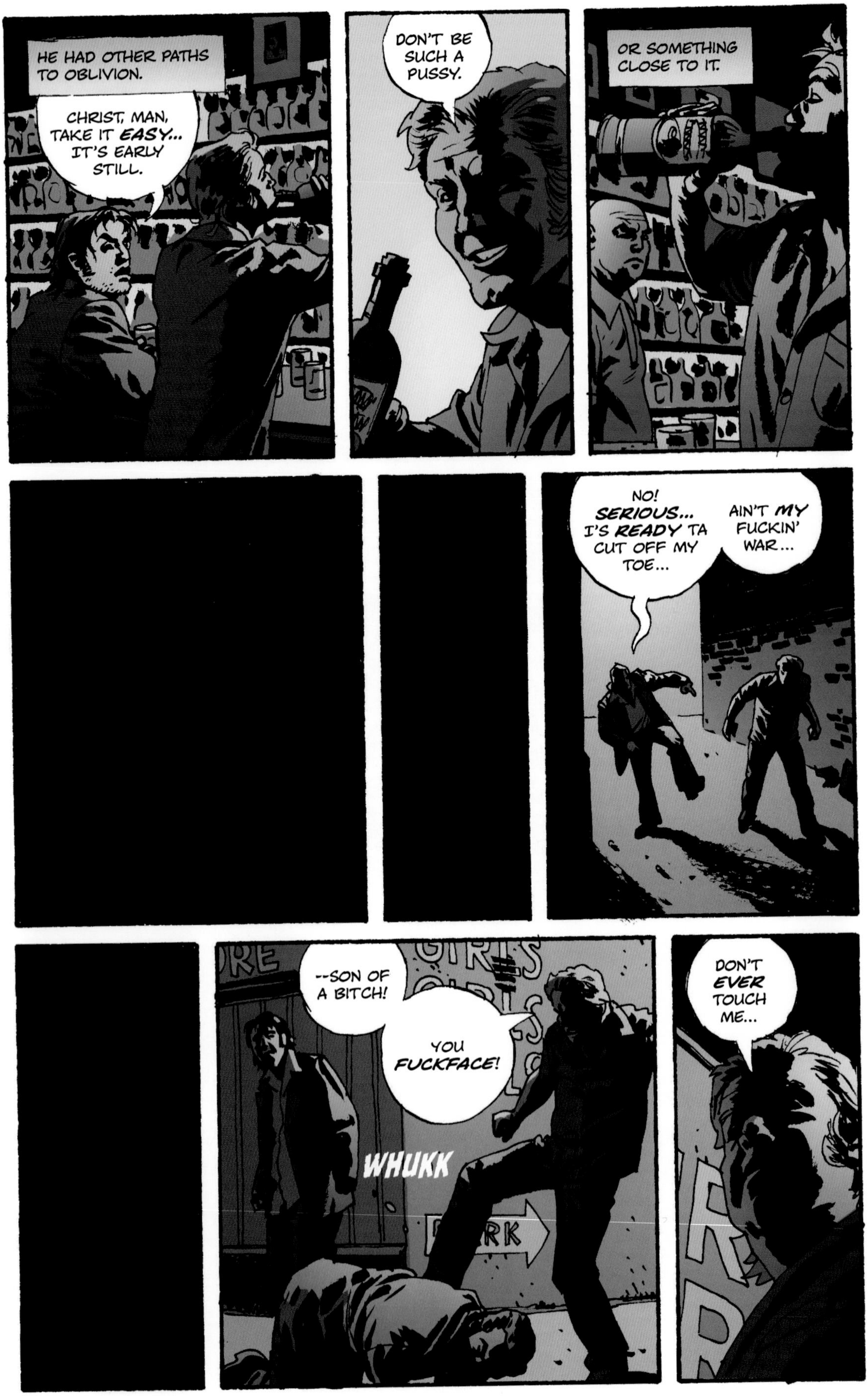
HE HAD OTHER PATHS TO OBLIVION.
CHRIST, MAN, TAKE IT EASY... IT'S EARLY STILL.
DON'T BE SUCH A PUSSY.
OR SOMETHING CLOSE TO IT.
NO! SERIOUS... I'S READY TA CUT OFF MY TOE...
AIN'T MY FUCKIN' WAR...
--SON OF A BITCH!
YOU FUCKFACE!
WHUKK
DON'T EVER TOUCH ME...

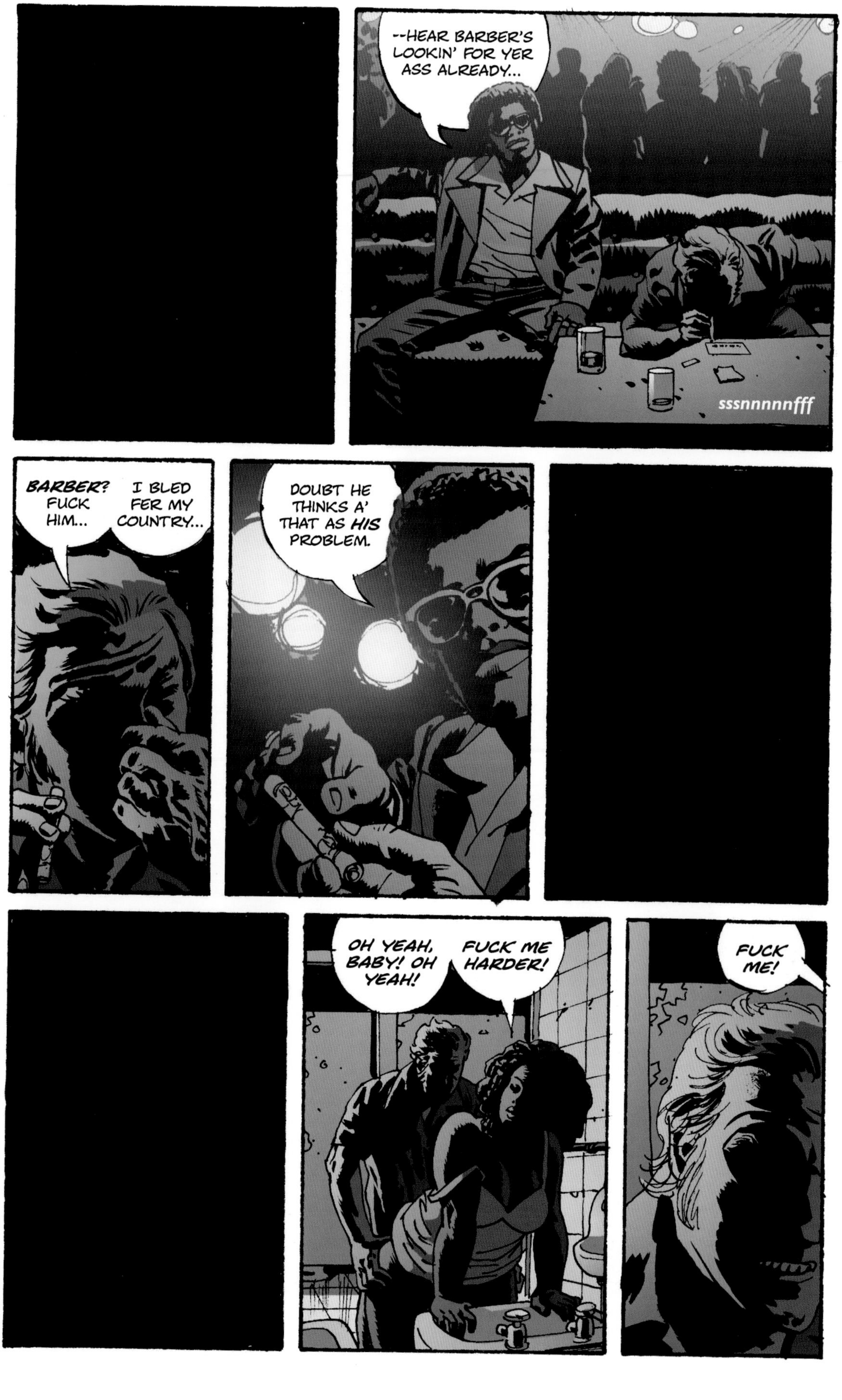
--HEAR BARBER'S LOOKIN' FOR YER ASS ALREADY...
sssnnnnnfff
BARBER? FUCK HIM...
I BLED FER MY COUNTRY...
DOUBT HE THINKS A' THAT AS HIS PROBLEM.
OH YEAH, BABY! OH YEAH!
FUCK ME HARDER!
FUCK ME!

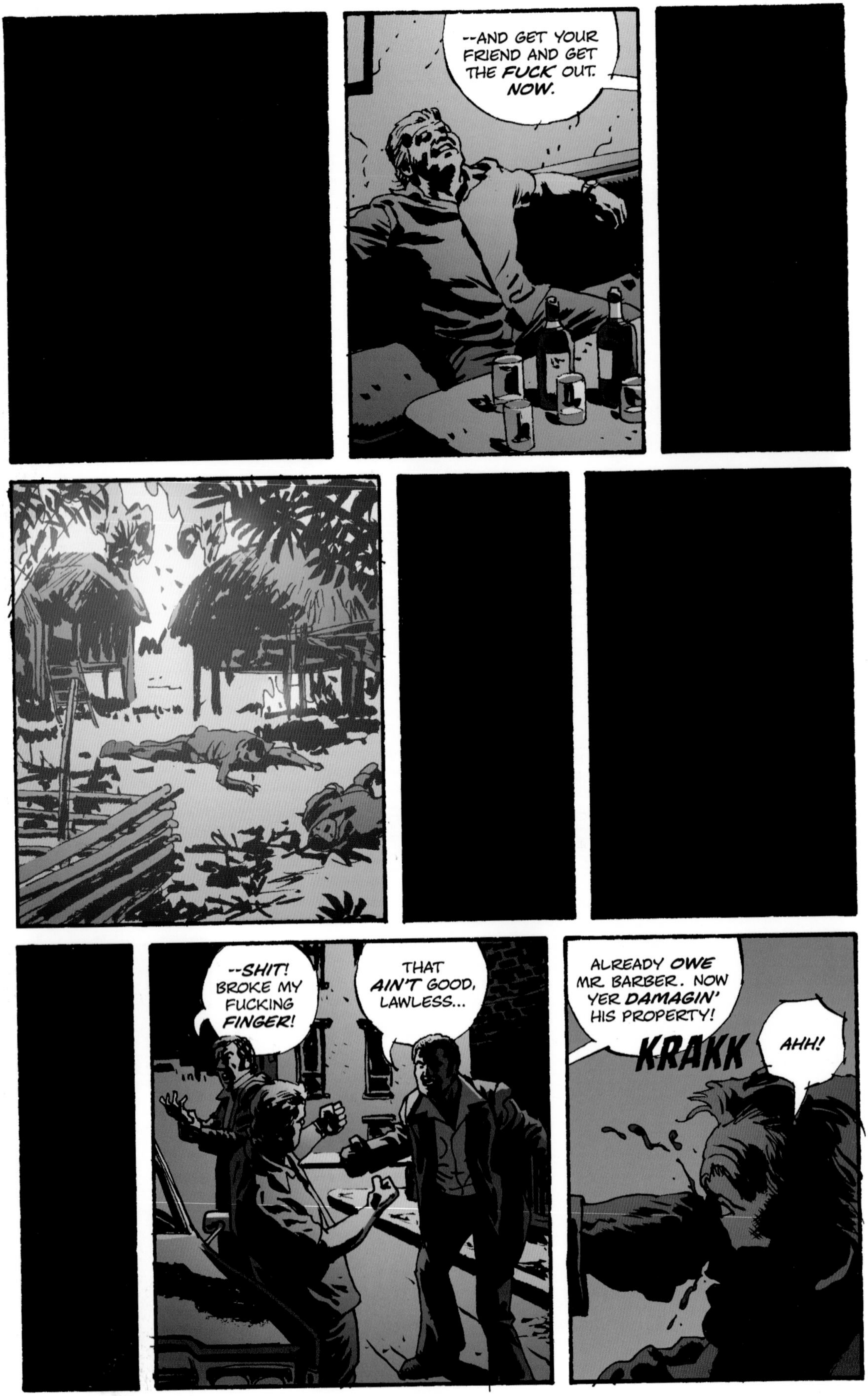
--AND GET YOUR FRIEND AND GET THE FUCK OUT. NOW.
--SHIT! BROKE MY FUCKING FINGER!
THAT AIN'T GOOD, LAWLESS...
ALREADY OWE MR. BARBER. NOW YER DAMAGIN' HIS PROPERTY!
KRAKK
AHH!

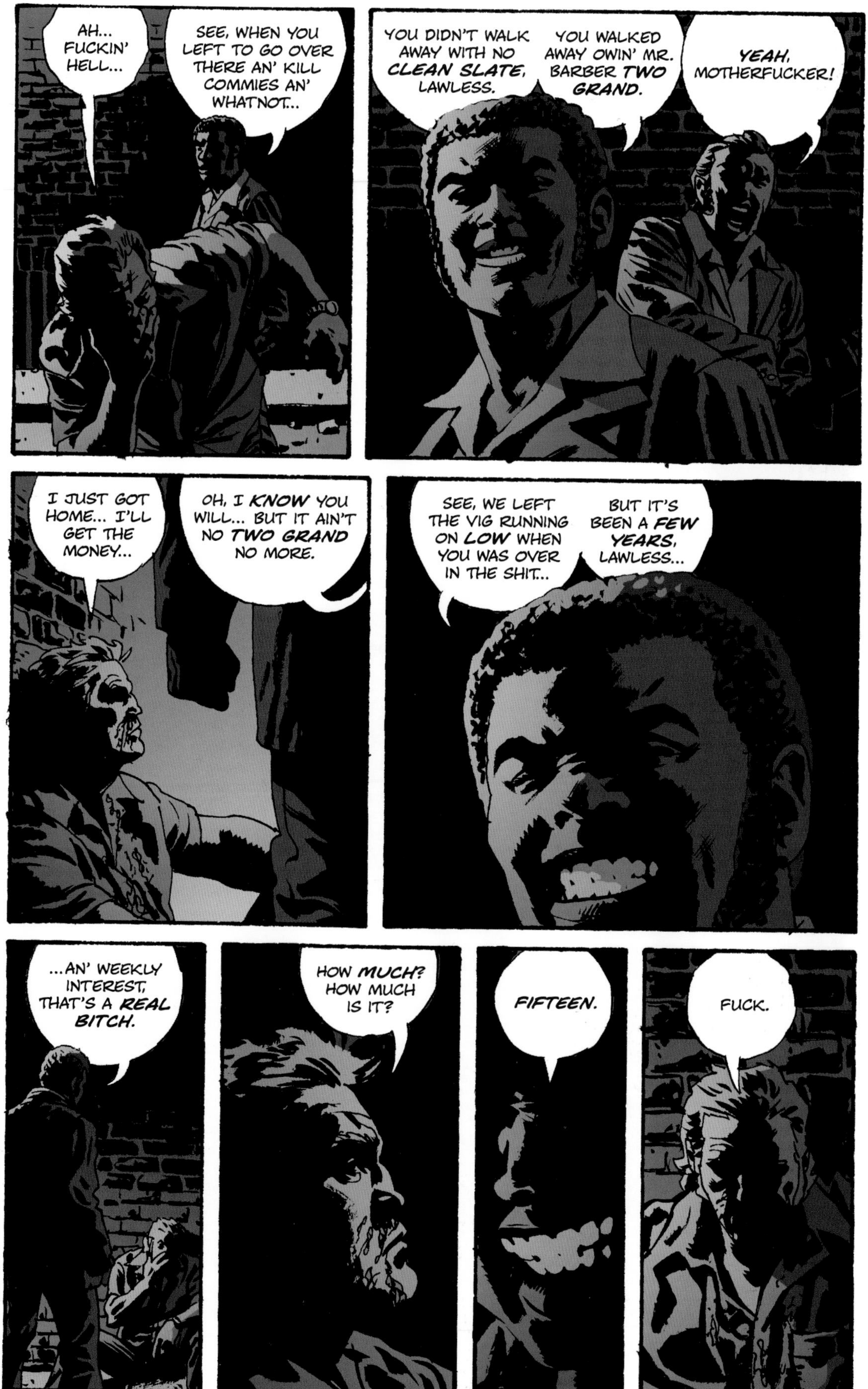
AH... FUCKIN' HELL...
SEE, WHEN YOU LEFT TO GO OVER THERE AN' KILL COMMIES AN' WHATNOT...
YOU DIDN'T WALK AWAY WITH NO CLEAN SLATE, LAWLESS.
YOU WALKED AWAY OWIN' MR. BARBER TWO GRAND.
YEAH, MOTHERFUCKER!
I JUST GOT HOME... I'LL GET THE MONEY...
OH, I KNOW YOU WILL... BUT IT AIN'T NO TWO GRAND NO MORE.
SEE, WE LEFT THE VIG RUNNING ON LOW WHEN YOU WAS OVER IN THE SHIT...
BUT IT'S BEEN A FEW YEARS, LAWLESS...
...AN' WEEKLY INTEREST, THAT'S A REAL BITCH.
HOW MUCH? HOW MUCH IS IT?
FIFTEEN.
FUCK.

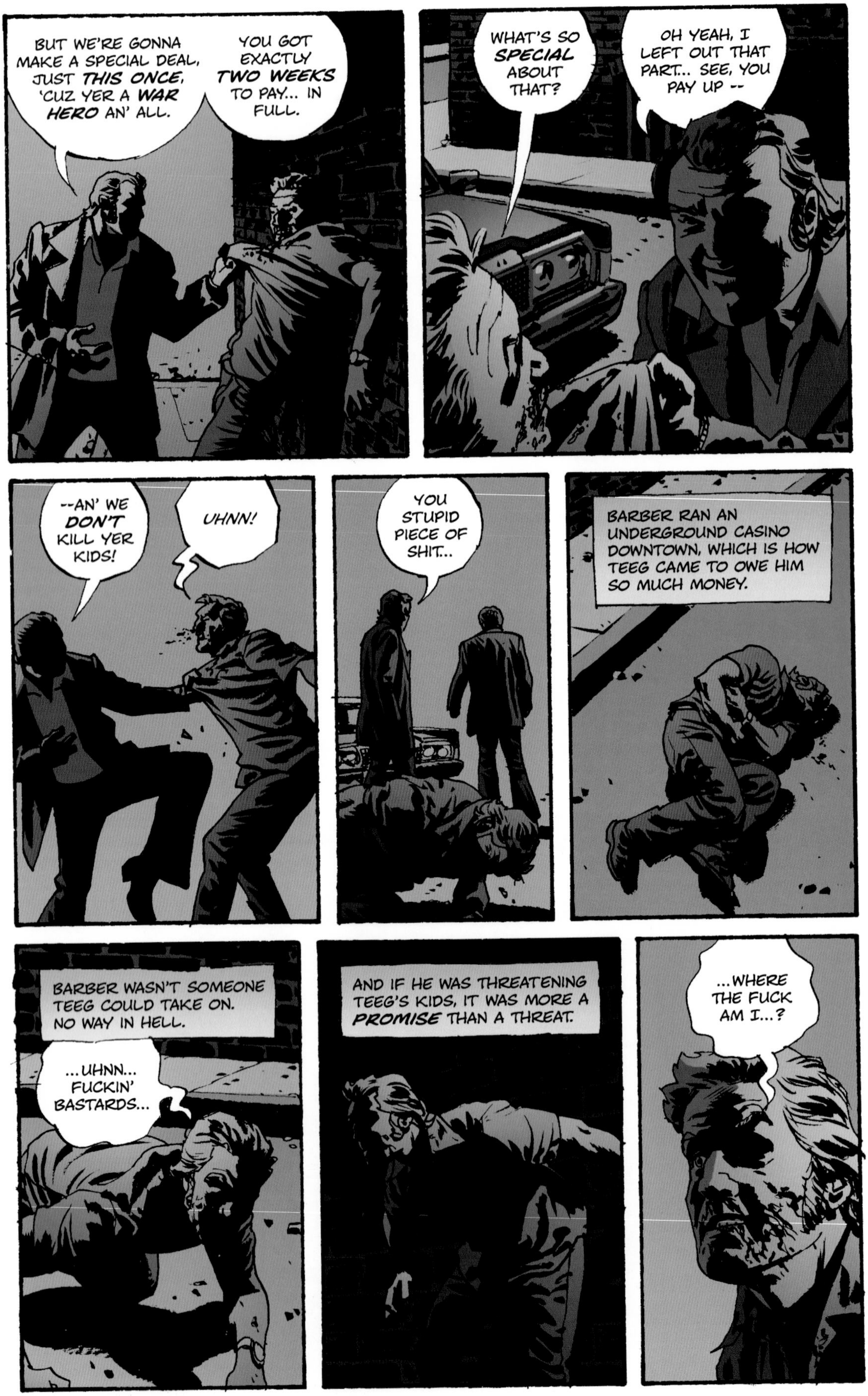
BUT WE'RE GONNA MAKE A SPECIAL DEAL, JUST THIS ONCE, 'CUZ YER A WAR HERO AN' ALL.
YOU GOT EXACTLY TWO WEEKS TO PAY... IN FULL.
WHAT'S SO SPECIAL ABOUT THAT?
OH YEAH, I LEFT OUT THAT PART... SEE, YOU PAY UP --
--AN' WE DON'T KILL YER KIDS!
UHNN!
YOU STUPID PIECE OF SHIT...
BARBER RAN AN UNDERGROUND CASINO DOWNTOWN, WHICH IS HOW TEEG CAME TO OWE HIM SO MUCH MONEY.
BARBER WASN'T SOMEONE TEEG COULD TAKE ON. NO WAY IN HELL.
...UHNN... FUCKIN' BASTARDS...
AND IF HE WAS THREATENING TEEG'S KIDS, IT WAS MORE A PROMISE THAN A THREAT.
...WHERE THE FUCK AM I...?

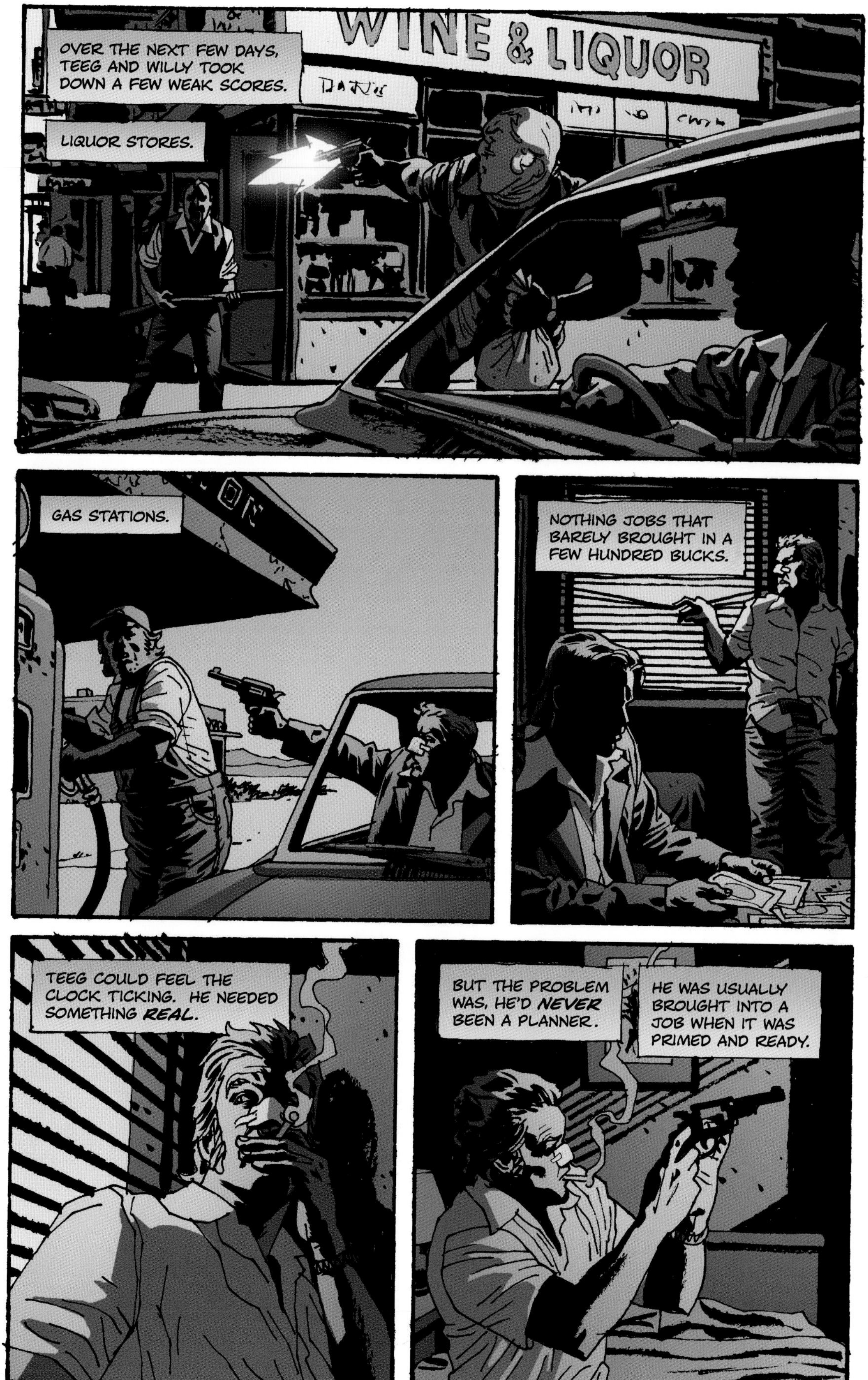
OVER THE NEXT FEW DAYS, TEEG AND WILLY TOOK DOWN A FEW WEAK SCORES.
LIQUOR STORES.
WINE & LIQUOR
GAS STATIONS.
NOTHING JOBS THAT BARELY BROUGHT IN A FEW HUNDRED BUCKS.
TEEG COULD FEEL THE CLOCK TICKING. HE NEEDED SOMETHING *REAL*.
BUT THE PROBLEM WAS, HE'D *NEVER* BEEN A PLANNER.
HE WAS USUALLY BROUGHT INTO A JOB WHEN IT WAS PRIMED AND READY.

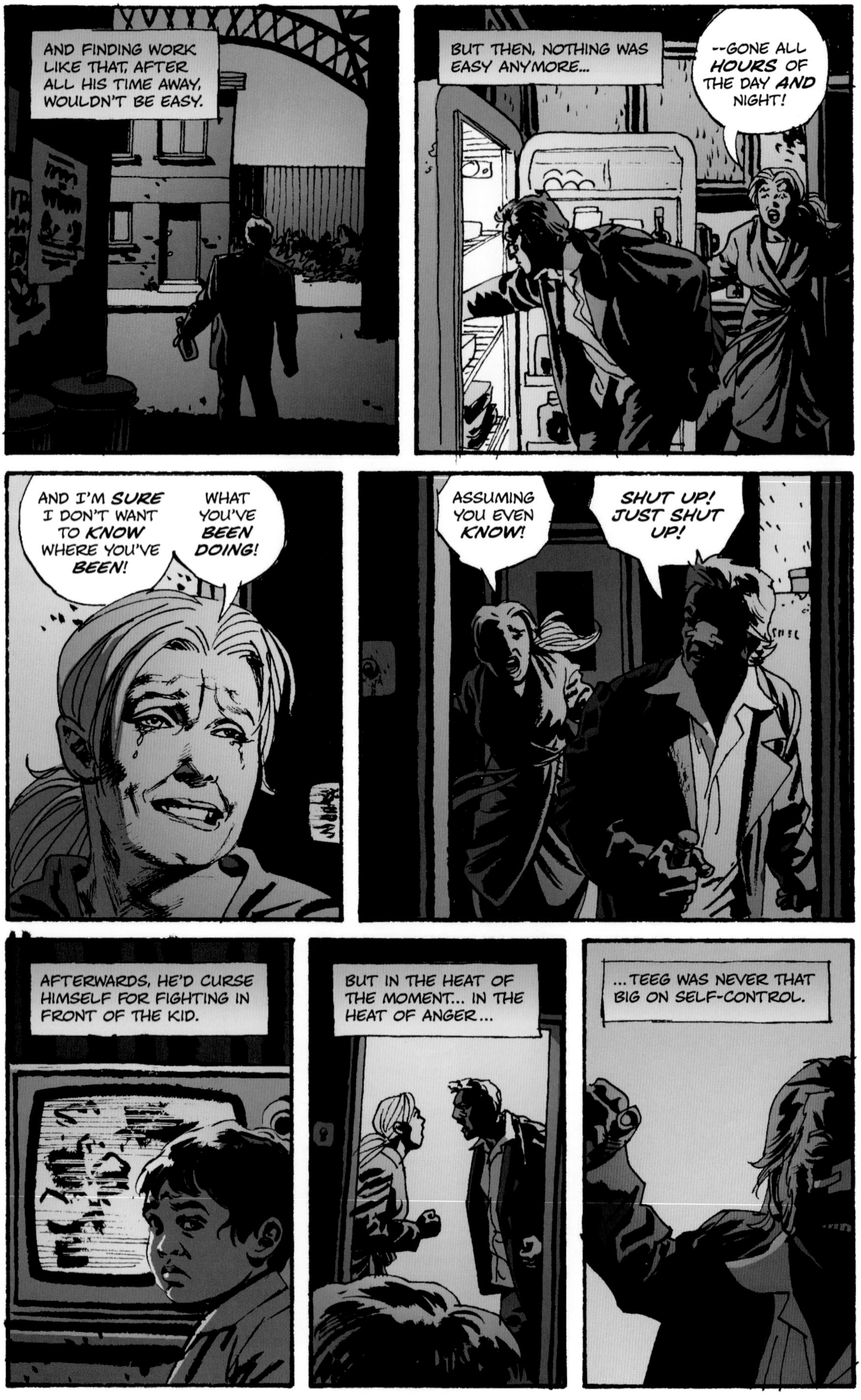
AND FINDING WORK LIKE THAT, AFTER ALL HIS TIME AWAY, WOULDN'T BE EASY.
BUT THEN, NOTHING WAS EASY ANYMORE...
--GONE ALL HOURS OF THE DAY AND NIGHT!
AND I'M SURE I DON'T WANT TO KNOW WHERE YOU'VE BEEN!
WHAT YOU'VE BEEN DOING!
ASSUMING YOU EVEN KNOW!
SHUT UP! JUST SHUT UP!
AFTERWARDS, HE'D CURSE HIMSELF FOR FIGHTING IN FRONT OF THE KID.
BUT IN THE HEAT OF THE MOMENT... IN THE HEAT OF ANGER...
...TEEG WAS NEVER THAT BIG ON SELF-CONTROL.

STILL, HIS REPUTATION FOR VIOLENCE WASN'T *ALWAYS* FROWNED ON...

WAY I HEAR IT, YOU TWO'RE LOOKIN' FOR A *MAJOR* SCORE.

AND WHERE'D YOU HEAR *THAT*, HAMSUNN?

SIT BEHIND THIS BAR *TWO HOURS*, YOU'LL HEAR EVERYTHING GOIN' ON IN THIS WHOLE CITY.

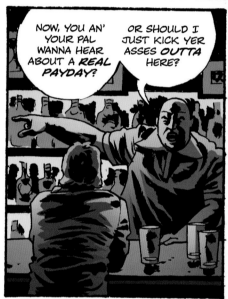

NOW, YOU AN' YOUR PAL WANNA HEAR ABOUT A *REAL PAYDAY*?

OR SHOULD I JUST KICK YER ASSES *OUTTA* HERE?

HAMSUNN, THE OWNER OF THE UNDERTOW, WAS AN EX-THIEF, BUT TEEG KNEW NO GOOD THIEF EVER *REALLY* RETIRED.

OKAY, LET'S HEAR IT.

SO HE LAID IT OUT... KEEPING THE DETAILS SUFFICIENTLY VAGUE.

THE TARGET WAS A UNIT IN AN APARTMENT BUILDING, WHERE ONCE A WEEK, DIRTY MONEY WAS COUNTED FOR PICK-UP.

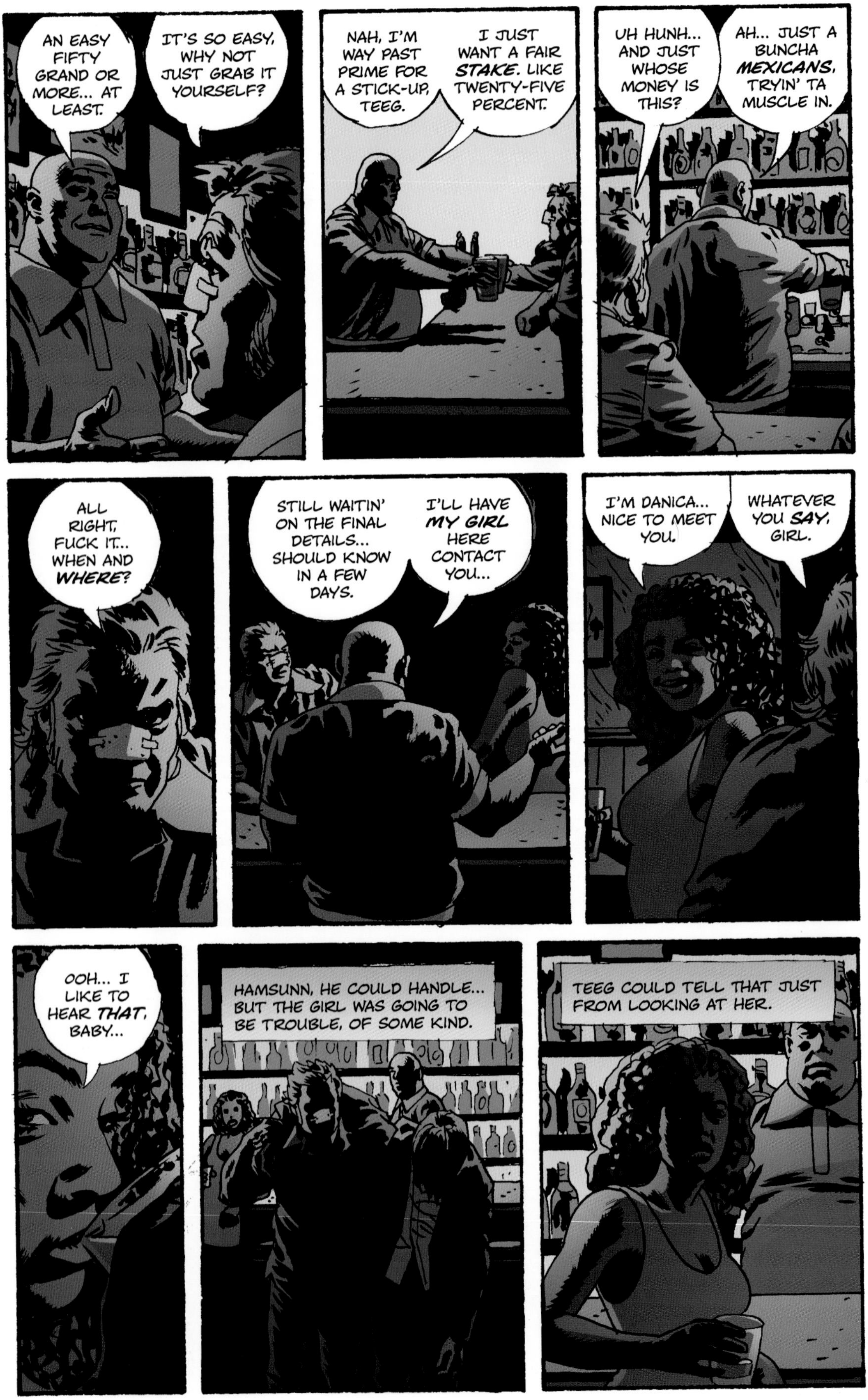
AN EASY FIFTY GRAND OR MORE... AT LEAST.
IT'S SO EASY, WHY NOT JUST GRAB IT YOURSELF?
NAH, I'M WAY PAST PRIME FOR A STICK-UP, TEEG.
I JUST WANT A FAIR *STAKE*. LIKE TWENTY-FIVE PERCENT.
UH HUNH... AND JUST WHOSE MONEY IS THIS?
AH... JUST A BUNCHA *MEXICANS*, TRYIN' TA MUSCLE IN.
ALL RIGHT, FUCK IT... WHEN AND *WHERE*?
STILL WAITIN' ON THE FINAL DETAILS... SHOULD KNOW IN A FEW DAYS.
I'LL HAVE *MY GIRL* HERE CONTACT YOU...
I'M DANICA... NICE TO MEET YOU.
WHATEVER YOU *SAY*, GIRL.
OOH... I LIKE TO HEAR *THAT*, BABY...
HAMSUNN, HE COULD HANDLE... BUT THE GIRL WAS GOING TO BE TROUBLE, OF SOME KIND.
TEEG COULD TELL THAT JUST FROM LOOKING AT HER.

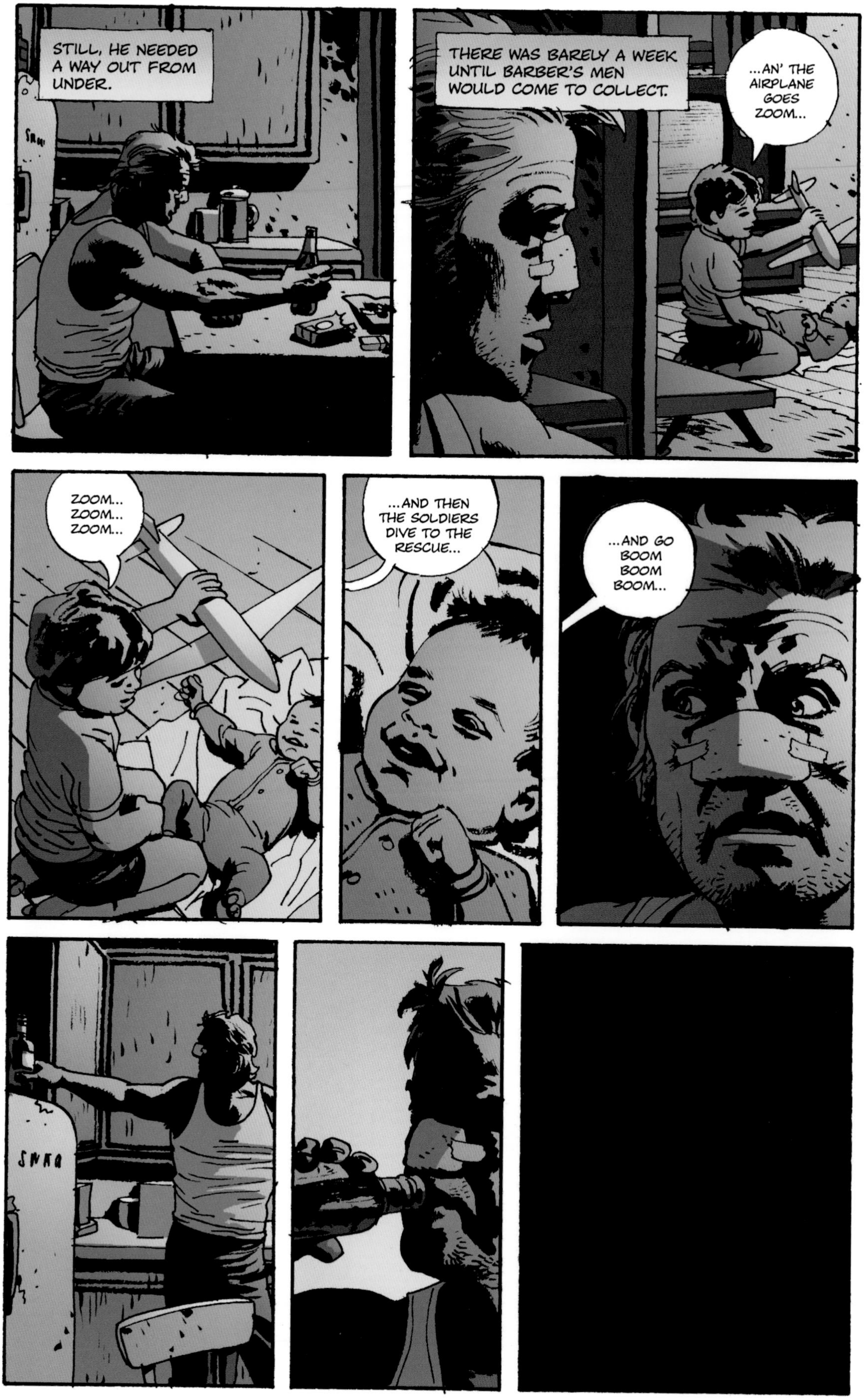
STILL, HE NEEDED A WAY OUT FROM UNDER.
THERE WAS BARELY A WEEK UNTIL BARBER'S MEN WOULD COME TO COLLECT.
...AN' THE AIRPLANE GOES ZOOM...
ZOOM... ZOOM... ZOOM...
...AND THEN THE SOLDIERS DIVE TO THE RESCUE...
...AND GO BOOM BOOM BOOM...

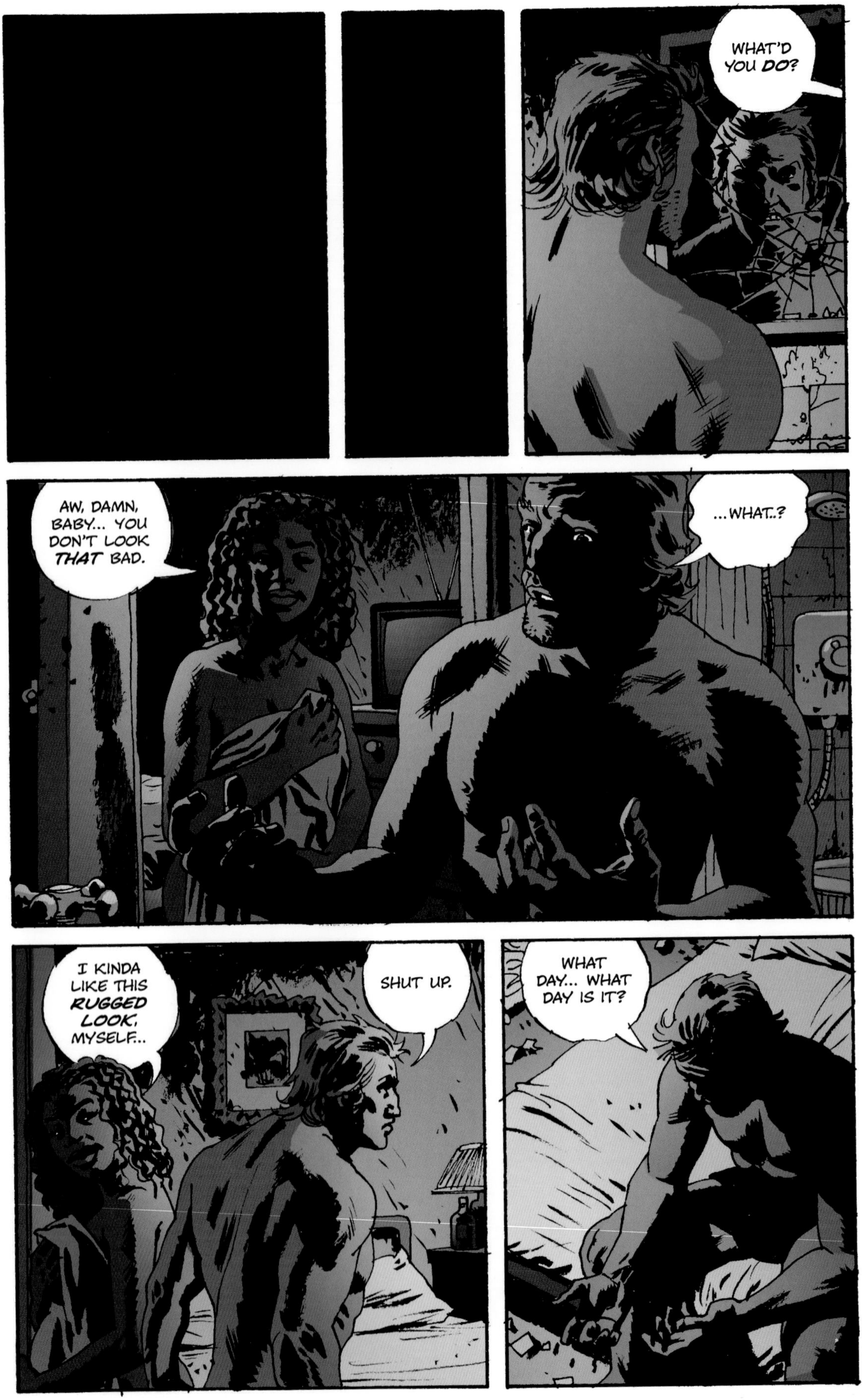
WHAT'D YOU DO?
AW, DAMN, BABY... YOU DON'T LOOK THAT BAD.
...WHAT..?
I KINDA LIKE THIS RUGGED LOOK, MYSELF...
SHUT UP.
WHAT DAY... WHAT DAY IS IT?

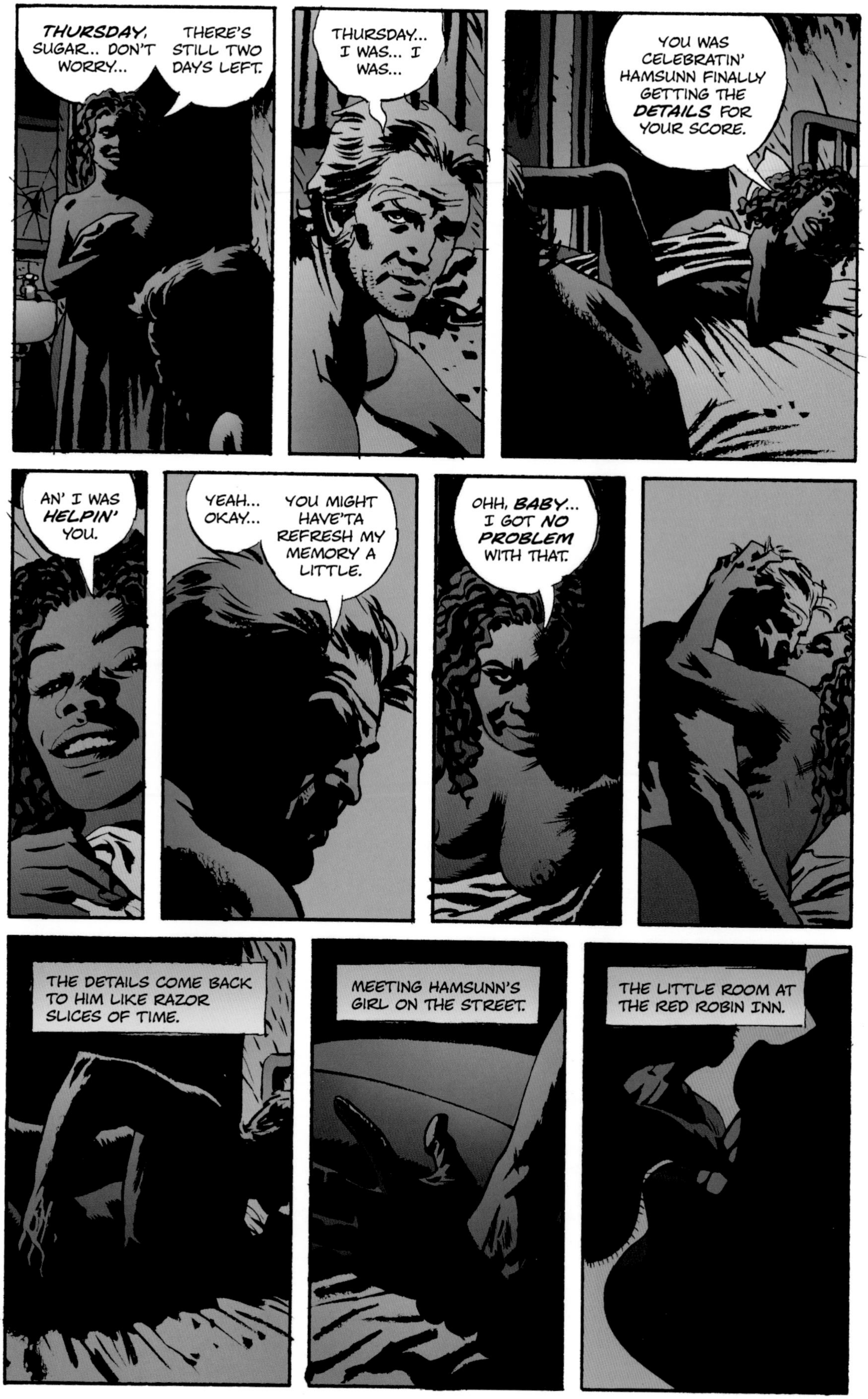
THURSDAY, SUGAR... DON'T WORRY...
THERE'S STILL TWO DAYS LEFT.
THURSDAY... I WAS... I WAS...
YOU WAS CELEBRATIN' HAMSUNN FINALLY GETTING THE DETAILS FOR YOUR SCORE.
AN' I WAS HELPIN' YOU.
YEAH... OKAY...
YOU MIGHT HAVE'TA REFRESH MY MEMORY A LITTLE.
OHH, BABY... I GOT NO PROBLEM WITH THAT.
THE DETAILS COME BACK TO HIM LIKE RAZOR SLICES OF TIME.
MEETING HAMSUNN'S GIRL ON THE STREET.
THE LITTLE ROOM AT THE RED ROBIN INN.

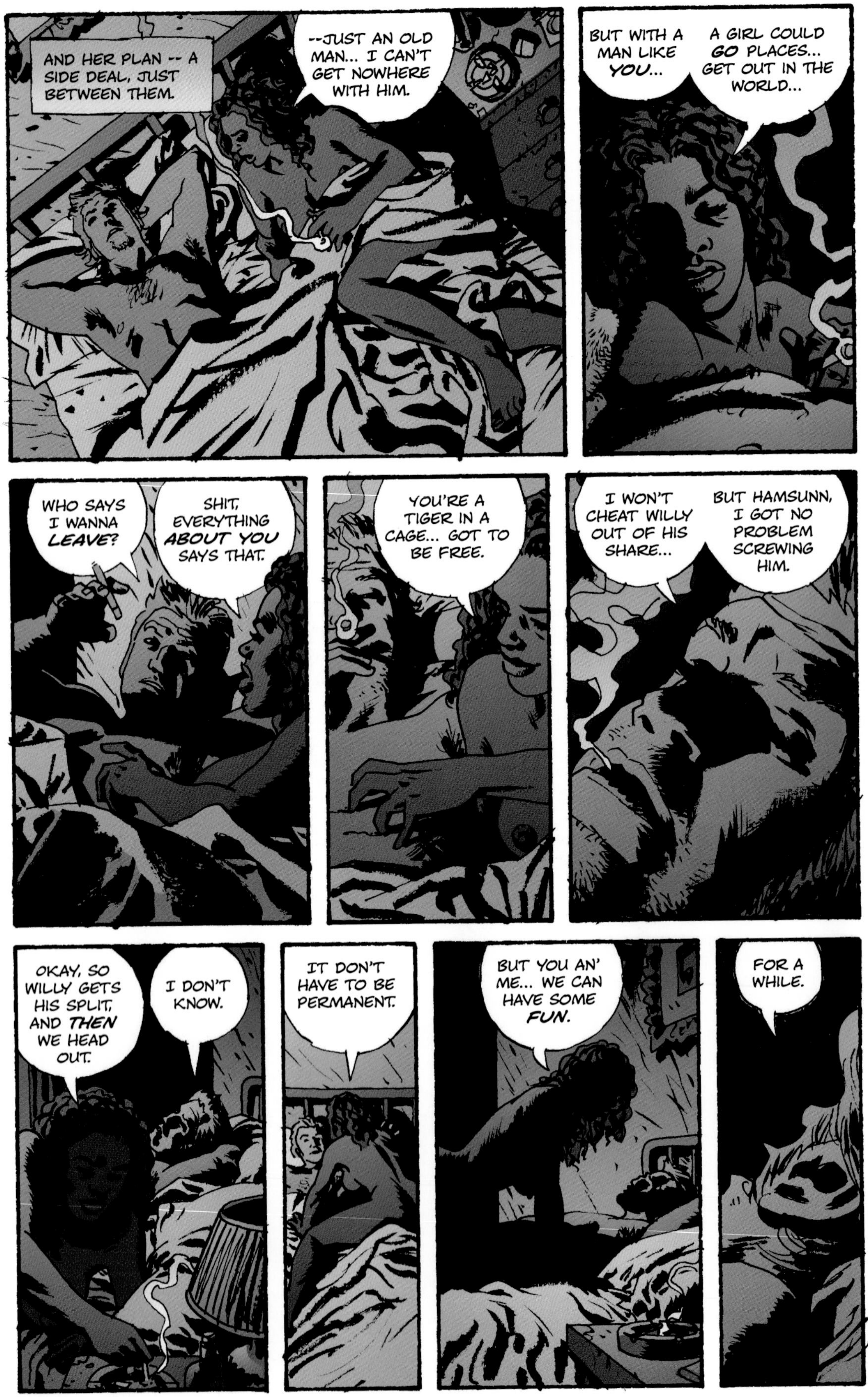
AND HER PLAN -- A SIDE DEAL, JUST BETWEEN THEM.
--JUST AN OLD MAN... I CAN'T GET NOWHERE WITH HIM.
BUT WITH A MAN LIKE YOU...
A GIRL COULD GO PLACES... GET OUT IN THE WORLD...
WHO SAYS I WANNA LEAVE?
SHIT, EVERYTHING ABOUT YOU SAYS THAT.
YOU'RE A TIGER IN A CAGE... GOT TO BE FREE.
I WON'T CHEAT WILLY OUT OF HIS SHARE...
BUT HAMSUNN, I GOT NO PROBLEM SCREWING HIM.
OKAY, SO WILLY GETS HIS SPLIT, AND THEN WE HEAD OUT.
I DON'T KNOW.
IT DON'T HAVE TO BE PERMANENT.
BUT YOU AN' ME... WE CAN HAVE SOME FUN.
FOR A WHILE.

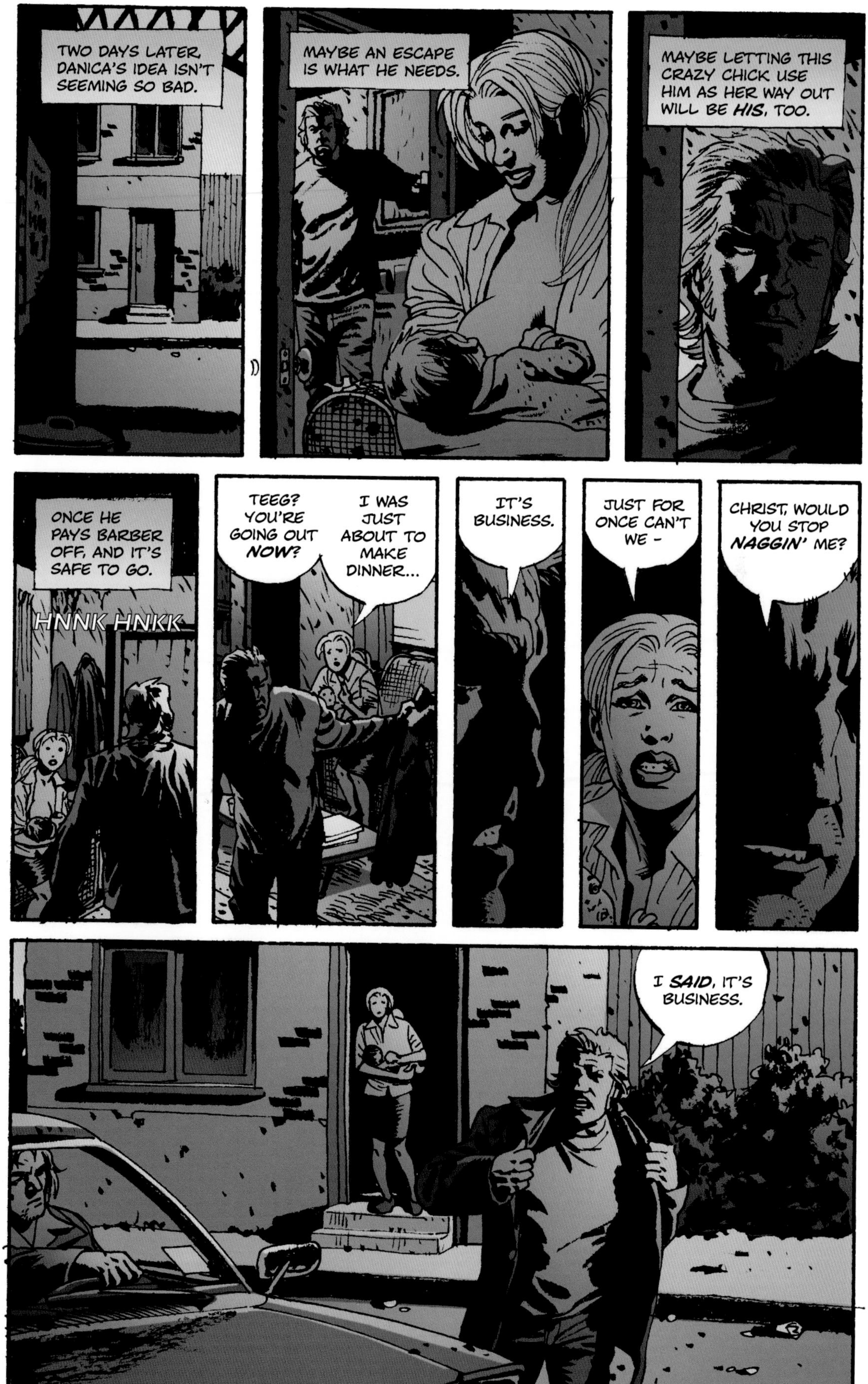
TWO DAYS LATER, DANICA'S IDEA ISN'T SEEMING SO BAD.
MAYBE AN ESCAPE IS WHAT HE NEEDS.
MAYBE LETTING THIS CRAZY CHICK USE HIM AS HER WAY OUT WILL BE HIS, TOO.
ONCE HE PAYS BARBER OFF, AND IT'S SAFE TO GO.
HNNK HNKK
TEEG? YOU'RE GOING OUT NOW?
I WAS JUST ABOUT TO MAKE DINNER...
IT'S BUSINESS.
JUST FOR ONCE CAN'T WE -
CHRIST, WOULD YOU STOP NAGGIN' ME?
I SAID, IT'S BUSINESS.

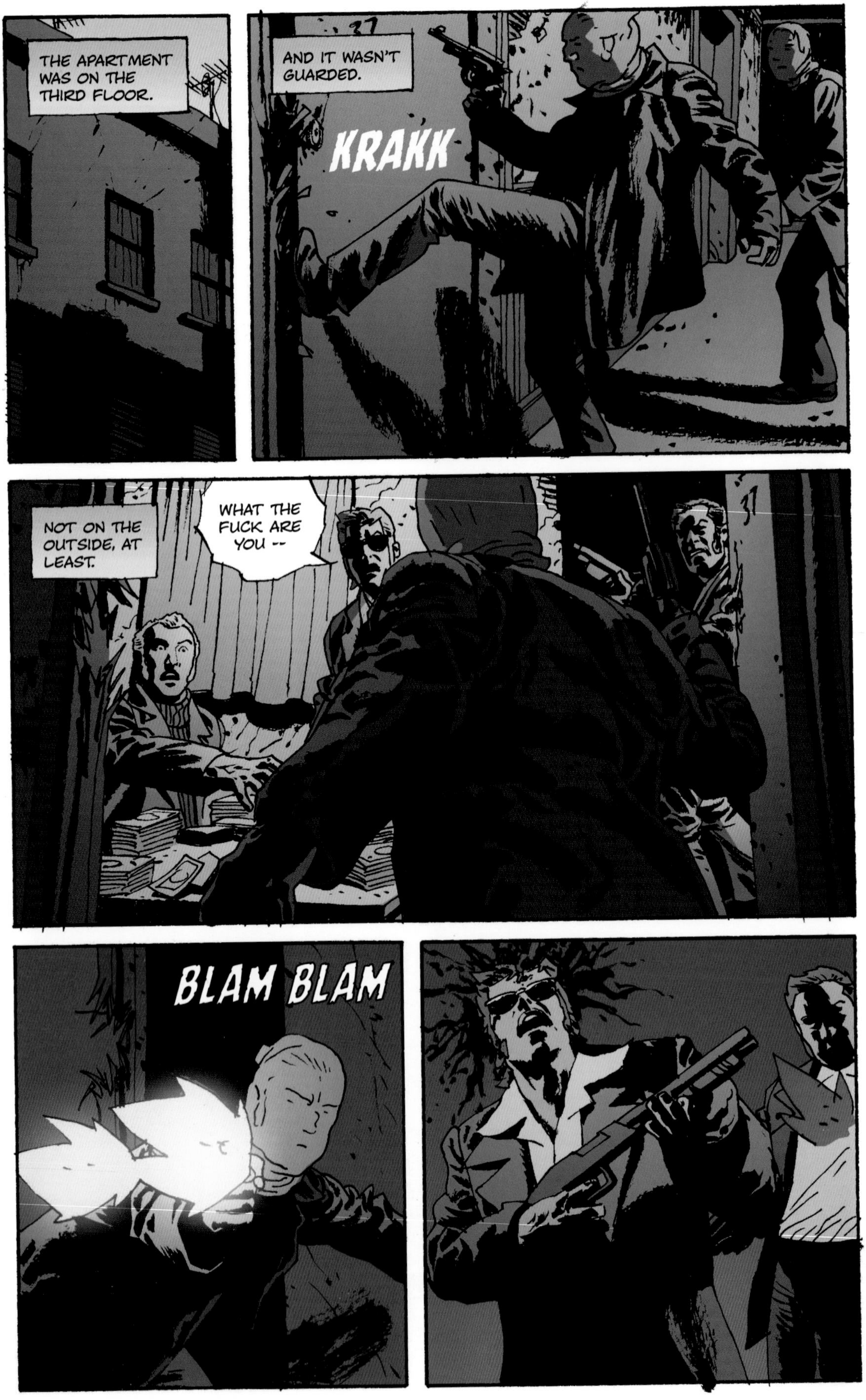
THE APARTMENT WAS ON THE THIRD FLOOR.
AND IT WASN'T GUARDED.
KRAKK
NOT ON THE OUTSIDE, AT LEAST.
WHAT THE FUCK ARE YOU --
BLAM BLAM

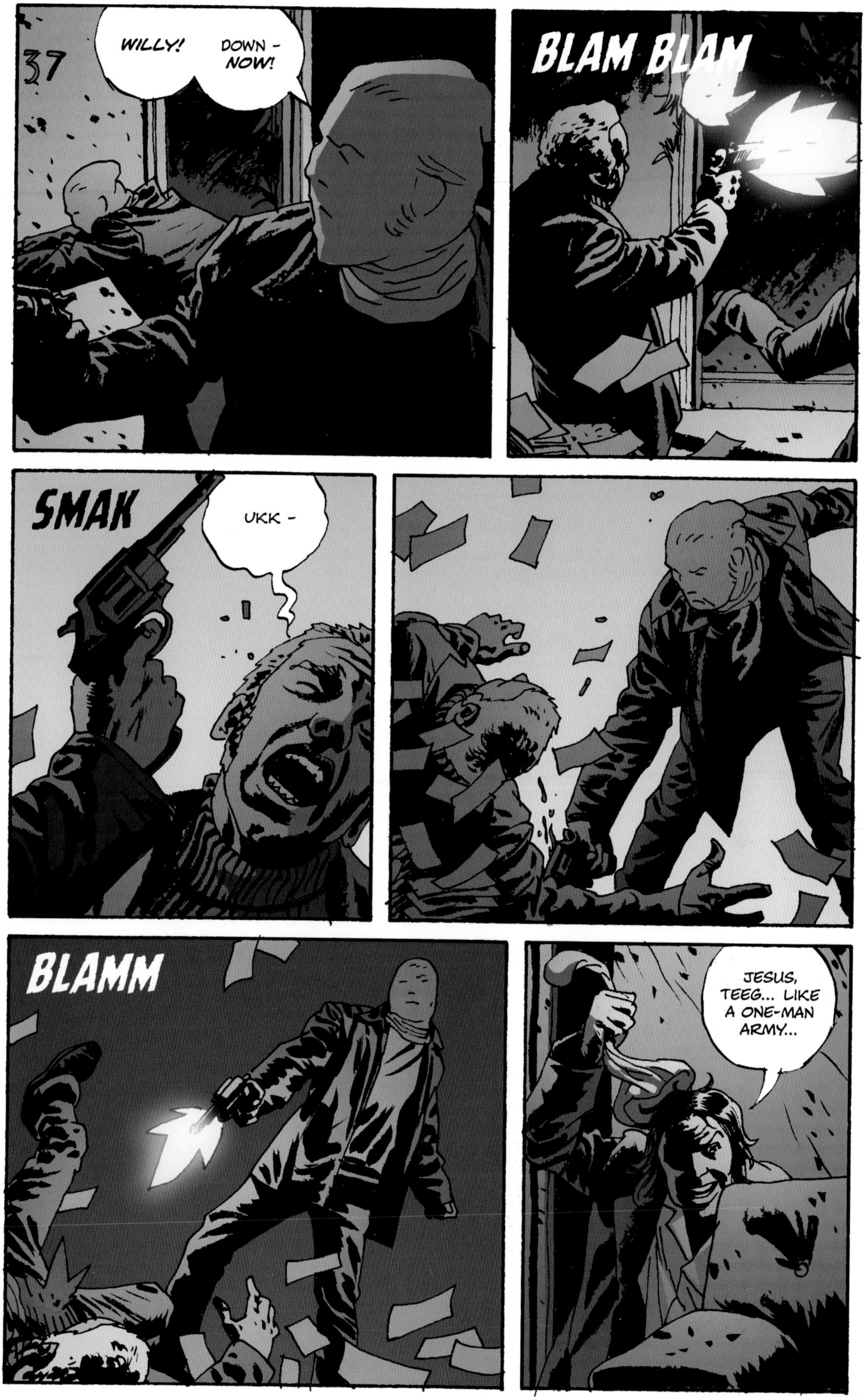
WILLY!
DOWN - NOW!
BLAM BLAM
SMAK
UKK -
BLAMM
JESUS, TEEG... LIKE A ONE-MAN ARMY...

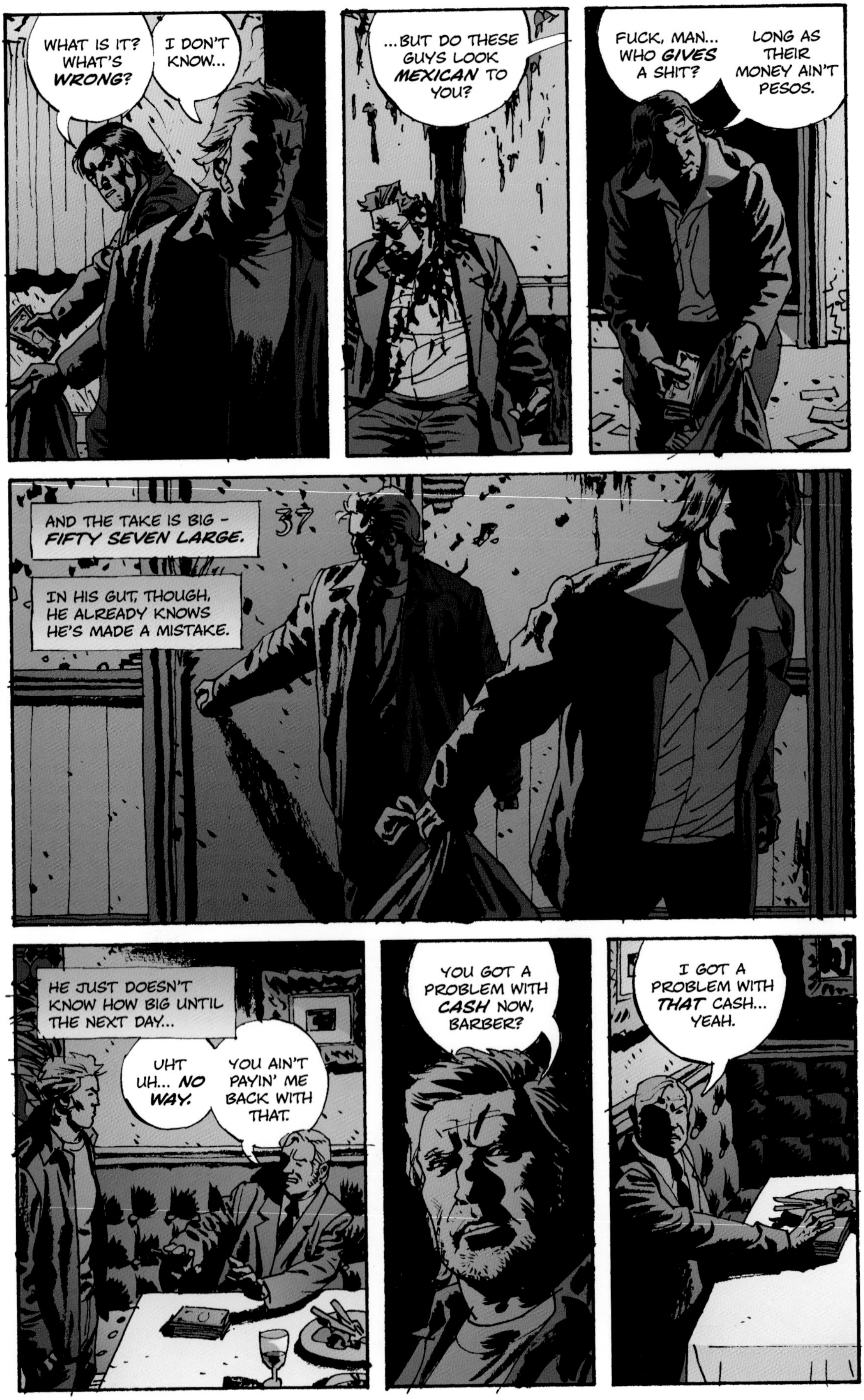
WHAT IS IT? WHAT'S *WRONG*?
I DON'T KNOW...
...BUT DO THESE GUYS LOOK *MEXICAN* TO YOU?
FUCK, MAN... WHO *GIVES* A SHIT?
LONG AS THEIR MONEY AIN'T PESOS.
AND THE TAKE IS BIG – *FIFTY SEVEN LARGE.*
37
IN HIS GUT, THOUGH, HE ALREADY KNOWS HE'S MADE A MISTAKE.
HE JUST DOESN'T KNOW HOW BIG UNTIL THE NEXT DAY...
UHT UH... *NO WAY.*
YOU AIN'T PAYIN' ME BACK WITH THAT.
YOU GOT A PROBLEM WITH *CASH* NOW, BARBER?
I GOT A PROBLEM WITH *THAT* CASH... YEAH.

MUST'A BEEN BURIED IN A *BOTTLE*, OR YOU'D'A HEARD THE HYDES GOT *HIT* YESTERDAY.

THE *HYDES?*

NO... *FUCK* NO.

JESUS... DON'T YA EVEN CHECK WHOSE MONEY YOU'RE *STEALIN'* ANYMORE, LAWLESS?

THEY HAD STOLEN THE HYDES' MONEY? WHAT THE HELL WAS HAMSUNN THINKING?

WALTER HYDE HAD BEEN THE TOP DOG IN THE CITY SINCE THE FIFTIES, AND YOU DIDN'T CROSS HIM.

BUT SOME SNIFFING AROUND LED TO WALTER'S SON, SEBASTIAN, WHO WAS TAKING OVER PARTS OF THE BUSINESS. IT WAS *HIS* STASH THEY'D HIT...

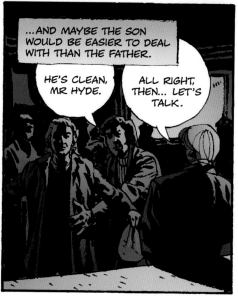

...AND MAYBE THE SON WOULD BE EASIER TO DEAL WITH THAN THE FATHER.

HE'S CLEAN, MR HYDE.

ALL RIGHT, THEN... LET'S TALK.

I WANNA GIVE IT BACK... THE MONEY.

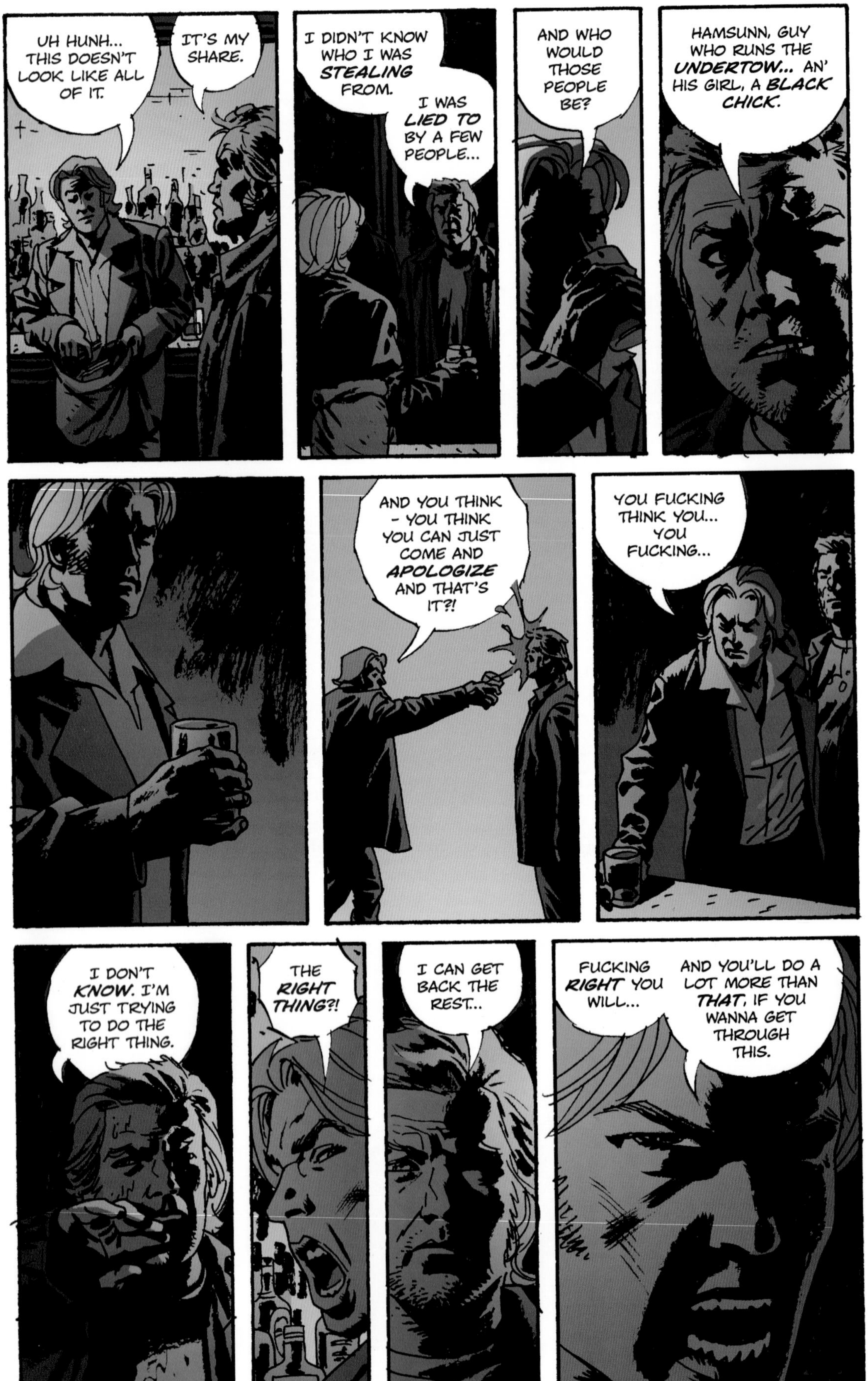
UH HUNH... THIS DOESN'T LOOK LIKE ALL OF IT.
IT'S MY SHARE.
I DIDN'T KNOW WHO I WAS STEALING FROM.
I WAS LIED TO BY A FEW PEOPLE...
AND WHO WOULD THOSE PEOPLE BE?
HAMSUNN, GUY WHO RUNS THE UNDERTOW... AN' HIS GIRL, A BLACK CHICK.
AND YOU THINK - YOU THINK YOU CAN JUST COME AND APOLOGIZE AND THAT'S IT?!
YOU FUCKING THINK YOU... YOU FUCKING...
I DON'T KNOW. I'M JUST TRYING TO DO THE RIGHT THING.
THE RIGHT THING?!
I CAN GET BACK THE REST...
FUCKING RIGHT YOU WILL...
AND YOU'LL DO A LOT MORE THAN THAT, IF YOU WANNA GET THROUGH THIS.

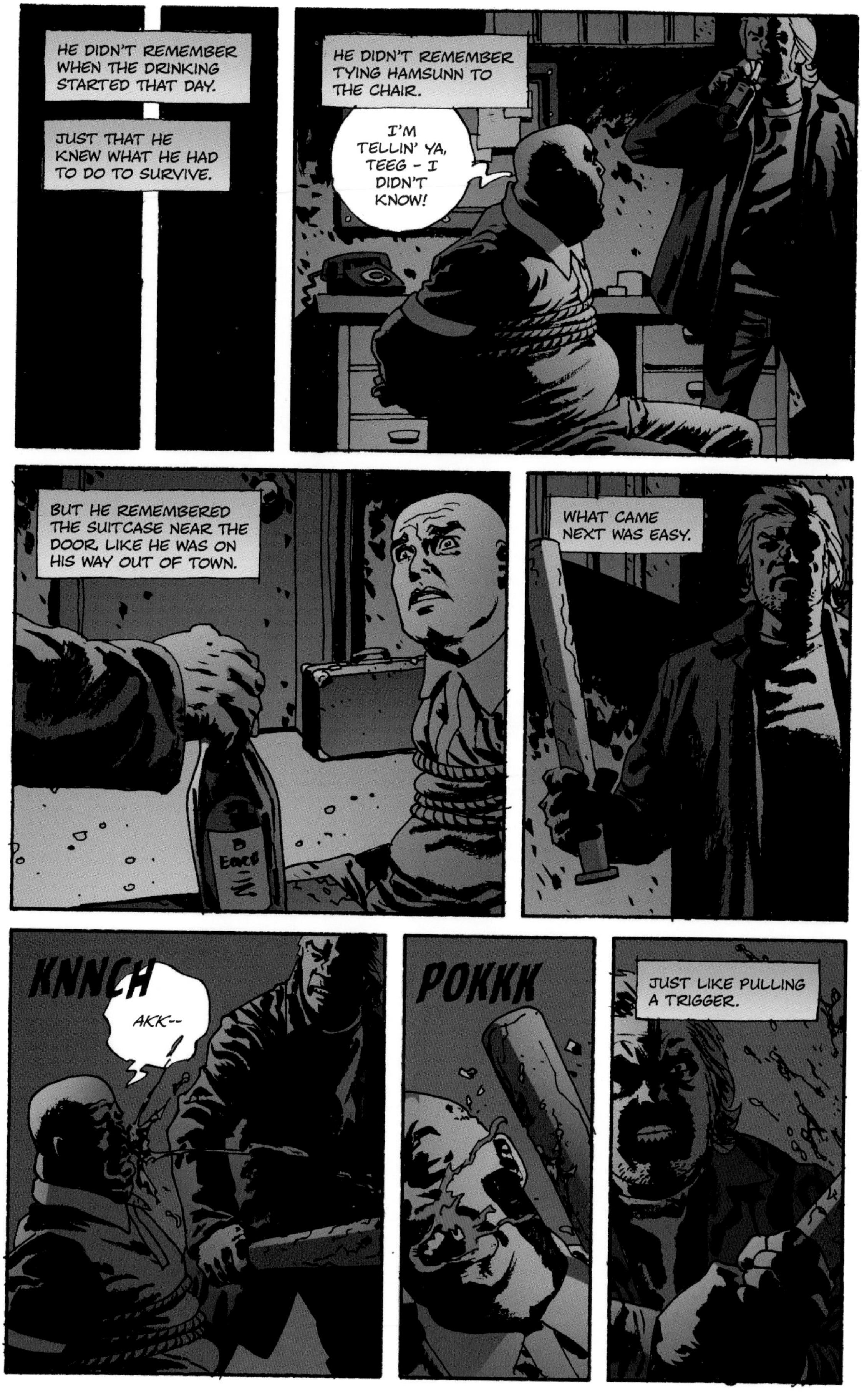

HE DIDN'T REMEMBER WHEN THE DRINKING STARTED THAT DAY.
JUST THAT HE KNEW WHAT HE HAD TO DO TO SURVIVE.
HE DIDN'T REMEMBER TYING HAMSUNN TO THE CHAIR.
I'M TELLIN' YA, TEEG - I DIDN'T KNOW!
BUT HE REMEMBERED THE SUITCASE NEAR THE DOOR, LIKE HE WAS ON HIS WAY OUT OF TOWN.
WHAT CAME NEXT WAS EASY.
KNNCH
AKK--
POKKK
JUST LIKE PULLING A TRIGGER.

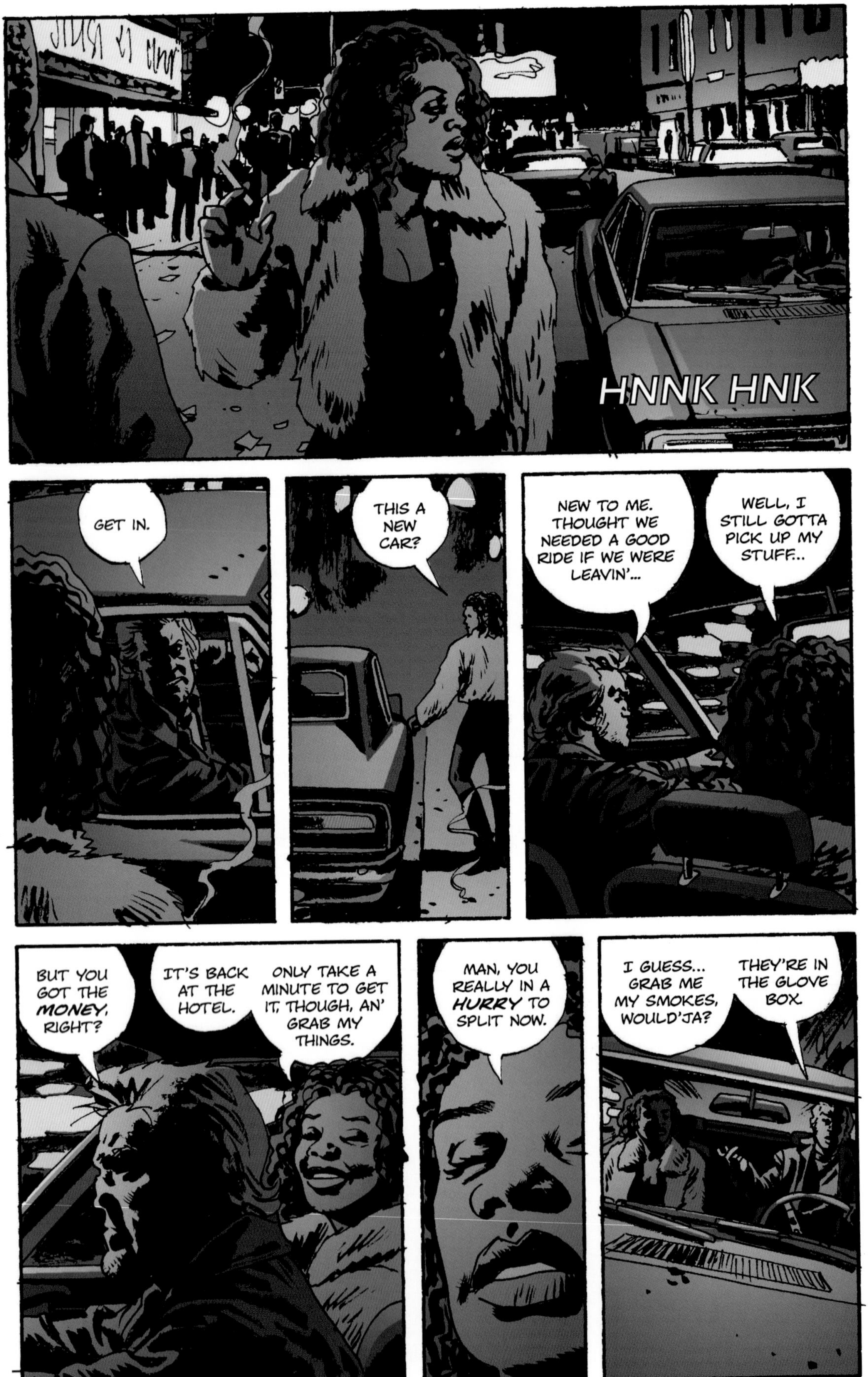
HNNK HNK
GET IN.
THIS A NEW CAR?
NEW TO ME. THOUGHT WE NEEDED A GOOD RIDE IF WE WERE LEAVIN'...
WELL, I STILL GOTTA PICK UP MY STUFF...
BUT YOU GOT THE MONEY, RIGHT?
IT'S BACK AT THE HOTEL.
ONLY TAKE A MINUTE TO GET IT, THOUGH, AN' GRAB MY THINGS.
MAN, YOU REALLY IN A HURRY TO SPLIT NOW.
I GUESS... GRAB ME MY SMOKES, WOULD'JA?
THEY'RE IN THE GLOVE BOX.

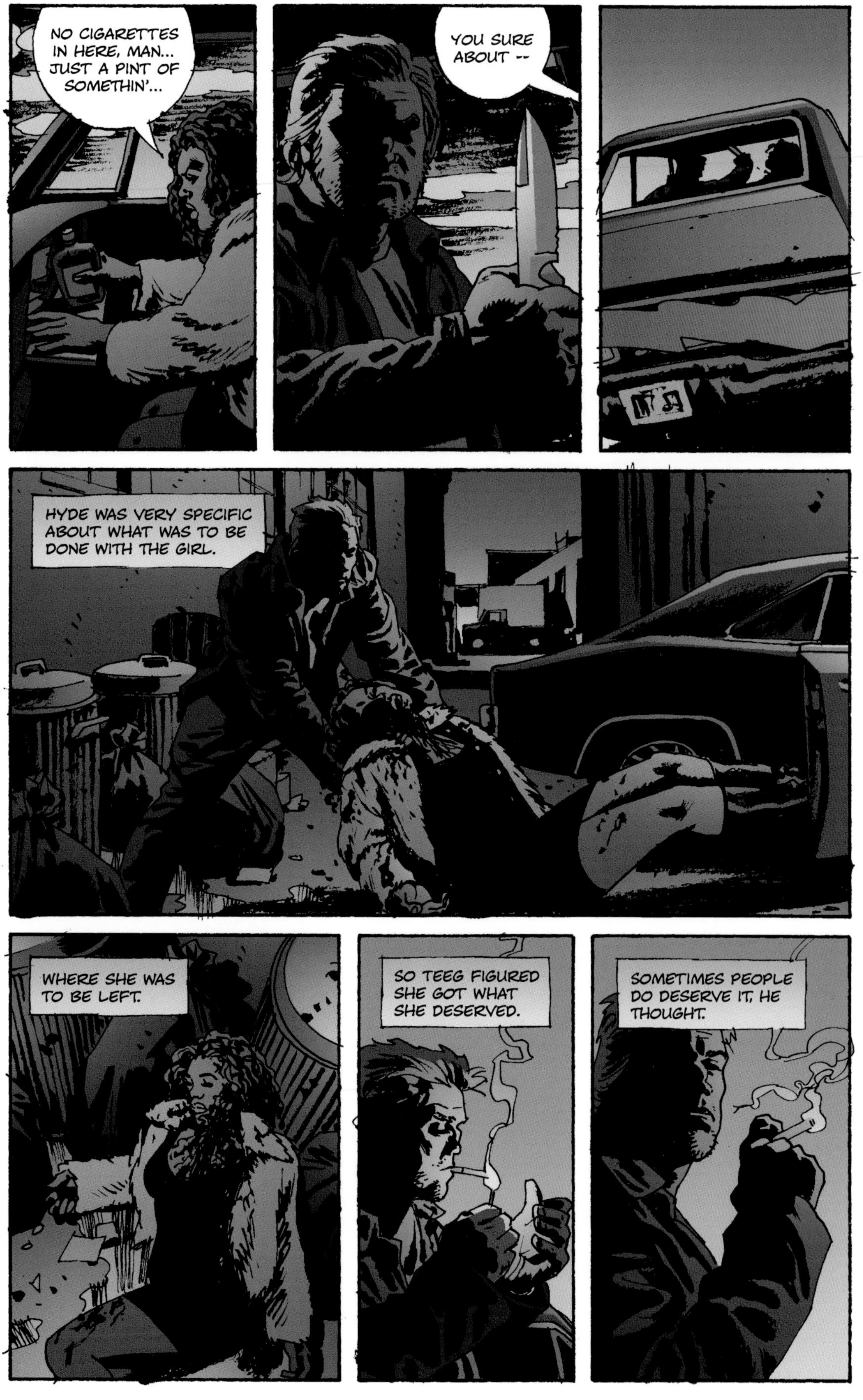
NO CIGARETTES IN HERE, MAN... JUST A PINT OF SOMETHIN'...
YOU SURE ABOUT --
HYDE WAS VERY SPECIFIC ABOUT WHAT WAS TO BE DONE WITH THE GIRL.
WHERE SHE WAS TO BE LEFT.
SO TEEG FIGURED SHE GOT WHAT SHE DESERVED.
SOMETIMES PEOPLE DO DESERVE IT, HE THOUGHT.

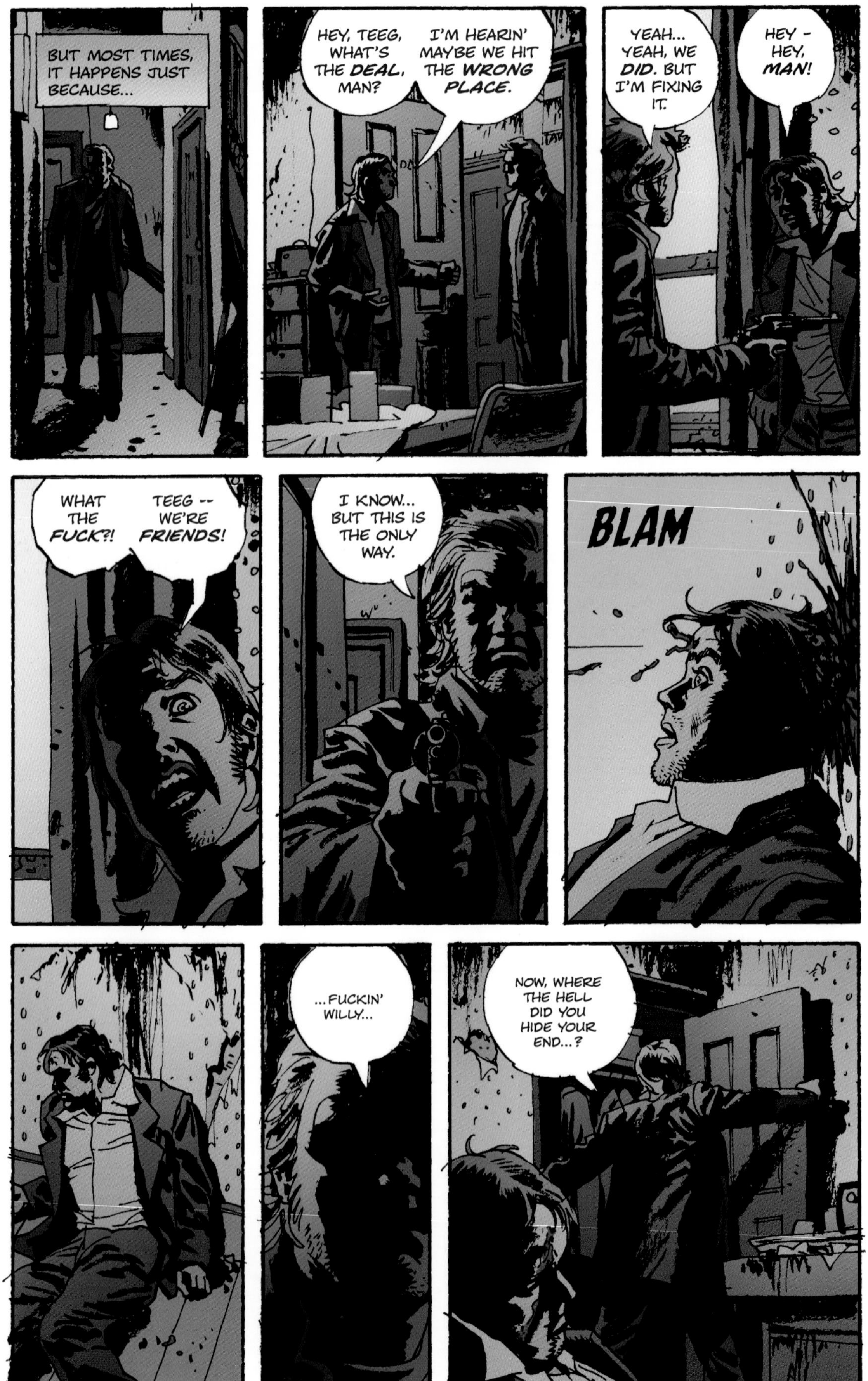
BUT MOST TIMES, IT HAPPENS JUST BECAUSE...
HEY, TEEG, WHAT'S THE DEAL, MAN?
I'M HEARIN' MAYBE WE HIT THE WRONG PLACE.
YEAH... YEAH, WE DID. BUT I'M FIXING IT.
HEY - HEY, MAN!
WHAT THE FUCK?!
TEEG -- WE'RE FRIENDS!
I KNOW... BUT THIS IS THE ONLY WAY.
BLAM
...FUCKIN' WILLY...
NOW, WHERE THE HELL DID YOU HIDE YOUR END...?

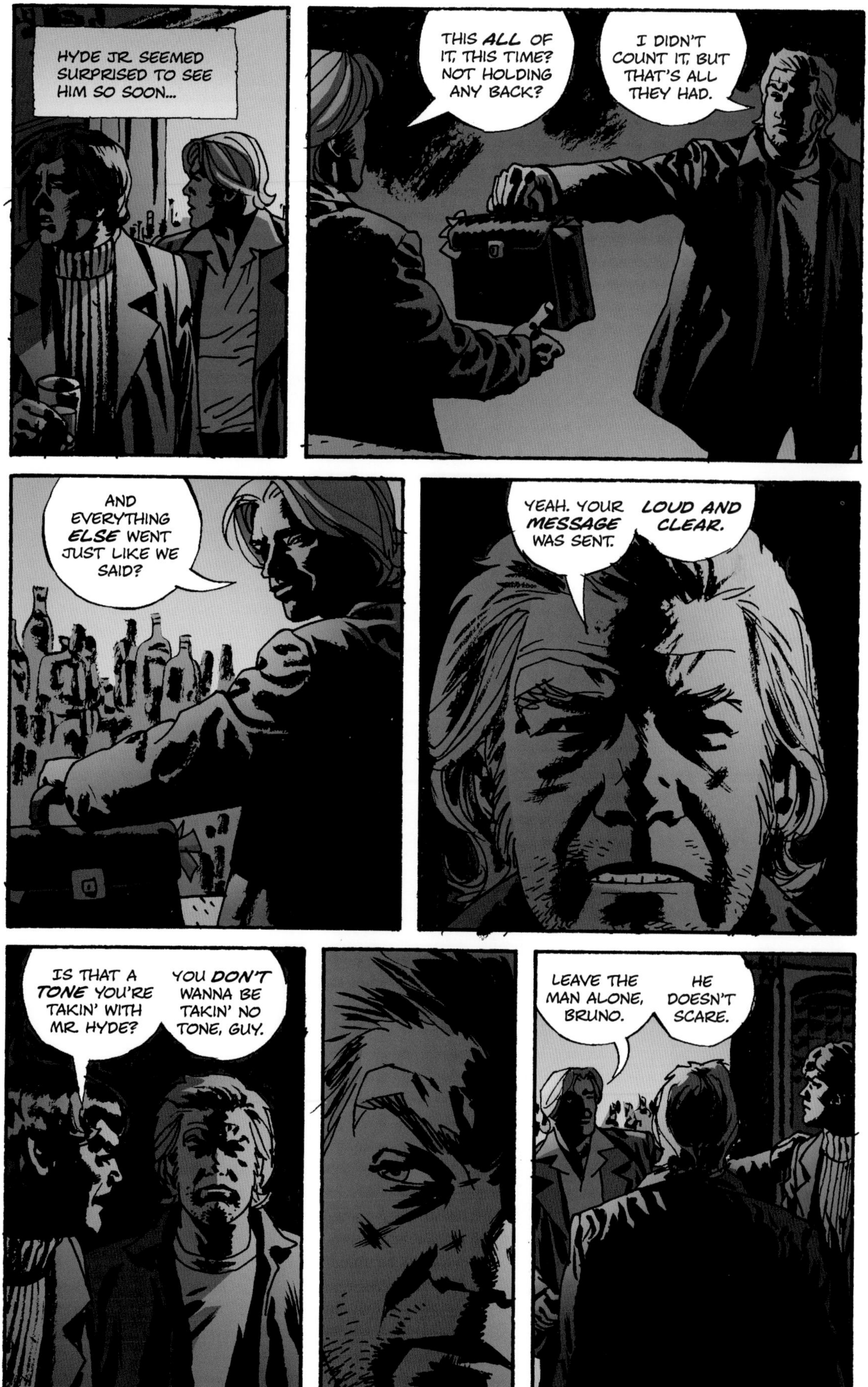
HYDE JR. SEEMED SURPRISED TO SEE HIM SO SOON...
THIS ALL OF IT, THIS TIME? NOT HOLDING ANY BACK?
I DIDN'T COUNT IT, BUT THAT'S ALL THEY HAD.
AND EVERYTHING ELSE WENT JUST LIKE WE SAID?
YEAH. YOUR MESSAGE WAS SENT.
LOUD AND CLEAR.
IS THAT A TONE YOU'RE TAKIN' WITH MR. HYDE?
YOU DON'T WANNA BE TAKIN' NO TONE, GUY.
LEAVE THE MAN ALONE, BRUNO.
HE DOESN'T SCARE.

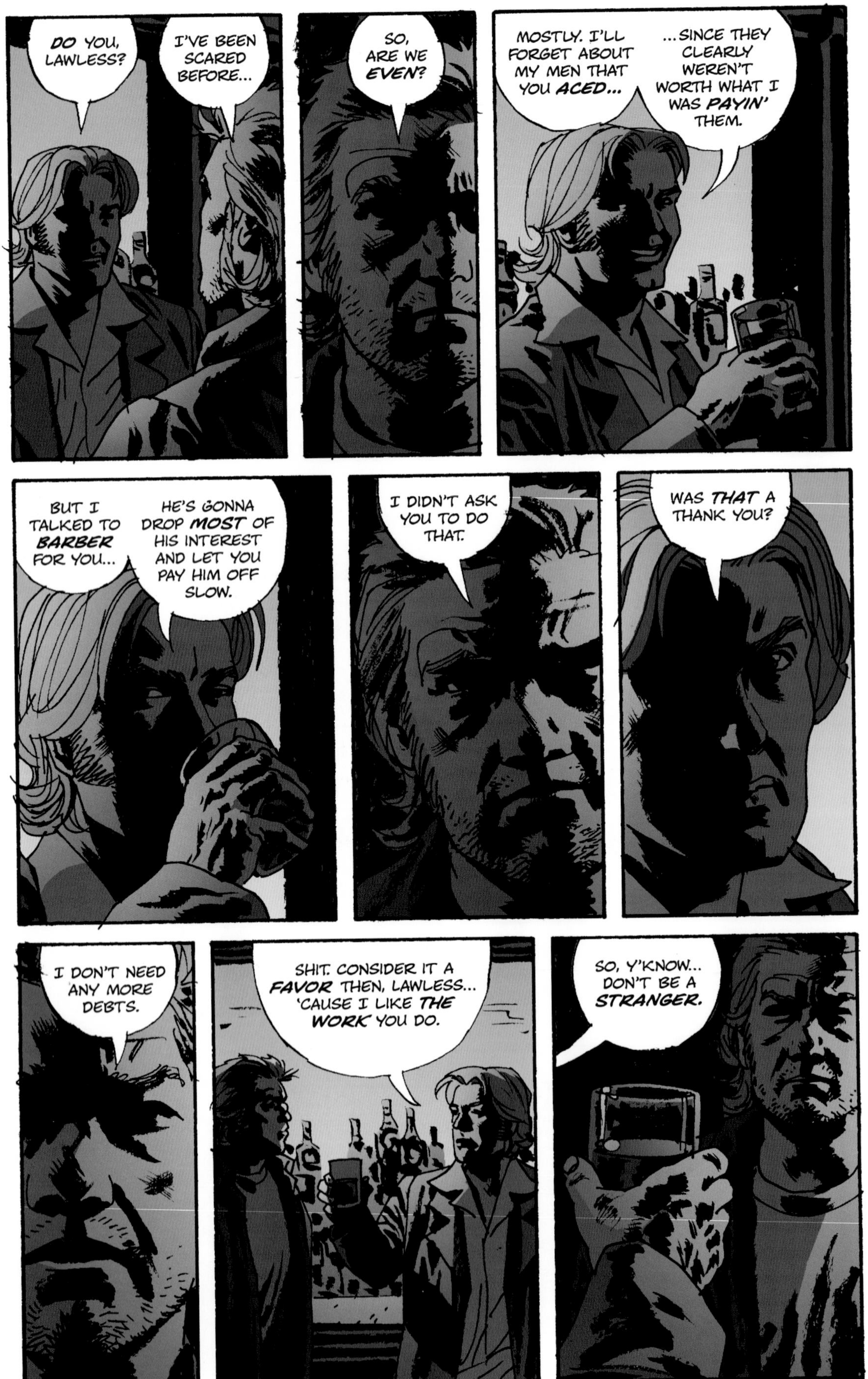
DO YOU, LAWLESS?
I'VE BEEN SCARED BEFORE...
SO, ARE WE EVEN?
MOSTLY. I'LL FORGET ABOUT MY MEN THAT YOU ACED...
...SINCE THEY CLEARLY WEREN'T WORTH WHAT I WAS PAYIN' THEM.
BUT I TALKED TO BARBER FOR YOU...
HE'S GONNA DROP MOST OF HIS INTEREST AND LET YOU PAY HIM OFF SLOW.
I DIDN'T ASK YOU TO DO THAT.
WAS THAT A THANK YOU?
I DON'T NEED ANY MORE DEBTS.
SHIT. CONSIDER IT A FAVOR THEN, LAWLESS... 'CAUSE I LIKE THE WORK YOU DO.
SO, Y'KNOW... DON'T BE A STRANGER.

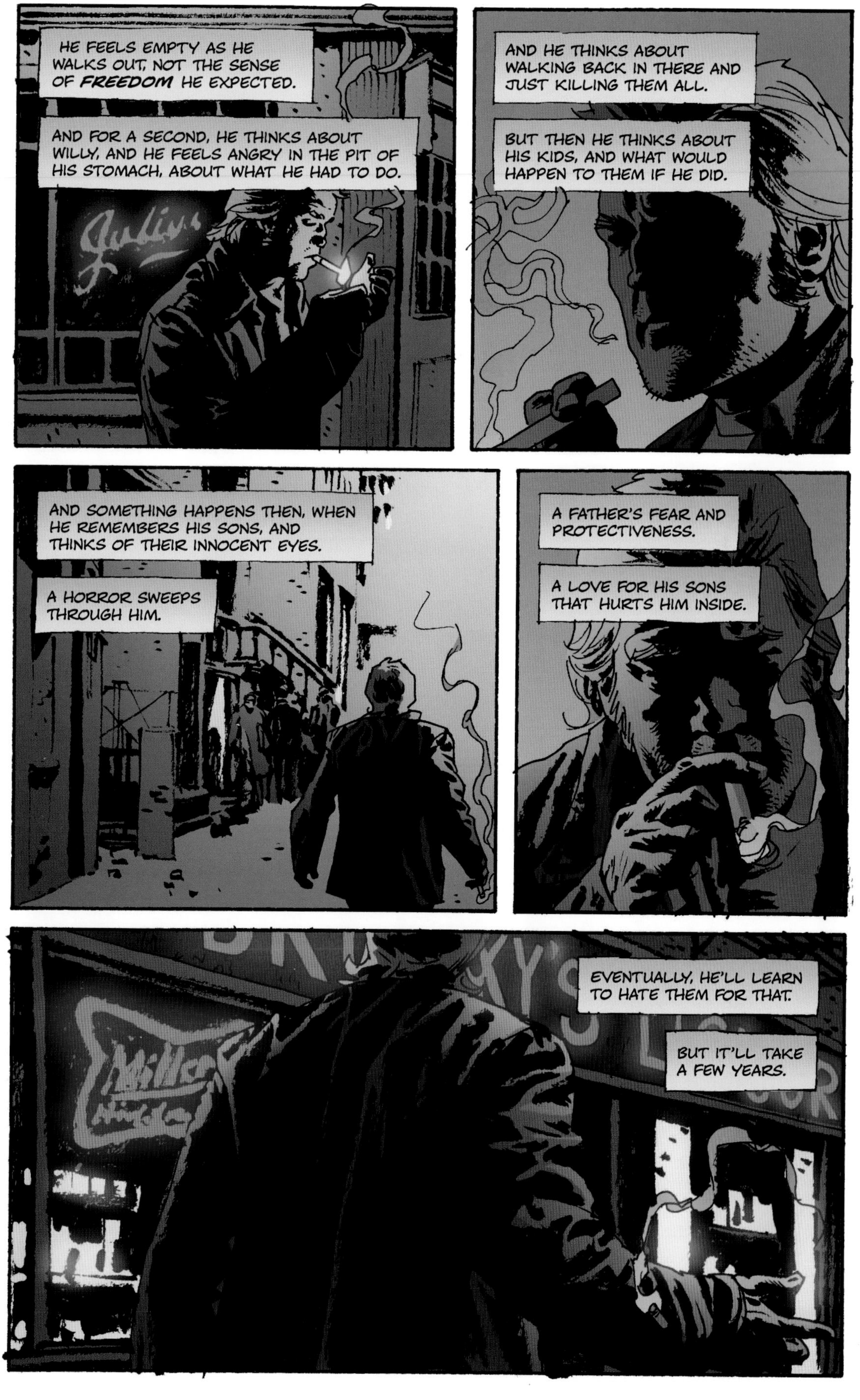
HE FEELS EMPTY AS HE WALKS OUT, NOT THE SENSE OF *FREEDOM* HE EXPECTED.
AND FOR A SECOND, HE THINKS ABOUT WILLY, AND HE FEELS ANGRY IN THE PIT OF HIS STOMACH, ABOUT WHAT HE HAD TO DO.
AND HE THINKS ABOUT WALKING BACK IN THERE AND JUST KILLING THEM ALL.
BUT THEN HE THINKS ABOUT HIS KIDS, AND WHAT WOULD HAPPEN TO THEM IF HE DID.
AND SOMETHING HAPPENS THEN, WHEN HE REMEMBERS HIS SONS, AND THINKS OF THEIR INNOCENT EYES.
A HORROR SWEEPS THROUGH HIM.
A FATHER'S FEAR AND PROTECTIVENESS.
A LOVE FOR HIS SONS THAT HURTS HIM INSIDE.
EVENTUALLY, HE'LL LEARN TO HATE THEM FOR THAT.
BUT IT'LL TAKE A FEW YEARS.

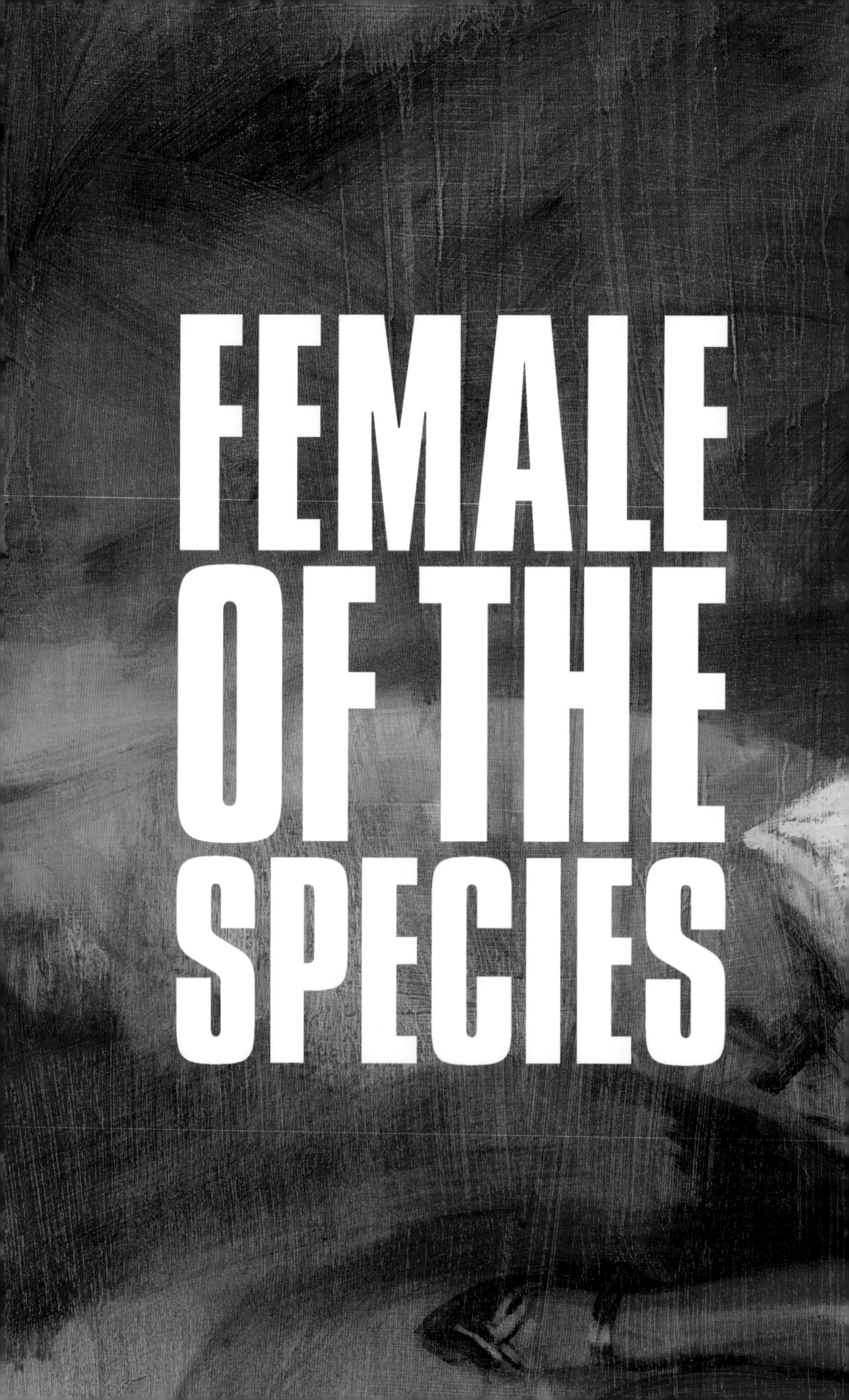
FEMALE
OF THE
SPECIES

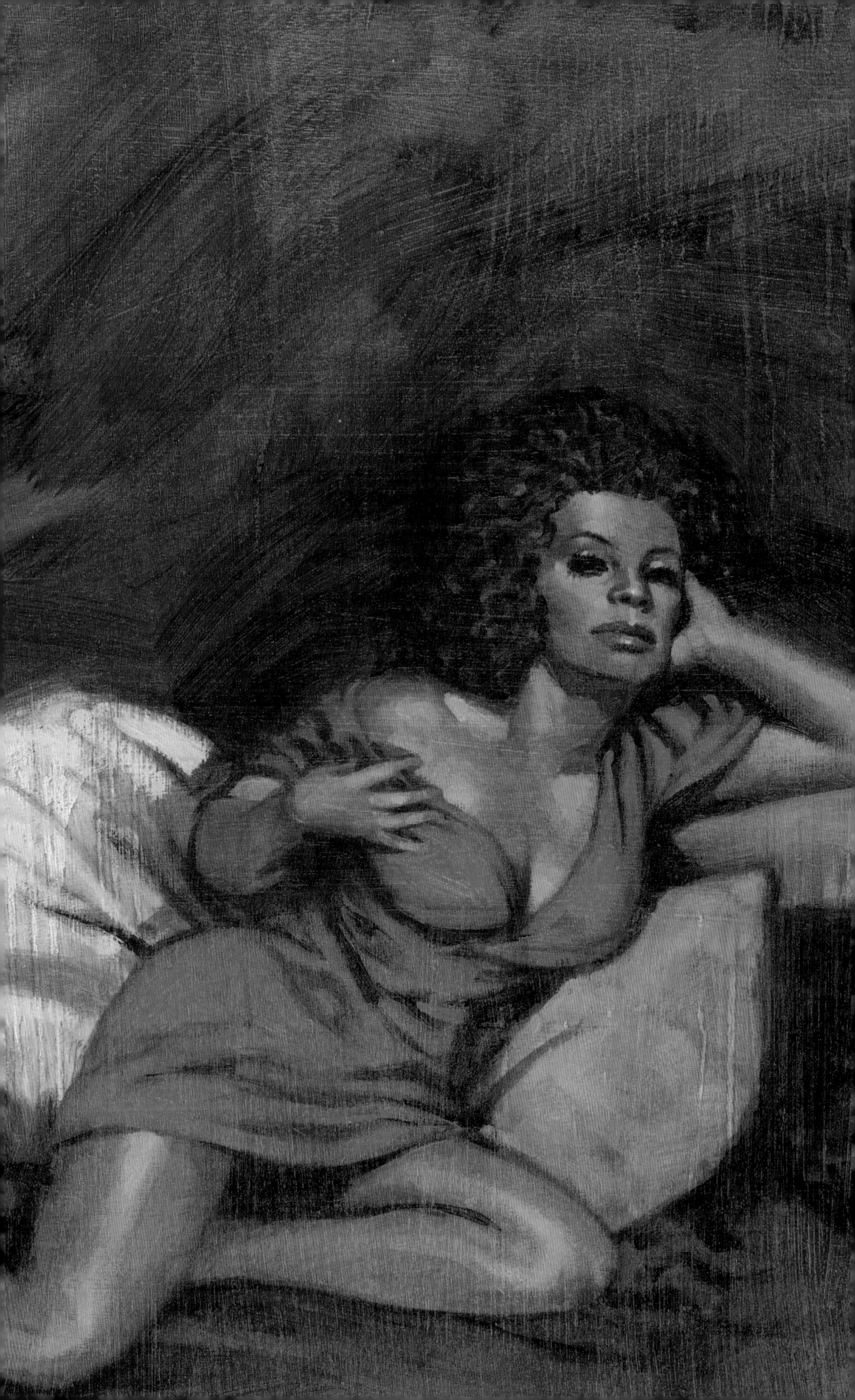

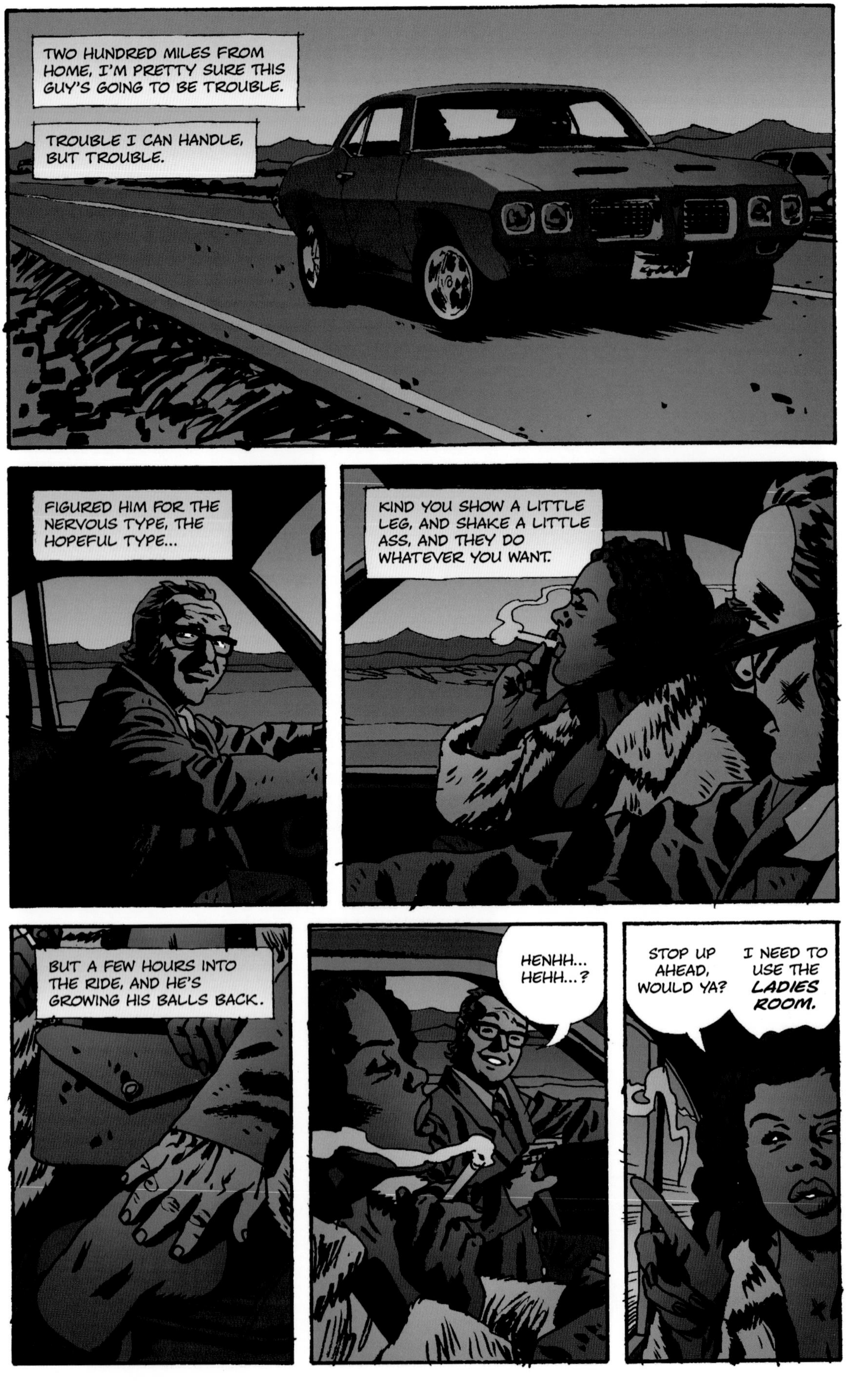
TWO HUNDRED MILES FROM HOME, I'M PRETTY SURE THIS GUY'S GOING TO BE TROUBLE.
TROUBLE I CAN HANDLE, BUT TROUBLE.
FIGURED HIM FOR THE NERVOUS TYPE, THE HOPEFUL TYPE...
KIND YOU SHOW A LITTLE LEG, AND SHAKE A LITTLE ASS, AND THEY DO WHATEVER YOU WANT.
BUT A FEW HOURS INTO THE RIDE, AND HE'S GROWING HIS BALLS BACK.
HENHH... HEHH...?
STOP UP AHEAD, WOULD YA?
I NEED TO USE THE LADIES ROOM.

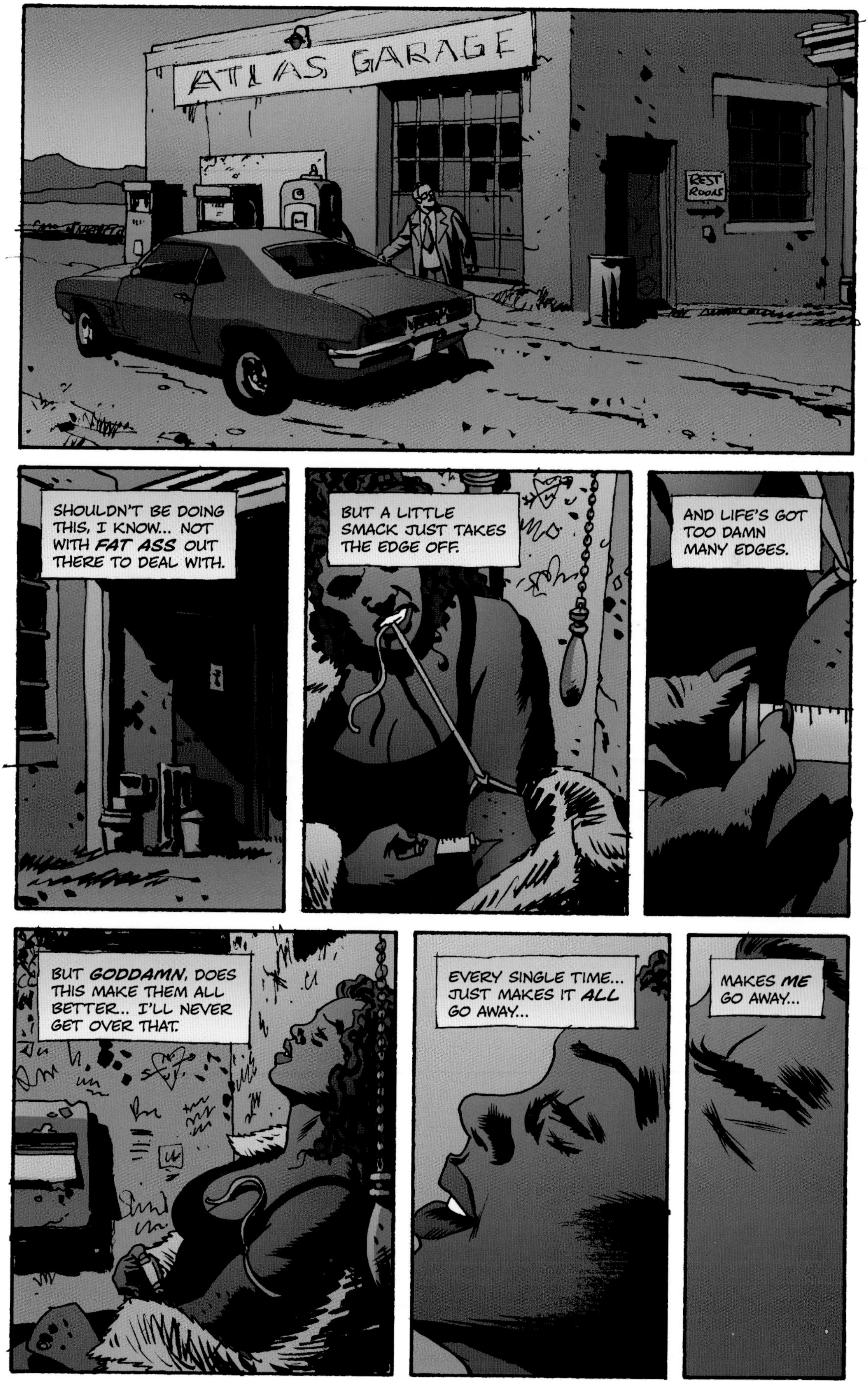
ATLAS GARAGE
REST ROOMS
SHOULDN'T BE DOING THIS, I KNOW... NOT WITH FAT ASS OUT THERE TO DEAL WITH.
BUT A LITTLE SMACK JUST TAKES THE EDGE OFF.
AND LIFE'S GOT TOO DAMN MANY EDGES.
BUT GODDAMN, DOES THIS MAKE THEM ALL BETTER.. I'LL NEVER GET OVER THAT.
EVERY SINGLE TIME... JUST MAKES IT ALL GO AWAY...
MAKES ME GO AWAY...

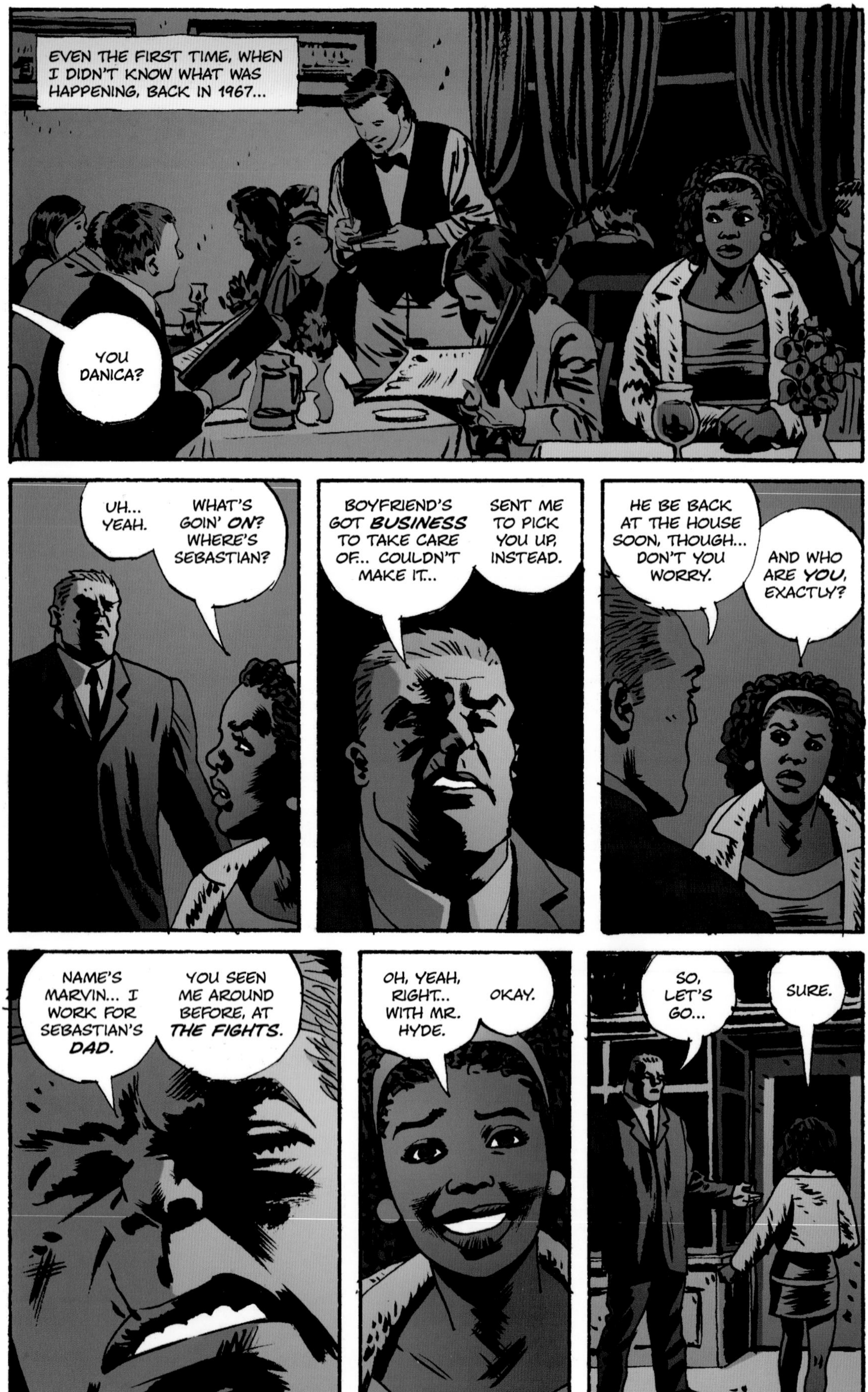
EVEN THE FIRST TIME, WHEN I DIDN'T KNOW WHAT WAS HAPPENING, BACK IN 1967...
YOU DANICA?
UH... YEAH.
WHAT'S GOIN' ON? WHERE'S SEBASTIAN?
BOYFRIEND'S GOT BUSINESS TO TAKE CARE OF... COULDN'T MAKE IT...
SENT ME TO PICK YOU UP, INSTEAD.
HE BE BACK AT THE HOUSE SOON, THOUGH... DON'T YOU WORRY.
AND WHO ARE YOU, EXACTLY?
NAME'S MARVIN... I WORK FOR SEBASTIAN'S DAD.
YOU SEEN ME AROUND BEFORE, AT THE FIGHTS.
OH, YEAH, RIGHT... WITH MR. HYDE.
OKAY.
SO, LET'S GO...
SURE.

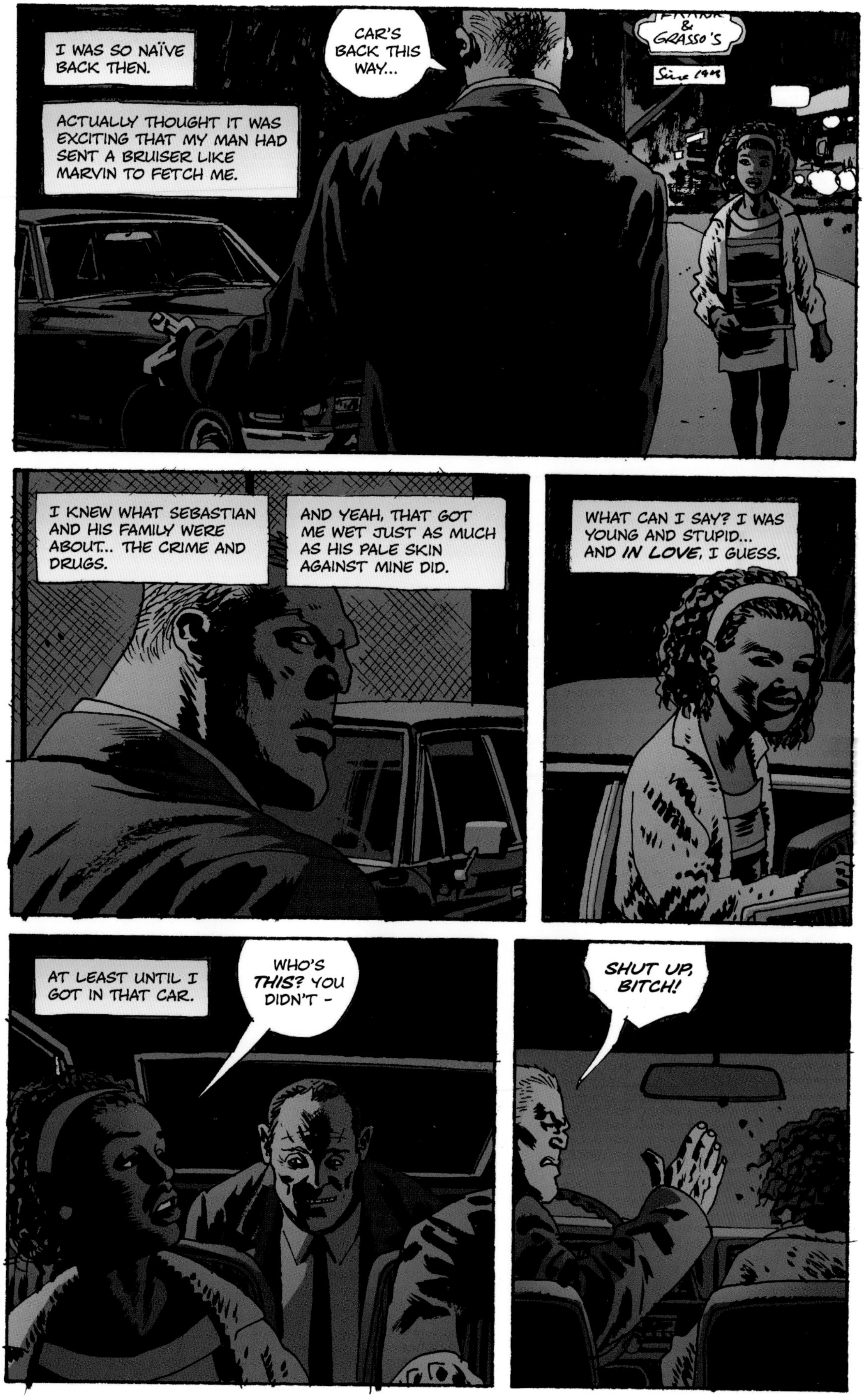
I WAS SO NAÏVE BACK THEN.
ACTUALLY THOUGHT IT WAS EXCITING THAT MY MAN HAD SENT A BRUISER LIKE MARVIN TO FETCH ME.
CAR'S BACK THIS WAY...
& GRASSO'S
I KNEW WHAT SEBASTIAN AND HIS FAMILY WERE ABOUT... THE CRIME AND DRUGS.
AND YEAH, THAT GOT ME WET JUST AS MUCH AS HIS PALE SKIN AGAINST MINE DID.
WHAT CAN I SAY? I WAS YOUNG AND STUPID... AND *IN LOVE*, I GUESS.
AT LEAST UNTIL I GOT IN THAT CAR.
WHO'S *THIS*? YOU DIDN'T -
SHUT UP, BITCH!

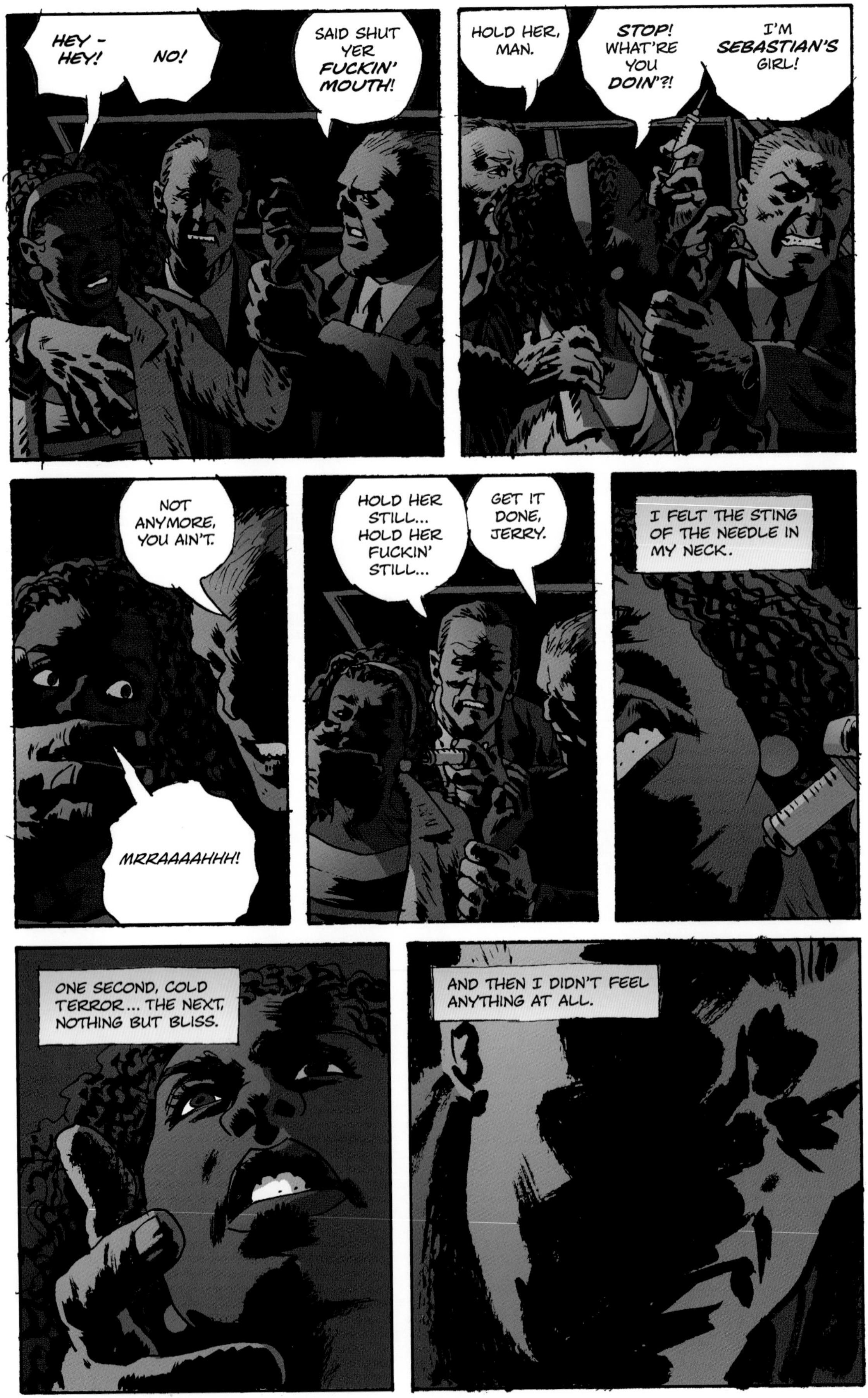
HEY - HEY!
NO!
SAID SHUT YER FUCKIN' MOUTH!
HOLD HER, MAN.
STOP! WHAT'RE YOU DOIN'?!
I'M SEBASTIAN'S GIRL!
NOT ANYMORE, YOU AIN'T.
MRRAAAAHHH!
HOLD HER STILL... HOLD HER FUCKIN' STILL...
GET IT DONE, JERRY.
I FELT THE STING OF THE NEEDLE IN MY NECK.
ONE SECOND, COLD TERROR... THE NEXT, NOTHING BUT BLISS.
AND THEN I DIDN'T FEEL ANYTHING AT ALL.

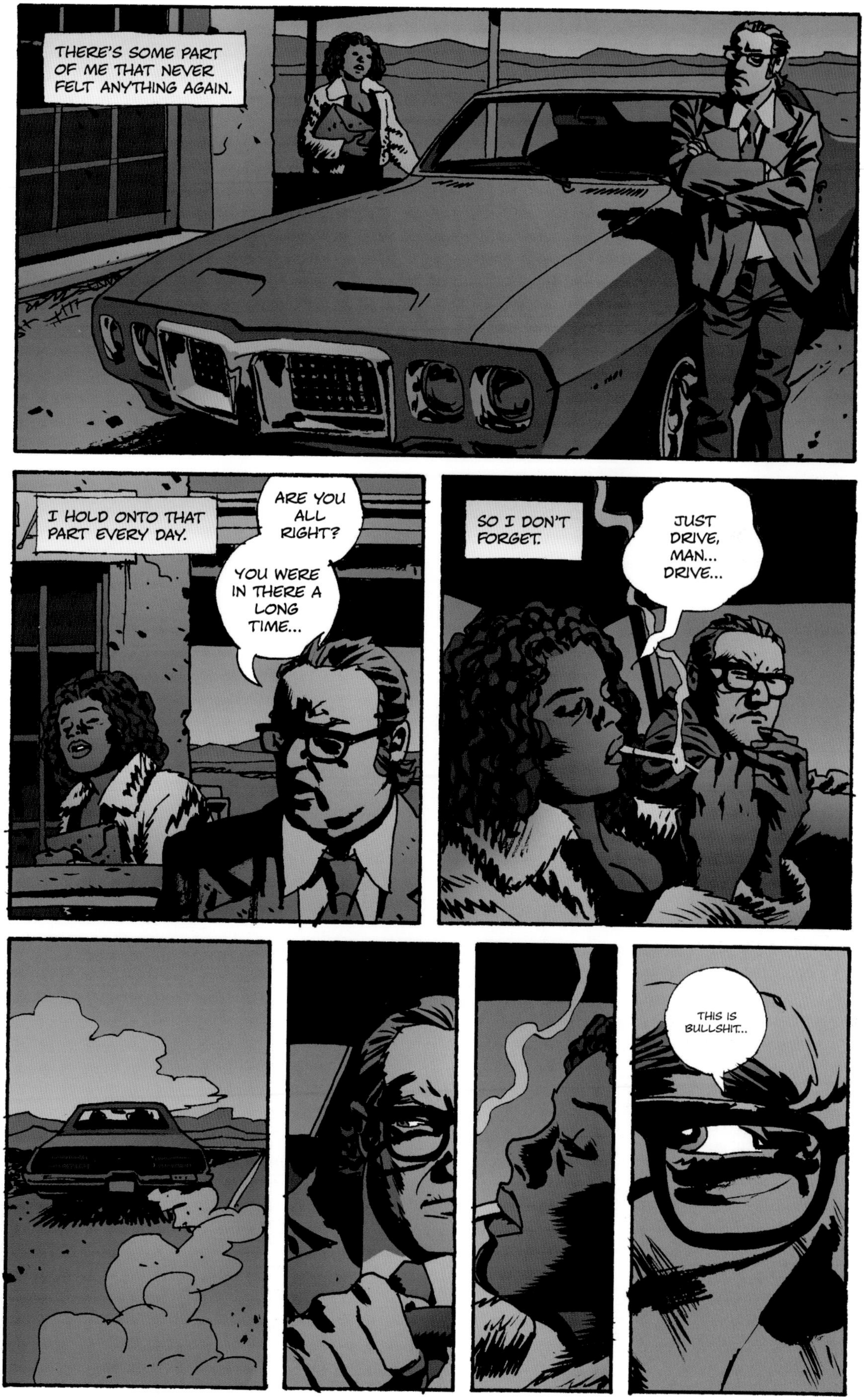
THERE'S SOME PART OF ME THAT NEVER FELT ANYTHING AGAIN.
I HOLD ONTO THAT PART EVERY DAY.
ARE YOU ALL RIGHT?
YOU WERE IN THERE A LONG TIME...
SO I DON'T FORGET.
JUST DRIVE, MAN... DRIVE...
THIS IS BULLSHIT...

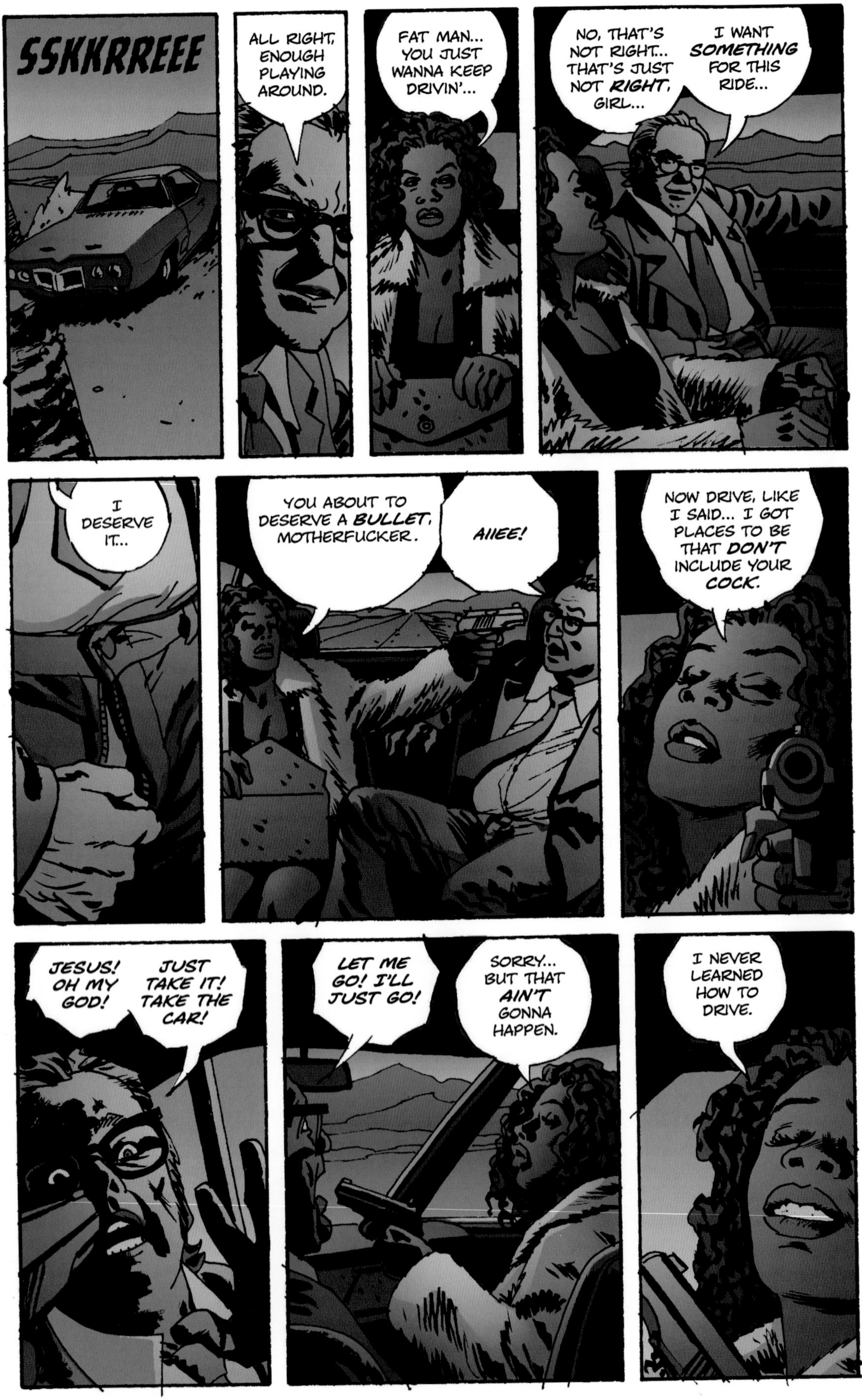

SSKKRREEE
ALL RIGHT, ENOUGH PLAYING AROUND.
FAT MAN... YOU JUST WANNA KEEP DRIVIN'...
NO, THAT'S NOT RIGHT.. THAT'S JUST NOT RIGHT, GIRL...
I WANT SOMETHING FOR THIS RIDE...
I DESERVE IT...
YOU ABOUT TO DESERVE A BULLET, MOTHERFUCKER.
AIIEE!
NOW DRIVE, LIKE I SAID... I GOT PLACES TO BE THAT DON'T INCLUDE YOUR COCK.
JESUS! OH MY GOD!
JUST TAKE IT! TAKE THE CAR!
LET ME GO! I'LL JUST GO!
SORRY... BUT THAT AIN'T GONNA HAPPEN.
I NEVER LEARNED HOW TO DRIVE.

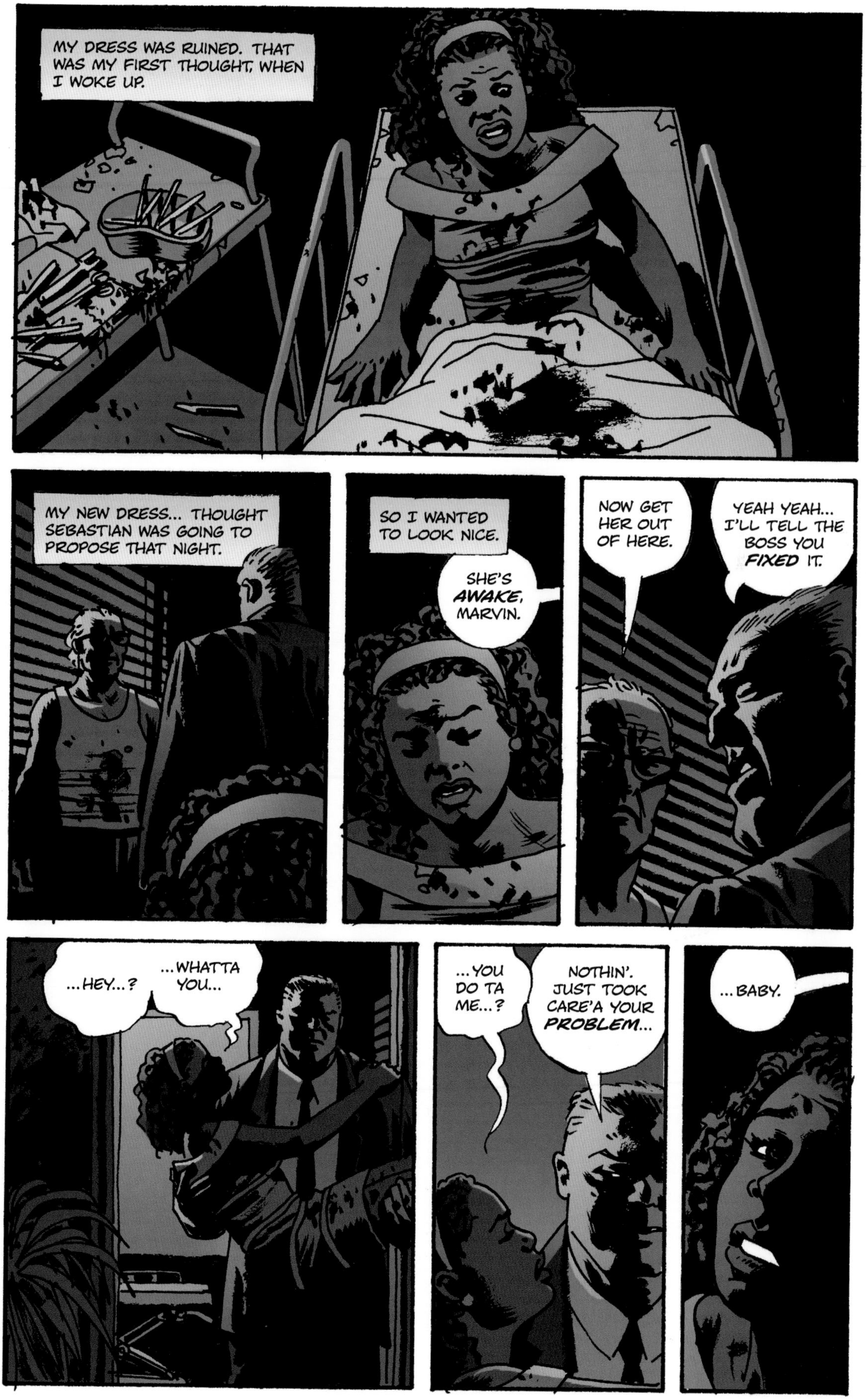
MY DRESS WAS RUINED. THAT WAS MY FIRST THOUGHT, WHEN I WOKE UP.
MY NEW DRESS... THOUGHT SEBASTIAN WAS GOING TO PROPOSE THAT NIGHT.
SO I WANTED TO LOOK NICE.
SHE'S AWAKE, MARVIN.
NOW GET HER OUT OF HERE.
YEAH YEAH... I'LL TELL THE BOSS YOU FIXED IT.
...HEY...?
...WHATTA YOU...
...YOU DO TA ME...?
NOTHIN'. JUST TOOK CARE'A YOUR PROBLEM...
...BABY.

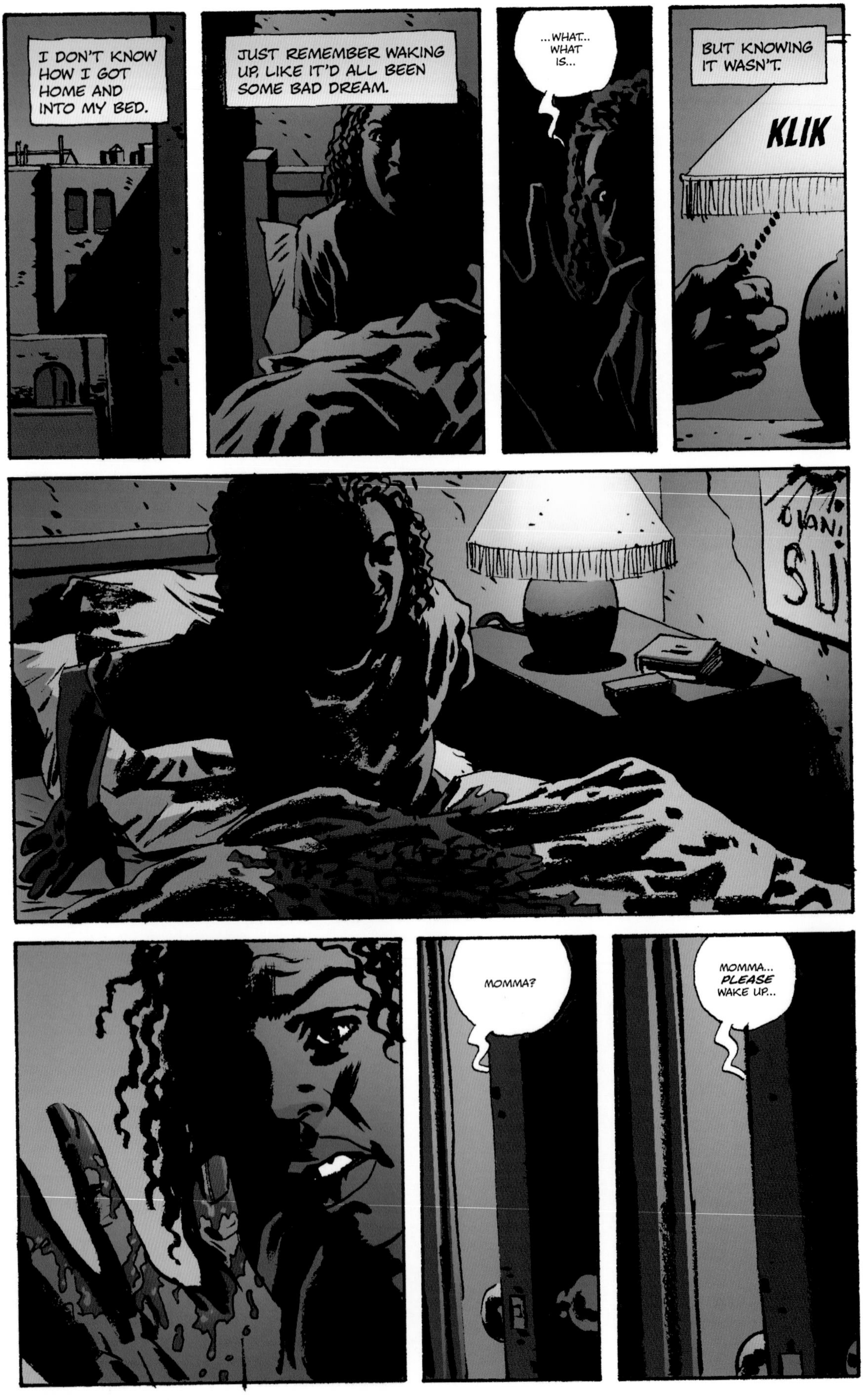
I DON'T KNOW HOW I GOT HOME AND INTO MY BED.
JUST REMEMBER WAKING UP, LIKE IT'D ALL BEEN SOME BAD DREAM.
...WHAT... WHAT IS...
BUT KNOWING IT WASN'T.
KLIK
MOMMA?
MOMMA... PLEASE WAKE UP...

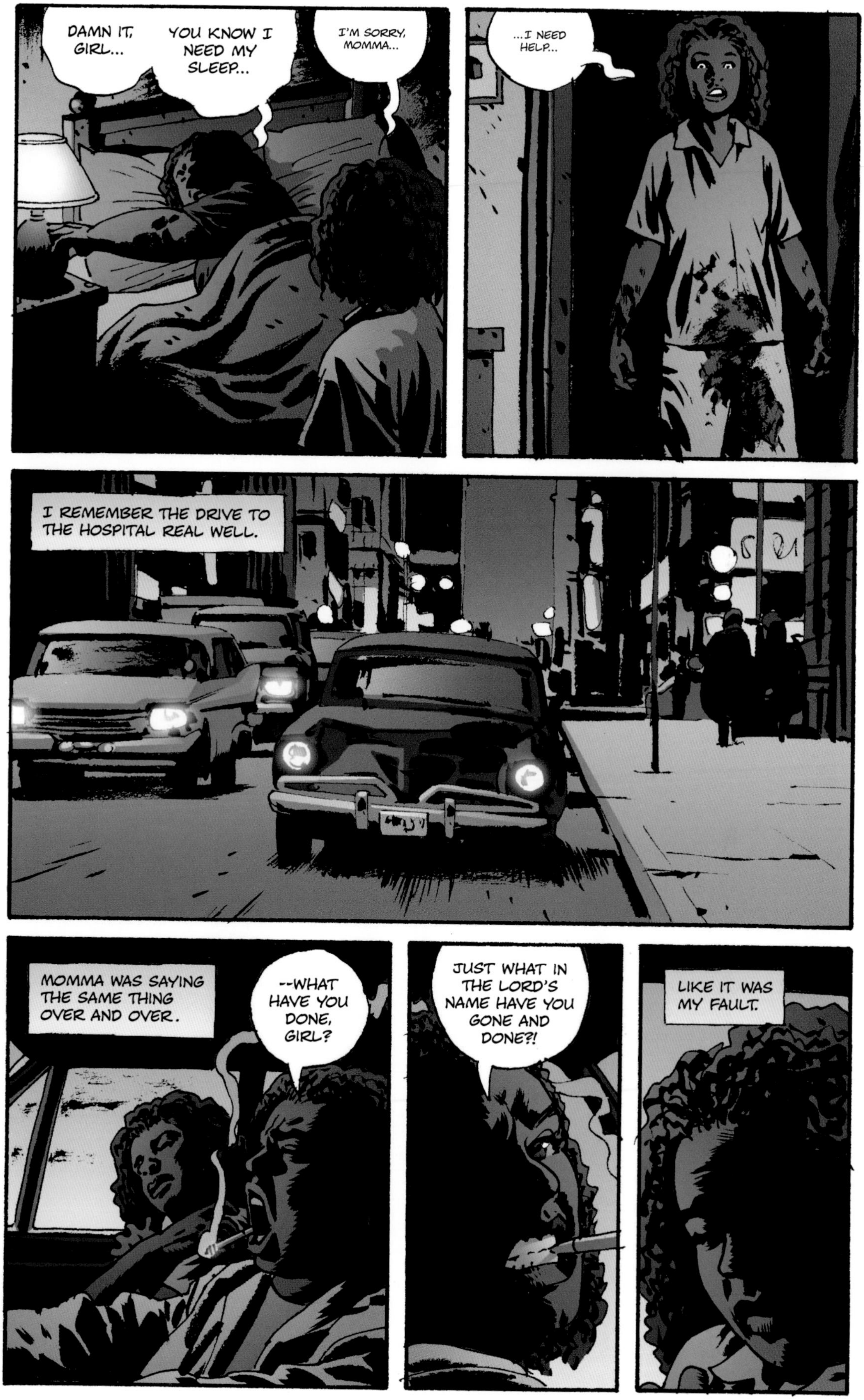
DAMN IT, GIRL...
YOU KNOW I NEED MY SLEEP...
I'M SORRY, MOMMA...
...I NEED HELP...
I REMEMBER THE DRIVE TO THE HOSPITAL REAL WELL.
MOMMA WAS SAYING THE SAME THING OVER AND OVER.
--WHAT HAVE YOU DONE, GIRL?
JUST WHAT IN THE LORD'S NAME HAVE YOU GONE AND DONE?!
LIKE IT WAS MY FAULT.

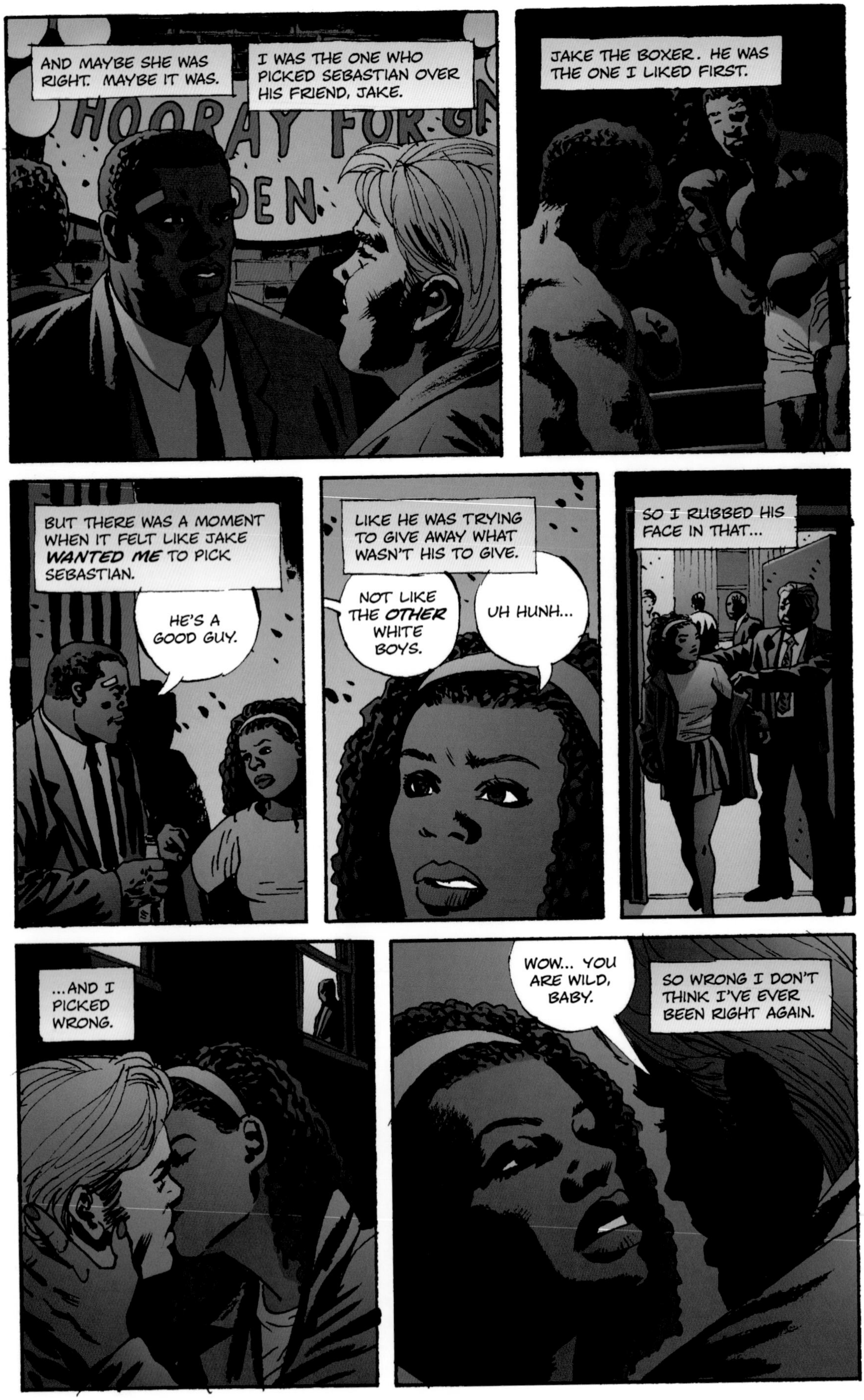
AND MAYBE SHE WAS RIGHT. MAYBE IT WAS.
I WAS THE ONE WHO PICKED SEBASTIAN OVER HIS FRIEND, JAKE.
JAKE THE BOXER. HE WAS THE ONE I LIKED FIRST.
BUT THERE WAS A MOMENT WHEN IT FELT LIKE JAKE WANTED ME TO PICK SEBASTIAN.
HE'S A GOOD GUY.
LIKE HE WAS TRYING TO GIVE AWAY WHAT WASN'T HIS TO GIVE.
NOT LIKE THE OTHER WHITE BOYS.
UH HUNH...
SO I RUBBED HIS FACE IN THAT...
...AND I PICKED WRONG.
WOW... YOU ARE WILD, BABY.
SO WRONG I DON'T THINK I'VE EVER BEEN RIGHT AGAIN.

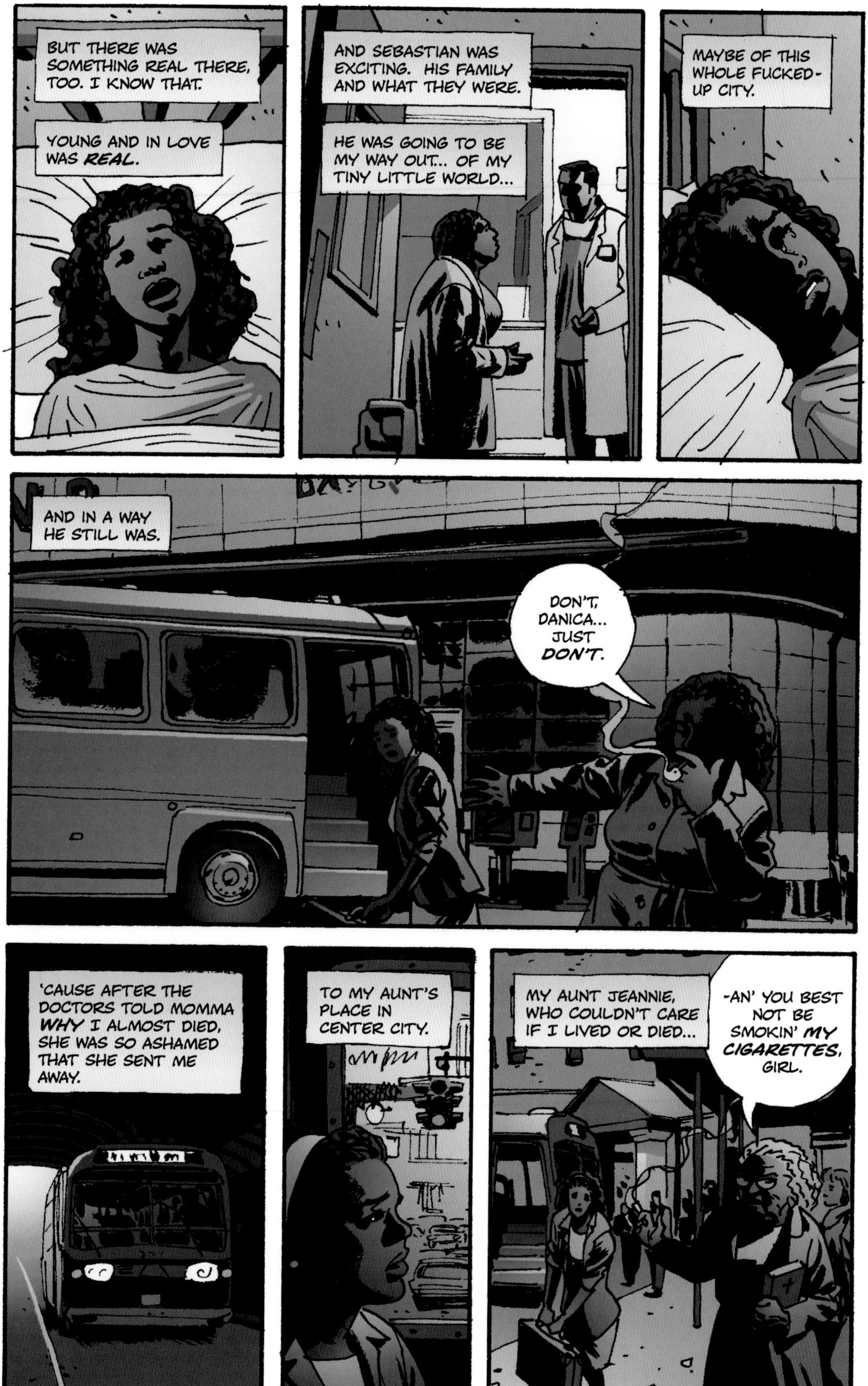
BUT THERE WAS SOMETHING REAL THERE, TOO. I KNOW THAT.
YOUNG AND IN LOVE WAS REAL.
AND SEBASTIAN WAS EXCITING. HIS FAMILY AND WHAT THEY WERE.
HE WAS GOING TO BE MY WAY OUT... OF MY TINY LITTLE WORLD...
MAYBE OF THIS WHOLE FUCKED-UP CITY.
AND IN A WAY HE STILL WAS.
DON'T, DANICA... JUST DON'T.
'CAUSE AFTER THE DOCTORS TOLD MOMMA WHY I ALMOST DIED, SHE WAS SO ASHAMED THAT SHE SENT ME AWAY.
TO MY AUNT'S PLACE IN CENTER CITY.
MY AUNT JEANNIE, WHO COULDN'T CARE IF I LIVED OR DIED...
-AN' YOU BEST NOT BE SMOKIN' MY CIGARETTES, GIRL.

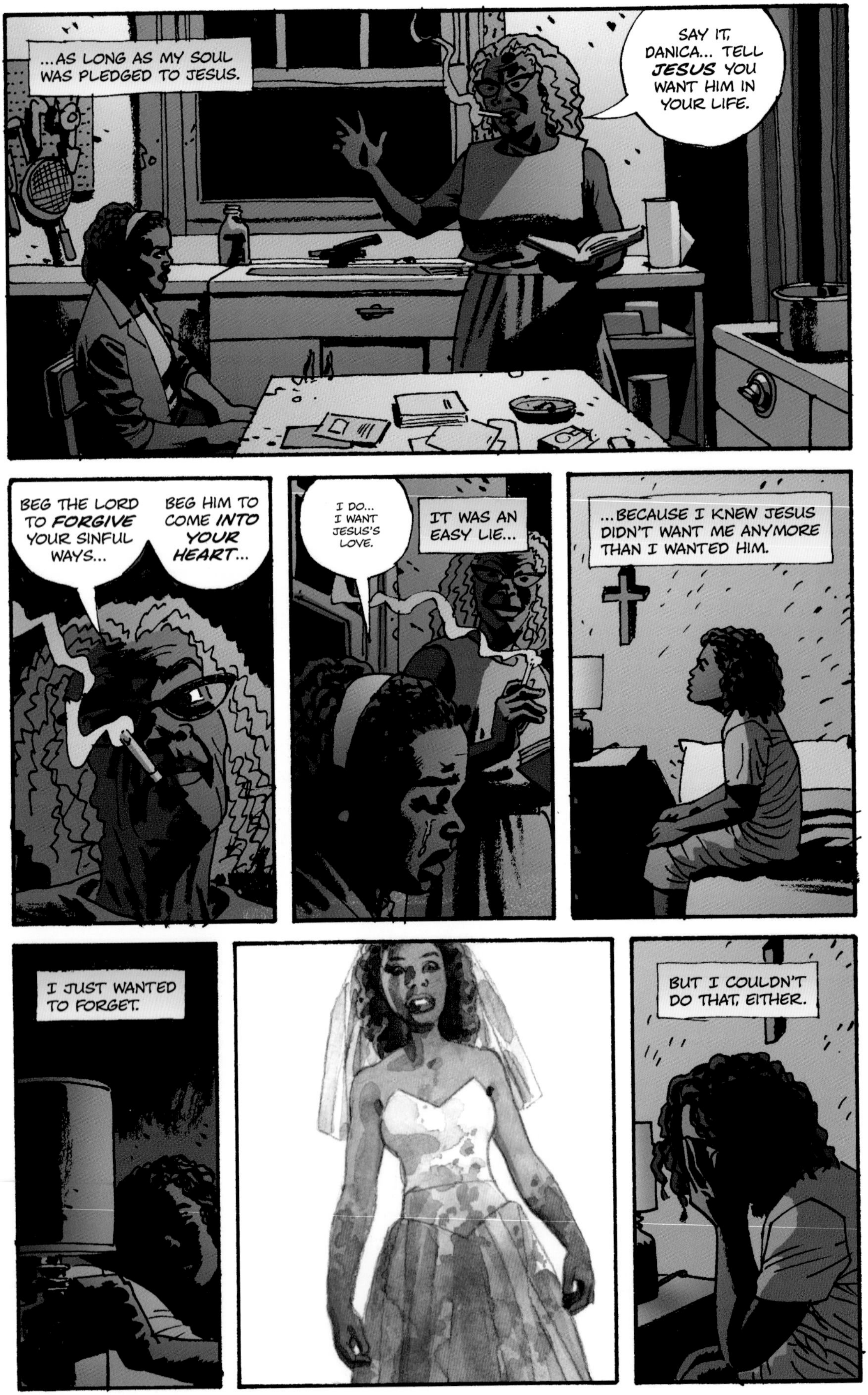
...AS LONG AS MY SOUL WAS PLEDGED TO JESUS.
SAY IT, DANICA... TELL JESUS YOU WANT HIM IN YOUR LIFE.
BEG THE LORD TO FORGIVE YOUR SINFUL WAYS...
BEG HIM TO COME INTO YOUR HEART...
I DO... I WANT JESUS'S LOVE.
IT WAS AN EASY LIE...
...BECAUSE I KNEW JESUS DIDN'T WANT ME ANYMORE THAN I WANTED HIM.
I JUST WANTED TO FORGET.
BUT I COULDN'T DO THAT, EITHER.

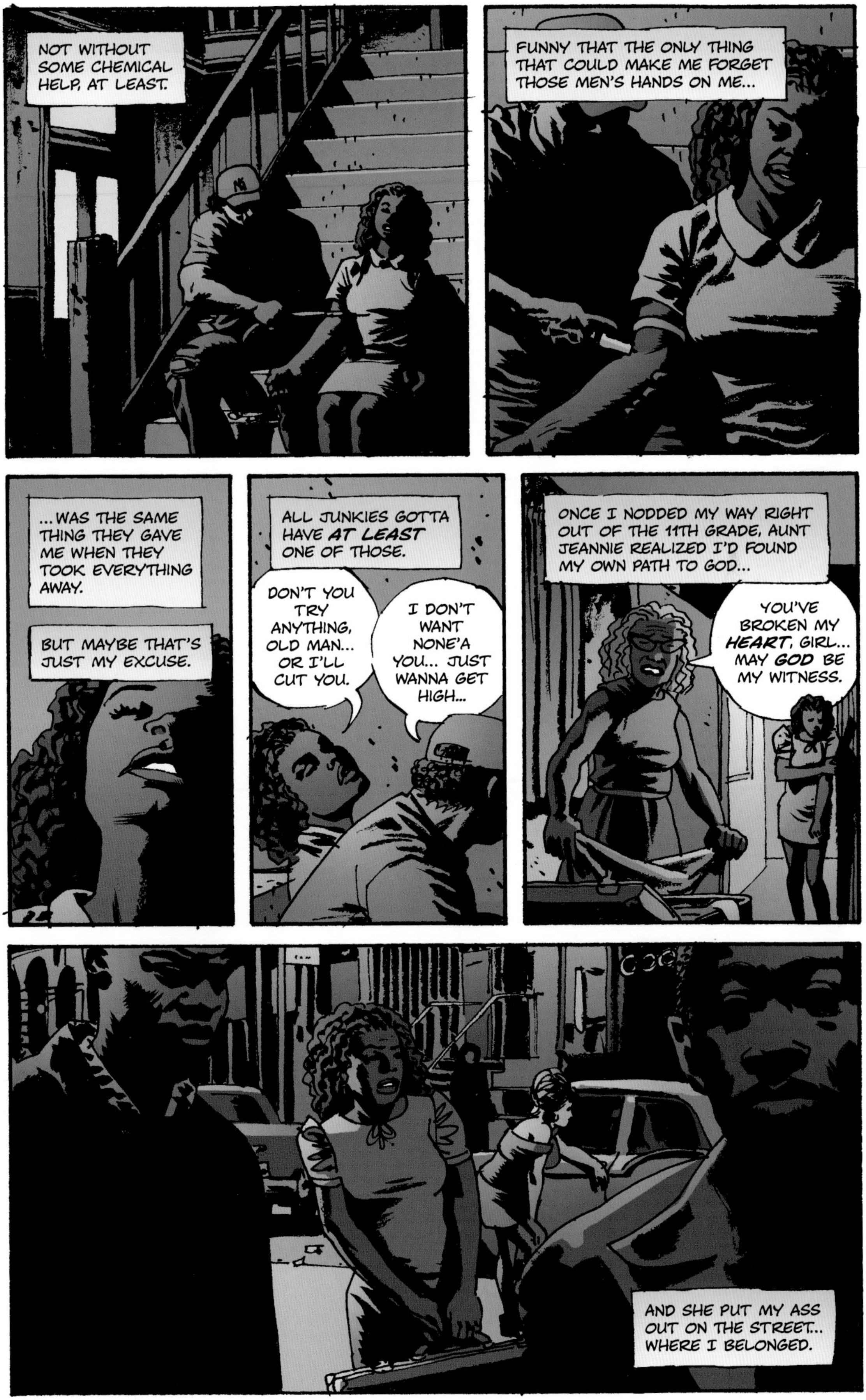
NOT WITHOUT SOME CHEMICAL HELP, AT LEAST.
FUNNY THAT THE ONLY THING THAT COULD MAKE ME FORGET THOSE MEN'S HANDS ON ME...
...WAS THE SAME THING THEY GAVE ME WHEN THEY TOOK EVERYTHING AWAY.
BUT MAYBE THAT'S JUST MY EXCUSE.
ALL JUNKIES GOTTA HAVE AT LEAST ONE OF THOSE.
DON'T YOU TRY ANYTHING, OLD MAN... OR I'LL CUT YOU.
I DON'T WANT NONE'A YOU... JUST WANNA GET HIGH...
ONCE I NODDED MY WAY RIGHT OUT OF THE 11TH GRADE, AUNT JEANNIE REALIZED I'D FOUND MY OWN PATH TO GOD...
YOU'VE BROKEN MY HEART, GIRL... MAY GOD BE MY WITNESS.
AND SHE PUT MY ASS OUT ON THE STREET... WHERE I BELONGED.

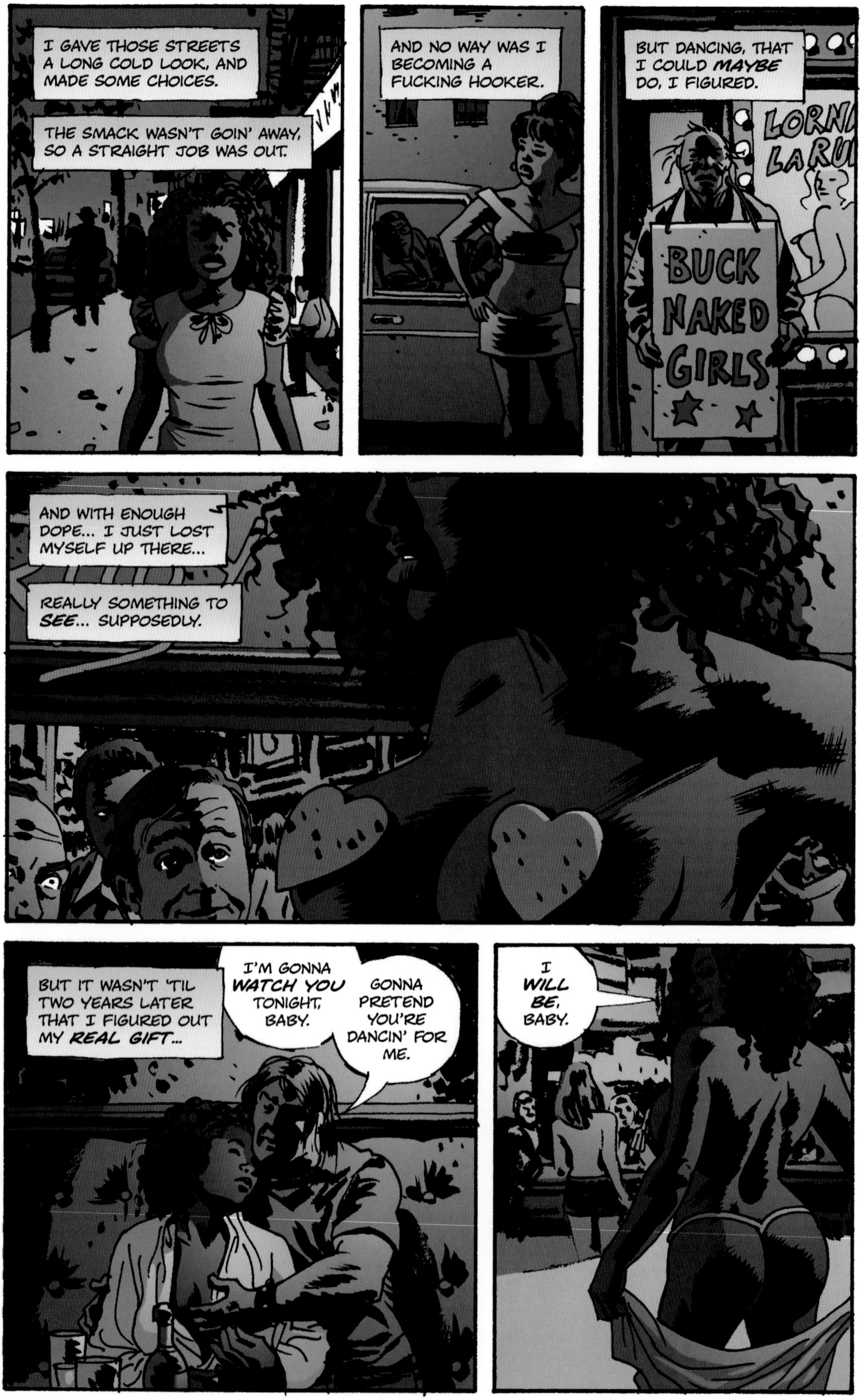
I GAVE THOSE STREETS A LONG COLD LOOK, AND MADE SOME CHOICES.
THE SMACK WASN'T GOIN' AWAY, SO A STRAIGHT JOB WAS OUT.
AND NO WAY WAS I BECOMING A FUCKING HOOKER.
BUT DANCING, THAT I COULD *MAYBE* DO, I FIGURED.
BUCK NAKED GIRLS
AND WITH ENOUGH DOPE... I JUST LOST MYSELF UP THERE...
REALLY SOMETHING TO *SEE*... SUPPOSEDLY.
BUT IT WASN'T 'TIL TWO YEARS LATER THAT I FIGURED OUT MY *REAL GIFT*...
I'M GONNA *WATCH YOU* TONIGHT, BABY.
GONNA PRETEND YOU'RE DANCIN' FOR ME.
I *WILL BE*, BABY.

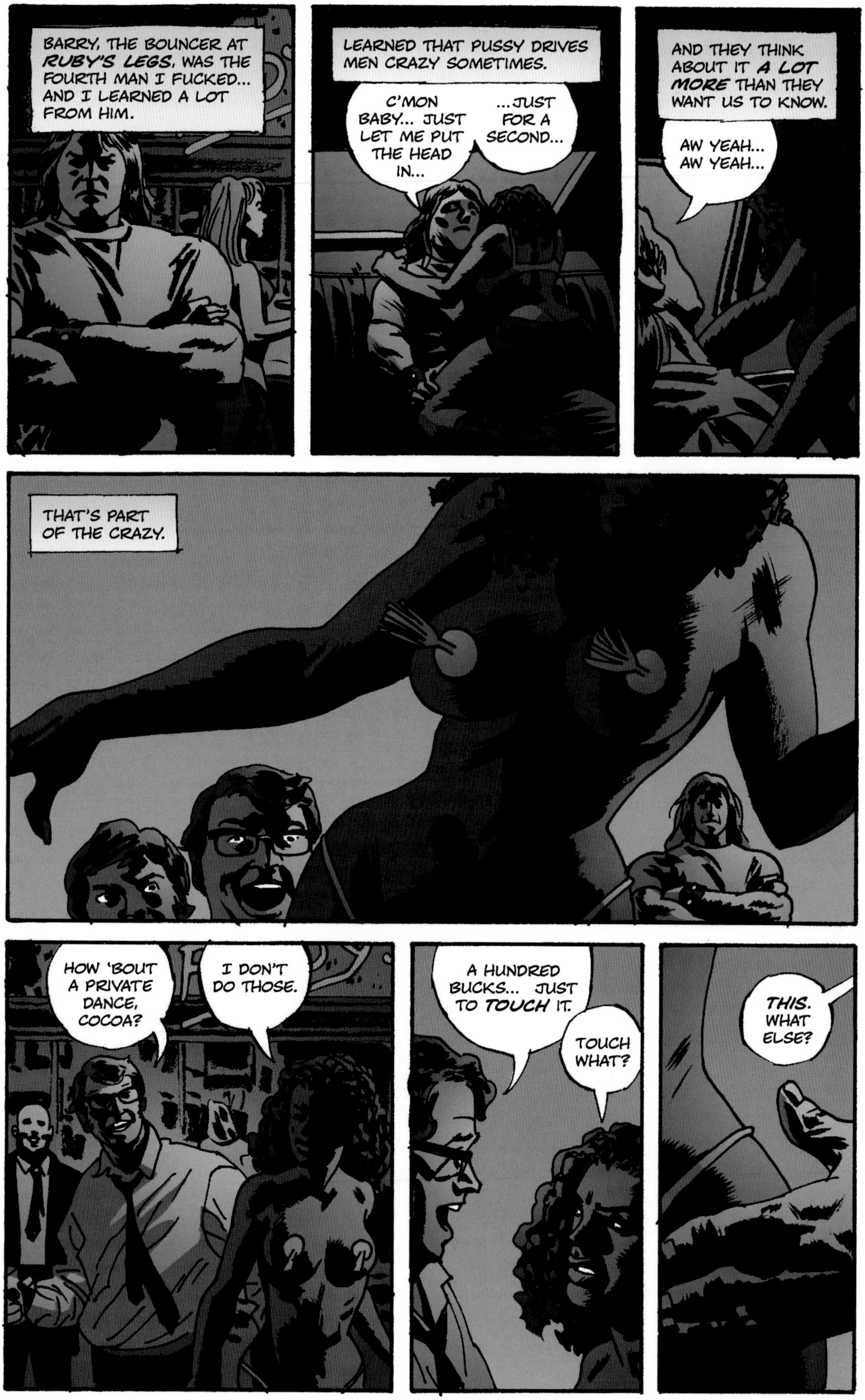
BARRY, THE BOUNCER AT *RUBY'S LEGS*, WAS THE FOURTH MAN I FUCKED... AND I LEARNED A LOT FROM HIM.
LEARNED THAT PUSSY DRIVES MEN CRAZY SOMETIMES.
C'MON BABY... JUST LET ME PUT THE HEAD IN...
...JUST FOR A SECOND...
AND THEY THINK ABOUT IT *A LOT MORE* THAN THEY WANT US TO KNOW.
AW YEAH... AW YEAH...
THAT'S PART OF THE CRAZY.
HOW 'BOUT A PRIVATE DANCE, COCOA?
I DON'T DO THOSE.
A HUNDRED BUCKS... JUST TO *TOUCH* IT.
TOUCH WHAT?
THIS. WHAT ELSE?

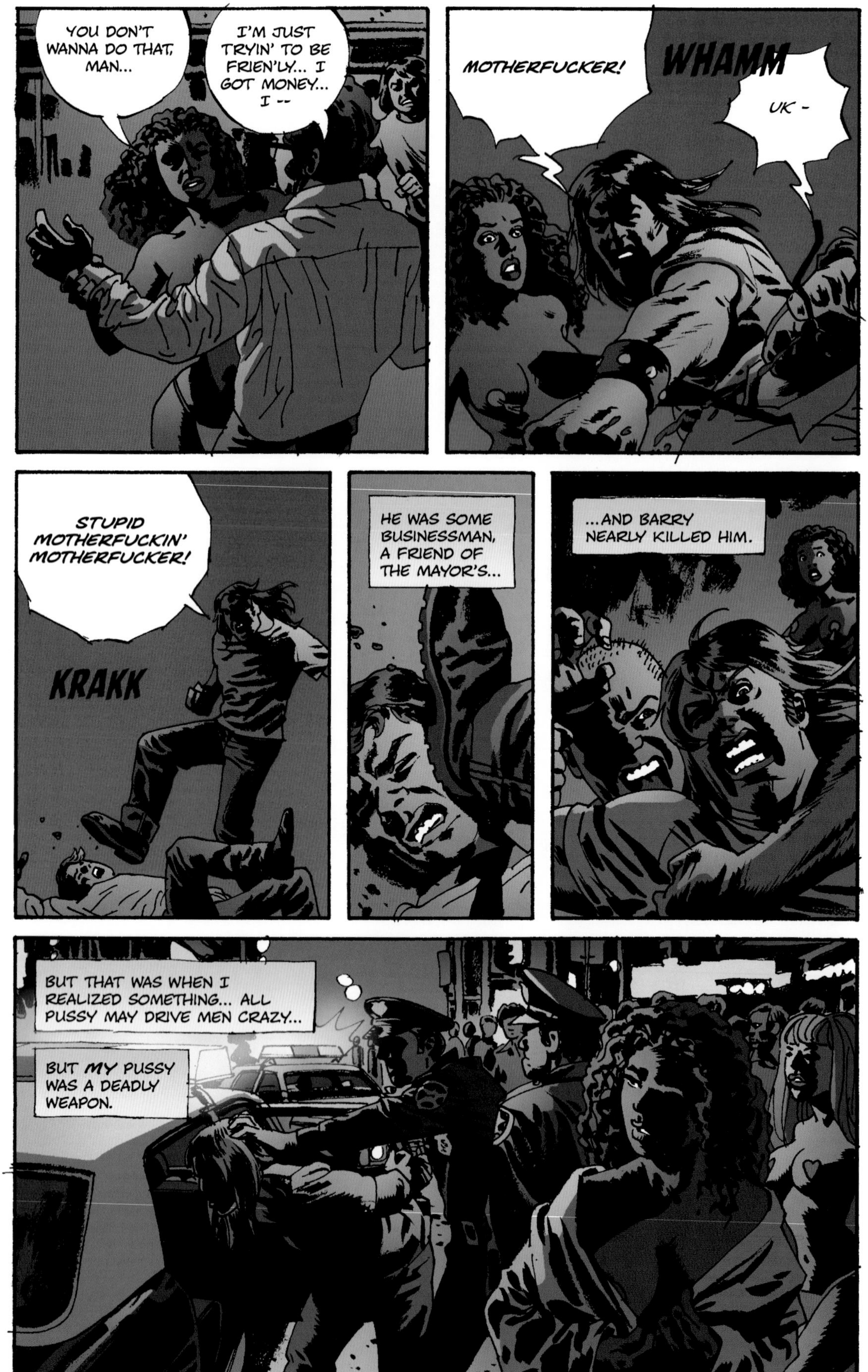
YOU DON'T WANNA DO THAT, MAN...
I'M JUST TRYIN' TO BE FRIEN'LY... I GOT MONEY... I --
MOTHERFUCKER!
WHAMM
UK -
STUPID MOTHERFUCKIN' MOTHERFUCKER!
KRAKK
HE WAS SOME BUSINESSMAN, A FRIEND OF THE MAYOR'S...
...AND BARRY NEARLY KILLED HIM.
BUT THAT WAS WHEN I REALIZED SOMETHING... ALL PUSSY MAY DRIVE MEN CRAZY...
BUT *MY* PUSSY WAS A DEADLY WEAPON.

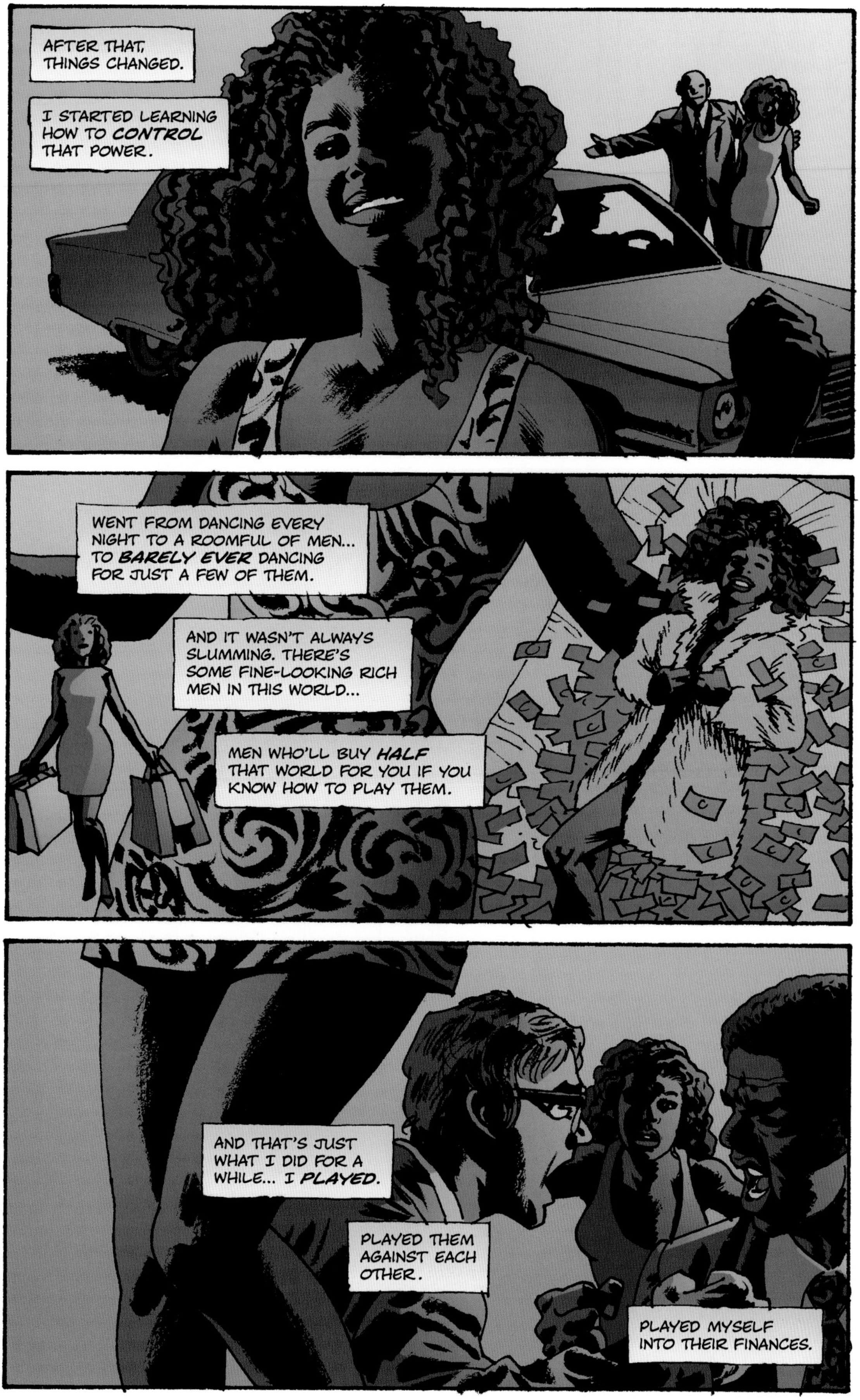
AFTER THAT, THINGS CHANGED.
I STARTED LEARNING HOW TO CONTROL THAT POWER.
WENT FROM DANCING EVERY NIGHT TO A ROOMFUL OF MEN... TO BARELY EVER DANCING FOR JUST A FEW OF THEM.
AND IT WASN'T ALWAYS SLUMMING. THERE'S SOME FINE-LOOKING RICH MEN IN THIS WORLD...
MEN WHO'LL BUY HALF THAT WORLD FOR YOU IF YOU KNOW HOW TO PLAY THEM.
AND THAT'S JUST WHAT I DID FOR A WHILE... I PLAYED.
PLAYED THEM AGAINST EACH OTHER.
PLAYED MYSELF INTO THEIR FINANCES.

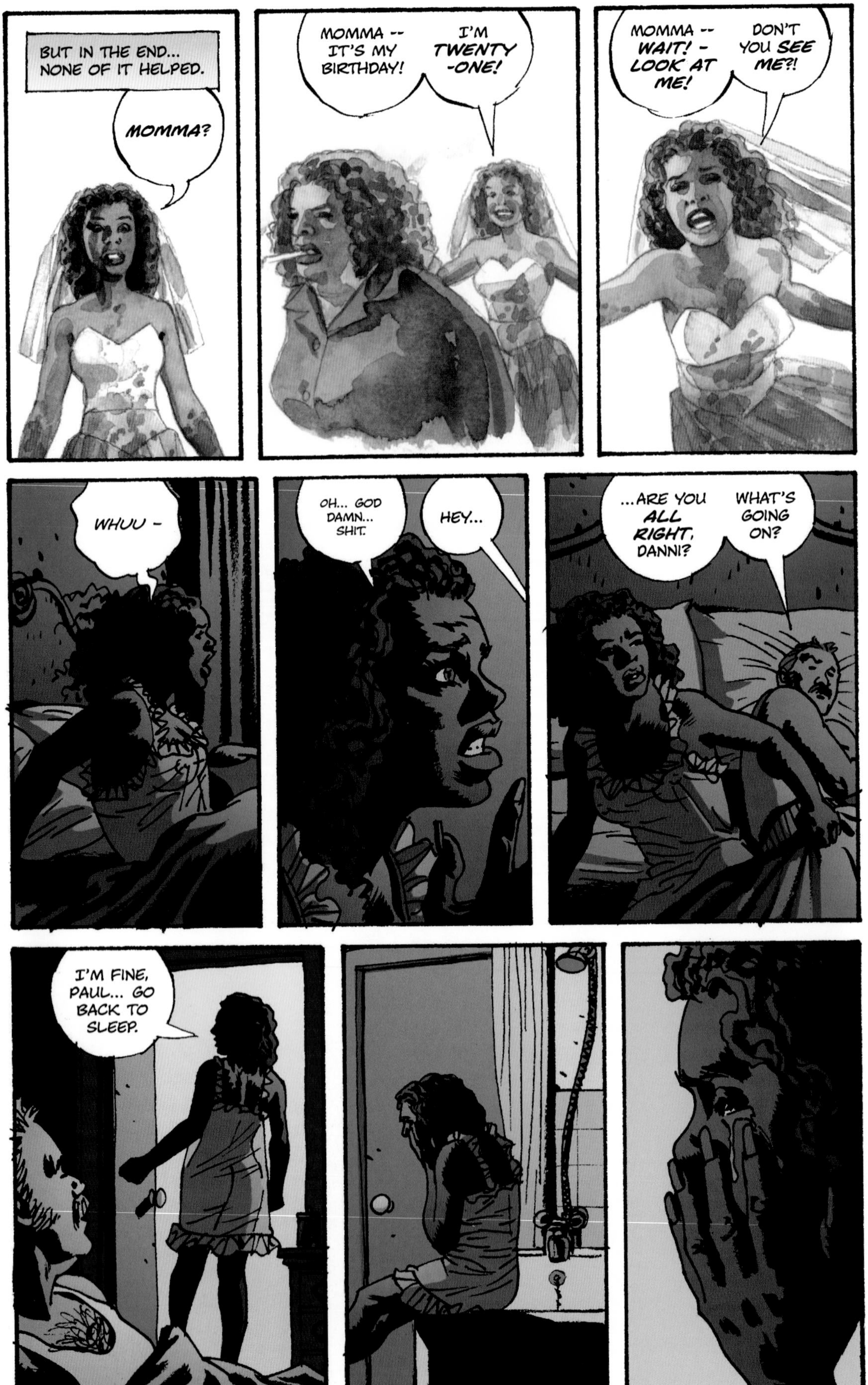
BUT IN THE END... NONE OF IT HELPED.
MOMMA?
MOMMA -- IT'S MY BIRTHDAY!
I'M TWENTY -ONE!
MOMMA -- WAIT! - LOOK AT ME!
DON'T YOU SEE ME?!
WHUU -
OH... GOD DAMN... SHIT.
HEY...
...ARE YOU ALL RIGHT, DANNI?
WHAT'S GOING ON?
I'M FINE, PAUL... GO BACK TO SLEEP.

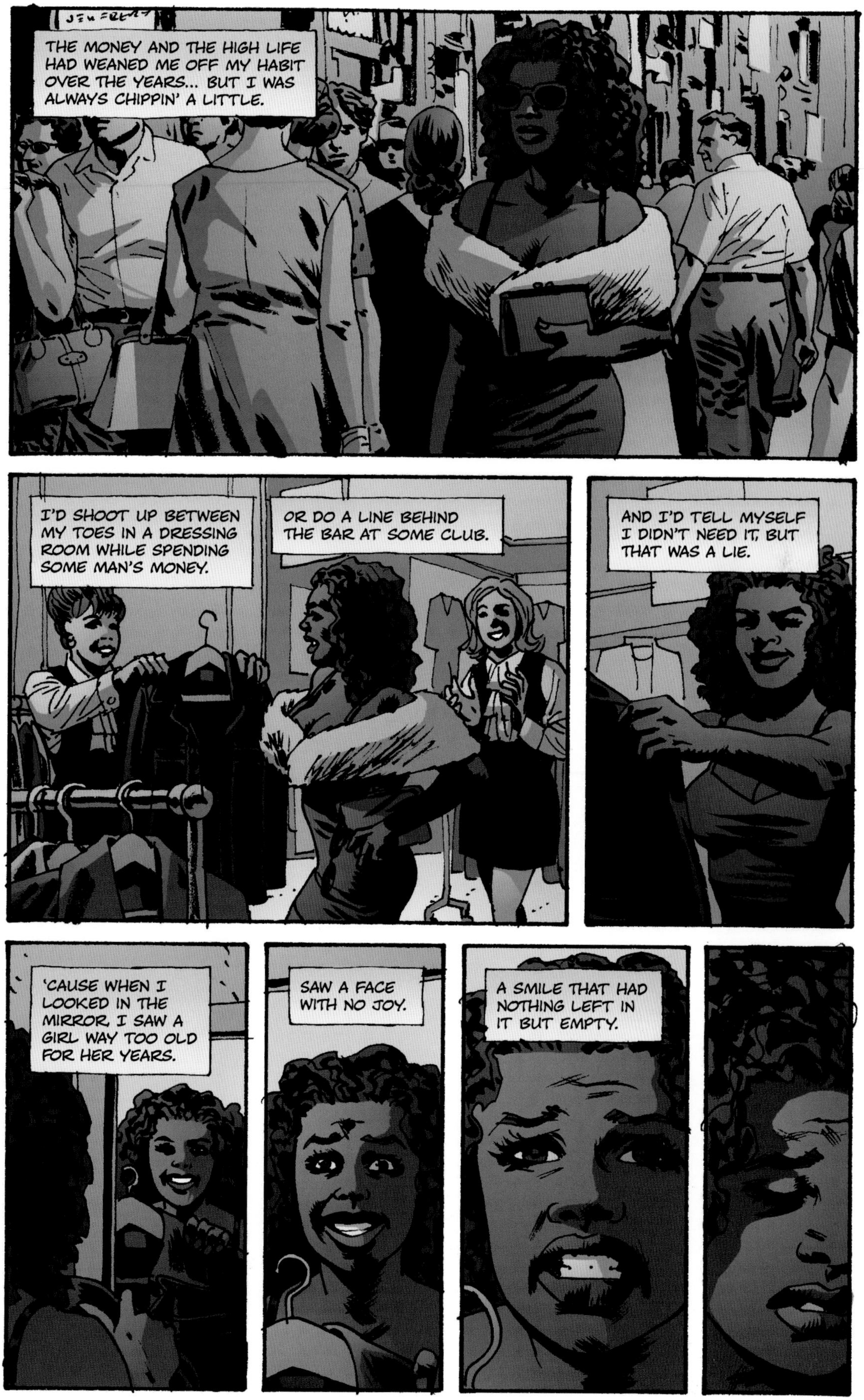
THE MONEY AND THE HIGH LIFE HAD WEANED ME OFF MY HABIT OVER THE YEARS... BUT I WAS ALWAYS CHIPPIN' A LITTLE.
I'D SHOOT UP BETWEEN MY TOES IN A DRESSING ROOM WHILE SPENDING SOME MAN'S MONEY.
OR DO A LINE BEHIND THE BAR AT SOME CLUB.
AND I'D TELL MYSELF I DIDN'T NEED IT, BUT THAT WAS A LIE.
'CAUSE WHEN I LOOKED IN THE MIRROR, I SAW A GIRL WAY TOO OLD FOR HER YEARS.
SAW A FACE WITH NO JOY.
A SMILE THAT HAD NOTHING LEFT IN IT BUT EMPTY.

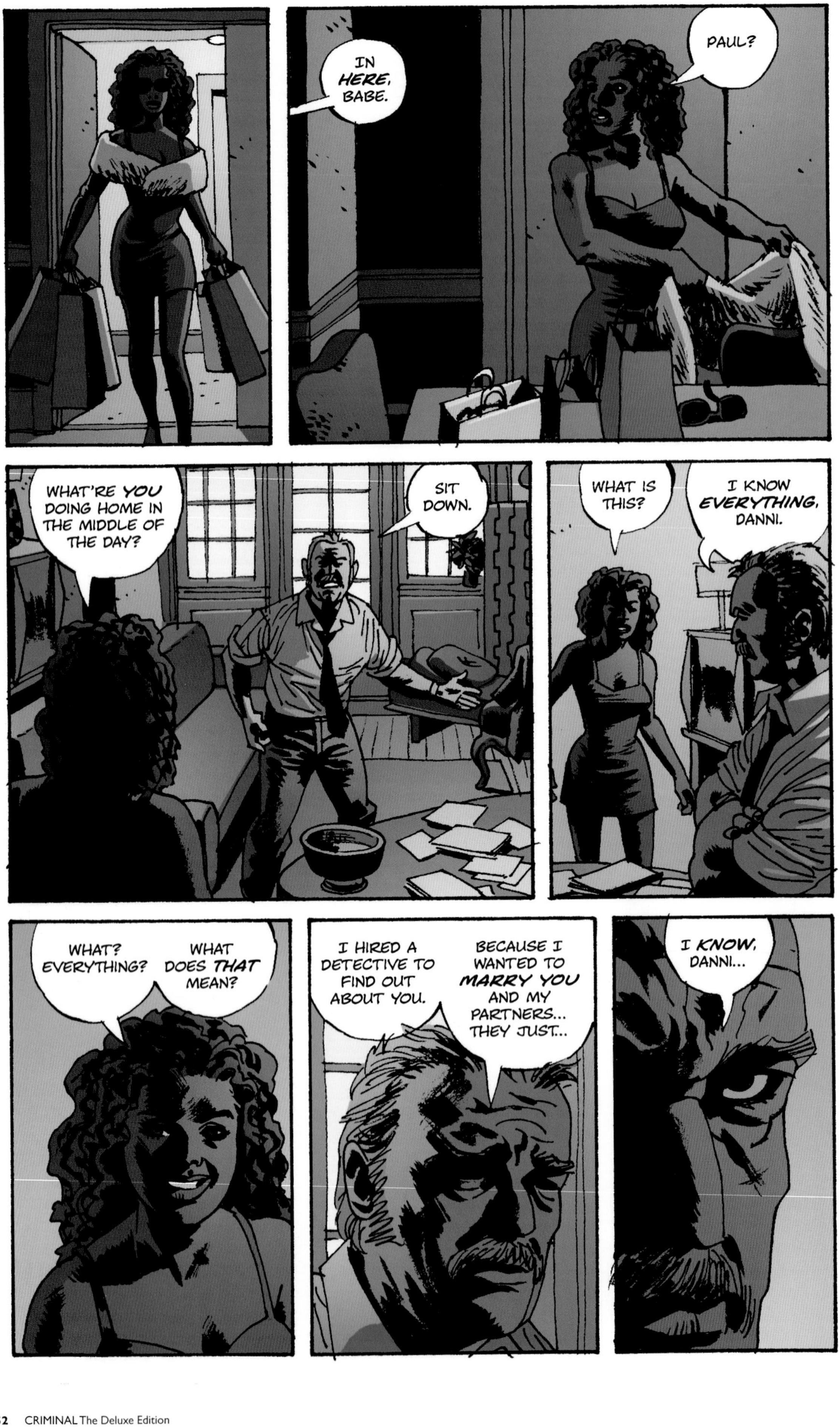
IN HERE, BABE.
PAUL?
WHAT'RE YOU DOING HOME IN THE MIDDLE OF THE DAY?
SIT DOWN.
WHAT IS THIS?
I KNOW EVERYTHING, DANNI.
WHAT? EVERYTHING?
WHAT DOES THAT MEAN?
I HIRED A DETECTIVE TO FIND OUT ABOUT YOU.
BECAUSE I WANTED TO MARRY YOU AND MY PARTNERS... THEY JUST...
I KNOW, DANNI...

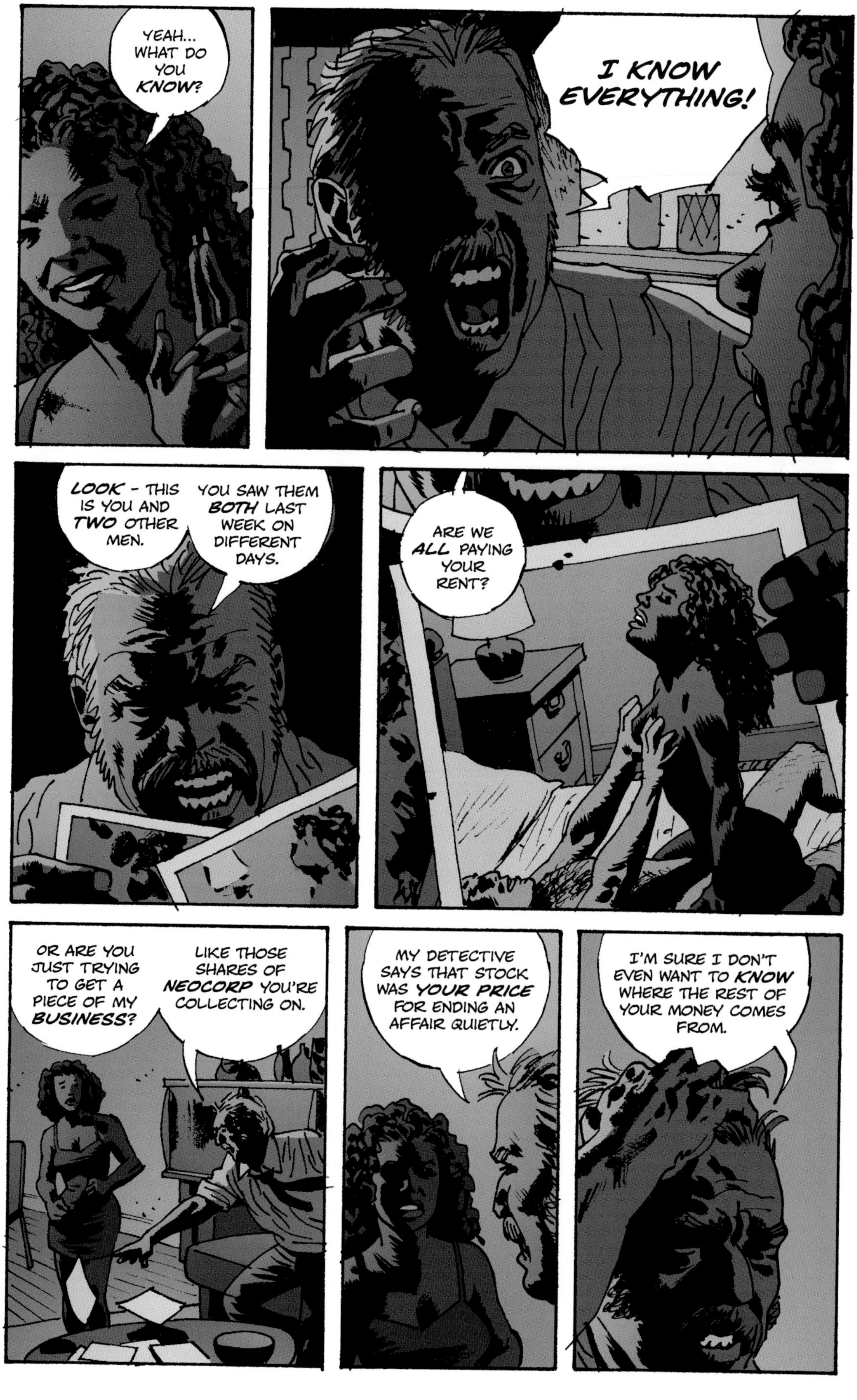
YEAH... WHAT DO YOU KNOW?
I KNOW EVERYTHING!
LOOK - THIS IS YOU AND TWO OTHER MEN.
YOU SAW THEM BOTH LAST WEEK ON DIFFERENT DAYS.
ARE WE ALL PAYING YOUR RENT?
OR ARE YOU JUST TRYING TO GET A PIECE OF MY BUSINESS?
LIKE THOSE SHARES OF NEOCORP YOU'RE COLLECTING ON.
MY DETECTIVE SAYS THAT STOCK WAS YOUR PRICE FOR ENDING AN AFFAIR QUIETLY.
I'M SURE I DON'T EVEN WANT TO KNOW WHERE THE REST OF YOUR MONEY COMES FROM.

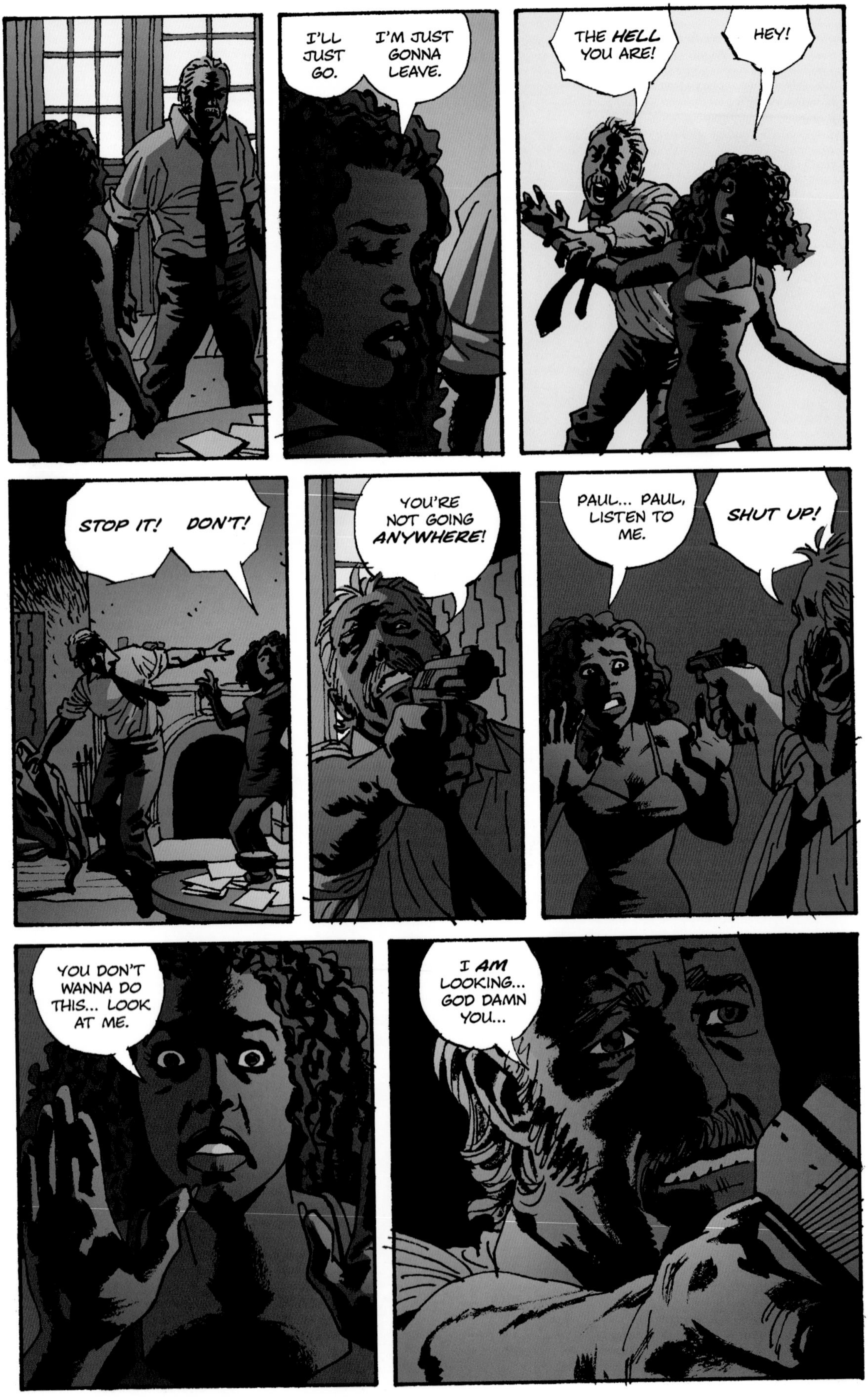
I'LL JUST GO.
I'M JUST GONNA LEAVE.
THE HELL YOU ARE!
HEY!
STOP IT!
DON'T!
YOU'RE NOT GOING ANYWHERE!
PAUL... PAUL, LISTEN TO ME.
SHUT UP!
YOU DON'T WANNA DO THIS... LOOK AT ME.
I AM LOOKING... GOD DAMN YOU...

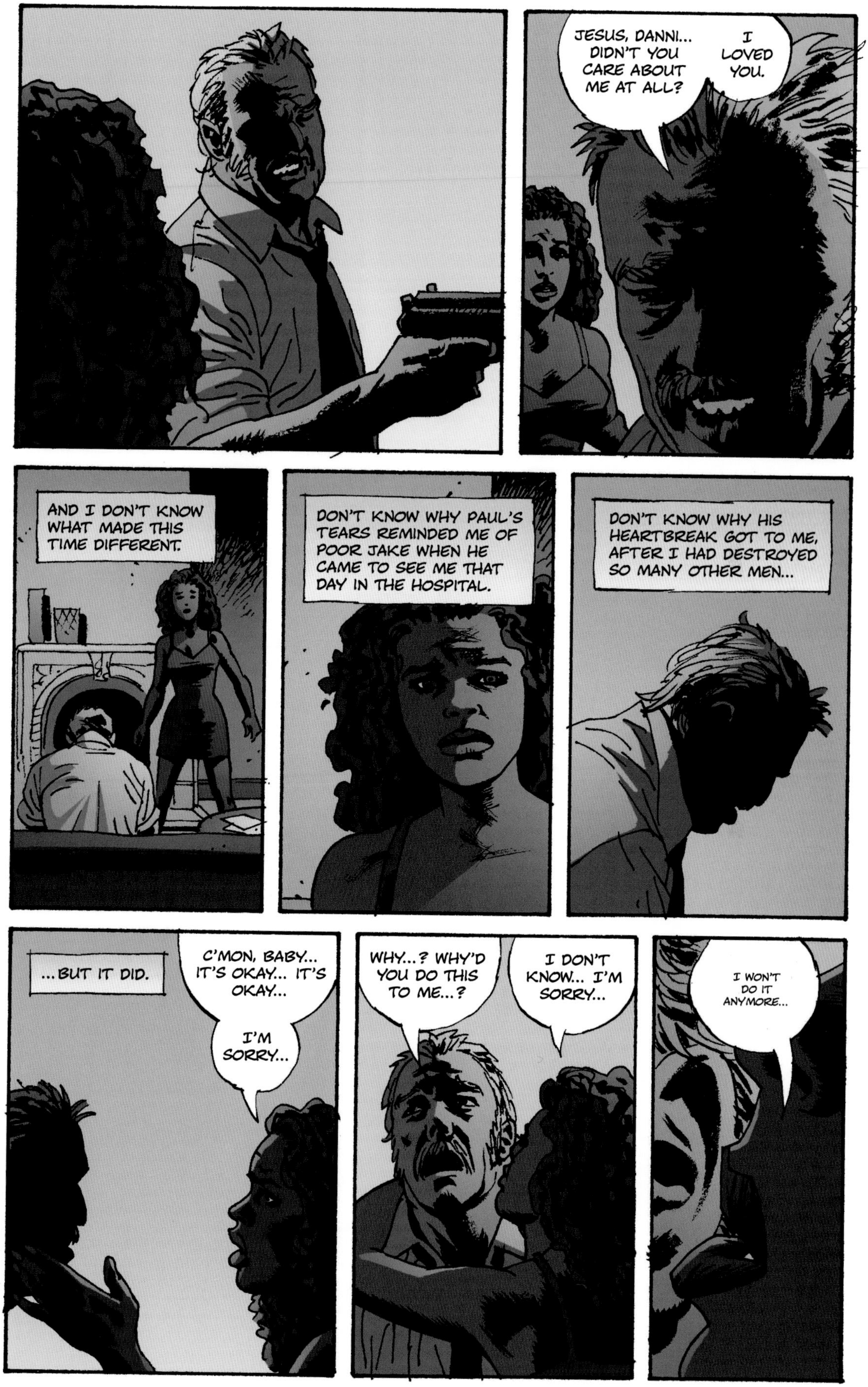
JESUS, DANNI... DIDN'T YOU CARE ABOUT ME AT ALL?
I LOVED YOU.
AND I DON'T KNOW WHAT MADE THIS TIME DIFFERENT.
DON'T KNOW WHY PAUL'S TEARS REMINDED ME OF POOR JAKE WHEN HE CAME TO SEE ME THAT DAY IN THE HOSPITAL.
DON'T KNOW WHY HIS HEARTBREAK GOT TO ME, AFTER I HAD DESTROYED SO MANY OTHER MEN...
...BUT IT DID.
C'MON, BABY... IT'S OKAY... IT'S OKAY...
I'M SORRY...
WHY...? WHY'D YOU DO THIS TO ME...?
I DON'T KNOW... I'M SORRY...
I WON'T DO IT ANYMORE...

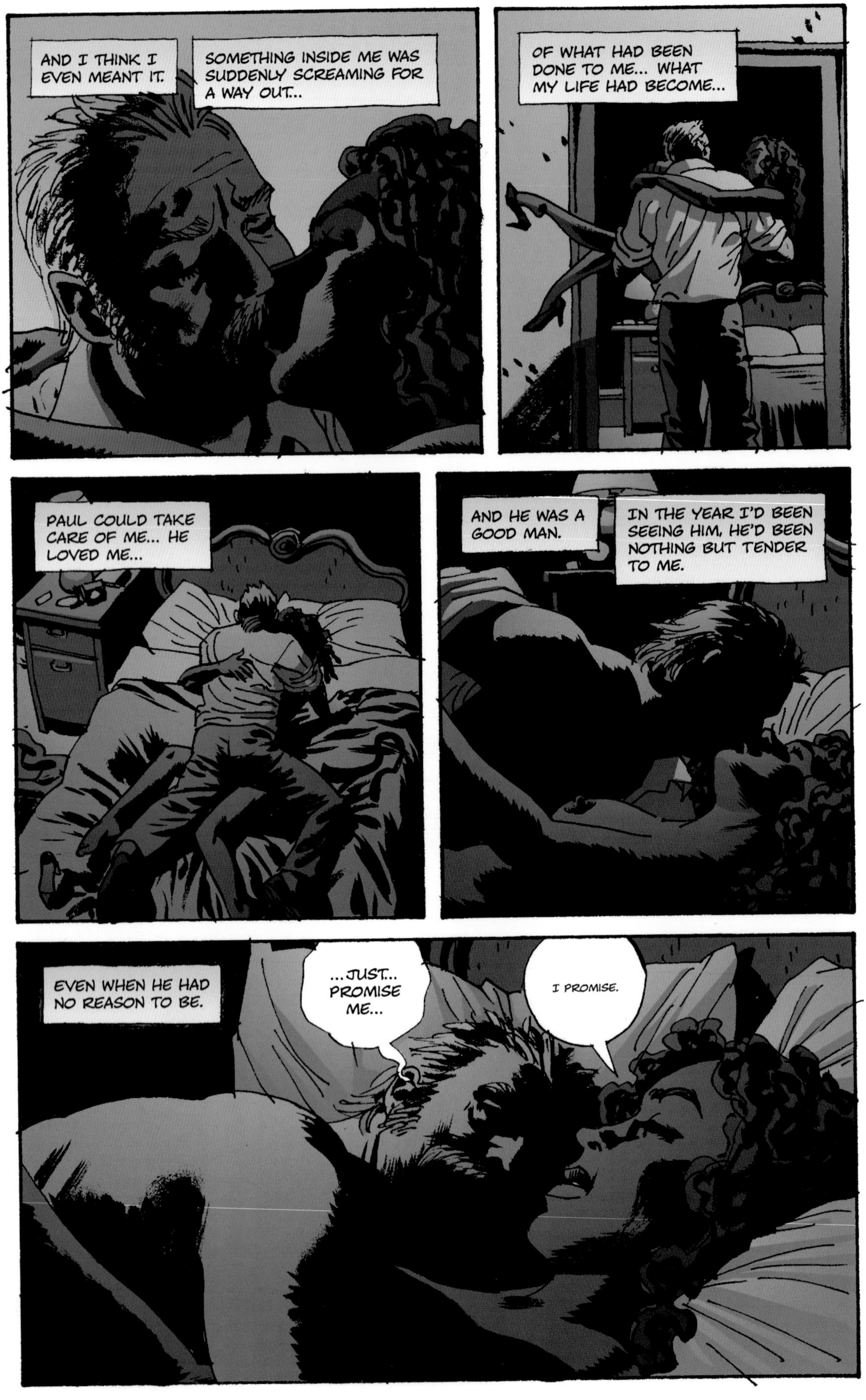

AND I THINK I EVEN MEANT IT.
SOMETHING INSIDE ME WAS SUDDENLY SCREAMING FOR A WAY OUT...
OF WHAT HAD BEEN DONE TO ME... WHAT MY LIFE HAD BECOME...
PAUL COULD TAKE CARE OF ME... HE LOVED ME...
AND HE WAS A GOOD MAN.
IN THE YEAR I'D BEEN SEEING HIM, HE'D BEEN NOTHING BUT TENDER TO ME.
EVEN WHEN HE HAD NO REASON TO BE.
...JUST... PROMISE ME...
I PROMISE.

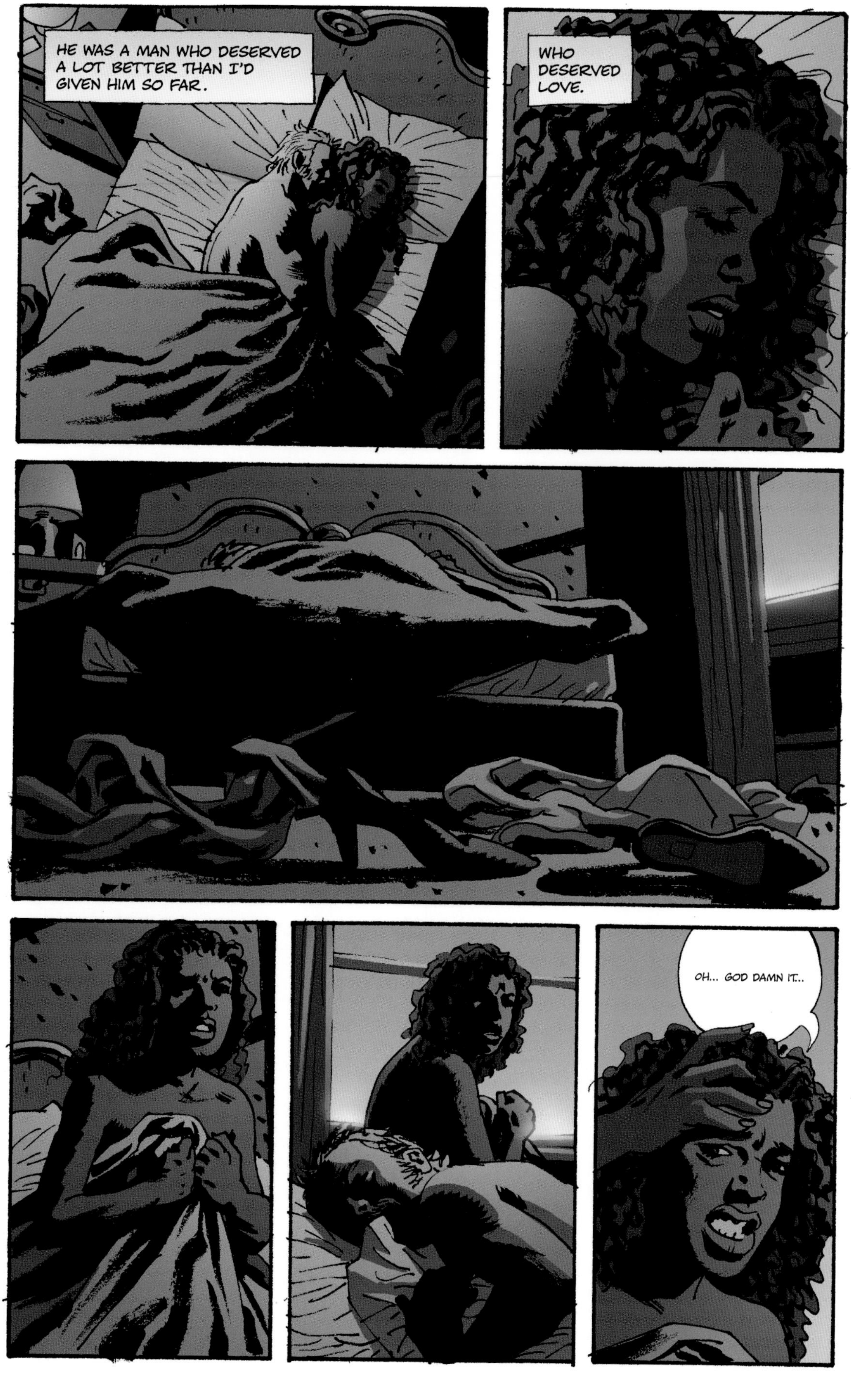
HE WAS A MAN WHO DESERVED A LOT BETTER THAN I'D GIVEN HIM SO FAR.
WHO DESERVED LOVE.
OH... GOD DAMN IT...

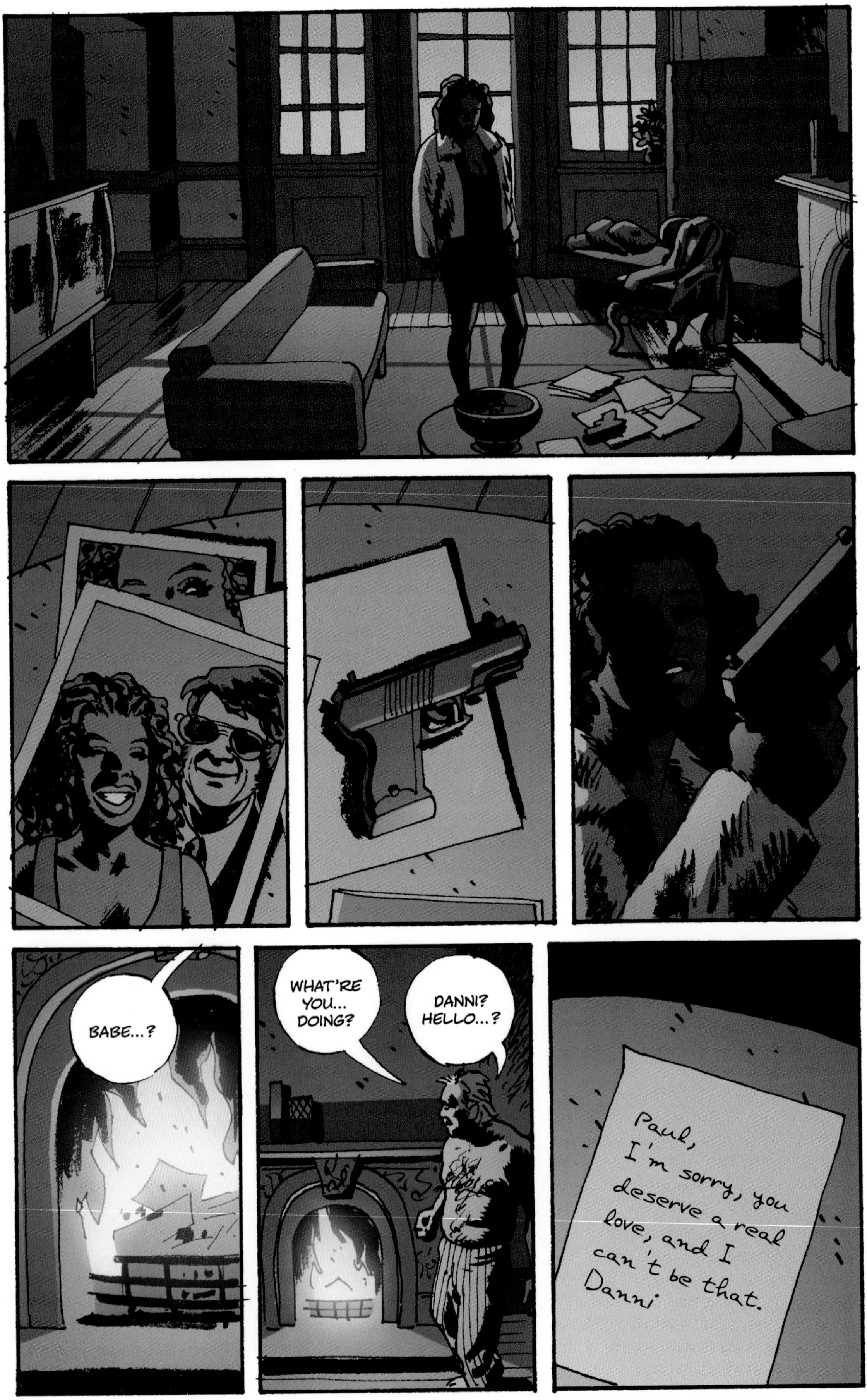
BABE...?
WHAT'RE YOU... DOING?
DANNI? HELLO...?
Paul,
I'm sorry, you deserve a real love, and I can't be that.
Danni

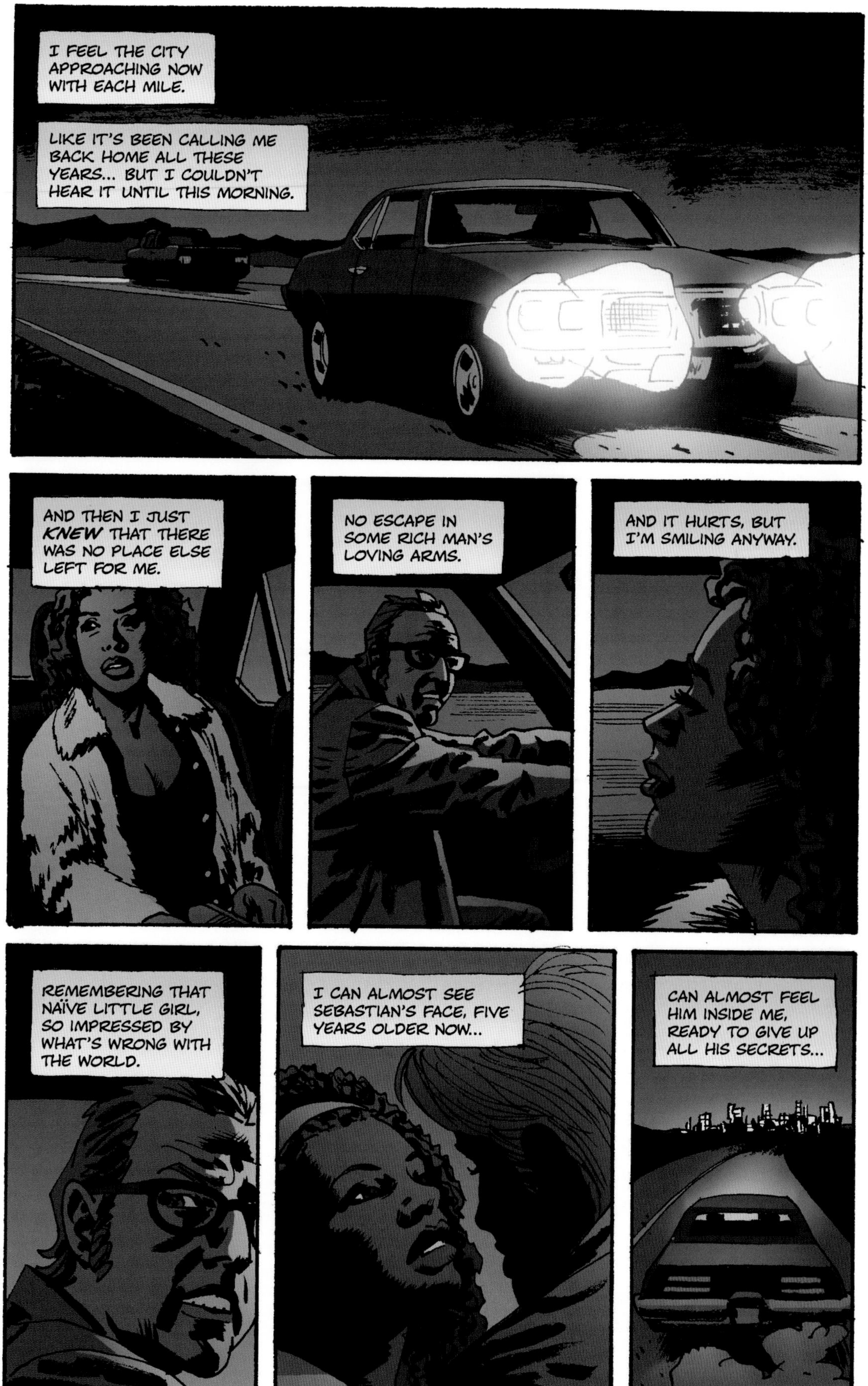
I FEEL THE CITY APPROACHING NOW WITH EACH MILE.
LIKE IT'S BEEN CALLING ME BACK HOME ALL THESE YEARS... BUT I COULDN'T HEAR IT UNTIL THIS MORNING.
AND THEN I JUST *KNEW* THAT THERE WAS NO PLACE ELSE LEFT FOR ME.
NO ESCAPE IN SOME RICH MAN'S LOVING ARMS.
AND IT HURTS, BUT I'M SMILING ANYWAY.
REMEMBERING THAT NAÏVE LITTLE GIRL, SO IMPRESSED BY WHAT'S WRONG WITH THE WORLD.
I CAN ALMOST SEE SEBASTIAN'S FACE, FIVE YEARS OLDER NOW...
CAN ALMOST FEEL HIM INSIDE ME, READY TO GIVE UP ALL HIS SECRETS...

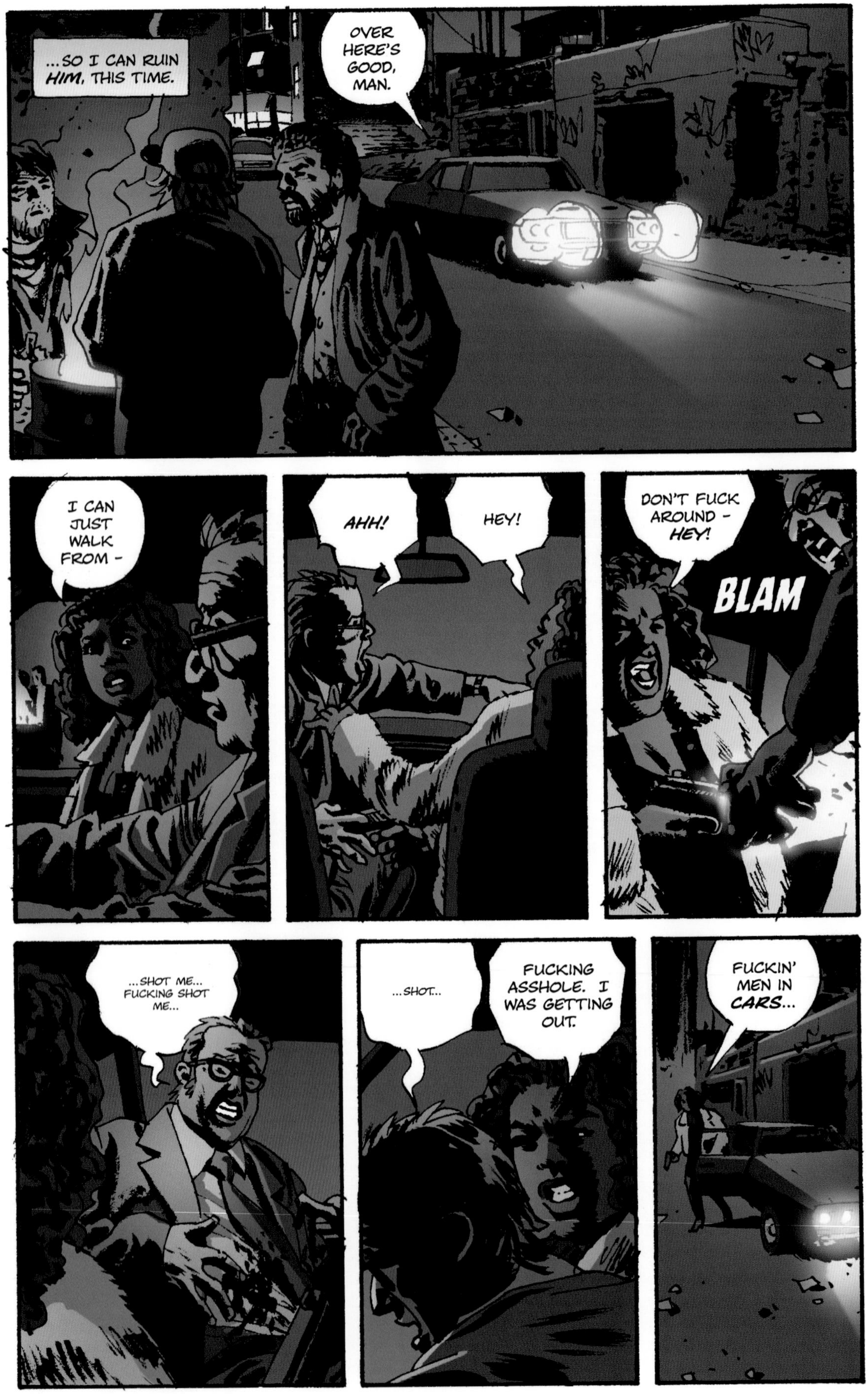
...SO I CAN RUIN HIM, THIS TIME.
OVER HERE'S GOOD, MAN.
I CAN JUST WALK FROM -
AHH!
HEY!
DON'T FUCK AROUND - HEY!
BLAM
...SHOT ME... FUCKING SHOT ME...
...SHOT...
FUCKING ASSHOLE. I WAS GETTING OUT.
FUCKIN' MEN IN CARS...

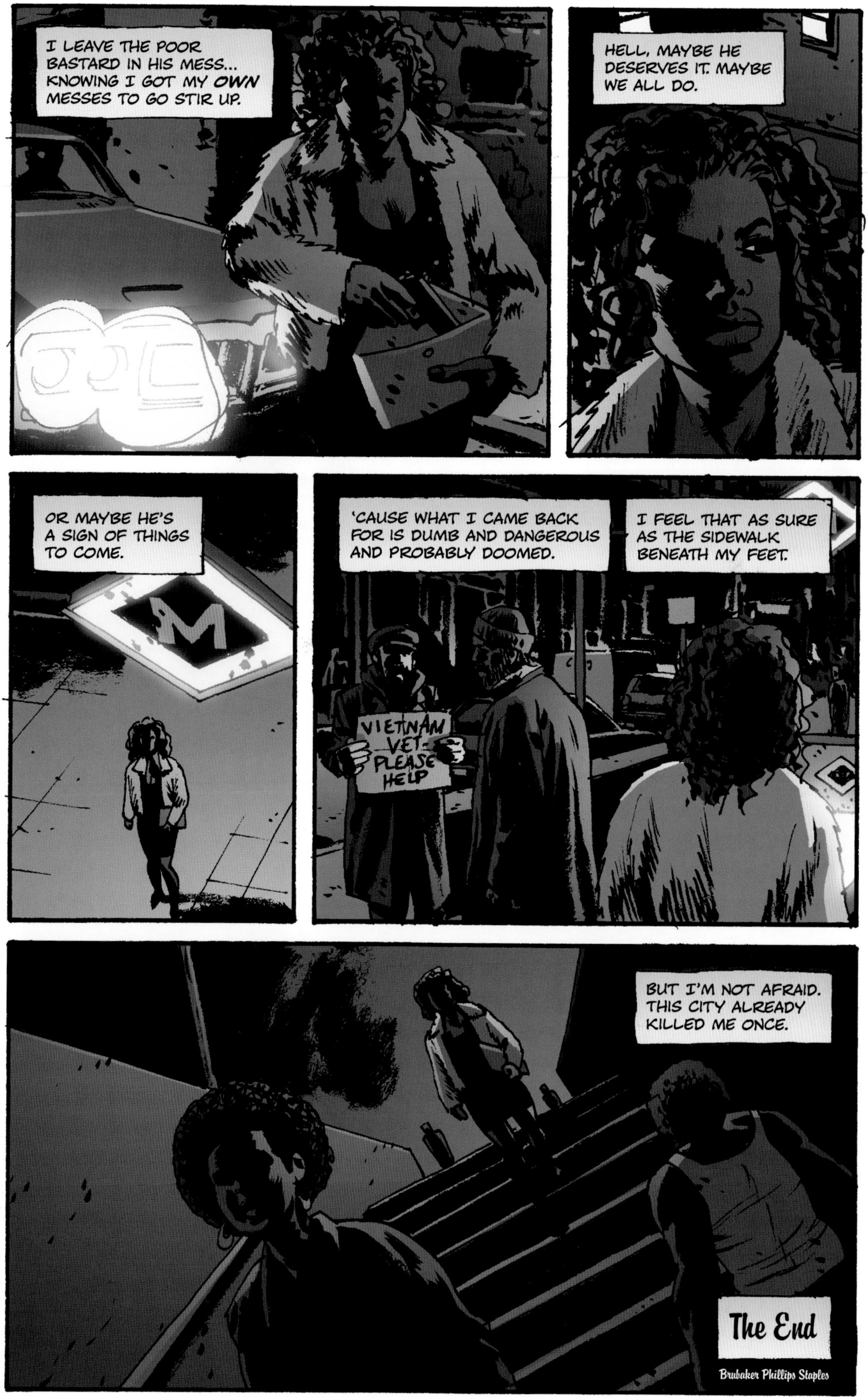
I LEAVE THE POOR BASTARD IN HIS MESS... KNOWING I GOT MY OWN MESSES TO GO STIR UP.
HELL, MAYBE HE DESERVES IT. MAYBE WE ALL DO.
OR MAYBE HE'S A SIGN OF THINGS TO COME.
M
'CAUSE WHAT I CAME BACK FOR IS DUMB AND DANGEROUS AND PROBABLY DOOMED.
I FEEL THAT AS SURE AS THE SIDEWALK BENEATH MY FEET.
VIETNAM VET- PLEASE HELP
BUT I'M NOT AFRAID. THIS CITY ALREADY KILLED ME ONCE.
The End
Brubaker Phillips Staples

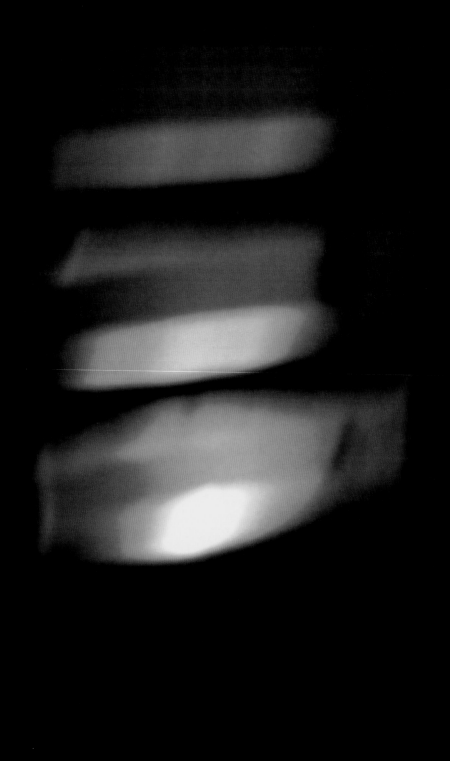

Extras

CRIMINAL #1 cover

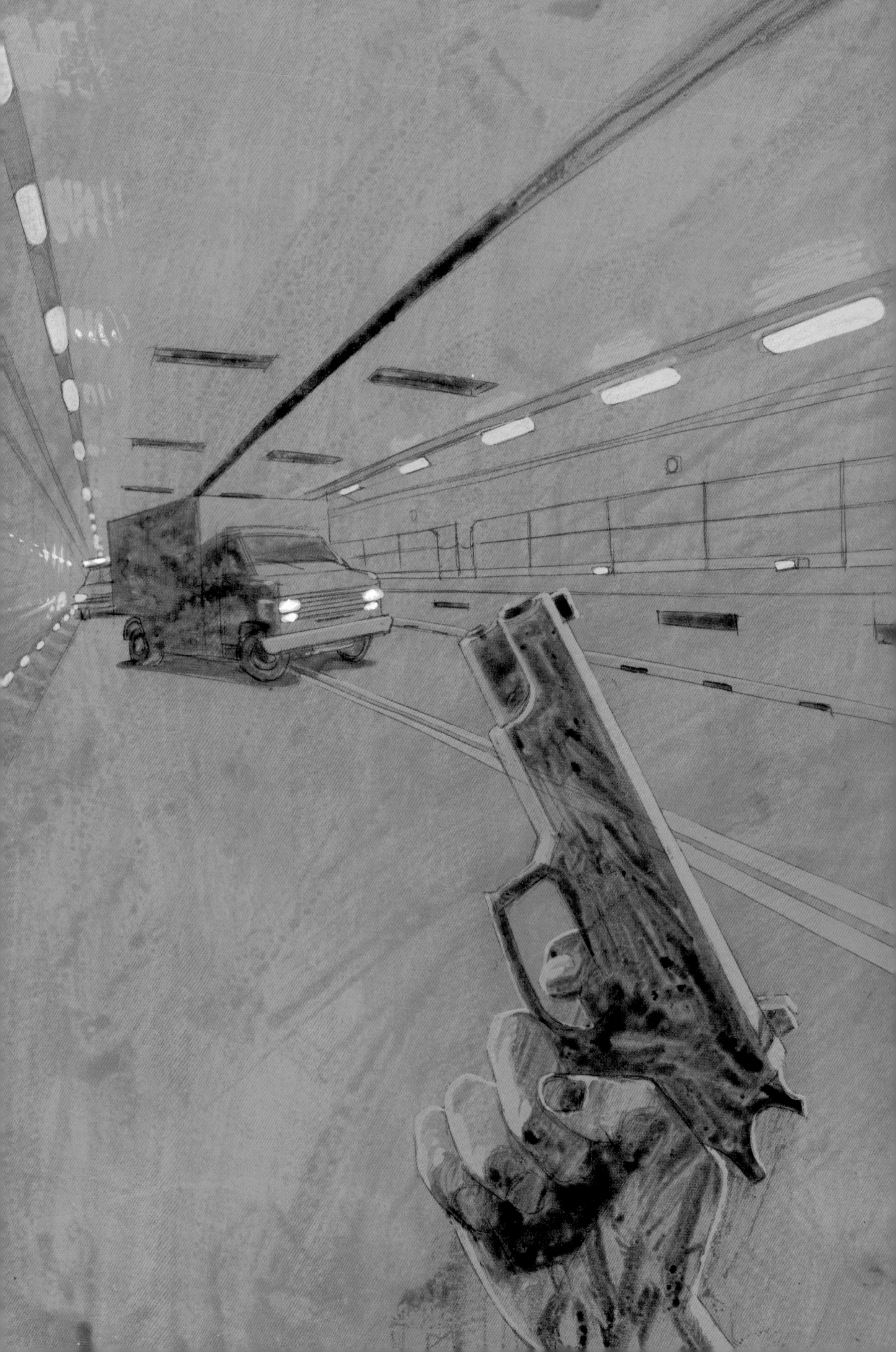

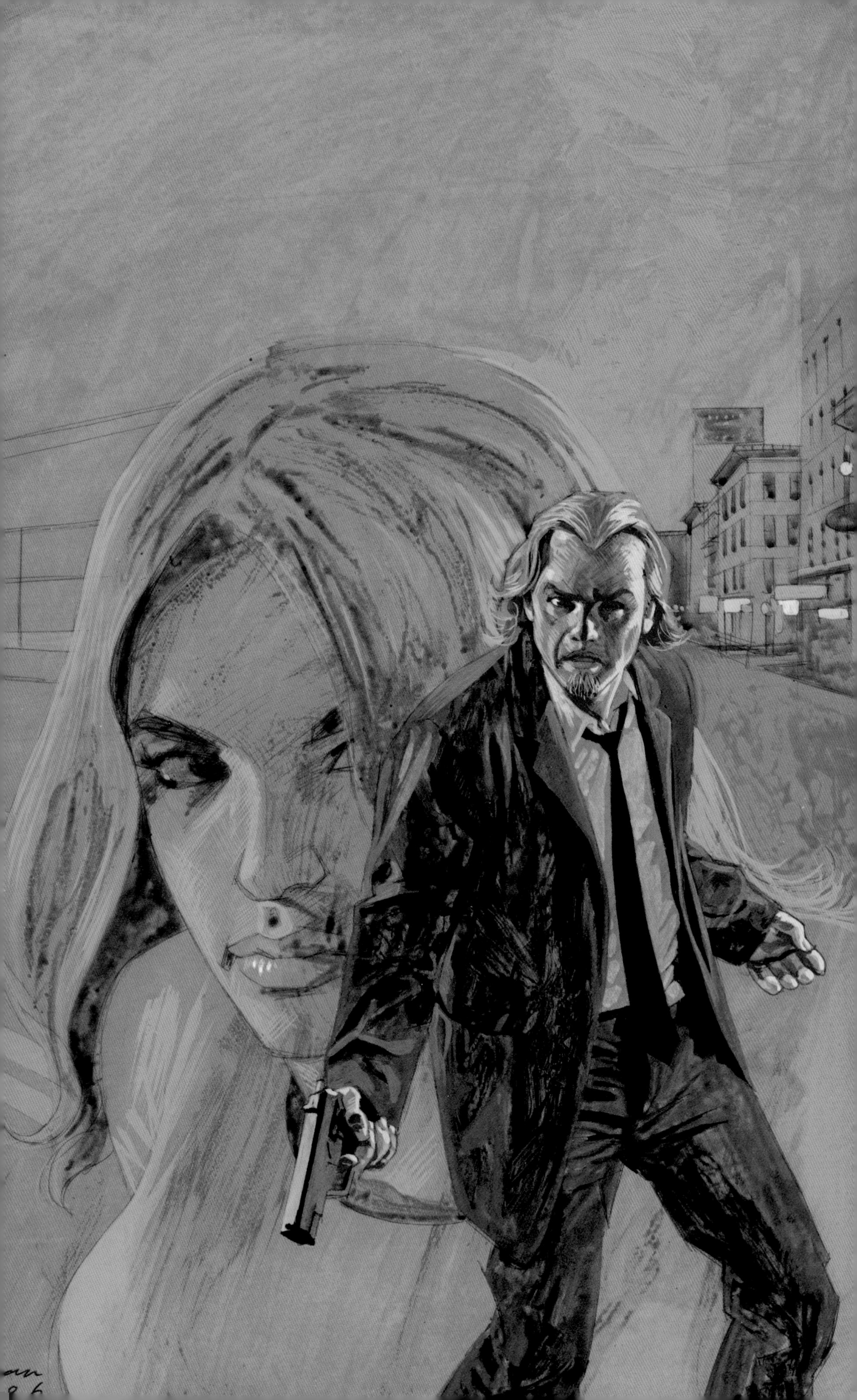

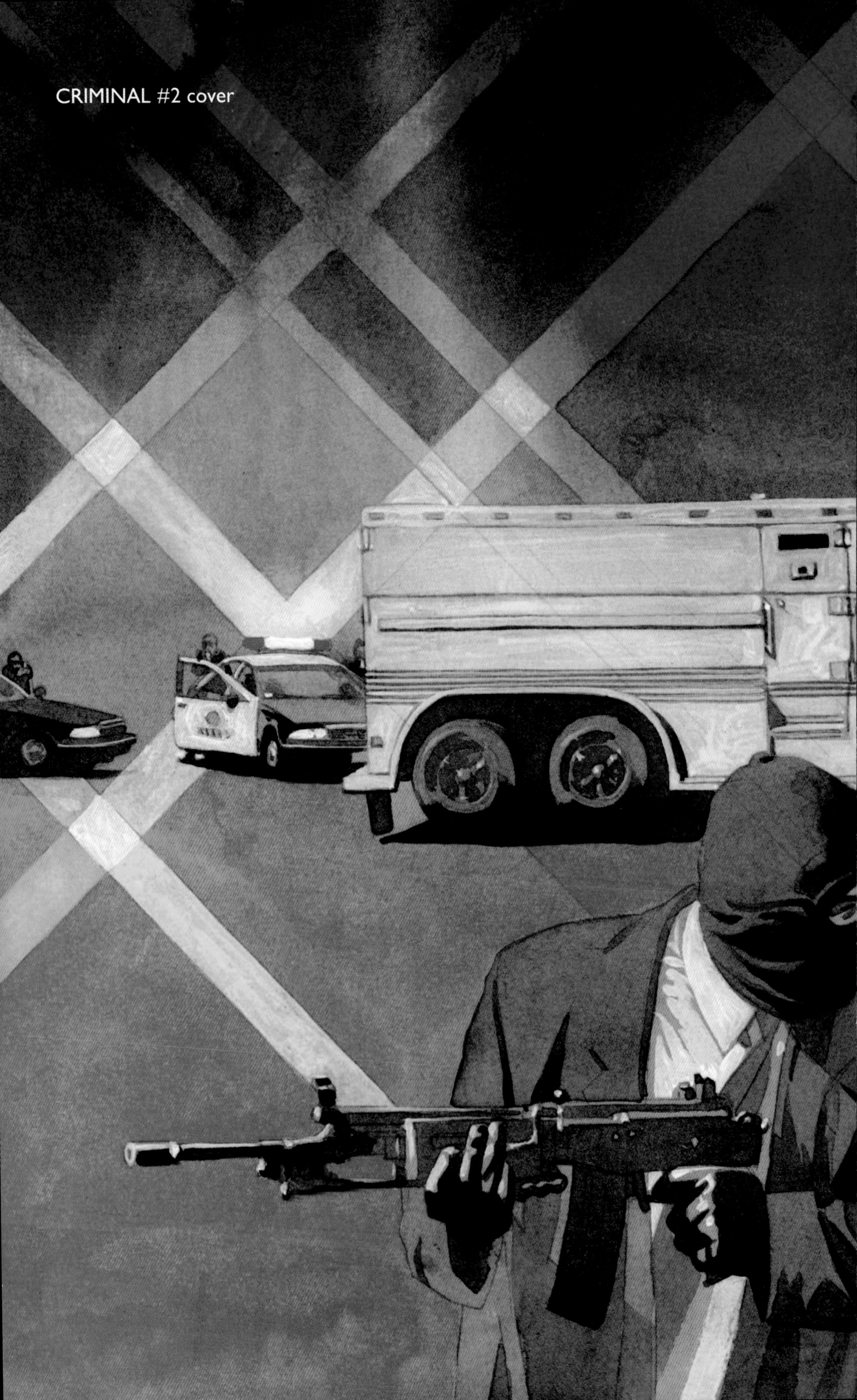
CRIMINAL #2 cover

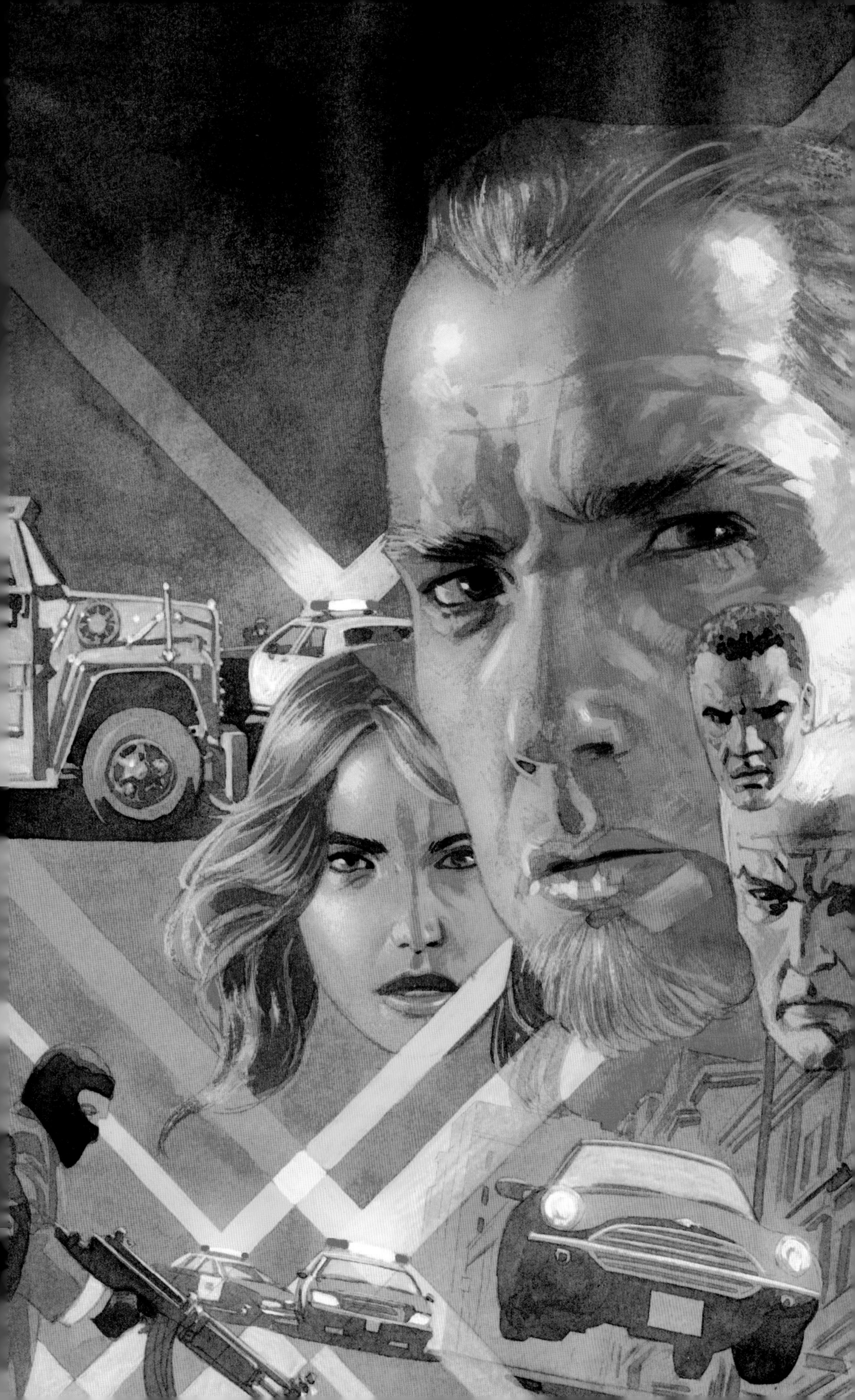

CRIMINAL #3 cover

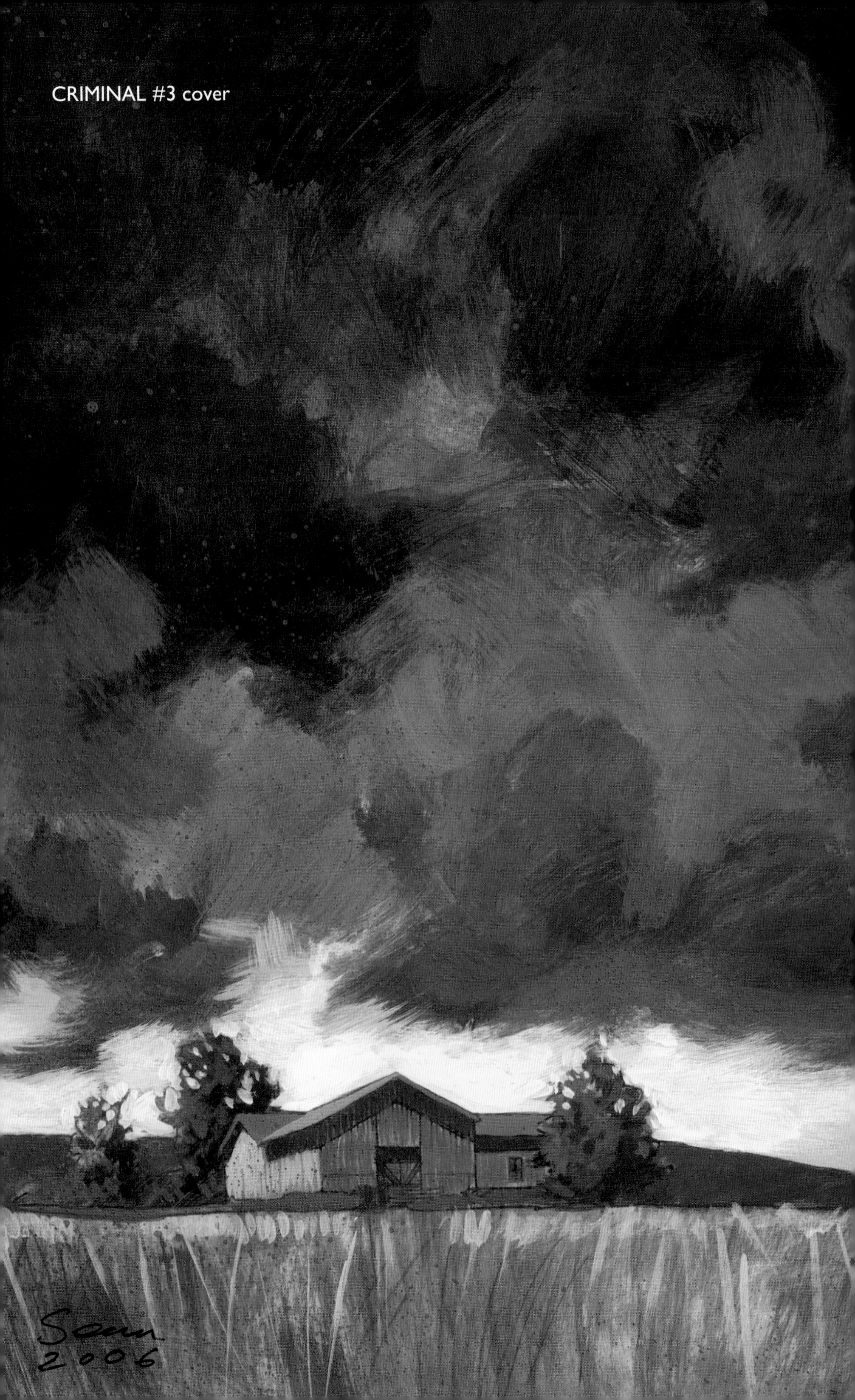
Sean
2006

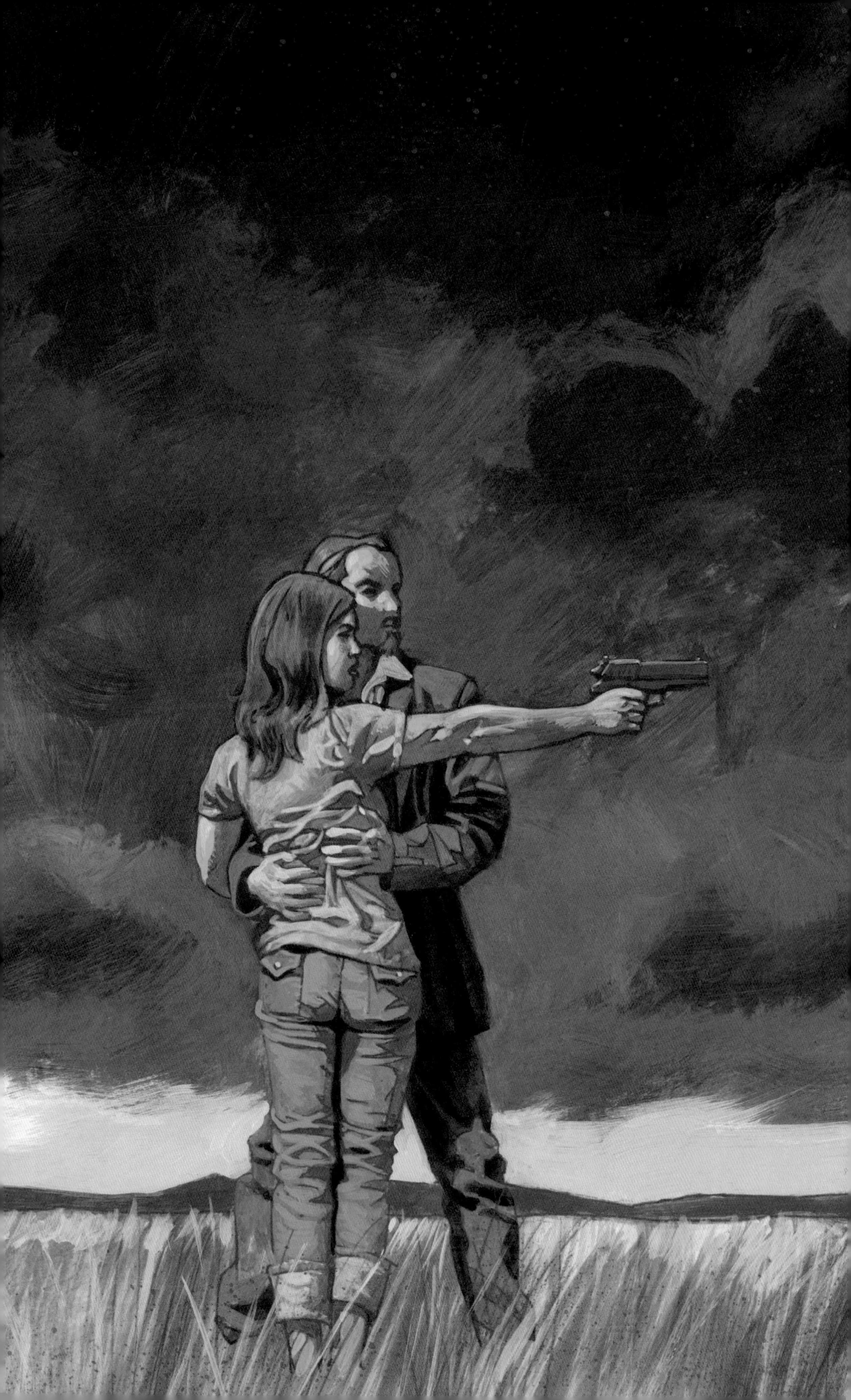

CRIMINAL #4 cover

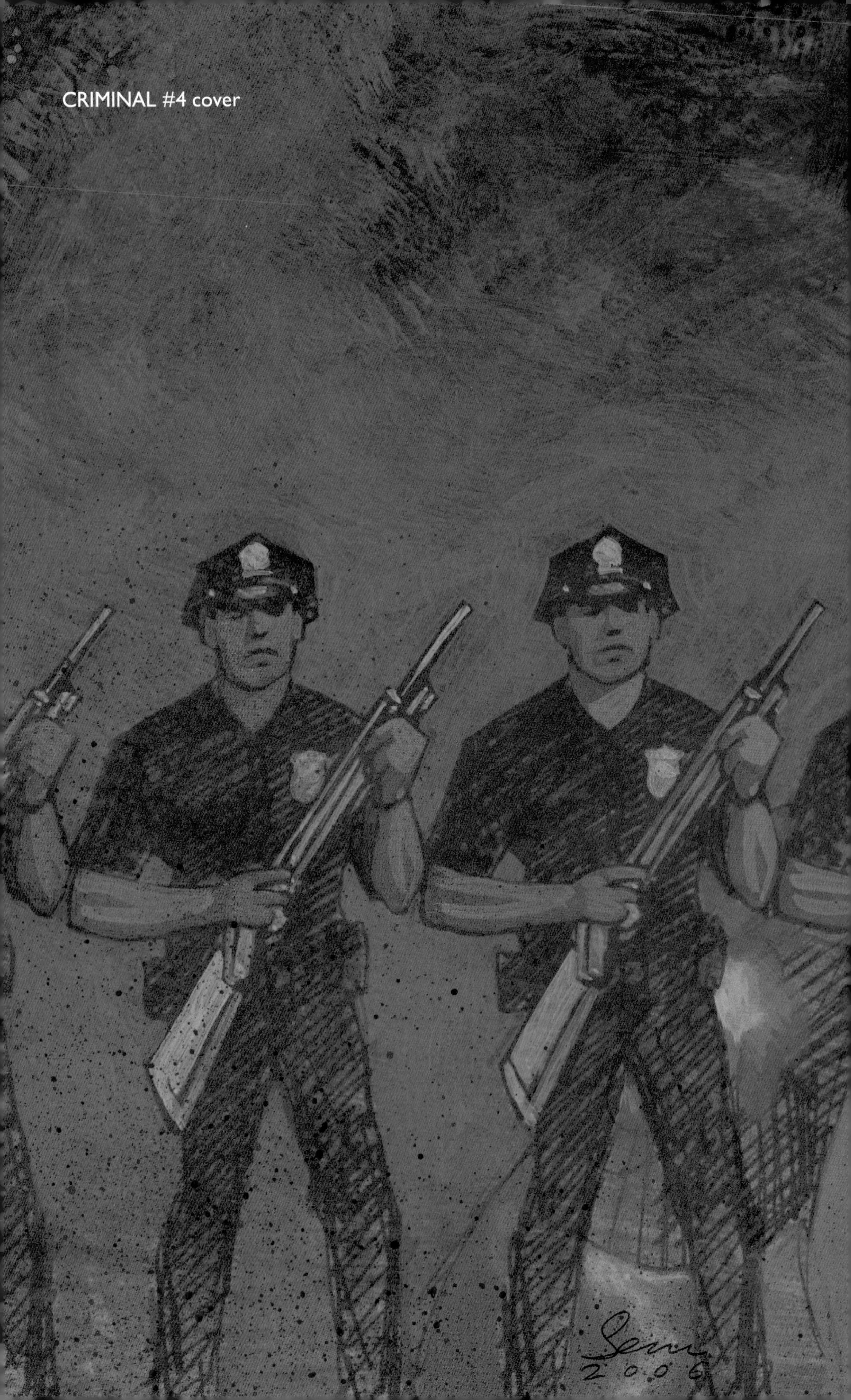

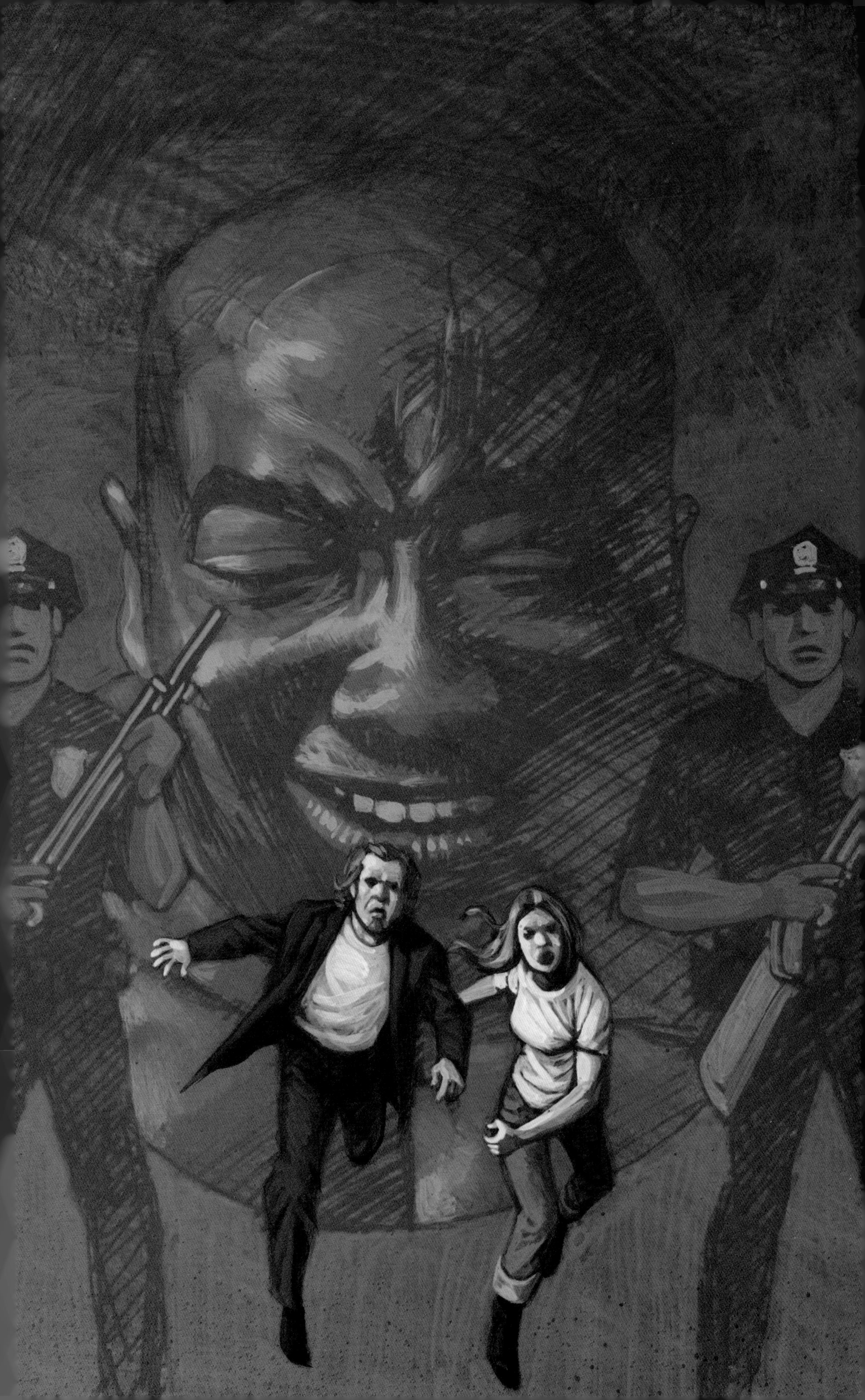

CRIMINAL #5 cover

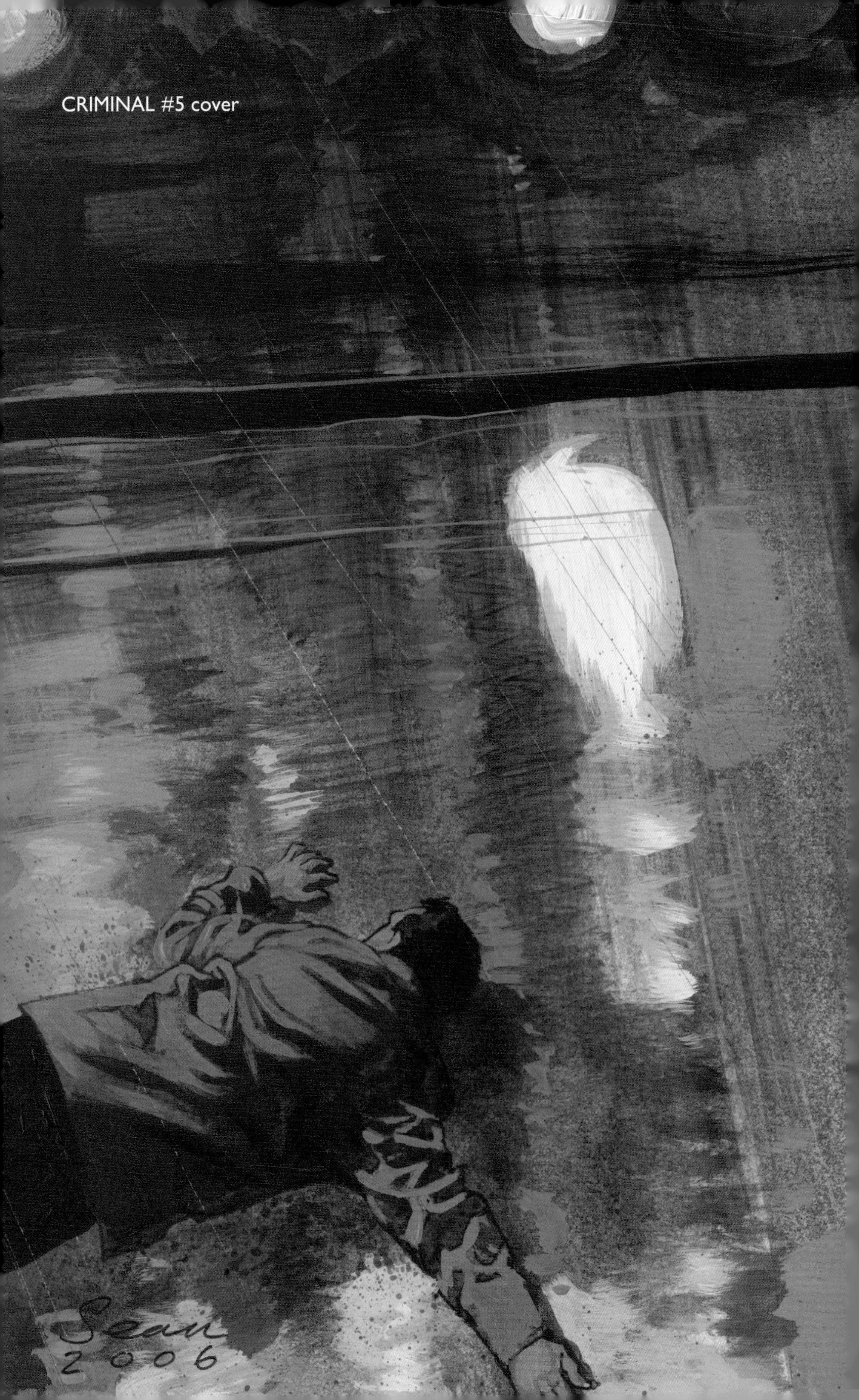
Sean
2006

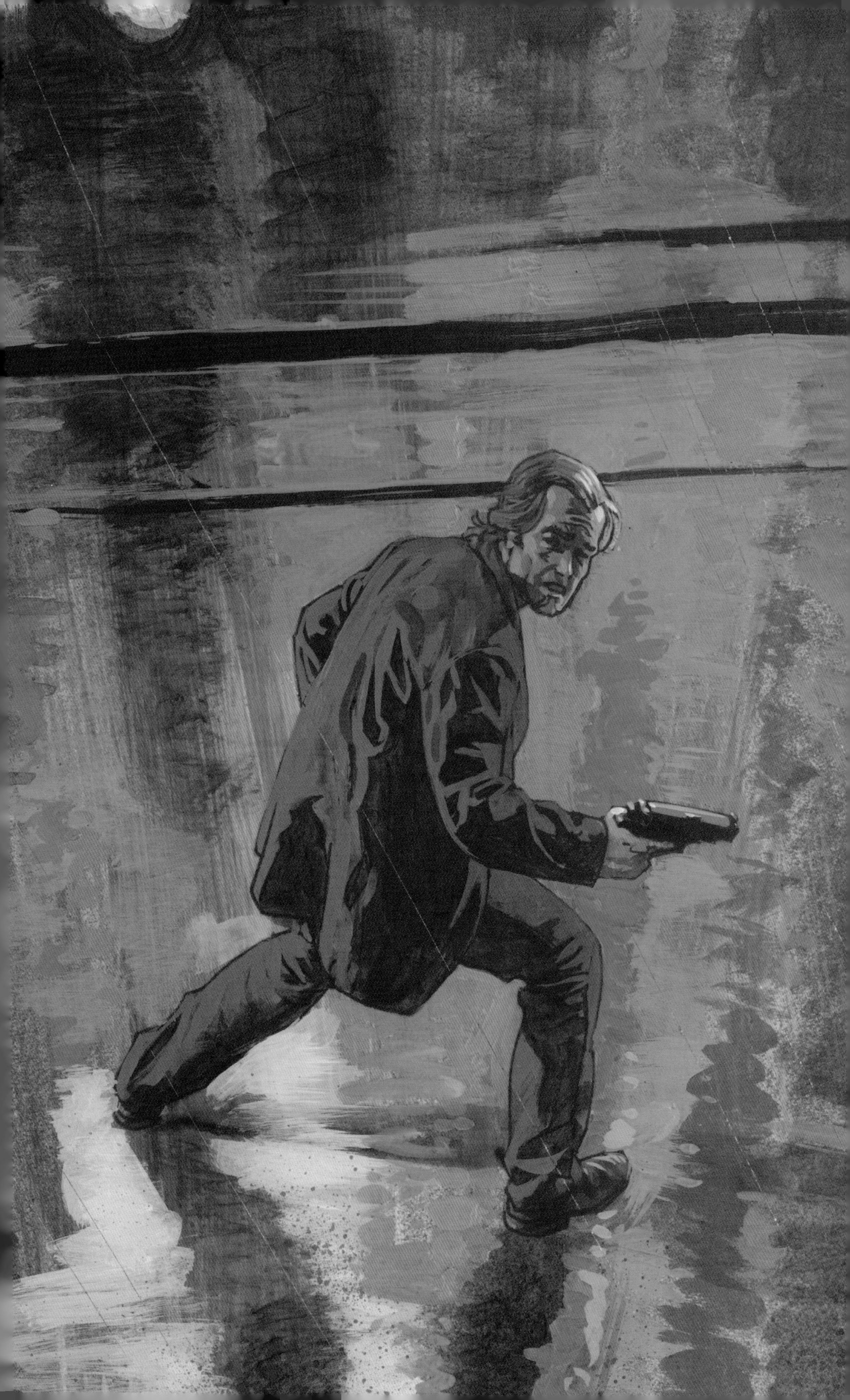

CRIMINAL #6 cover

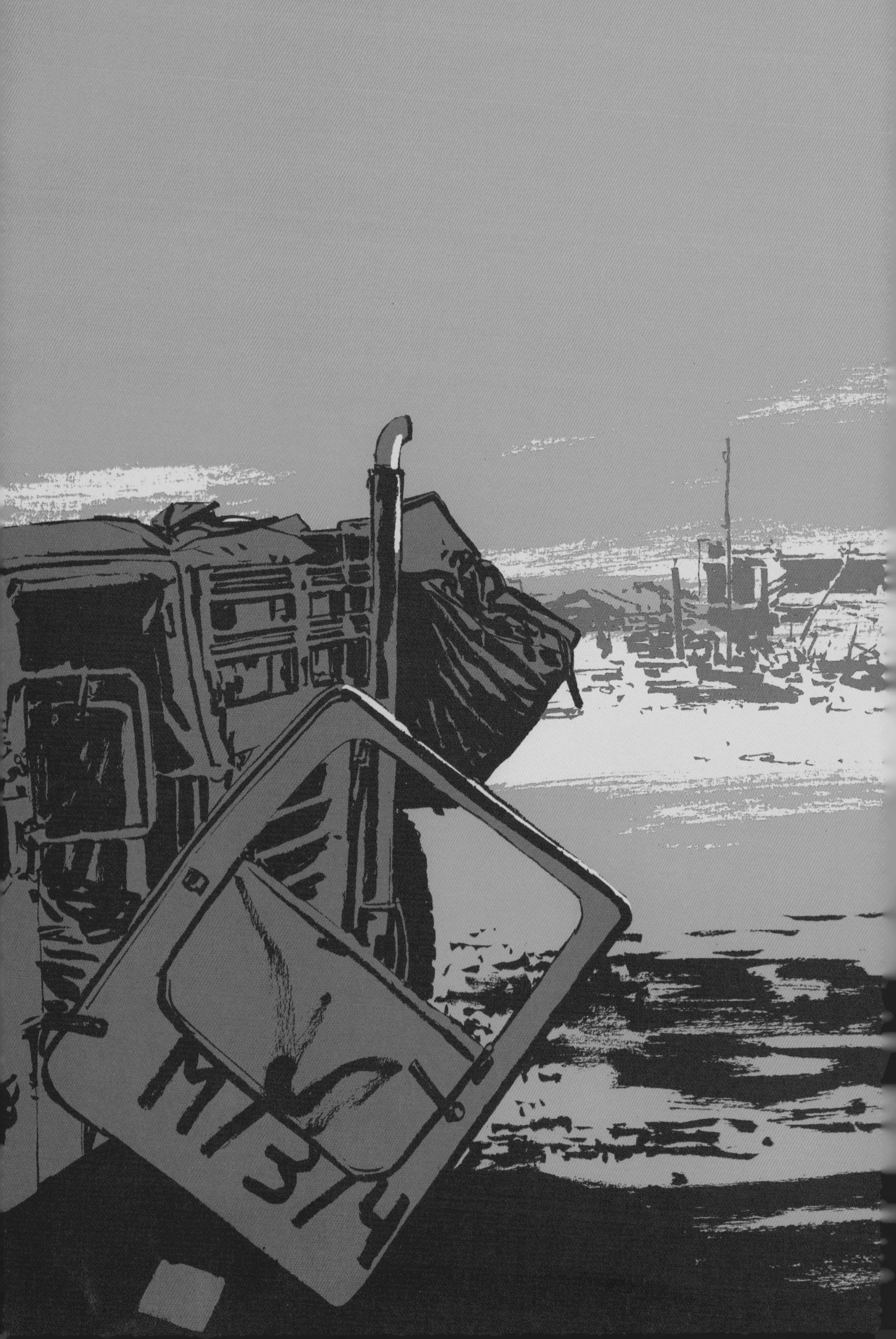

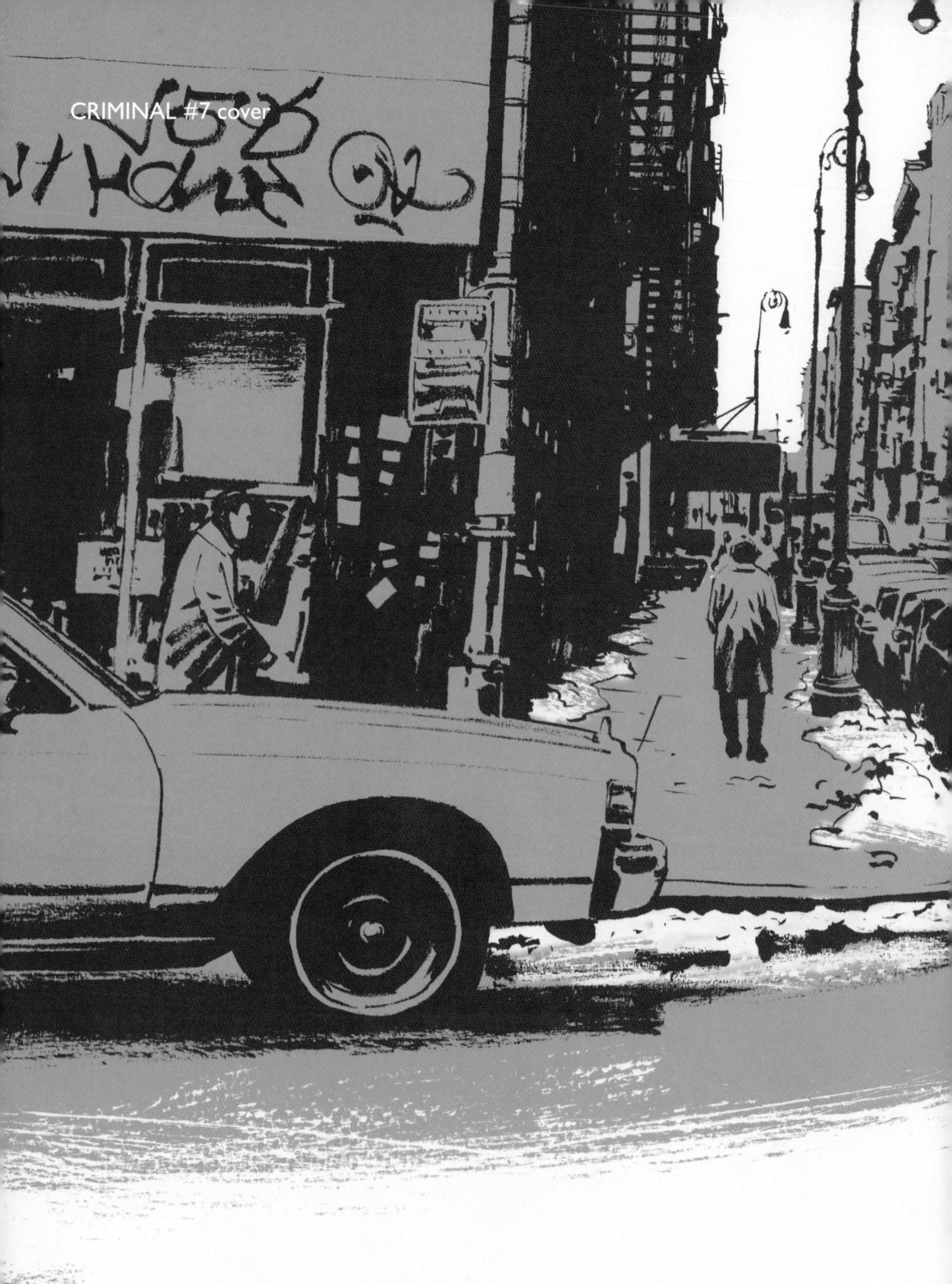

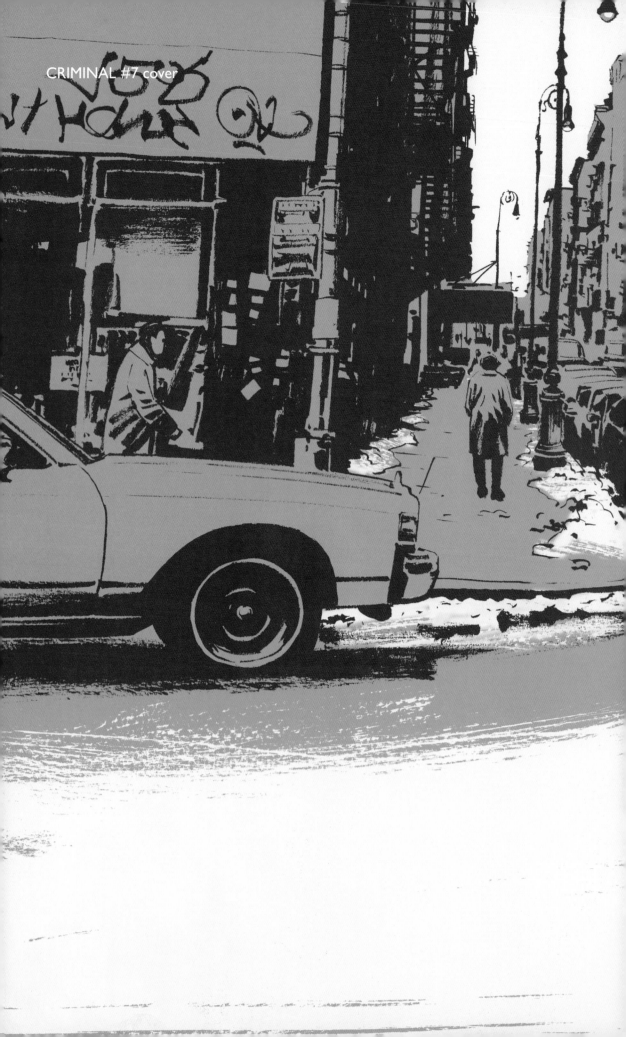

CRIMINAL #7 cover

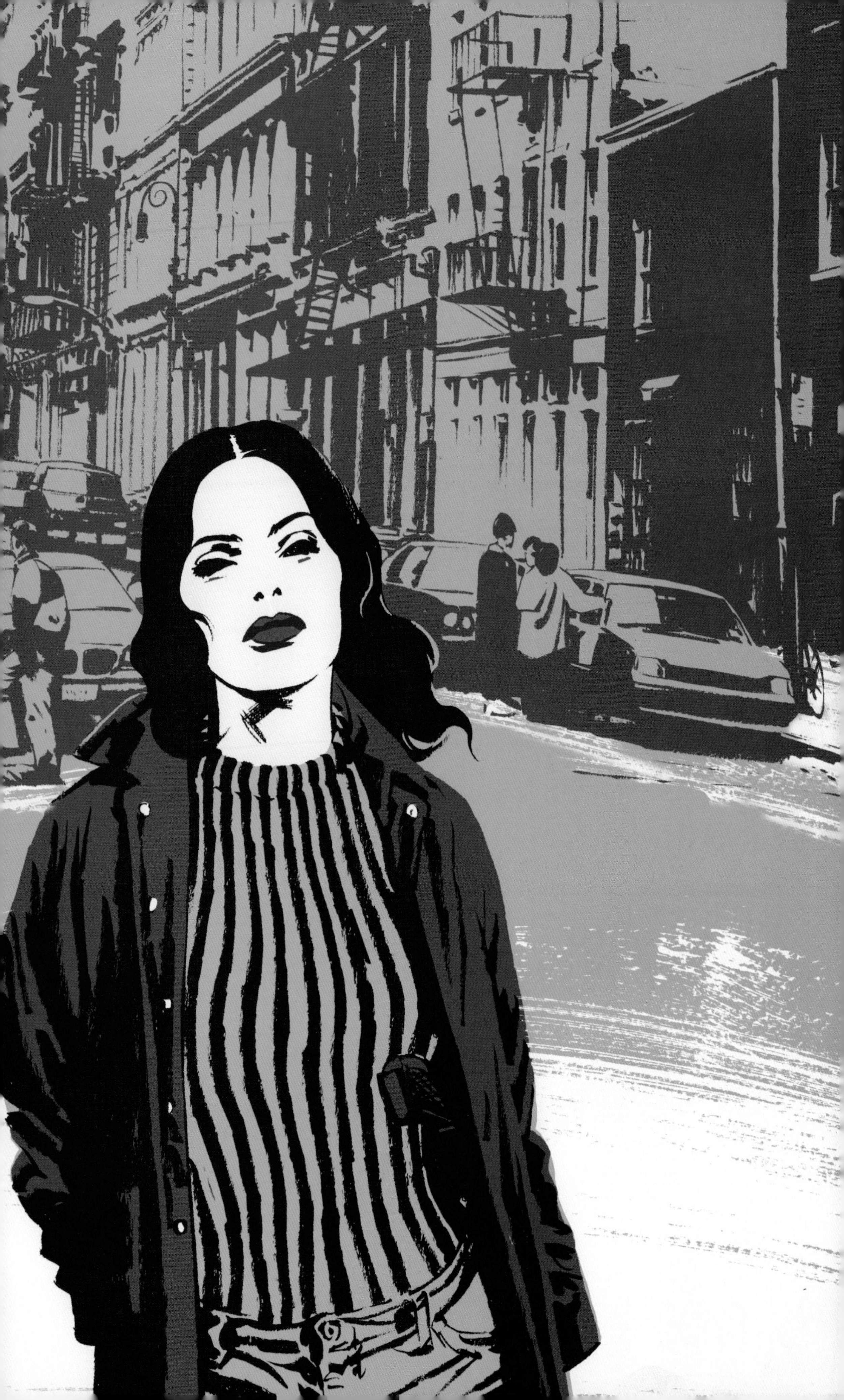

CRIMINAL #8 cover

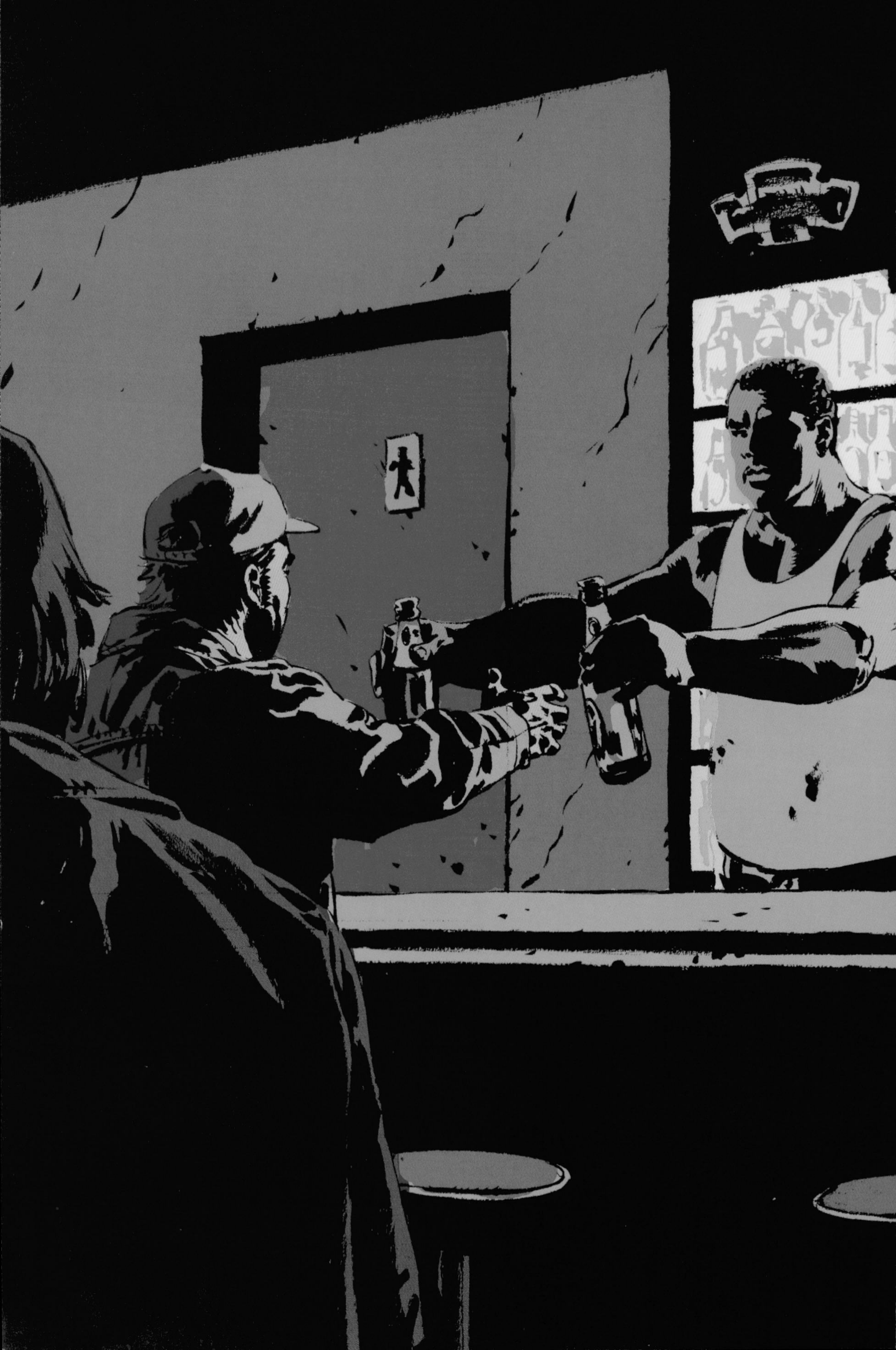

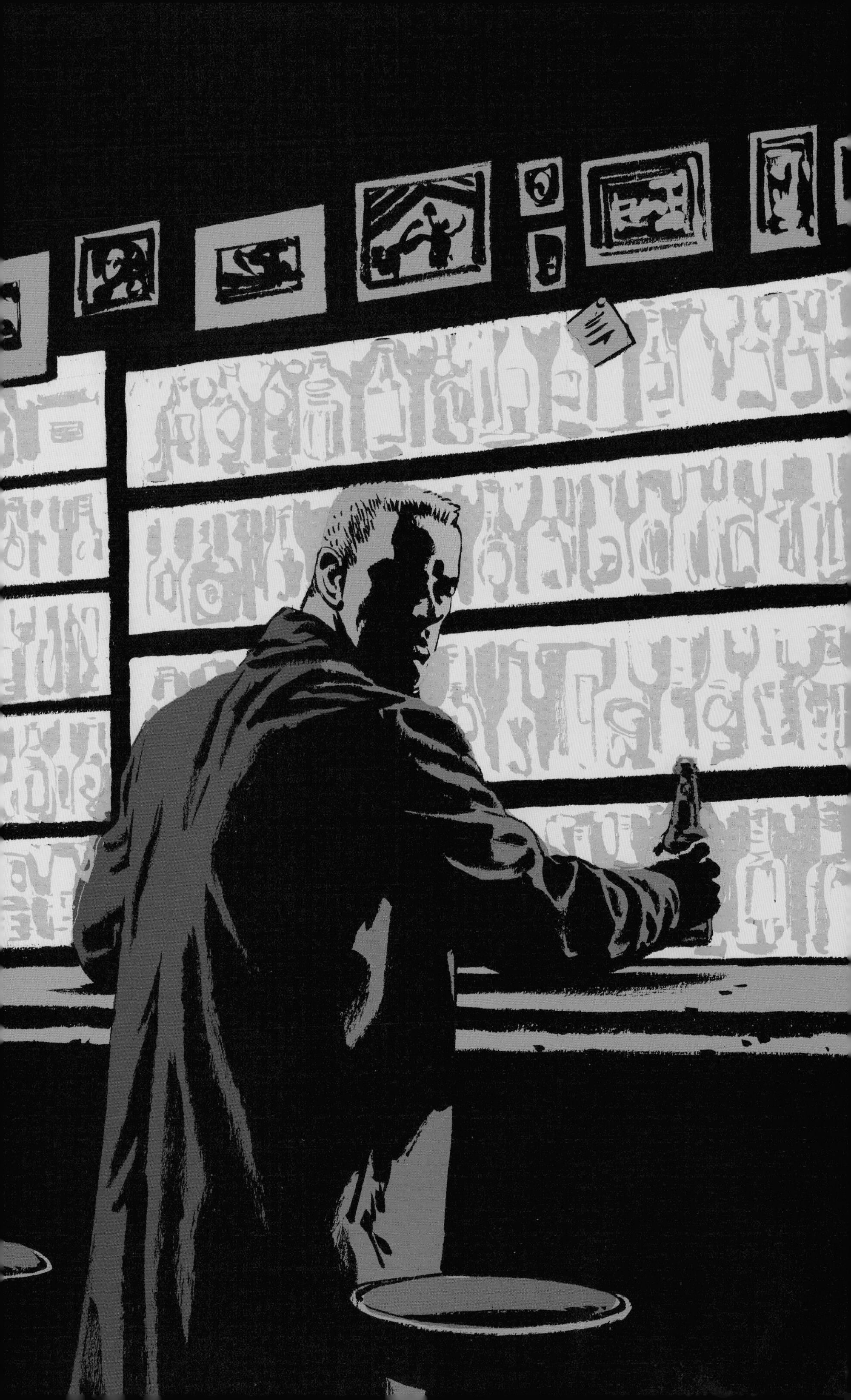

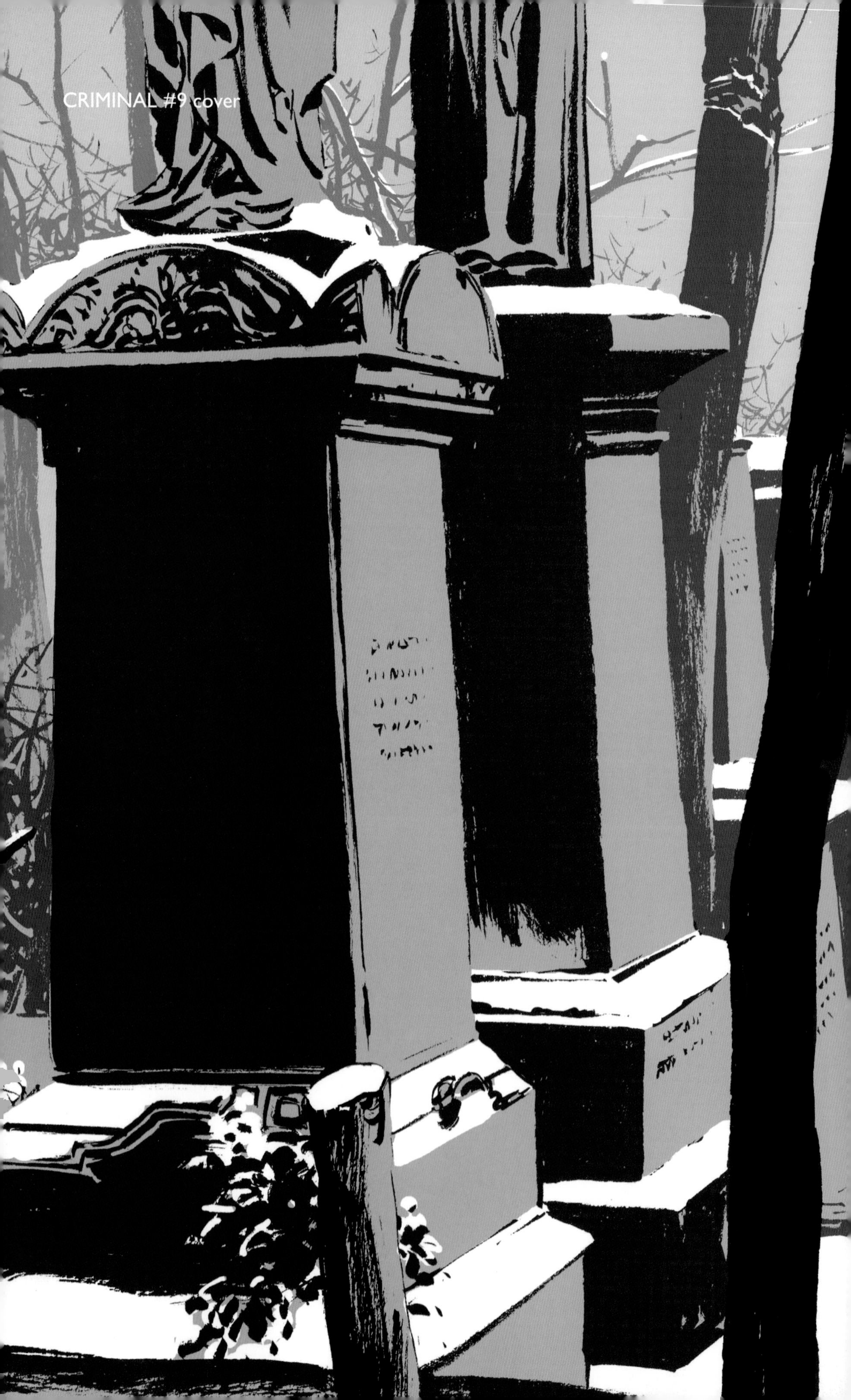
CRIMINAL #9 cover

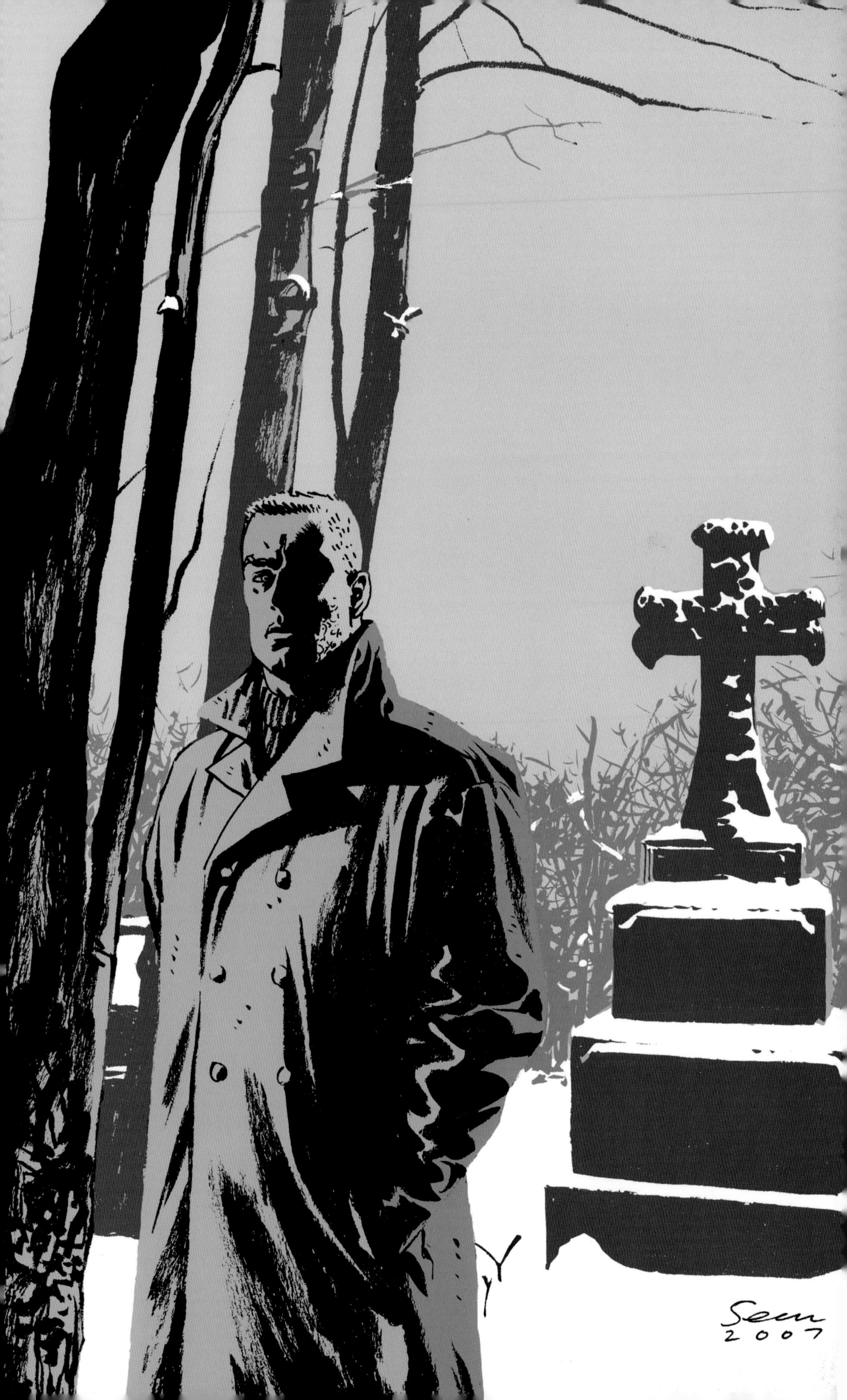
Sean
2007

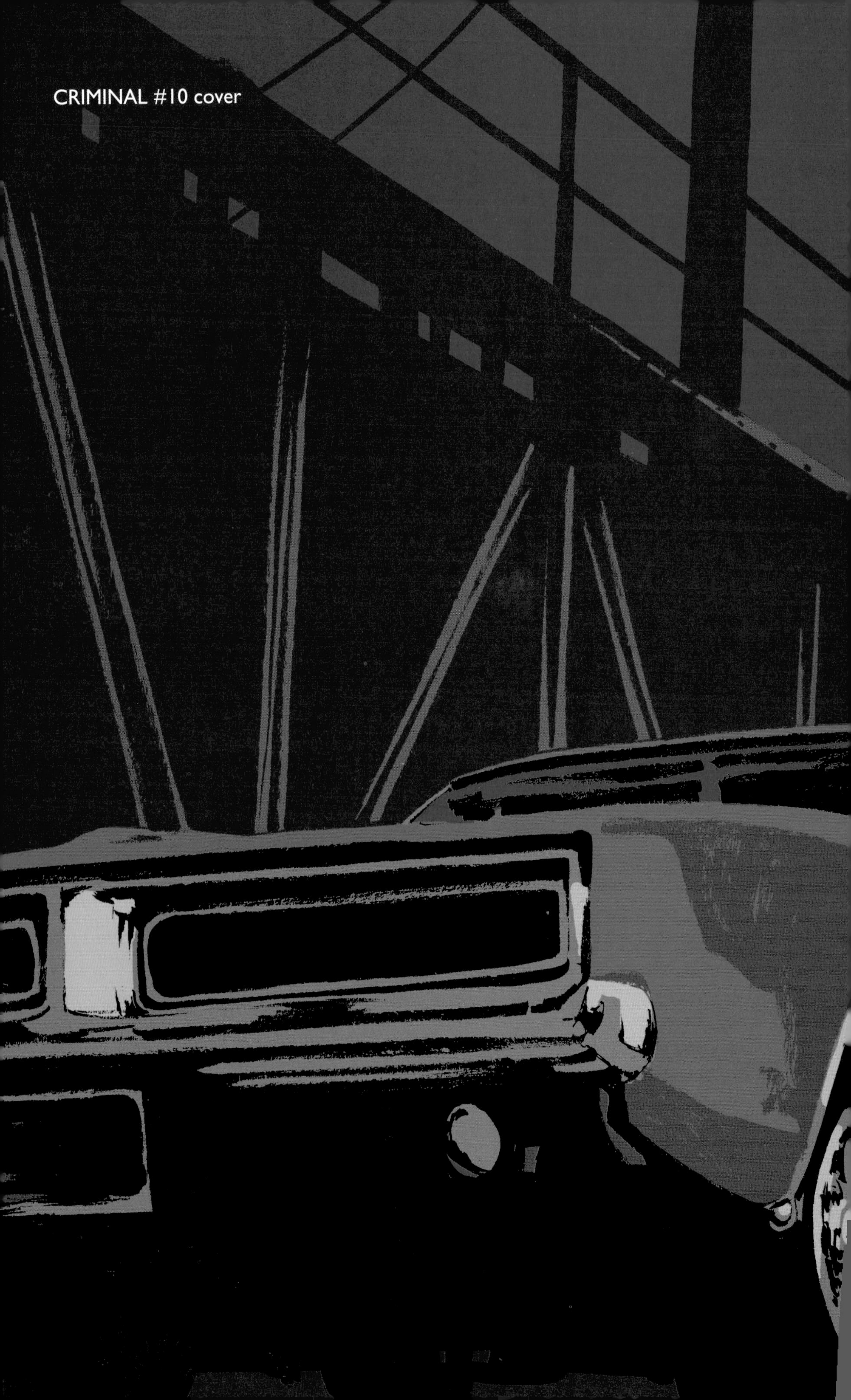
CRIMINAL #10 cover

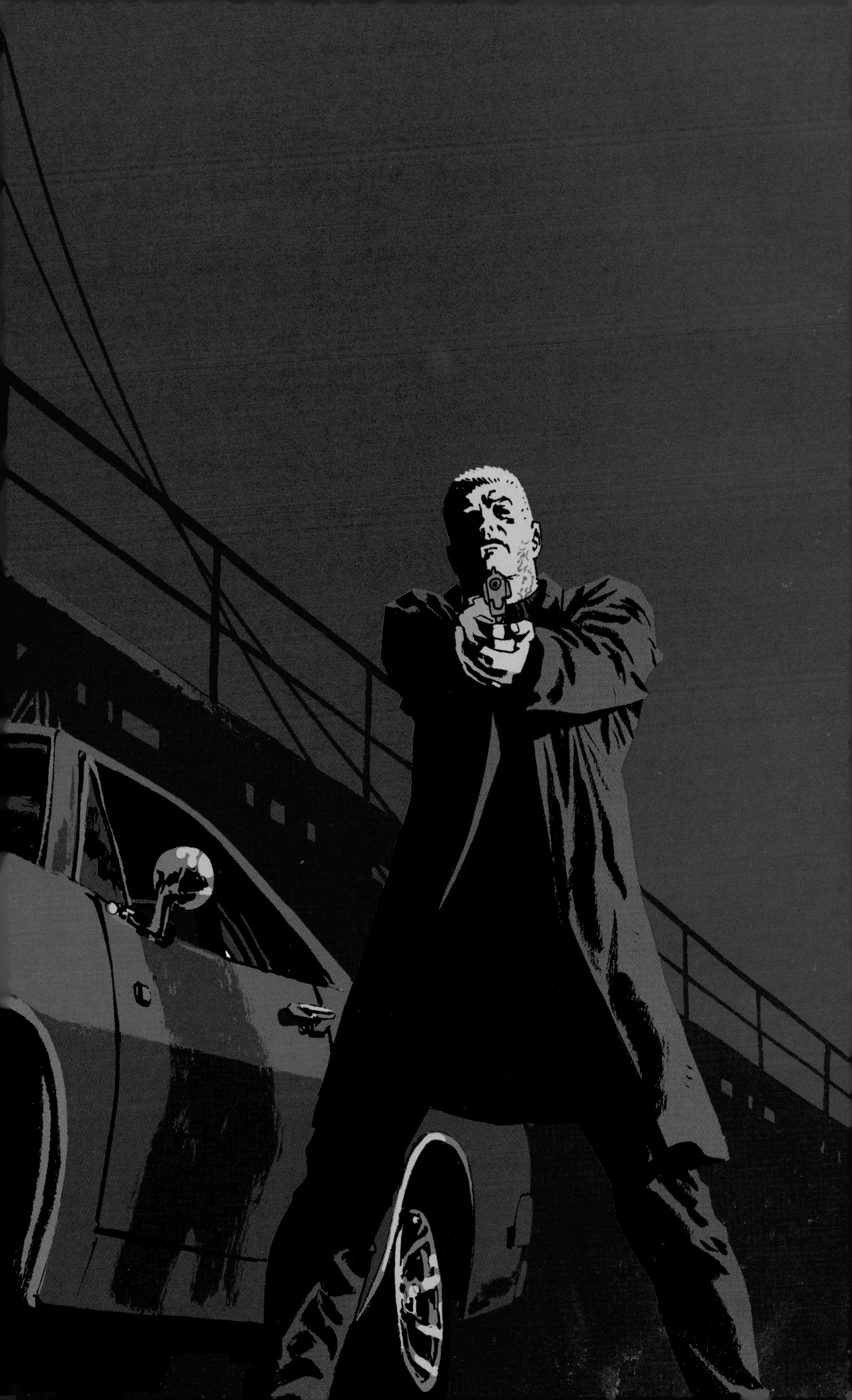

When Sean and I first decided to do **CRIMINAL** I suggested we do something different to announce and promote it, a sort of "movie trailer in comics form" that would tease the first book, **Coward**. To my knowledge, nothing like this had been done in comics, and it was fun to do, because I knew every beat of that first story even though I hadn't written it yet. As you can see, some things changed from the teaser to the actual story, and you can also spot a few panels that Sean was able to use again. Although not as many as he'd hoped, I bet.

We distributed this "trailer" all over the internet, and many readers downloaded it and printed copies to take in to their stores and give to the managers and owners there, to help support the series. This is the first time it's ever been printed in one of our books.

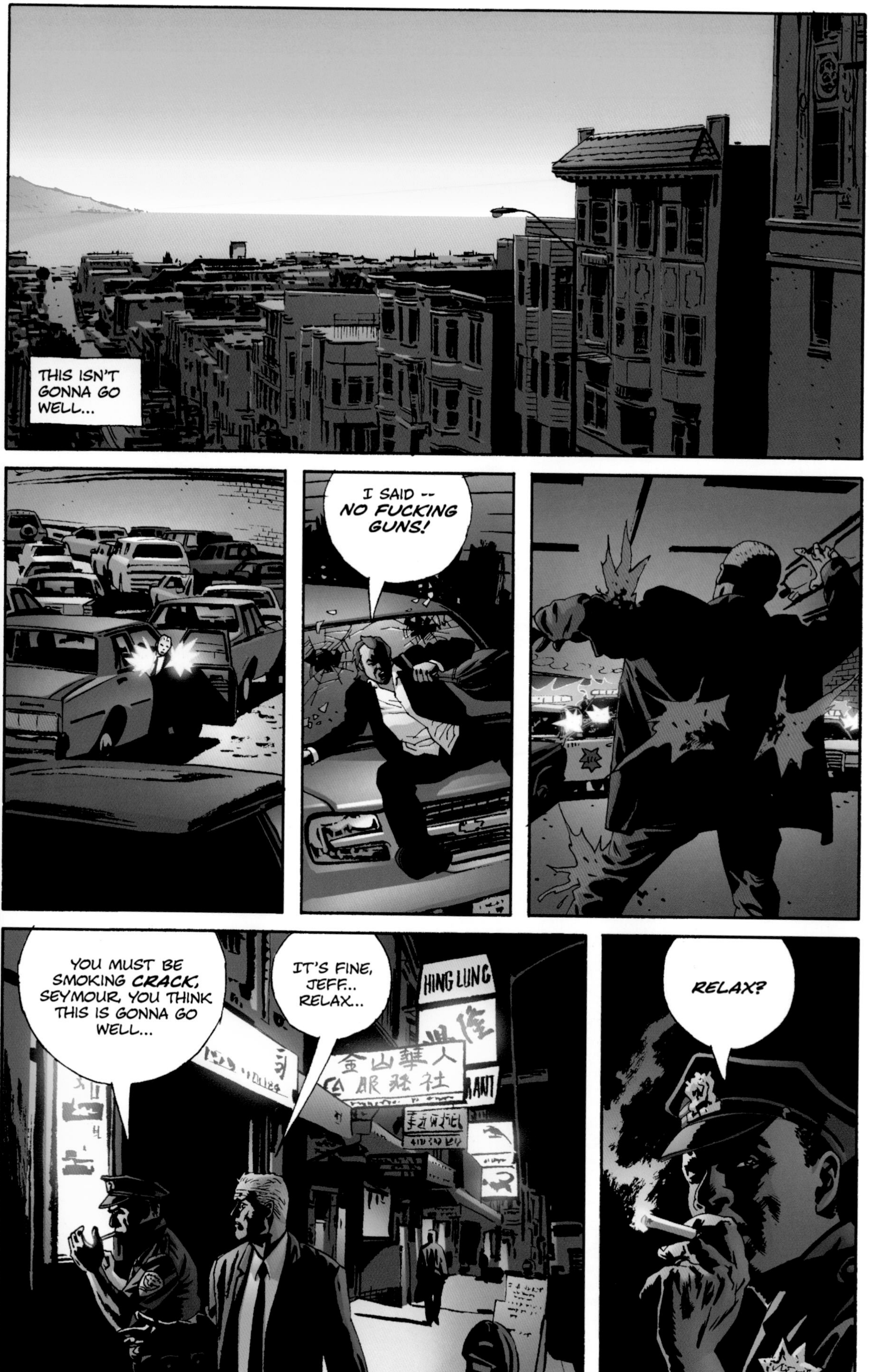
THIS ISN'T GONNA GO WELL...
I SAID -- NO FUCKING GUNS!
YOU MUST BE SMOKING CRACK, SEYMOUR, YOU THINK THIS IS GONNA GO WELL...
IT'S FINE, JEFF... RELAX...
HING LUNG
RELAX?

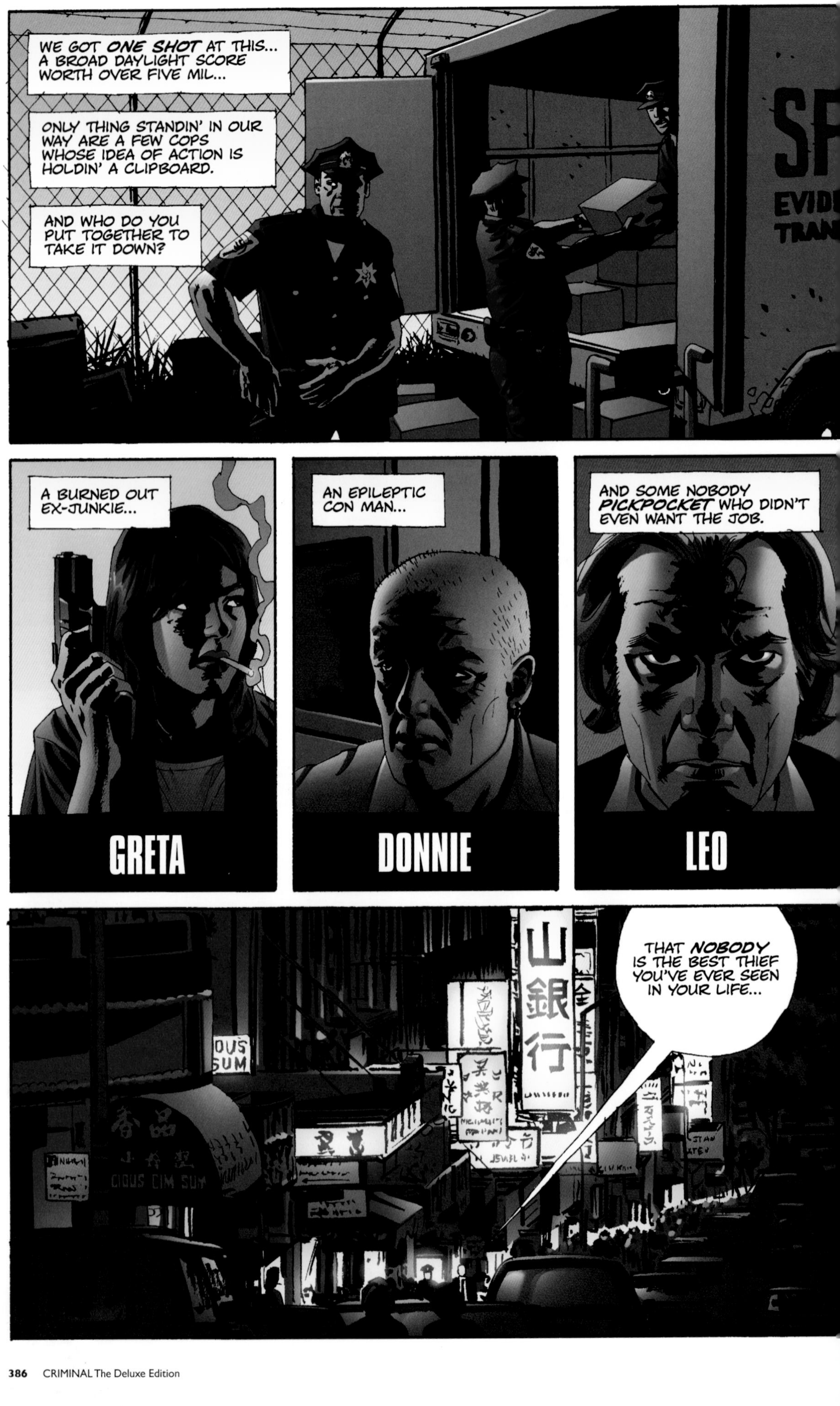
WE GOT ONE SHOT AT THIS... A BROAD DAYLIGHT SCORE WORTH OVER FIVE MIL...
ONLY THING STANDIN' IN OUR WAY ARE A FEW COPS WHOSE IDEA OF ACTION IS HOLDIN' A CLIPBOARD.
AND WHO DO YOU PUT TOGETHER TO TAKE IT DOWN?
A BURNED OUT EX-JUNKIE...
GRETA
AN EPILEPTIC CON MAN...
DONNIE
AND SOME NOBODY PICKPOCKET WHO DIDN'T EVEN WANT THE JOB.
LEO
THAT NOBODY IS THE BEST THIEF YOU'VE EVER SEEN IN YOUR LIFE...

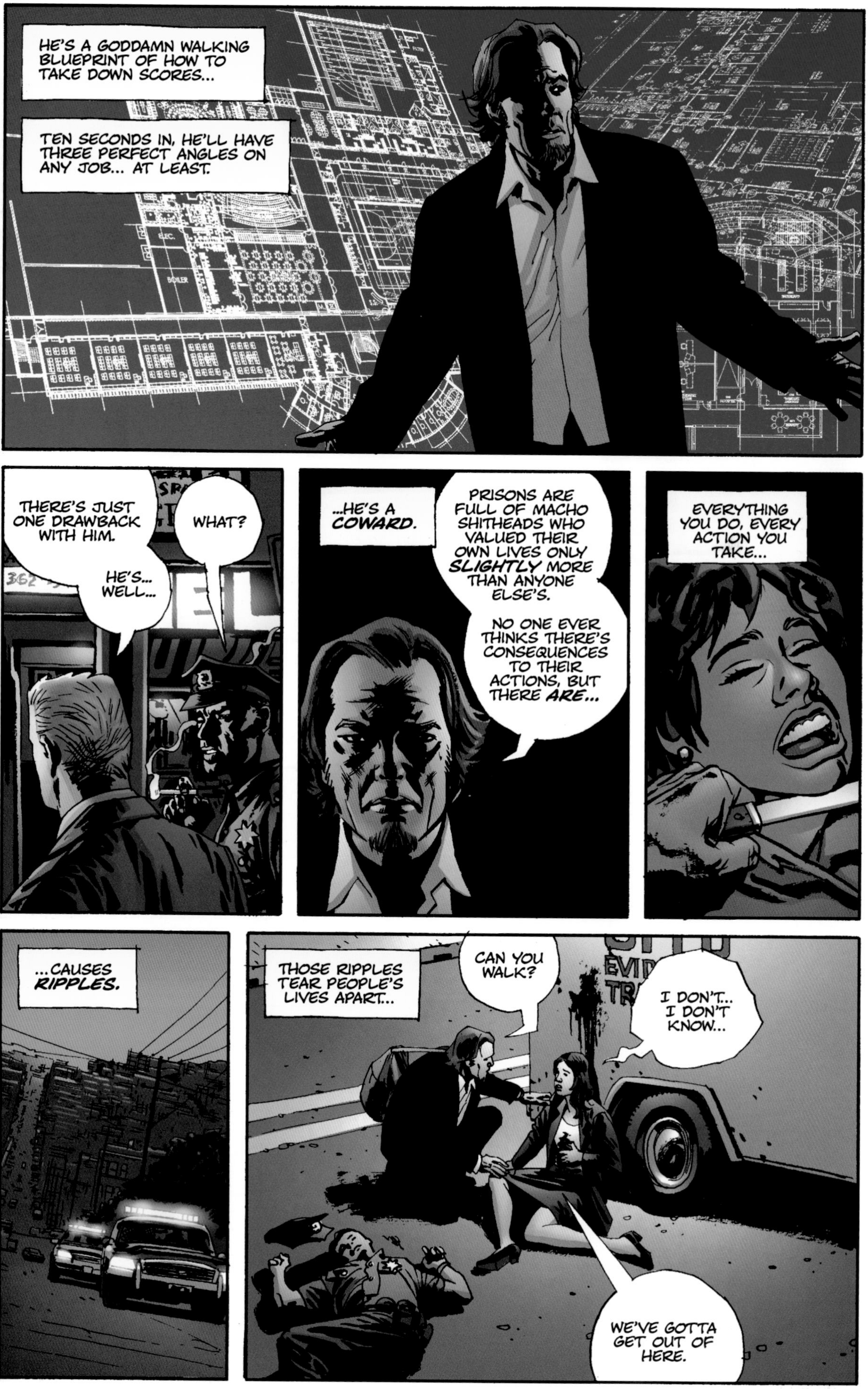
HE'S A GODDAMN WALKING BLUEPRINT OF HOW TO TAKE DOWN SCORES...
TEN SECONDS IN, HE'LL HAVE THREE PERFECT ANGLES ON ANY JOB... AT LEAST.
THERE'S JUST ONE DRAWBACK WITH HIM.
WHAT?
HE'S... WELL...
...HE'S A COWARD.
PRISONS ARE FULL OF MACHO SHITHEADS WHO VALUED THEIR OWN LIVES ONLY SLIGHTLY MORE THAN ANYONE ELSE'S.
NO ONE EVER THINKS THERE'S CONSEQUENCES TO THEIR ACTIONS, BUT THERE ARE...
EVERYTHING YOU DO, EVERY ACTION YOU TAKE...
...CAUSES RIPPLES.
THOSE RIPPLES TEAR PEOPLE'S LIVES APART...
CAN YOU WALK?
I DON'T... I DON'T KNOW...
WE'VE GOTTA GET OUT OF HERE.

...AND THEN THEY SUCK YOURS DOWN THE DRAIN WITH THEM.

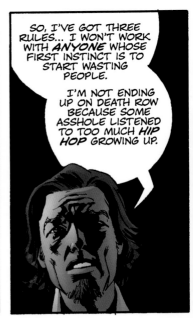

SO, I'VE GOT THREE RULES... I WON'T WORK WITH *ANYONE* WHOSE FIRST INSTINCT IS TO START WASTING PEOPLE.

I'M NOT ENDING UP ON DEATH ROW BECAUSE SOME ASSHOLE LISTENED TO TOO MUCH *HIP HOP* GROWING UP.

SECOND RULE... NO GUNS.

PEOPLE TEND TO GET *STUPID* AROUND GUNS...

...THEY OPEN TOO MANY OF THE WRONG DOORS, THE WRONG POSSIBILITIES...

...AND THEN THINGS GENERALLY GO TO HELL.

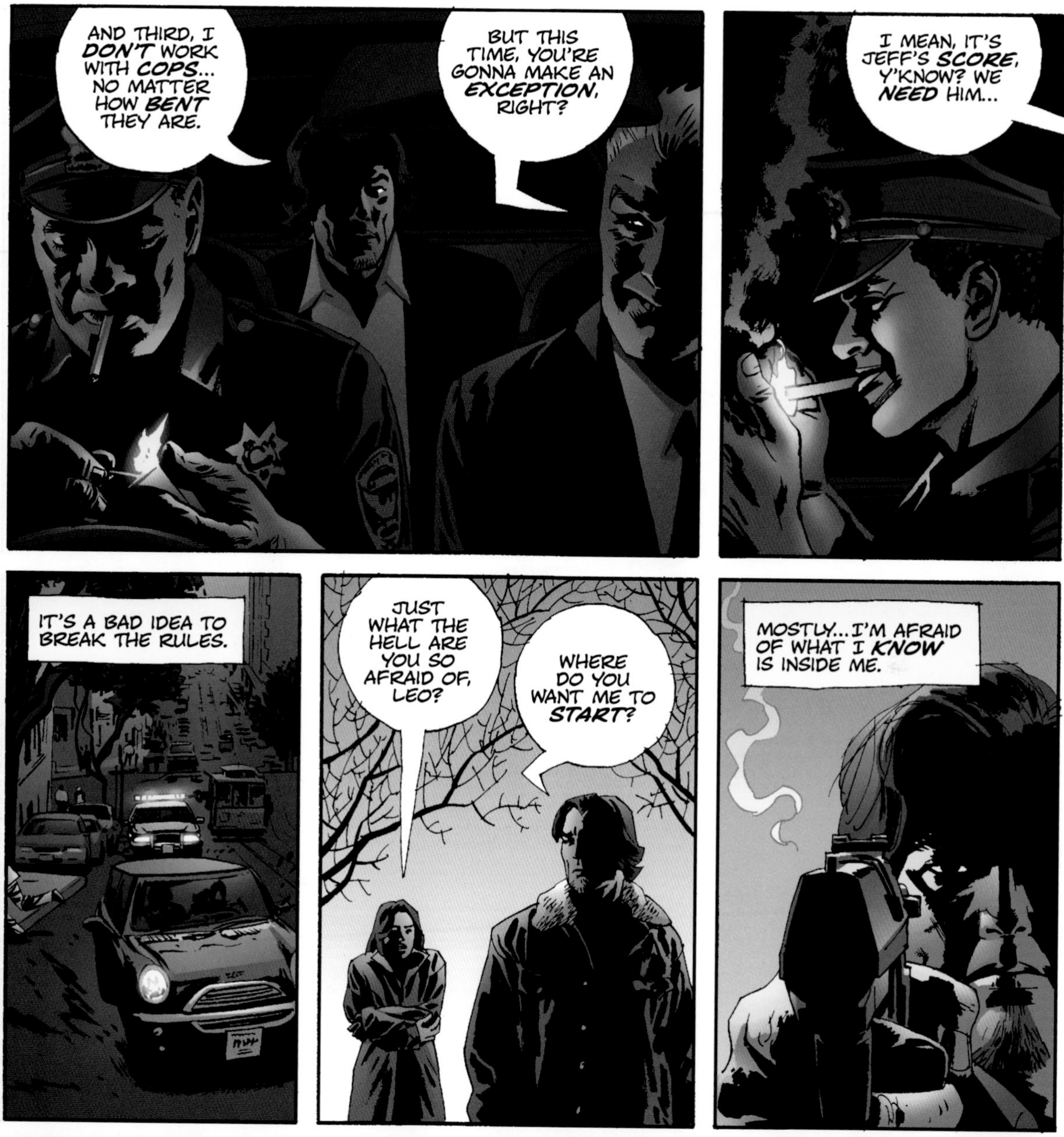
AND THIRD, I DON'T WORK WITH COPS... NO MATTER HOW BENT THEY ARE.
BUT THIS TIME, YOU'RE GONNA MAKE AN EXCEPTION, RIGHT?
I MEAN, IT'S JEFF'S SCORE, Y'KNOW? WE NEED HIM...
IT'S A BAD IDEA TO BREAK THE RULES.
JUST WHAT THE HELL ARE YOU SO AFRAID OF, LEO?
WHERE DO YOU WANT ME TO START?
MOSTLY...I'M AFRAID OF WHAT I KNOW IS INSIDE ME.

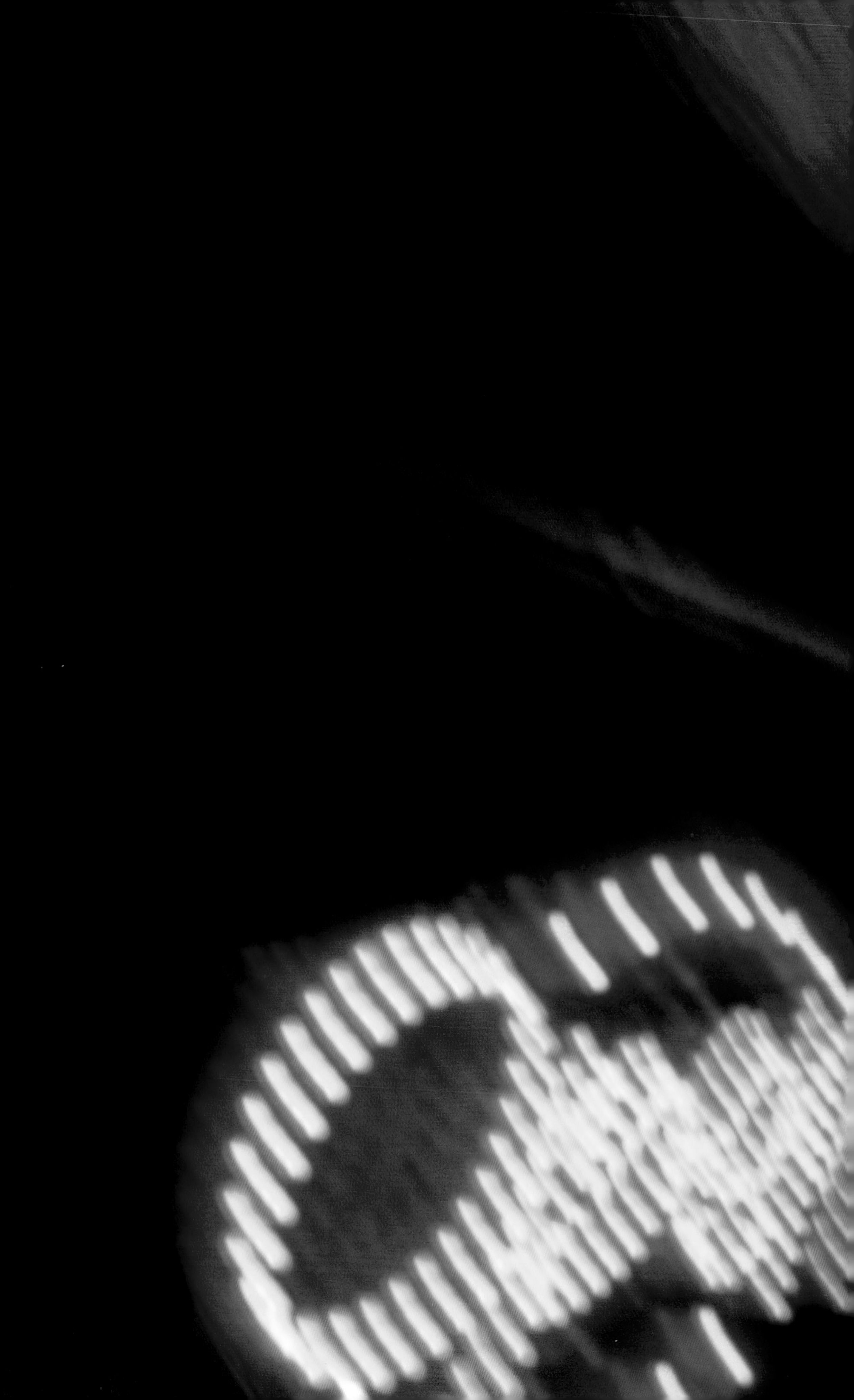

Essays

In the **Criminal** single issues, where we originally serialized these stories, we have a lot of extras at the back of the issues. I consider **Criminal** to be a magazine, in many ways, a place for me and Sean to put our stories, but also a place to write about the crime genre itself, too. I generally ramble about whatever I'm reading or researching, or print a few letters, and then we have articles that are longer and more serious. Informal essays, sort of.

These are usually pieces about old movies or books, or sometimes both, and if they aren't written by me, they're done by friends of mine as a favor. It's something that makes the single issues a special thing, and gives Sean a chance to do some illustrations to enhance these pieces.

I often get asked why we haven't collected these articles in the trade paperbacks, and my usual answer is that you don't get to the end of a crime novel and find a bunch of articles by the author's friends about 70s crime movies or Noir films from the 40s and 50s. But in addition to that, **Criminal** is a bit like Public Radio or TV – it's *reader-funded* – so we want to make sure we're rewarding those readers who have helped make it all possible. And as I said, most of the articles are done by friends of mine as favors, and I wouldn't want to abuse their charity, since they've helped make **Criminal** what it is.

That said, the following are Sean's illustrations for the articles in the 13 issues collected here, as well as a few of the pieces I've written for the series about some of my favorite crime films.

Out Of The Past

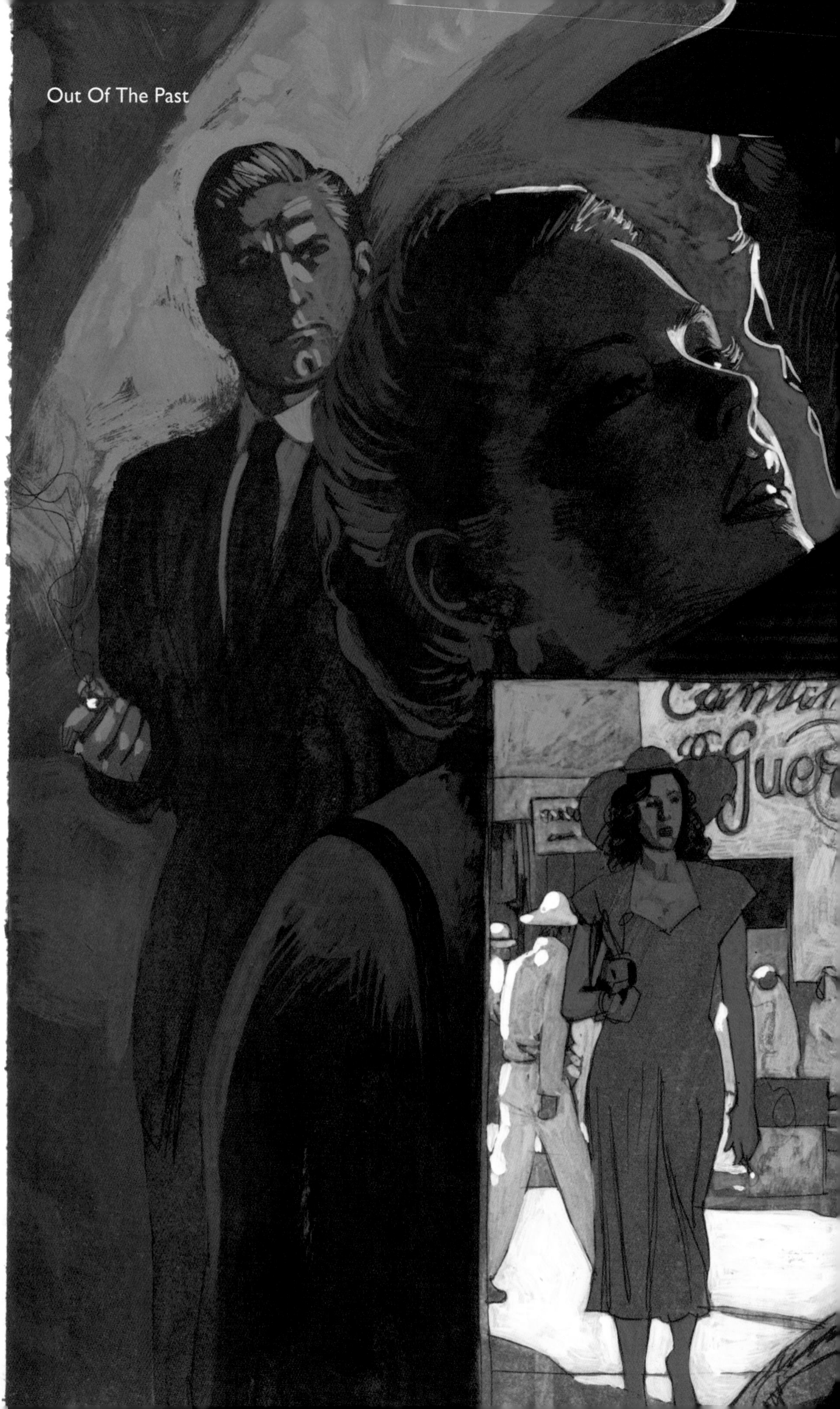

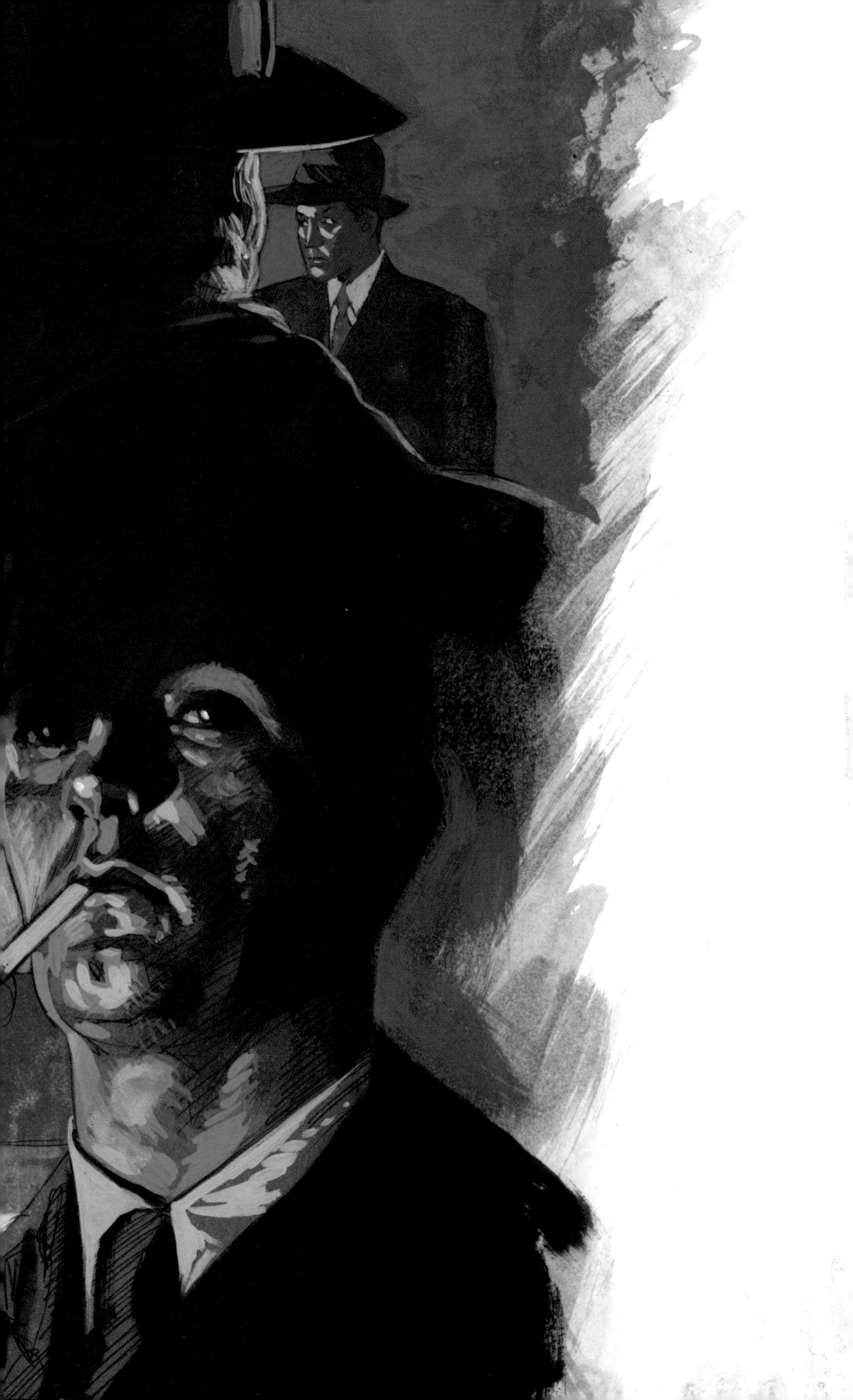

Out Of The Past

For years, since I first saw it in a theater in 1989, if you asked me to name my favorite films, Out of the Past would have been at the top of the list, if not in the number one slot. I've ceased having a list of favorite films, probably because it's a bit of a Sophie's Choice getting it under a top ten or twenty these days, but Out of the Past still ranks as the finest noir film I've ever seen. It also has the distinction of containing my second favorite performance by Robert Mitchum – my favorite being his truly terrifying role in Night of the Hunter.

But in Out of the Past Mitchum plays the good guy, and a more noir good guy you'd be hard-pressed to find. His character, Jeff Markham, is a private eye that isn't too clean to take a job from a gambler/mobster (played by Kirk Douglas) that he's got some kind of sorted history with. And when the job turns out to be tracking a beautiful woman halfway around the world to Acapulco, he's not too good a guy not to fall in love with her and run off, leaving an angry client and partner waiting behind in the States. That's just one small reason that I love this film. The good guy is a shady character who thinks with his dick instead of his wallet when confronted with the beautiful mystery that is Kathie Moffett, played brilliantly by Jane Greer... But we'll get to her later.

The first thing that really grabbed me about the movie was the way it was structured. It opens with Jeff living under an assumed name, running a gas station in a small town outside Reno, and dating the woman who runs the local diner. He's making an attempt at living the clean life, and one under the radar, which is highlighted by the fact that his best friend is a deaf-mute. But almost immediately, someone who knew Jeff in his previous life stumbles across his trail, and things begin to get complicated. We learn how complicated in a long flashback sequence where Jeff tells his current girl, Ann (the Betty to Kathie Moffett's Veronica) of his fall from... well, from somewhere a bit further down the ladder than grace, at least.

The flashback almost unfolds like a dream, through the direction of Jacques Tourneur and the cinematography of Nicholas Musuraca, with Mitchum's pot-smoker drawl narrating his hunt for the vixen who shot a man and ran away with a pile of his cash. When he finally meets her, it's never exactly explained why he gives up his task and takes up with her. It needs no explanation, though, because every single time I've watched it, I've understood. He had to have her, and in his place, I'd probably have felt the same way. And that is really the heart of what I find fascinating in this film. The story of Jeff and Kathie falling for each other and going on the run for a few years, until ultimately, their love tears them apart and ends in murder is just a vehicle, as far as I'm concerned, to explore the complete, utter, and incomprehensible desperation of Kathie Moffett.

Kathie has often been called the ultimate Femme Fatale, but to me, she's so much more than that. Because I can understand Barbara Stanwyck's motives in Double Indemnity — she wants out of her loveless marriage, and she wants to be rich — but Kathie Moffett remains an enigma. Why is Kathie doing any of the things she's doing? What made her so alone and afraid that she'll turn on almost anyone, even trying to murder people she loves? It's that beautiful chaotic desperation that elevates Kathie Moffett, and Out of the Past to a level most noir films never achieve. Early on, when Jeff and Kathy are revealing their truths to each other, she tearfully tells him that Whit (Kirk Douglas) has lied, and that she never took his money. You have no idea whether to believe her or not, but Mitchum, in possibly the single finest moment of his career, just mumbles, "Baby, I don't care," and leans in for a kiss that will take him all the way to hell and back. And it's a kiss I fully understand, because Kathie is a fragile thing at that moment, vulnerable yet sexy, and sharp as a whip on top of it. In short, she's not just a Femme Fatale, she's also the original fucked-up girlfriend. The kind that breaks your heart, but that you can never say no to, even when you know that you should. Kathie's only motive appears to be survival, and yet with Jeff, she finds both happiness and passion, as well. That she's willing to give the latter up for the former is her undoing, but it's a peculiar kind of human failure, and one again, which comes from desperation.

Long after any viewing of Out of the Past, I will find myself wondering what is really going on behind Kathie's wild eyes, and where this desperation came from. We'll never know, but in post-WW2 America, it's not hard to see why people would feel desperate to live, to feel passion, and to be free. Even if they have to kill for it.

There are many other reasons to watch Out of the Past, and I won't list them and ruin the movie any more than I already have. I do want to point out two small details that help make it great, though. Good noir often has an element of disability layered into it. It's symbolism and character all at once — the old man in the wheelchair who hires Bogart in The Big Sleep, the Professor's sexual hang-ups in Asphalt Jungle, the reporter with two canes in Lady From Shanghai, the G.I. with shell-shock in The Blue Dahlia, just to name a few off the top of my head. Noir is showing us a fractured world full of damaged people, who nonetheless try to survive, but who mostly fail. And in sketching out that world, the camera never shies away from the symbolism of people crippled by war or disease. In fact, the camera loves them, and uses them to flesh out the world around the main characters. The mute kid that Jeff Markham befriends fits that noir theme here, serving as both a supporting character, and a symbol for Jeff's need to keep his past a secret. That alone would have been a great noir beat to hit, but the final stroke of genius of this film is that only the mute boy and the audience ever know the truth about Jeff and why he does the things he does. No one else in the film does, not even the girl who loves him. That silent pact between movie and viewer echoes long after the final credits have rolled.

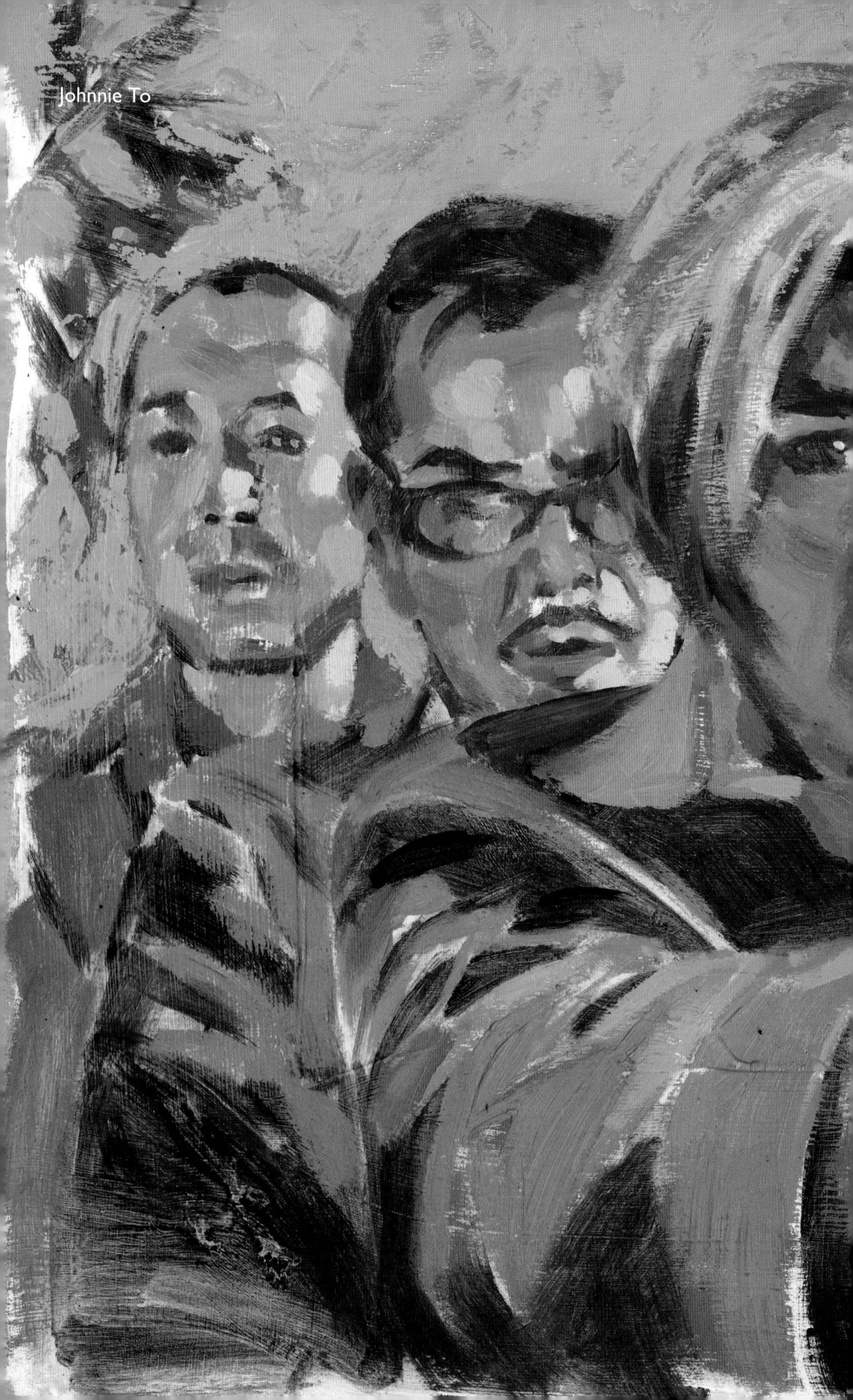
Johnnie To

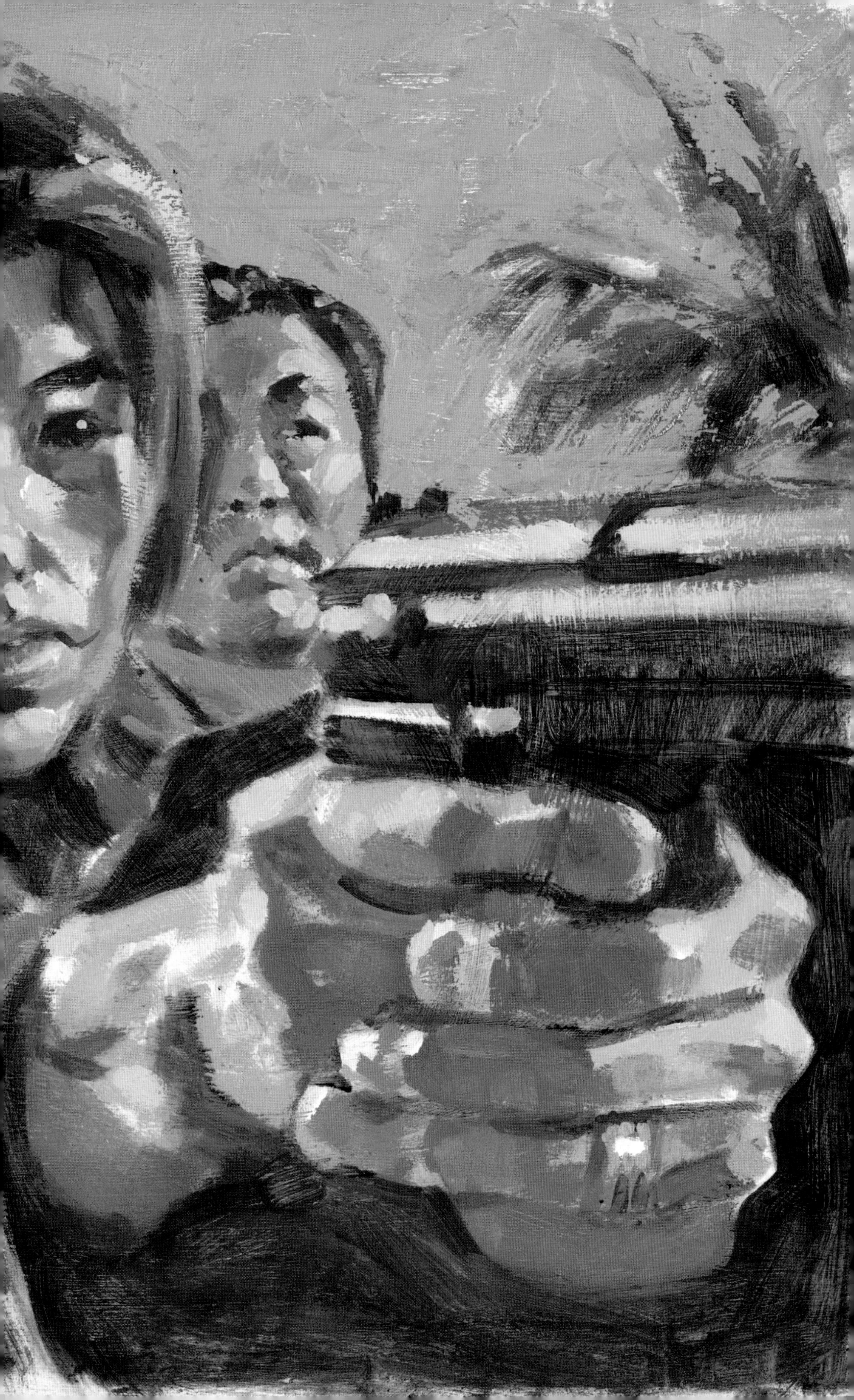

Two By To

I'm not nearly as well-versed in Asian cinema as I would like to be. I have a passing knowledge of it, and have seen a fair amount of the best films from the region over the years, but I've never been a fanatic like many of my friends have been. I never saw a Jackie Chan movie when it was cool to, for example. My following of Asian cinema has been sporadic at best, generally with me stumbling onto some genius of a film-maker and tracking down as much of their work as I can after that. So yes, I've seen plenty of John Woo, and I've seen almost all of Akira Kurosawa's films, and Lady Snowblood, and many great movies in between, but I would never claim to be any kind of authority on film from the region in any era.

That said, there is one thing that I've found a true love for in Hong Kong films, and that's the "bad but honorable men who stick together against all odds" genre. It's a kind of macho brotherhood and loyalty that really works in crime films, and we see it over here in everything from Butch and Sundance to the more recent Kiss Kiss Bang Bang, but no one seems to have grasped this strange hybrid genre quite like they do in Hong Kong. John Woo's The Killer wouldn't be any good if the hitman and the cop didn't have such a deep respect for each other, if their nobility weren't such a huge part of the equation. City on Fire, the film that was of some inspiration to Reservoir Dogs, is the same way -- you feel the pain of the bad guy when he realizes the friend he's trying to save is an undercover cop.

But where John Woo was more like Sam Peckinpah at times, with his carefully choreographed bloodbaths, Johnnie To seems to have quietly become Hong Kong's own Sergio Leone. At least, when he wants to be, and when the material calls for it. In two films, The Mission and Exiled, To has taken the silence and pace and mood of Leone's westerns and seamlessly integrated it all into the modern style of Hong Kong cinema, and at the same time he's written the book on honor and loyalty and the bonds that tie bad men together.

The first thing that leaps out at you when watching The Mission are the risks taken by the director. He skips right over a huge action scene that would have been the explosive opening of most movies (lesser movies) and instead pans over the aftermath. The smoke-filled air of a restaurant full of dead men, the camera slowly moving through the scene until it finds Boss Lung, the mobster this hit was intended to take out. He's hiding in a freezer in the kitchen, quietly calling for back-up from his right-hand man.

After being extricated from his near-death experience, Boss Lung hires five bodyguards, and it's these five men the film is really about. The murder plot against their boss is little more than an excuse for a film about the brotherhood that grows among these bad men. And that's where the silence comes in, and the humor, which isn't something you're used to seeing in crime movies in the US. But Hong Kong cinema often has moments of slapstick humor, or deadpan, or even outrageous shocks that US viewers have a tendency to reject. But it's the same kind of humor you find in a Spaghetti Western, really, and something that enriches the bonds between the main characters and allows us to get to like them quickly.

There's a scene in The Mission, not long before a harrowing gunfight in a mall, that says everything about the movie, and it's a simple moment -- an innocent moment, even. Our heroes are waiting for Boss Lung in his office lobby, and they begin quietly playing soccer from their seats with a wadded-up ball of paper. Stretching their legs while not leaving their chairs, kicking this wad of paper back and forth between them. It's silly, I know, but there's something both tense and lighthearted about that scene, especially when the defacto leader of the group, Curtis (played brilliantly by Anthony Wong) notices what the others are doing. Is he going to snarl at them to quit? But instead, he steps out of his role for just a moment and kicks the ball, too. And then the second their boss appears, these men are cold professionals again, as if the whole scene never happened. This is a movie about those quiet moments.

Strangely, the real heart of the Mission comes after these men's mission is actually over, when it turns out that one of our heroes has done something stupid (I don't want to spoil it so I'm being vague) and Boss Lung has ordered his death. It turns out the first two acts were really just building towards the moment when these men of honor are forced to turn on each other. Do they kill their comrade, their friend, or do they turn on the life they know? I won't ruin it for you, but I will say that Francis Ng, who plays Roy, is simply amazing here. The kind of soulful actor the US could use a lot more of in our cinema.

Johnny To made The Mission in 1999, and then last year he made what is generally referred to as it's sequel, Exiled. In another touch of Sergio Leone inspiration, Exiled is more of a spiritual sequel than a literal one, much as the Good, the Bad, and the Ugly is a spiritual sequel to Fistful of Dollars and For a Few Dollars More. Eastwood appears to play the same character in them all, but his name is different in each film (which has somehow led to people thinking his character had no name in any of them, which is untrue) just as the Lee Van Cleef of Good Bad is not the same character he plays in Few Dollars More.

In Exiled, most of the actors who starred in the Mission return, and Francis Ng and Anthony Wong appear to be the exact same characters, but their names are different, and the young friend they fought so hard to save in the previous film is here again, but in a different role. Personally, I like it more because it's not a literal sequel. It makes you think about the artistry and the themes it circles around more that way, I think. Instead of just wondering what happened next, you get to see a master director approaching a favorite theme from yet another angle.

Exiled opens with two men sent to Macau to execute a guy they used to work with a long time ago, who was never supposed to come back. But when these two arrive in Macau, they are met by two other old friends, who are there to save their exiled brother. It feels like what would have probably happened next in the Mission, had the story been slightly different. And again, Francis Ng is the friend who refuses to let his old partner just be killed, just as he was in the Mission, while Anthony Wong is the hardened professional who can't turn down his boss's orders, even if it means killing someone who is like family to him.

This of course leads to some beautiful and ridiculous moments, such as a gunfight where the three participants try as hard as possible not to shoot each other, while their old friend's baby cries in an adjoining room. And that humor I spoke of rears its head again at the same time outside in the street, with a truly funny slapstick moment – a killer scaring off a cowardly cop by shooting a tin can off the ground and ricocheting it into the cop's head and bouncing it off his car. But that comedy isn't just there for relief, it's got a deeper message that parallels the shootout going on upstairs -- These are men who hit what they aim at, so when the smoke clears and nothing but the apartment is damaged, you know they're in a really shitty spot. So what do they do? They start fixing up the apartment and cook a big meal and catch up over dinner, just like old friends.

From there they realize that their friend is doomed, and that the only thing to do is figure out how to provide for his wife and kid after his death. So the five old comrades reunite to take on one last hit to earn a big score, and to say everything goes flying off the rails at that point would be a giant understatement. Exiled is far more brutal and violent than the Mission, with several gun fights that are like a bloody ballet being performed onscreen. When bullets hit their mark, dust clouds of blood explode. There were a few times I found myself going "oh fuck" at the sheer weight of the action as our five friends careen from one ill-fated move to another. Where the Mission was about brotherhood and the mob and honor, Exiled is much more of a noir story. These characters feel their own doom, and given the chance to escape it, they still can't, because of the bonds that tie them together.

And again, like a Leone movie, silence and small scenes are as important, maybe more important, than the action. Johnnie To never forgets that, and he lets his narrative wander, and linger on that silence. When our heroes continually have to push-start all the cars they end up with, and choose their path by flipping coins once they're on the run, you feel you're wandering the barren wasteland with them. When they stumble upon a gold heist in that wilderness, too, it just feels right. It fits. Just as their goofing around the camp fire does.

And it's those moments that will rip you apart inside, eventually, as all the strands of the story all come together. Johnnie To's deft hand, and his understanding of the weight of history carries you through it, though, all the way to the final haunting frames.

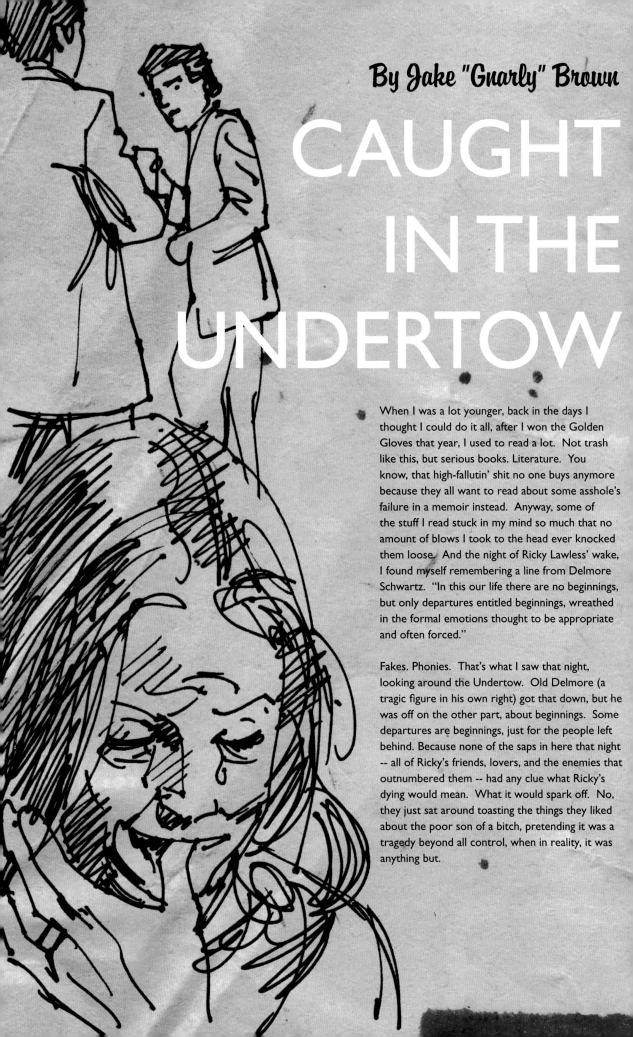

By Jake "Gnarly" Brown

CAUGHT IN THE UNDERTOW

When I was a lot younger, back in the days I thought I could do it all, after I won the Golden Gloves that year, I used to read a lot. Not trash like this, but serious books. Literature. You know, that high-fallutin' shit no one buys anymore because they all want to read about some asshole's failure in a memoir instead. Anyway, some of the stuff I read stuck in my mind so much that no amount of blows I took to the head ever knocked them loose. And the night of Ricky Lawless' wake, I found myself remembering a line from Delmore Schwartz. "In this our life there are no beginnings, but only departures entitled beginnings, wreathed in the formal emotions thought to be appropriate and often forced."

Fakes. Phonies. That's what I saw that night, looking around the Undertow. Old Delmore (a tragic figure in his own right) got that down, but he was off on the other part, about beginnings. Some departures are beginnings, just for the people left behind. Because none of the saps in here that night -- all of Ricky's friends, lovers, and the enemies that outnumbered them -- had any clue what Ricky's dying would mean. What it would spark off. No, they just sat around toasting the things they liked about the poor son of a bitch, pretending it was a tragedy beyond all control, when in reality, it was anything but.

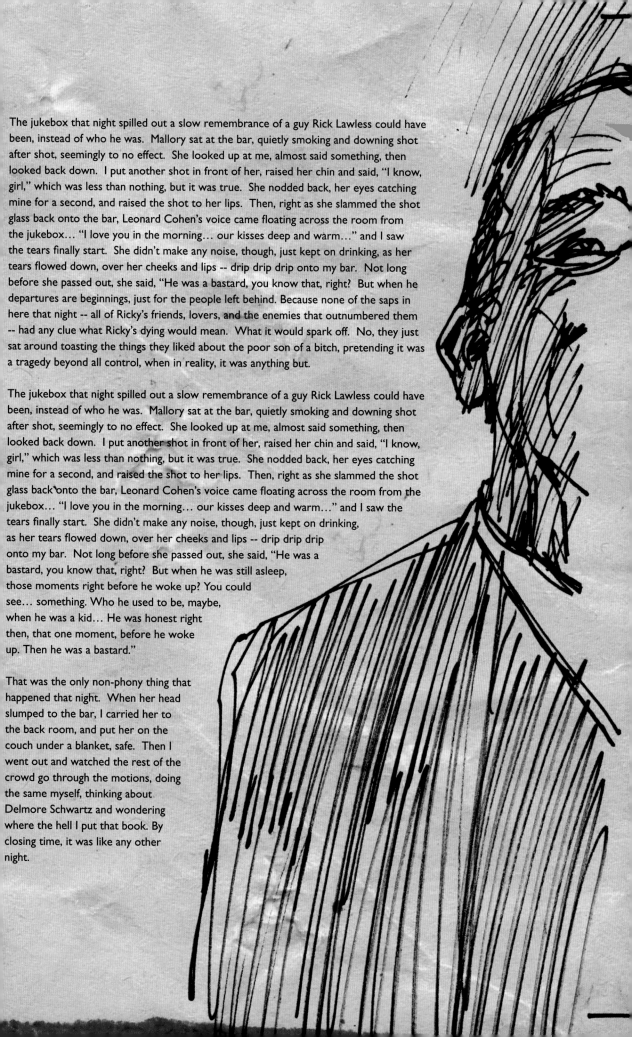

The jukebox that night spilled out a slow remembrance of a guy Rick Lawless could have been, instead of who he was. Mallory sat at the bar, quietly smoking and downing shot after shot, seemingly to no effect. She looked up at me, almost said something, then looked back down. I put another shot in front of her, raised her chin and said, "I know, girl," which was less than nothing, but it was true. She nodded back, her eyes catching mine for a second, and raised the shot to her lips. Then, right as she slammed the shot glass back onto the bar, Leonard Cohen's voice came floating across the room from the jukebox… "I love you in the morning… our kisses deep and warm…" and I saw the tears finally start. She didn't make any noise, though, just kept on drinking, as her tears flowed down, over her cheeks and lips -- drip drip drip onto my bar. Not long before she passed out, she said, "He was a bastard, you know that, right? But when he departures are beginnings, just for the people left behind. Because none of the saps in here that night -- all of Ricky's friends, lovers, and the enemies that outnumbered them -- had any clue what Ricky's dying would mean. What it would spark off. No, they just sat around toasting the things they liked about the poor son of a bitch, pretending it was a tragedy beyond all control, when in reality, it was anything but.

The jukebox that night spilled out a slow remembrance of a guy Rick Lawless could have been, instead of who he was. Mallory sat at the bar, quietly smoking and downing shot after shot, seemingly to no effect. She looked up at me, almost said something, then looked back down. I put another shot in front of her, raised her chin and said, "I know, girl," which was less than nothing, but it was true. She nodded back, her eyes catching mine for a second, and raised the shot to her lips. Then, right as she slammed the shot glass back onto the bar, Leonard Cohen's voice came floating across the room from the jukebox… "I love you in the morning… our kisses deep and warm…" and I saw the tears finally start. She didn't make any noise, though, just kept on drinking, as her tears flowed down, over her cheeks and lips -- drip drip drip onto my bar. Not long before she passed out, she said, "He was a bastard, you know that, right? But when he was still asleep, those moments right before he woke up? You could see… something. Who he used to be, maybe, when he was a kid… He was honest right then, that one moment, before he woke up. Then he was a bastard."

That was the only non-phony thing that happened that night. When her head slumped to the bar, I carried her to the back room, and put her on the couch under a blanket, safe. Then I went out and watched the rest of the crowd go through the motions, doing the same myself, thinking about Delmore Schwartz and wondering where the hell I put that book. By closing time, it was like any other night.

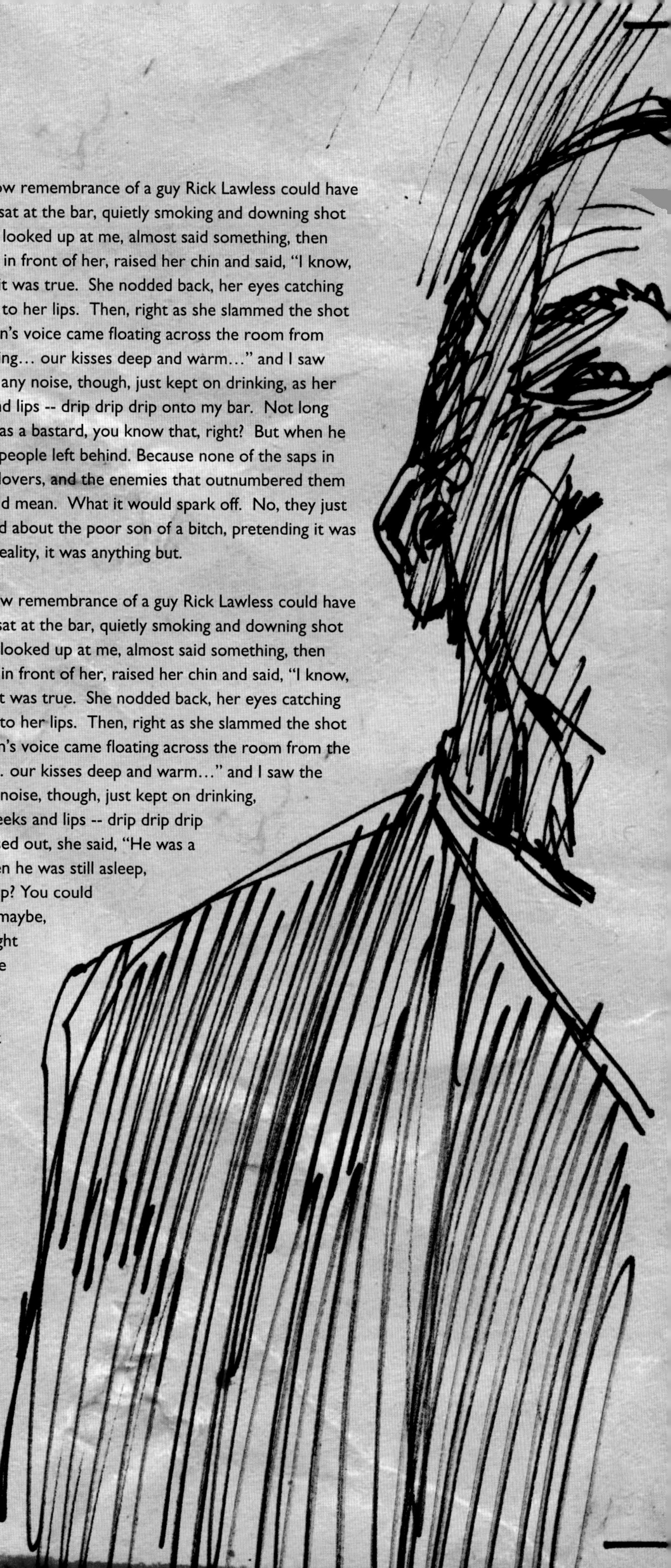

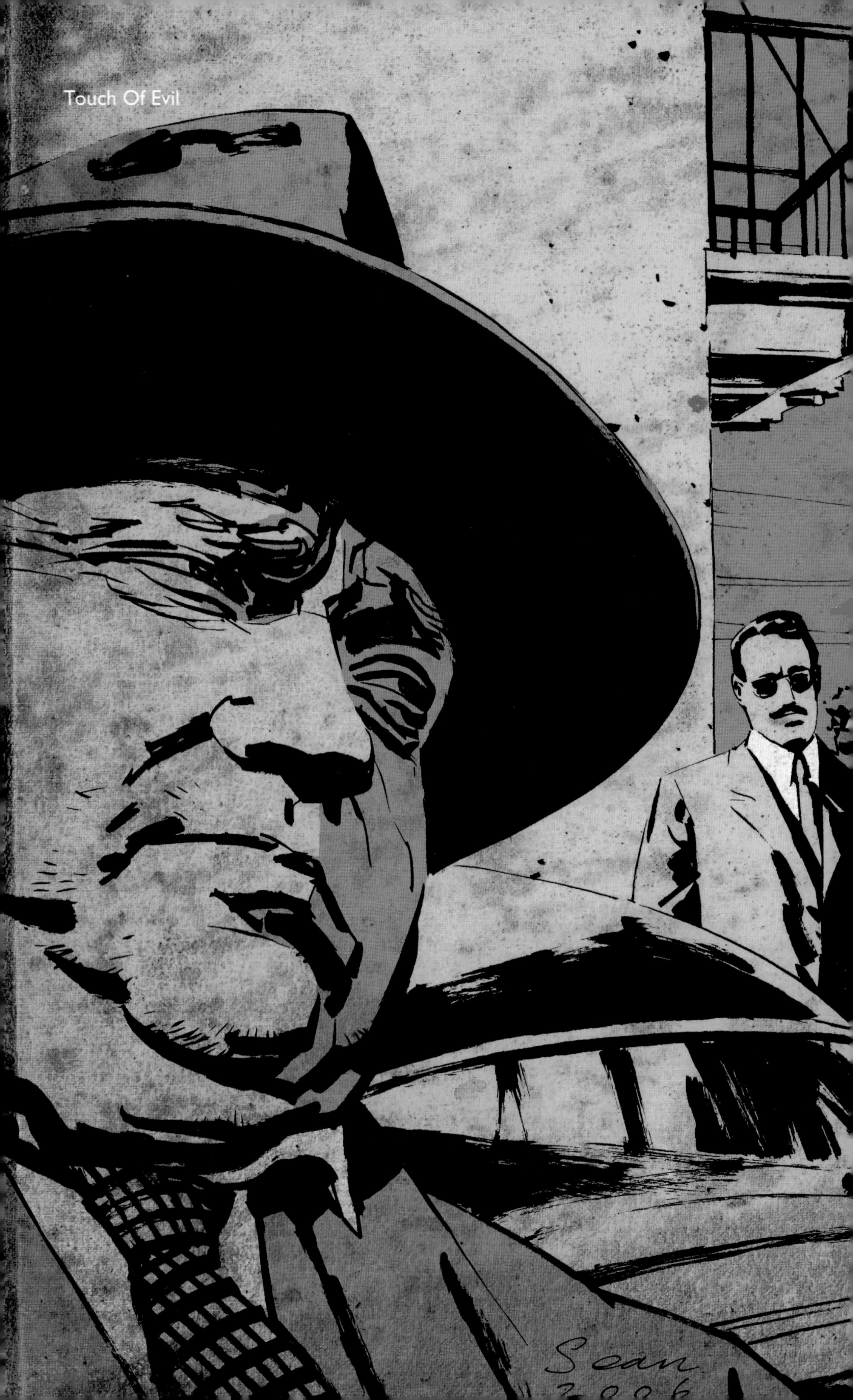
Touch Of Evil
Sean

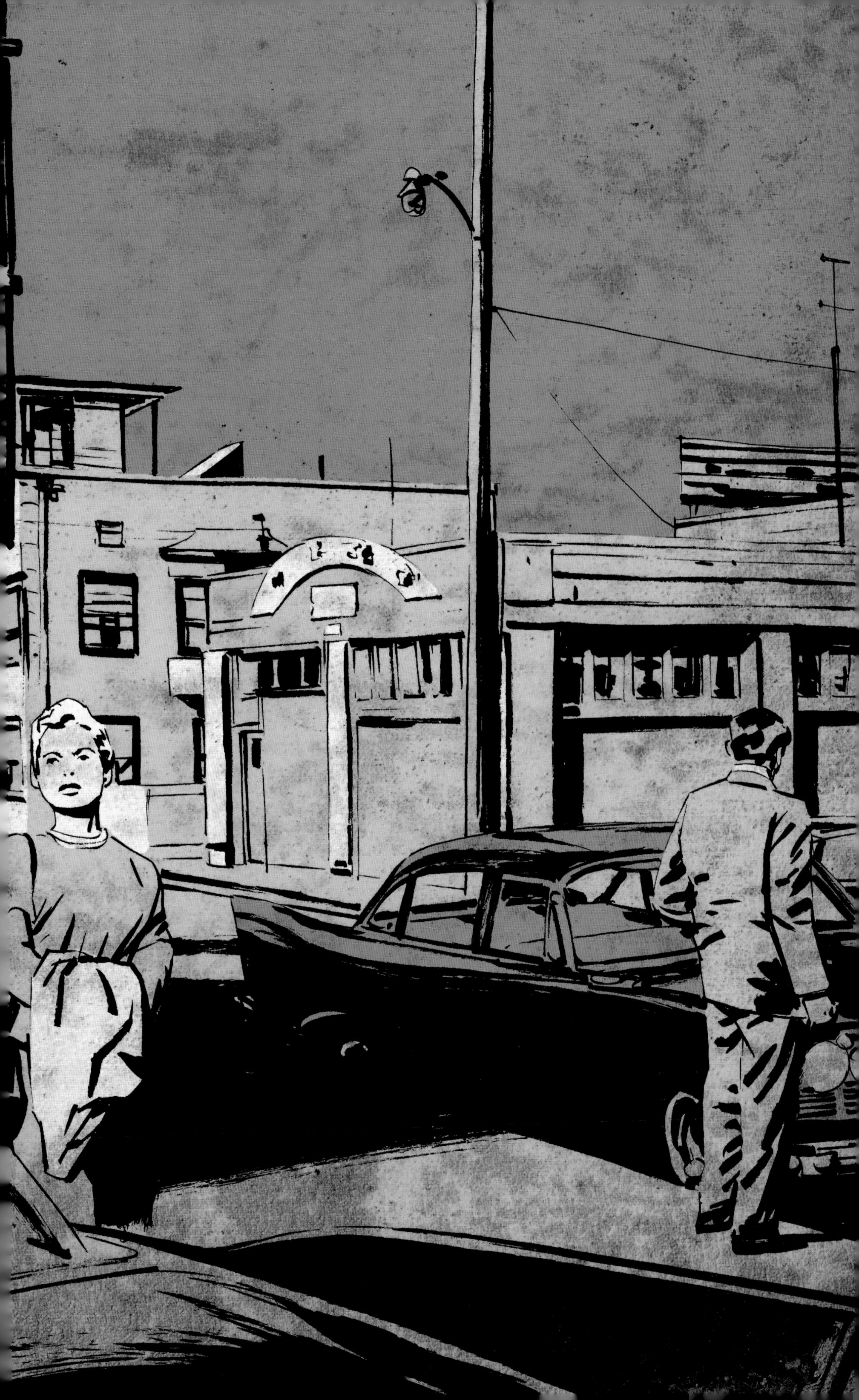

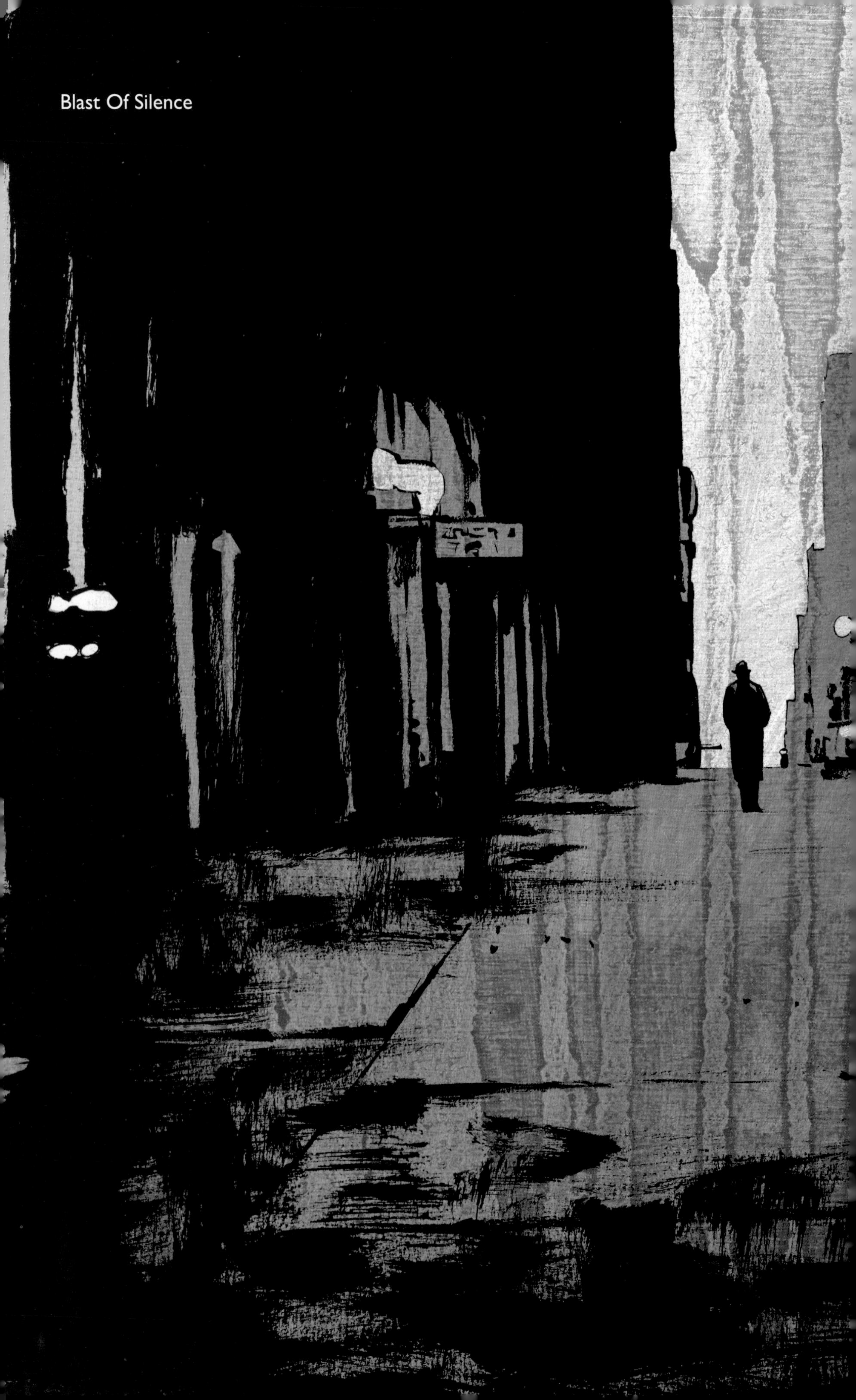

Blast Of Silence

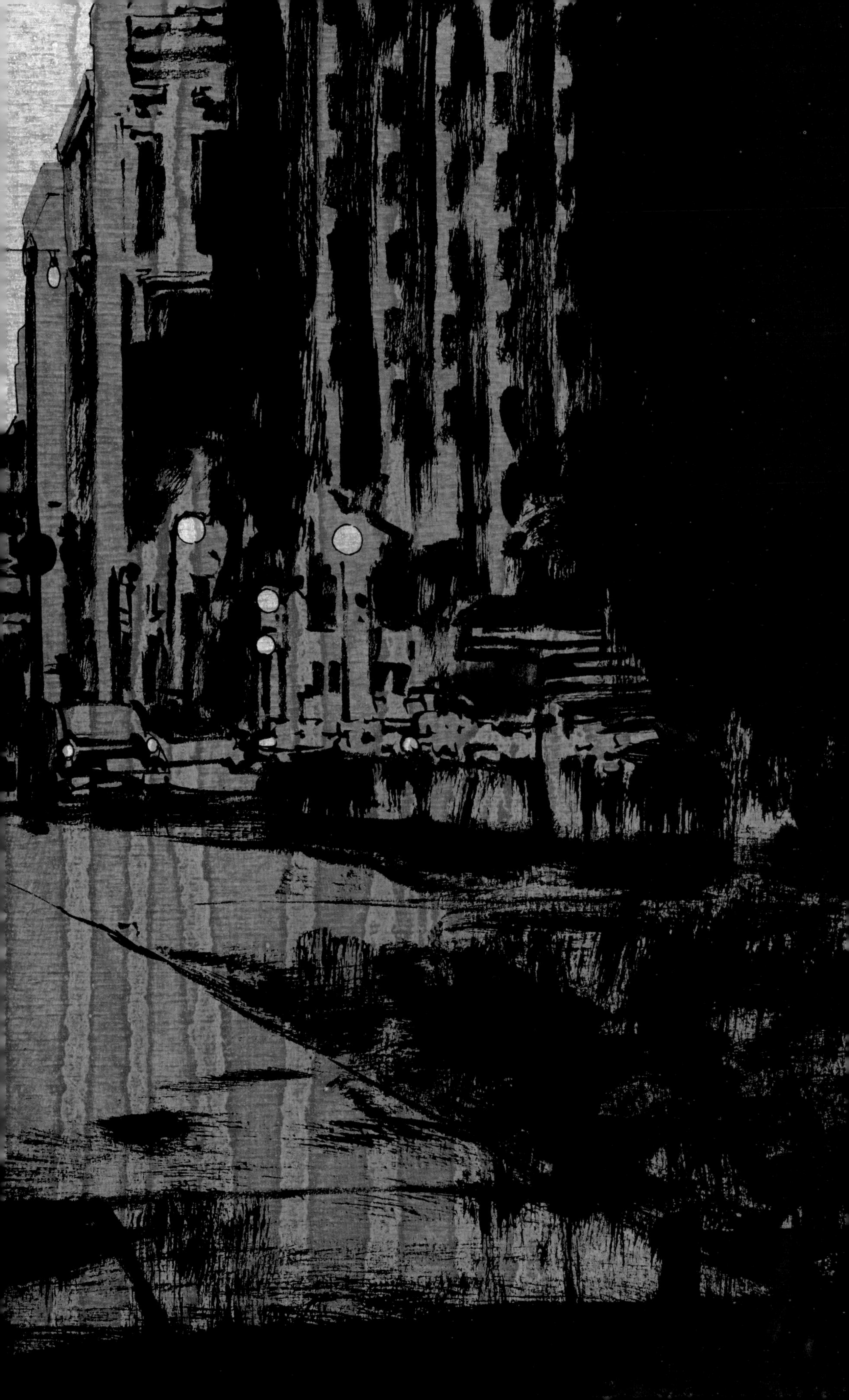

The Neo-Noir

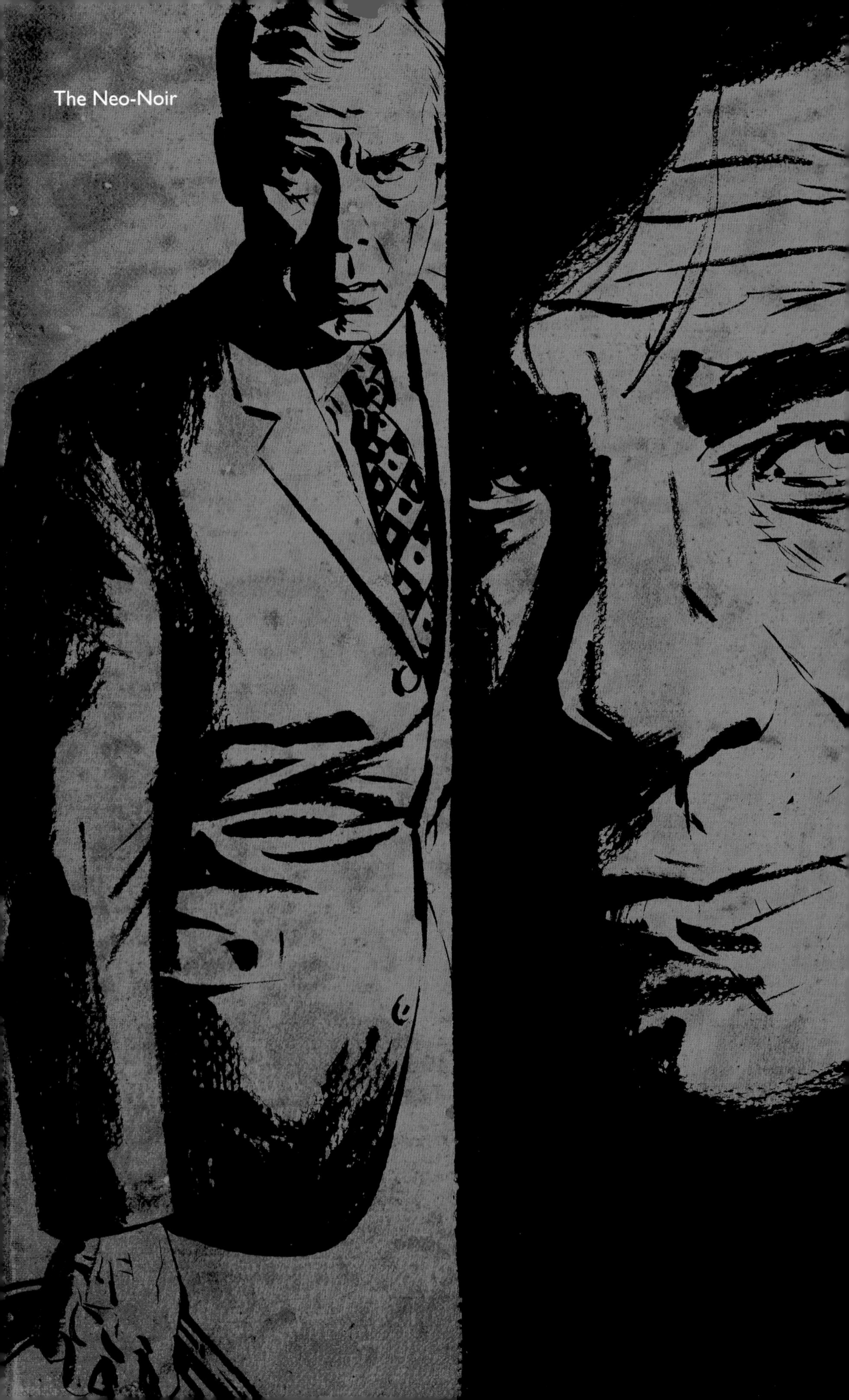

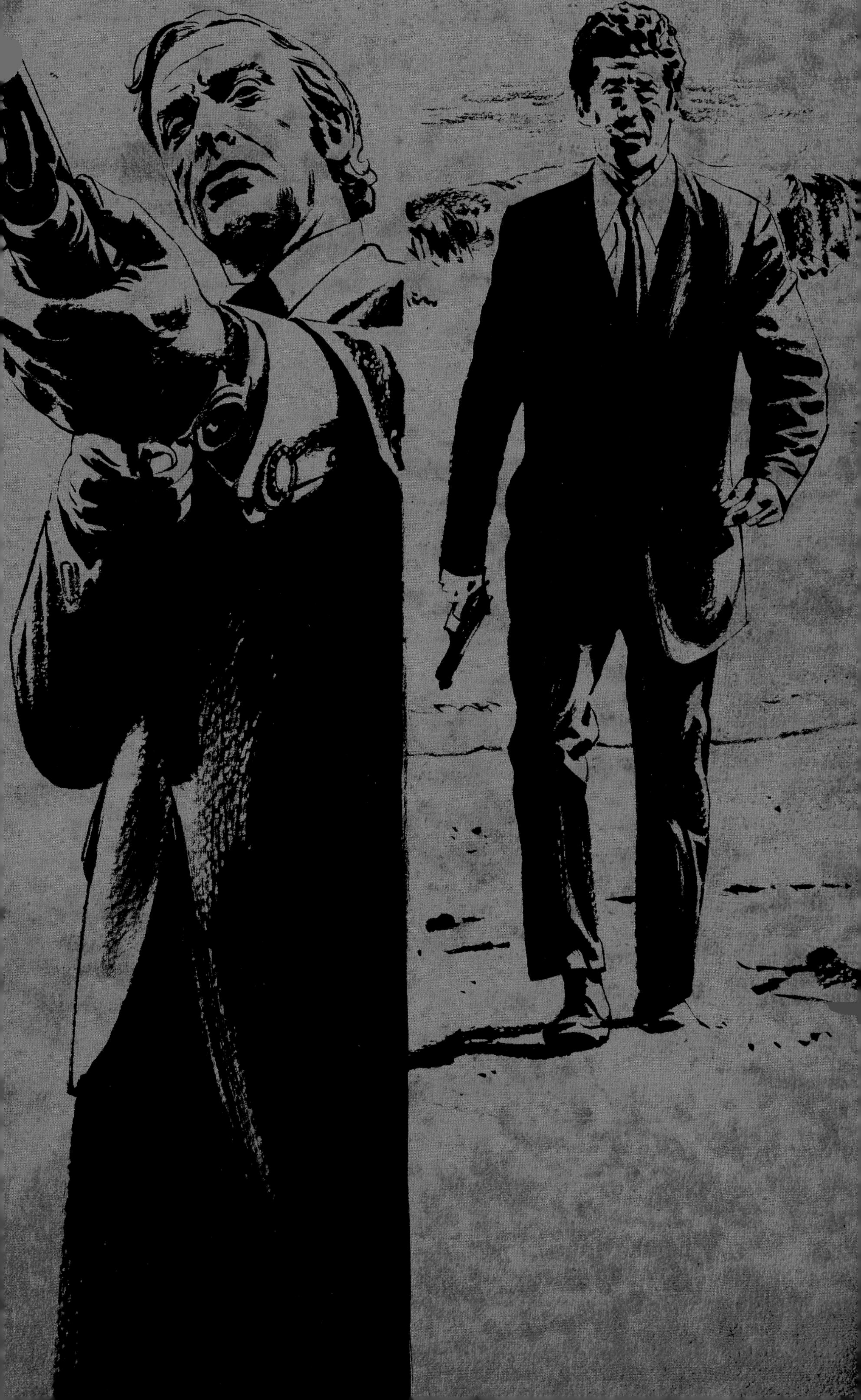

The Long Goodbye

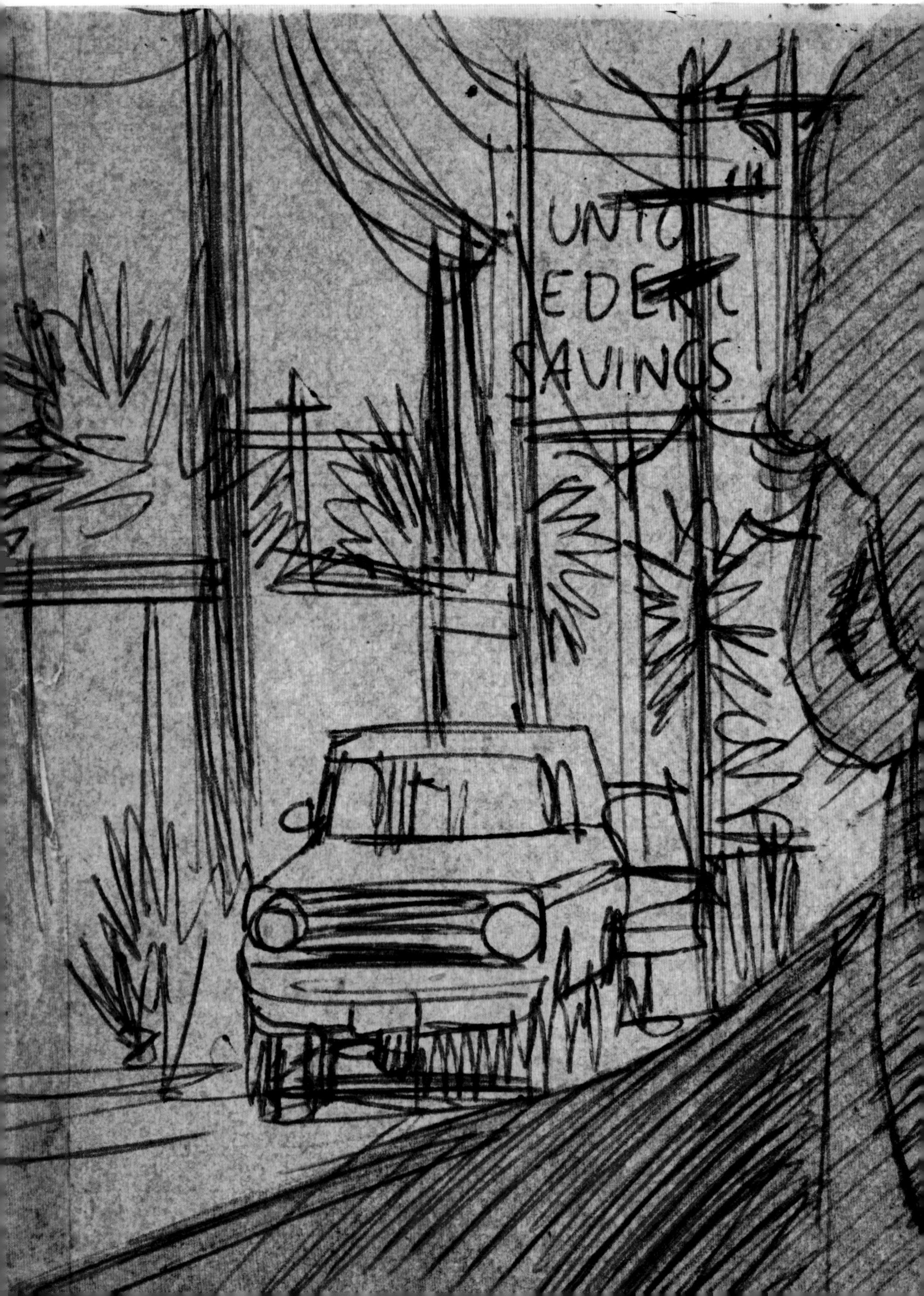
UNTO
SAVINGS

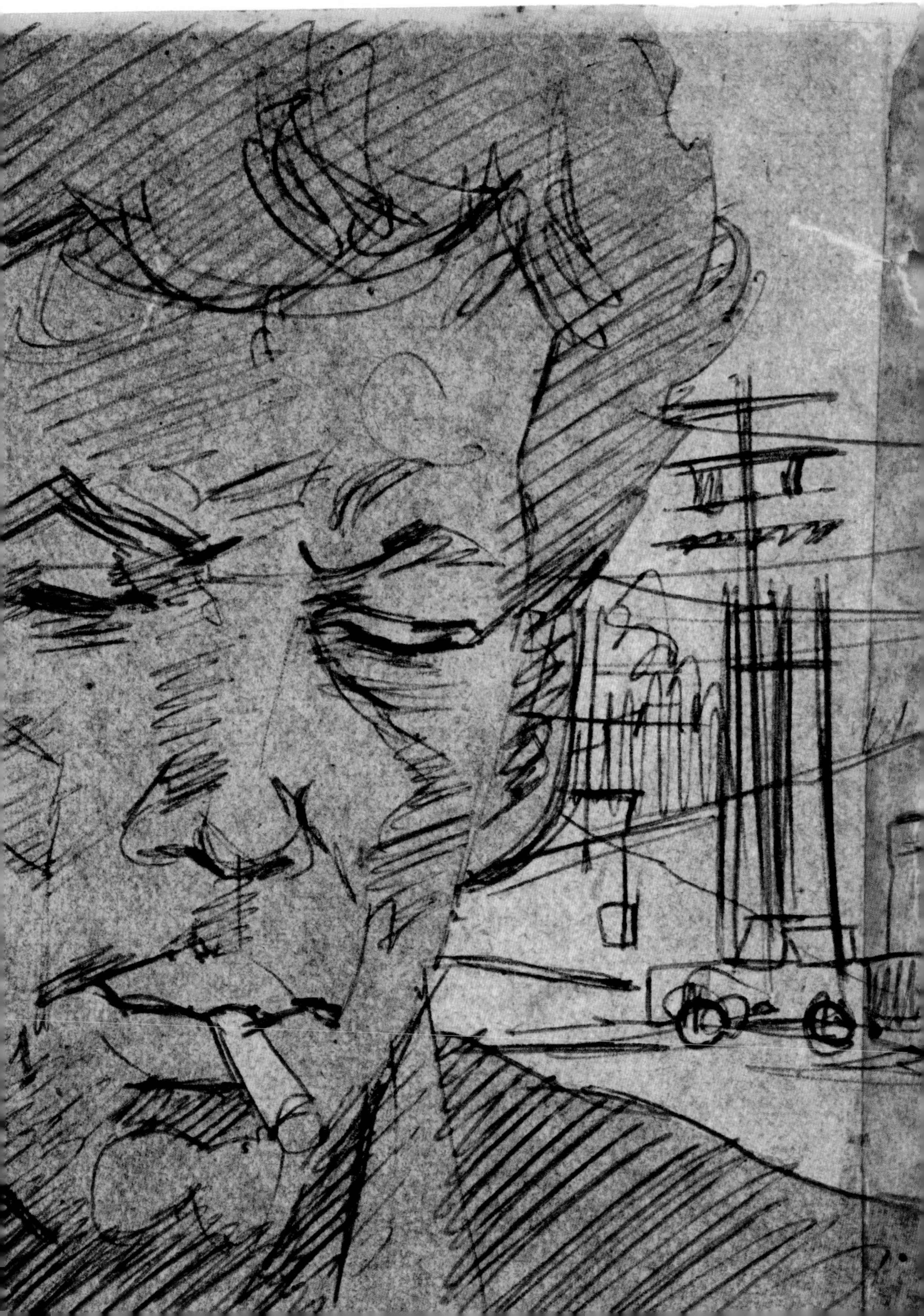

Blaxploitation

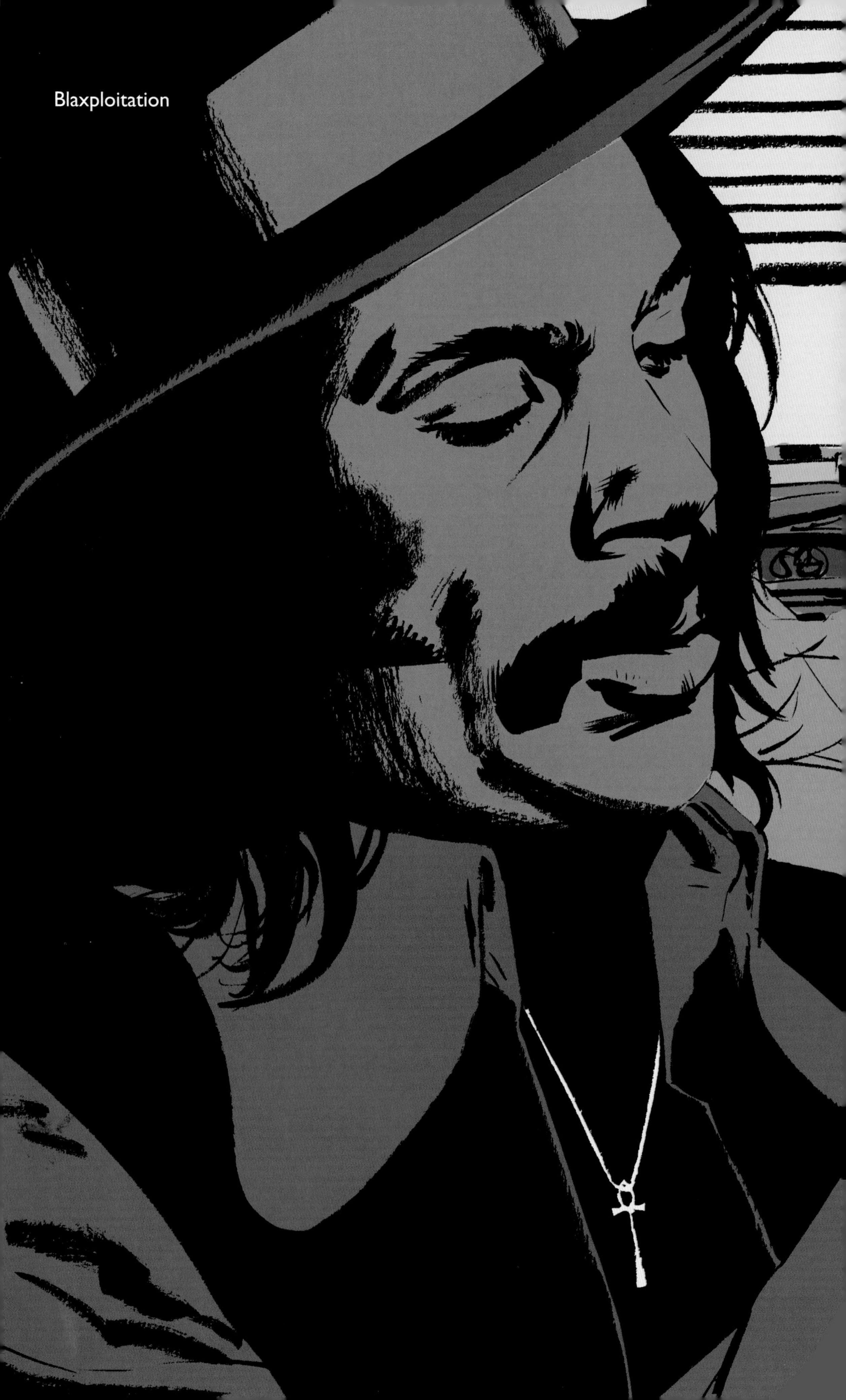

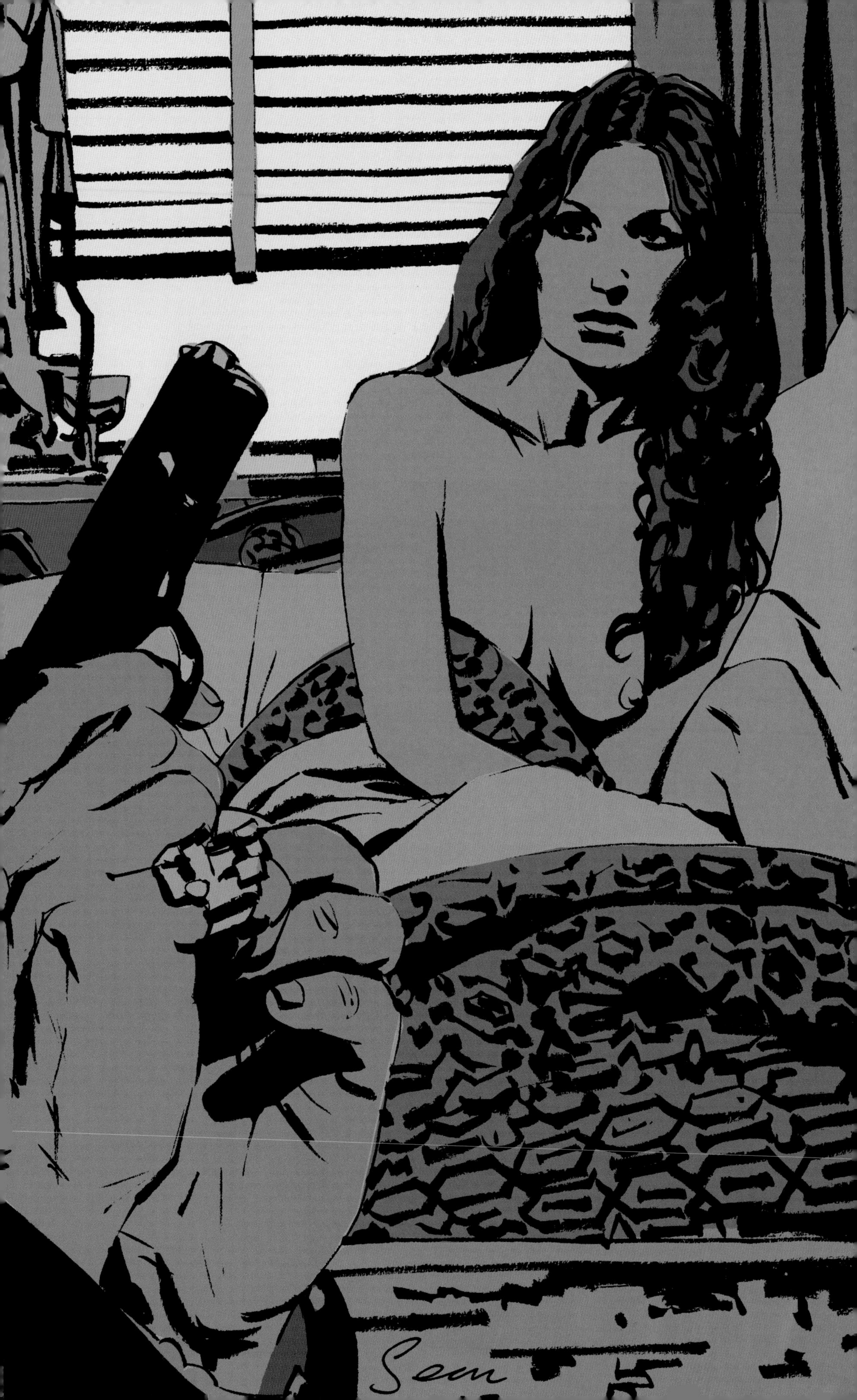
Sean

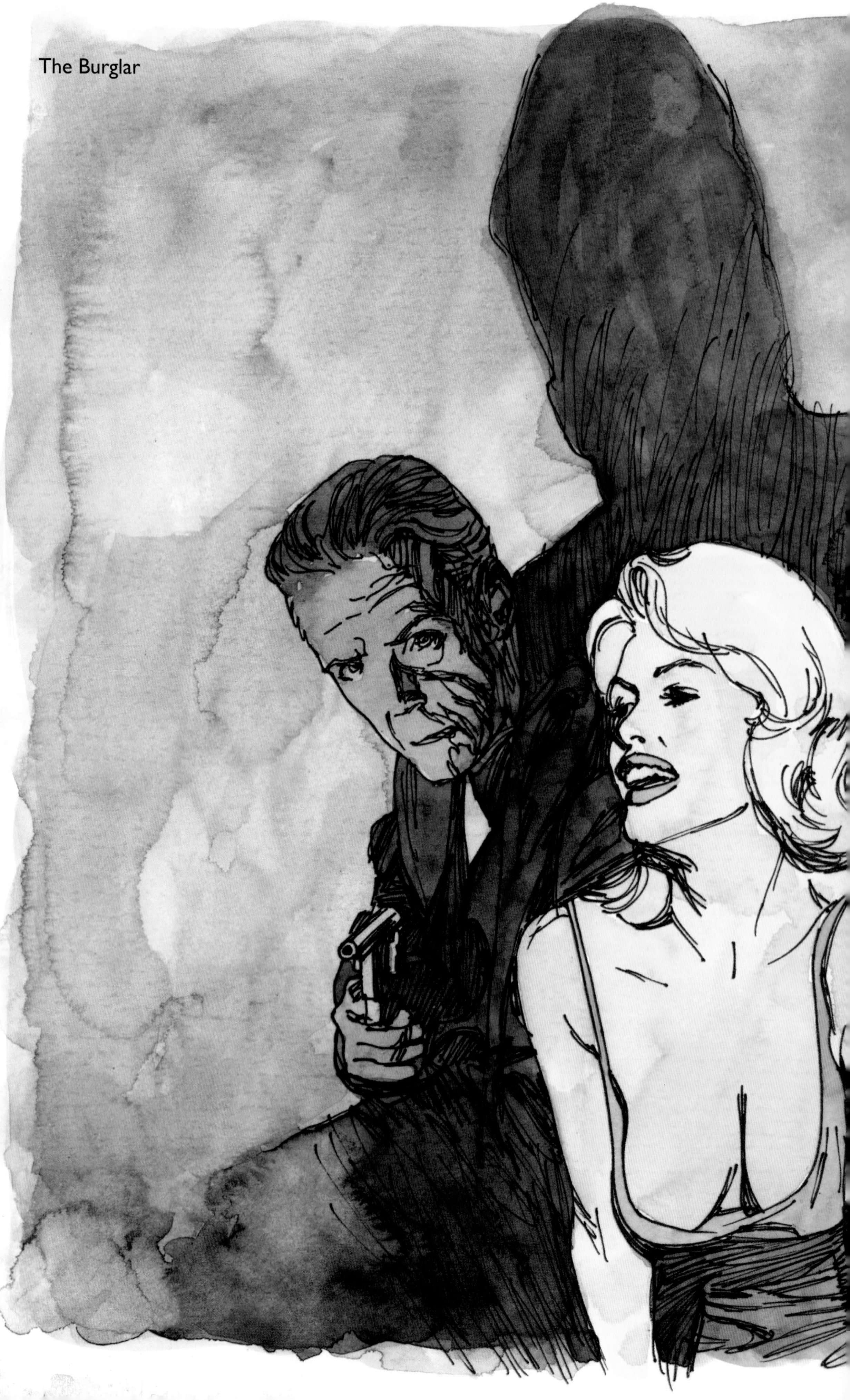

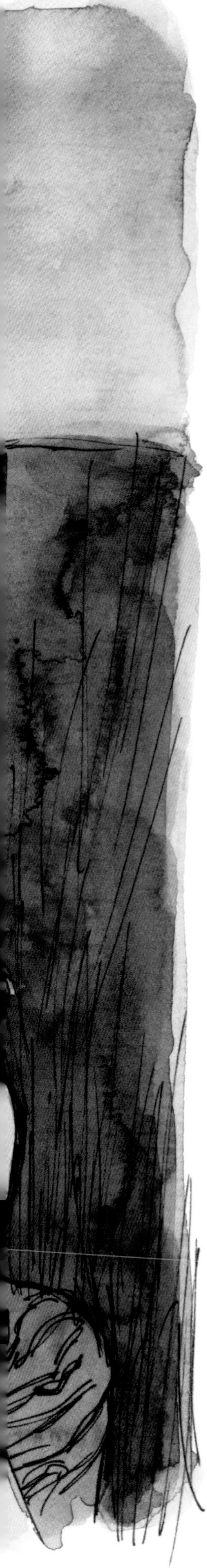

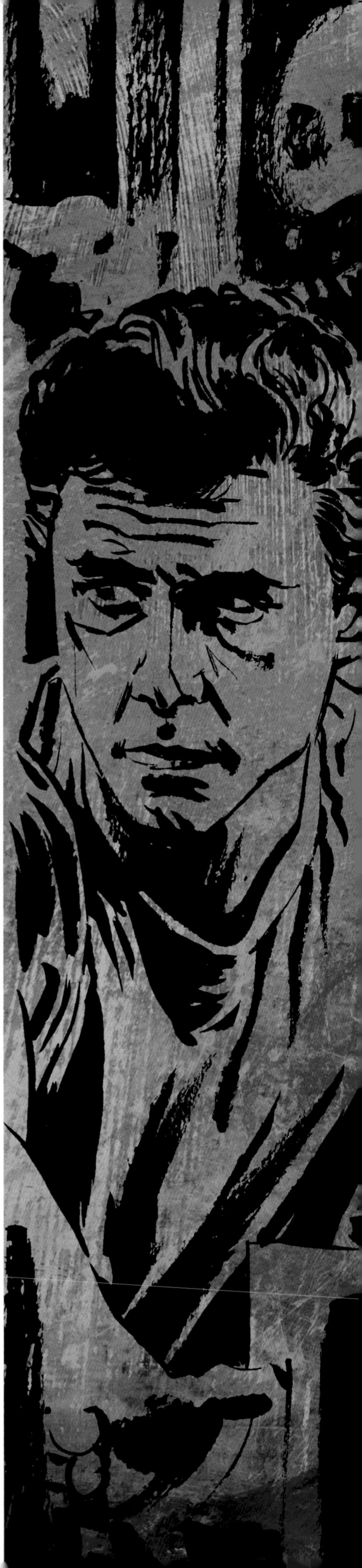

TV Cops and Movie Tough Guys

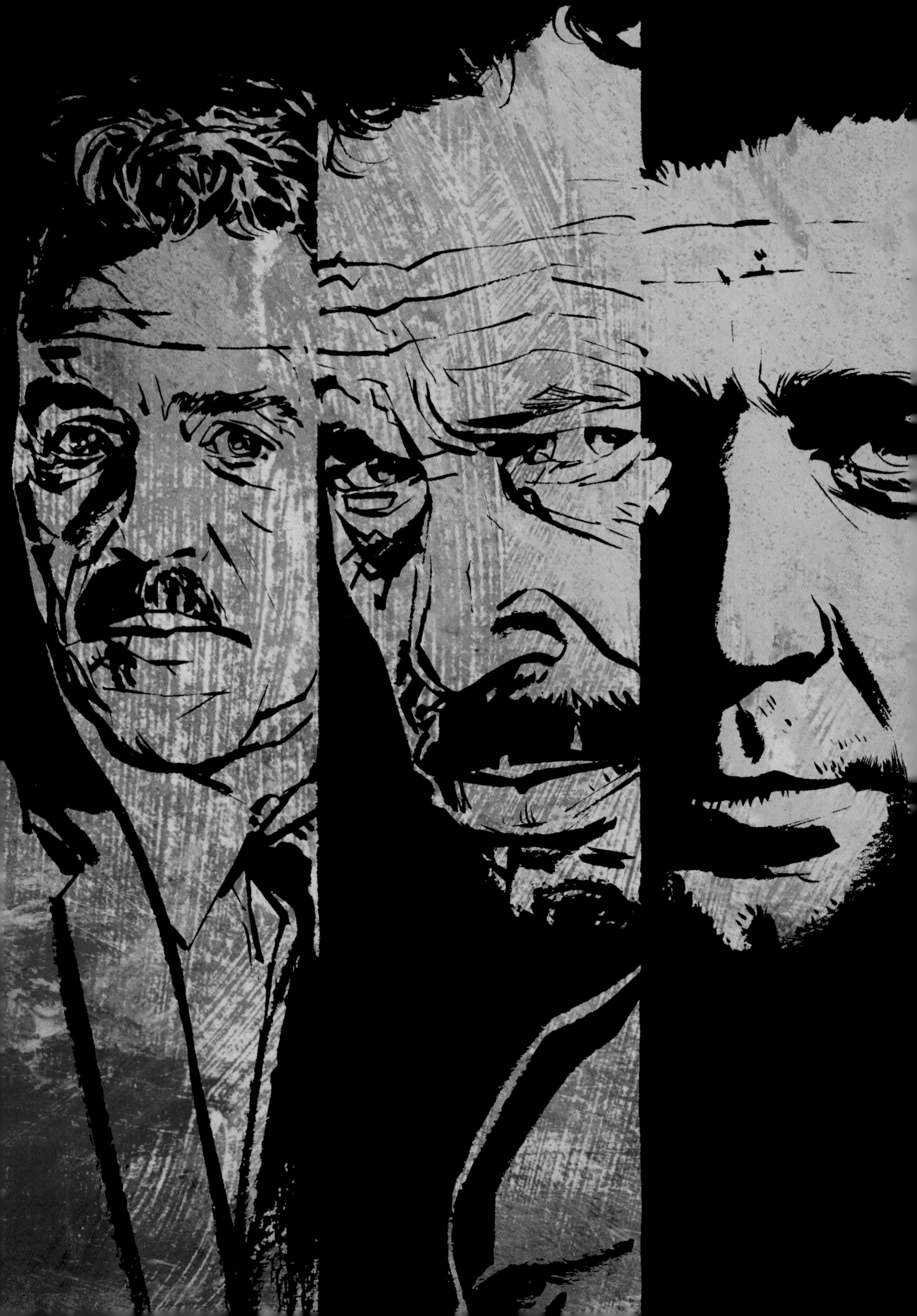

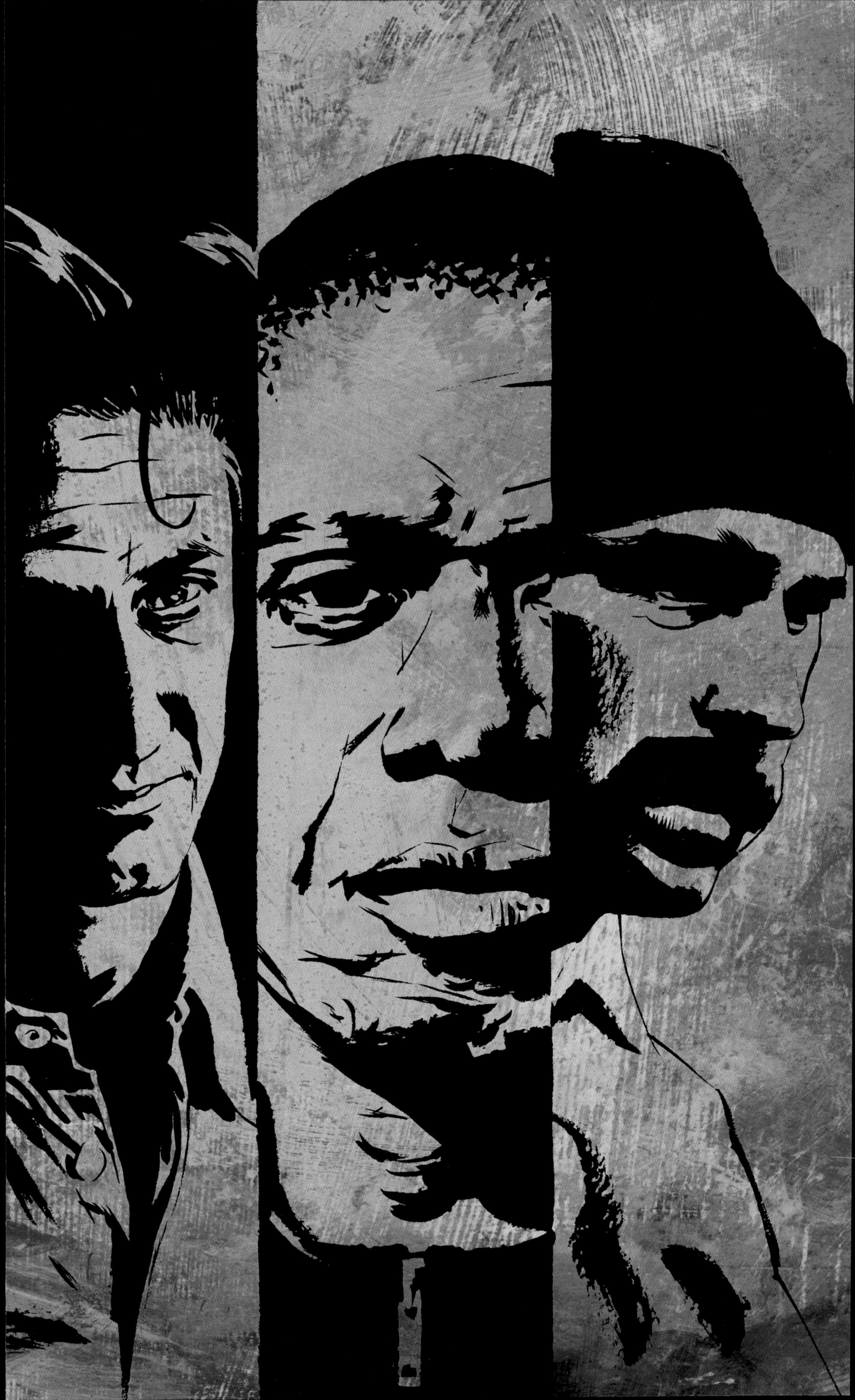

The Yakuza

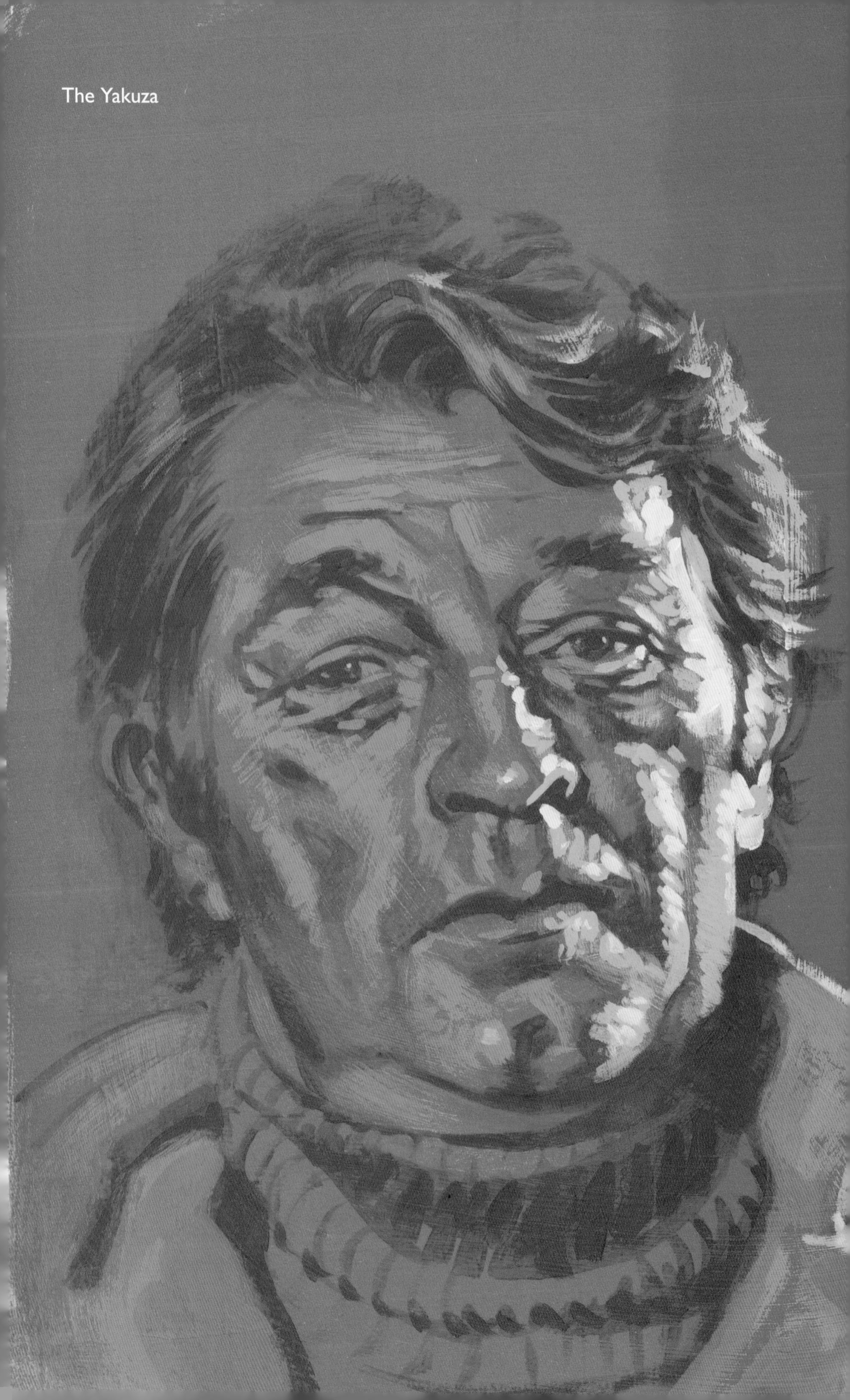

On the following pages you'll find the short story NO ONE RIDES FOR FREE which was originally done for a CBLDF benefit book in 2008.

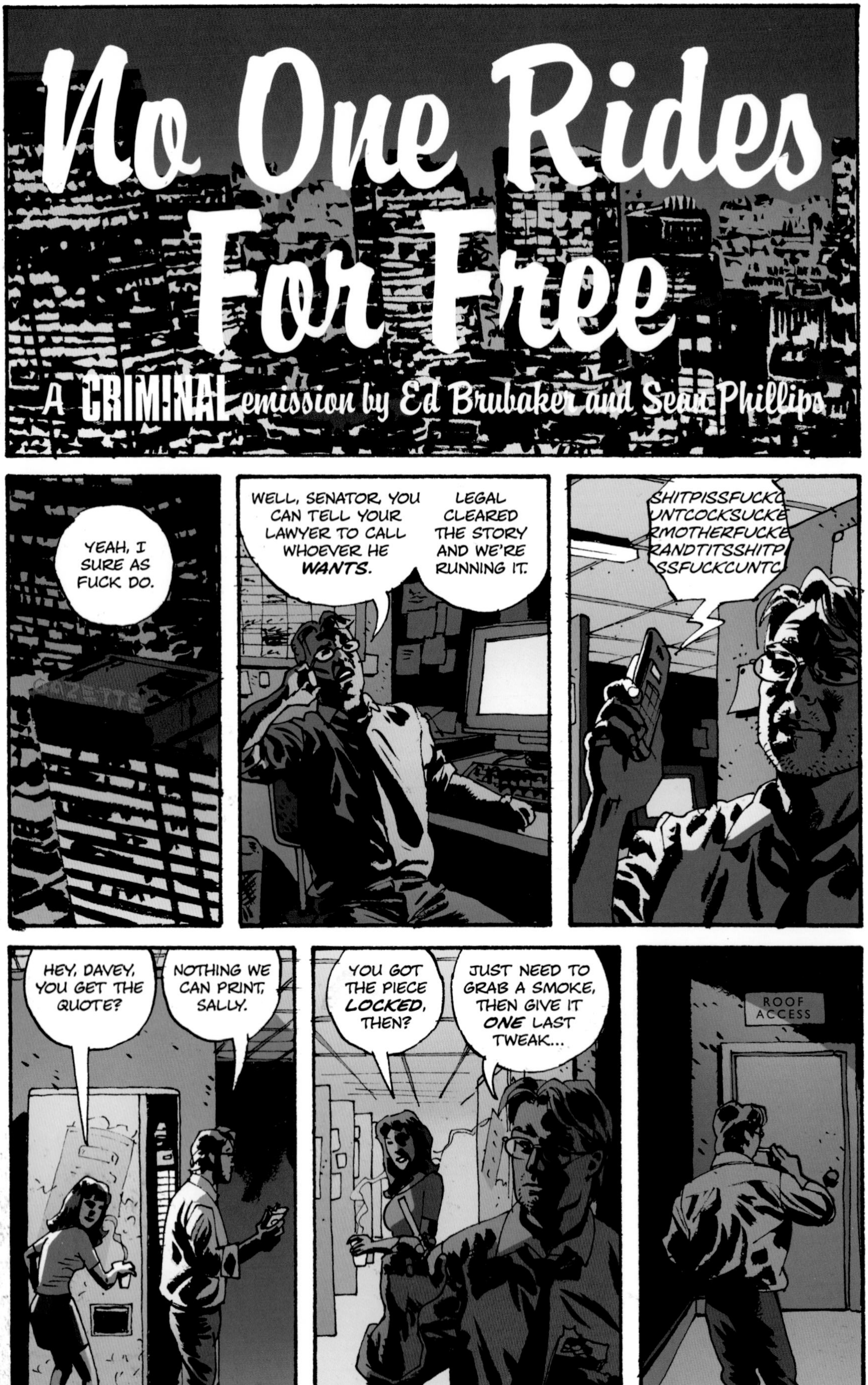
No One Rides For Free
A CRIMINAL emission by Ed Brubaker and Sean Phillips
YEAH, I SURE AS FUCK DO.
GAZETTE
WELL, SENATOR, YOU CAN TELL YOUR LAWYER TO CALL WHOEVER HE WANTS.
LEGAL CLEARED THE STORY AND WE'RE RUNNING IT.
SHITPISSFUCKC UNTCOCKSUCKE RMOTHERFUCKE RANDTITSSHITP SSFUCKCUNTC
HEY, DAVEY, YOU GET THE QUOTE?
NOTHING WE CAN PRINT, SALLY.
YOU GOT THE PIECE LOCKED, THEN?
JUST NEED TO GRAB A SMOKE, THEN GIVE IT ONE LAST TWEAK...
ROOF ACCESS

OH — HEY, I DON'T THINK YOU'RE SUPPOSED TO --

WAIT! NO –

FUHH... FF...

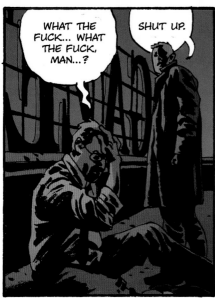
WHAT THE FUCK... WHAT THE FUCK, MAN...?

SHUT UP.

WHERE THE... WHERE ARE WE? IS THIS --

YEAH, THE ROOF...

AND YOU'VE GOT ONE CHANCE OF MAKING IT OFF OF HERE ALIVE.

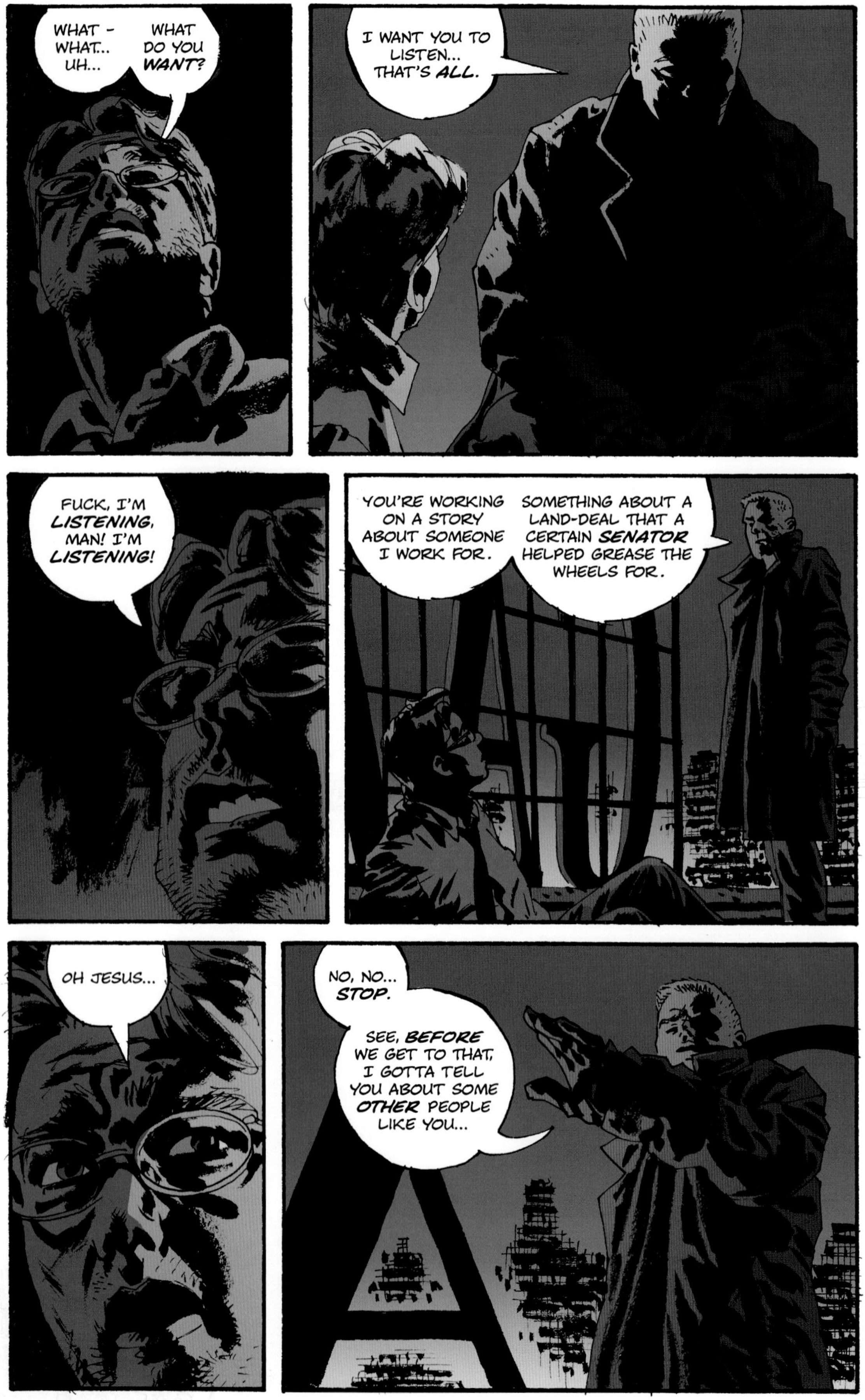
WHAT - WHAT... UH...
WHAT DO YOU WANT?
I WANT YOU TO LISTEN... THAT'S ALL.
FUCK, I'M LISTENING, MAN! I'M LISTENING!
YOU'RE WORKING ON A STORY ABOUT SOMEONE I WORK FOR.
SOMETHING ABOUT A LAND-DEAL THAT A CERTAIN SENATOR HELPED GREASE THE WHEELS FOR.
OH JESUS...
NO, NO... STOP.
SEE, BEFORE WE GET TO THAT, I GOTTA TELL YOU ABOUT SOME OTHER PEOPLE LIKE YOU...

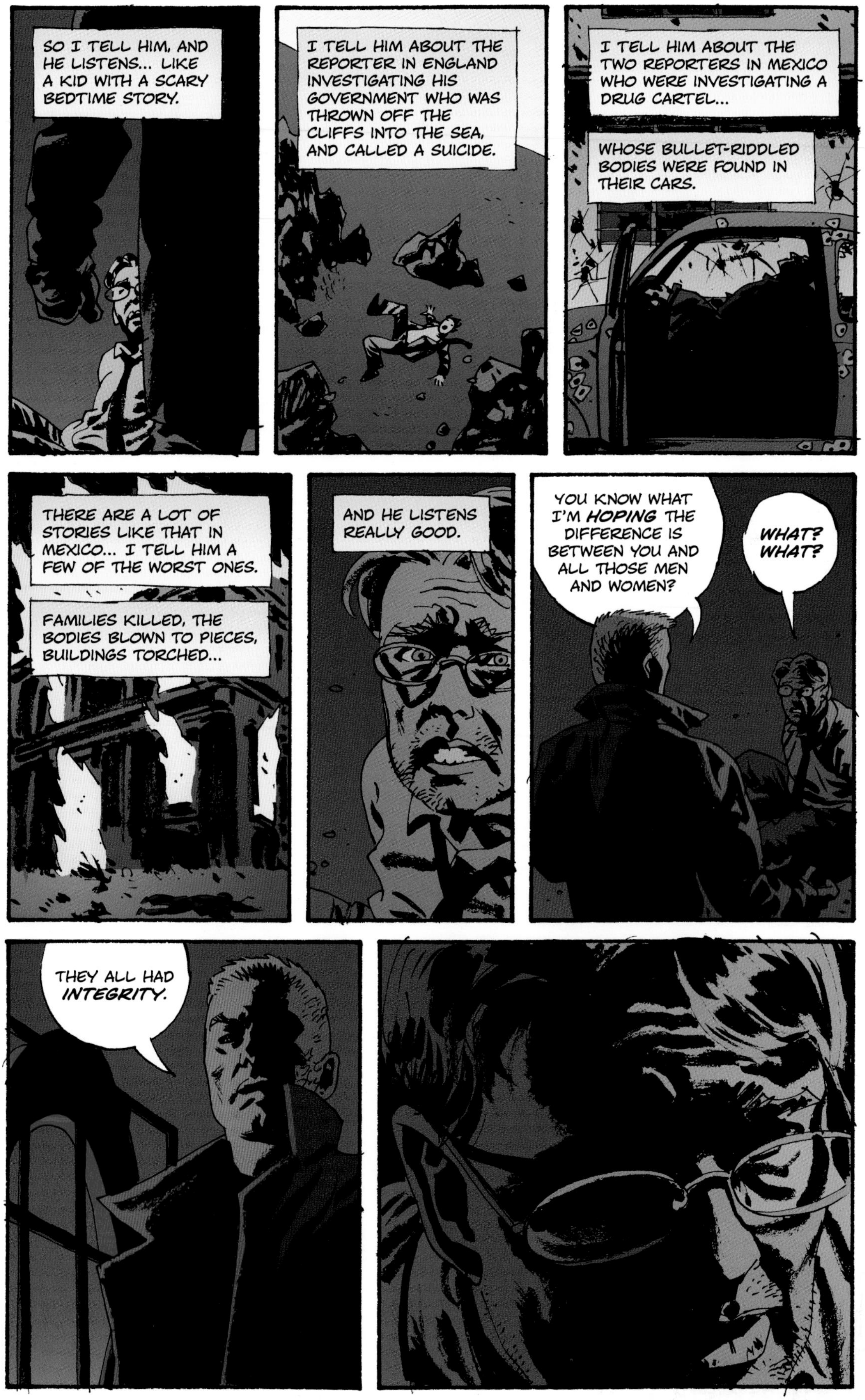
SO I TELL HIM, AND HE LISTENS... LIKE A KID WITH A SCARY BEDTIME STORY.
I TELL HIM ABOUT THE REPORTER IN ENGLAND INVESTIGATING HIS GOVERNMENT WHO WAS THROWN OFF THE CLIFFS INTO THE SEA, AND CALLED A SUICIDE.
I TELL HIM ABOUT THE TWO REPORTERS IN MEXICO WHO WERE INVESTIGATING A DRUG CARTEL...
WHOSE BULLET-RIDDLED BODIES WERE FOUND IN THEIR CARS.
THERE ARE A LOT OF STORIES LIKE THAT IN MEXICO... I TELL HIM A FEW OF THE WORST ONES.
FAMILIES KILLED, THE BODIES BLOWN TO PIECES, BUILDINGS TORCHED...
AND HE LISTENS REALLY GOOD.
YOU KNOW WHAT I'M *HOPING* THE DIFFERENCE IS BETWEEN YOU AND ALL THOSE MEN AND WOMEN?
WHAT? WHAT?
THEY ALL HAD *INTEGRITY*.

JESUS, DAVE... YOU SMOKING THE WHOLE PACK UP THERE?

?

C'MON... DELETE... DE-FUCKIN' -LETE.

SSSSKKKKKKKKKNKSKKKKKKKK

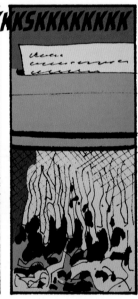

DAVE, IS EVERYTHING OKAY?

YEAH, JUST... TWEAKING...

HYDE CORP. NOT LINKED TO LAND DEAL

The End

Brubaker Phillips Staples

Process

The cover is usually the first thing I do for any comic, sometimes even before the script has been written. At this stage I don't know what's happening in the story, I asked Ed to never tell me before I get the script. It keeps it fresh for me and also means I don't get too distracted by something difficult I'll have to draw in a few months time.

Ed usually has a clear idea of what he wants, for this cover for Criminal #3, he asked for Leo and Greta with a gun in a field running away from the bad guys. I'd been looking at a lot of old paperback covers by Robert McGinnis and wanted to try something like he might have done, so I decided on a variation on the classic 'clinch' style cover. I did a few very rough sketches to decide on the positions of the figures and then worked up a more detailed sketch of Leo and Greta and also a rough of the farmhouse they were holed up in. These were scanned into Photoshop together and a couple of colour roughs produced. The first was a night time scene with flat colours which I quite liked, but then I tried a daytime version with an impending ominous storm approaching.

This was much more successful, so my wife grudgingly posed for some photo ref with me and I started painting. The painting was done the same size as the printed comic rather than the more normal 50% larger, partly because I thought it might make it quicker to paint and partly to help with painting the rough swirling sky. The finished painting was scanned into Photoshop and the contrast tweaked slightly.

Also on this sketchbook page are thumbnails for a couple of the Frank Kafka newspaper strips. These were always drawn separately and dropped into the story pages later.

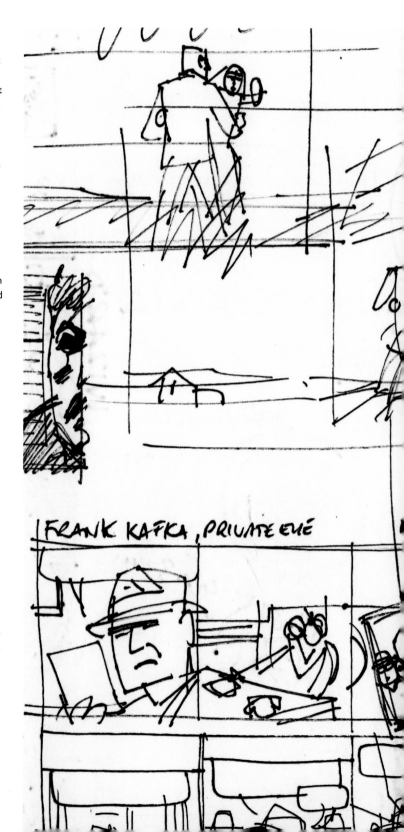

FRANK KAFKA, PRIVATE EYE

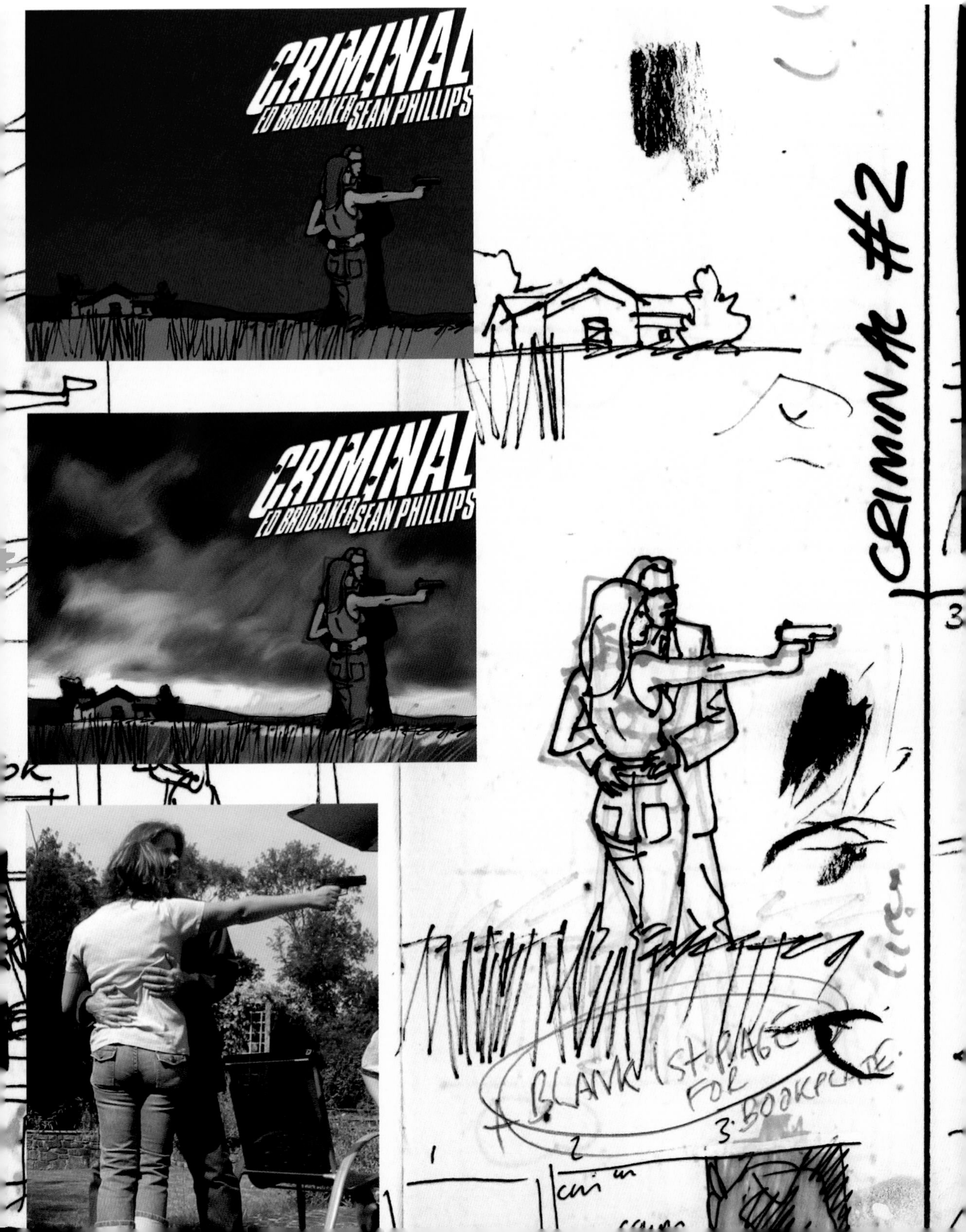
CRIMINAL
ED BRUBAKER SEAN PHILLIPS
CRIMINAL
ED BRUBAKER SEAN PHILLIPS
CRIMINAL #2
BLANK 1st PAGE FOR
3: BOOKPLATE

It all starts with the script.

Then, after telling Ed how great it is, I get to work.

After reading the script through a couple of times, I know just how to make it better! Usually this just consists of adding a few extra panels to help the dialogue flow a little easier. Because Criminal pages always follow a three tier grid, sometimes an extra panel is necessary to get a panel on the tier I want. Also those talky pages look more interesting with more panels on, so I often break the dialogue up into more panels especially if more than one person is talking. Even it's it one person with two dialogue balloons I'll break it up into two panels if a change in their expression will have more impact.

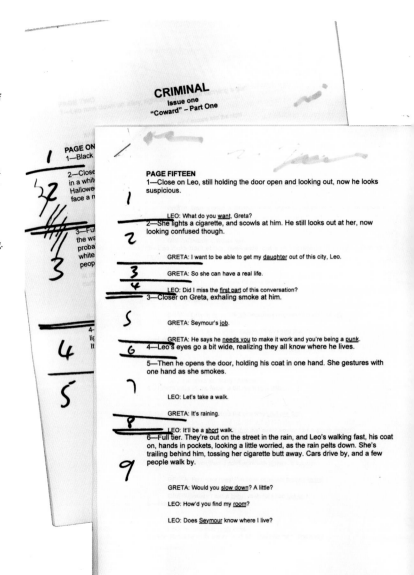

CRIMINAL
Issue one
"Coward" – Part One

PAGE FIFTEEN
1—Close on Leo, still holding the door open and looking out, now he looks suspicious.

LEO: What do you want, Greta?
2—She lights a cigarette, and scowls at him. He still looks out at her, now looking confused though.

GRETA: I want to be able to get my daughter out of this city, Leo.

GRETA: So she can have a real life.

LEO: Did I miss the first part of this conversation?
3—Closer on Greta, exhaling smoke at him.

GRETA: Seymour's job.

GRETA: He says he needs you to make it work and you're being a punk.
4—Leo's eyes go a bit wide, realizing they all know where he lives.

5—Then he opens the door, holding his coat in one hand. She gestures with one hand as she smokes.

LEO: Let's take a walk.

GRETA: It's raining.

LEO: It'll be a short walk.
6—Full tier. They're out on the street in the rain, and Leo's walking fast, his coat on, hands in pockets, looking a little worried, as the rain pelts down. She's trailing behind him, tossing her cigarette butt away. Cars drive by, and a few people walk by.

GRETA: Would you slow down? A little?

LEO: How'd you find my room?

LEO: Does Seymour know where I live?

I usually draw small two inch high thumbnails of each page, following my amended script for placement of panels. Before drawing anything in the panels, I'll indicate the balloons and captions. This makes sure the words are read in the right order and that there is enough room left for them. As I also letter Criminal it's easy for me to control that from the beginning.

Then drawing very crudely I indicate what will be in each panel just for rough placement and composition. I'm not interested in making a nice drawing yet, I worry about that later.

After thumbnailing I gather any reference photos I need of people and places. Most of the people photos I take of myself with my camera on a tripod and a timer. I occasionally use other models for particular characters and in this story I used my son Fred as a model for Greta, mainly because he had long hair at the time and he was easy to boss around.

The orange scribbles on the thumbnails are made after I've taken each photo. I also look through my extensive library of books on New York and other cities and photos taken in places I've visited for any street scenes.

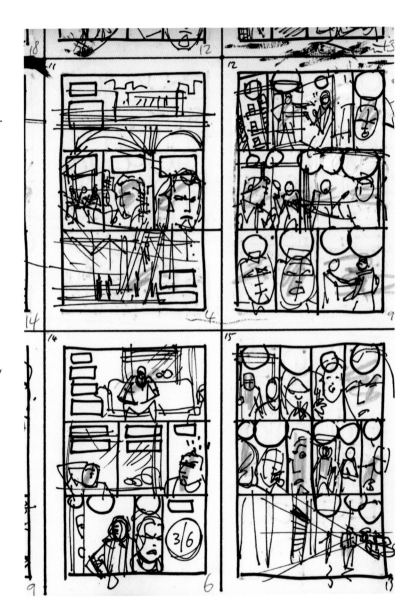

Okay, then the hard part begins.

In Illustrator on my Mac I open up my page template. I always start with this file as it ensures every page is the same size and the lettering all matches. I drop in the gutters first and then get on with the lettering using a font Comicraft made of my hand lettering samples. For Criminal the balloons are always circular and almost always touch the edge of the panels. The captions are always in the top left corner though they don't touch the panel edges. If the lettering is a tight fit I can always move the gutters to make for a better fit. In the last panel I also dropped in a photo I found of I think a San Francisco strret.

All this is then printed out at 125% of print size in pale blue onto a thin watercolour paper. I then rule in the panel borders with a pen and roughly hand draw the balloons and captions boxes with a steel nib. On this page I also outlined a couple of figures in the last panel to make them stand out a little better against the blue photo.

Then, using a pale blue marker I start pencilling the page. As I ink my own pencils, I don't need to add to much detail here, just basic construction lines. The broad tip of the marker stops me doing that anyway.

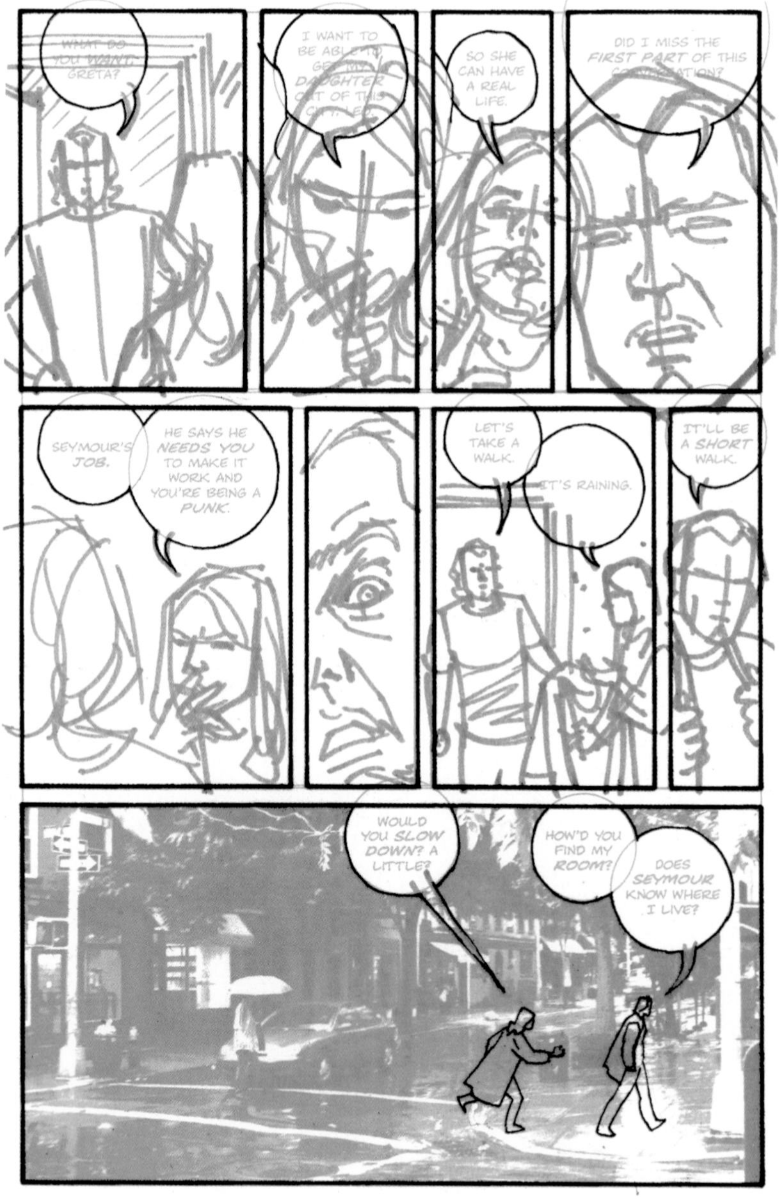

WHAT DO YOU WANT, GRETA?
I WANT TO BE ABLE TO GET MY DAUGHTER OUT OF THIS CITY, LEE.
SO SHE CAN HAVE A REAL LIFE.
DID I MISS THE FIRST PART OF THIS CONVERSATION?
SEYMOUR'S JOB.
HE SAYS HE NEEDS YOU TO MAKE IT WORK AND YOU'RE BEING A PUNK.
LET'S TAKE A WALK.
IT'S RAINING.
IT'LL BE A SHORT WALK.
WOULD YOU SLOW DOWN? A LITTLE?
HOW'D YOU FIND MY ROOM?
DOES SEYMOUR KNOW WHERE I LIVE?

Most of the work is then done in the inking. I use a Faber-Castell Pitt pen for outlines and fiddly things like fingers and eyes. Then just straight in with a Pentel Color Brush trying to keep the marks impressionistic and loose. A few slashes of a white-out pen for the rain in the last panel and then I'm done.

Easy really!

The inks are scanned back into Illustrator and the lettering is added to the balloons. Then I send the file to Val the day before the deadline and he works his magic at the last minute...

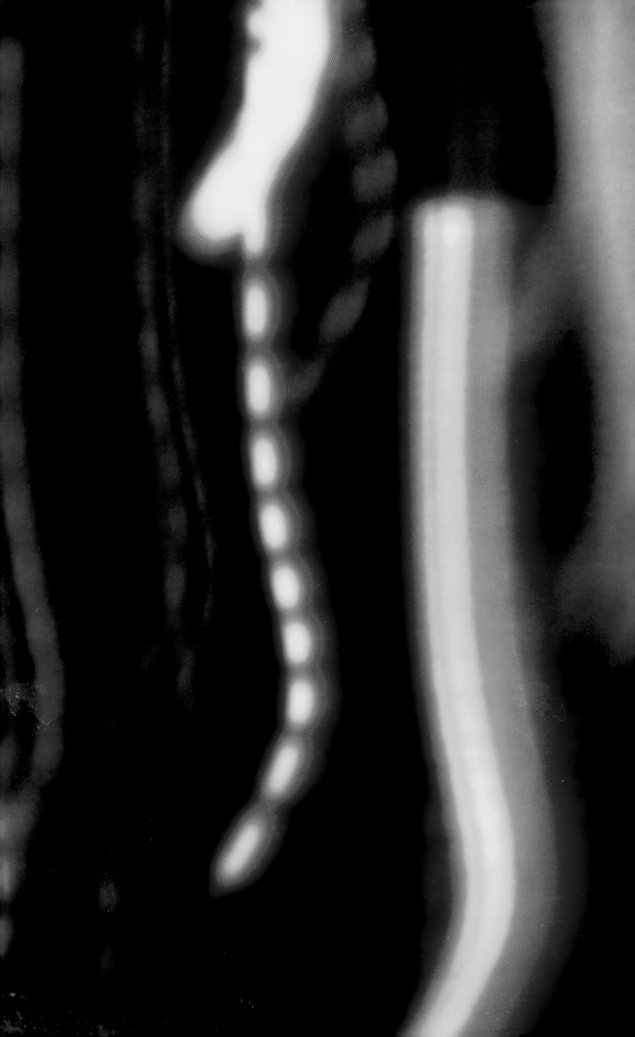

Afterword

A long time ago, when I first met my wife, she asked me what kind of books I wanted to write… what would I do if I could do anything I wanted, regardless of the market or sales or editors or publishers, or anything? (She probably won't remember this, it was so long ago). And that morning was the beginning of **Criminal**, even though I didn't know it at the time. But I knew I wanted to do crime and mystery stories, and I knew I wanted to have the freedom to create a book that would be whatever I wanted it to be, where the main character could change every story-arc.

Around that same time, Sean Phillips and I began collaborating on a book called **GOTHAM NOIR** for Mike Carlin at DC. A sort of Batman comic, that was really an insane detective story about a guy losing his mind. And then we created a series called **SLEEPER** for Scott Dunbier and Jim Lee at DC's Wildstorm label, about a super-powered double-agent which garnered a lot of critical acclaim and film interest, with Tom Cruise now attached to star (I'll believe that when I'm sitting at the movies watching it, though).

Sean and I were becoming a team, and we liked to do the same kind of comics. Smoky rooms, people standing around talking, gunfire and girls, lots and lots of shadows. Sean likes Munoz and Sampayo's **Alack Sinner** books as much as I do. We both dig weird European crime comics and we both had a desire to do something that would be like that, but be our own thing, too. And so when I finally got the chance to do something at **Marvel Comics' ICON line**, I knew the time was right to do the book I'd always wanted and I knew there was no artist other than Sean to do it with. Soon we found Val Staples, who's now become Sean's primary colorist, and we were off and running.

So far it's been a success, and even though we've been at it a few years now, it feels like we're just getting started. I hope we are, honestly, because I want to do stories like this with Sean for the rest of my life.

I'd like to take a moment to thank some of the people who've helped make **Criminal** possible (and if I leave anyone out, I hope they'll forgive the oversight) – Brian Bendis, Matt Fraction, Michael Lark, Dan Buckley, Jeff Youngquist, Robert Kirkman, Warren Ellis, John Layman, Joe Quesada, Jim McCann, Arune Singh, Ruwan Jayatilleke, Charles Meyer, David Bogart, David Gabriel, and of course, my lovely wife Melanie Tomlin, without whom nothing would be the same.

Ed Brubaker
July 2009

Biographies

Ed Brubaker was born in 1966 in the Bethesda Naval Hospital, and was a navy brat for most of his childhood. Comics were often his only friend, and he grew up wanting to be a penciler for Marvel. Instead, he ended up an acclaimed writer, with four awards for **Best Writer** (Two Harvey Awards and Two Eisner Awards) as well as many other awards for his work on **Criminal** and other series. His work has been translated into many languages around the world and optioned for film. In 2009 his internet project **Angel of Death** became the first internet production to be sold to cable TV for broadcast and re-edited into a feature for DVD. He currently lives in Seattle with his wife and a cat named Little Guy and a dog named Watson.

Sean Phillips has been drawing comics professionally for nearly thirty years. It's all been downhill since **Bunty**.

Val Staples got into comics when he was a teen. Then he got out of comics and into girls instead. Then he got back into comics in college and enjoyed the best of both worlds. Soon after he tried to break in as a colorist instead of a writer, figuring it would be easier. It wasn't. He colored comics for a couple years, then published comics for a few years, then returned to coloring. He somehow conned Ed and Sean into letting him color Criminal; the only title where Val feels completely at home as a colorist. The only downside is that the Criminal gig hasn't come with groupies.